WOTAKOI:
LOVE IS HARD FOR OTAKU

FUJITA

Episode....31

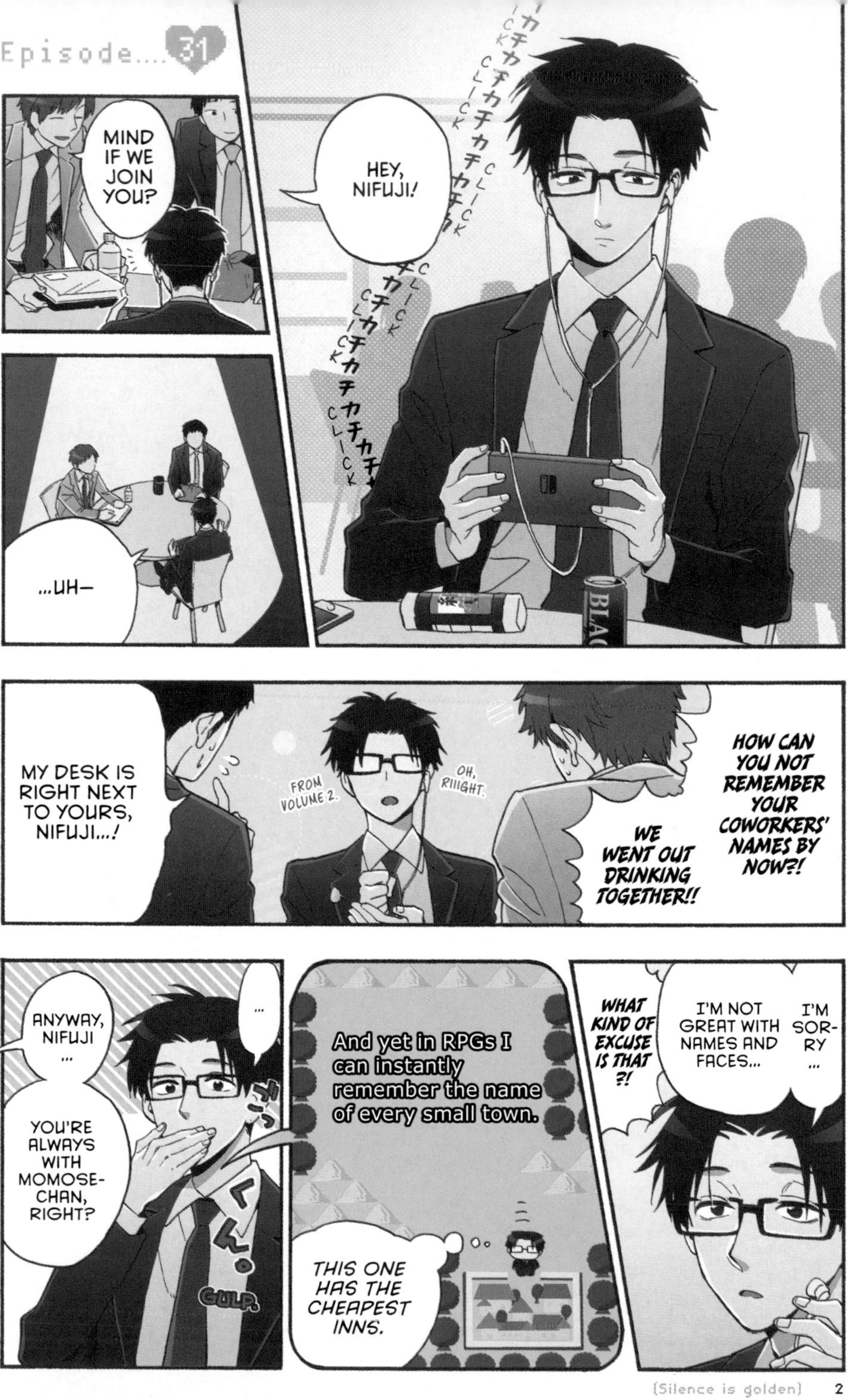

HEY, NIFUJI!
CLICK CLICK CLICK CLICK CLICK
MIND IF WE JOIN YOU?
...UH—
HOW CAN YOU NOT REMEMBER YOUR COWORKERS' NAMES BY NOW?!
WE WENT OUT DRINKING TOGETHER!!
OH, RIIIGHT.
FROM VOLUME 2.
MY DESK IS RIGHT NEXT TO YOURS, NIFUJI...!
I'M SORRY...
I'M NOT GREAT WITH NAMES AND FACES...
WHAT KIND OF EXCUSE IS THAT?!
And yet in RPGs I can instantly remember the name of every small town.
THIS ONE HAS THE CHEAPEST INNS.
...
ANYWAY, NIFUJI...
YOU'RE ALWAYS WITH MOMOSE-CHAN, RIGHT?
GULP.

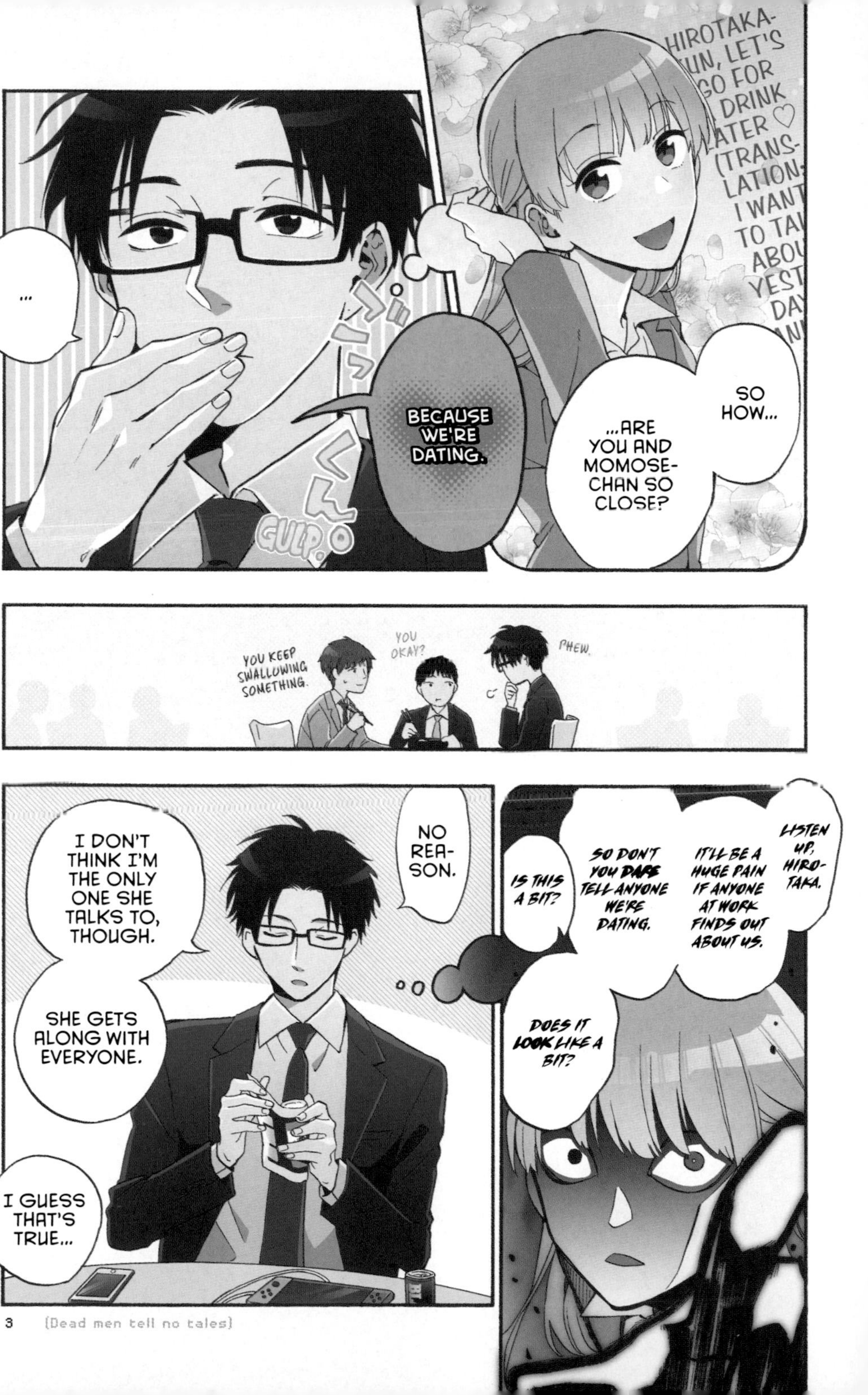
HIROTAKA-KUN, LET'S GO FOR A DRINK LATER ♡ (TRANS-LATION: I WANT TO TA ABOU YEST DAY
SO HOW...
...ARE YOU AND MOMOSE-CHAN SO CLOSE?
BECAUSE WE'RE DATING.
GULP.
...
PHEW.
YOU OKAY?
YOU KEEP SWALLOWING SOMETHING.
LISTEN UP, HIRO-TAKA.
IT'LL BE A HUGE PAIN IF ANYONE AT WORK FINDS OUT ABOUT US.
SO DON'T YOU DARE TELL ANYONE WE'RE DATING.
IS THIS A BIT?
DOES IT LOOK LIKE A BIT?
NO REA-SON.
I DON'T THINK I'M THE ONLY ONE SHE TALKS TO, THOUGH.
SHE GETS ALONG WITH EVERYONE.
I GUESS THAT'S TRUE...

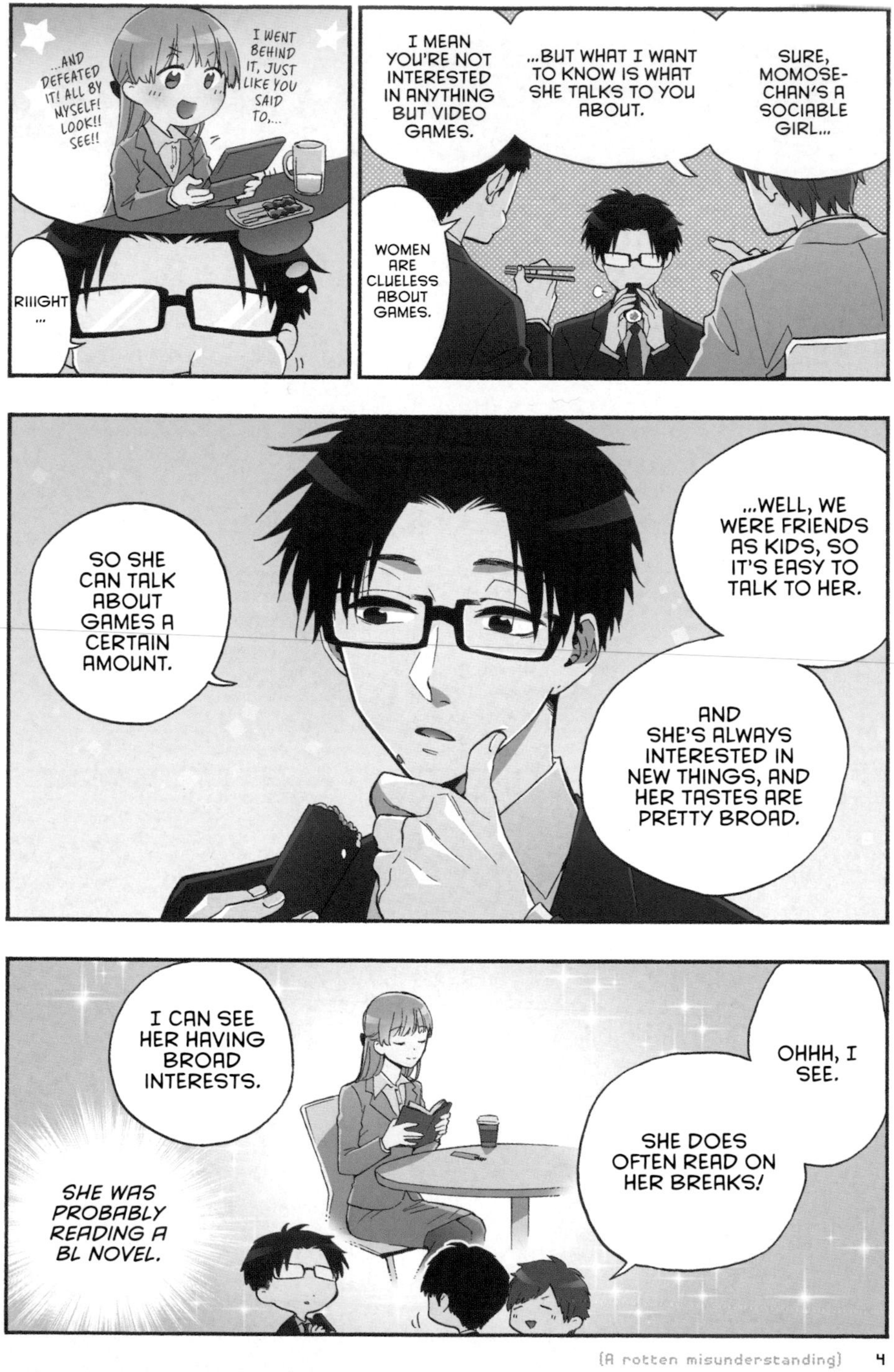
SURE, MOMOSE-CHAN'S A SOCIABLE GIRL...
...BUT WHAT I WANT TO KNOW IS WHAT SHE TALKS TO YOU ABOUT.
I MEAN YOU'RE NOT INTERESTED IN ANYTHING BUT VIDEO GAMES.
WOMEN ARE CLUELESS ABOUT GAMES.
I WENT BEHIND IT, JUST LIKE YOU SAID TO,...
...AND DEFEATED IT! ALL BY MYSELF! LOOK!! SEE!!
RIIIGHT ...
...WELL, WE WERE FRIENDS AS KIDS, SO IT'S EASY TO TALK TO HER.
AND SHE'S ALWAYS INTERESTED IN NEW THINGS, AND HER TASTES ARE PRETTY BROAD.
SO SHE CAN TALK ABOUT GAMES A CERTAIN AMOUNT.
OHHH, I SEE.
SHE DOES OFTEN READ ON HER BREAKS!
I CAN SEE HER HAVING BROAD INTERESTS.
SHE WAS PROBABLY READING A BL NOVEL.

(A rotten misunderstanding)

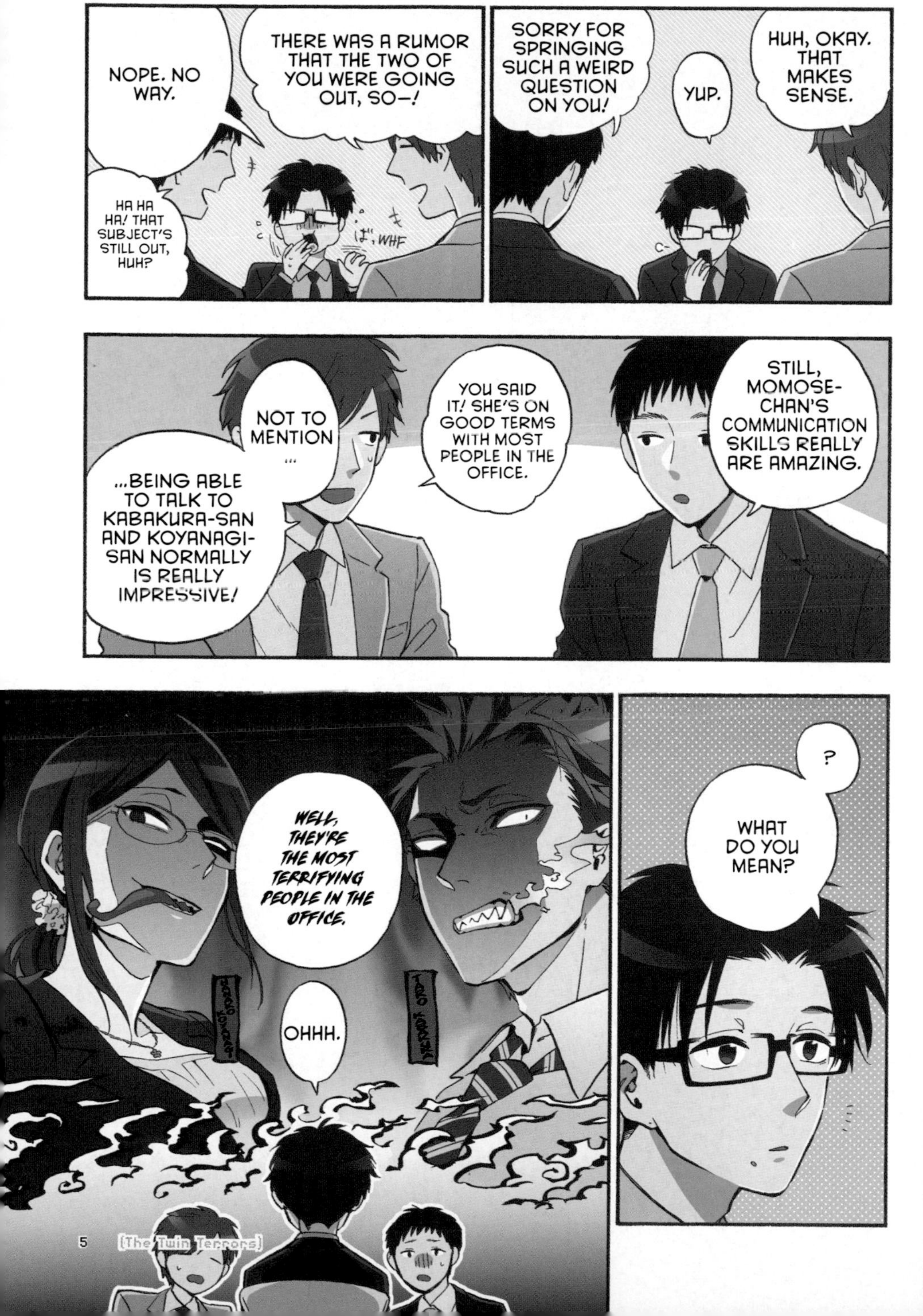
HUH, OKAY. THAT MAKES SENSE.
YUP.
SORRY FOR SPRINGING SUCH A WEIRD QUESTION ON YOU!
THERE WAS A RUMOR THAT THE TWO OF YOU WERE GOING OUT, SO—!
NOPE. NO WAY.
HA HA HA! THAT SUBJECT'S STILL OUT, HUH?
WHF
STILL, MOMOSE-CHAN'S COMMUNICATION SKILLS REALLY ARE AMAZING.
YOU SAID IT! SHE'S ON GOOD TERMS WITH MOST PEOPLE IN THE OFFICE.
NOT TO MENTION...
...BEING ABLE TO TALK TO KABAKURA-SAN AND KOYANAGI-SAN NORMALLY IS REALLY IMPRESSIVE!
?
WHAT DO YOU MEAN?
WELL, THEY'RE THE MOST TERRIFYING PEOPLE IN THE OFFICE.
TARO KABAKURA
OHHH.
[The Twin Terrors]

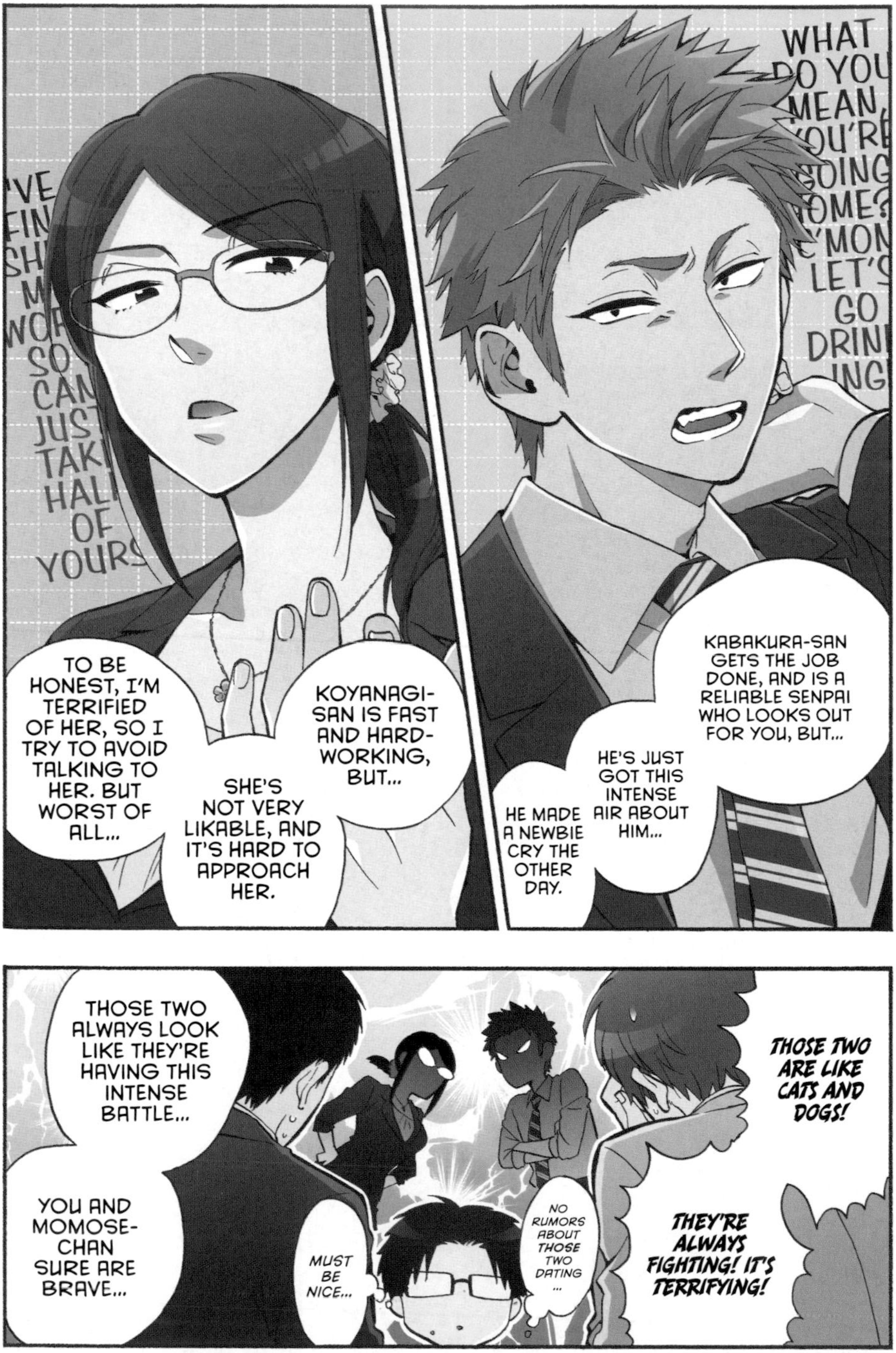
WHAT DO YOU MEAN, YOU'RE GOING HOME? C'MON LET'S GO DRINKING
KABAKURA-SAN GETS THE JOB DONE, AND IS A RELIABLE SENPAI WHO LOOKS OUT FOR YOU, BUT...
HE'S JUST GOT THIS INTENSE AIR ABOUT HIM...
HE MADE A NEWBIE CRY THE OTHER DAY.
KOYANAGI-SAN IS FAST AND HARD-WORKING, BUT...
SHE'S NOT VERY LIKABLE, AND IT'S HARD TO APPROACH HER.
TO BE HONEST, I'M TERRIFIED OF HER, SO I TRY TO AVOID TALKING TO HER. BUT WORST OF ALL...
THOSE TWO ARE LIKE CATS AND DOGS!
THEY'RE ALWAYS FIGHTING! IT'S TERRIFYING!
NO RUMORS ABOUT THOSE TWO DATING...
MUST BE NICE...
THOSE TWO ALWAYS LOOK LIKE THEY'RE HAVING THIS INTENSE BATTLE...
YOU AND MOMOSE-CHAN SURE ARE BRAVE...

[Scary faces, scary words]

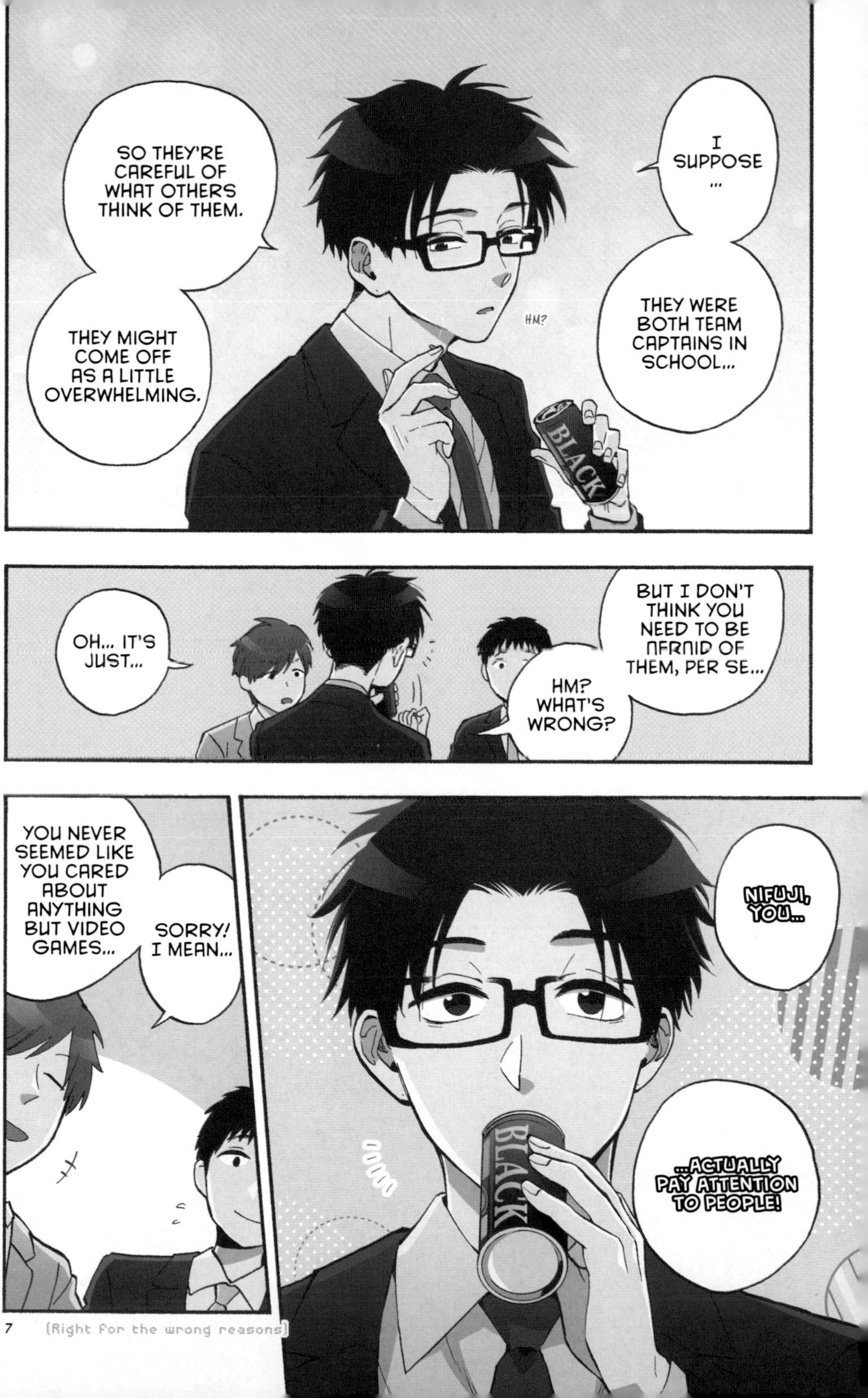
I SUPPOSE ...
THEY WERE BOTH TEAM CAPTAINS IN SCHOOL...
HM?
SO THEY'RE CAREFUL OF WHAT OTHERS THINK OF THEM.
THEY MIGHT COME OFF AS A LITTLE OVERWHELMING.
BUT I DON'T THINK YOU NEED TO BE AFRAID OF THEM, PER SE...
HM? WHAT'S WRONG?
OH... IT'S JUST...
NIFUJI, YOU...
...ACTUALLY PAY ATTENTION TO PEOPLE!
SORRY! I MEAN...
YOU NEVER SEEMED LIKE YOU CARED ABOUT ANYTHING BUT VIDEO GAMES...

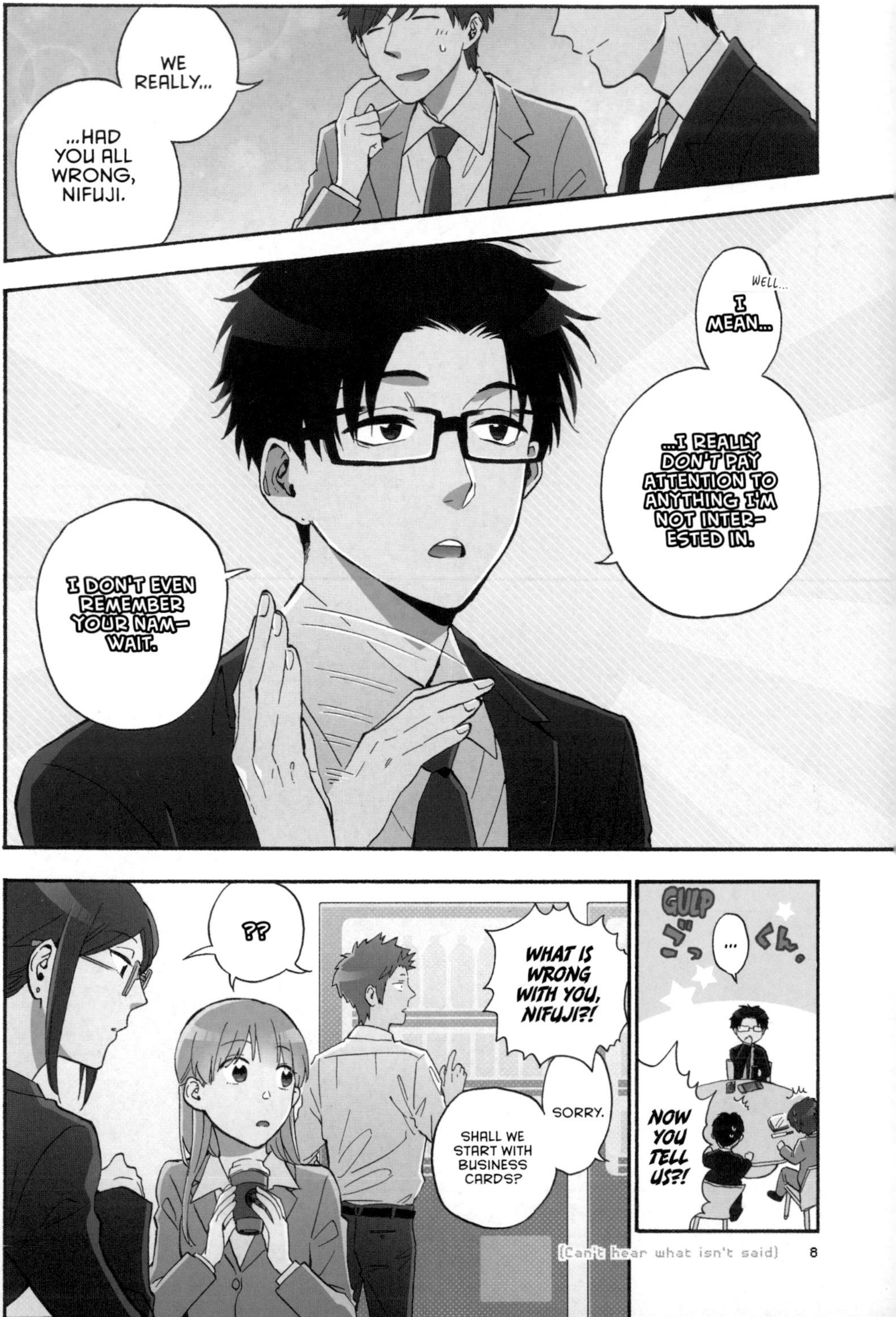
WE REALLY...
...HAD YOU ALL WRONG, NIFUJI.
WELL...
I MEAN...
...I REALLY DON'T PAY ATTENTION TO ANYTHING I'M NOT INTER-ESTED IN.
I DON'T EVEN REMEMBER YOUR NAM— WAIT.
GULP
ごっくん。
...
NOW YOU TELL US?!
WHAT IS WRONG WITH YOU, NIFUJI?!
SORRY.
SHALL WE START WITH BUSINESS CARDS?
??

(Can't hear what isn't said)

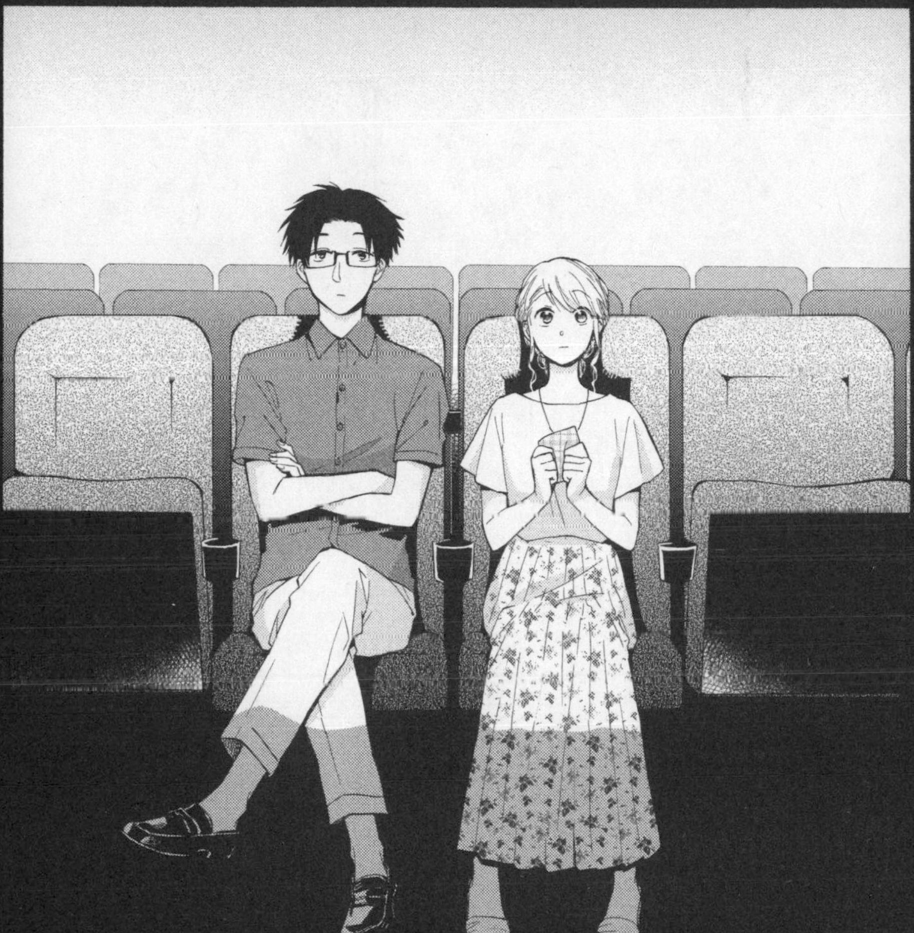

Episode.... 32

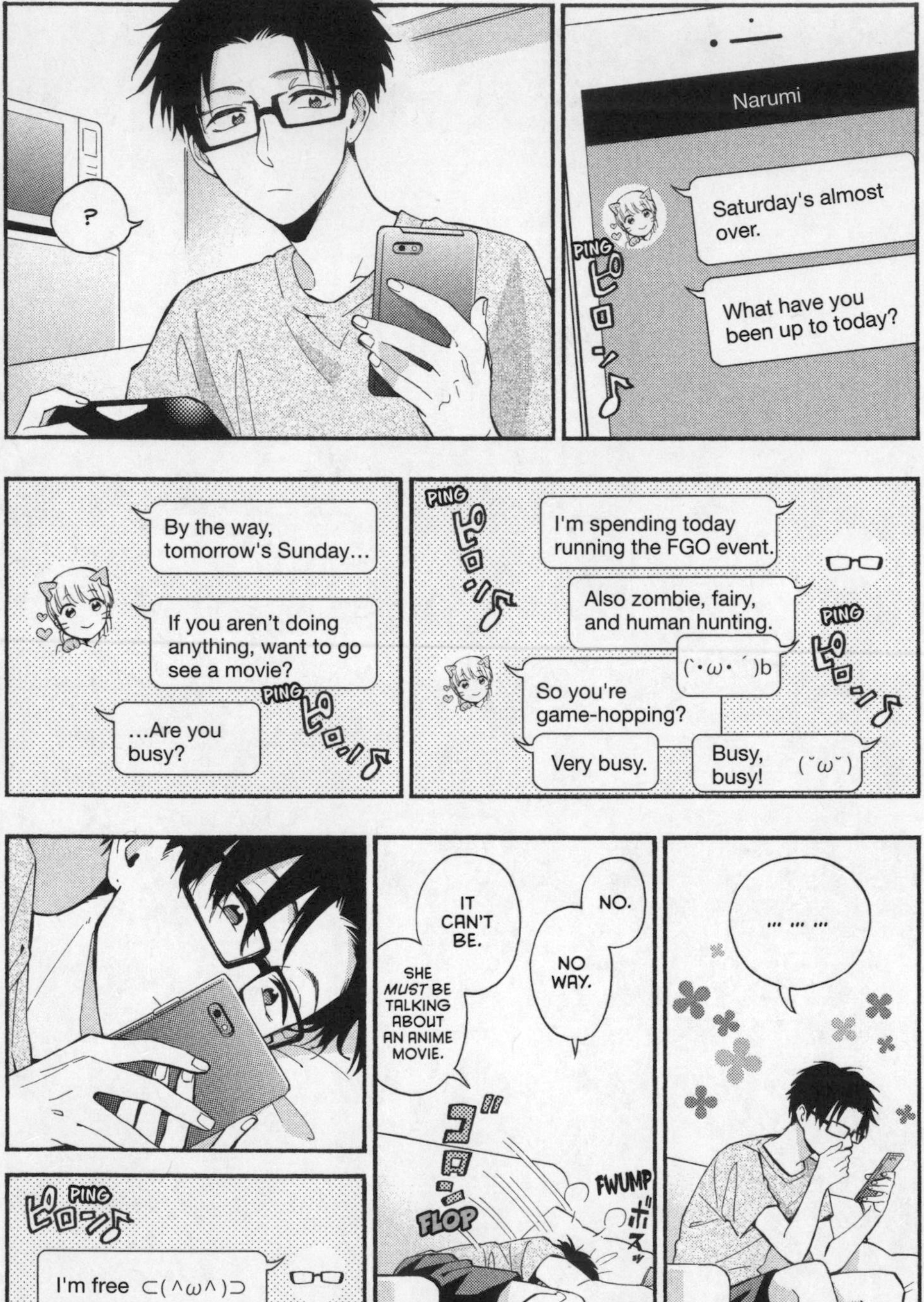
Narumi
PING
Saturday's almost over.
What have you been up to today?
?
PING
I'm spending today running the FGO event.
Also zombie, fairy, and human hunting.
PING
(`・ω・´)b
So you're game-hopping?
Very busy.
Busy, busy! (˘ω˘)
PING
By the way, tomorrow's Sunday…
If you aren't doing anything, want to go see a movie?
PING
…Are you busy?
… … …
NO.
NO WAY.
IT CAN'T BE.
SHE *MUST* BE TALKING ABOUT AN ANIME MOVIE.
FWUMP
FLOP
PING
I'm free ⊂(＾ω＾)⊃

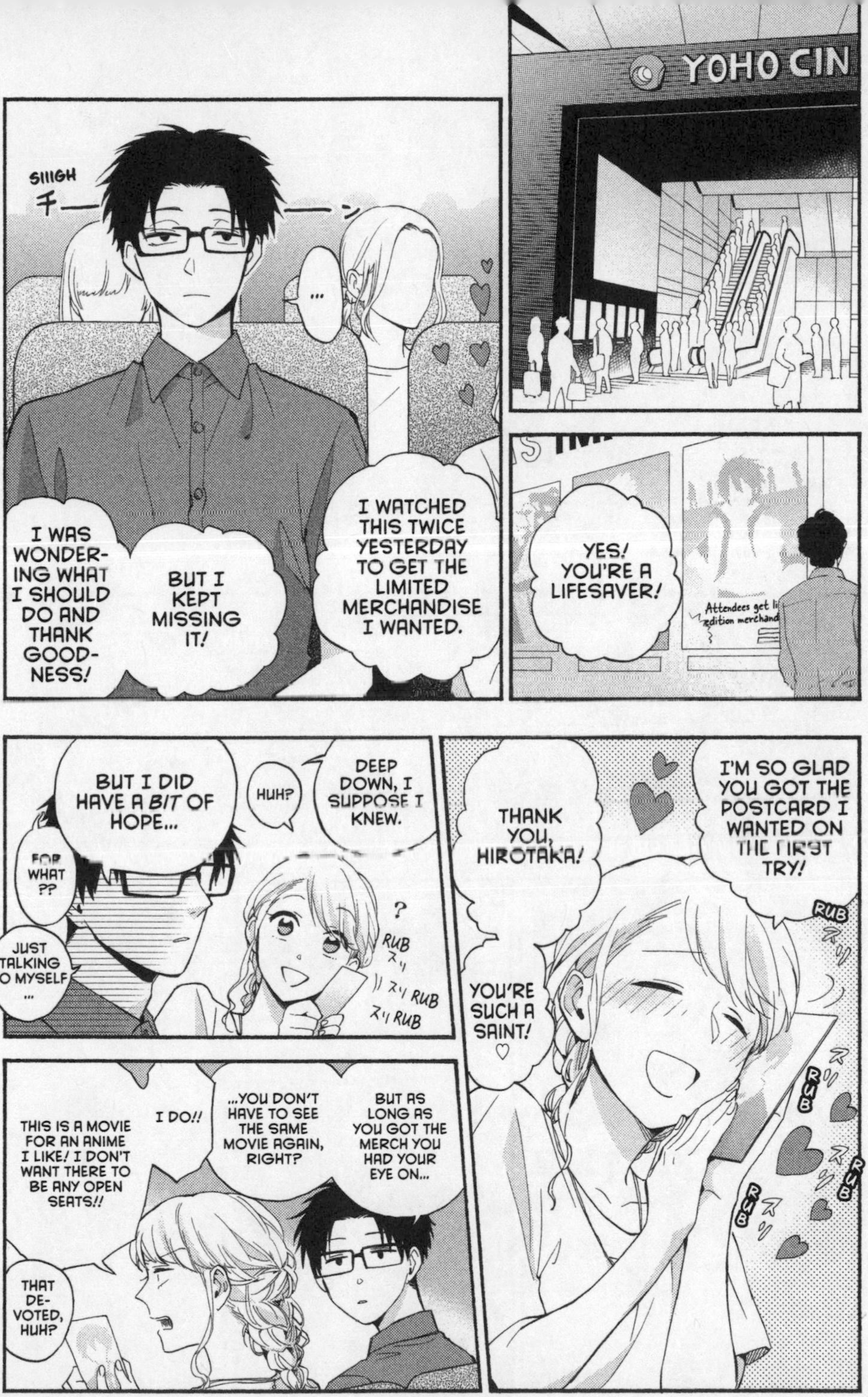
YOHO CIN
YES! YOU'RE A LIFESAVER!
Attendees get li... edition merchand...
I WATCHED THIS TWICE YESTERDAY TO GET THE LIMITED MERCHANDISE I WANTED.
BUT I KEPT MISSING IT!
I WAS WONDER-ING WHAT I SHOULD DO AND THANK GOOD-NESS!
...
SIIIGH
I'M SO GLAD YOU GOT THE POSTCARD I WANTED ON THE FIRST TRY!
THANK YOU, HIROTAKA!
YOU'RE SUCH A SAINT! ♡
RUB
RUB
RUB
RUB
DEEP DOWN, I SUPPOSE I KNEW.
HUH?
BUT I DID HAVE A *BIT* OF HOPE...
FOR WHAT??
JUST TALKING TO MYSELF...
?
RUB
RUB
RUB
BUT AS LONG AS YOU GOT THE MERCH YOU HAD YOUR EYE ON...
...YOU DON'T HAVE TO SEE THE SAME MOVIE AGAIN, RIGHT?
I DO!!
THIS IS A MOVIE FOR AN ANIME I LIKE! I DON'T WANT THERE TO BE ANY OPEN SEATS!!
THAT DE-VOTED, HUH?

(All for a postcard)

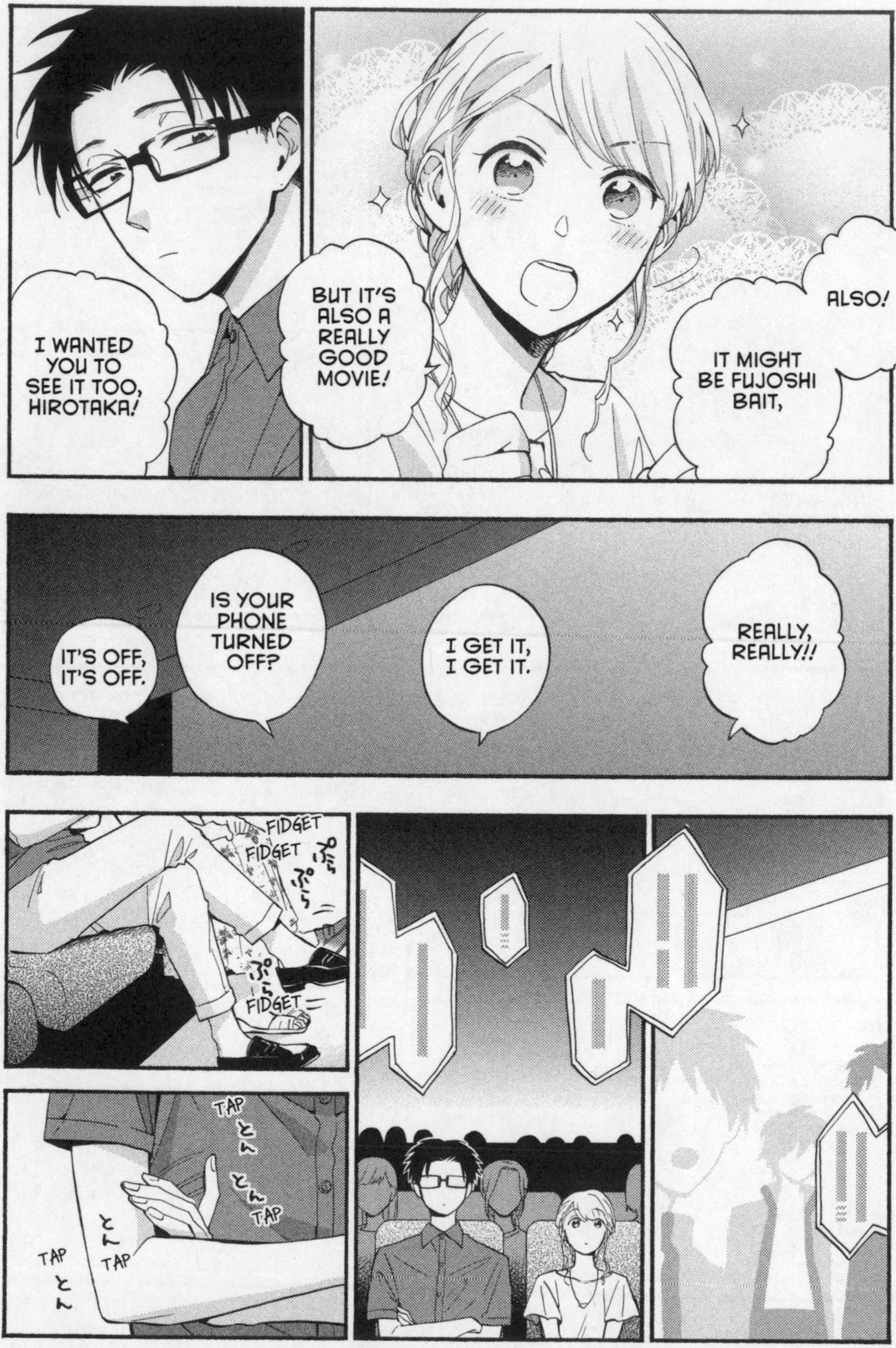
ALSO!
IT MIGHT BE FUJOSHI BAIT,
BUT IT'S ALSO A REALLY GOOD MOVIE!
I WANTED YOU TO SEE IT TOO, HIROTAKA!
REALLY, REALLY!!
I GET IT, I GET IT.
IS YOUR PHONE TURNED OFF?
IT'S OFF, IT'S OFF.
FIDGET
FIDGET
ぷら
ぷら
ぷら
FIDGET
TAP
とん
とん
TAP
とん
TAP
TAP
とん

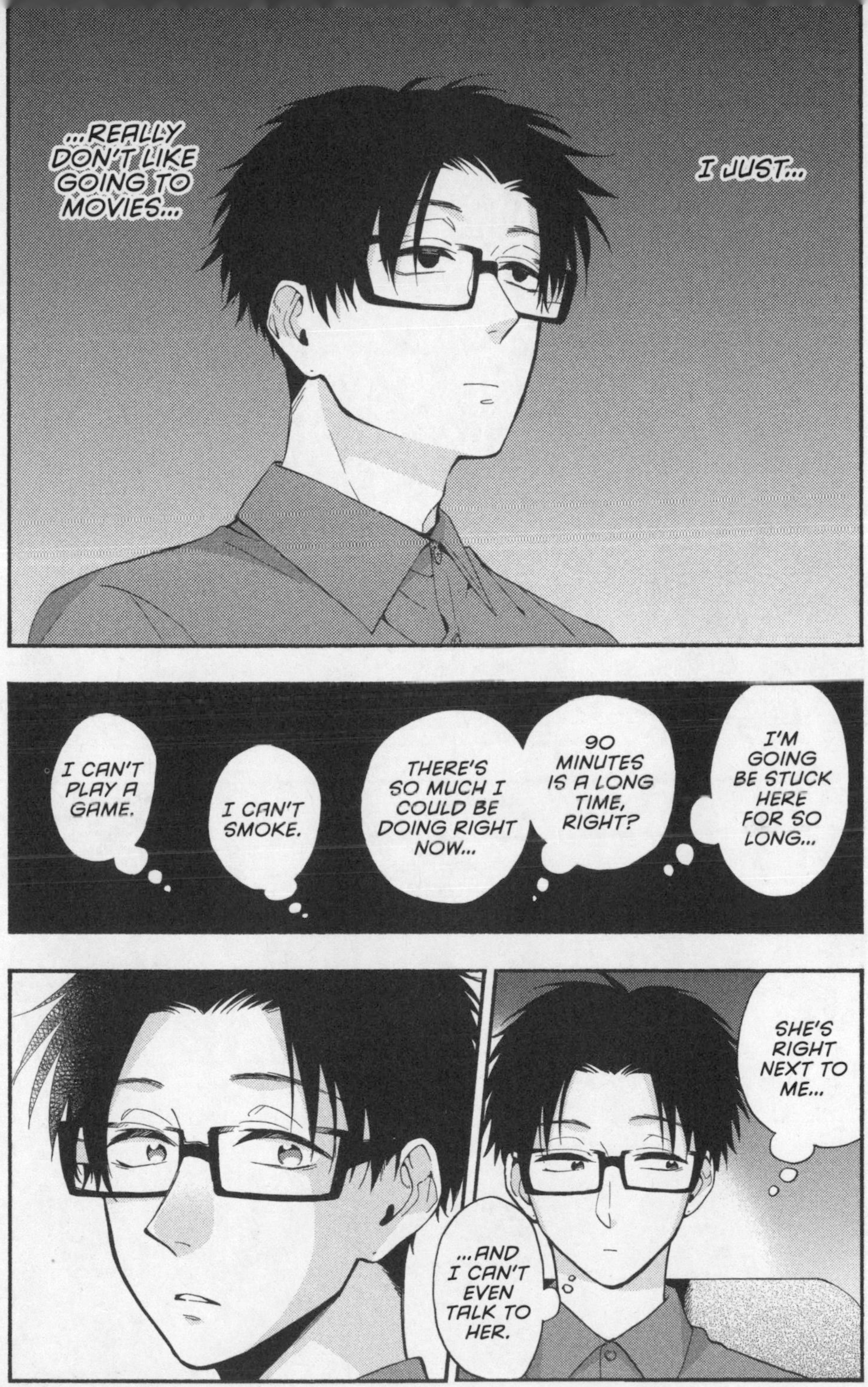
I JUST...
...REALLY DON'T LIKE GOING TO MOVIES...
I'M GOING BE STUCK HERE FOR SO LONG...
90 MINUTES IS A LONG TIME, RIGHT?
THERE'S SO MUCH I COULD BE DOING RIGHT NOW...
I CAN'T SMOKE.
I CAN'T PLAY A GAME.
SHE'S RIGHT NEXT TO ME...
...AND I CAN'T EVEN TALK TO HER.

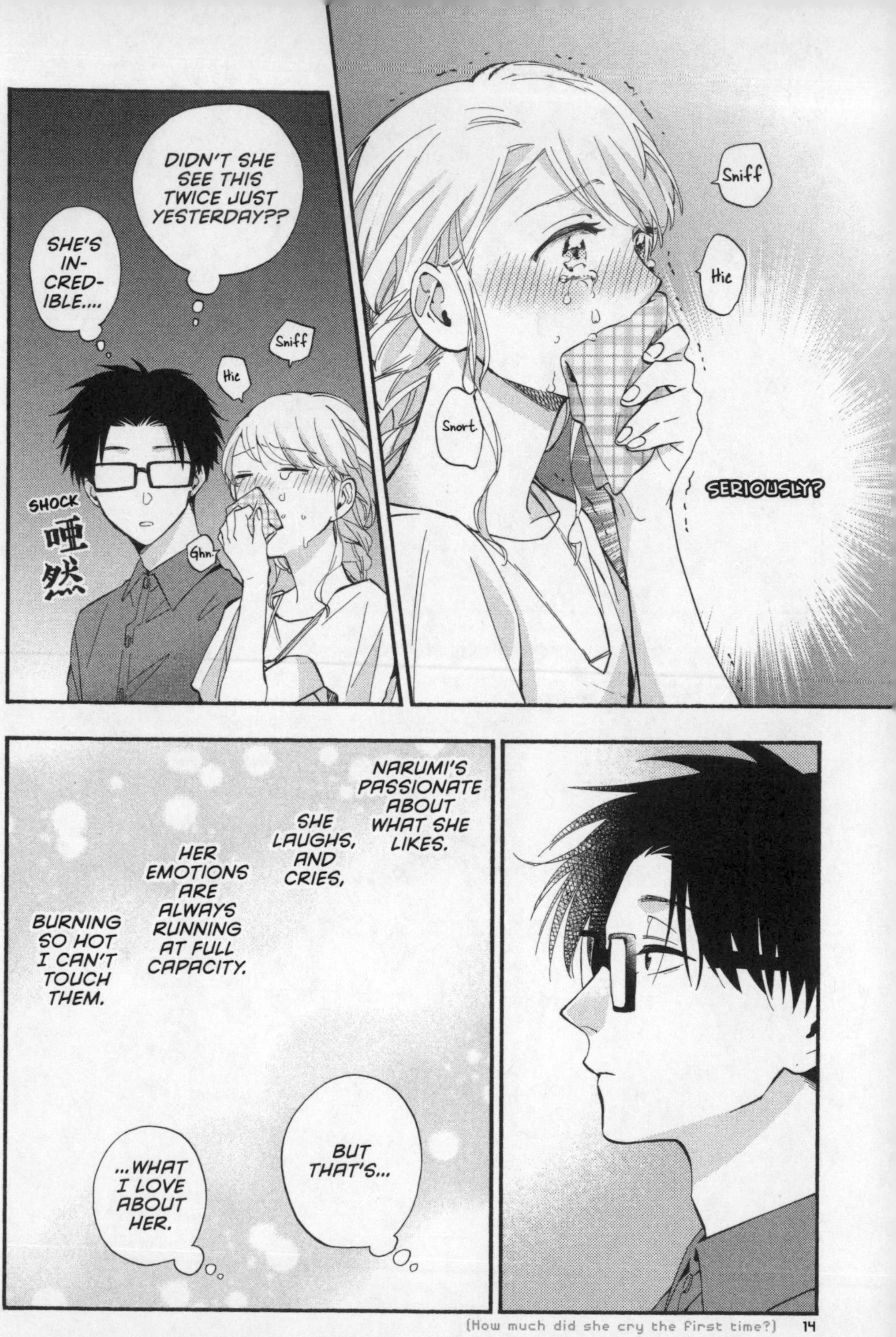
Sniff
Hic
Snort.
SERIOUSLY?
DIDN'T SHE SEE THIS TWICE JUST YESTERDAY??
SHE'S IN-CRED-IBLE....
Sniff
Hic
SHOCK 唖然
Ghn.
NARUMI'S PASSIONATE ABOUT WHAT SHE LIKES.
SHE LAUGHS, AND CRIES,
HER EMOTIONS ARE ALWAYS RUNNING AT FULL CAPACITY.
BURNING SO HOT I CAN'T TOUCH THEM.
BUT THAT'S...
...WHAT I LOVE ABOUT HER.

(How much did she cry the first time?)

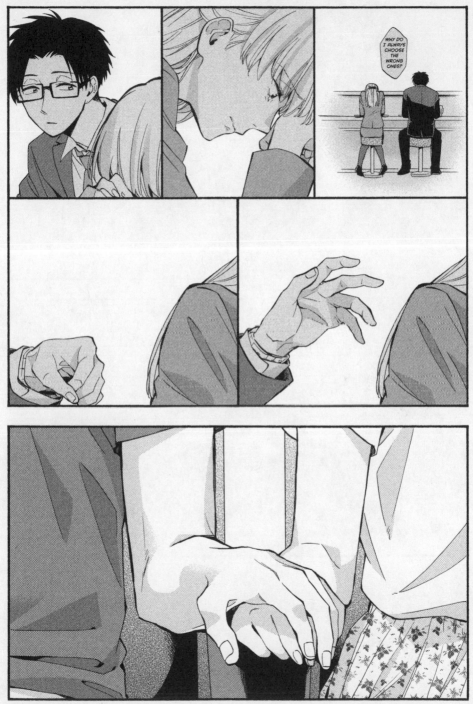

WHY DO
I *ALWAYS*
CHOOSE
THE
WRONG
ONES?

[This time for sure]

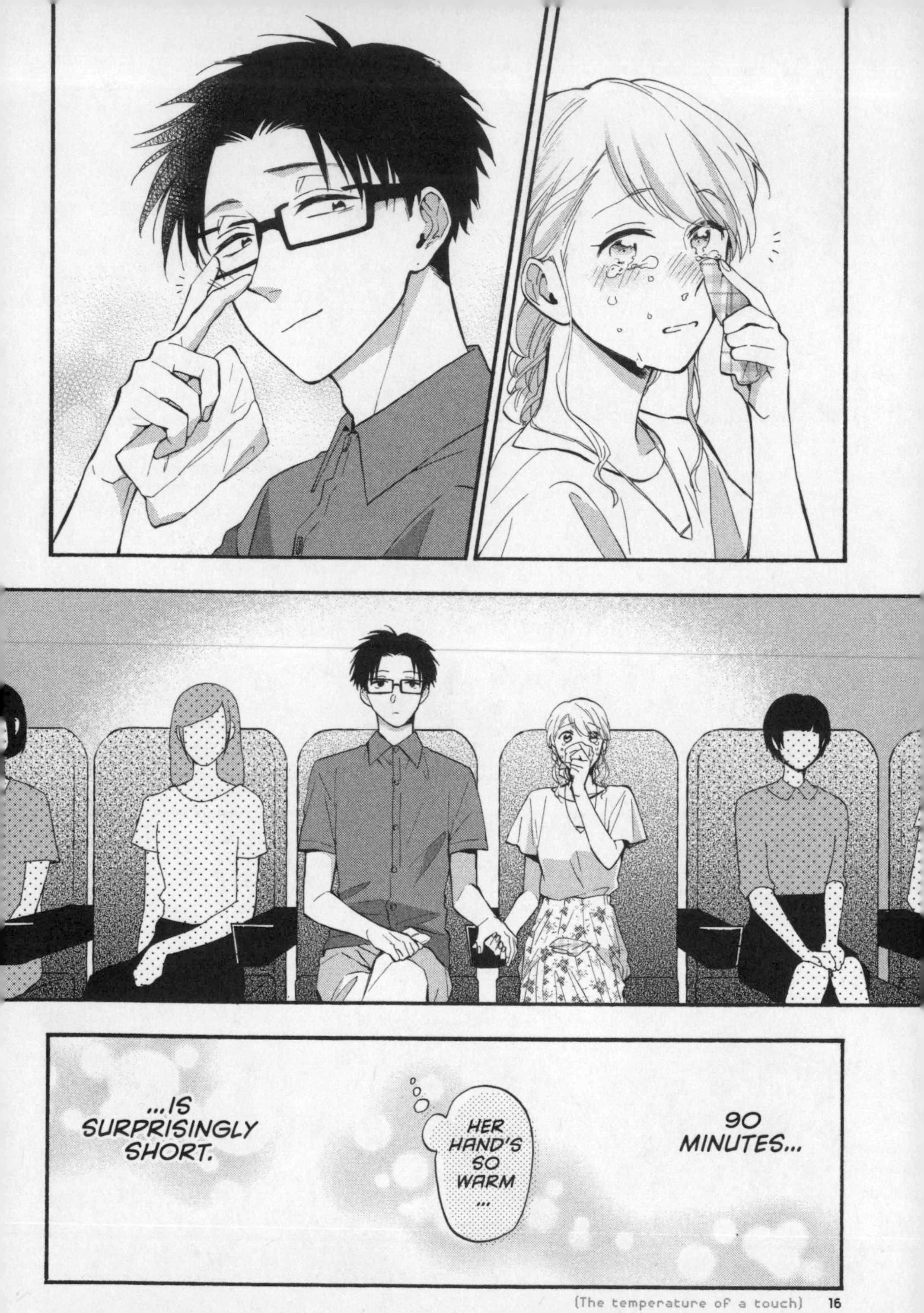
90 MINUTES...
HER HAND'S SO WARM ...
...IS SURPRISINGLY SHORT.

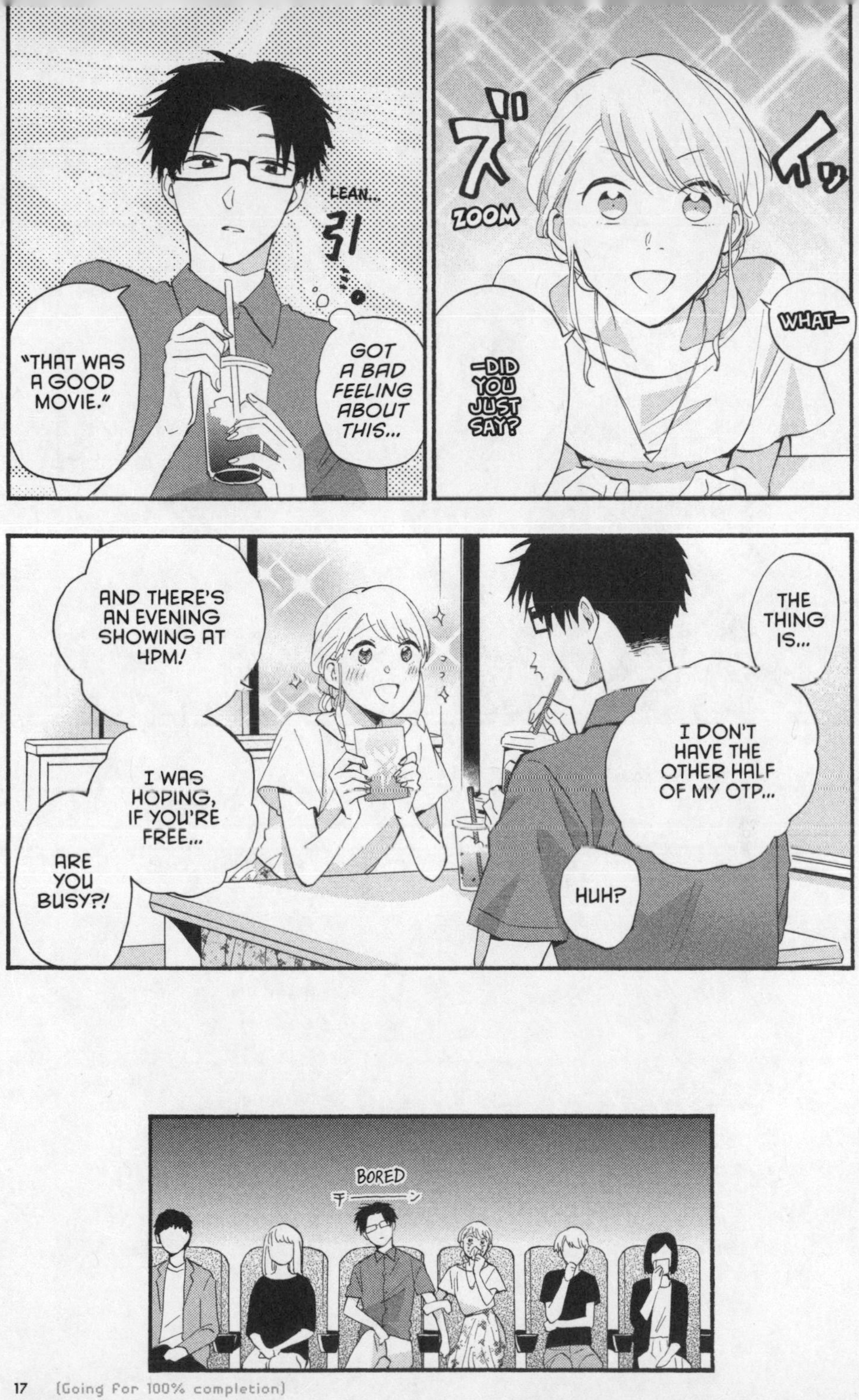
ズ
ZOOM
イッ
WHAT—
—DID YOU JUST SAY?
LEAN...
引
GOT A BAD FEELING ABOUT THIS...
"THAT WAS A GOOD MOVIE."
THE THING IS...
I DON'T HAVE THE OTHER HALF OF MY OTP...
HUH?
AND THERE'S AN EVENING SHOWING AT 4PM!
I WAS HOPING, IF YOU'RE FREE...
ARE YOU BUSY?!
BORED
チーン

CHARACTERS

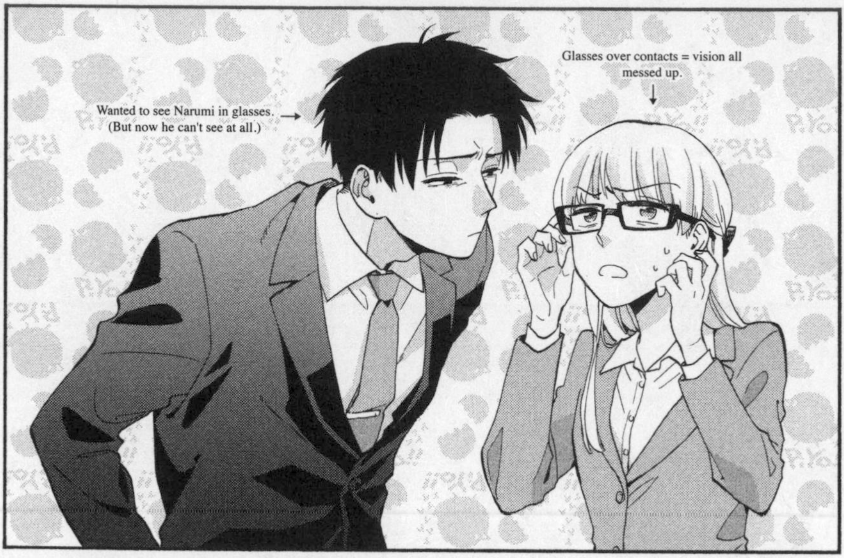
Wanted to see Narumi in glasses. (But now he can't see at all.)
Glasses over contacts = vision all messed up.

FAN REQUEST

"NARUMI IS SAYING 'URK' TO HOW BLIND HIROTAKA IS AFTER BORROWING HIS GLASSES, AND HIROTAKA IS BEHIND HER GOING 'I CAN'T SEE'."

☞ HIROTAKA NIFUJI

- GAMER.
- HAS HAD GLASSES FOR AS LONG AS HE CAN REMEMBER.
- HE ISN'T PARTICULARLY INTO WEARING GLASSES, BUT IS COMPLETELY LOST WITHOUT THEM.
- DOESN'T HAVE A THING FOR GIRLS IN GLASSES, BUT DOES WANT TO SEE NARUMI IN THEM.

☞ NARUMI MOMOSE

- SECRET FUJOSHI.
- HATES GOING OUTSIDE IN GLASSES.
- SOMETIMES FALLS ASLEEP WITH CONTACTS IN AND LOOKS LIKE HELL THE NEXT DAY.
- DOESN'T PARTICULARLY HAVE A THING FOR GUYS IN GLASSES.

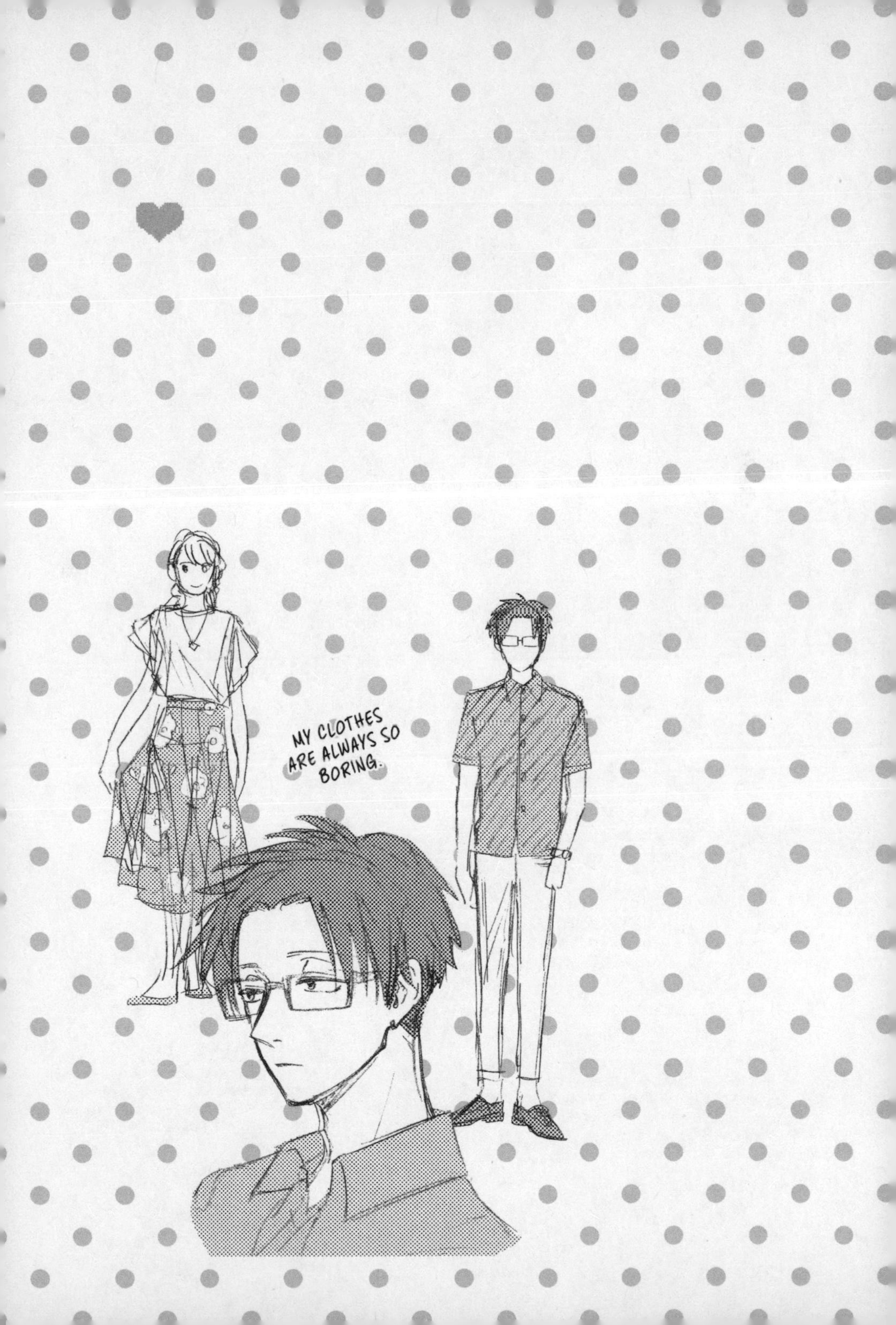
MY CLOTHES ARE ALWAYS SO BORING.

MESSY HAIR (HIS HAIR IS STILL MESSY)
LOOKED LIKE HE WAS GLARING, NOT SHY, BAD EXPRESSION.
HIROTAKA NOW
SOFTER LOOK.
HAIR TRIMMED CLOSE UP THE BACK OF HIS NECK.
HIS TIE ALSO HAS A WEIRD TONE.
HIROTAKA'S ORIGINAL DESIGN.
HIS GLASSES WERE A WEIRD SHADE.
IN GOOD SHAPE, SUIT BULGING.

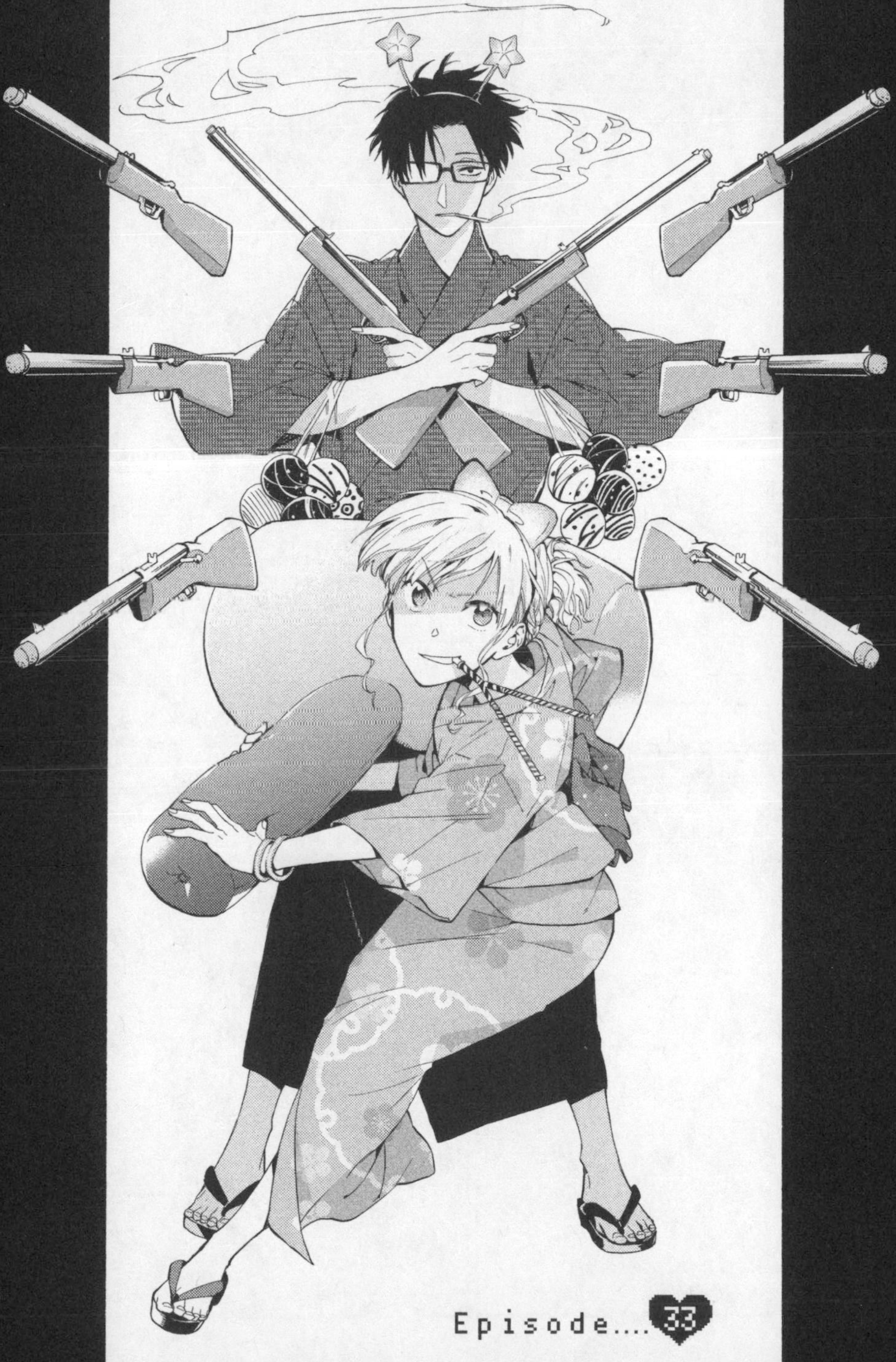
Episode....33

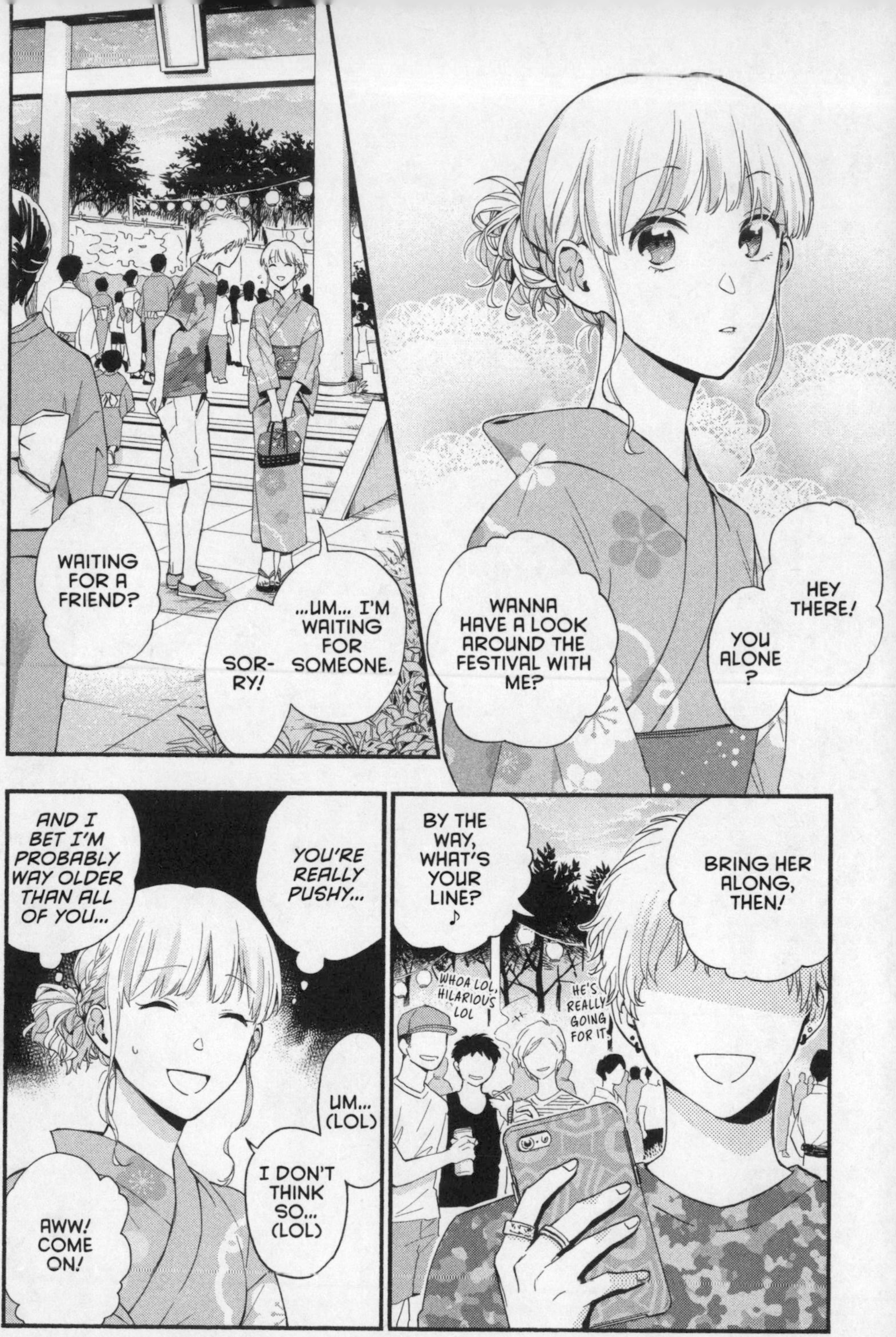
HEY THERE! YOU ALONE?
WANNA HAVE A LOOK AROUND THE FESTIVAL WITH ME?
...UM... I'M WAITING FOR SOMEONE.
SORRY!
WAITING FOR A FRIEND?
BRING HER ALONG, THEN!
BY THE WAY, WHAT'S YOUR LINE? ♪
HE'S REALLY GOING FOR IT.
WHOA LOL, HILARIOUS LOL
YOU'RE REALLY PUSHY...
AND I BET I'M PROBABLY WAY OLDER THAN ALL OF YOU...
UM... (LOL)
I DON'T THINK SO... (LOL)
AWW! COME ON!

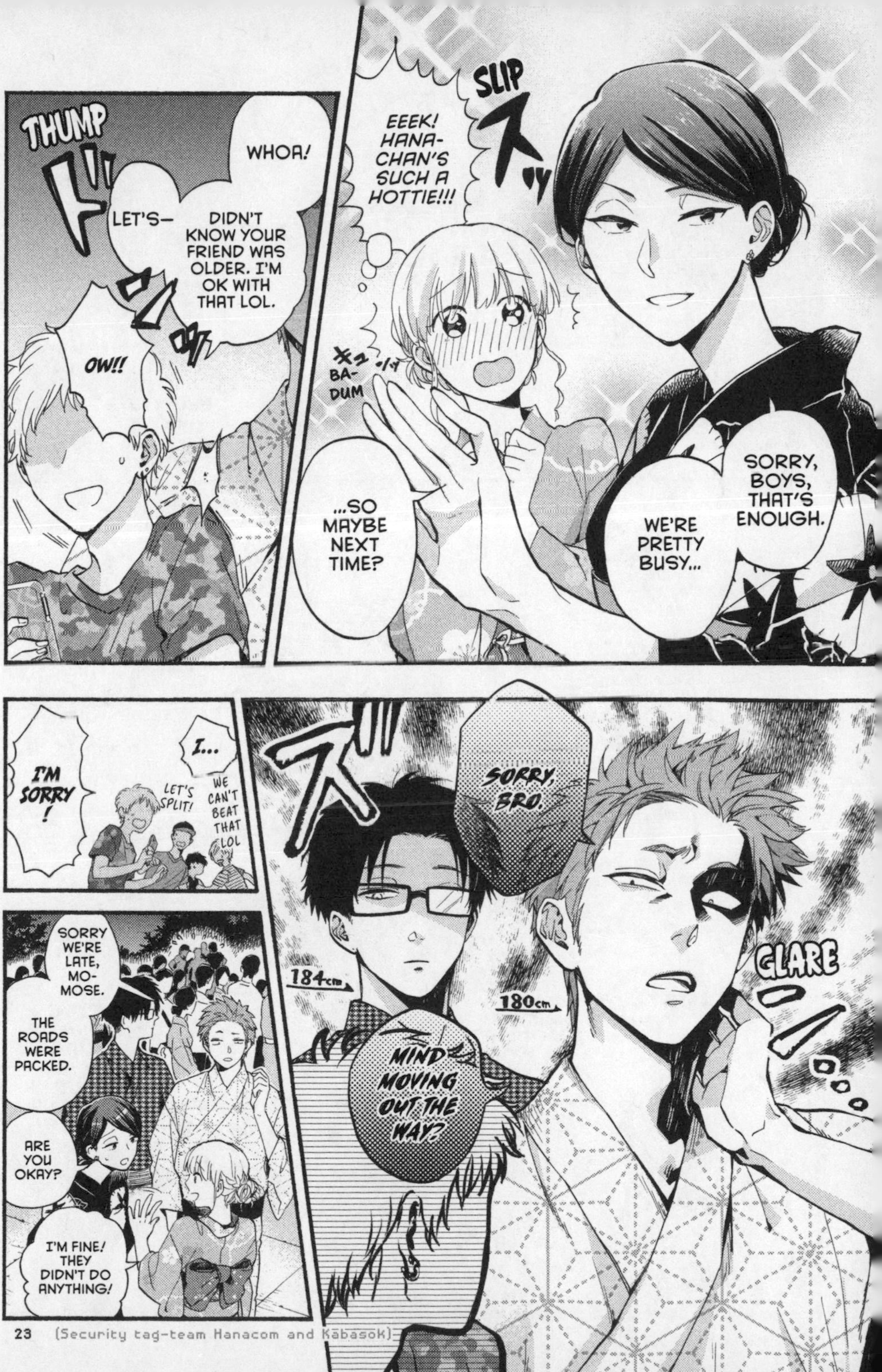
SLIP
EEEK! HANA-CHAN'S SUCH A HOTTIE!!!
SORRY, BOYS, THAT'S ENOUGH.
WE'RE PRETTY BUSY...
BA-DUM
...SO MAYBE NEXT TIME?
WHOA!
DIDN'T KNOW YOUR FRIEND WAS OLDER. I'M OK WITH THAT LOL.
THUMP
LET'S—
OW!!
SORRY, BRO.
GLARE
184cm
180cm
MIND MOVING OUT THE WAY?
I...
WE CAN'T BEAT THAT LOL
LET'S SPLIT!
I'M SORRY!
SORRY WE'RE LATE, MO-MOSE.
THE ROADS WERE PACKED.
ARE YOU OKAY?
I'M FINE! THEY DIDN'T DO ANYTHING!

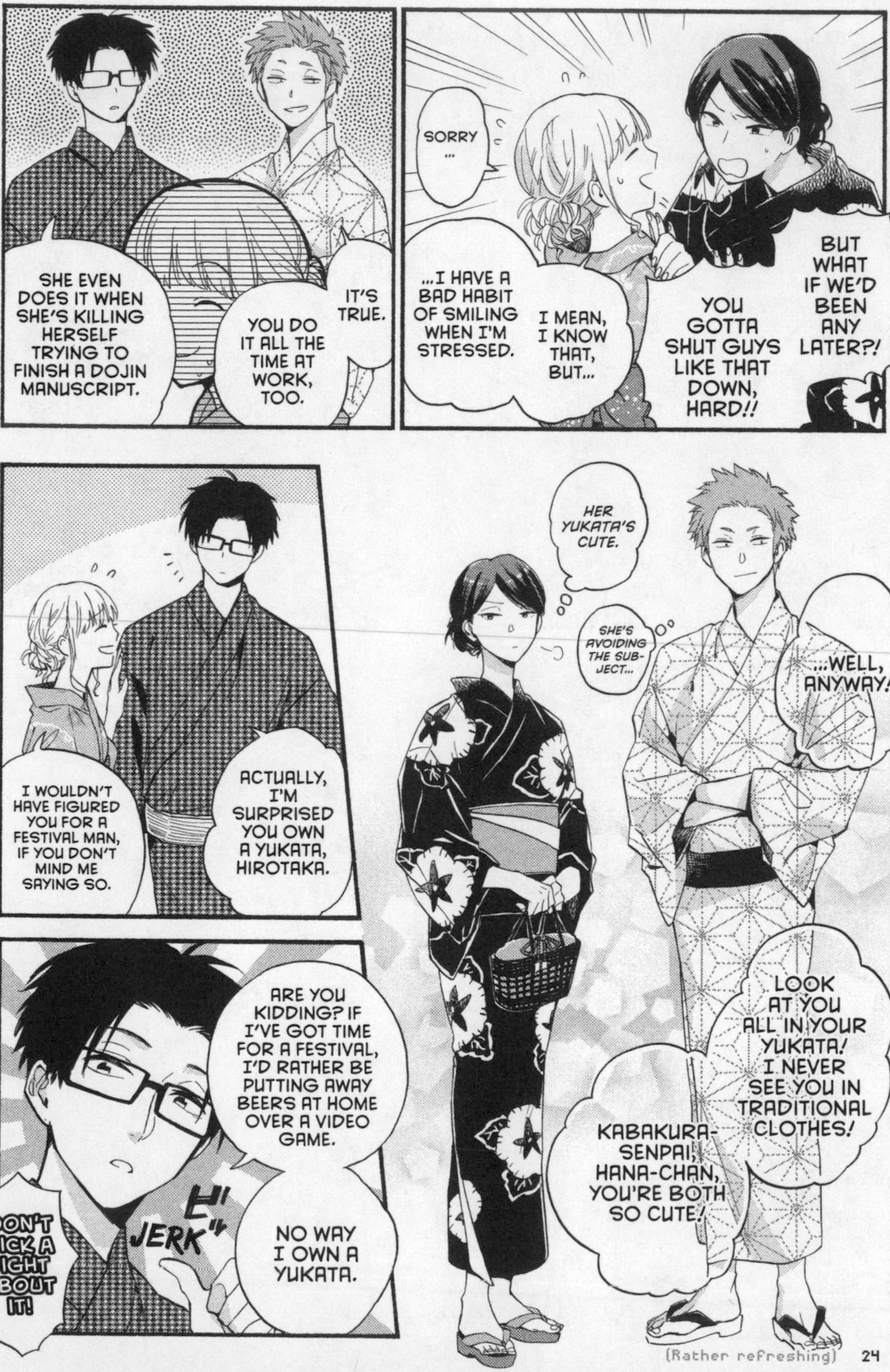
BUT WHAT IF WE'D BEEN ANY LATER?!
YOU GOTTA SHUT GUYS LIKE THAT DOWN, HARD!!
SORRY...
I MEAN, I KNOW THAT, BUT...
...I HAVE A BAD HABIT OF SMILING WHEN I'M STRESSED.
IT'S TRUE.
YOU DO IT ALL THE TIME AT WORK, TOO.
SHE EVEN DOES IT WHEN SHE'S KILLING HERSELF TRYING TO FINISH A DOJIN MANUSCRIPT.
HER YUKATA'S CUTE.
SHE'S AVOIDING THE SUB-JECT...
...WELL, ANYWAY!
LOOK AT YOU ALL IN YOUR YUKATA! I NEVER SEE YOU IN TRADITIONAL CLOTHES!
KABAKURA-SENPAI, HANA-CHAN, YOU'RE BOTH SO CUTE!
ACTUALLY, I'M SURPRISED YOU OWN A YUKATA, HIROTAKA.
I WOULDN'T HAVE FIGURED YOU FOR A FESTIVAL MAN, IF YOU DON'T MIND ME SAYING SO.
ARE YOU KIDDING? IF I'VE GOT TIME FOR A FESTIVAL, I'D RATHER BE PUTTING AWAY BEERS AT HOME OVER A VIDEO GAME.
NO WAY I OWN A YUKATA.
JERK
DON'T PICK A FIGHT ABOUT IT!

(Rather refreshing)

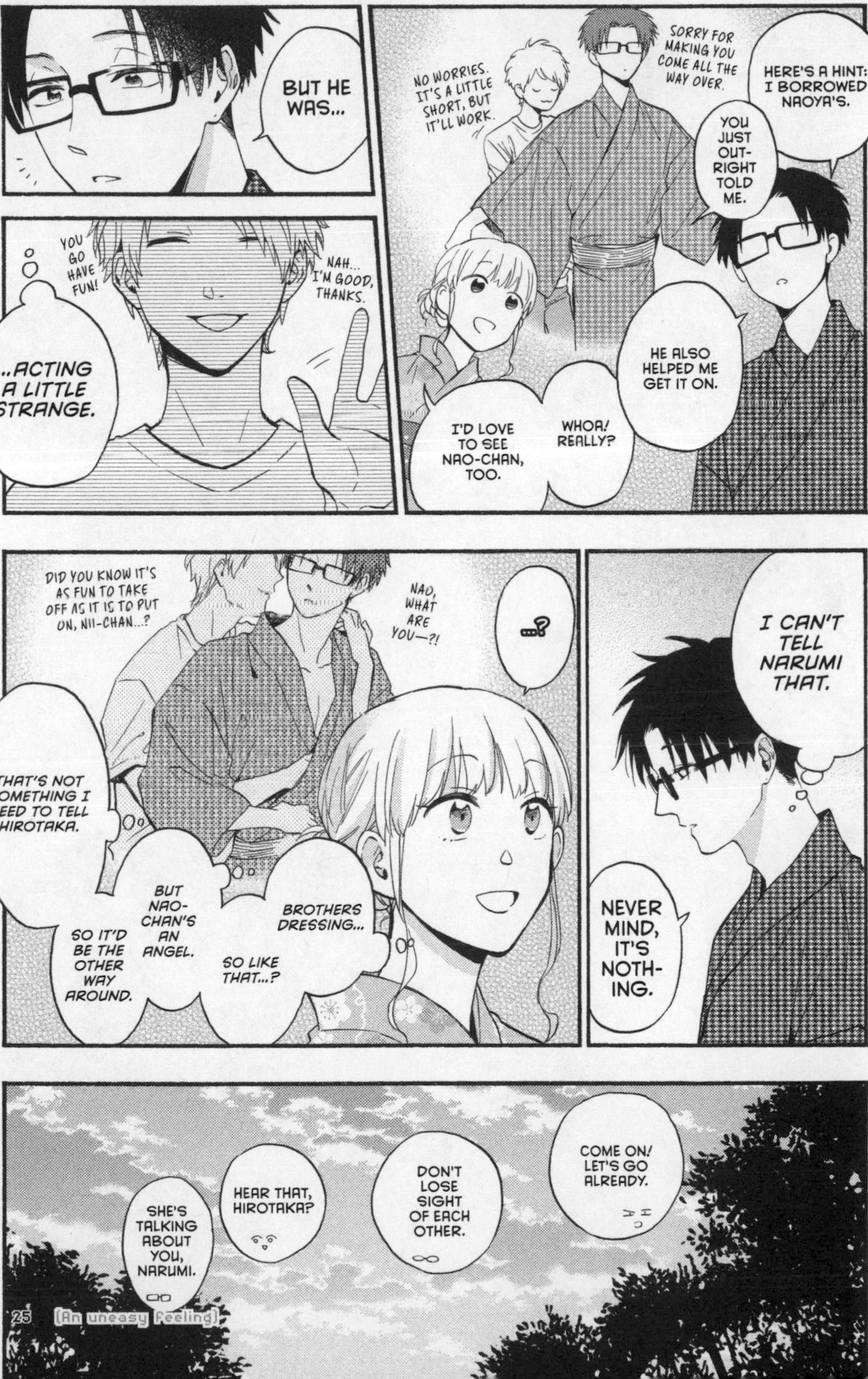
HERE'S A HINT: I BORROWED NAOYA'S.
YOU JUST OUT-RIGHT TOLD ME.
SORRY FOR MAKING YOU COME ALL THE WAY OVER.
NO WORRIES. IT'S A LITTLE SHORT, BUT IT'LL WORK.
HE ALSO HELPED ME GET IT ON.
WHOA! REALLY?
I'D LOVE TO SEE NAO-CHAN, TOO.
BUT HE WAS...
NAH... I'M GOOD, THANKS.
YOU GO HAVE FUN!
...ACTING A LITTLE STRANGE.
I CAN'T TELL NARUMI THAT.
NEVER MIND, IT'S NOTH-ING.
...?
NAO, WHAT ARE YOU—?!
DID YOU KNOW IT'S AS FUN TO TAKE OFF AS IT IS TO PUT ON, NII-CHAN...?
BROTHERS DRESSING...
SO LIKE THAT...?
BUT NAO-CHAN'S AN ANGEL.
SO IT'D BE THE OTHER WAY AROUND.
THAT'S NOT SOMETHING I NEED TO TELL HIROTAKA.
COME ON! LET'S GO ALREADY.
DON'T LOSE SIGHT OF EACH OTHER.
HEAR THAT, HIROTAKA?
SHE'S TALKING ABOUT YOU, NARUMI.

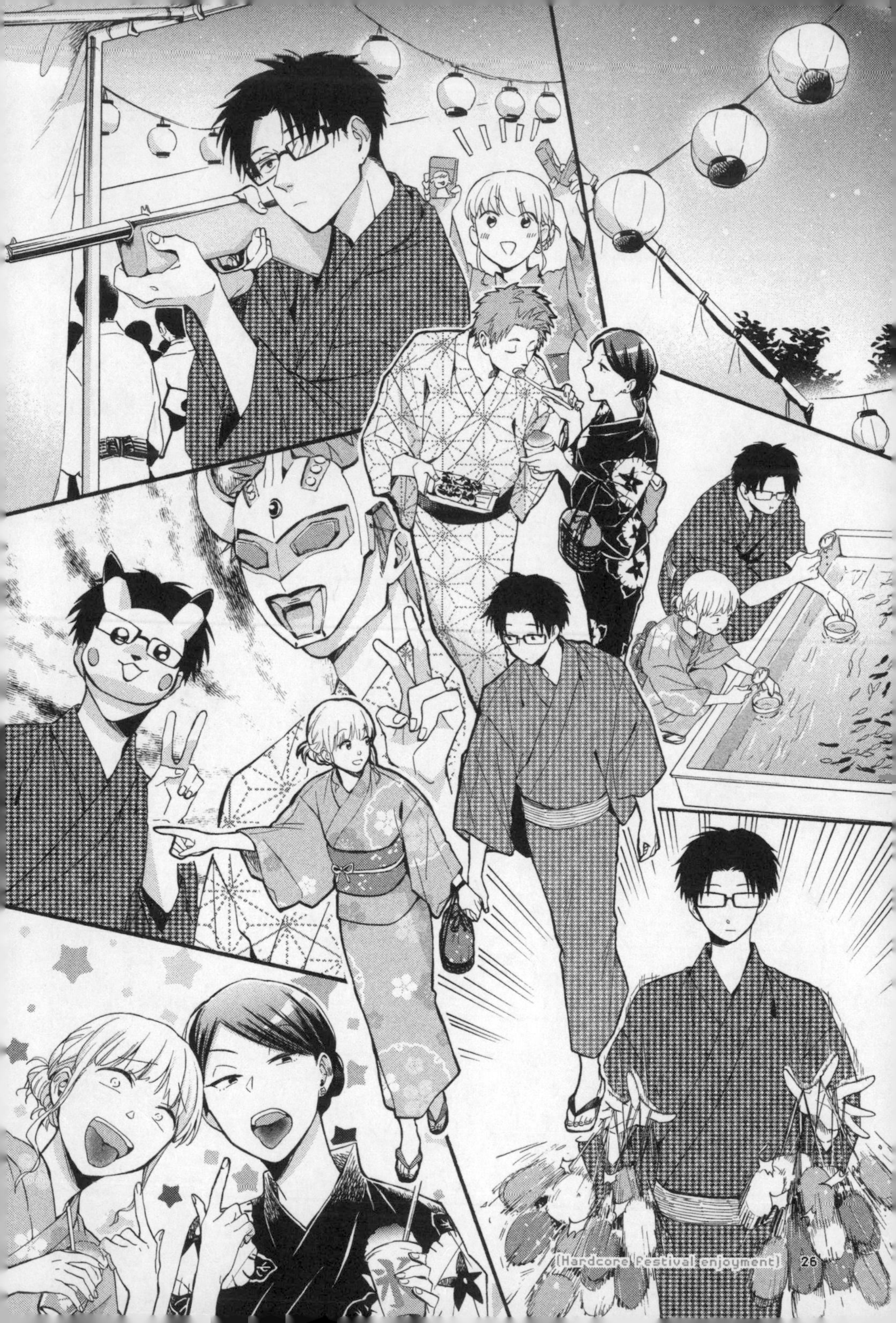
(Hardcore Festival enjoyment)

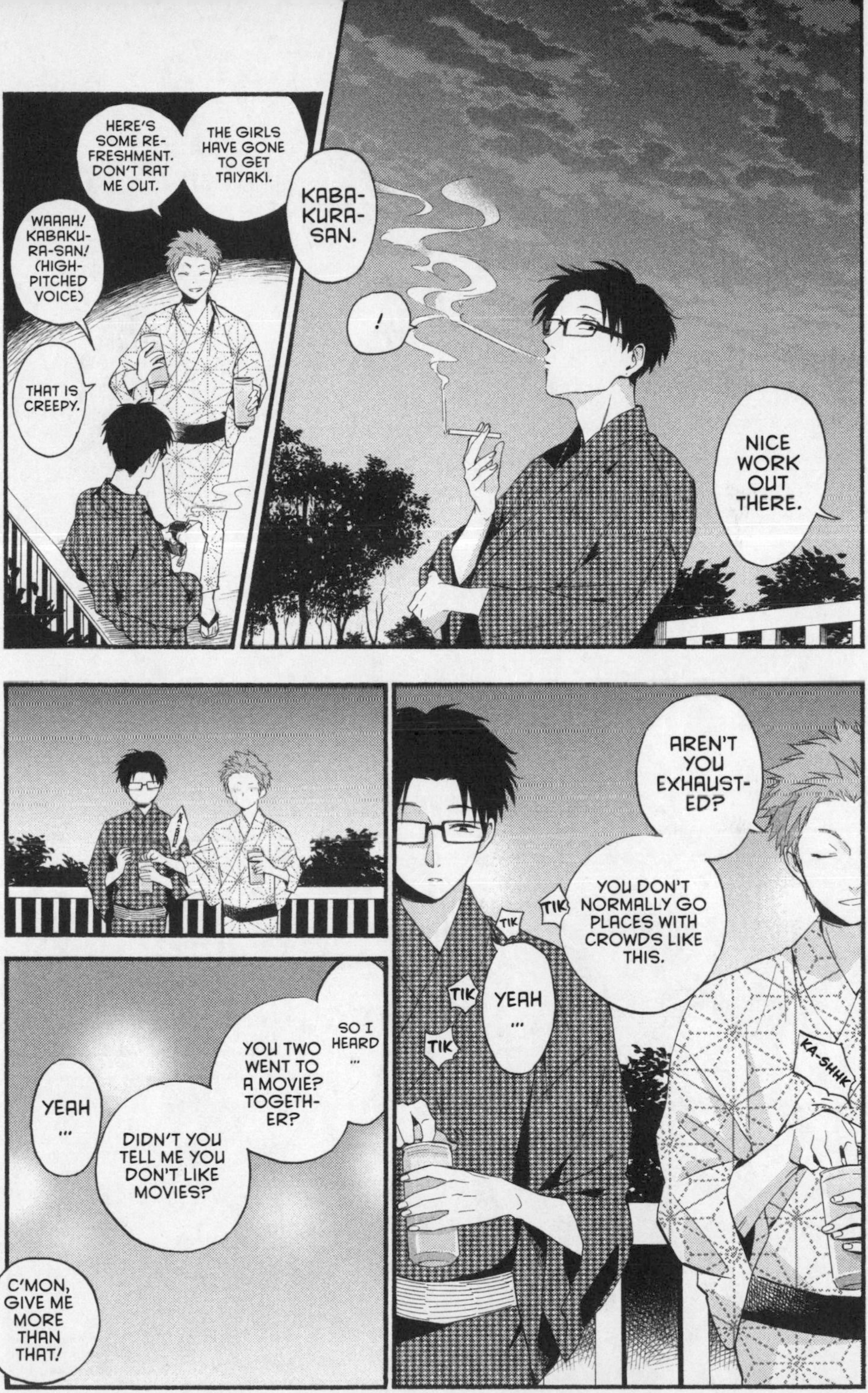
KABA-KURA-SAN.
!
NICE WORK OUT THERE.
THE GIRLS HAVE GONE TO GET TAIYAKI.
HERE'S SOME RE-FRESHMENT. DON'T RAT ME OUT.
WAAAH! KABAKU-RA-SAN! (HIGH-PITCHED VOICE)
THAT IS CREEPY.
AREN'T YOU EXHAUST-ED?
YOU DON'T NORMALLY GO PLACES WITH CROWDS LIKE THIS.
TIK
TIK
YEAH ...
TIK
TIK
KA-SHHK
SO I HEARD ...
YOU TWO WENT TO A MOVIE? TOGETH-ER?
YEAH ...
DIDN'T YOU TELL ME YOU DON'T LIKE MOVIES?
C'MON, GIVE ME MORE THAN THAT!

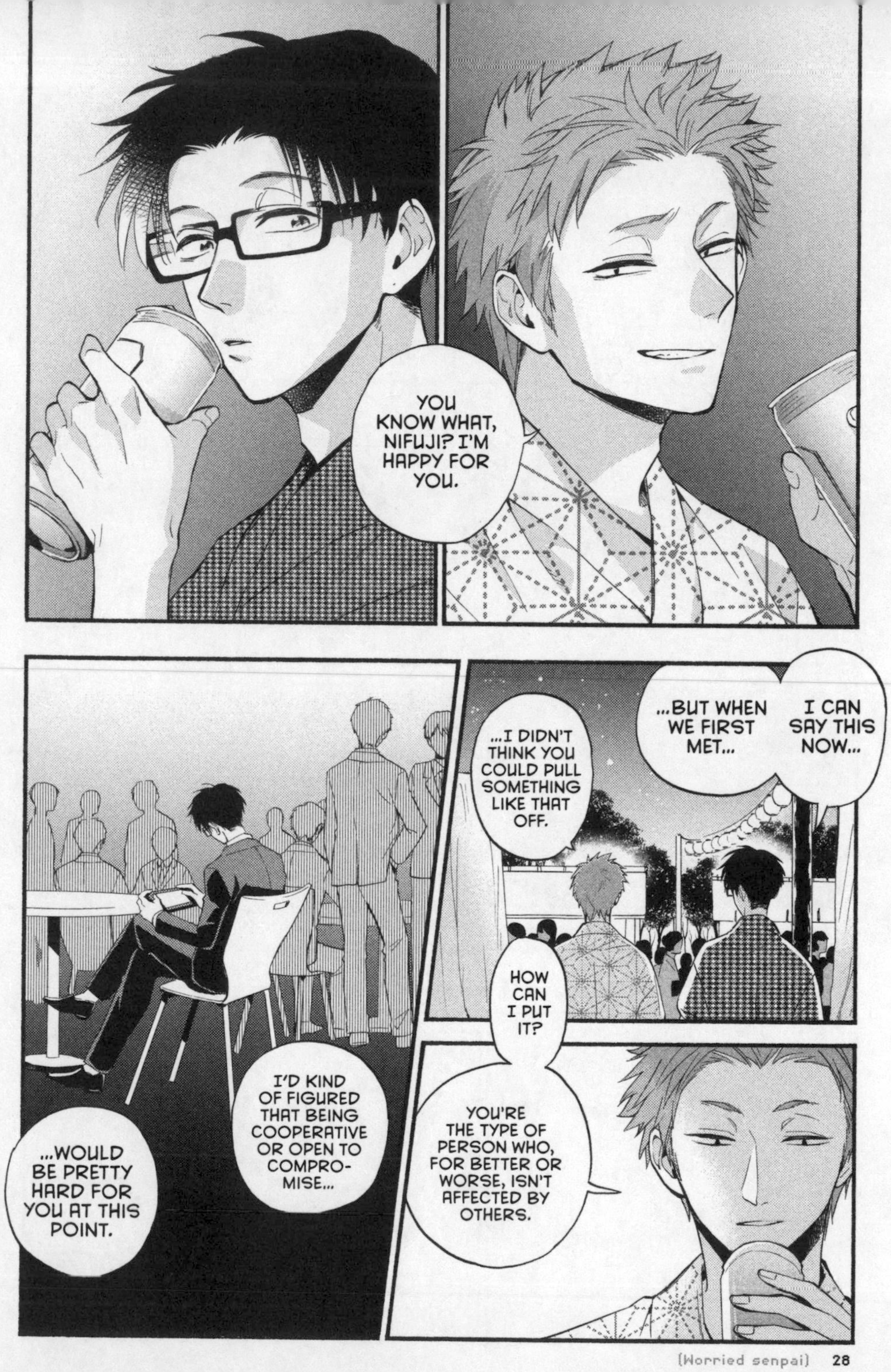
YOU KNOW WHAT, NIFUJI? I'M HAPPY FOR YOU.
I CAN SAY THIS NOW...
...BUT WHEN WE FIRST MET...
...I DIDN'T THINK YOU COULD PULL SOMETHING LIKE THAT OFF.
HOW CAN I PUT IT?
YOU'RE THE TYPE OF PERSON WHO, FOR BETTER OR WORSE, ISN'T AFFECTED BY OTHERS.
I'D KIND OF FIGURED THAT BEING COOPERATIVE OR OPEN TO COMPROMISE...
...WOULD BE PRETTY HARD FOR YOU AT THIS POINT.

(Worried senpai)

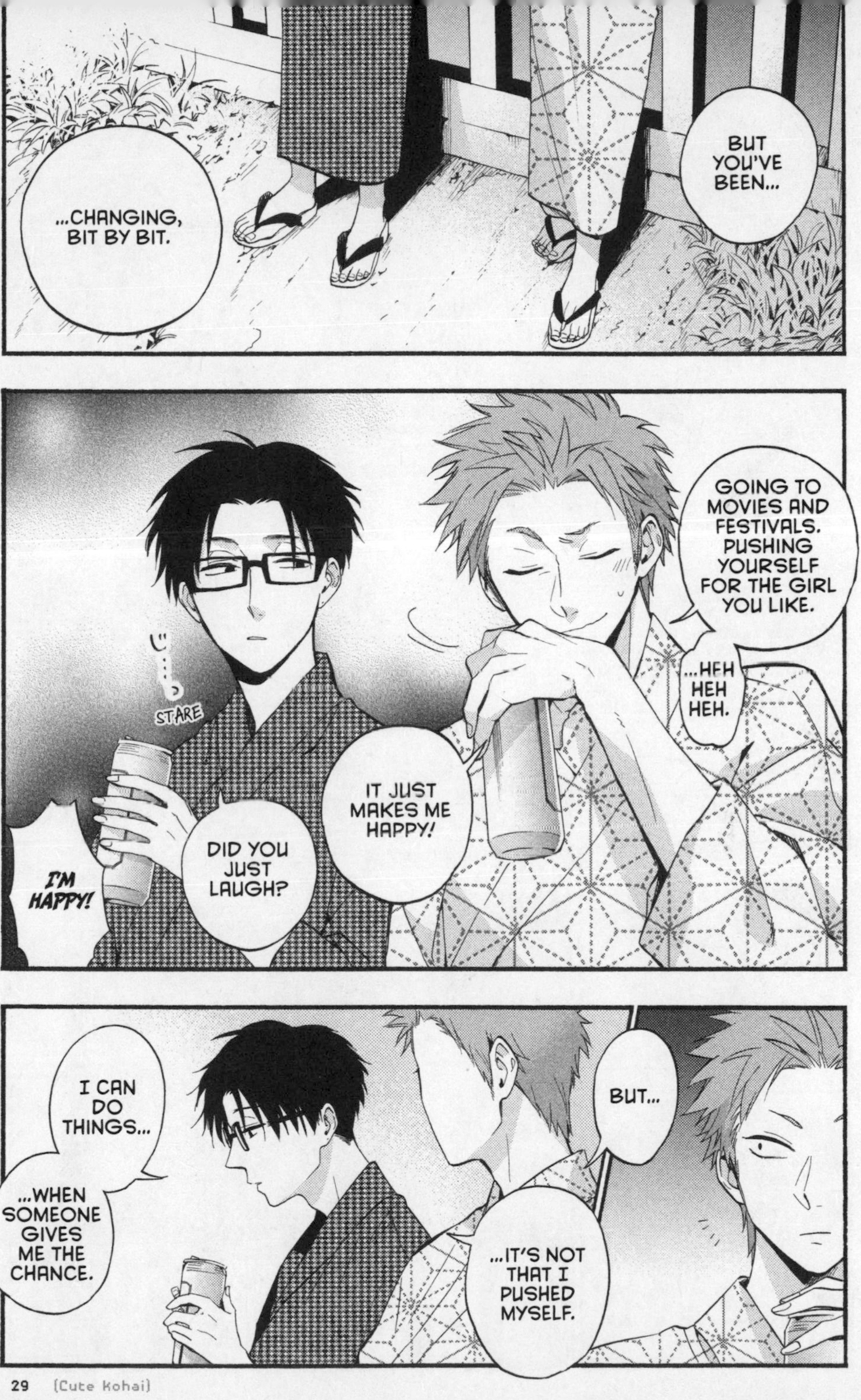
BUT YOU'VE BEEN...
...CHANGING, BIT BY BIT.
GOING TO MOVIES AND FESTIVALS. PUSHING YOURSELF FOR THE GIRL YOU LIKE.
...HEH HEH HEH.
IT JUST MAKES ME HAPPY!
STARE
DID YOU JUST LAUGH?
I'M HAPPY!
BUT...
...IT'S NOT THAT I PUSHED MYSELF.
I CAN DO THINGS...
...WHEN SOMEONE GIVES ME THE CHANCE.

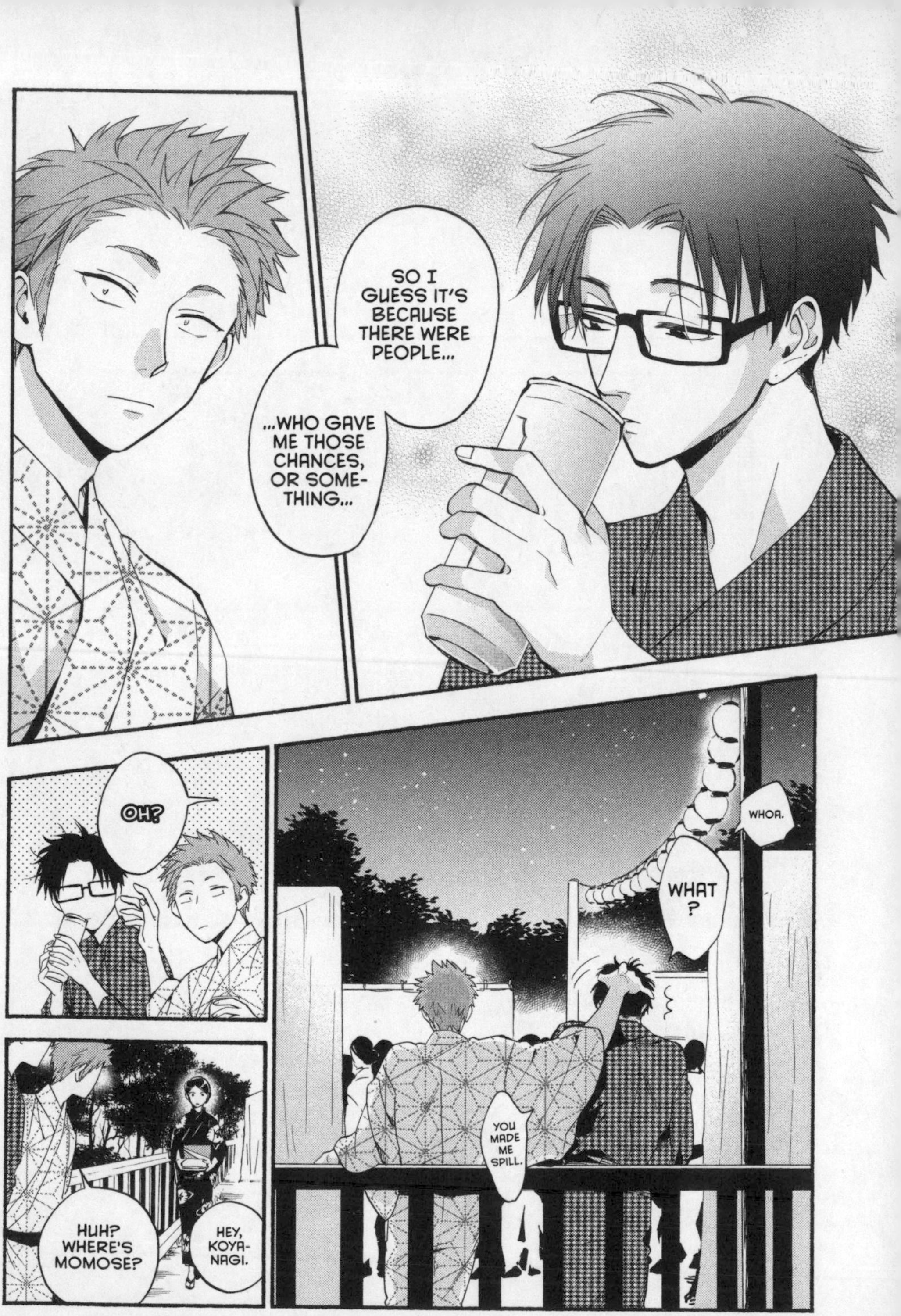
SO I GUESS IT'S BECAUSE THERE WERE PEOPLE...
...WHO GAVE ME THOSE CHANCES, OR SOME-THING...
WHOA.
WHAT?
YOU MADE ME SPILL.
OH?
HEY, KOYA-NAGI.
HUH? WHERE'S MOMOSE?

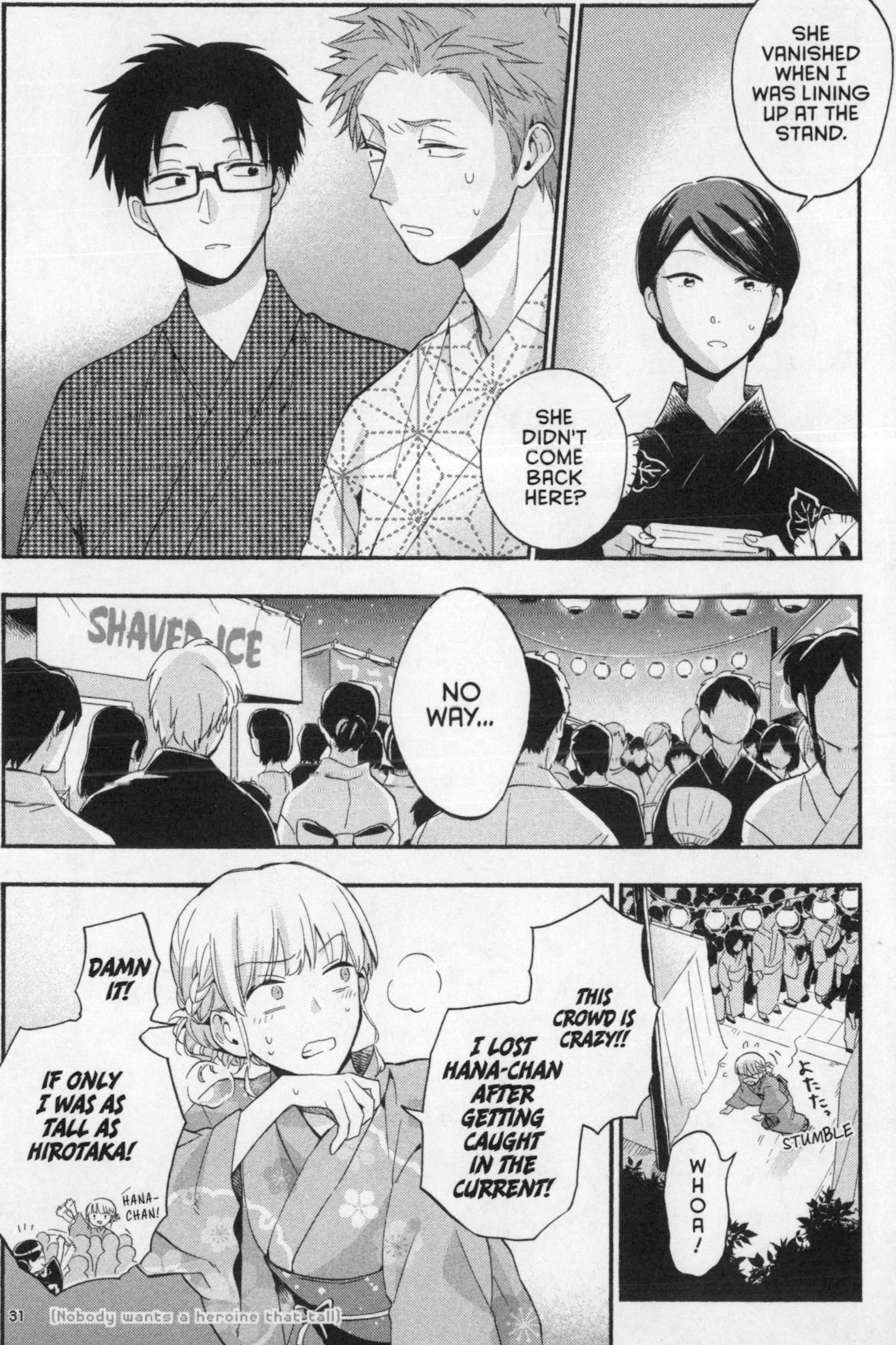
SHE VANISHED WHEN I WAS LINING UP AT THE STAND.
SHE DIDN'T COME BACK HERE?
NO WAY...
SHAVED ICE
よたたっ
STUMBLE
WHOA!
THIS CROWD IS CRAZY!!
I LOST HANA-CHAN AFTER GETTING CAUGHT IN THE CURRENT!
DAMN IT!
IF ONLY I WAS AS TALL AS HIROTAKA!
HANA-CHAN!

(Nobody wants a heroine that tall)

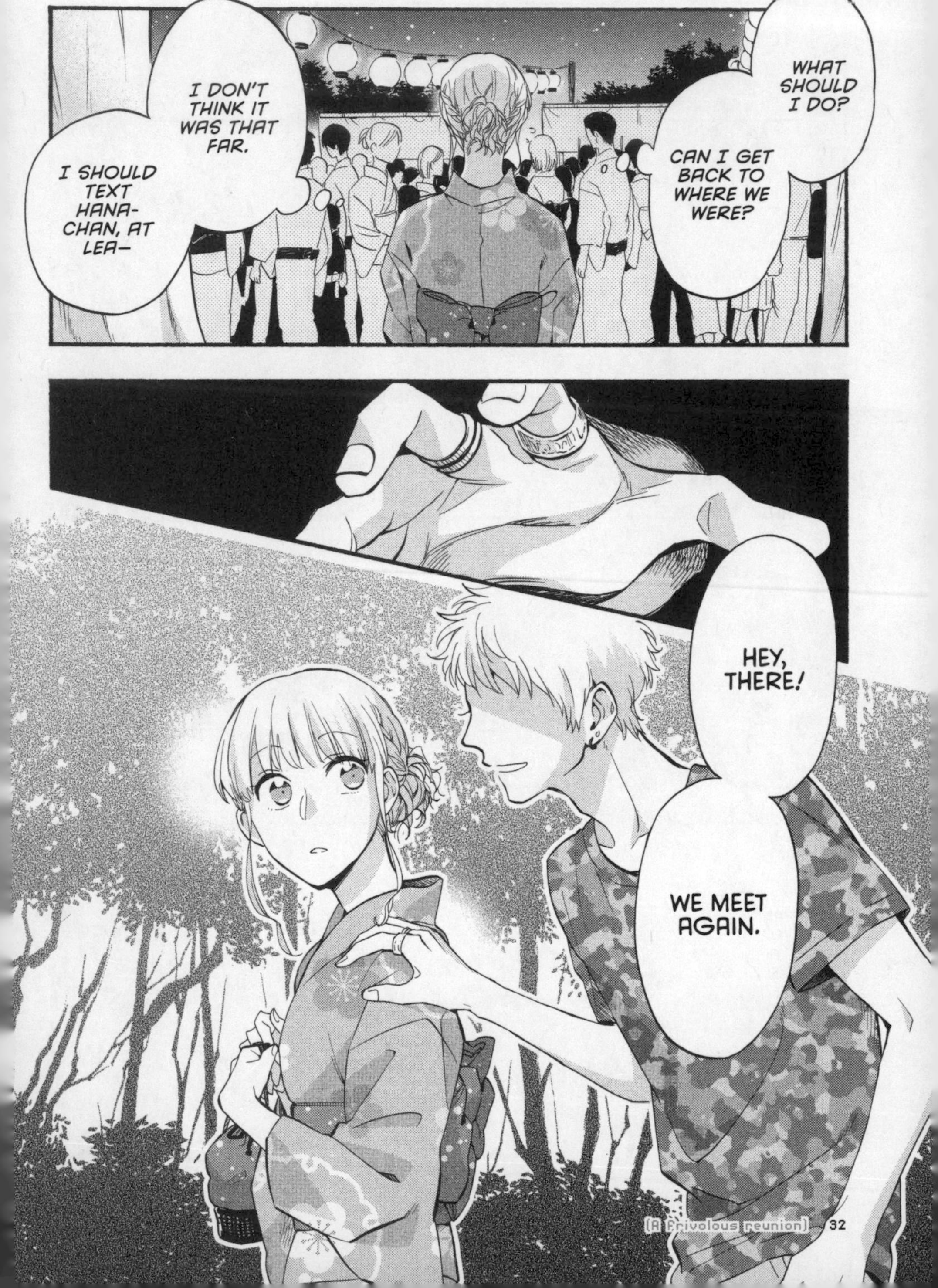
WHAT SHOULD I DO?
CAN I GET BACK TO WHERE WE WERE?
I DON'T THINK IT WAS THAT FAR.
I SHOULD TEXT HANA-CHAN, AT LEA—
HEY, THERE!
WE MEET AGAIN.
[A frivolous reunion]

CHARACTERS

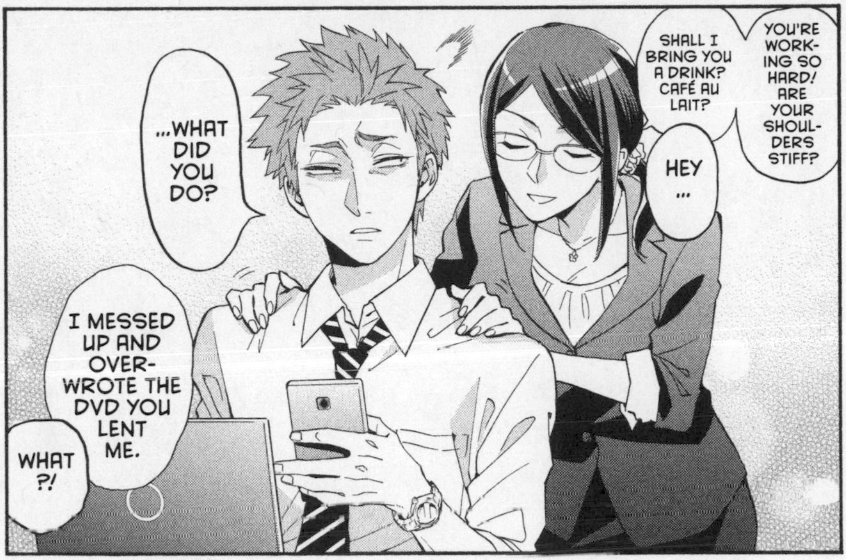
YOU'RE WORKING SO HARD! ARE YOUR SHOULDERS STIFF?
SHALL I BRING YOU A DRINK? CAFÉ AU LAIT?
HEY ...
...WHAT DID YOU DO?
I MESSED UP AND OVERWROTE THE DVD YOU LENT ME.
WHAT ?!

▼ FAN REQUEST

"KABAKURA GETTING CREEPED OUT BECAUSE KOYANAGI IS ACTING STRANGELY NICE."

☞ TARO KABAKURA

- ANIME OTAKU.
- FORGIVES EASILY WHEN PEOPLE APOLOGIZE TO HIM—BUT THERE ARE SOME THINGS THAT A MAN CANNOT FORGIVE.
- SURPRISINGLY, HE DOESN'T MAKE MANY MISTAKES. (HE'D BE EMBARRASSED BY THEM)

☞ HANAKO KOYANAGI

- CROSSPLAYER.
- WHEN SHE ACTS NICE TO KABAKURA, 90% OF THE TIME IT'S BECAUSE IT'S JUST BEFORE PAYDAY OR BECAUSE SHE DID SOMETHING.
- SURPRISINGLY, SHE MAKES A LOT OF CARELESS MISTAKES.

SKETCHES FROM BEFORE VOLUME 2.

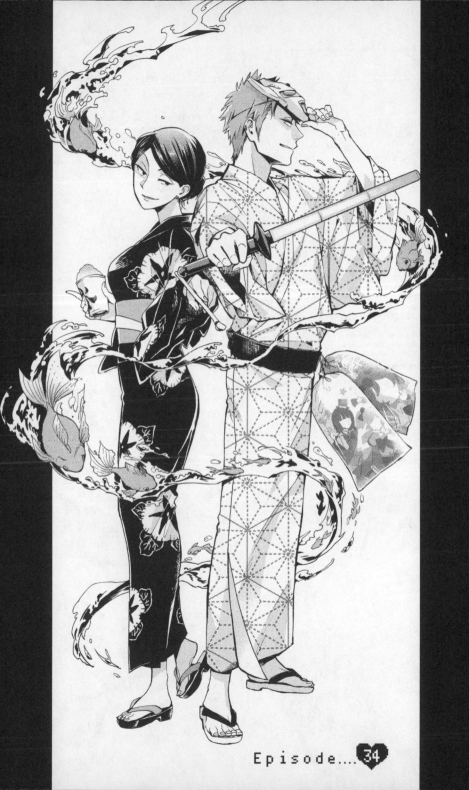

Episode....34

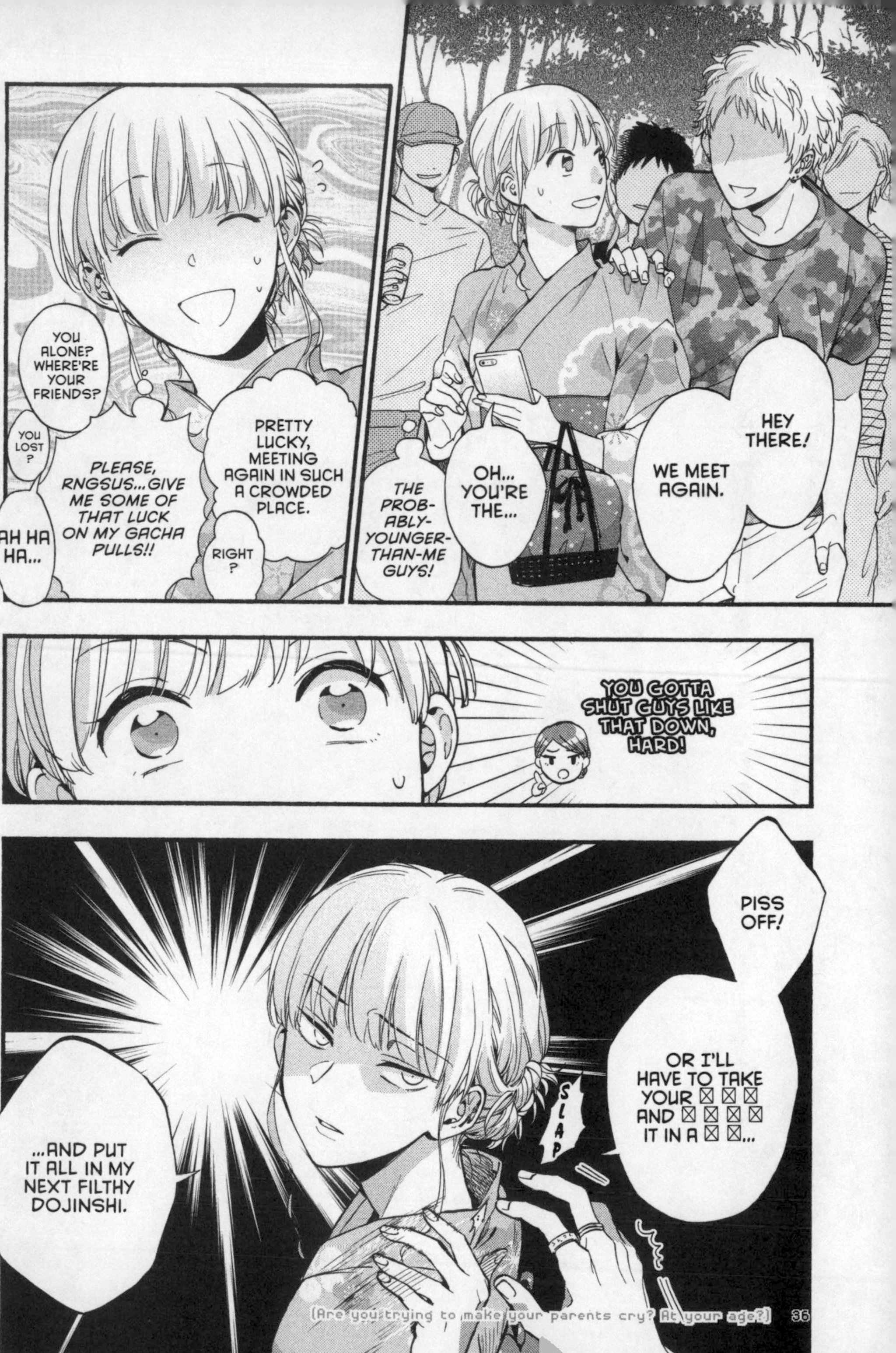
HEY THERE!
WE MEET AGAIN.
OH... YOU'RE THE...
THE PROBABLY-YOUNGER-THAN-ME GUYS!
PRETTY LUCKY, MEETING AGAIN IN SUCH A CROWDED PLACE.
RIGHT?
YOU ALONE? WHERE'RE YOUR FRIENDS?
YOU LOST?
PLEASE, RNGSUS...GIVE ME SOME OF THAT LUCK ON MY GACHA PULLS!!
AH HA HA...
YOU GOTTA SHUT GUYS LIKE THAT DOWN, HARD!
PISS OFF!
OR I'LL HAVE TO TAKE YOUR ☒☒☒ AND ☒☒☒☒ IT IN A ☒☒...
SLAP
...AND PUT IT ALL IN MY NEXT FILTHY DOJINSHI.
(Are you trying to make your parents cry? At your age?)

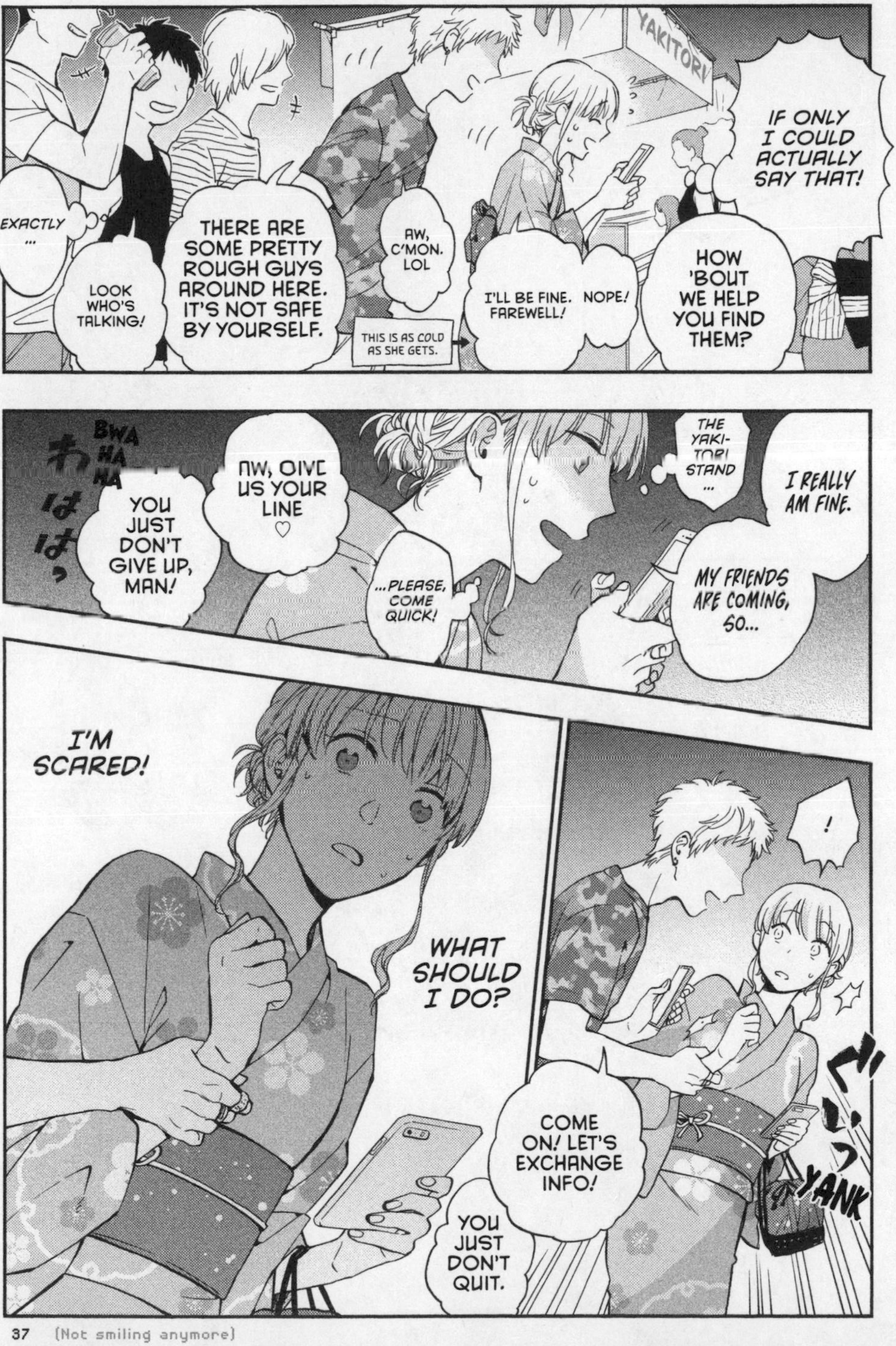
YAKITORI
IF ONLY I COULD ACTUALLY SAY THAT!
HOW 'BOUT WE HELP YOU FIND THEM?
NOPE!
I'LL BE FINE. FAREWELL!
THIS IS AS COLD AS SHE GETS.
AW, C'MON. LOL
THERE ARE SOME PRETTY ROUGH GUYS AROUND HERE. IT'S NOT SAFE BY YOURSELF.
LOOK WHO'S TALKING!
EXACTLY ...
I REALLY AM FINE.
MY FRIENDS ARE COMING, SO...
THE YAKITORI STAND ...
...PLEASE, COME QUICK!
AW, GIVE US YOUR LINE ♡
YOU JUST DON'T GIVE UP, MAN!
わははっ
BWA HA HA
!
ぐいっ
YANK
COME ON! LET'S EXCHANGE INFO!
YOU JUST DON'T QUIT.
WHAT SHOULD I DO?
I'M SCARED!

(Not smiling anymore)

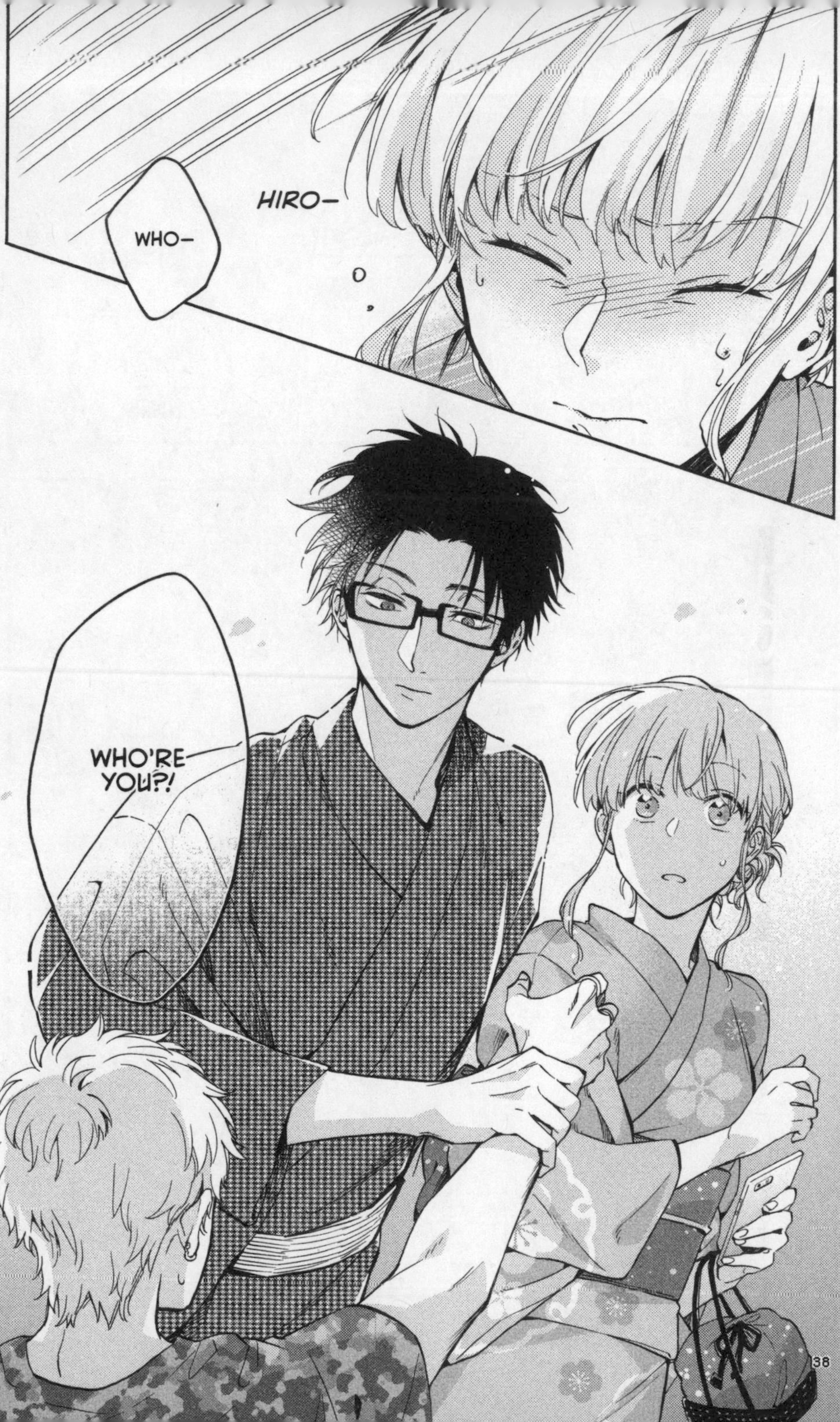
HIRO—
WHO—
WHO'RE YOU?!

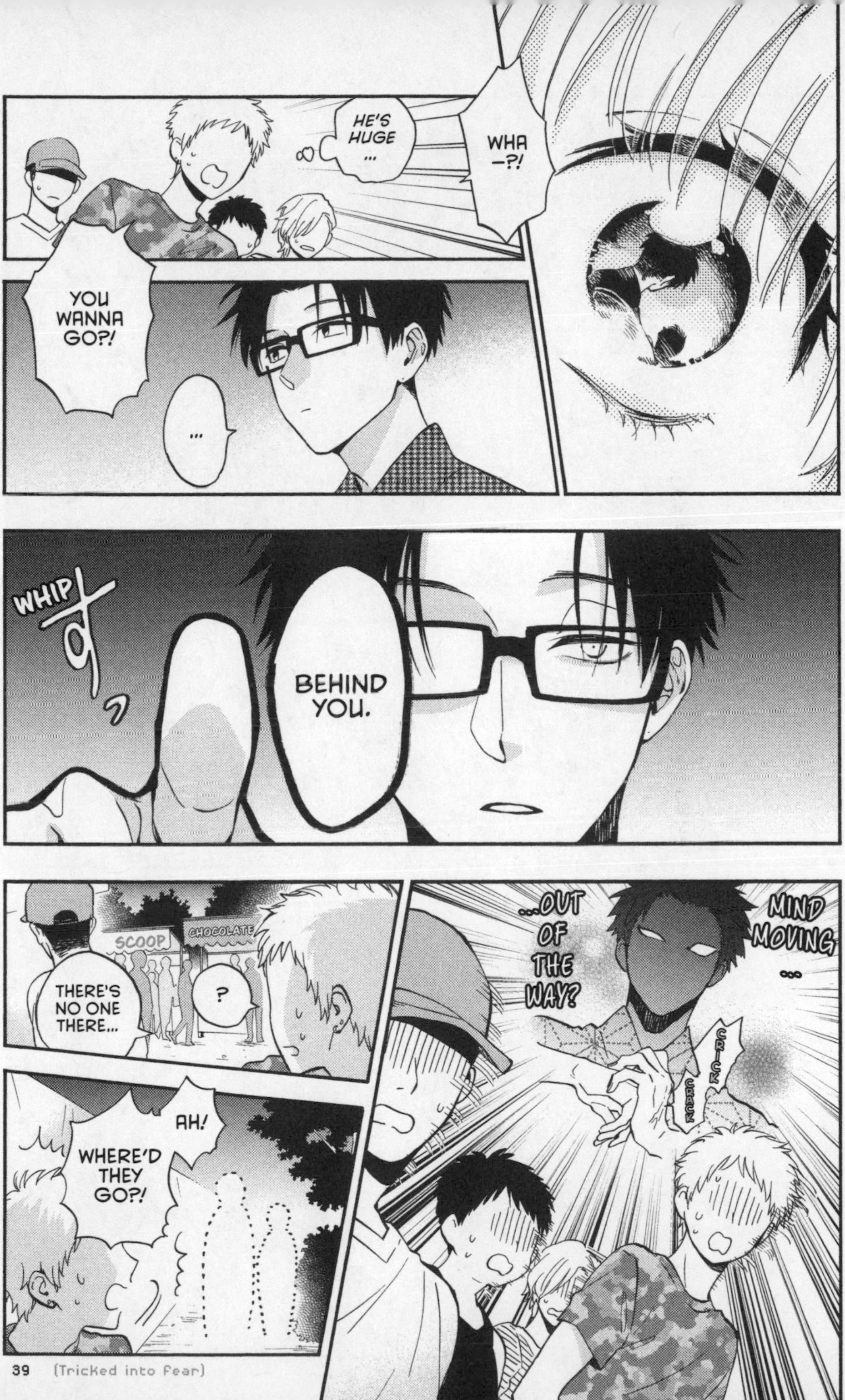
WHA —?!
HE'S HUGE ...
YOU WANNA GO?!
...
WHIP
す
BEHIND YOU.
MIND MOVING ...
...OUT OF THE WAY?
CRICK
CRACK
CHOCOLATE
SCOOP
THERE'S NO ONE THERE...
?
AH!
WHERE'D THEY GO?!

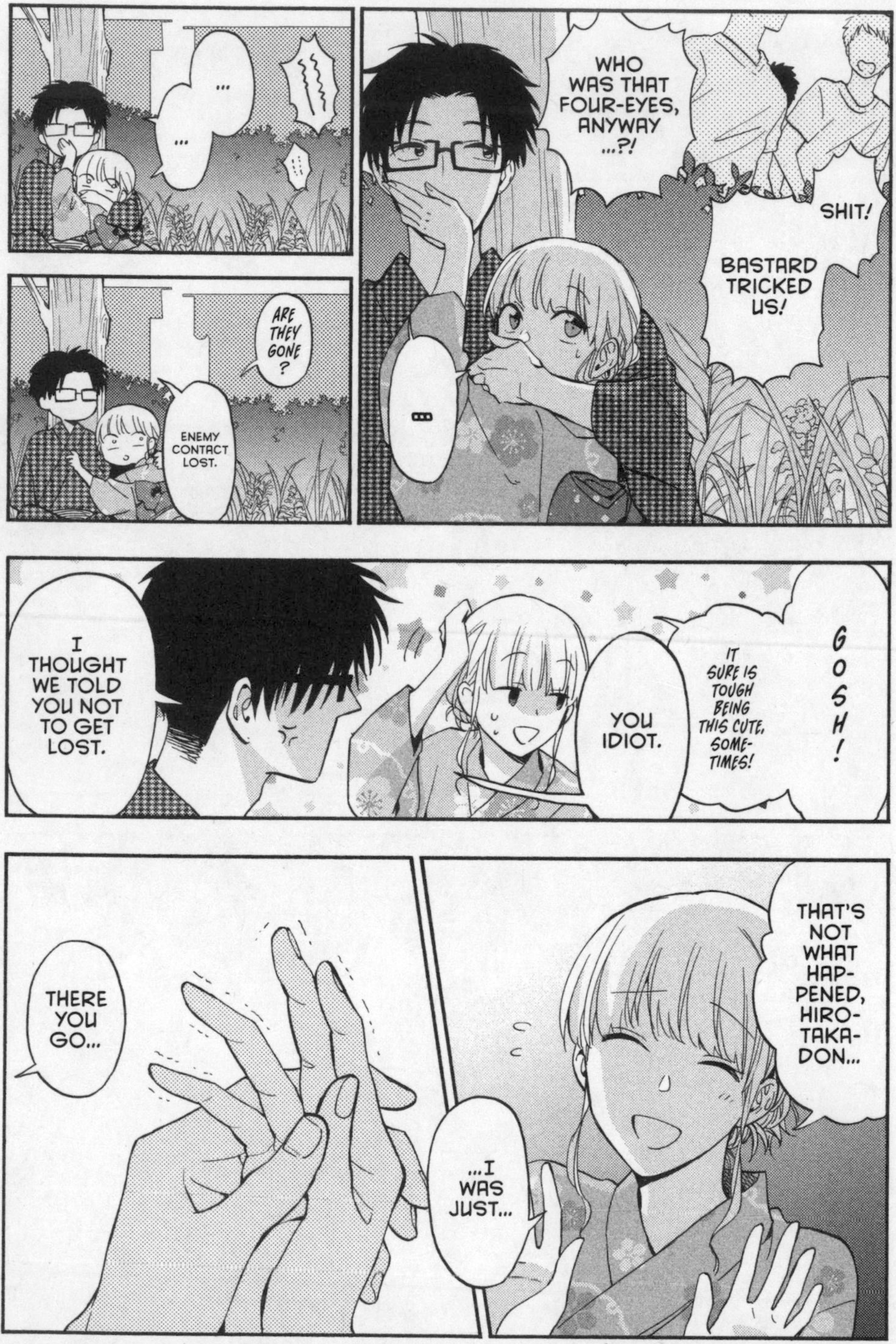
WHO WAS THAT FOUR-EYES, ANYWAY ...?!
SHIT!
BASTARD TRICKED US!
...
...
...
ARE THEY GONE?
ENEMY CONTACT LOST.
GOSH!
IT SURE IS TOUGH BEING THIS CUTE, SOME-TIMES!
YOU IDIOT.
I THOUGHT WE TOLD YOU NOT TO GET LOST.
THAT'S NOT WHAT HAP-PENED, HIRO-TAKA-DON...
...I WAS JUST...
THERE YOU GO...

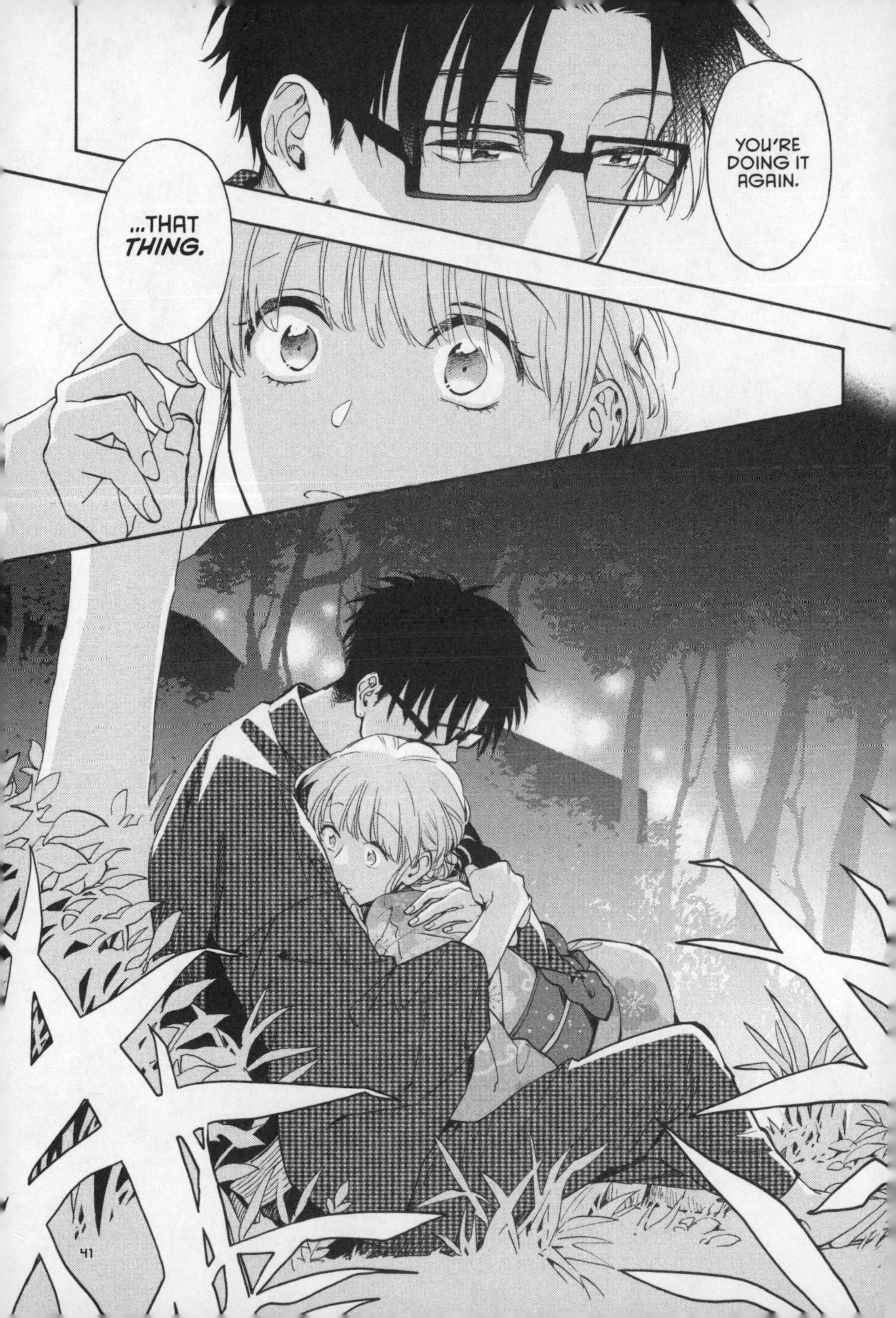
YOU'RE DOING IT AGAIN.
...THAT *THING.*

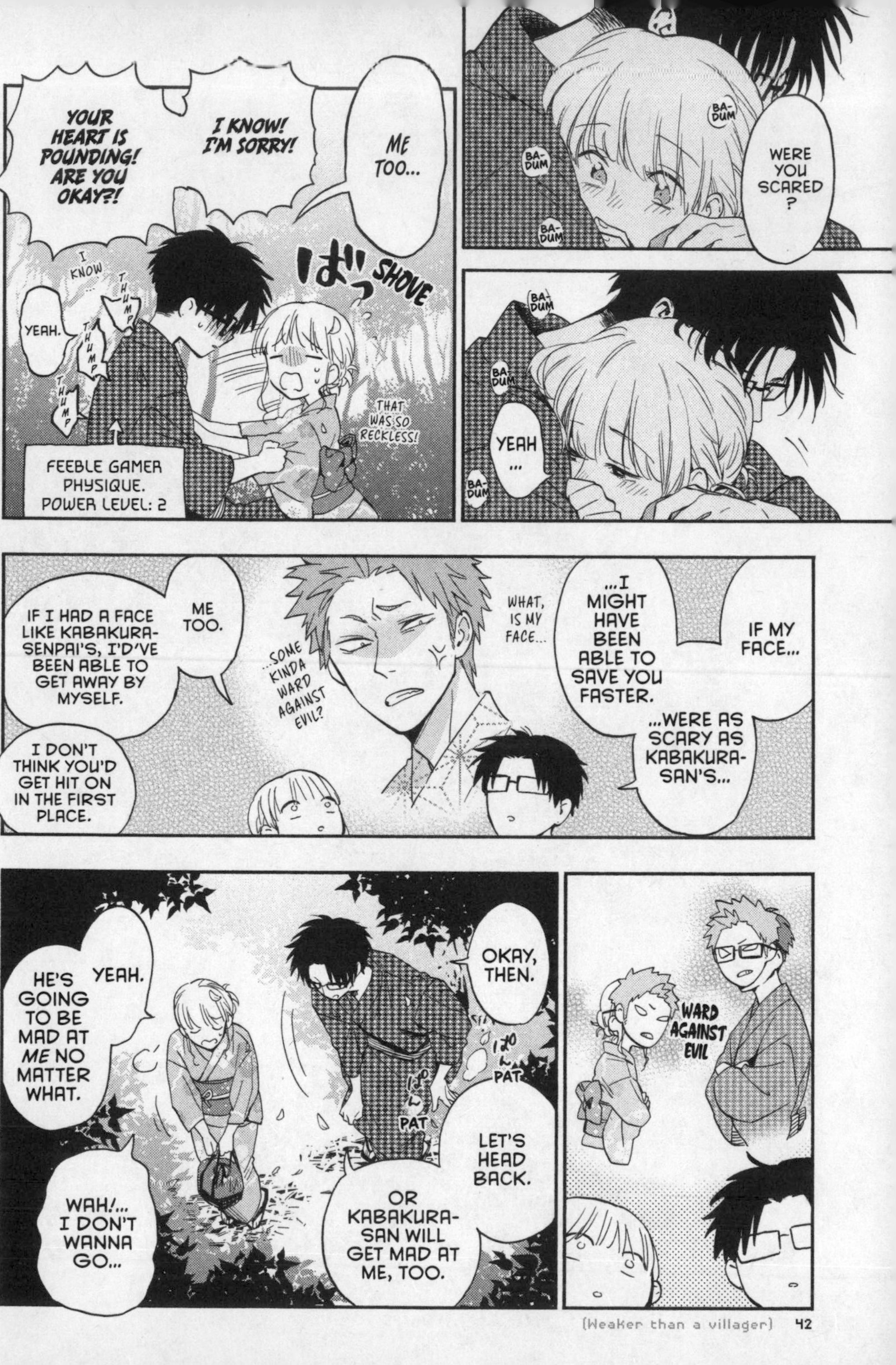
BA-DUM
BA-DUM
BA-DUM
WERE YOU SCARED?
BA-DUM
BA-DUM
BA-DUM
YEAH...
ME TOO...
I KNOW! I'M SORRY!
YOUR HEART IS POUNDING! ARE YOU OKAY?!
ばっ SHOVE
THAT WAS SO RECKLESS!
I KNOW...
THUMP THUMP THUMP
YEAH.
FEEBLE GAMER PHYSIQUE. POWER LEVEL: 2
IF MY FACE...
...WERE AS SCARY AS KABAKURA-SAN'S...
...I MIGHT HAVE BEEN ABLE TO SAVE YOU FASTER.
WHAT, IS MY FACE...
...SOME KINDA WARD AGAINST EVIL?
ME TOO.
IF I HAD A FACE LIKE KABAKURA-SENPAI'S, I'D'VE BEEN ABLE TO GET AWAY BY MYSELF.
I DON'T THINK YOU'D GET HIT ON IN THE FIRST PLACE.
WARD AGAINST EVIL
OKAY, THEN.
PAT
PAT
LET'S HEAD BACK.
OR KABAKURA-SAN WILL GET MAD AT ME, TOO.
YEAH.
HE'S GOING TO BE MAD AT ME NO MATTER WHAT.
WAH!... I DON'T WANNA GO...

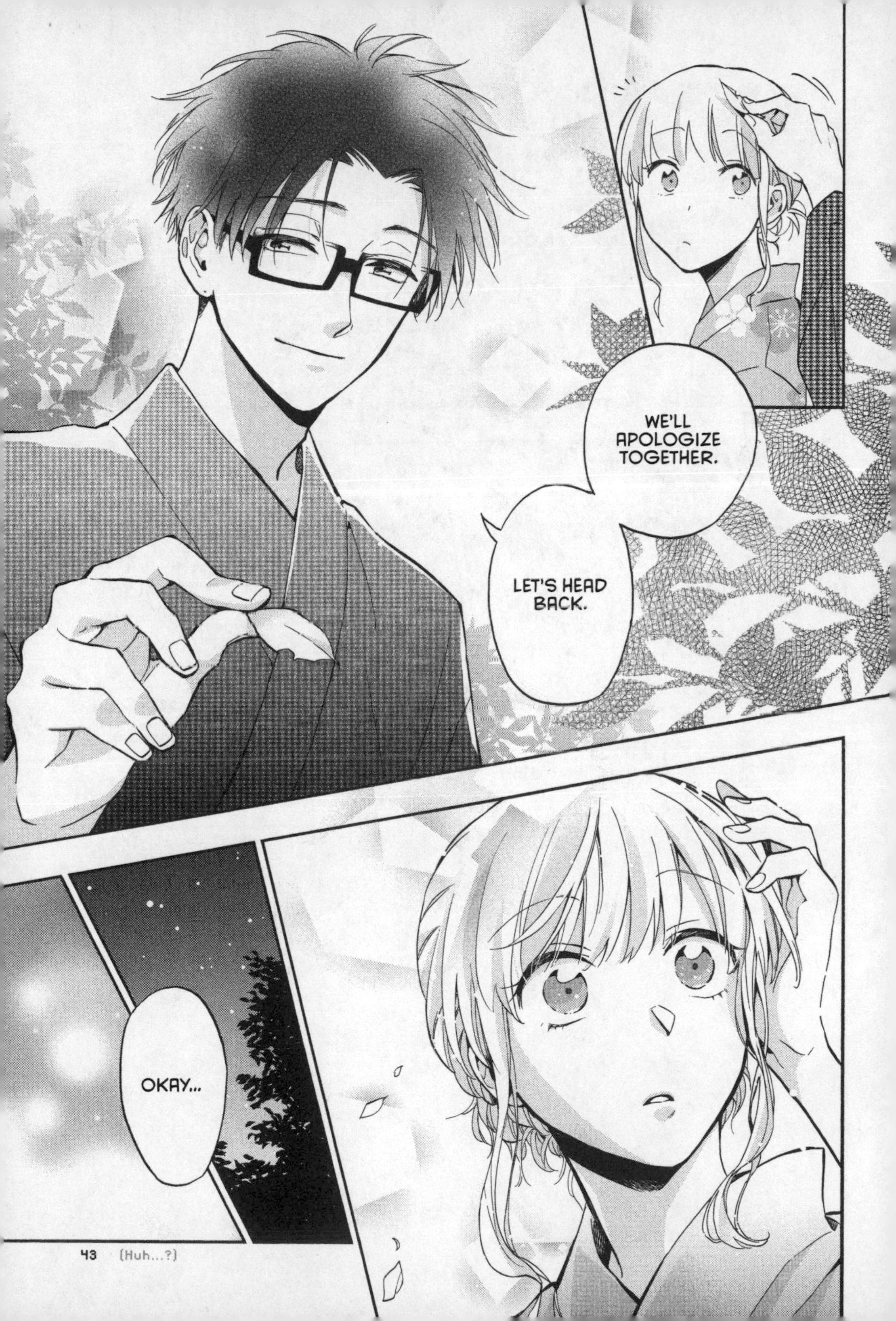
WE'LL APOLOGIZE TOGETHER.
LET'S HEAD BACK.
OKAY...
(Huh...?)

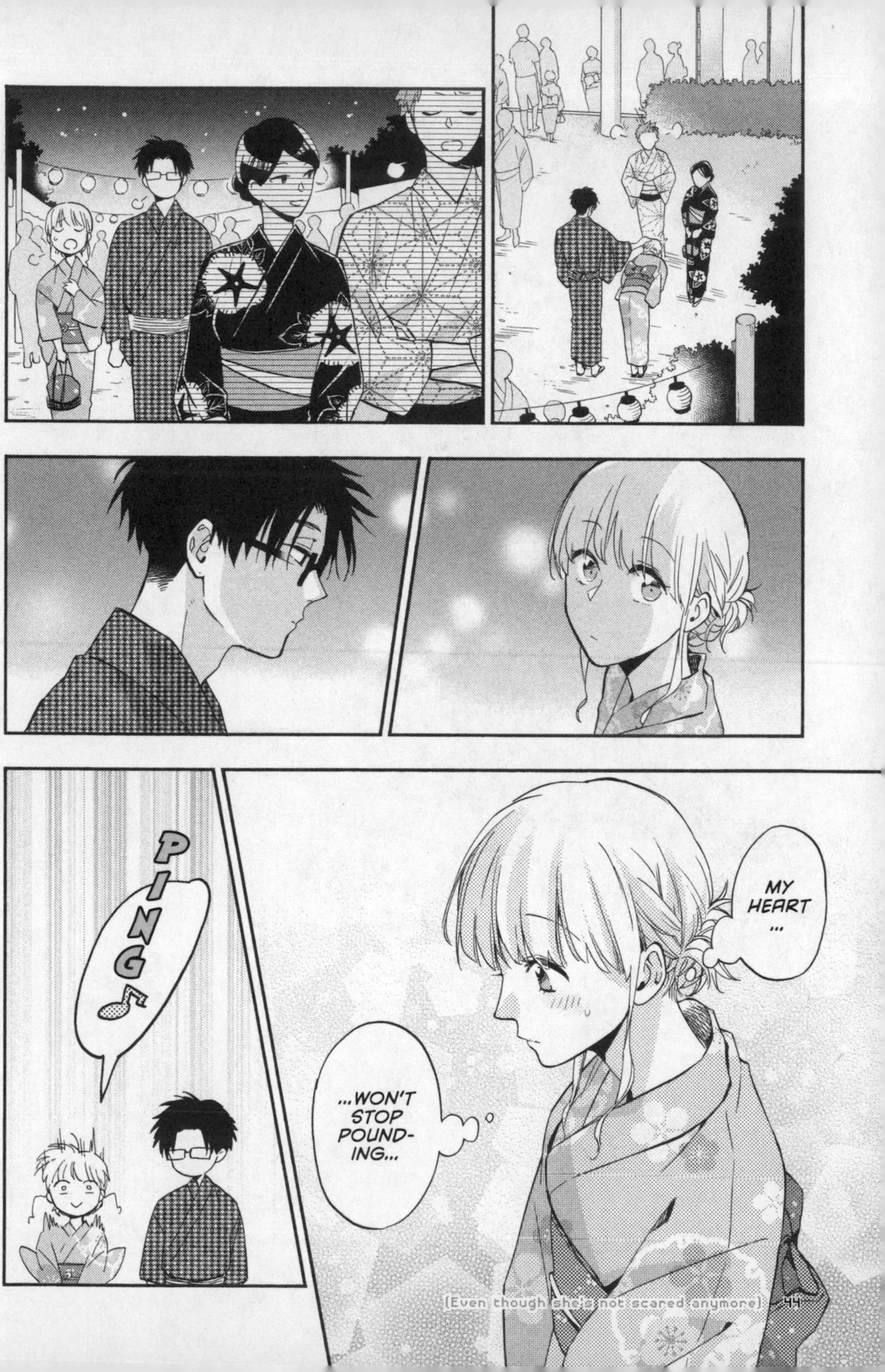
MY HEART ...
...WON'T STOP POUND-ING...
PING
(Even though she's not scared anymore)

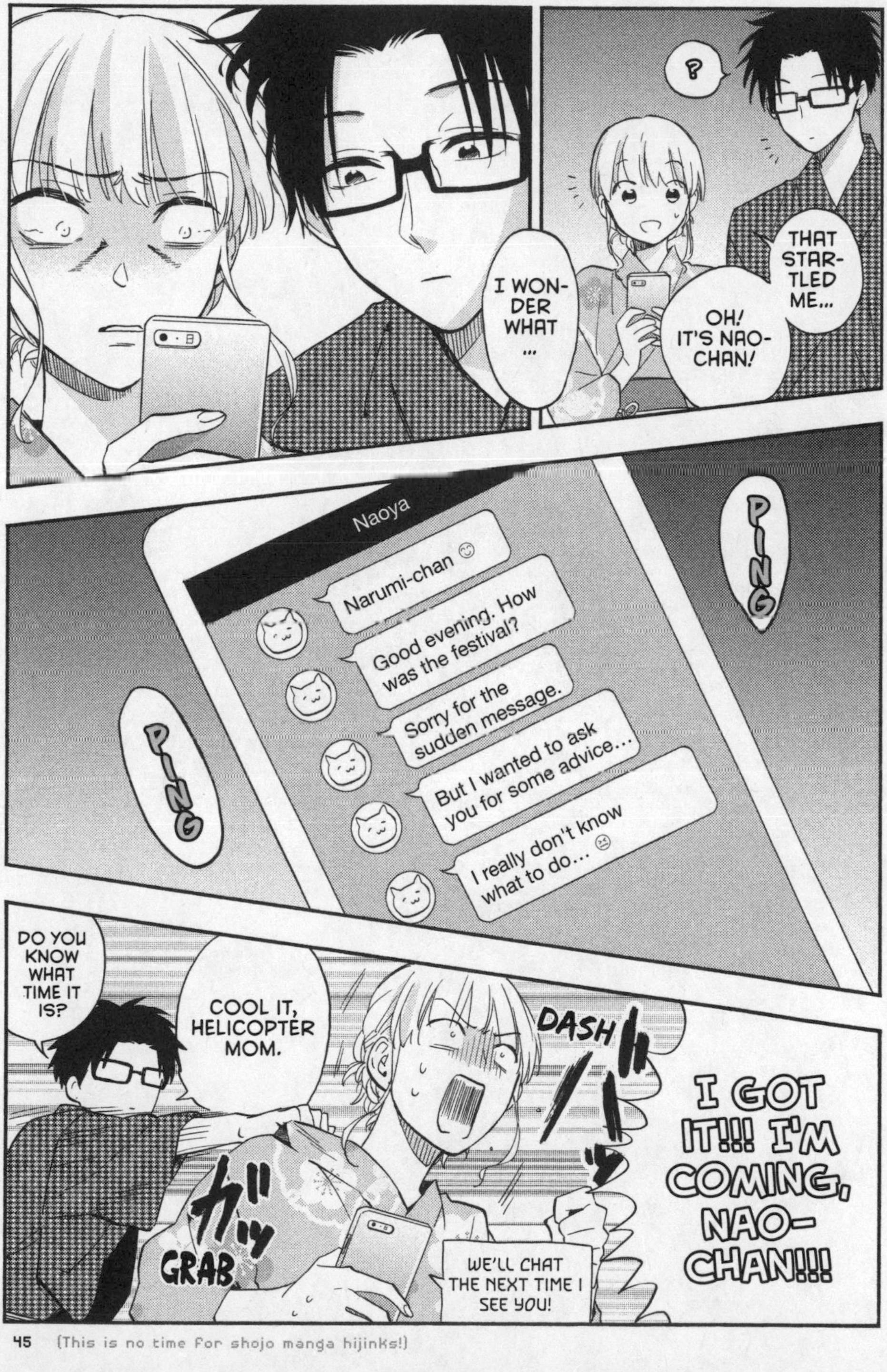
?
THAT STARTLED ME...
OH! IT'S NAO-CHAN!
I WONDER WHAT ...
PING
Naoya
Narumi-chan
Good evening. How was the festival?
Sorry for the sudden message.
But I wanted to ask you for some advice...
I really don't know what to do...
PING
I GOT IT!!! I'M COMING, NAO-CHAN!!!
DASH
WE'LL CHAT THE NEXT TIME I SEE YOU!
COOL IT, HELICOPTER MOM.
DO YOU KNOW WHAT TIME IT IS?
GRAB

 (This is no time for shojo manga hijinks!)

Wotakoi: Love is Hard for Otaku

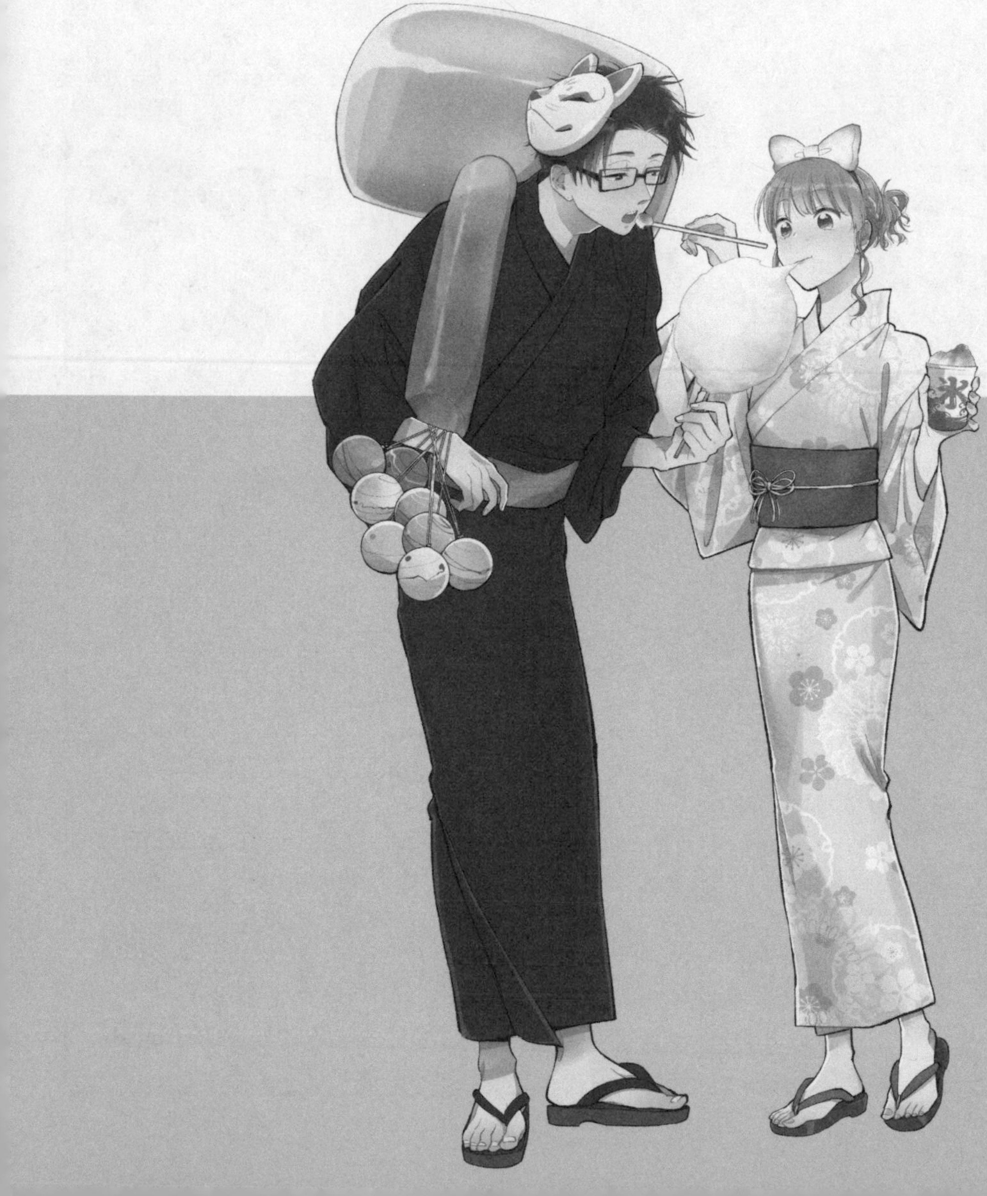
氷

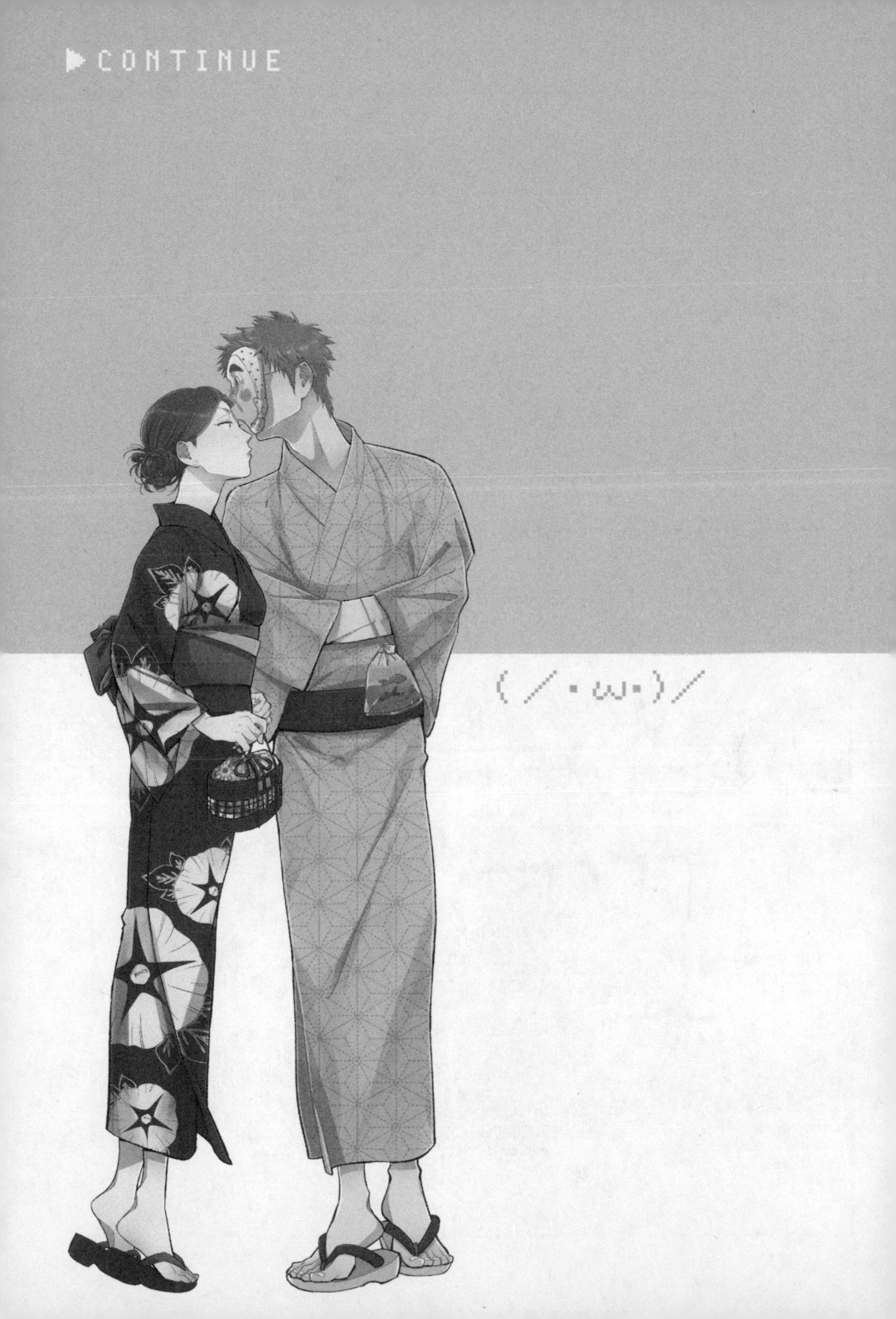
▶CONTINUE
(/・ω・)/

Episode....35
friends...1

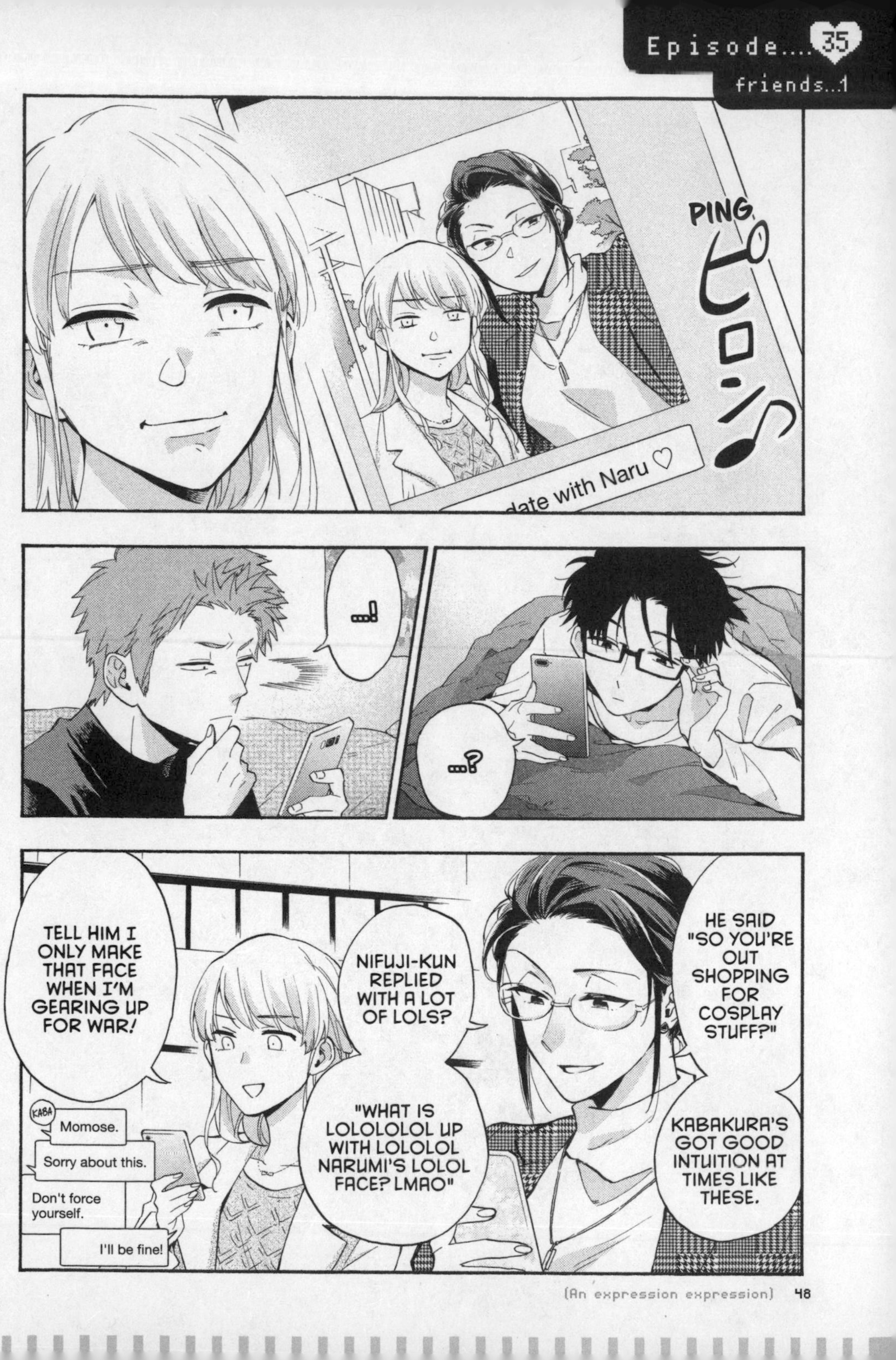
PING
ピロン♪
date with Naru ♡
...?
...!
HE SAID "SO YOU'RE OUT SHOPPING FOR COSPLAY STUFF?"
KABAKURA'S GOT GOOD INTUITION AT TIMES LIKE THESE.
NIFUJI-KUN REPLIED WITH A LOT OF LOLS?
"WHAT IS LOLOLOLOL UP WITH LOLOLOL NARUMI'S LOLOL FACE? LMAO"
TELL HIM I ONLY MAKE THAT FACE WHEN I'M GEARING UP FOR WAR!
KABA
Momose.
Sorry about this.
Don't force yourself.
I'll be fine!

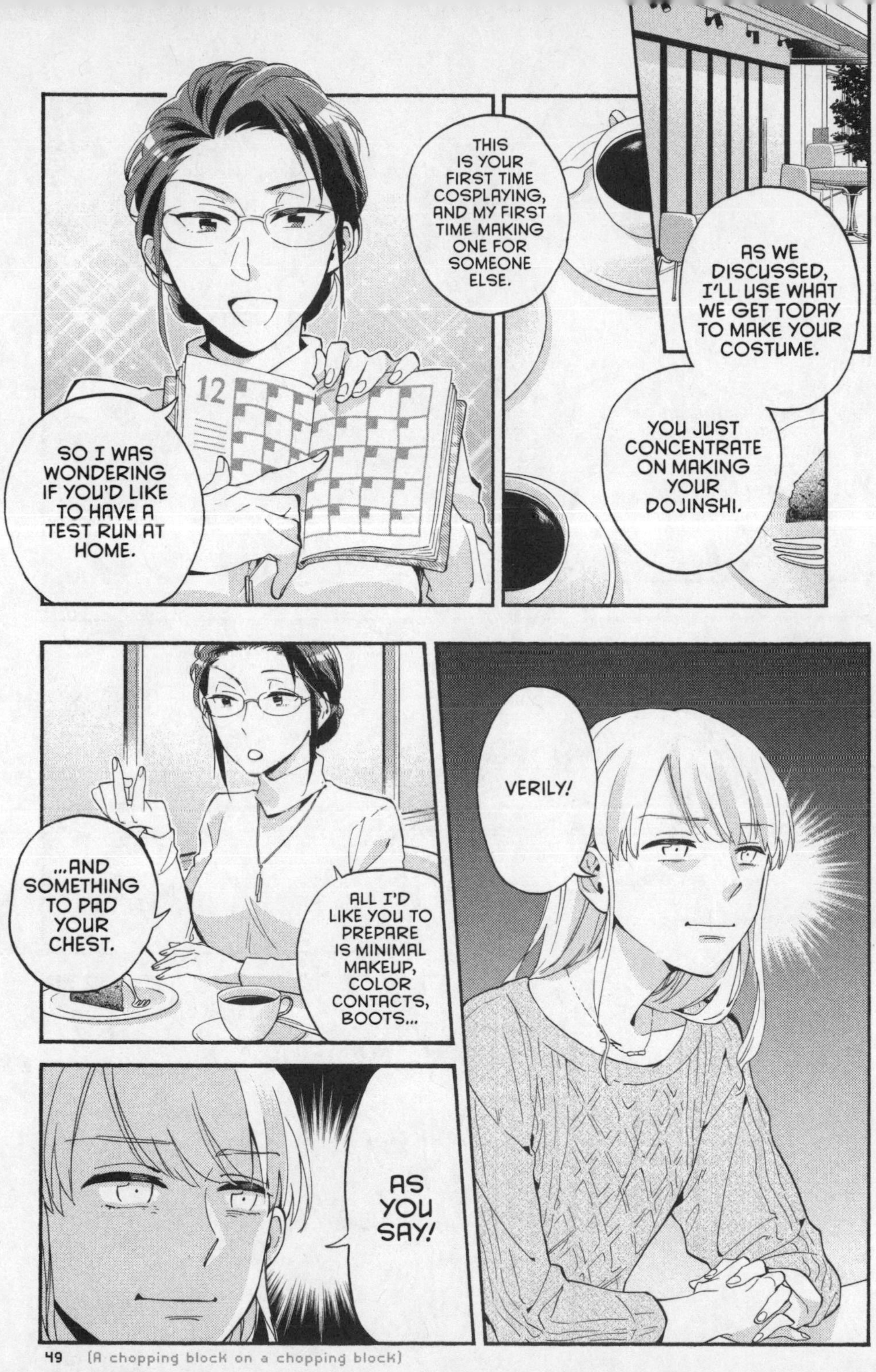
AS WE DISCUSSED, I'LL USE WHAT WE GET TODAY TO MAKE YOUR COSTUME.
YOU JUST CONCENTRATE ON MAKING YOUR DOJINSHI.
THIS IS YOUR FIRST TIME COSPLAYING, AND MY FIRST TIME MAKING ONE FOR SOMEONE ELSE.
12
SO I WAS WONDERING IF YOU'D LIKE TO HAVE A TEST RUN AT HOME.
VERILY!
ALL I'D LIKE YOU TO PREPARE IS MINIMAL MAKEUP, COLOR CONTACTS, BOOTS...
...AND SOMETHING TO PAD YOUR CHEST.
AS YOU SAY!

 (A chopping block on a chopping block)

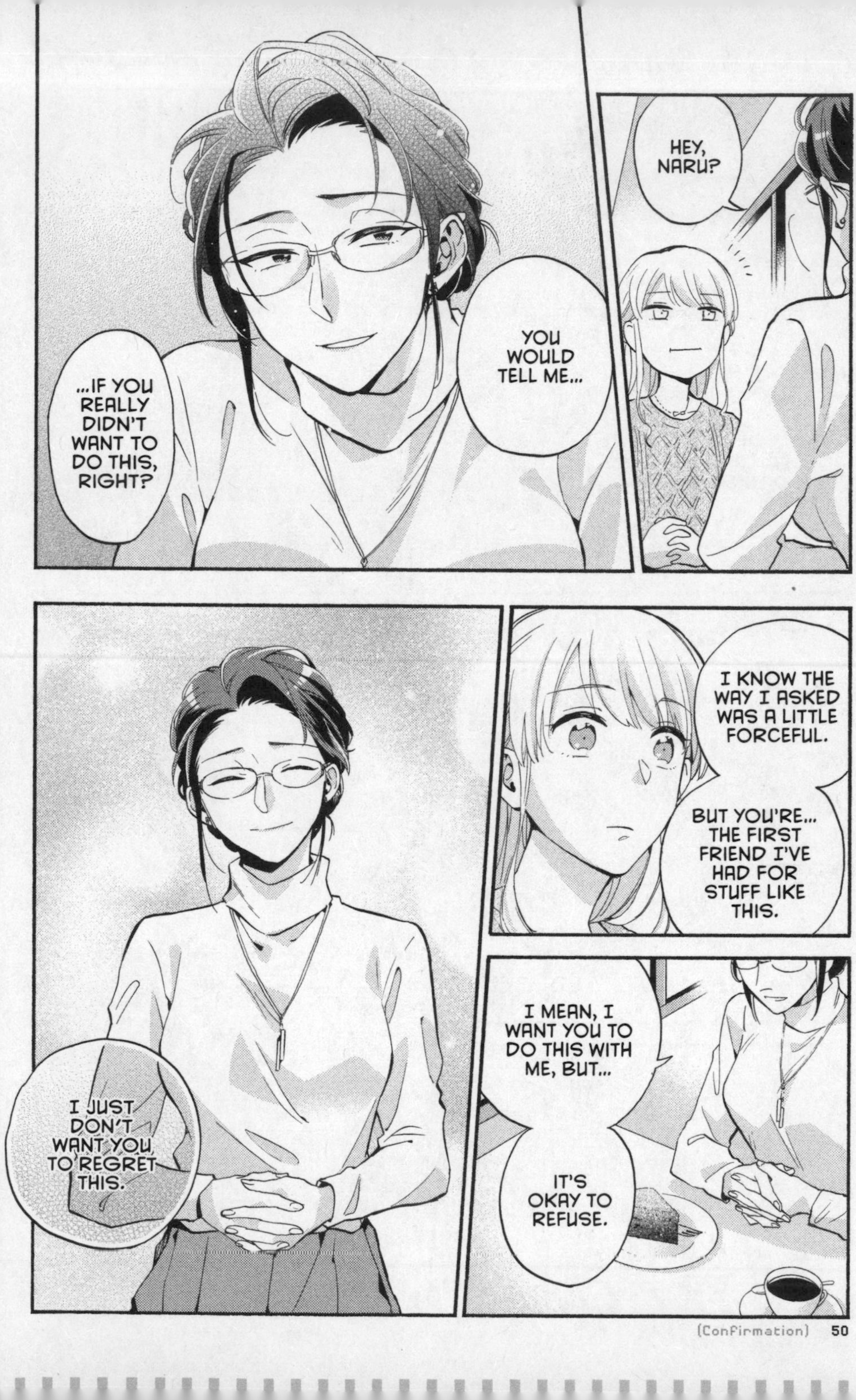
HEY, NARU?
YOU WOULD TELL ME...
...IF YOU REALLY DIDN'T WANT TO DO THIS, RIGHT?
I KNOW THE WAY I ASKED WAS A LITTLE FORCEFUL.
BUT YOU'RE... THE FIRST FRIEND I'VE HAD FOR STUFF LIKE THIS.
I MEAN, I WANT YOU TO DO THIS WITH ME, BUT...
IT'S OKAY TO REFUSE.
I JUST DON'T WANT YOU TO REGRET THIS.

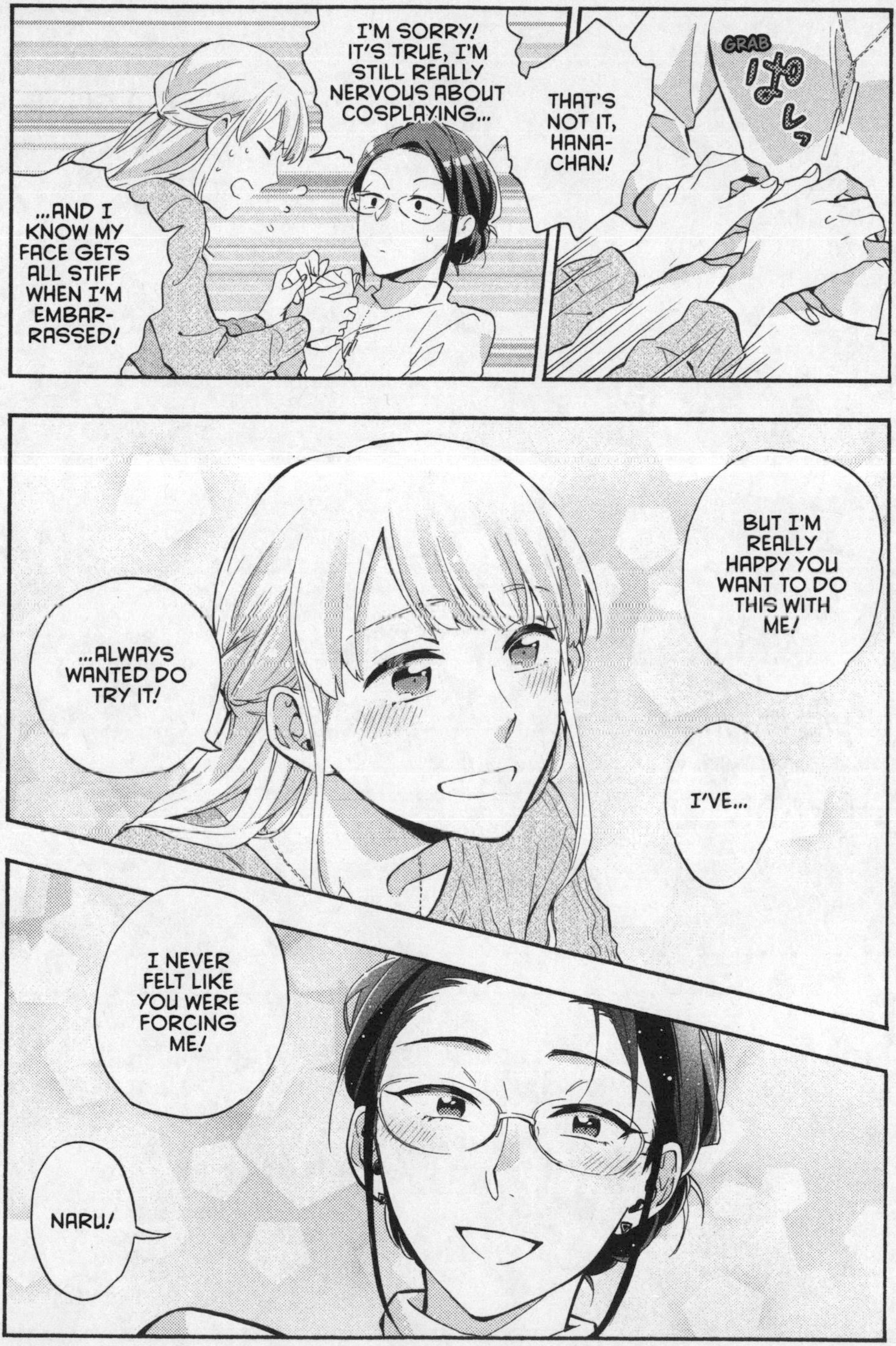
GRAB
ぱしっ
THAT'S NOT IT, HANA-CHAN!
I'M SORRY! IT'S TRUE, I'M STILL REALLY NERVOUS ABOUT COSPLAYING...
...AND I KNOW MY FACE GETS ALL STIFF WHEN I'M EMBARRASSED!
BUT I'M REALLY HAPPY YOU WANT TO DO THIS WITH ME!
I'VE...
...ALWAYS WANTED DO TRY IT!
I NEVER FELT LIKE YOU WERE FORCING ME!
NARU!

 (No hesitation)

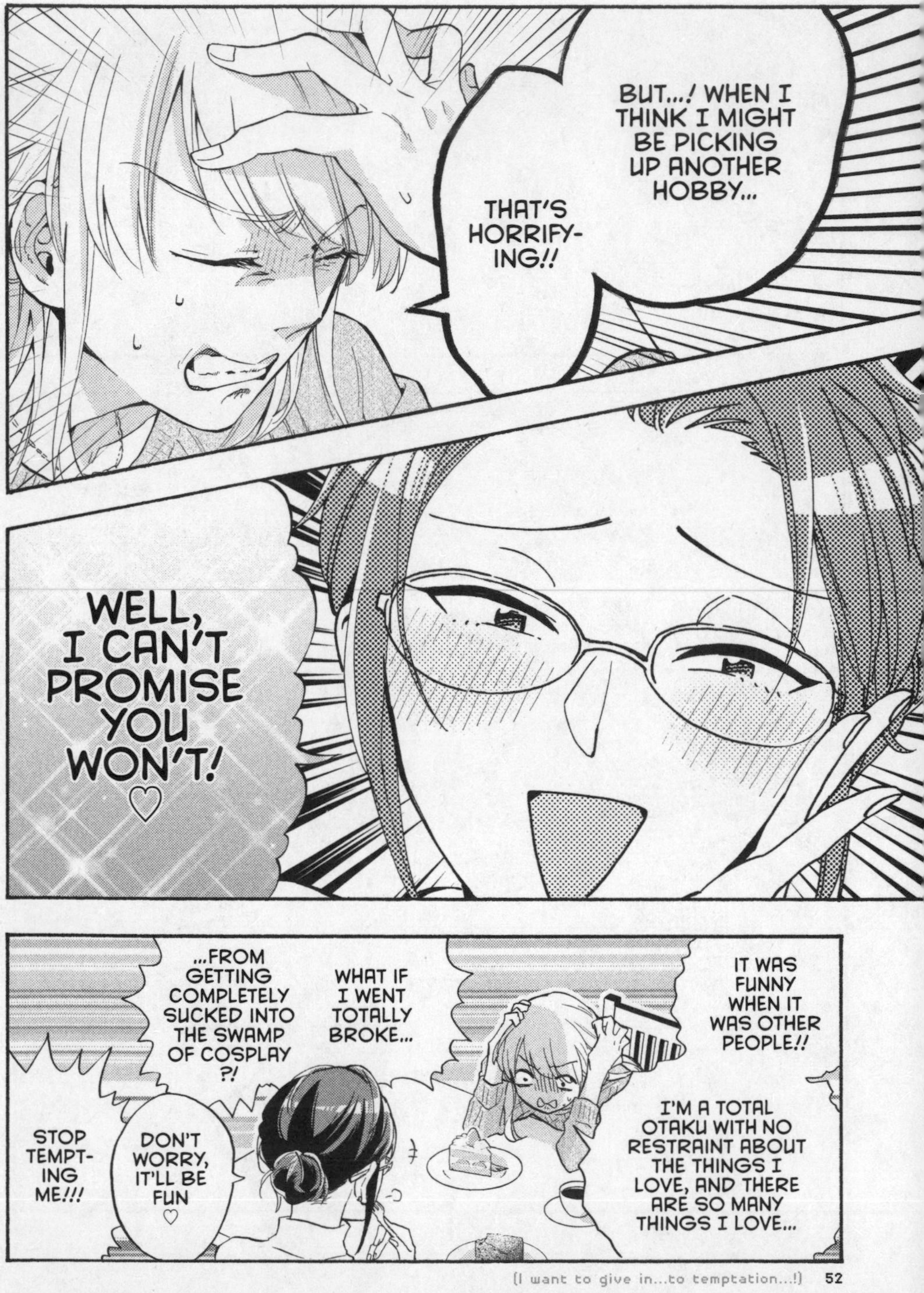

BUT...! WHEN I THINK I MIGHT BE PICKING UP ANOTHER HOBBY...
THAT'S HORRIFY-ING!!
WELL, I CAN'T PROMISE YOU WON'T! ♡
IT WAS FUNNY WHEN IT WAS OTHER PEOPLE!!
I'M A TOTAL OTAKU WITH NO RESTRAINT ABOUT THE THINGS I LOVE, AND THERE ARE SO MANY THINGS I LOVE...
WHAT IF I WENT TOTALLY BROKE...
...FROM GETTING COMPLETELY SUCKED INTO THE SWAMP OF COSPLAY?!
DON'T WORRY, IT'LL BE FUN ♡
STOP TEMPT-ING ME!!!

(I want to give in...to temptation...!)

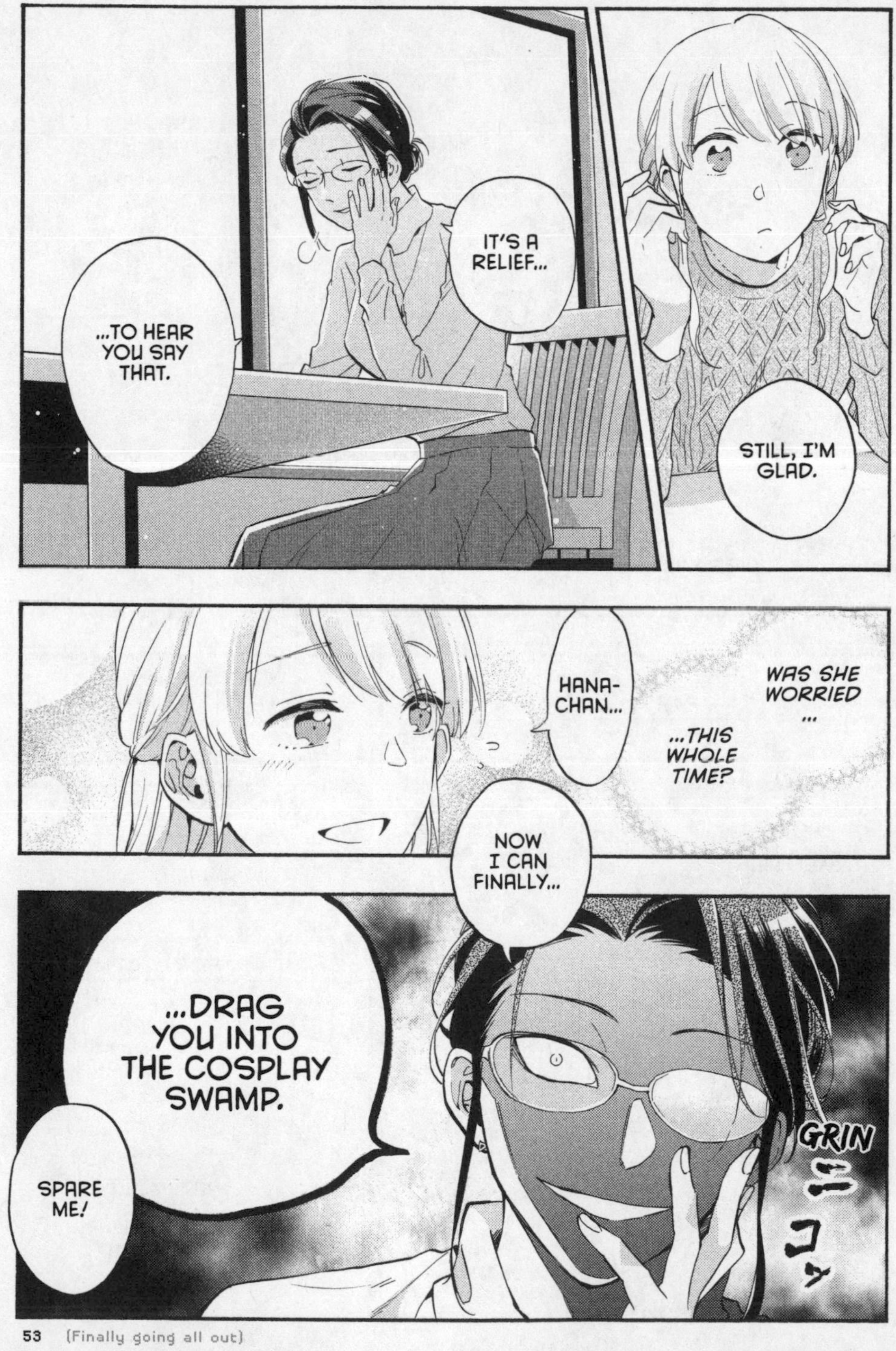
STILL, I'M GLAD.
IT'S A RELIEF...
...TO HEAR YOU SAY THAT.
WAS SHE WORRIED ...
...THIS WHOLE TIME?
HANA-CHAN...
NOW I CAN FINALLY...
GRIN
ニコッ
...DRAG YOU INTO THE COSPLAY SWAMP.
SPARE ME!

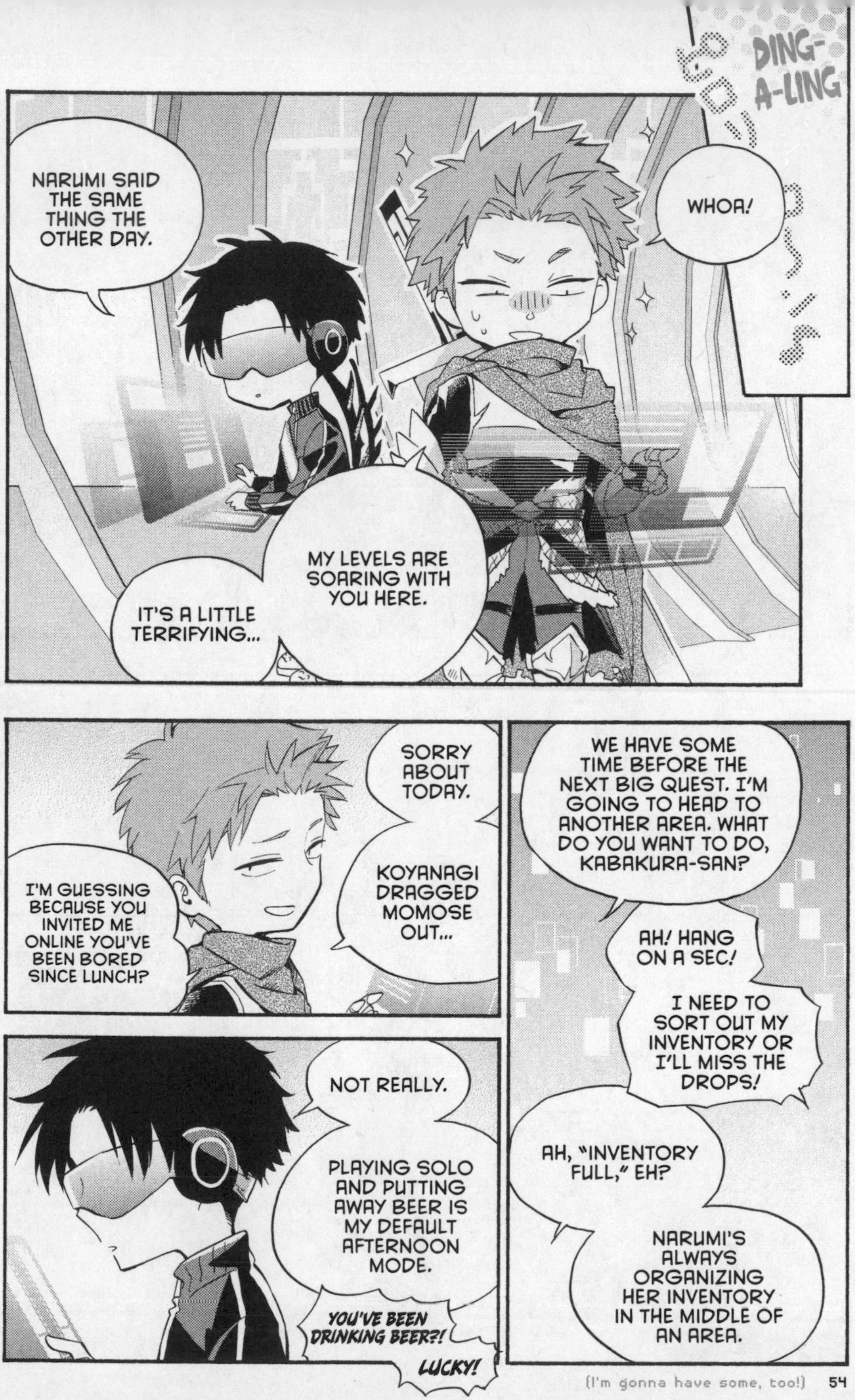
DING-A-LING
WHOA!
MY LEVELS ARE SOARING WITH YOU HERE.
IT'S A LITTLE TERRIFYING...
NARUMI SAID THE SAME THING THE OTHER DAY.
WE HAVE SOME TIME BEFORE THE NEXT BIG QUEST. I'M GOING TO HEAD TO ANOTHER AREA. WHAT DO YOU WANT TO DO, KABAKURA-SAN?
AH! HANG ON A SEC!
I NEED TO SORT OUT MY INVENTORY OR I'LL MISS THE DROPS!
AH, "INVENTORY FULL," EH?
NARUMI'S ALWAYS ORGANIZING HER INVENTORY IN THE MIDDLE OF AN AREA.
SORRY ABOUT TODAY.
KOYANAGI DRAGGED MOMOSE OUT...
I'M GUESSING BECAUSE YOU INVITED ME ONLINE YOU'VE BEEN BORED SINCE LUNCH?
NOT REALLY.
PLAYING SOLO AND PUTTING AWAY BEER IS MY DEFAULT AFTERNOON MODE.
YOU'VE BEEN DRINKING BEER?!
LUCKY!

(I'm gonna have some, too!)

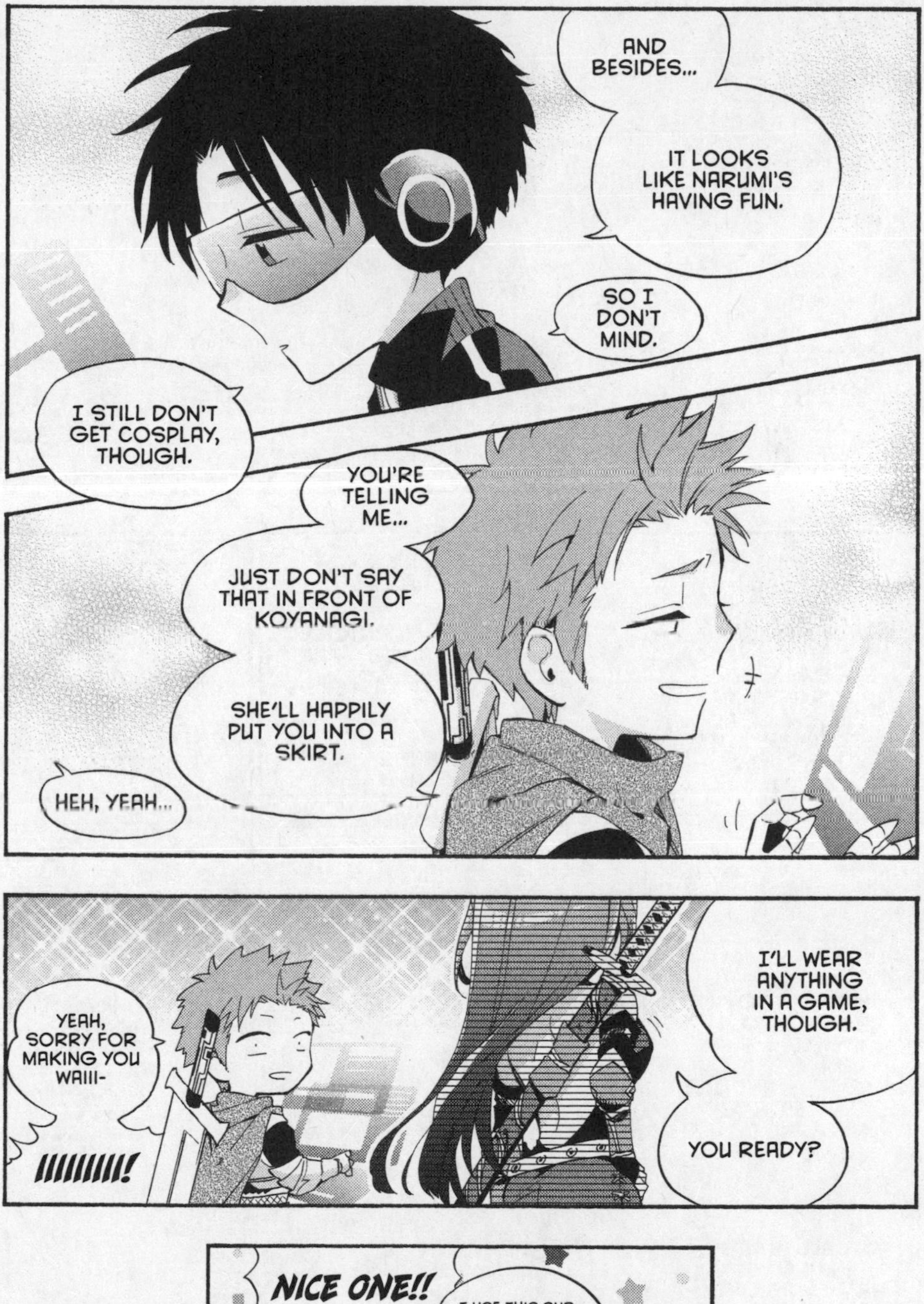
AND BESIDES...
IT LOOKS LIKE NARUMI'S HAVING FUN.
SO I DON'T MIND.
I STILL DON'T GET COSPLAY, THOUGH.
YOU'RE TELLING ME...
JUST DON'T SAY THAT IN FRONT OF KOYANAGI.
SHE'LL HAPPILY PUT YOU INTO A SKIRT.
HEH, YEAH...
I'LL WEAR ANYTHING IN A GAME, THOUGH.
YOU READY?
YEAH, SORRY FOR MAKING YOU WAIIII-
IIIIIIIII!
NICE ONE!!
I USE THIS SUB-CHARACTER WHEN I PLAY SOLO.
WHAT'S UP WITH THAT AVATAR?!

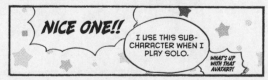

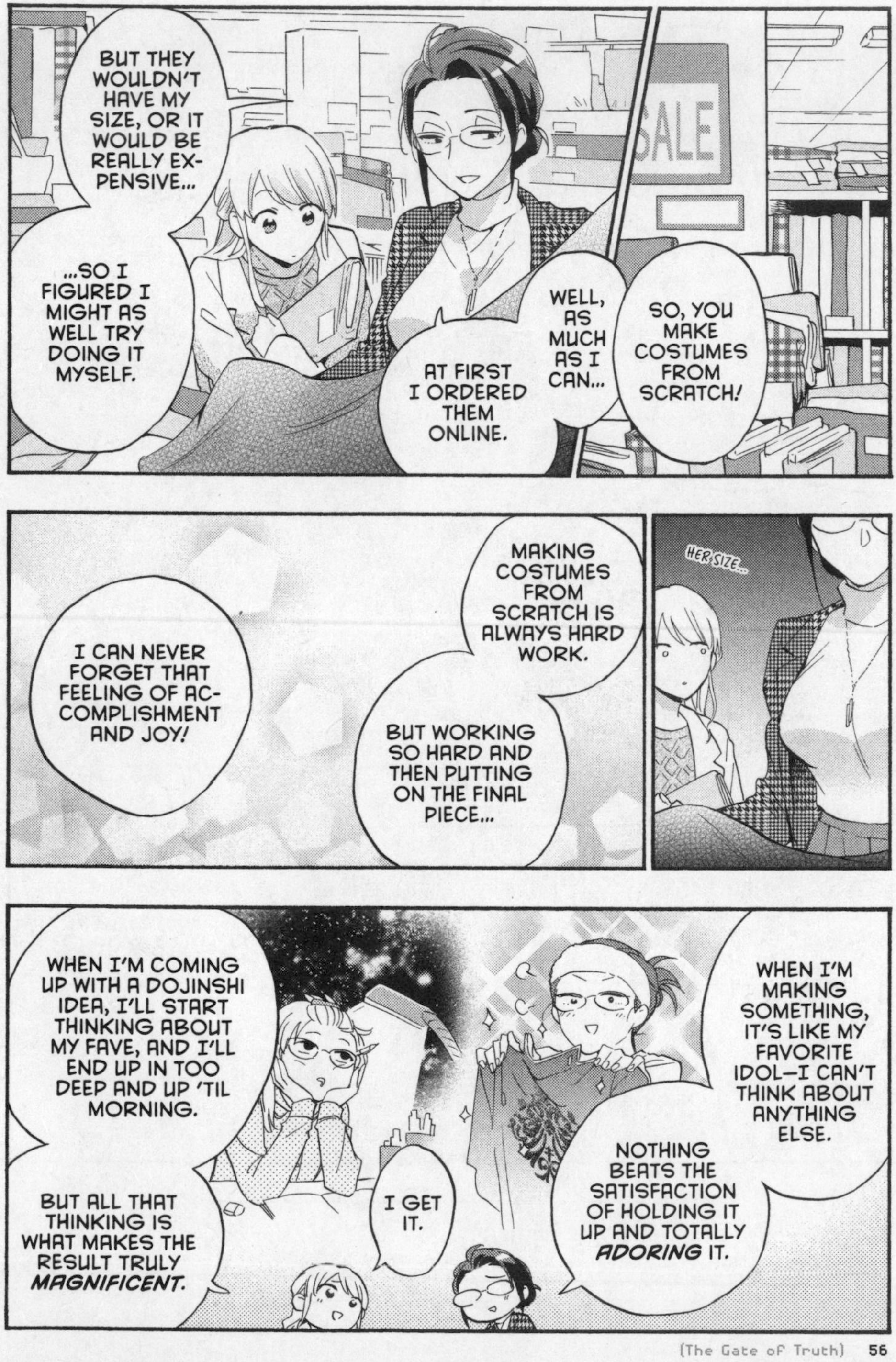
SO, YOU MAKE COSTUMES FROM SCRATCH!
WELL, AS MUCH AS I CAN...
AT FIRST I ORDERED THEM ONLINE.
BUT THEY WOULDN'T HAVE MY SIZE, OR IT WOULD BE REALLY EXPENSIVE...
...SO I FIGURED I MIGHT AS WELL TRY DOING IT MYSELF.
SALE
HER SIZE...
MAKING COSTUMES FROM SCRATCH IS ALWAYS HARD WORK.
BUT WORKING SO HARD AND THEN PUTTING ON THE FINAL PIECE...
I CAN NEVER FORGET THAT FEELING OF ACCOMPLISHMENT AND JOY!
WHEN I'M MAKING SOMETHING, IT'S LIKE MY FAVORITE IDOL—I CAN'T THINK ABOUT ANYTHING ELSE.
NOTHING BEATS THE SATISFACTION OF HOLDING IT UP AND TOTALLY *ADORING* IT.
WHEN I'M COMING UP WITH A DOJINSHI IDEA, I'LL START THINKING ABOUT MY FAVE, AND I'LL END UP IN TOO DEEP AND UP 'TIL MORNING.
BUT ALL THAT THINKING IS WHAT MAKES THE RESULT TRULY *MAGNIFICENT*.
I GET IT.

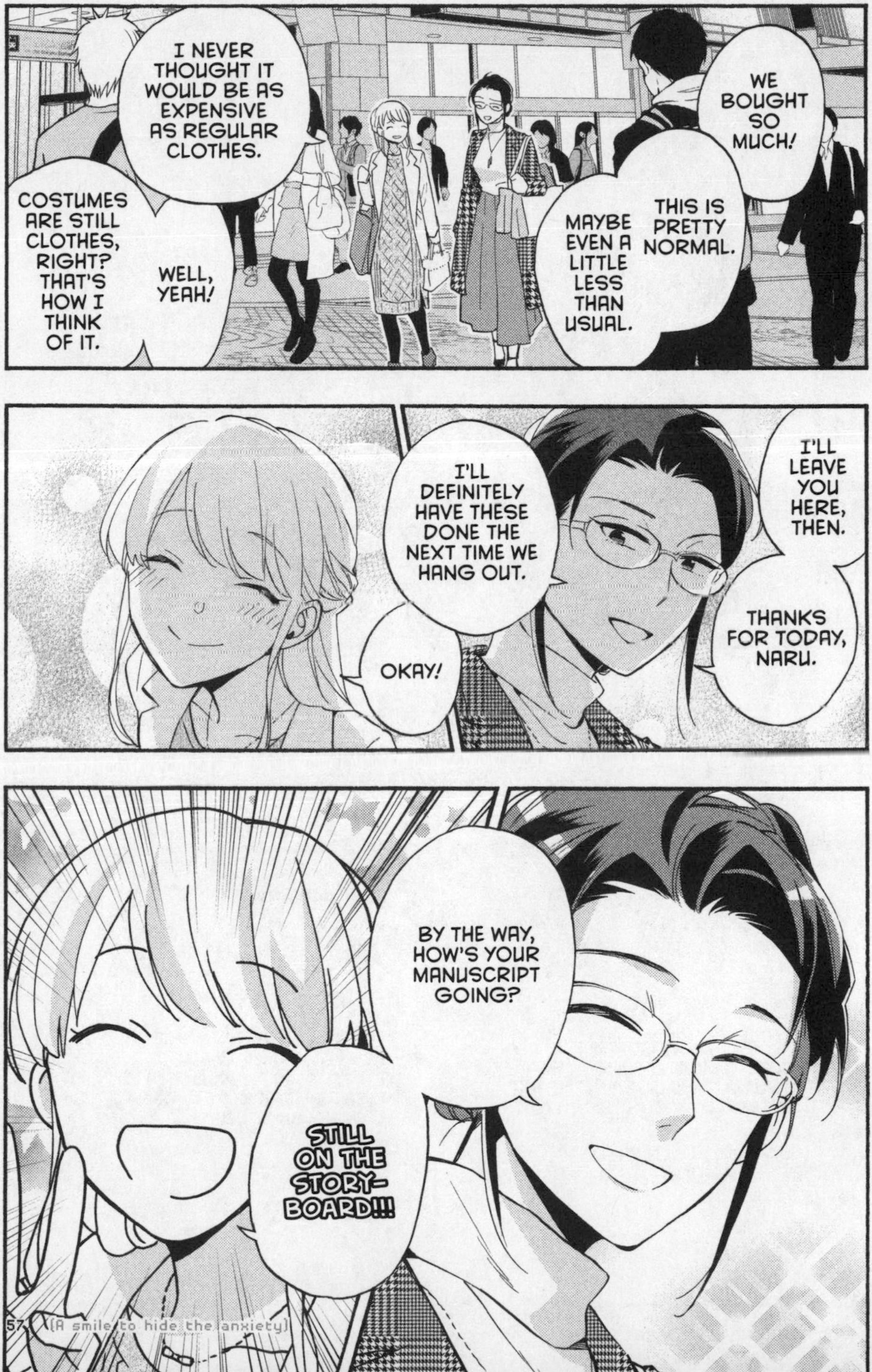
WE BOUGHT SO MUCH!
THIS IS PRETTY NORMAL.
MAYBE EVEN A LITTLE LESS THAN USUAL.
I NEVER THOUGHT IT WOULD BE AS EXPENSIVE AS REGULAR CLOTHES.
WELL, YEAH!
COSTUMES ARE STILL CLOTHES, RIGHT? THAT'S HOW I THINK OF IT.
I'LL LEAVE YOU HERE, THEN.
THANKS FOR TODAY, NARU.
I'LL DEFINITELY HAVE THESE DONE THE NEXT TIME WE HANG OUT.
OKAY!
BY THE WAY, HOW'S YOUR MANUSCRIPT GOING?
STILL ON THE STORY-BOARD!!!

(A smile to hide the anxiety)

CHARACTERS

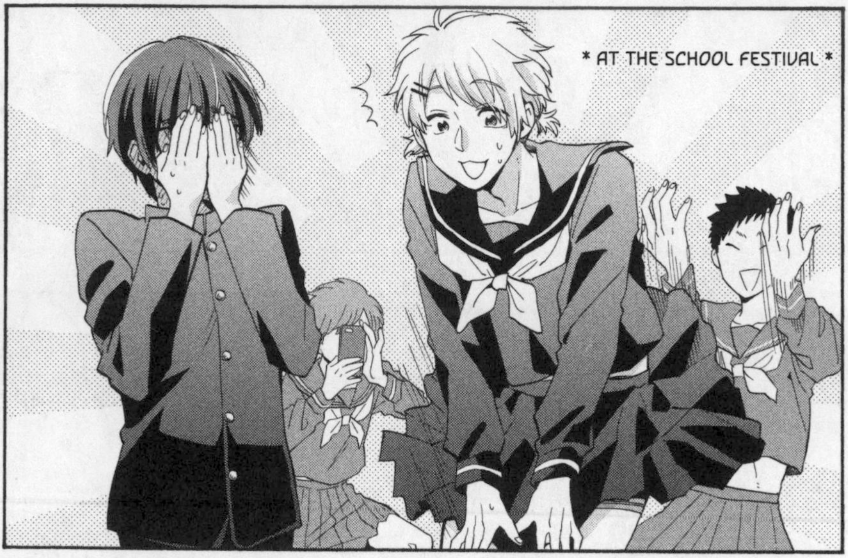
* AT THE SCHOOL FESTIVAL *

▼ FAN REQUEST

"NAO-CHAN IN GIRLS' CLOTHES"

☞ KO SAKURAGI

*GAMER WITH SOCIAL ANXIETY.
*I WAS ORIGINALLY GOING TO HAVE HER IN A GIRL'S UNIFORM, TOO, BUT DECIDED TO GO WITH THIS INSTEAD.

☞ NAOYA NIFUJI

*NON-OTAKU.
*THANK YOU FOR THE SIMPLE REQUEST. I TRIED TO ADD PLENTY OF NICE BONUS DETAILS.
*EVERYONE'S WEARING GIRLS' CLOTHES, SO HE'S NOT EMBARRASSED AT ALL.

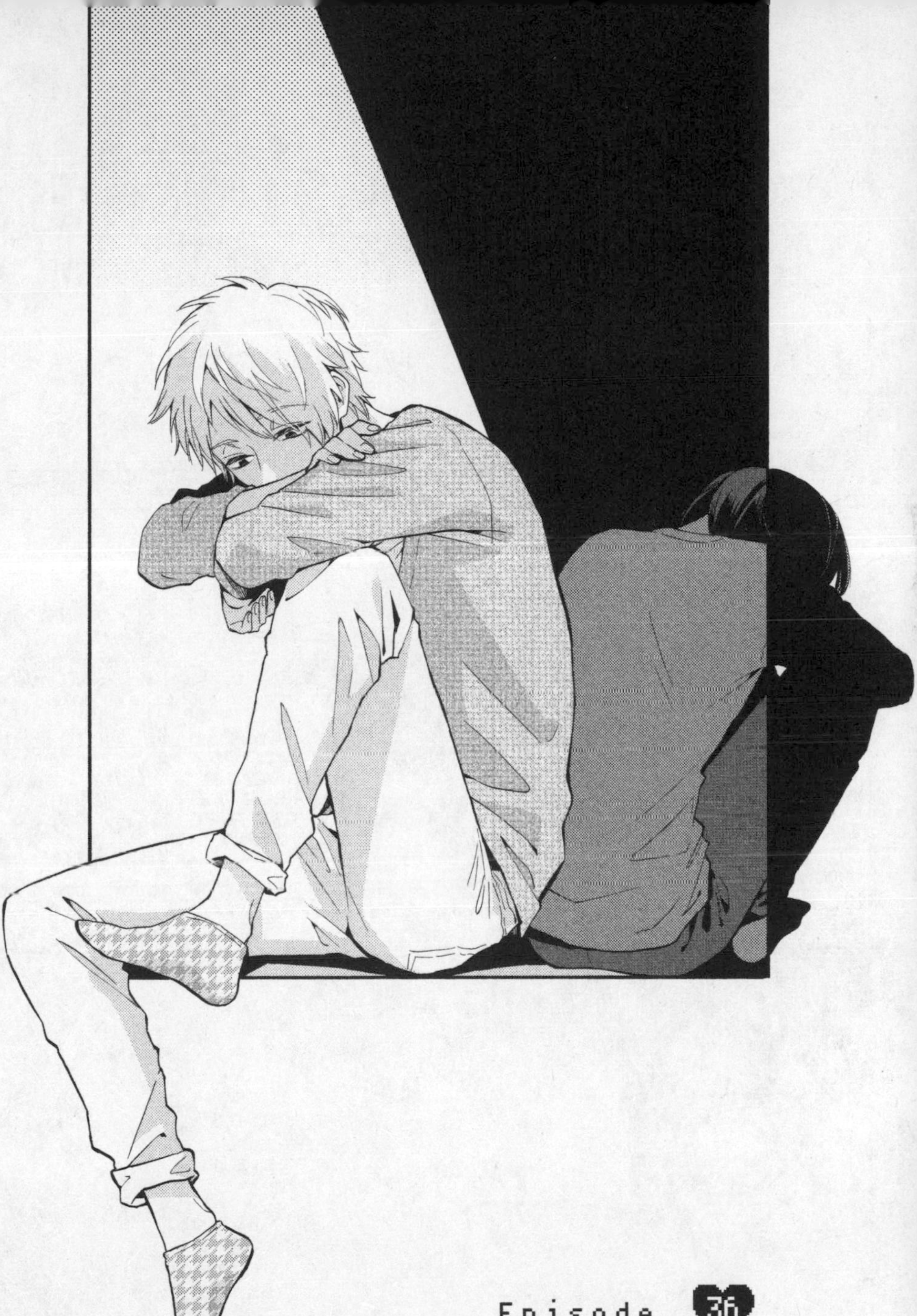

Episode.... 36

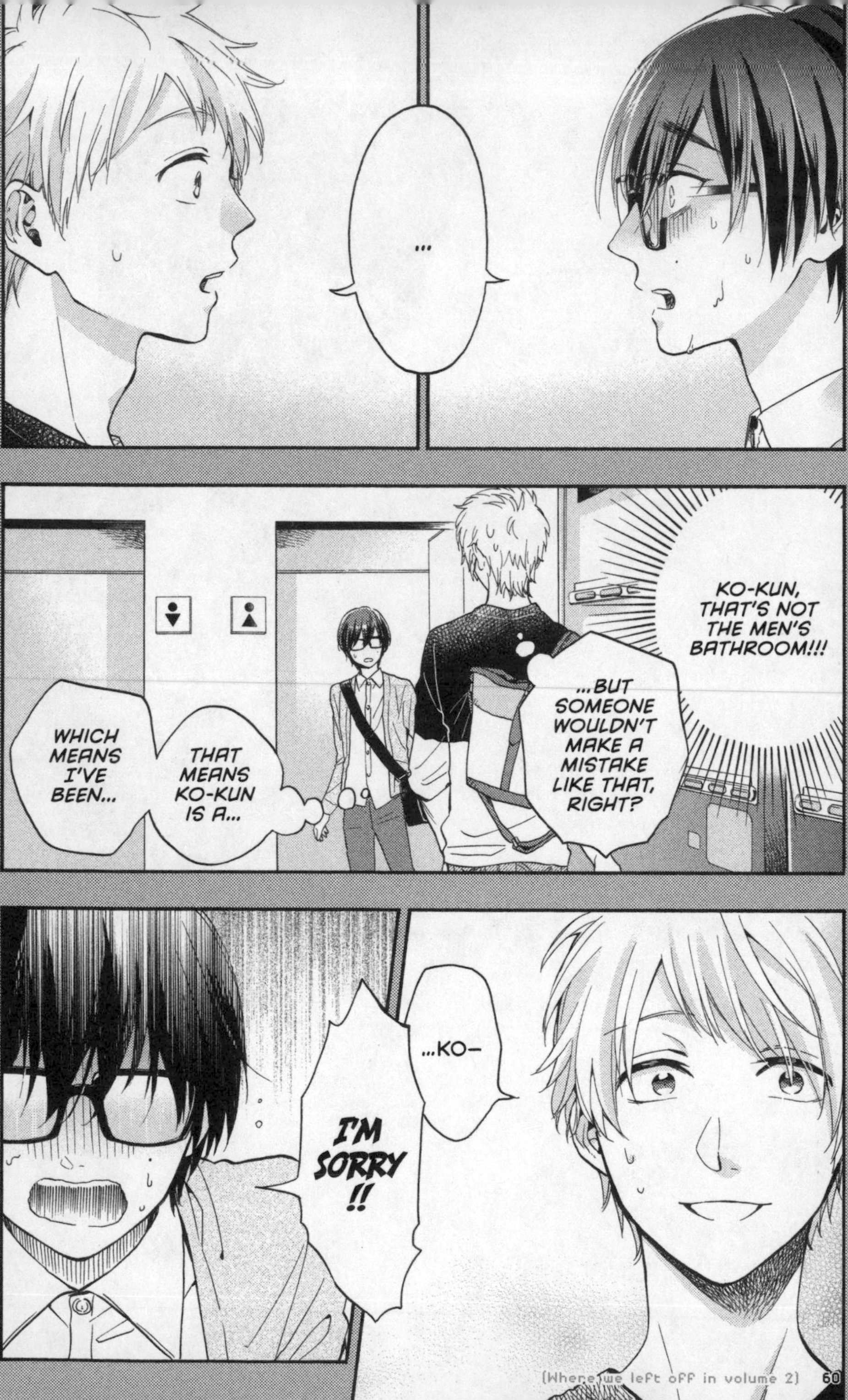
...
KO-KUN, THAT'S NOT THE MEN'S BATHROOM!!!
...BUT SOMEONE WOULDN'T MAKE A MISTAKE LIKE THAT, RIGHT?
THAT MEANS KO-KUN IS A...
WHICH MEANS I'VE BEEN...
...KO-
I'M SORRY!!

(Where we left off in volume 2)

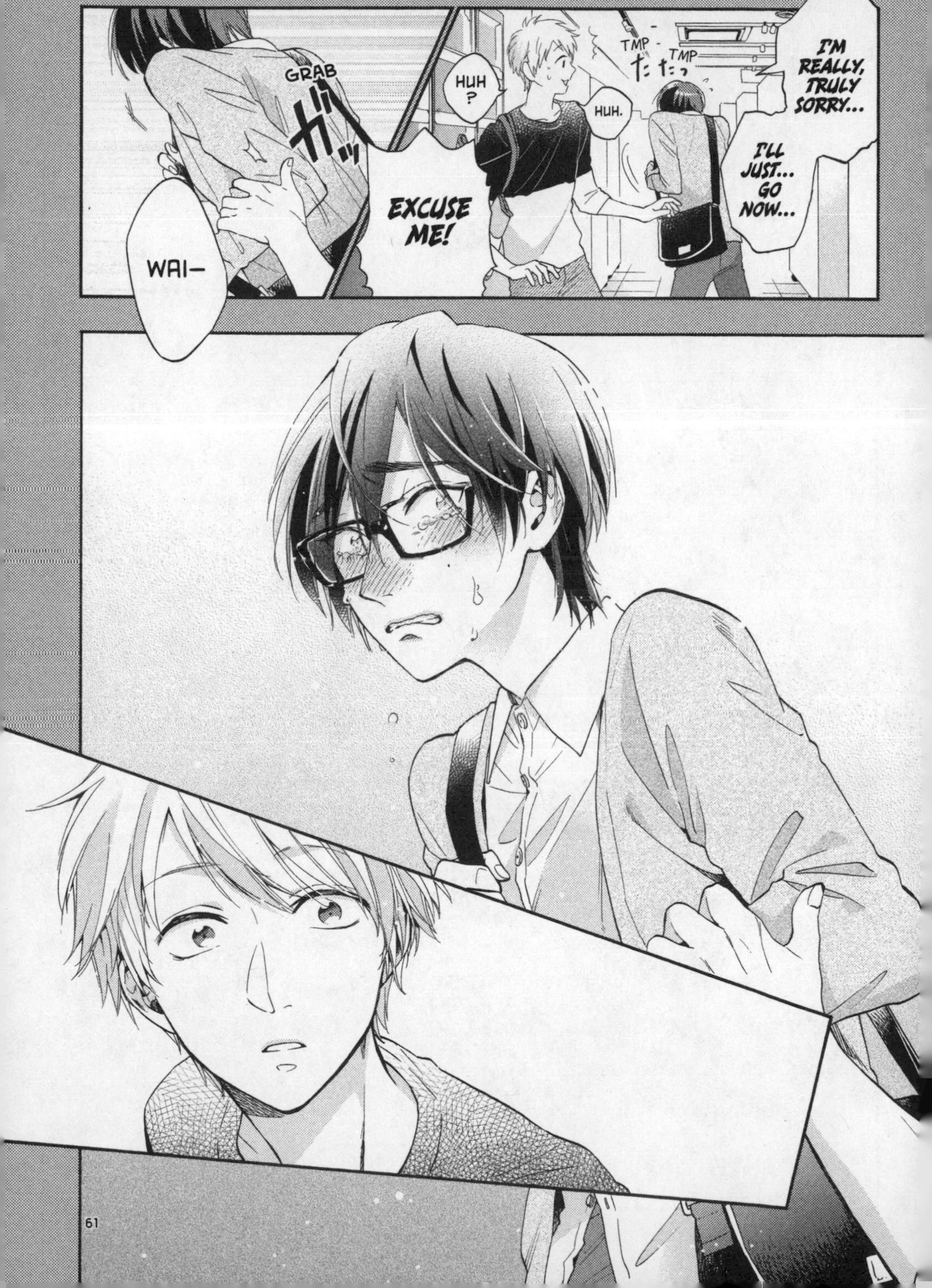
I'M REALLY, TRULY SORRY...
I'LL JUST... GO NOW...
TMP TMP
たたっ
HUH?
HUH.
GRAB
ガッ
EXCUSE ME!
WAI—

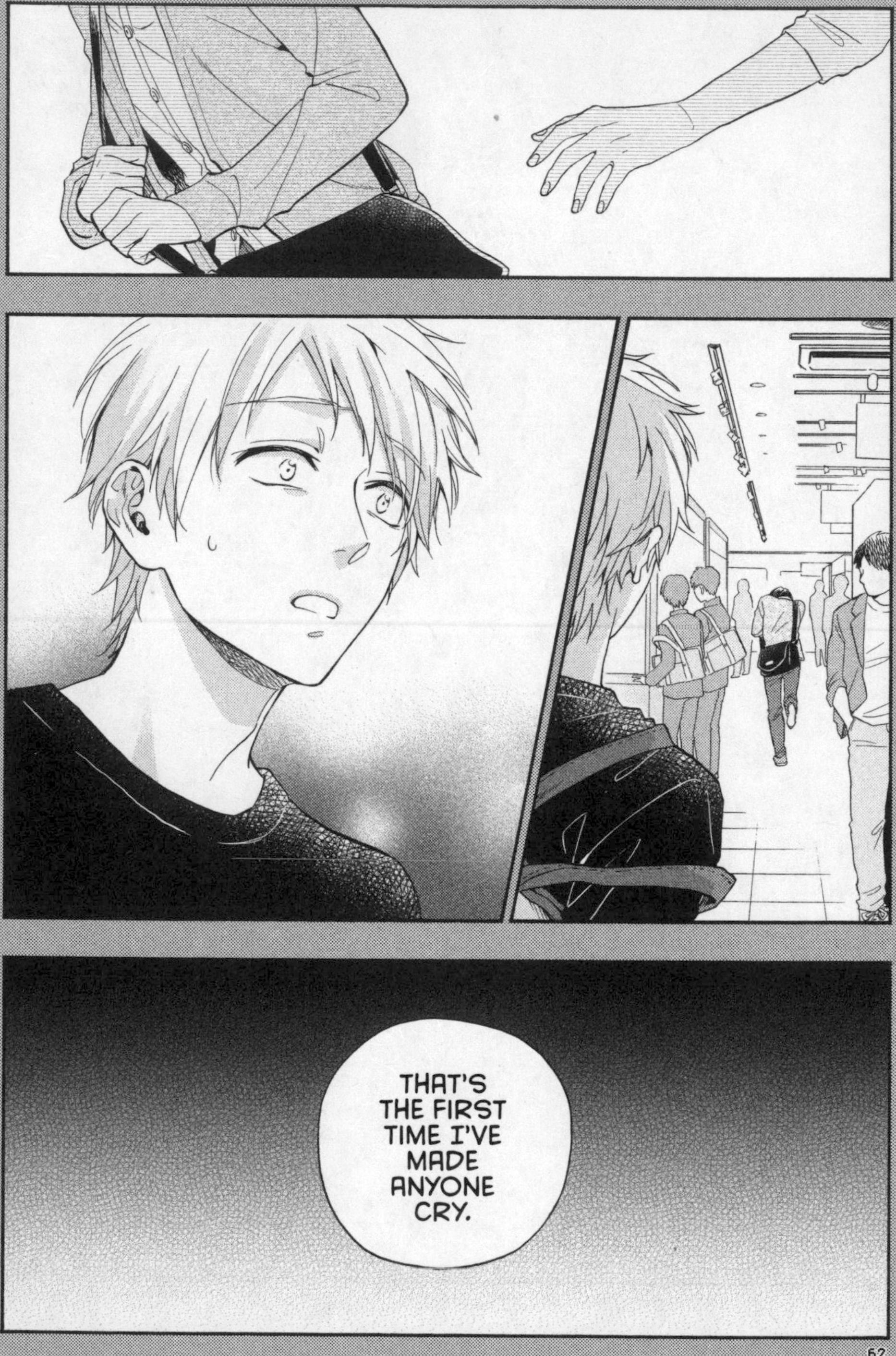
THAT'S THE FIRST TIME I'VE MADE ANYONE CRY.

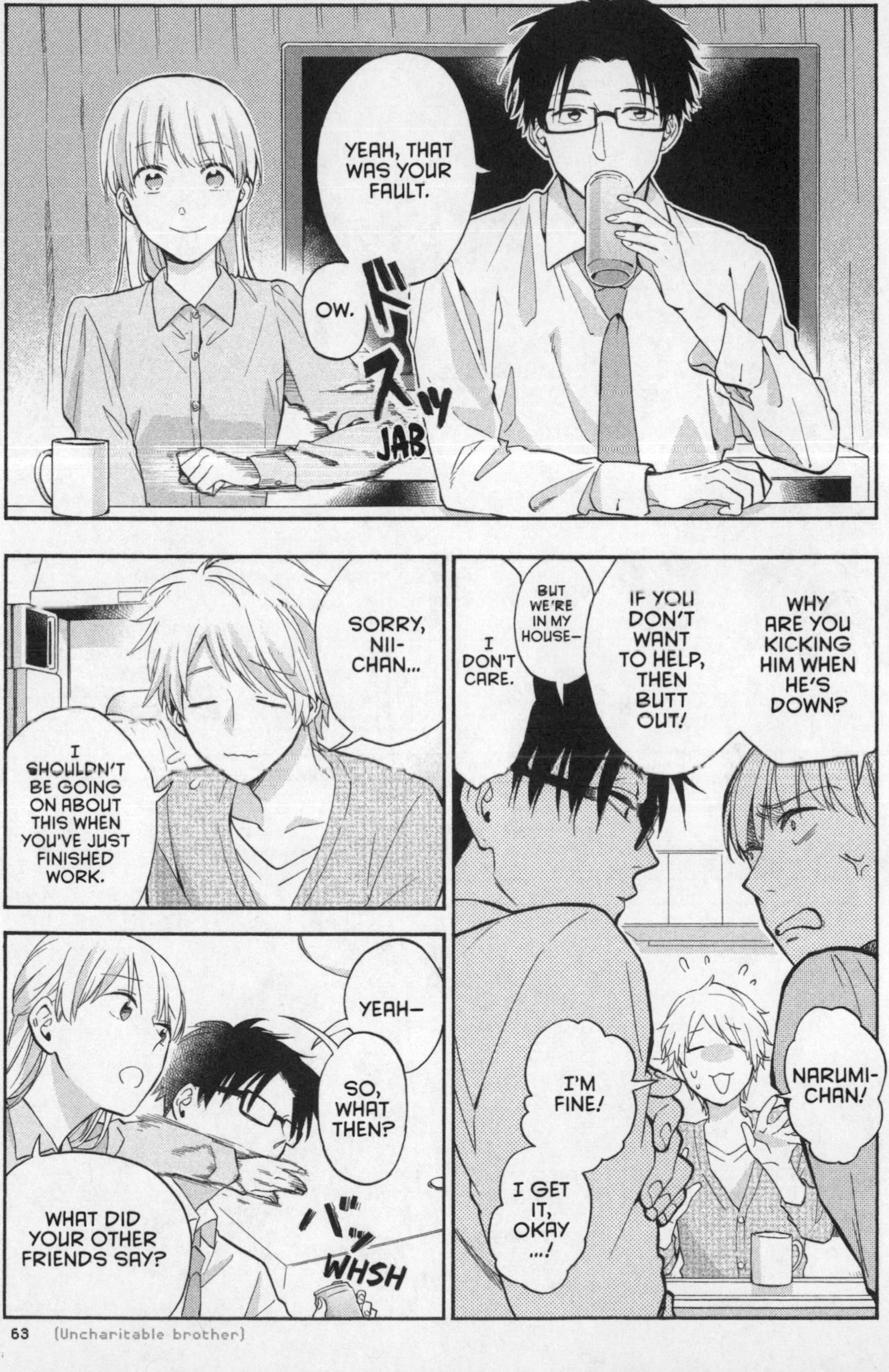
YEAH, THAT WAS YOUR FAULT.
OW.
ドスッ
JAB
WHY ARE YOU KICKING HIM WHEN HE'S DOWN?
IF YOU DON'T WANT TO HELP, THEN BUTT OUT!
BUT WE'RE IN MY HOUSE—
I DON'T CARE.
NARUMI-CHAN!
I'M FINE!
I GET IT, OKAY...!
SORRY, NII-CHAN...
I SHOULDN'T BE GOING ON ABOUT THIS WHEN YOU'VE JUST FINISHED WORK.
YEAH—
SO, WHAT THEN?
WHAT DID YOUR OTHER FRIENDS SAY?
バッ
WHSH

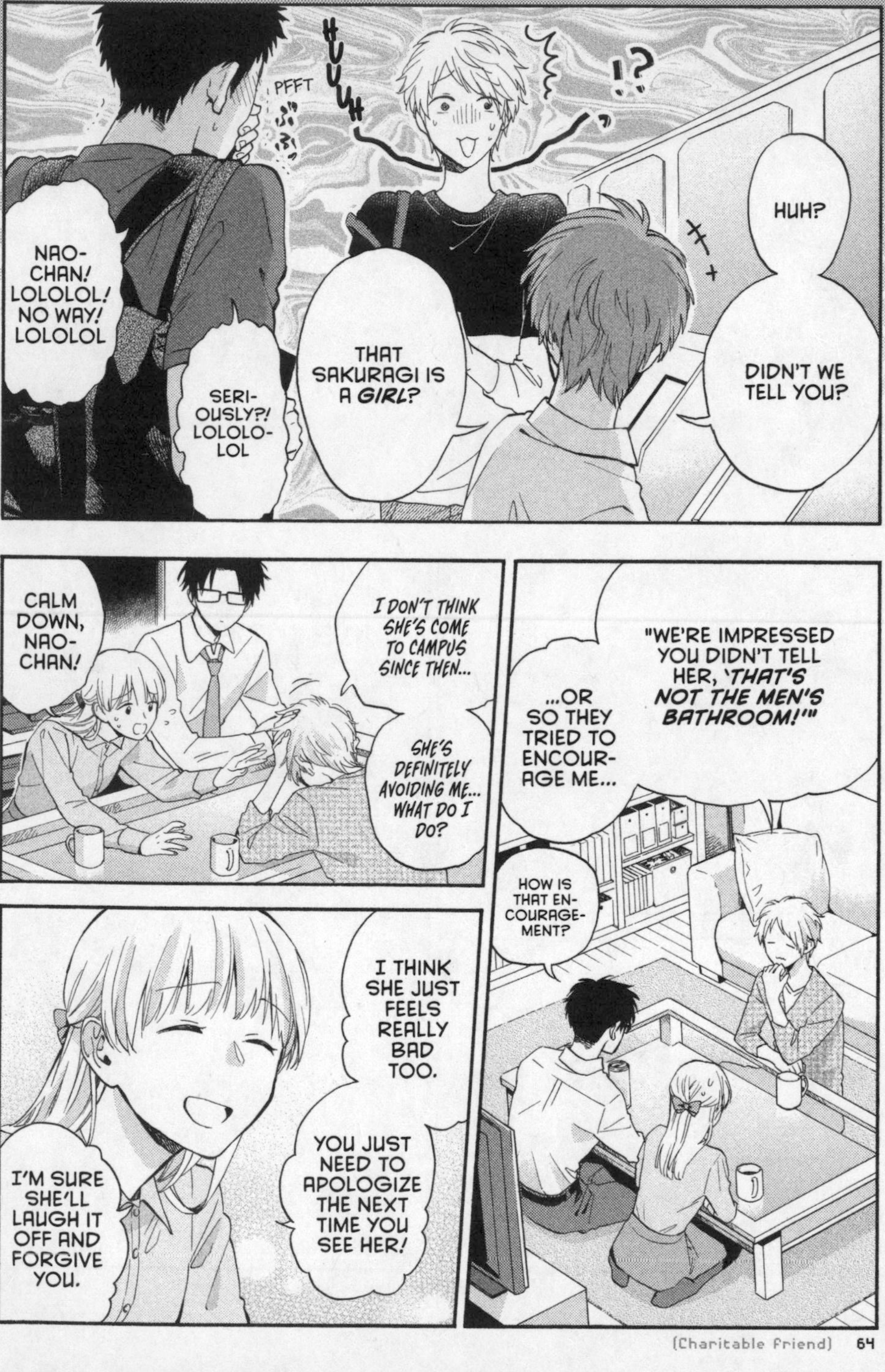
!?
HUUUH
PFFT
HUH?
DIDN'T WE TELL YOU?
THAT SAKURAGI IS A *GIRL*?
NAO-CHAN! LOLOLOL! NO WAY! LOLOLOL
SERI-OUSLY?! LOLOLO-LOL
"WE'RE IMPRESSED YOU DIDN'T TELL HER, '*THAT'S NOT THE MEN'S BATHROOM!*'"
...OR SO THEY TRIED TO ENCOURAGE ME...
HOW IS THAT EN-COURAGE-MENT?
I DON'T THINK SHE'S COME TO CAMPUS SINCE THEN...
SHE'S DEFINITELY AVOIDING ME... WHAT DO I DO?
CALM DOWN, NAO-CHAN!
I THINK SHE JUST FEELS REALLY BAD TOO.
YOU JUST NEED TO APOLOGIZE THE NEXT TIME YOU SEE HER!
I'M SURE SHE'LL LAUGH IT OFF AND FORGIVE YOU.

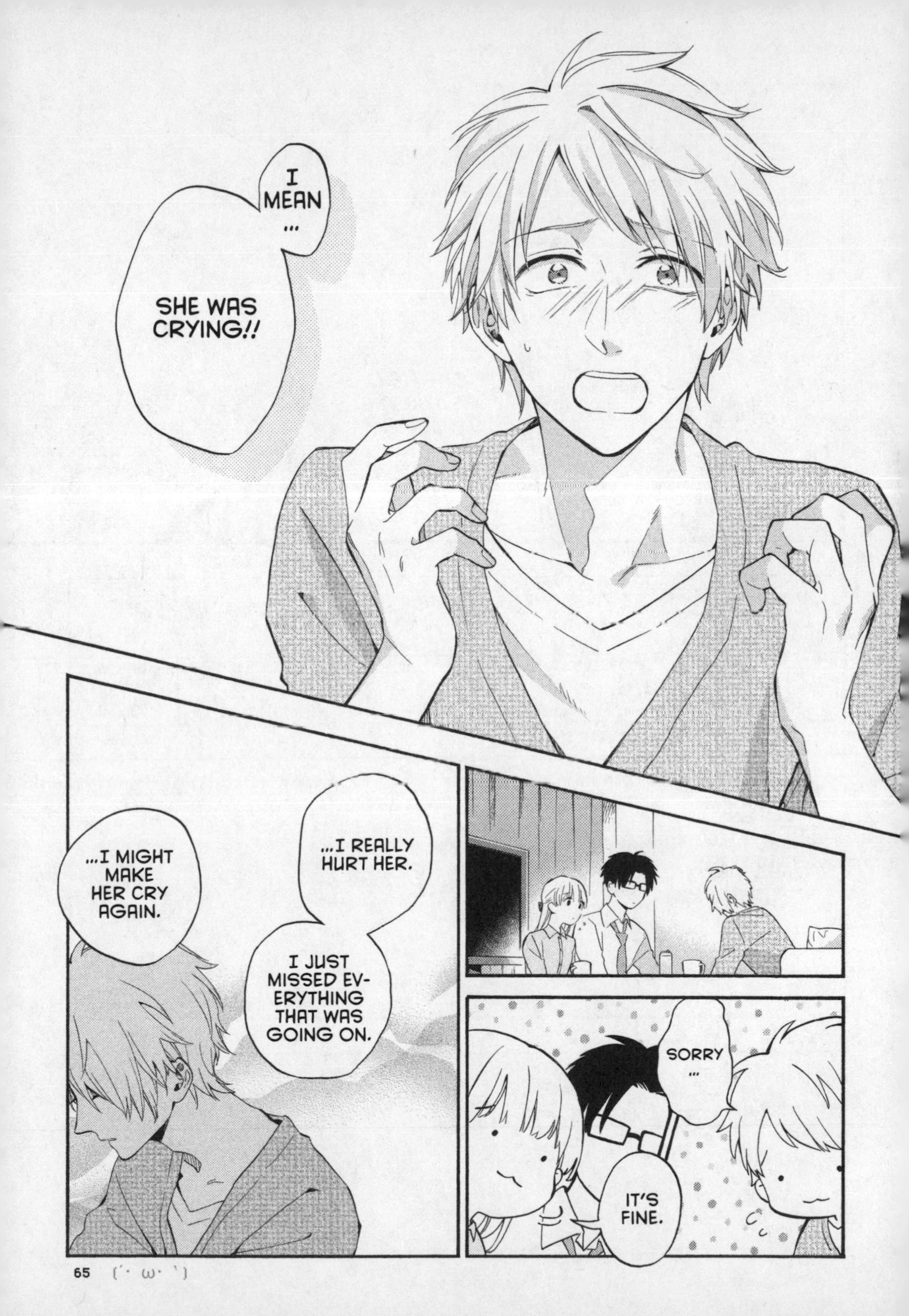
I MEAN ...
SHE WAS CRYING!!
SORRY ...
IT'S FINE.
...I REALLY HURT HER.
I JUST MISSED EV-ERYTHING THAT WAS GOING ON.
...I MIGHT MAKE HER CRY AGAIN.

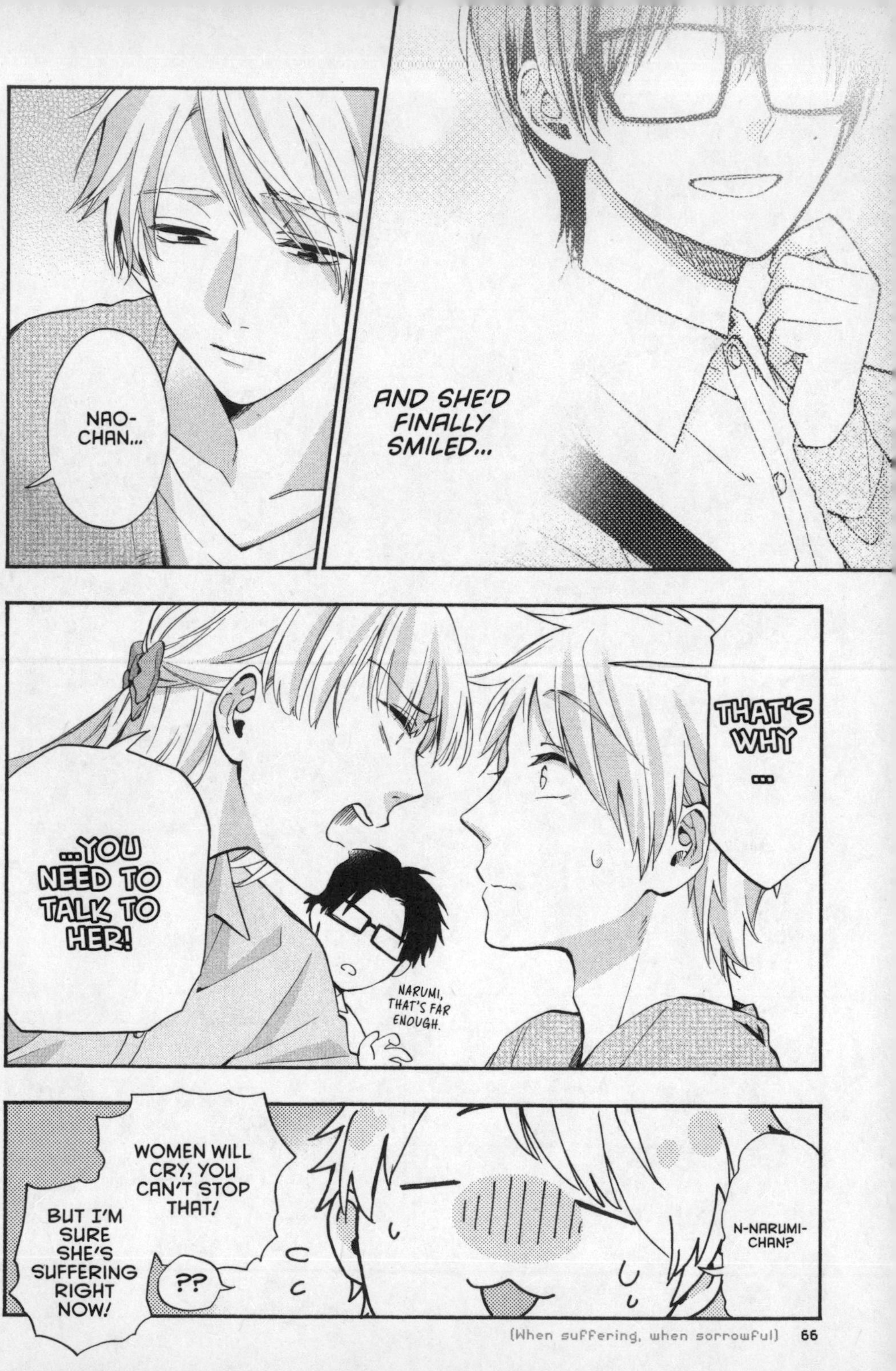
AND SHE'D FINALLY SMILED...
NAO-CHAN...
THAT'S WHY ...
...YOU NEED TO TALK TO HER!
NARUMI, THAT'S FAR ENOUGH.
N-NARUMI-CHAN?
WOMEN WILL CRY, YOU CAN'T STOP THAT!
??
BUT I'M SURE SHE'S SUFFERING RIGHT NOW!

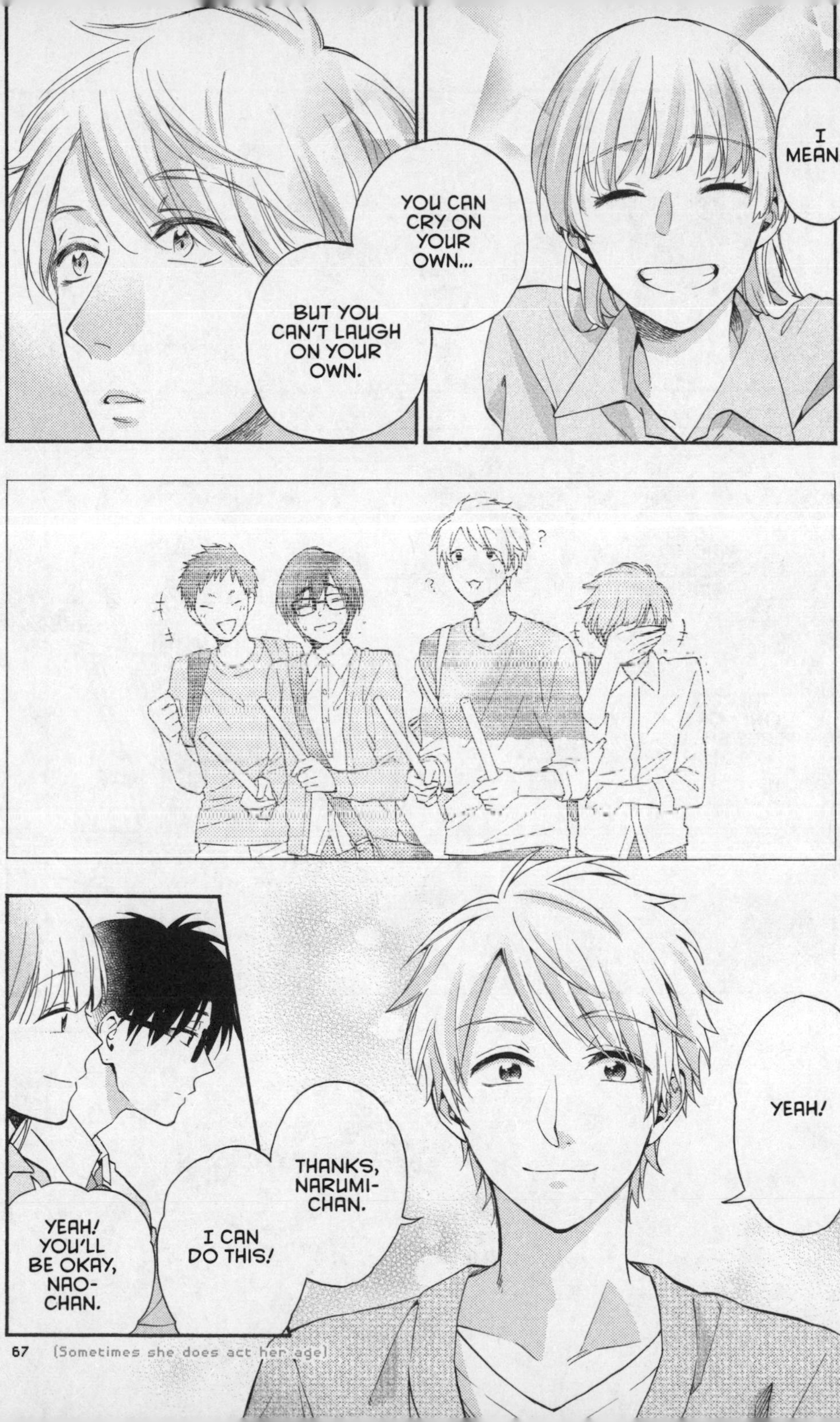
I MEAN...
YOU CAN CRY ON YOUR OWN...
BUT YOU CAN'T LAUGH ON YOUR OWN.
YEAH!
THANKS, NARUMI-CHAN.
I CAN DO THIS!
YEAH! YOU'LL BE OKAY, NAO-CHAN.

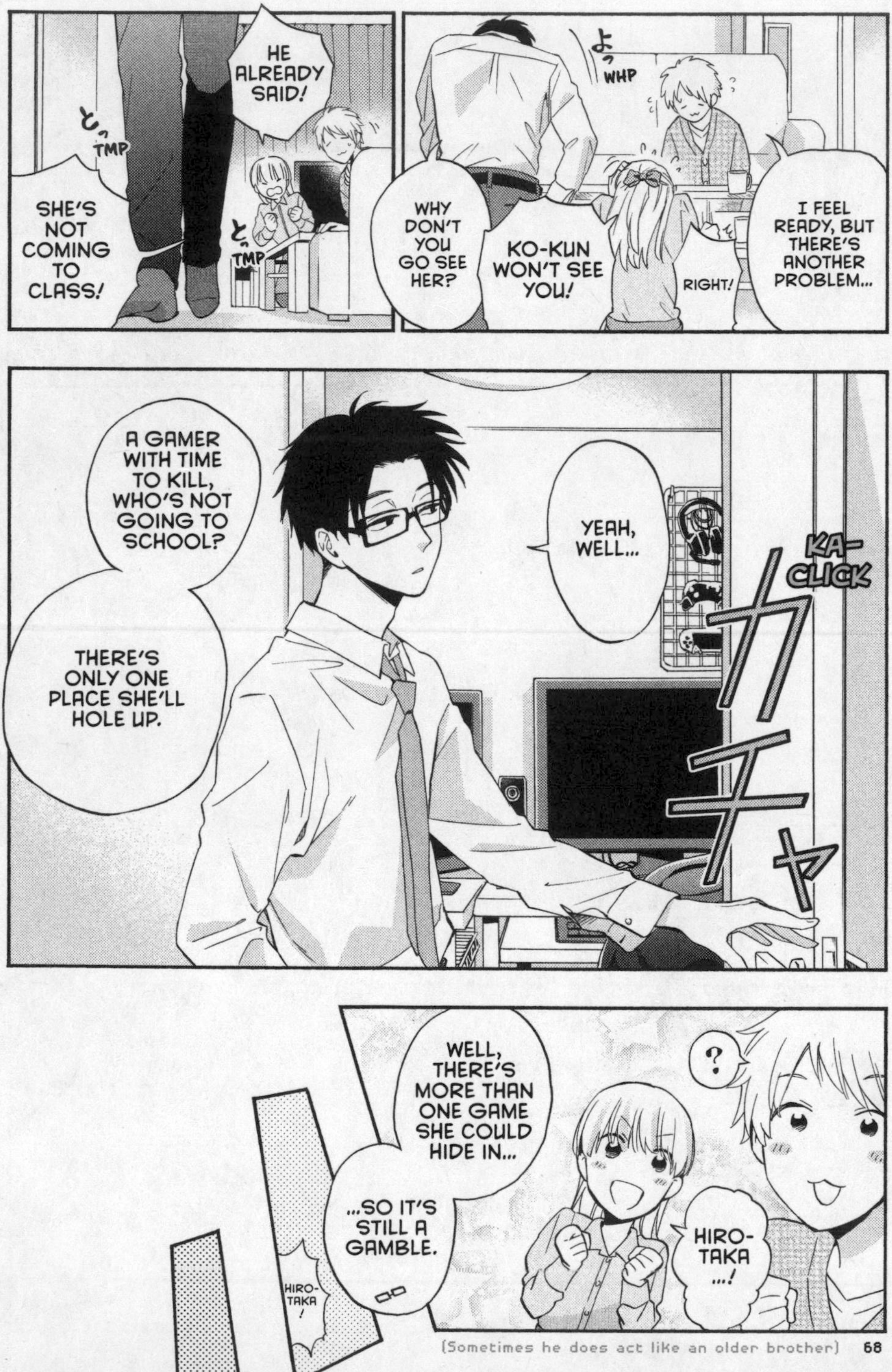
I FEEL READY, BUT THERE'S ANOTHER PROBLEM...
よっ WHP
RIGHT!
KO-KUN WON'T SEE YOU!
WHY DON'T YOU GO SEE HER?
HE ALREADY SAID!
とっ TMP
とっ TMP
SHE'S NOT COMING TO CLASS!
KA-CLICK
カチャ
YEAH, WELL...
A GAMER WITH TIME TO KILL, WHO'S NOT GOING TO SCHOOL?
THERE'S ONLY ONE PLACE SHE'LL HOLE UP.
?
HIRO-TAKA ...!
WELL, THERE'S MORE THAN ONE GAME SHE COULD HIDE IN...
...SO IT'S STILL A GAMBLE.
HIRO-TAKA!

(Sometimes he does act like an older brother)

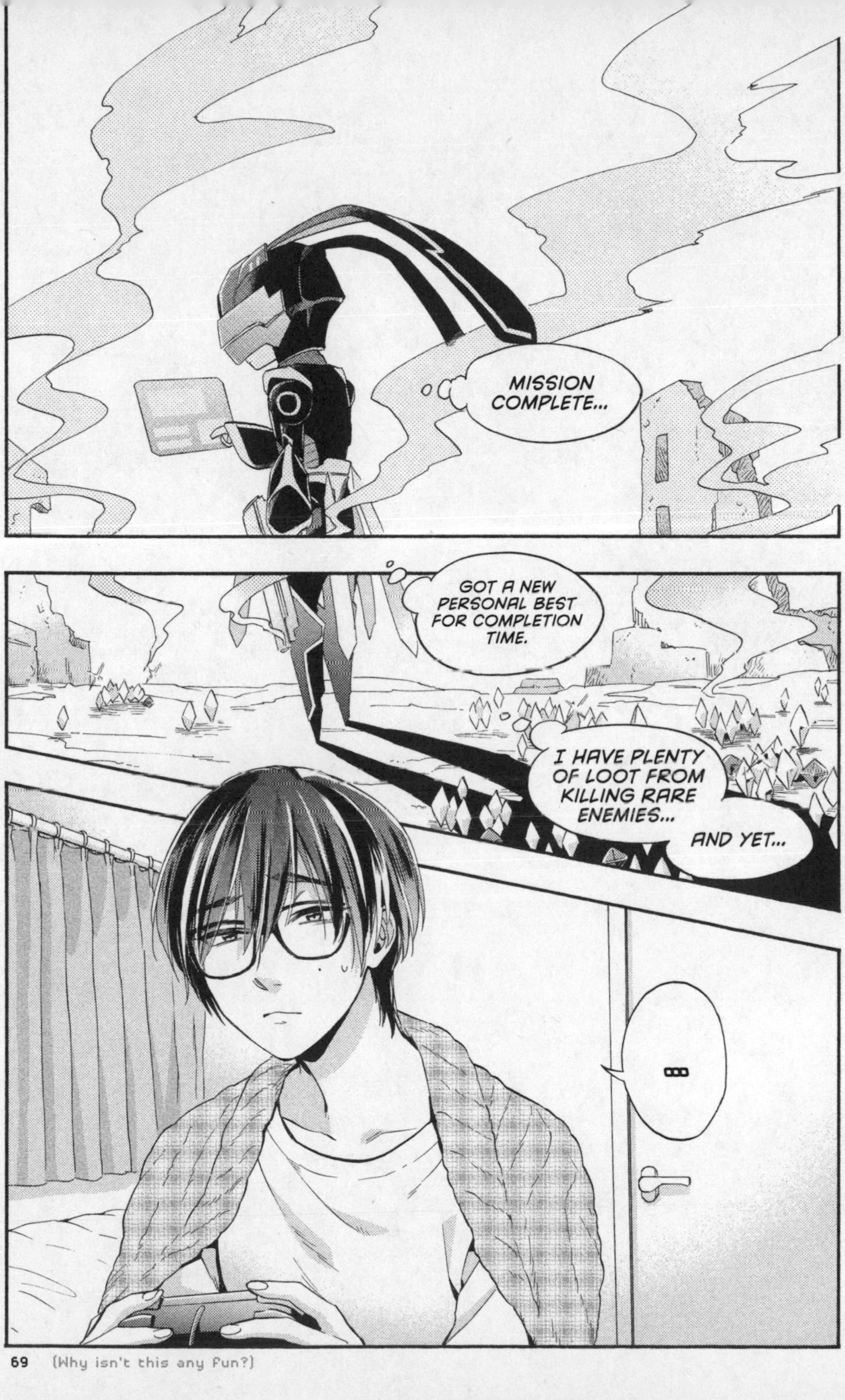
MISSION COMPLETE...
GOT A NEW PERSONAL BEST FOR COMPLETION TIME.
I HAVE PLENTY OF LOOT FROM KILLING RARE ENEMIES...
AND YET...
...

HIS ORIGINAL DESIGNS WERE A LITTLE DIFFERENT.

HER ORIGINAL DESIGN WAS REALLY DIFFERENT.

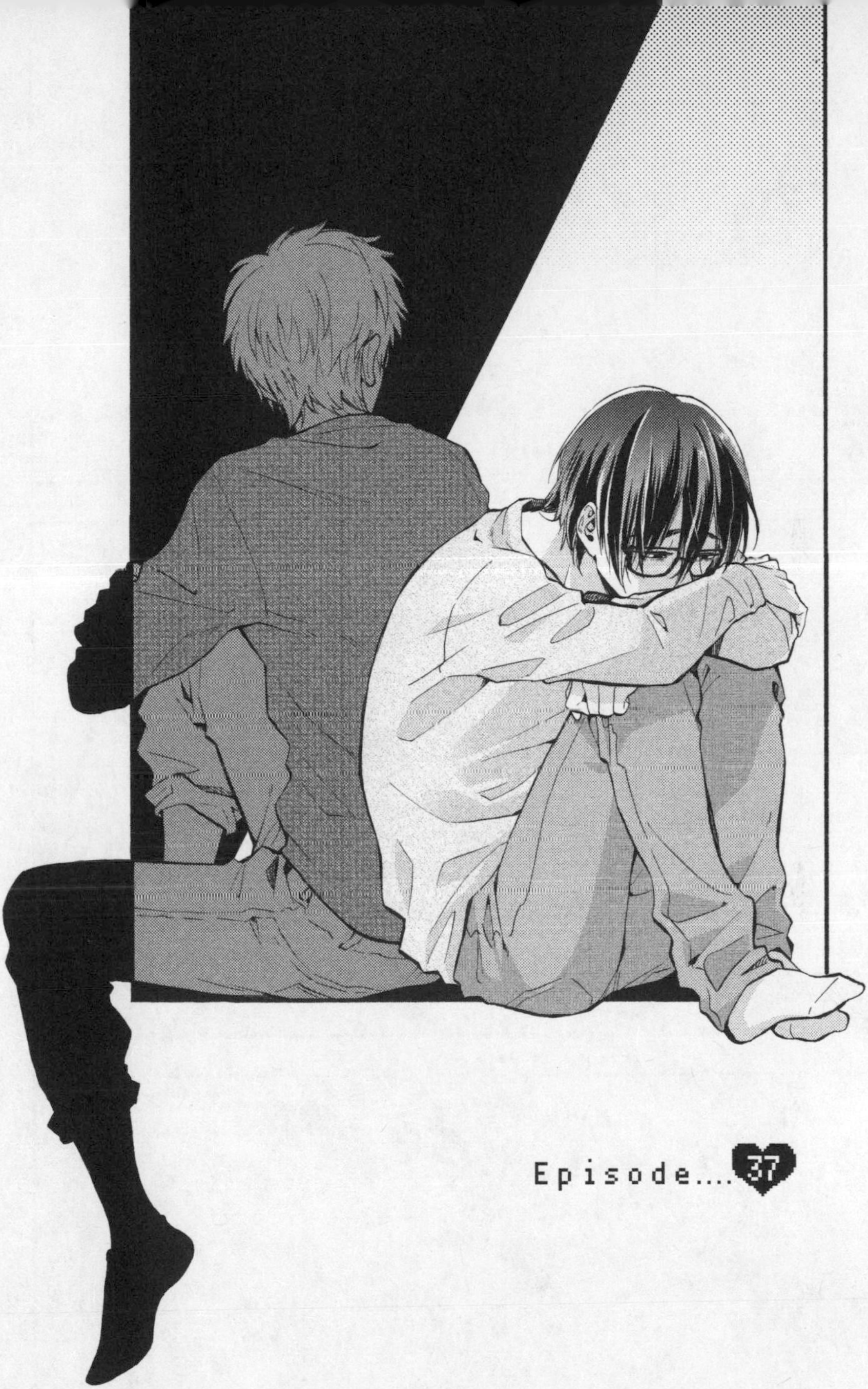

Episode.... 37

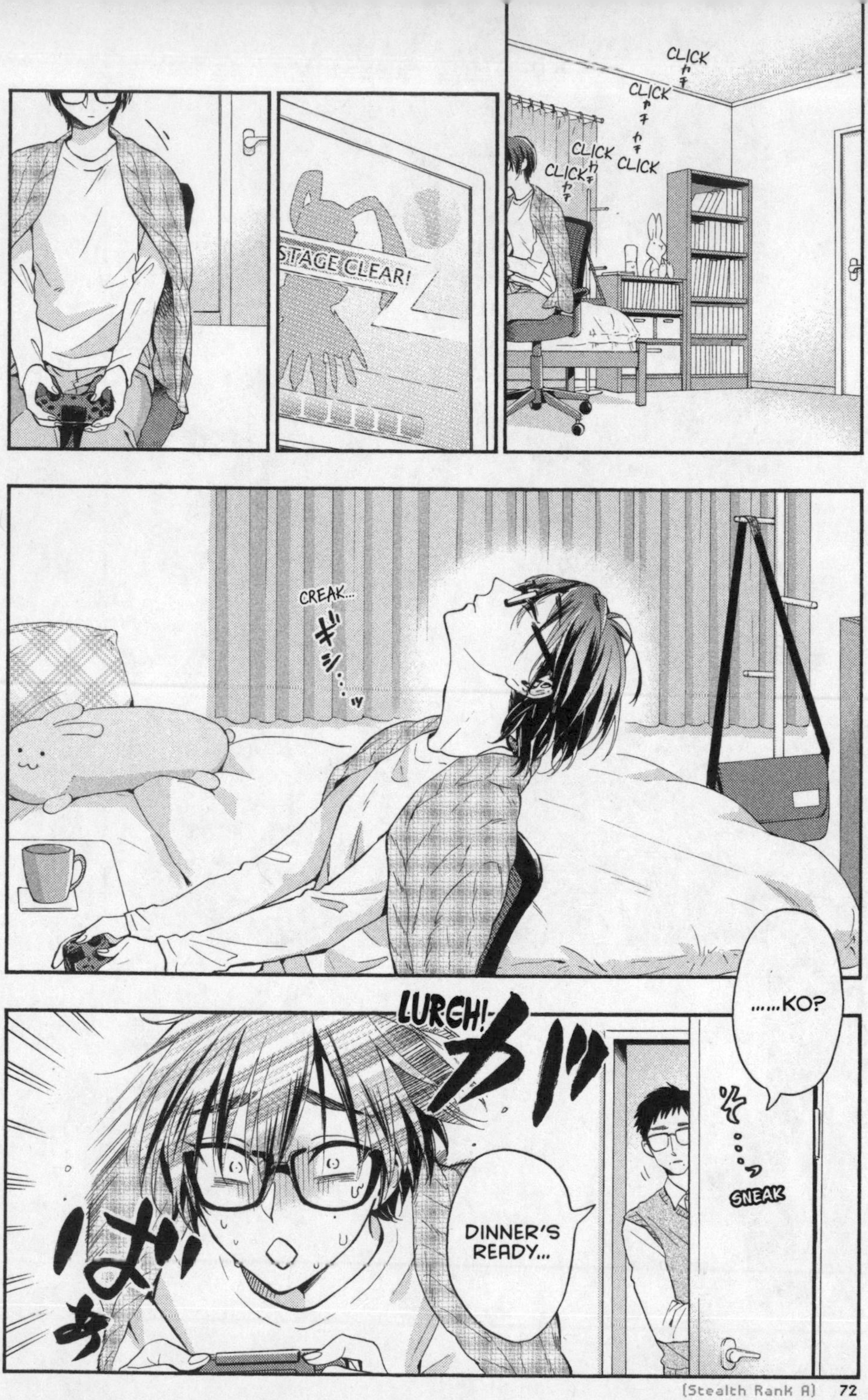
CLICK
CLICK
CLICK
CLICK
CLICK
STAGE CLEAR!
CREAK...
ギシ...
......KO?
SNEAK
LURCH!
DINNER'S READY...

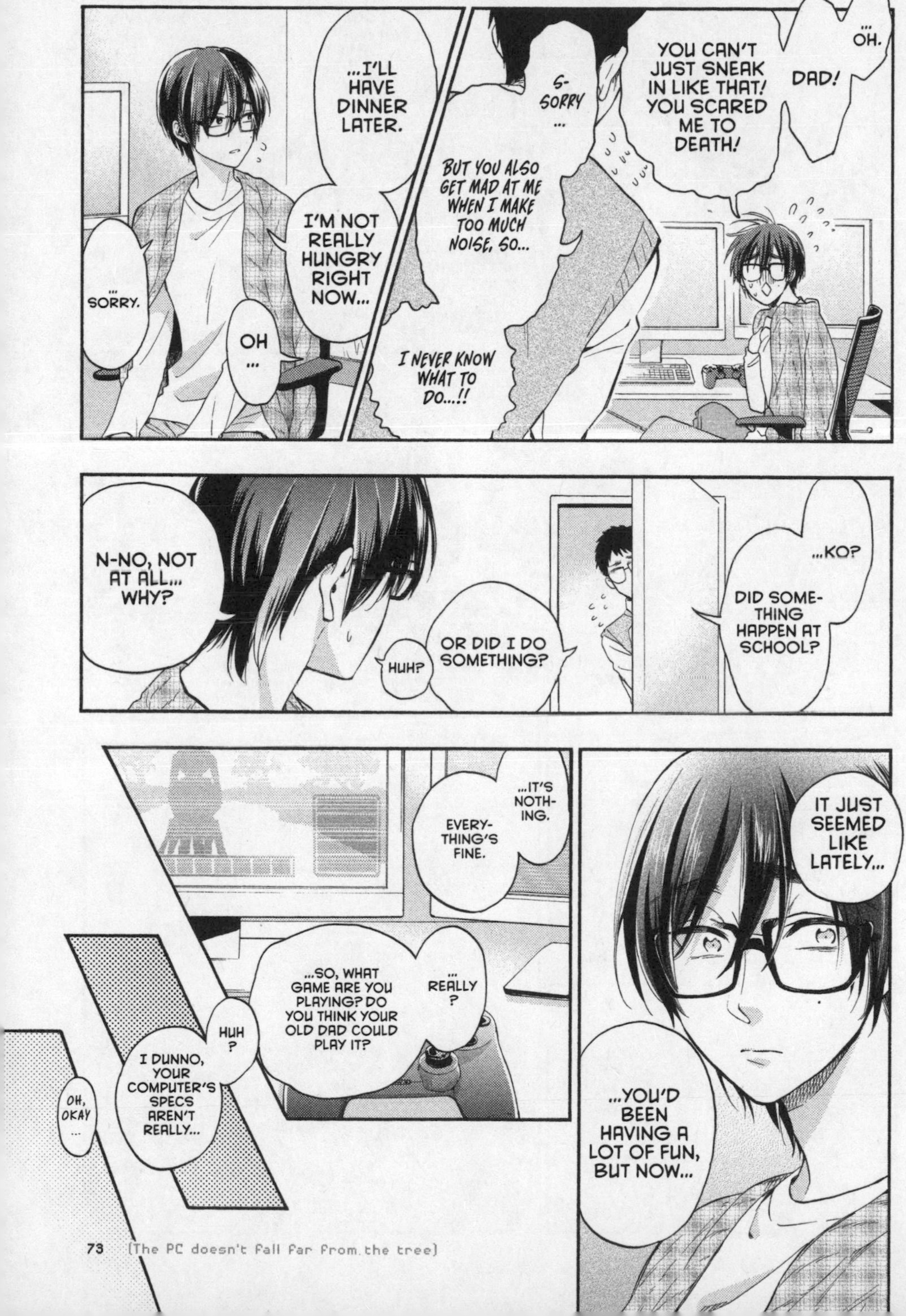
...OH.
DAD!
YOU CAN'T JUST SNEAK IN LIKE THAT! YOU SCARED ME TO DEATH!
S-SORRY...
BUT YOU ALSO GET MAD AT ME WHEN I MAKE TOO MUCH NOISE, SO...
I NEVER KNOW WHAT TO DO...!!
...I'LL HAVE DINNER LATER.
I'M NOT REALLY HUNGRY RIGHT NOW...
OH...
...SORRY.
...KO?
DID SOMETHING HAPPEN AT SCHOOL?
OR DID I DO SOMETHING?
HUH?
N-NO, NOT AT ALL... WHY?
IT JUST SEEMED LIKE LATELY...
...YOU'D BEEN HAVING A LOT OF FUN, BUT NOW...
...IT'S NOTHING.
EVERYTHING'S FINE.
...REALLY?
...SO, WHAT GAME ARE YOU PLAYING? DO YOU THINK YOUR OLD DAD COULD PLAY IT?
HUH?
I DUNNO, YOUR COMPUTER'S SPECS AREN'T REALLY...
OH, OKAY...

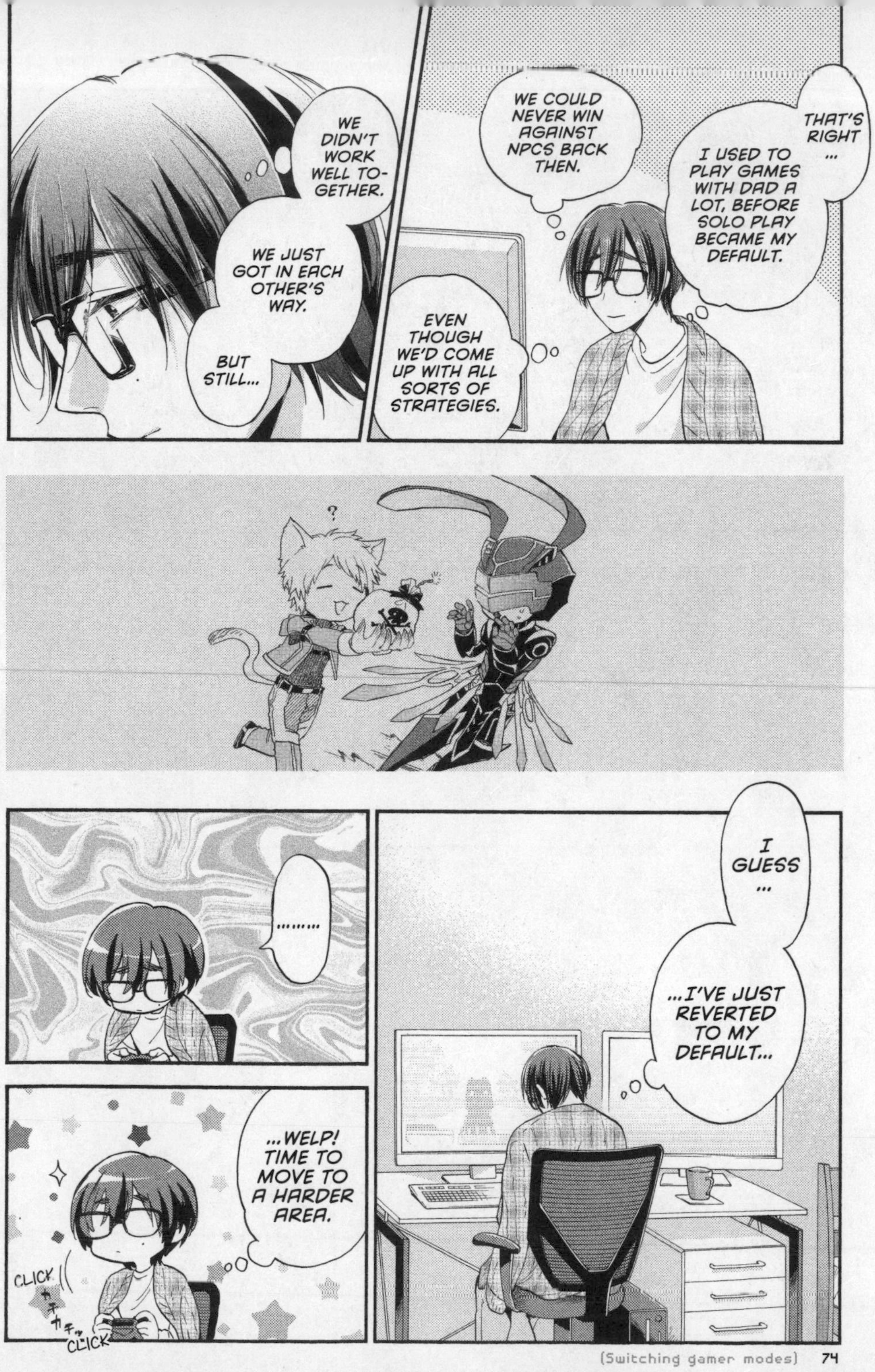
THAT'S RIGHT ...
I USED TO PLAY GAMES WITH DAD A LOT, BEFORE SOLO PLAY BECAME MY DEFAULT.
WE COULD NEVER WIN AGAINST NPCS BACK THEN.
EVEN THOUGH WE'D COME UP WITH ALL SORTS OF STRATEGIES.
WE DIDN'T WORK WELL TO-GETHER.
WE JUST GOT IN EACH OTHER'S WAY.
BUT STILL...
?
I GUESS ...
...I'VE JUST REVERTED TO MY DEFAULT...
....
...WELP! TIME TO MOVE TO A HARDER AREA.
CLICK
カチカチ
CLICK

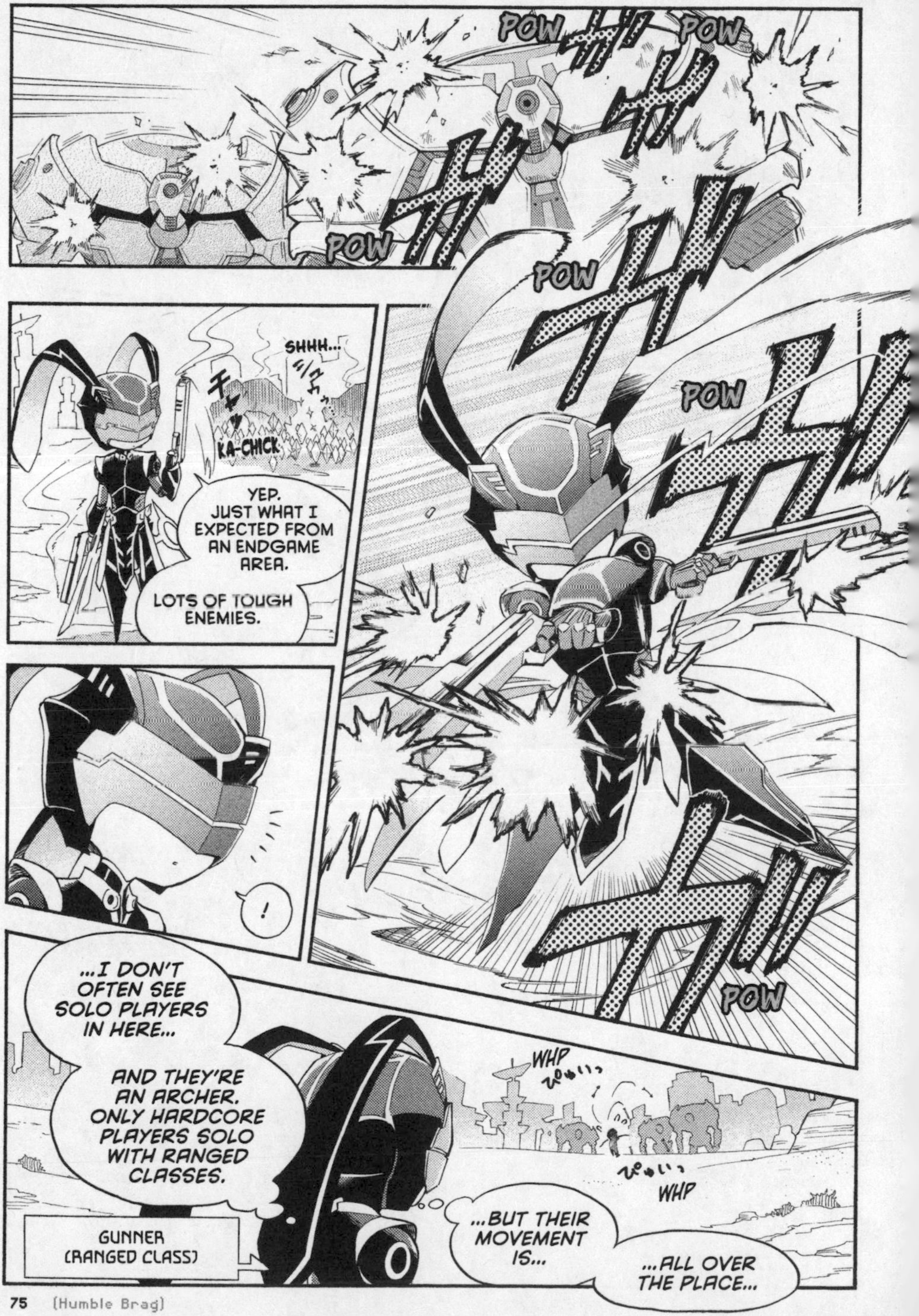
POW
POW
POW
POW
POW
POW
SHHH...
KA-CHICK
YEP. JUST WHAT I EXPECTED FROM AN ENDGAME AREA.
LOTS OF TOUGH ENEMIES.
!
...I DON'T OFTEN SEE SOLO PLAYERS IN HERE...
AND THEY'RE AN ARCHER. ONLY HARDCORE PLAYERS SOLO WITH RANGED CLASSES.
GUNNER (RANGED CLASS)
WHP
ぴゅいっ
ぴゅいっ
WHP
...BUT THEIR MOVEMENT IS...
...ALL OVER THE PLACE...

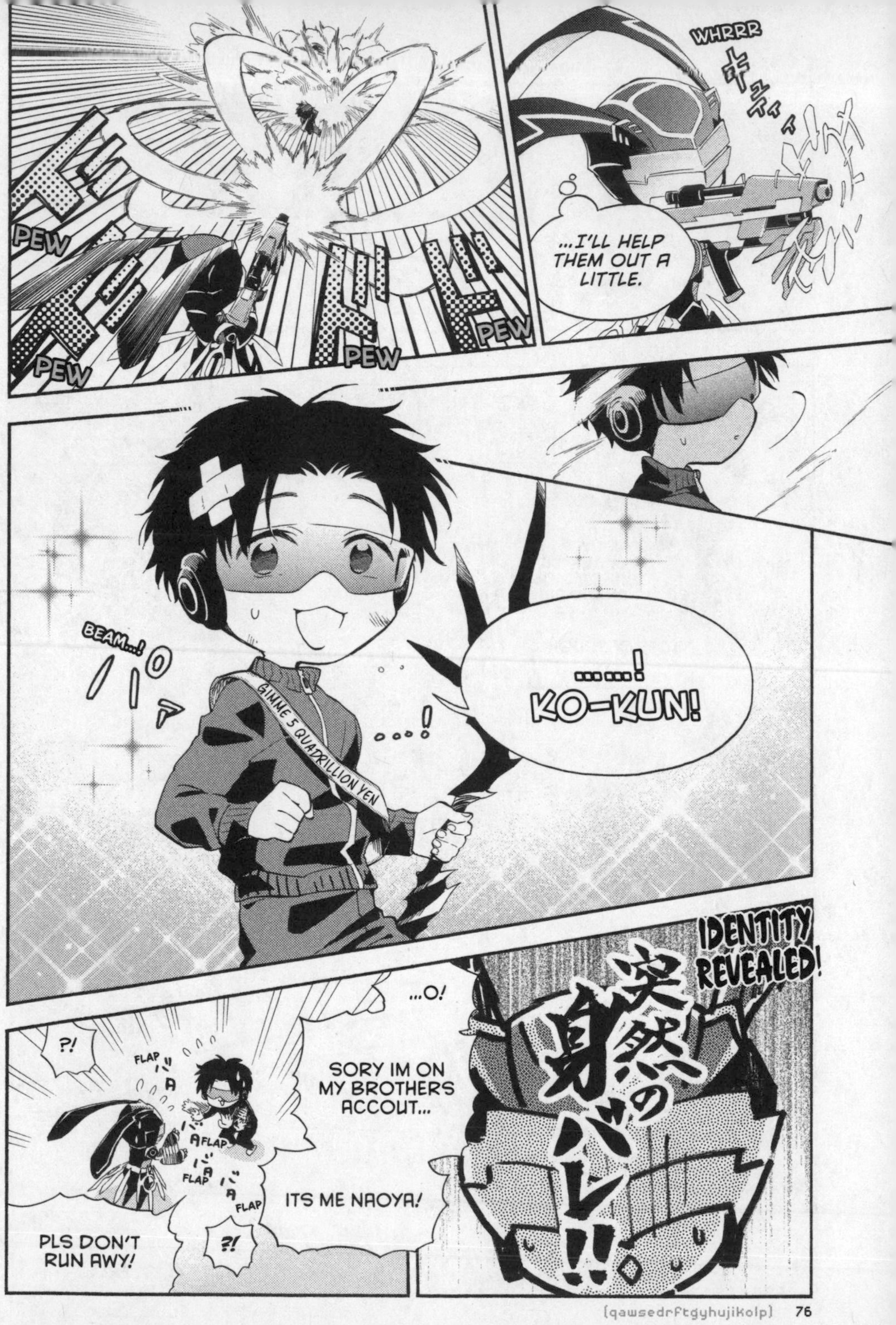
WHRRR
...I'LL HELP THEM OUT A LITTLE.
PEW
PEW
PEW
PEW
......! KO-KUN!
...!
BEAM...!
IDENTITY REVEALED!
突然の身バレ!!
...O!
SORY IM ON MY BROTHERS ACCOUT...
ITS ME NAOYA!
?!
FLAP
FLAP
FLAP
FLAP
?!
PLS DON'T RUN AWY!

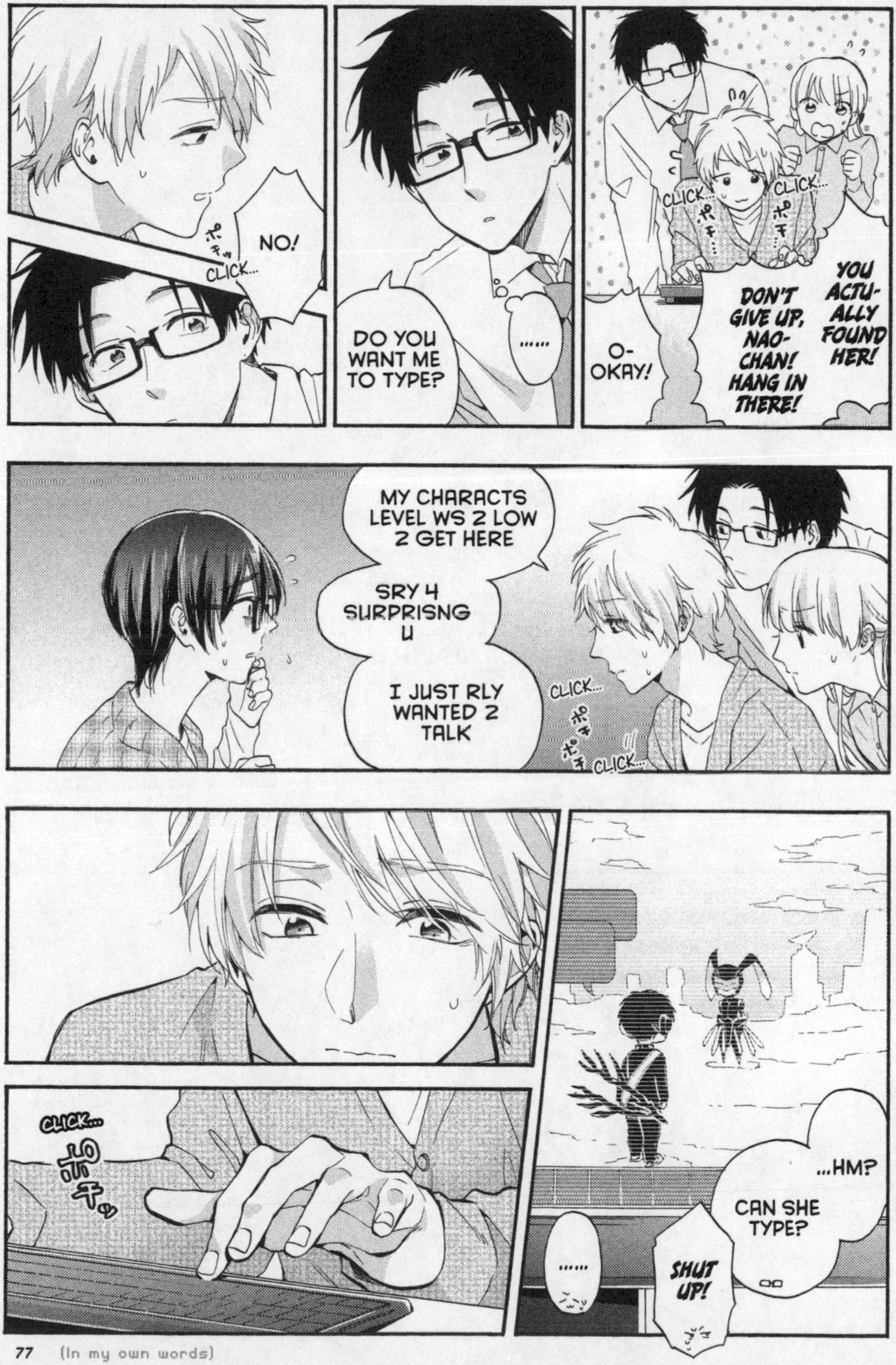
YOU ACTUALLY FOUND HER!
DON'T GIVE UP, NAO-CHAN! HANG IN THERE!
CLICK...
CLICK...
O-OKAY!
......
DO YOU WANT ME TO TYPE?
NO!
CLICK...
MY CHARACTS LEVEL WS 2 LOW 2 GET HERE
SRY 4 SURPRISNG U
I JUST RLY WANTED 2 TALK
CLICK...
CLICK...
...HM?
CAN SHE TYPE?
SHUT UP!
......
CLICK...

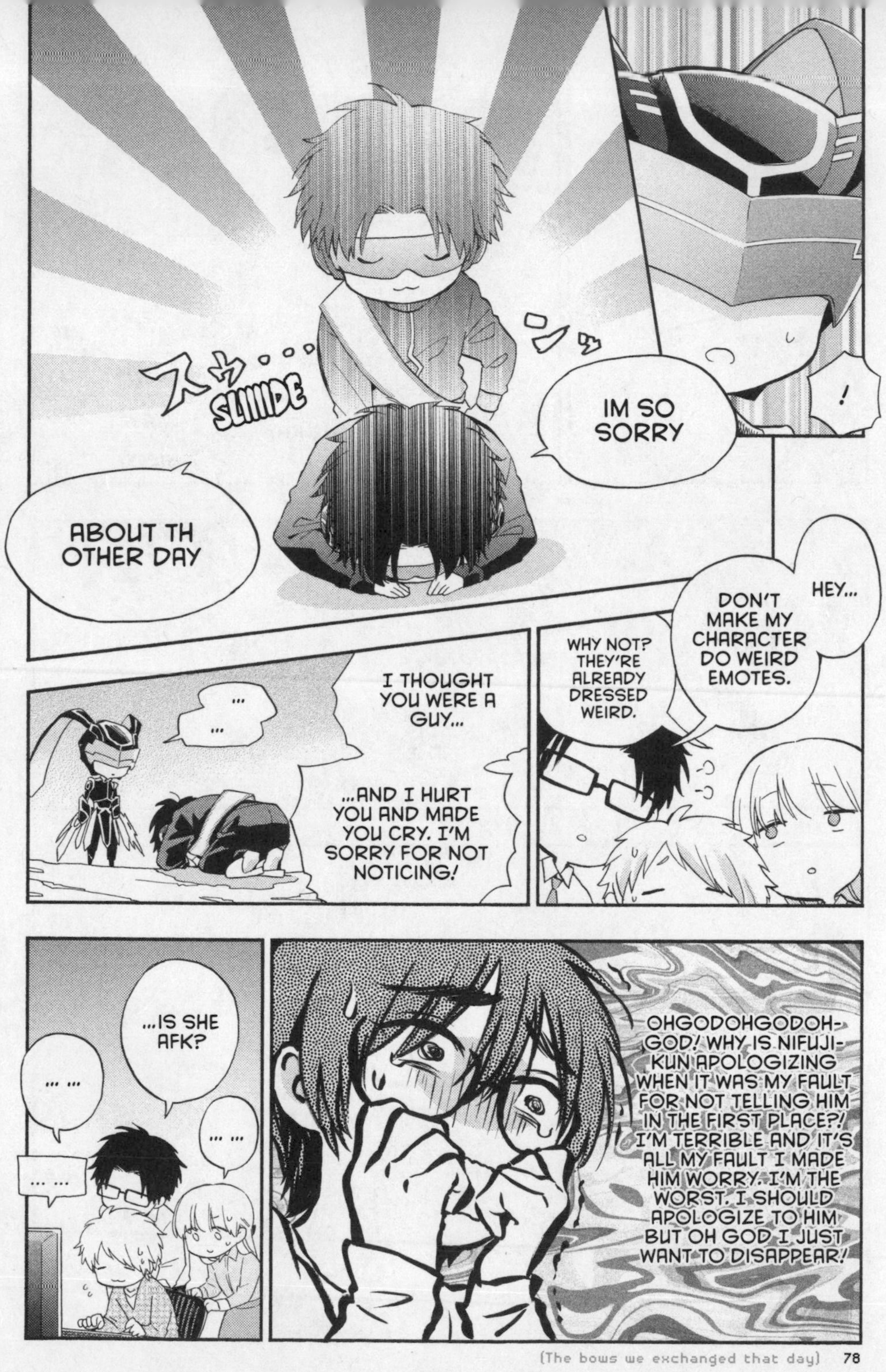
!
スゥ...
SLIIIIDE
IM SO SORRY
ABOUT TH OTHER DAY
HEY...
DON'T MAKE MY CHARACTER DO WEIRD EMOTES.
WHY NOT? THEY'RE ALREADY DRESSED WEIRD.
I THOUGHT YOU WERE A GUY...
...AND I HURT YOU AND MADE YOU CRY. I'M SORRY FOR NOT NOTICING!
... ...
OHGODOHGODOH-GOD! WHY IS NIFUJI-KUN APOLOGIZING WHEN IT WAS MY FAULT FOR NOT TELLING HIM IN THE FIRST PLACE?! I'M TERRIBLE AND IT'S ALL MY FAULT I MADE HIM WORRY. I'M THE WORST. I SHOULD APOLOGIZE TO HIM BUT OH GOD I JUST WANT TO DISAPPEAR!
...IS SHE AFK?
... ...
... ...
... ...

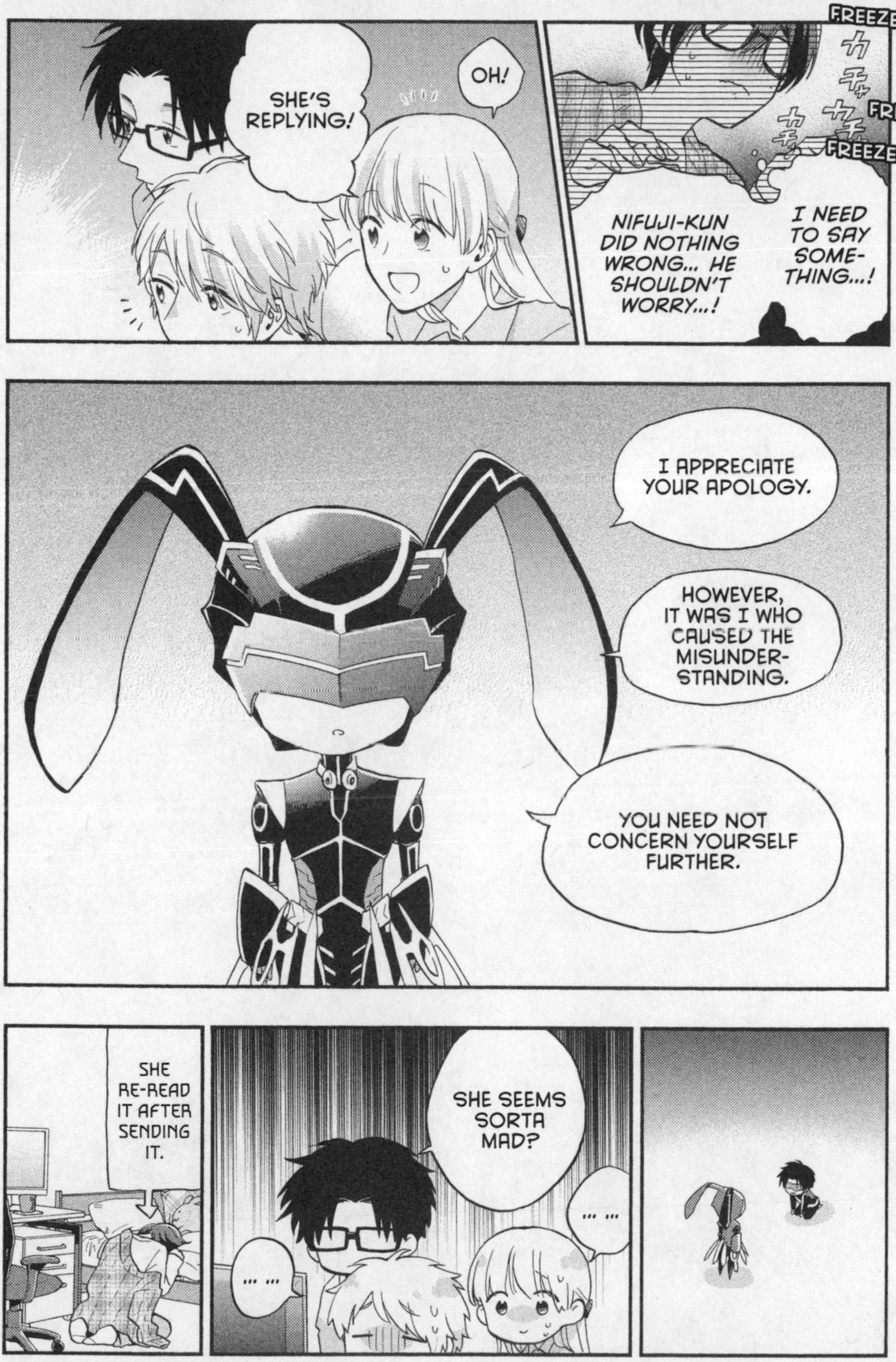
FREEZE
FREEZE
FREEZE
I NEED TO SAY SOME-THING...!
NIFUJI-KUN DID NOTHING WRONG... HE SHOULDN'T WORRY...!
OH!
SHE'S REPLYING!
I APPRECIATE YOUR APOLOGY.
HOWEVER, IT WAS I WHO CAUSED THE MISUNDER-STANDING.
YOU NEED NOT CONCERN YOURSELF FURTHER.
SHE SEEMS SORTA MAD?
... ...
... ...
SHE RE-READ IT AFTER SENDING IT.

(Painfully awkward)

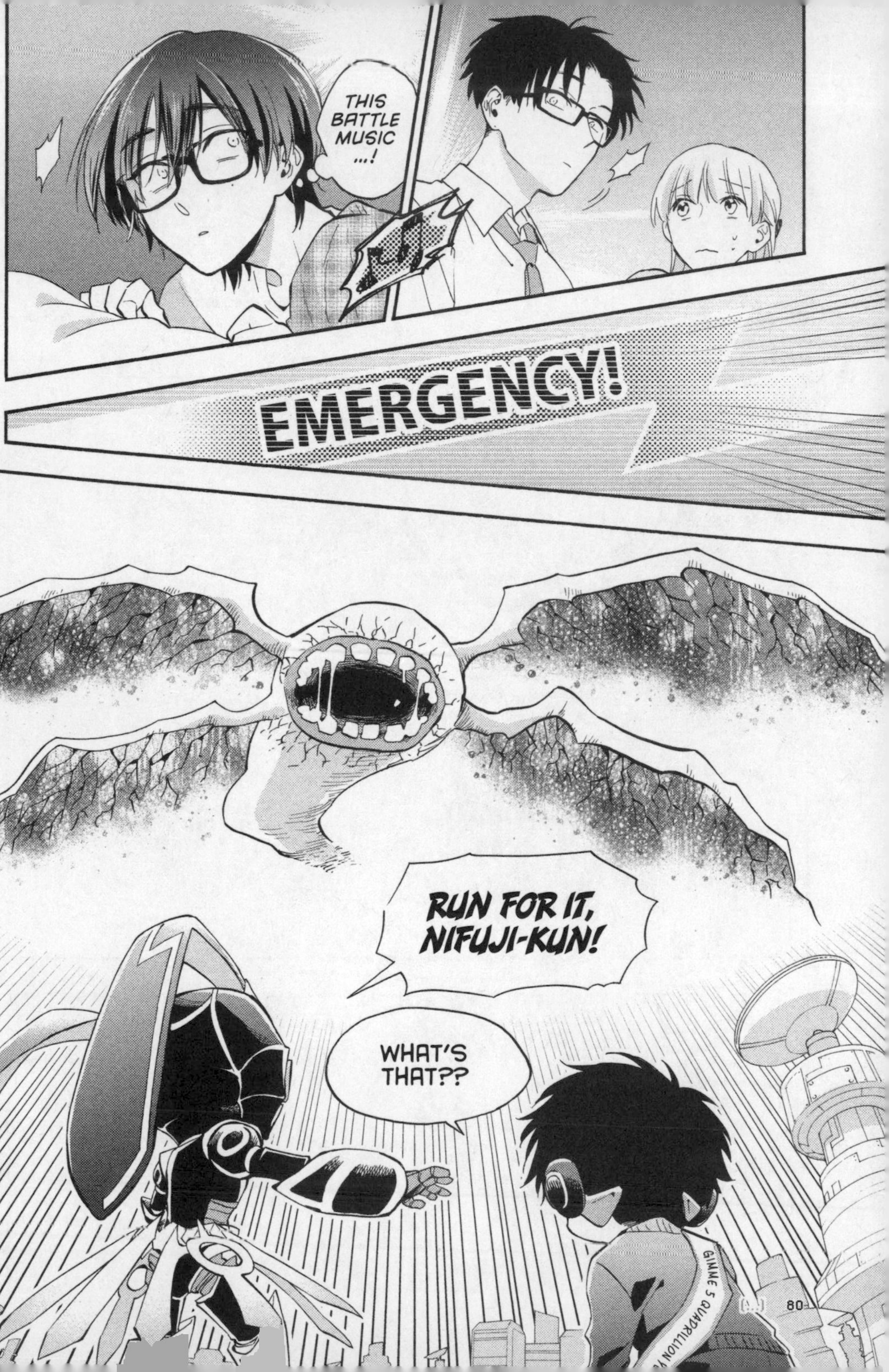
THIS BATTLE MUSIC ...!
EMERGENCY!
RUN FOR IT, NIFUJI-KUN!
WHAT'S THAT??
GIMME 5 QUADRILLION

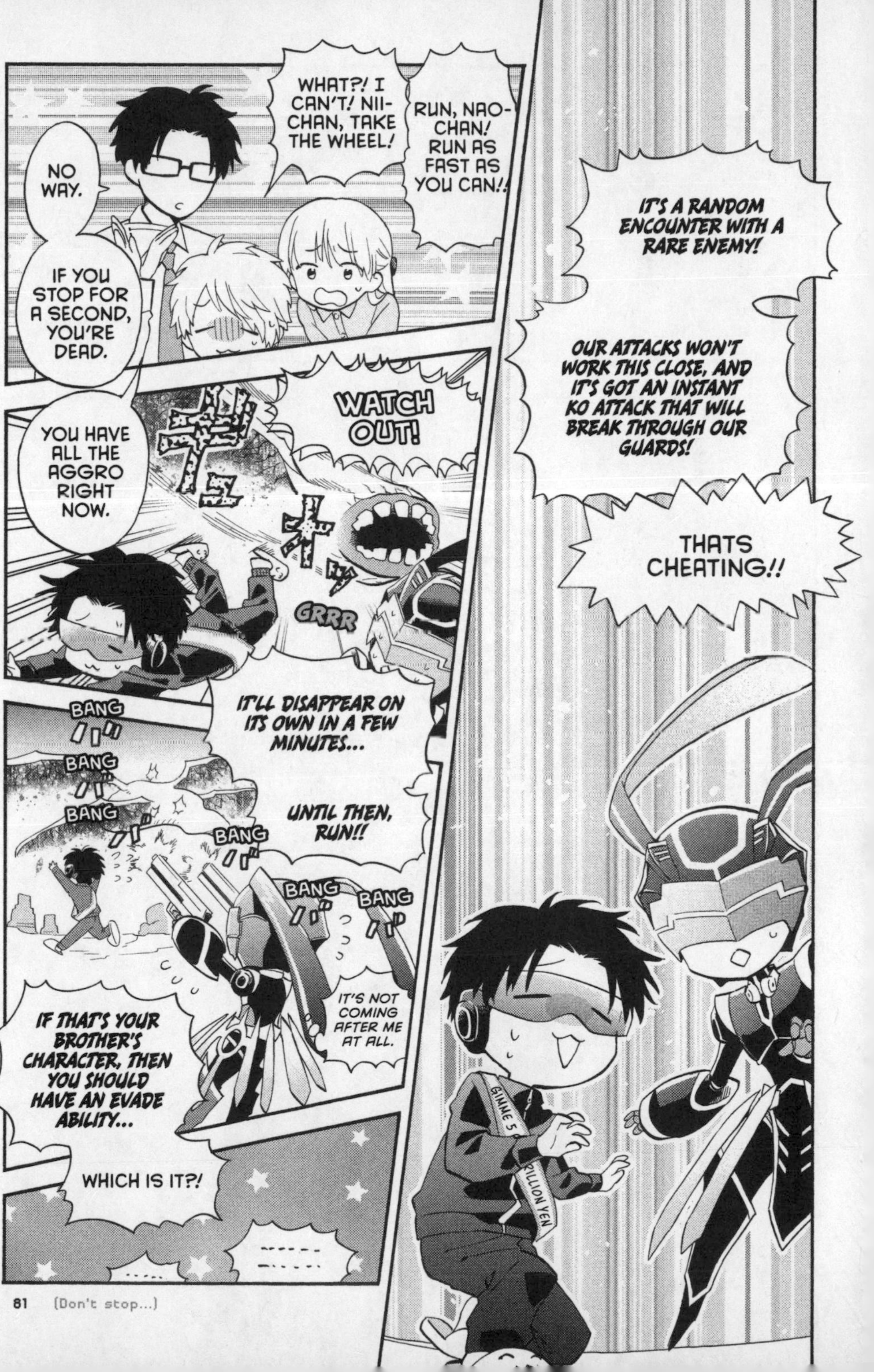
IT'S A RANDOM ENCOUNTER WITH A RARE ENEMY!
OUR ATTACKS WON'T WORK THIS CLOSE, AND IT'S GOT AN INSTANT KO ATTACK THAT WILL BREAK THROUGH OUR GUARDS!
THATS CHEATING!!
RUN, NAO-CHAN! RUN AS FAST AS YOU CAN!!
WHAT?! I CAN'T! NII-CHAN, TAKE THE WHEEL!
NO WAY.
IF YOU STOP FOR A SECOND, YOU'RE DEAD.
WATCH OUT!
YOU HAVE ALL THE AGGRO RIGHT NOW.
GRRR
IT'LL DISAPPEAR ON ITS OWN IN A FEW MINUTES...
UNTIL THEN, RUN!!
BANG
BANG
BANG
BANG
BANG
BANG
IT'S NOT COMING AFTER ME AT ALL.
IF THAT'S YOUR BROTHER'S CHARACTER, THEN YOU SHOULD HAVE AN EVADE ABILITY...
WHICH IS IT?!

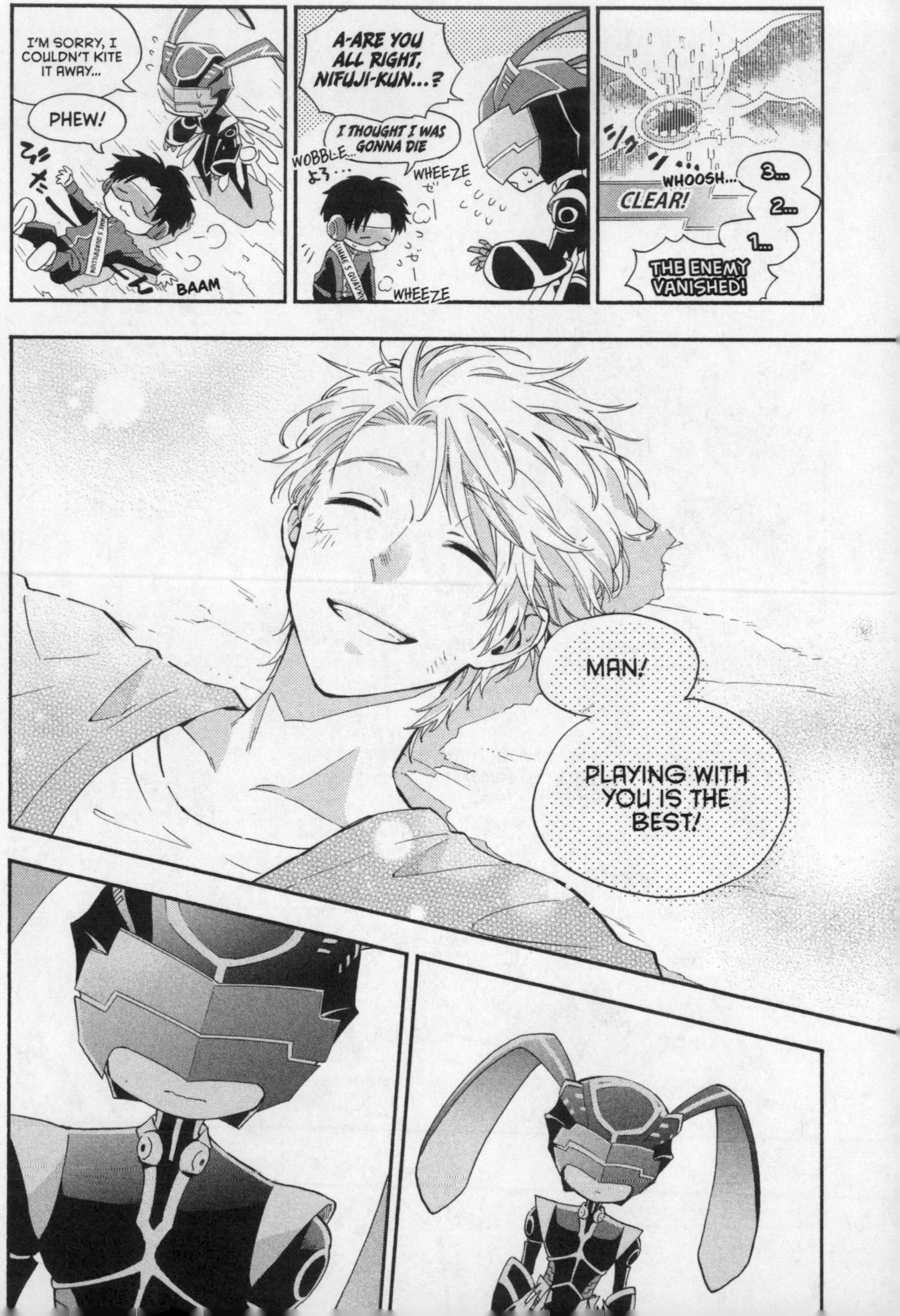
3...
2...
1...
WHOOSH...
CLEAR!
THE ENEMY VANISHED!
A-ARE YOU ALL RIGHT, NIFUJI-KUN...?
I THOUGHT I WAS GONNA DIE
WHEEZE
WOBBLE...
WHEEZE
I'M SORRY, I COULDN'T KITE IT AWAY...
PHEW!
BAAM
MAN!
PLAYING WITH YOU IS THE BEST!

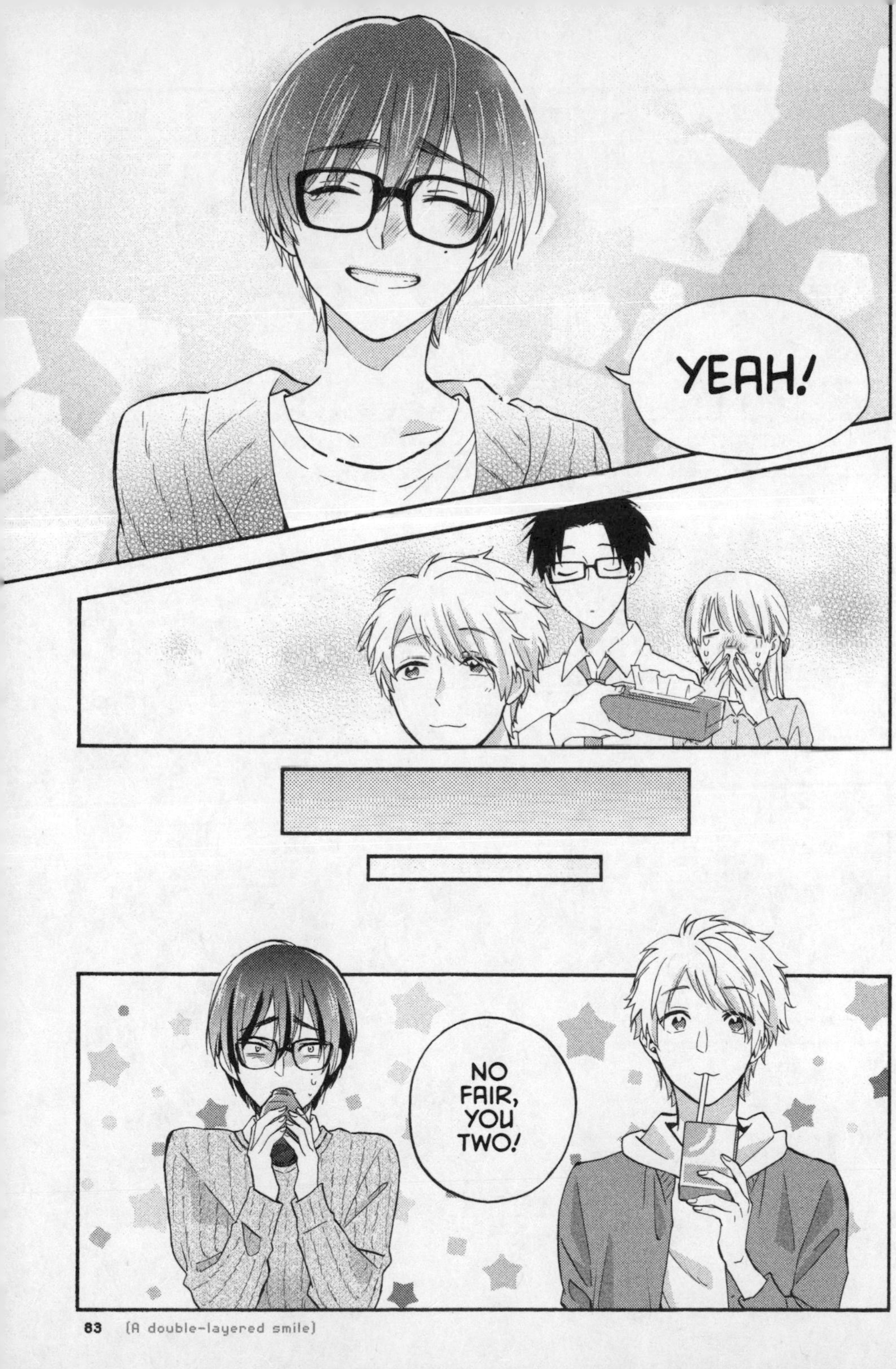
YEAH!
NO FAIR, YOU TWO!

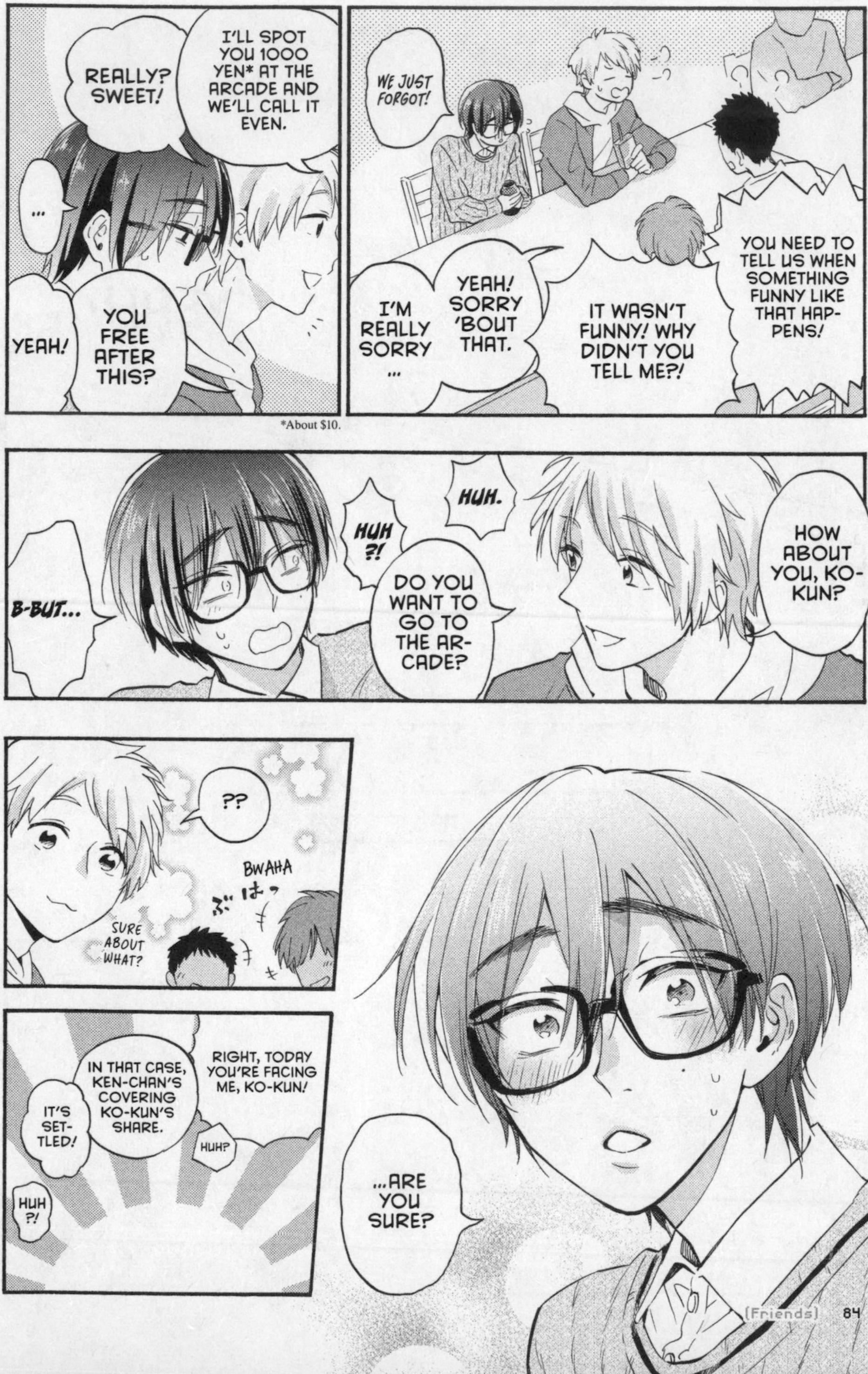

YOU NEED TO TELL US WHEN SOMETHING FUNNY LIKE THAT HAP-PENS!
IT WASN'T FUNNY! WHY DIDN'T YOU TELL ME?!
WE JUST FORGOT!
YEAH! SORRY 'BOUT THAT.
I'M REALLY SORRY ...
I'LL SPOT YOU 1000 YEN* AT THE ARCADE AND WE'LL CALL IT EVEN.
REALLY? SWEET!
...
YOU FREE AFTER THIS?
YEAH!
HOW ABOUT YOU, KO-KUN?
HUH.
HUH ?!
DO YOU WANT TO GO TO THE AR-CADE?
B-BUT...
...ARE YOU SURE?
??
BWAHA
ぶはっ
SURE ABOUT WHAT?
RIGHT, TODAY YOU'RE FACING ME, KO-KUN!
IN THAT CASE, KEN-CHAN'S COVERING KO-KUN'S SHARE.
HUH?
IT'S SET-TLED!
HUH ?!

*About $10.

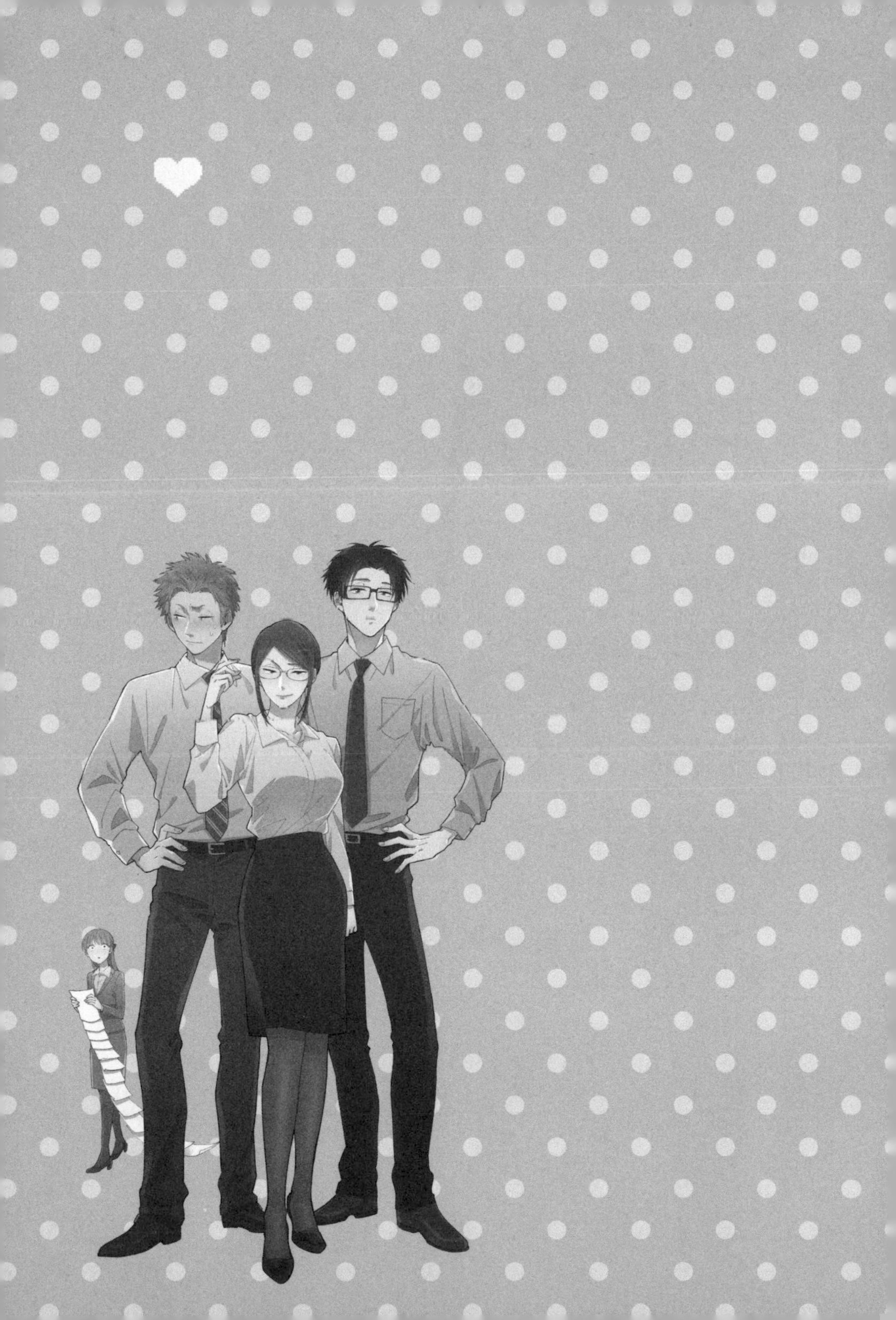

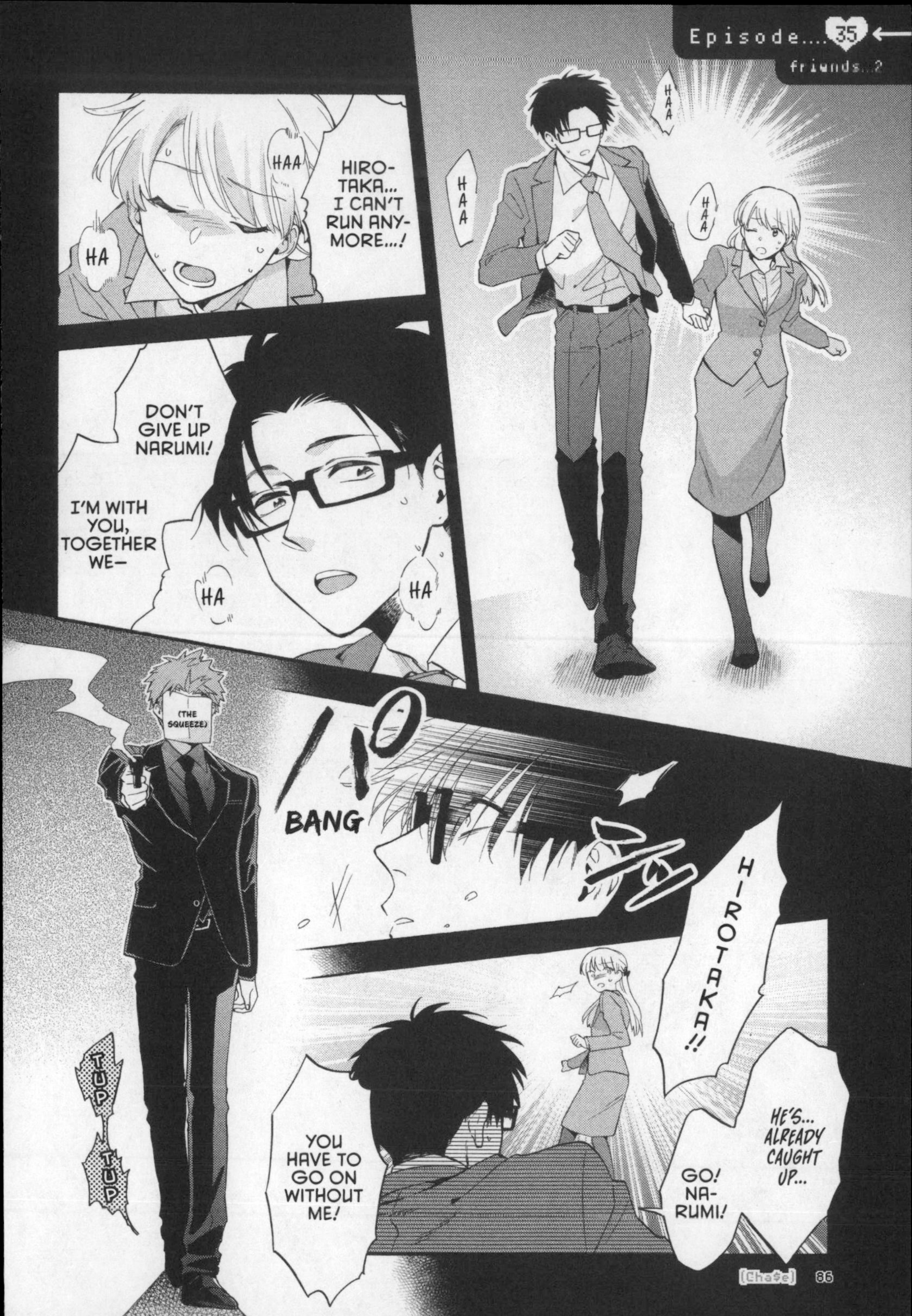
HAA
HAA
HAA
HAA
HIRO-TAKA... I CAN'T RUN ANY-MORE...!
HA
DON'T GIVE UP NARUMI!
I'M WITH YOU, TOGETHER WE—
HA
HA
BANG
HIROTAKA!!
HE'S... ALREADY CAUGHT UP...
GO! NA-RUMI!
YOU HAVE TO GO ON WITHOUT ME!
(THE SQUEEZE)
TUP
TUP

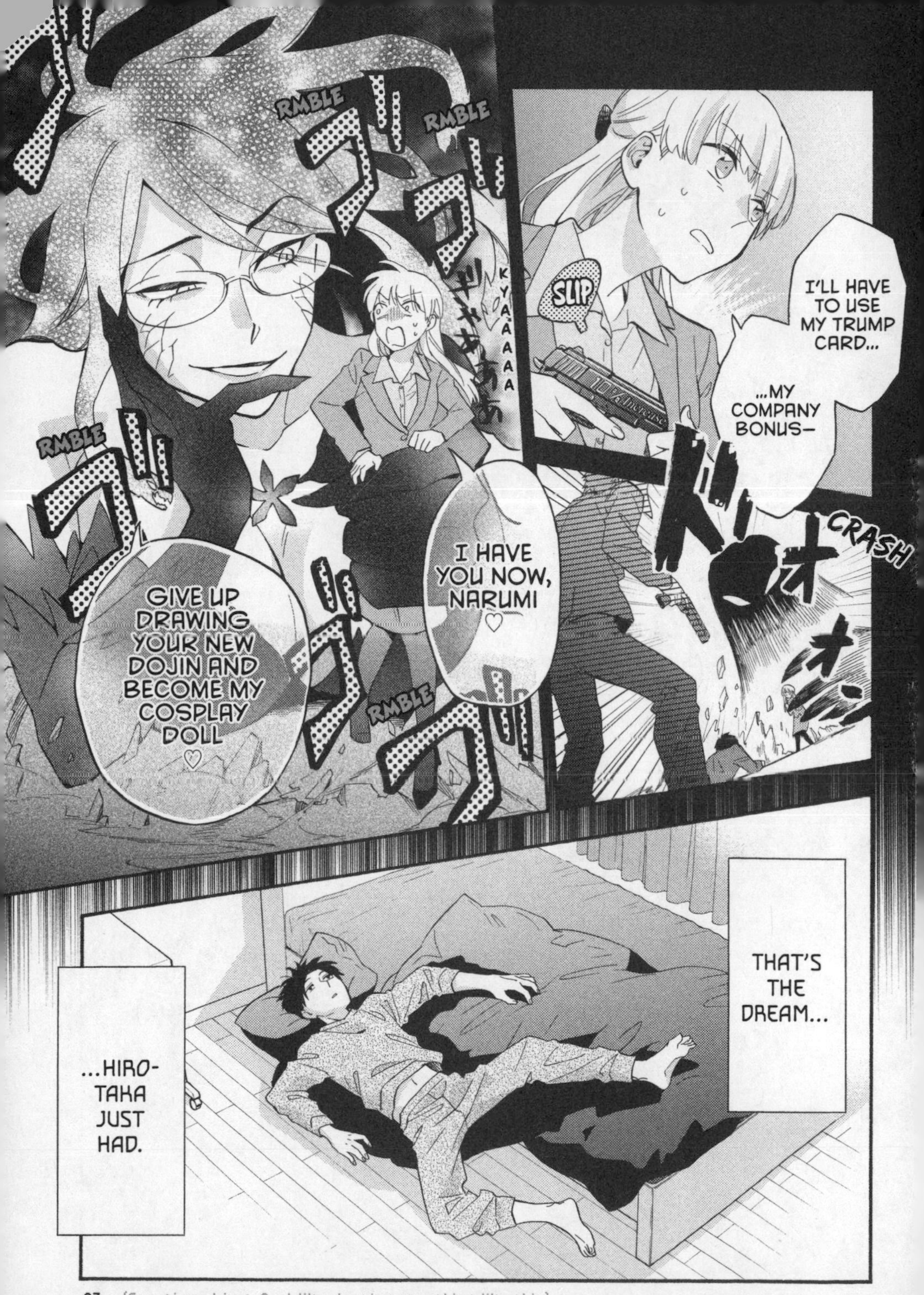
SLIP
I'LL HAVE TO USE MY TRUMP CARD...
...MY COMPANY BONUS—
CRASH
RMBLE
RMBLE
KYAAAAA
RMBLE
I HAVE YOU NOW, NARUMI ♡
GIVE UP DRAWING YOUR NEW DOJIN AND BECOME MY COSPLAY DOLL ♡
RMBLE
THAT'S THE DREAM...
...HIRO-TAKA JUST HAD.

 (Sometimes I just feel like drawing something like this)

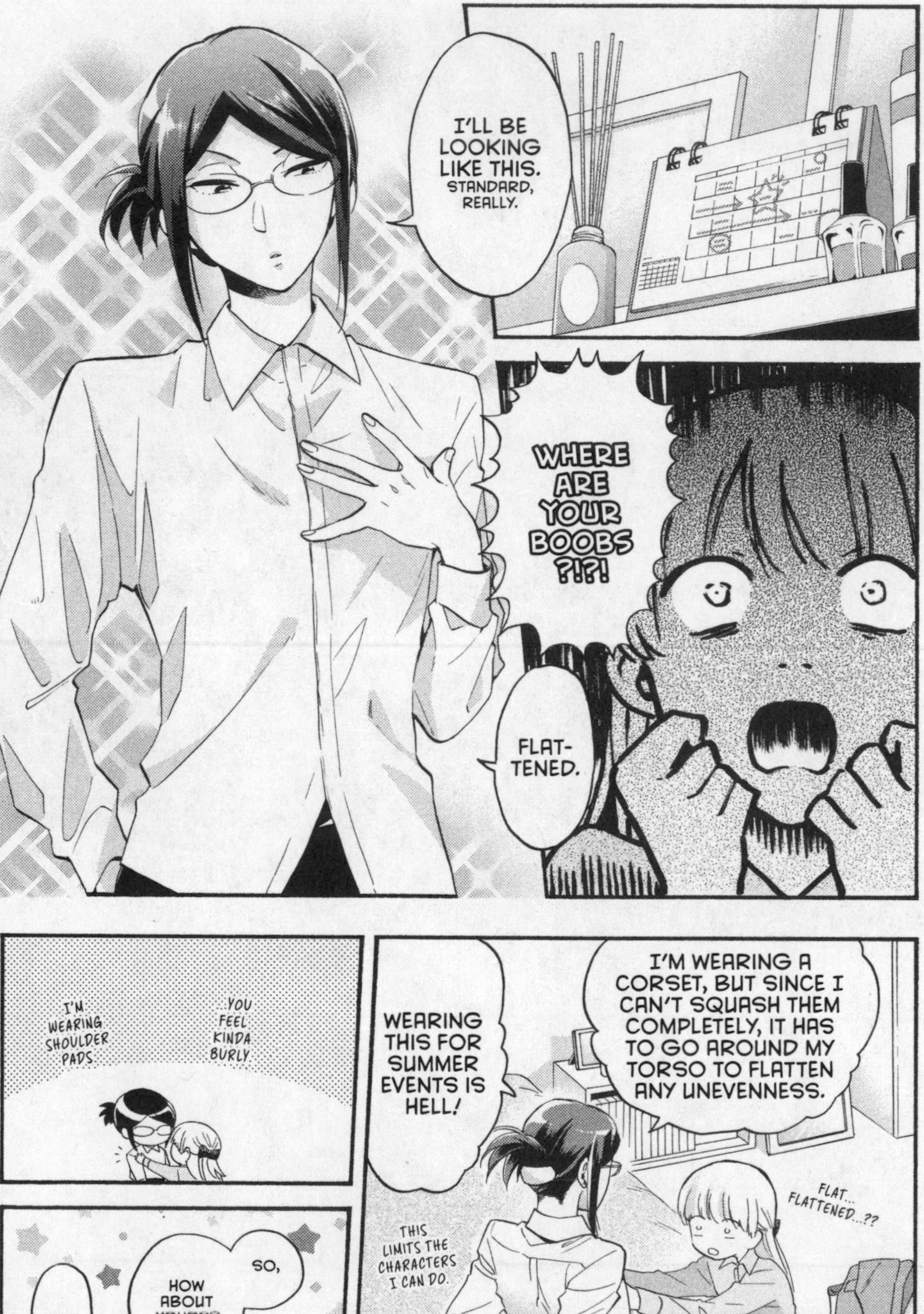
I'LL BE LOOKING LIKE THIS. STANDARD, REALLY.
WHERE ARE YOUR BOOBS?!?!
FLAT-TENED.
I'M WEARING A CORSET, BUT SINCE I CAN'T SQUASH THEM COMPLETELY, IT HAS TO GO AROUND MY TORSO TO FLATTEN ANY UNEVENNESS.
WEARING THIS FOR SUMMER EVENTS IS HELL!
FLAT... FLATTENED...??
THIS LIMITS THE CHARACTERS I CAN DO.
YOU FEEL KINDA BURLY
I'M WEARING SHOULDER PADS.
SO,
HOW ABOUT YOURS?
....

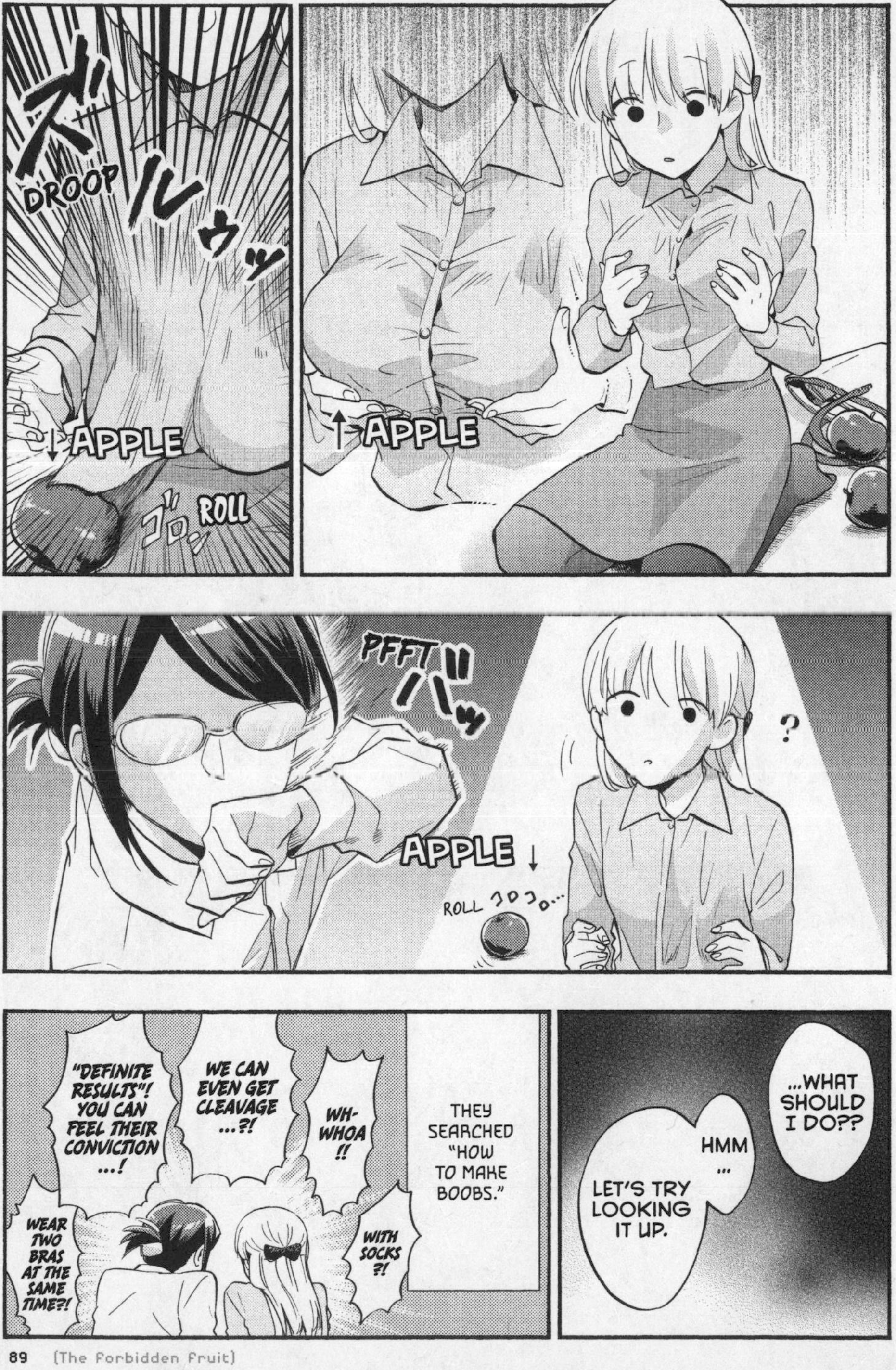
↑APPLE
ズルウッ
DROOP
↓APPLE
ゴロン
ROLL
PFFT
バッ
?
APPLE ↓
ROLL
コロコロ…
...WHAT SHOULD I DO??
HMM ...
LET'S TRY LOOKING IT UP.
THEY SEARCHED "HOW TO MAKE BOOBS."
WH-WHOA!!
WE CAN EVEN GET CLEAVAGE ...?!
"DEFINITE RESULTS"! YOU CAN FEEL THEIR CONVICTION ...!
WITH SOCKS?!
WEAR TWO BRAS AT THE SAME TIME?!

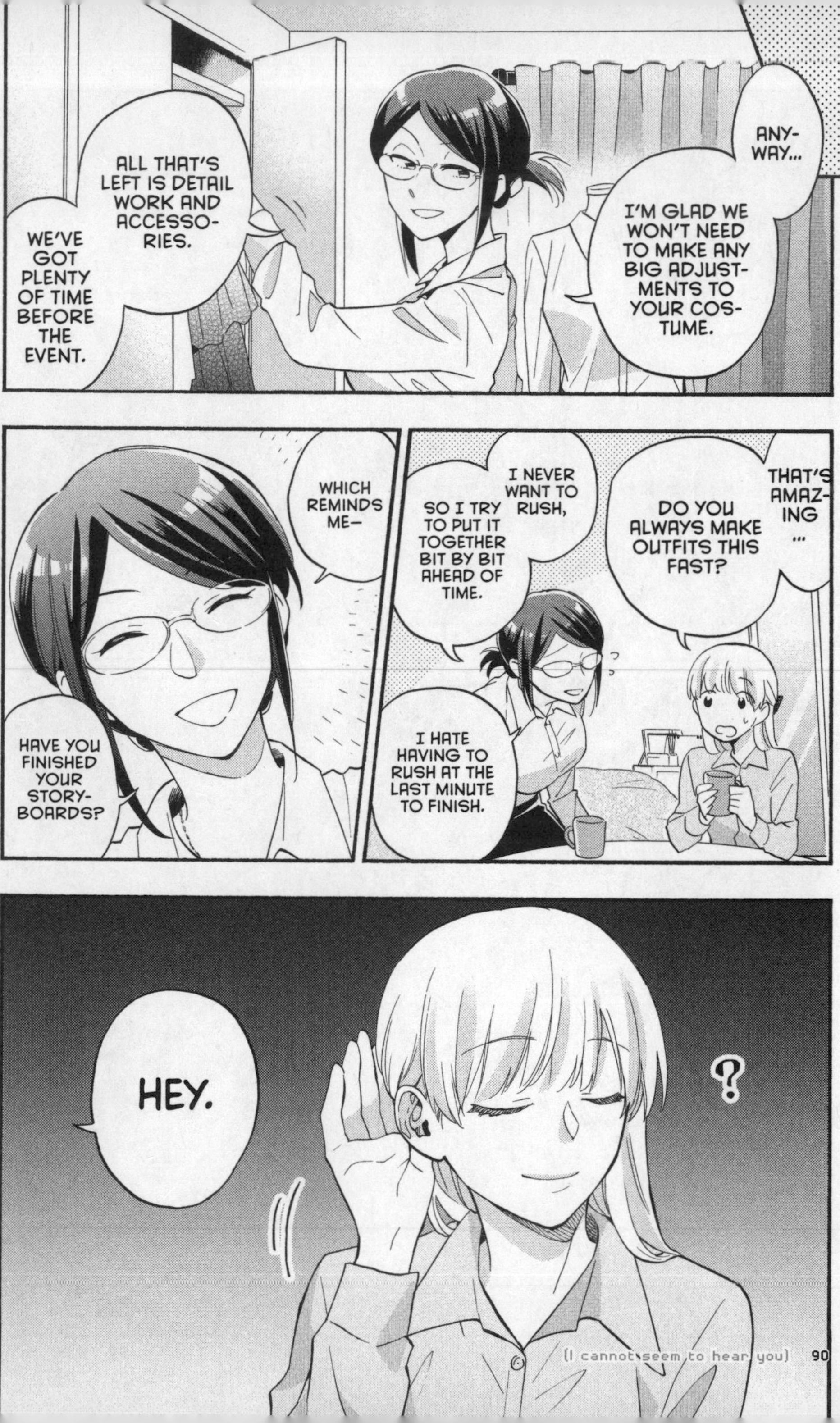
ANYWAY...
I'M GLAD WE WON'T NEED TO MAKE ANY BIG ADJUSTMENTS TO YOUR COSTUME.
ALL THAT'S LEFT IS DETAIL WORK AND ACCESSORIES.
WE'VE GOT PLENTY OF TIME BEFORE THE EVENT.
THAT'S AMAZING...
DO YOU ALWAYS MAKE OUTFITS THIS FAST?
I NEVER WANT TO RUSH,
SO I TRY TO PUT IT TOGETHER BIT BY BIT AHEAD OF TIME.
I HATE HAVING TO RUSH AT THE LAST MINUTE TO FINISH.
WHICH REMINDS ME—
HAVE YOU FINISHED YOUR STORYBOARDS?
?
HEY.
(I cannot seem to hear you)

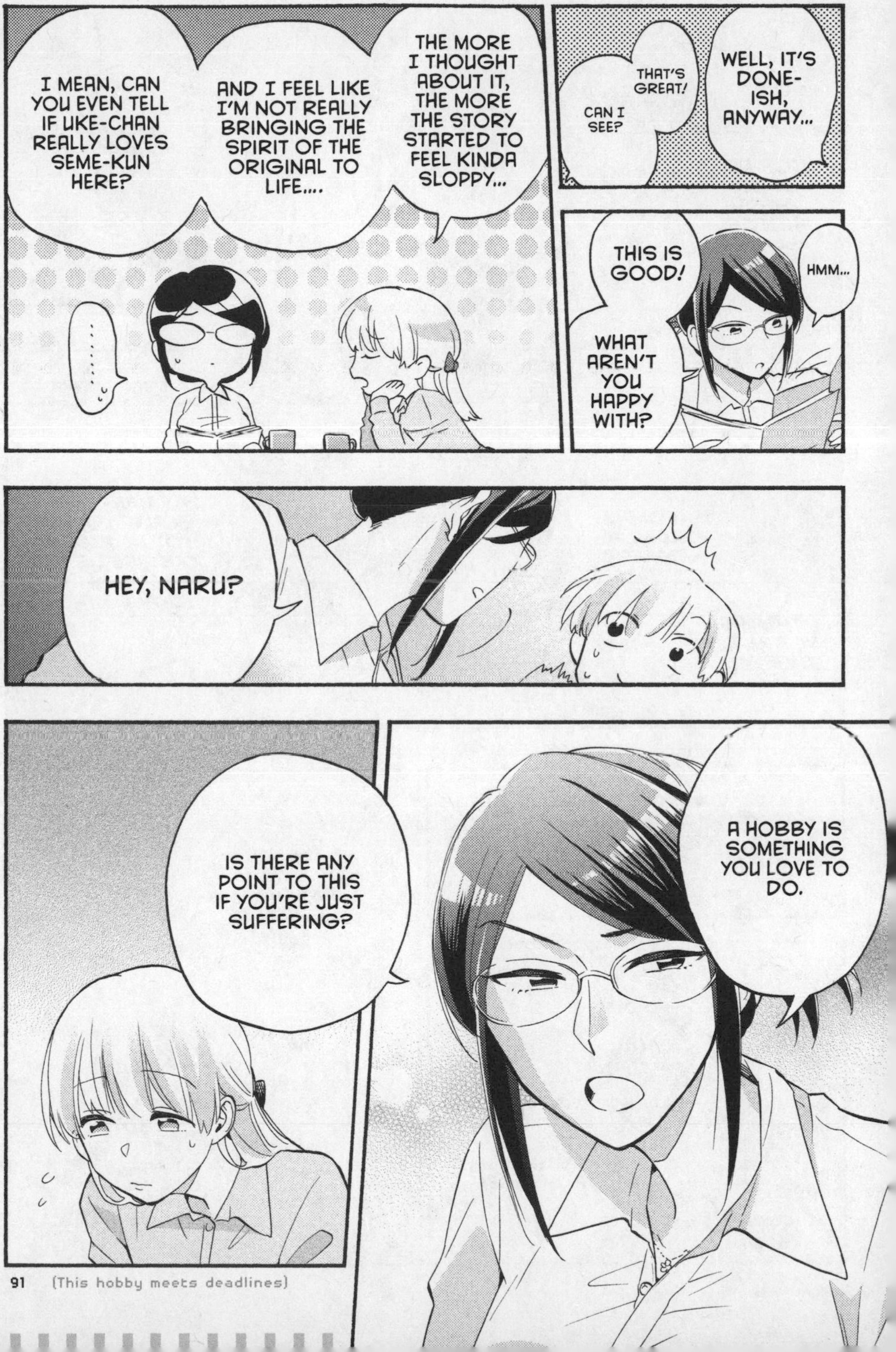
WELL, IT'S DONE-ISH, ANYWAY...
THAT'S GREAT!
CAN I SEE?
HMM...
THIS IS GOOD!
WHAT AREN'T YOU HAPPY WITH?
THE MORE I THOUGHT ABOUT IT, THE MORE THE STORY STARTED TO FEEL KINDA SLOPPY...
AND I FEEL LIKE I'M NOT REALLY BRINGING THE SPIRIT OF THE ORIGINAL TO LIFE....
I MEAN, CAN YOU EVEN TELL IF UKE-CHAN REALLY LOVES SEME-KUN HERE?
....
HEY, NARU?
A HOBBY IS SOMETHING YOU LOVE TO DO.
IS THERE ANY POINT TO THIS IF YOU'RE JUST SUFFERING?

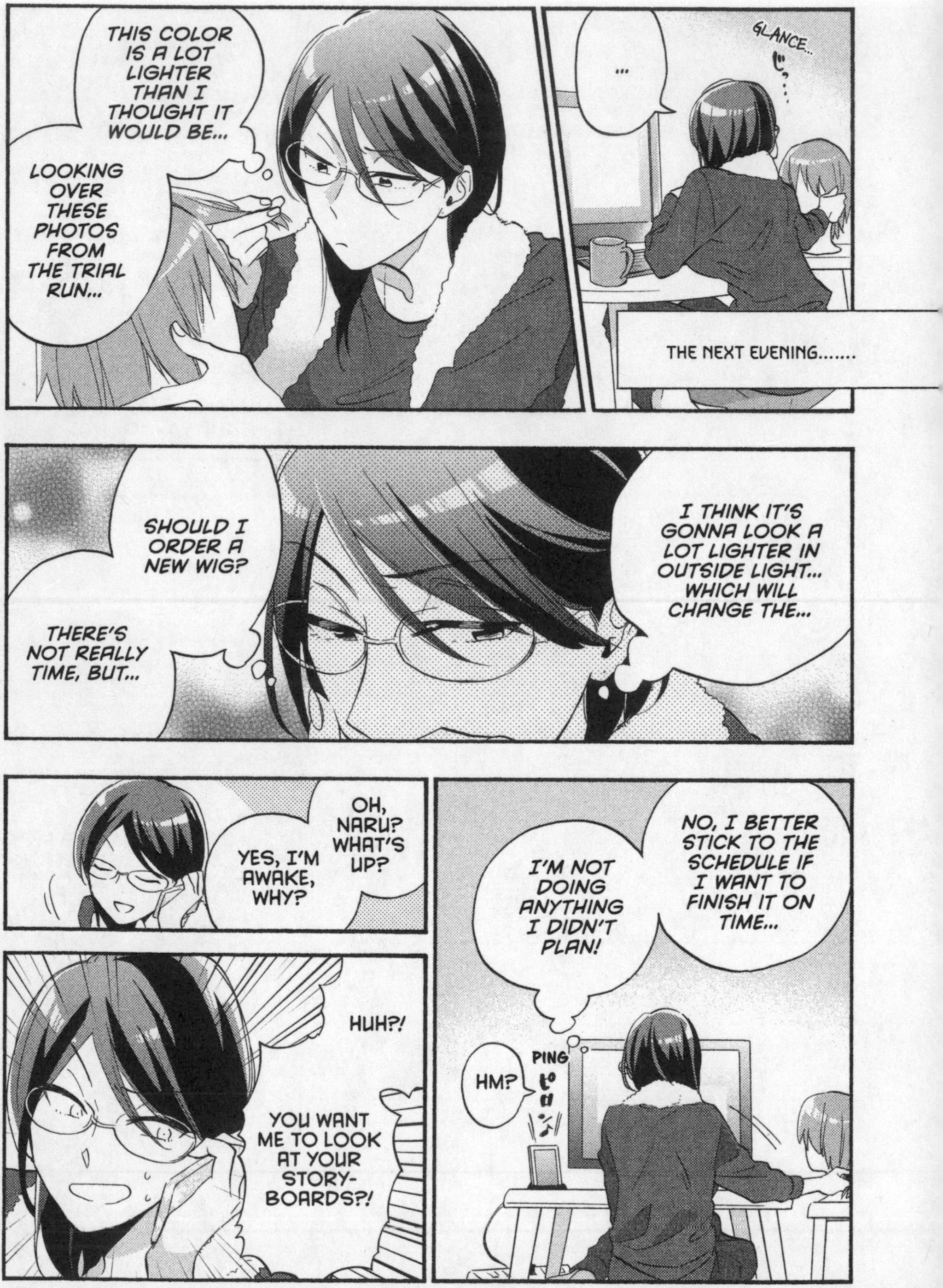
...
GLANCE...
THE NEXT EVENING.......
THIS COLOR IS A LOT LIGHTER THAN I THOUGHT IT WOULD BE...
LOOKING OVER THESE PHOTOS FROM THE TRIAL RUN...
I THINK IT'S GONNA LOOK A LOT LIGHTER IN OUTSIDE LIGHT... WHICH WILL CHANGE THE...
SHOULD I ORDER A NEW WIG?
THERE'S NOT REALLY TIME, BUT...
NO, I BETTER STICK TO THE SCHEDULE IF I WANT TO FINISH IT ON TIME...
I'M NOT DOING ANYTHING I DIDN'T PLAN!
PING
HM?
OH, NARU? WHAT'S UP?
YES, I'M AWAKE, WHY?
HUH?!
YOU WANT ME TO LOOK AT YOUR STORY-BOARDS?!

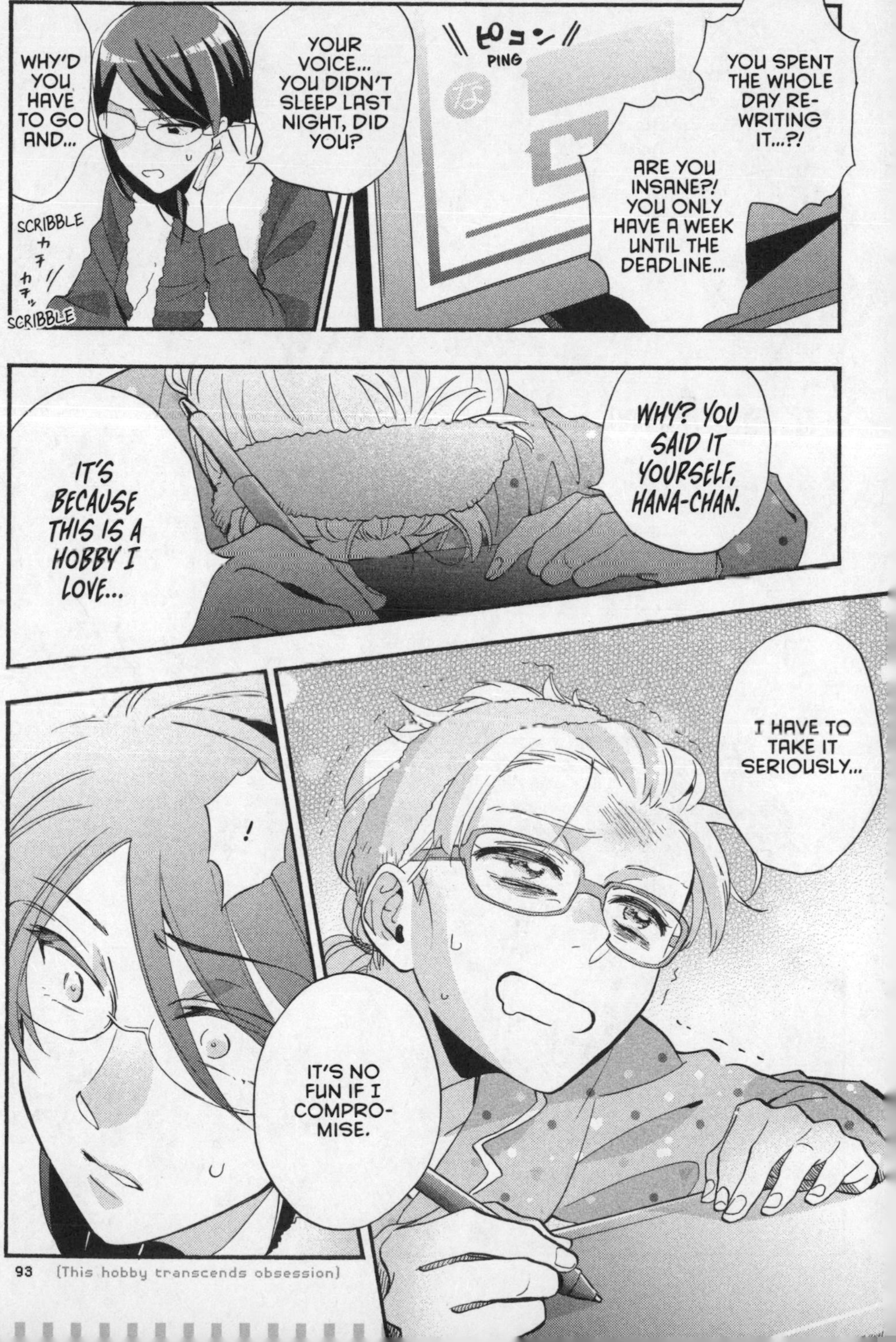
YOU SPENT THE WHOLE DAY RE-WRITING IT...?!
ARE YOU INSANE?! YOU ONLY HAVE A WEEK UNTIL THE DEADLINE...
ピコン
PING
YOUR VOICE... YOU DIDN'T SLEEP LAST NIGHT, DID YOU?
WHY'D YOU HAVE TO GO AND...
SCRIBBLE
カチカチッ
SCRIBBLE
WHY? YOU SAID IT YOURSELF, HANA-CHAN.
IT'S BECAUSE THIS IS A HOBBY I LOVE...
I HAVE TO TAKE IT SERIOUSLY...
IT'S NO FUN IF I COMPROMISE.
!

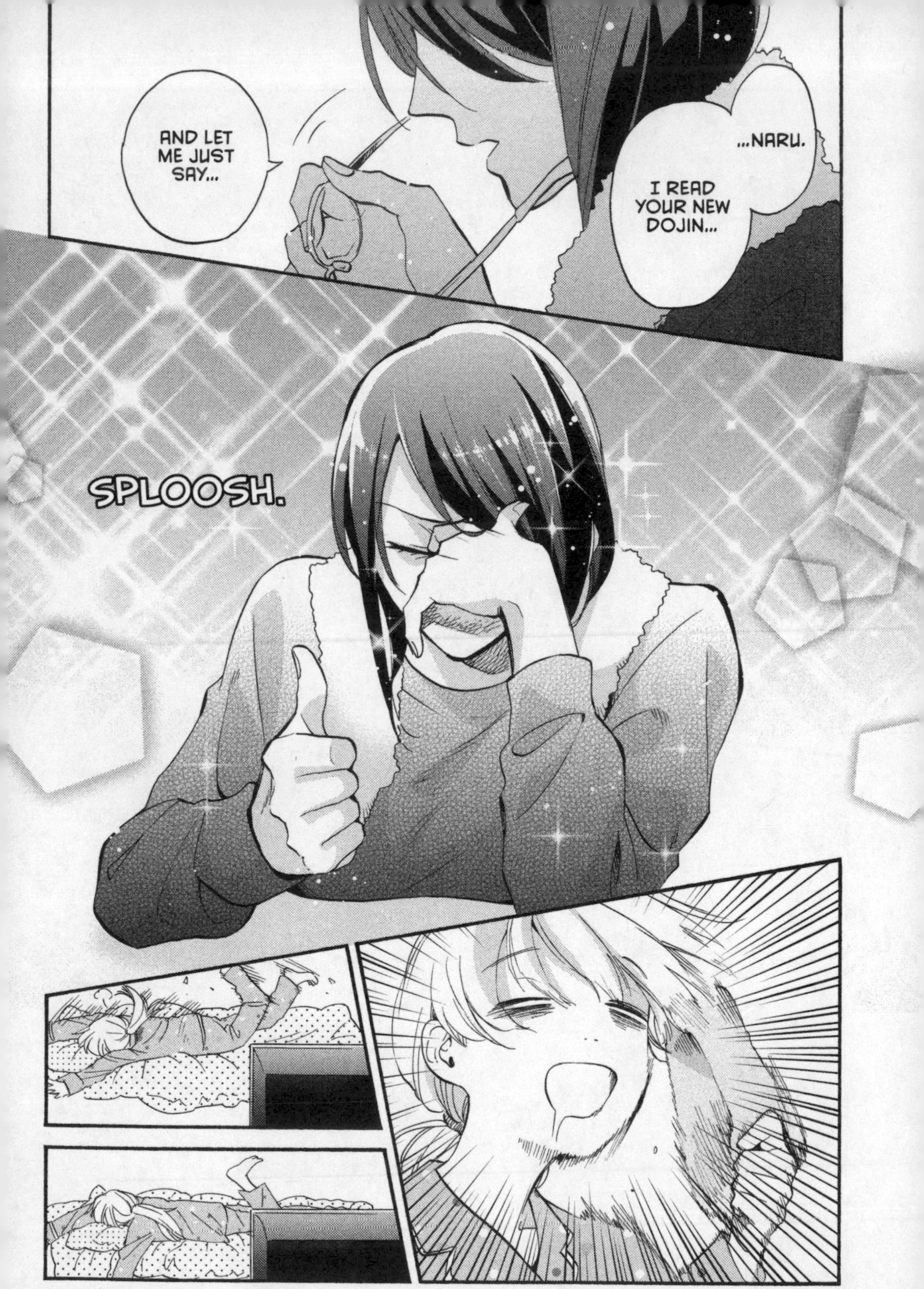
...NARU.
I READ YOUR NEW DOJIN...
AND LET ME JUST SAY...
SPLOOSH.

(Instant KO)

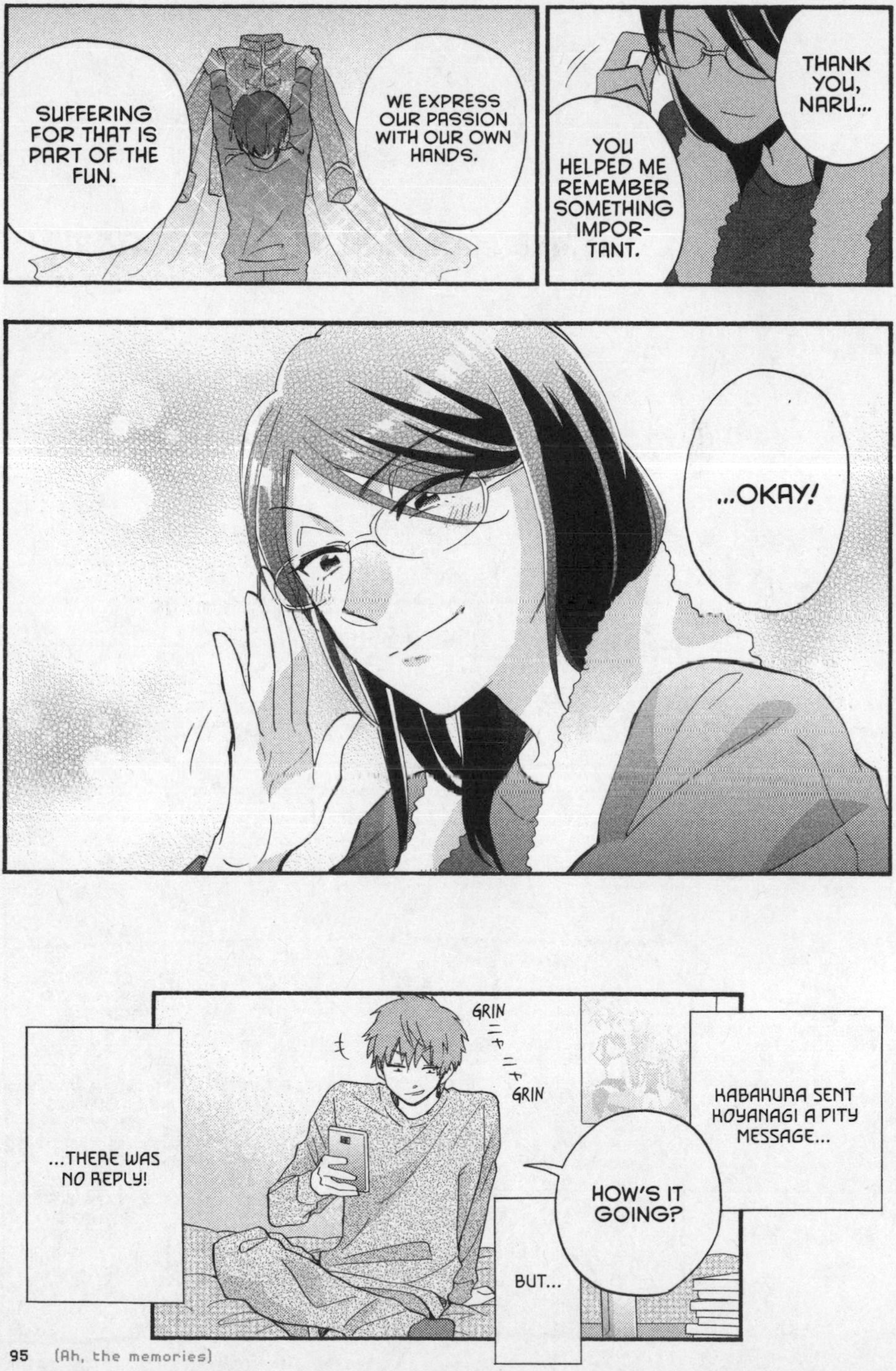
THANK YOU, NARU...
YOU HELPED ME REMEMBER SOMETHING IMPORTANT.
WE EXPRESS OUR PASSION WITH OUR OWN HANDS.
SUFFERING FOR THAT IS PART OF THE FUN.
...OKAY!
KABAKURA SENT KOYANAGI A PITY MESSAGE...
HOW'S IT GOING?
GRIN
GRIN
BUT...
...THERE WAS NO REPLY!

THE WEB MANGA GENERAL ELECTION!

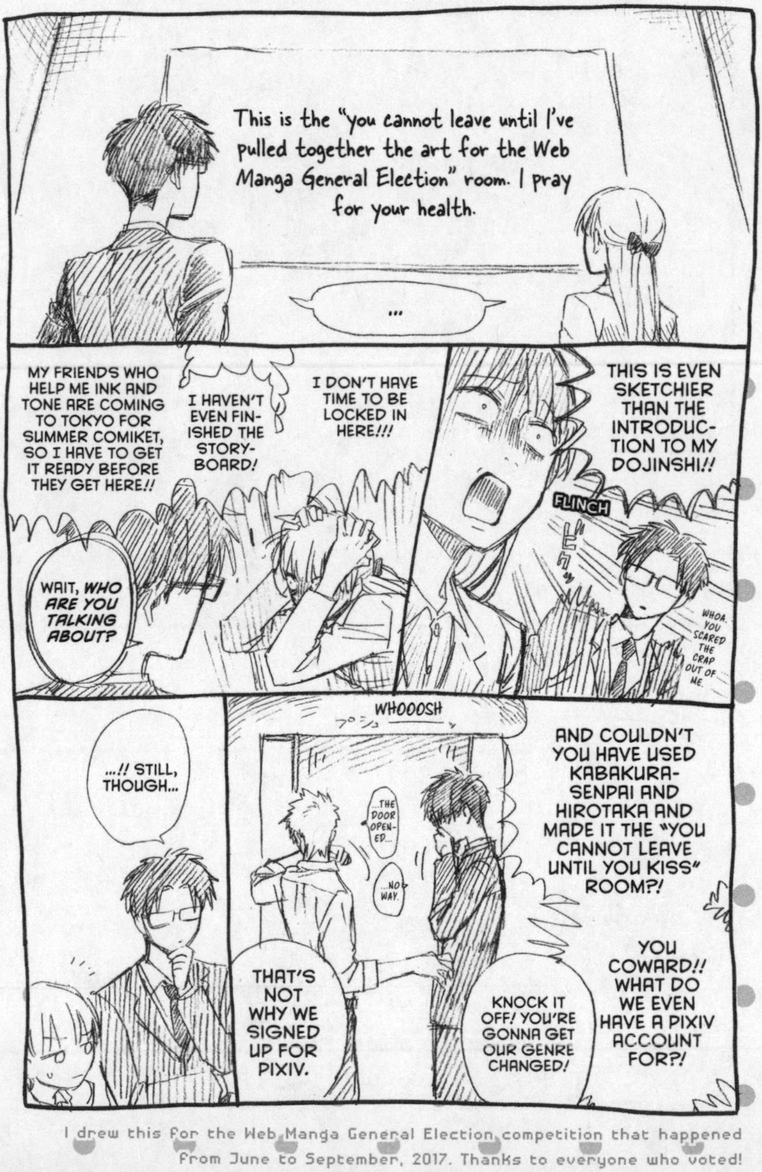
This is the "you cannot leave until I've pulled together the art for the Web Manga General Election" room. I pray for your health.
...
THIS IS EVEN SKETCHIER THAN THE INTRODUCTION TO MY DOJINSHI!!
FLINCH
WHOA. YOU SCARED THE CRAP OUT OF ME.
I DON'T HAVE TIME TO BE LOCKED IN HERE!!!
I HAVEN'T EVEN FINISHED THE STORYBOARD!
MY FRIENDS WHO HELP ME INK AND TONE ARE COMING TO TOKYO FOR SUMMER COMIKET, SO I HAVE TO GET IT READY BEFORE THEY GET HERE!!
WAIT, WHO ARE YOU TALKING ABOUT?
WHOOOSH
AND COULDN'T YOU HAVE USED KABAKURA-SENPAI AND HIROTAKA AND MADE IT THE "YOU CANNOT LEAVE UNTIL YOU KISS" ROOM?!
...THE DOOR OPENED...
...NO WAY.
YOU COWARD!! WHAT DO WE EVEN HAVE A PIXIV ACCOUNT FOR?!
KNOCK IT OFF! YOU'RE GONNA GET OUR GENRE CHANGED!
THAT'S NOT WHY WE SIGNED UP FOR PIXIV.
...!! STILL, THOUGH...

I drew this for the Web Manga General Election competition that happened from June to September, 2017. Thanks to everyone who voted!

Wotakoi: Love is Hard for Otaku

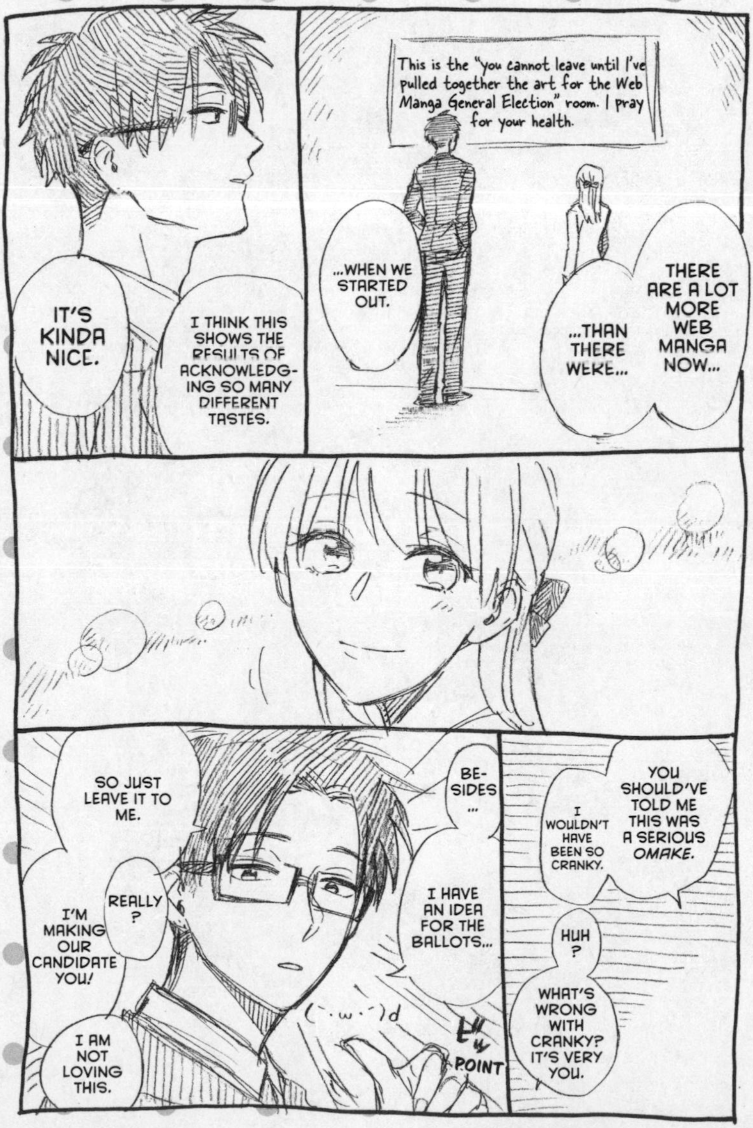
This is the "you cannot leave until I've pulled together the art for the Web Manga General Election" room. I pray for your health.
THERE ARE A LOT MORE WEB MANGA NOW...
...THAN THERE WERE...
...WHEN WE STARTED OUT.
I THINK THIS SHOWS THE RESULTS OF ACKNOWLEDGING SO MANY DIFFERENT TASTES.
IT'S KINDA NICE.
YOU SHOULD'VE TOLD ME THIS WAS A SERIOUS *OMAKE.*
I WOULDN'T HAVE BEEN SO CRANKY.
HUH?
WHAT'S WRONG WITH CRANKY? IT'S VERY YOU.
BESIDES...
I HAVE AN IDEA FOR THE BALLOTS...
SO JUST LEAVE IT TO ME.
REALLY?
I'M MAKING OUR CANDIDATE YOU!
(´・ω・`)d
POINT
I AM NOT LOVING THIS.

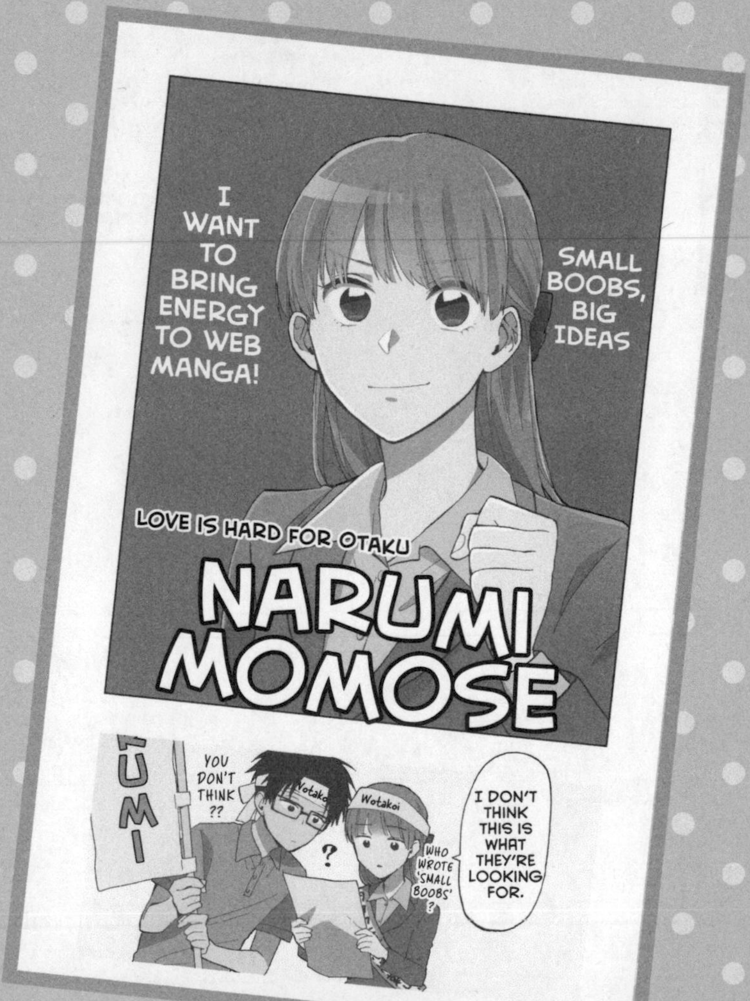
I WANT TO BRING ENERGY TO WEB MANGA!
SMALL BOOBS, BIG IDEAS
LOVE IS HARD FOR OTAKU
NARUMI MOMOSE
I DON'T THINK THIS IS WHAT THEY'RE LOOKING FOR.
WHO WROTE 'SMALL BOOBS'?
Wotakoi
?
YOU DON'T THINK ??
RUMI

Episode.... 38

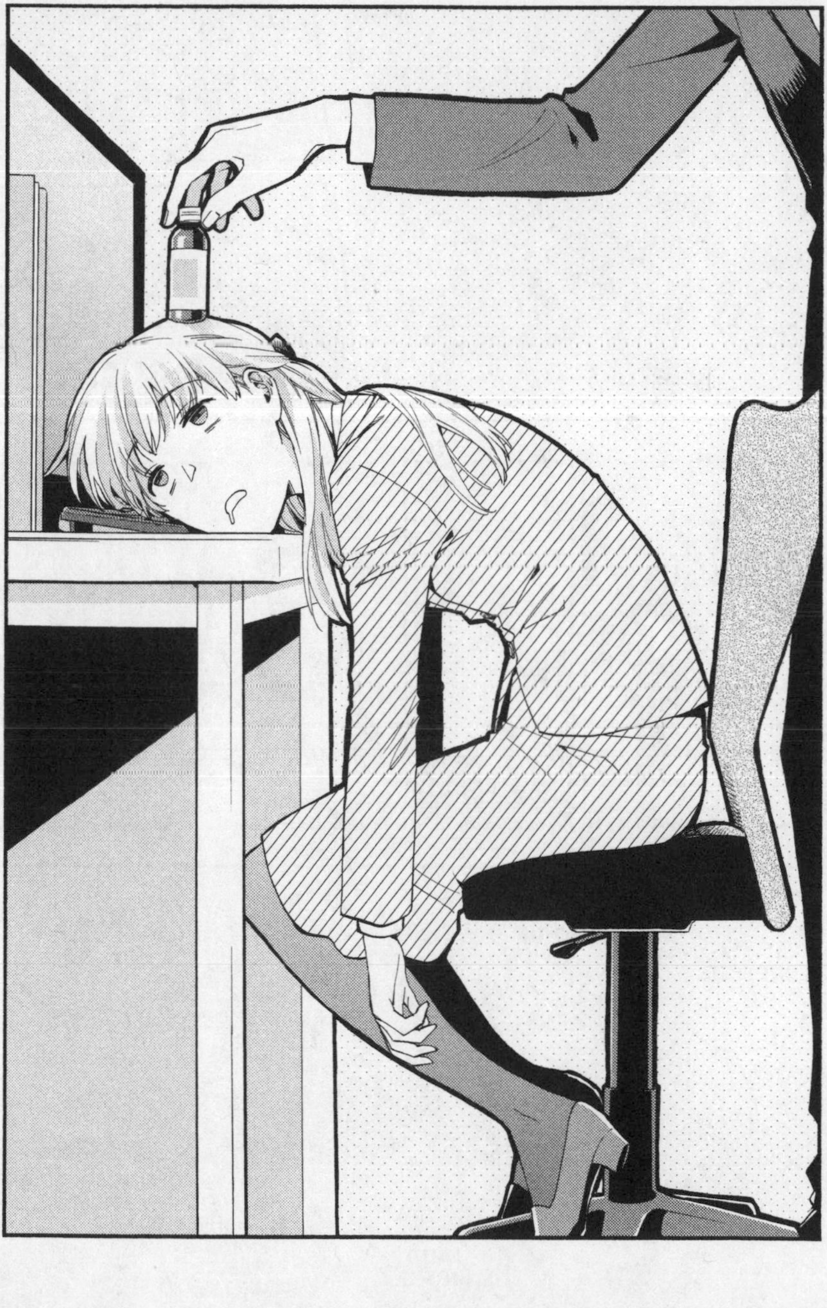

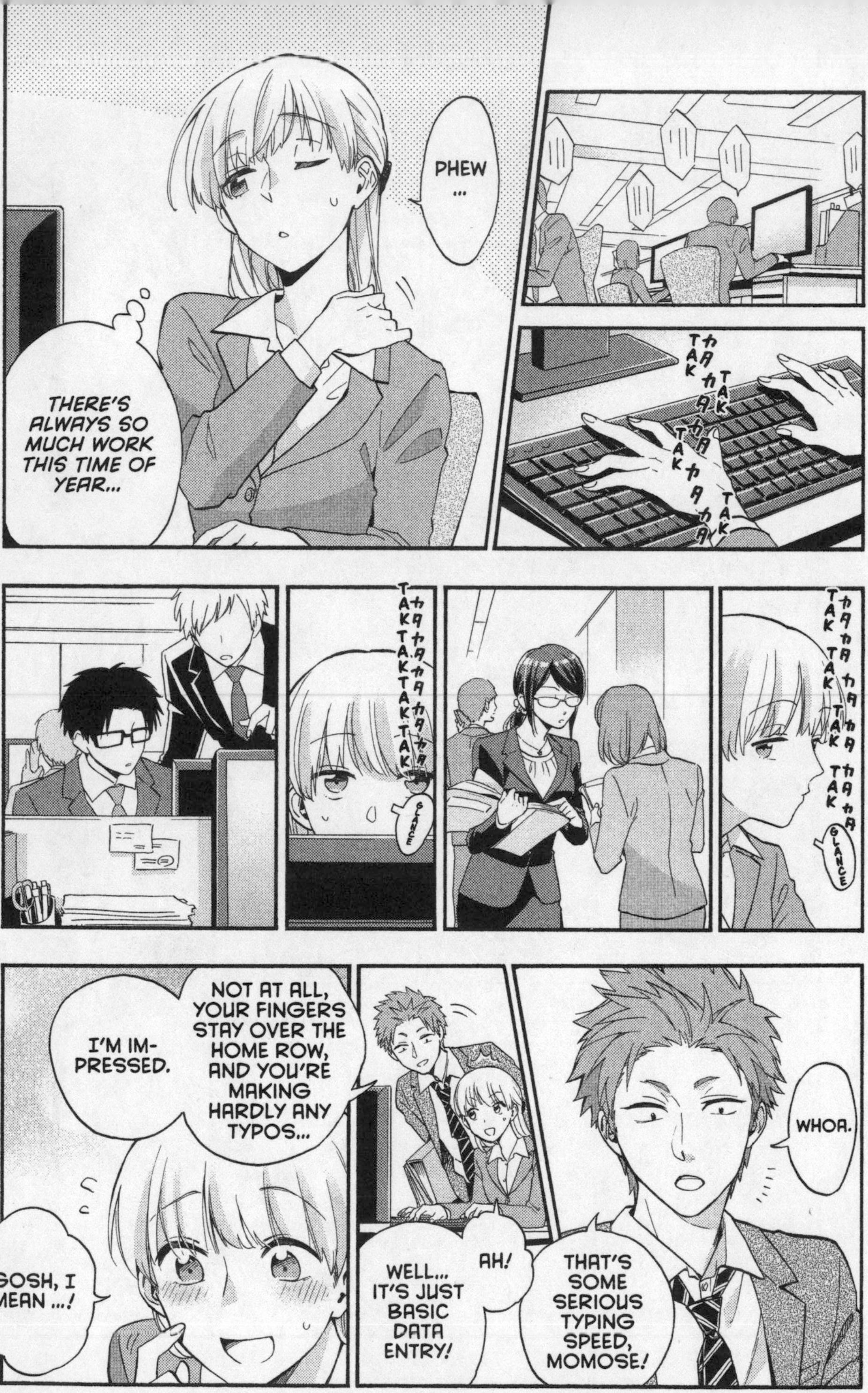
TAK TAKA TAK TAKA TAK TAKA TAK TAKA TAK
PHEW ...
THERE'S ALWAYS SO MUCH WORK THIS TIME OF YEAR...
TAK TAKA TAK TAKA TAK TAKA TAK TAKA
GLANCE
TAK TAKA TAK TAKA TAK TAKA TAK TAKA
GLANCE
WHOA.
THAT'S SOME SERIOUS TYPING SPEED, MOMOSE!
AH!
WELL... IT'S JUST BASIC DATA ENTRY!
NOT AT ALL, YOUR FINGERS STAY OVER THE HOME ROW, AND YOU'RE MAKING HARDLY ANY TYPOS...
I'M IM-PRESSED.
GOSH, I MEAN ...!

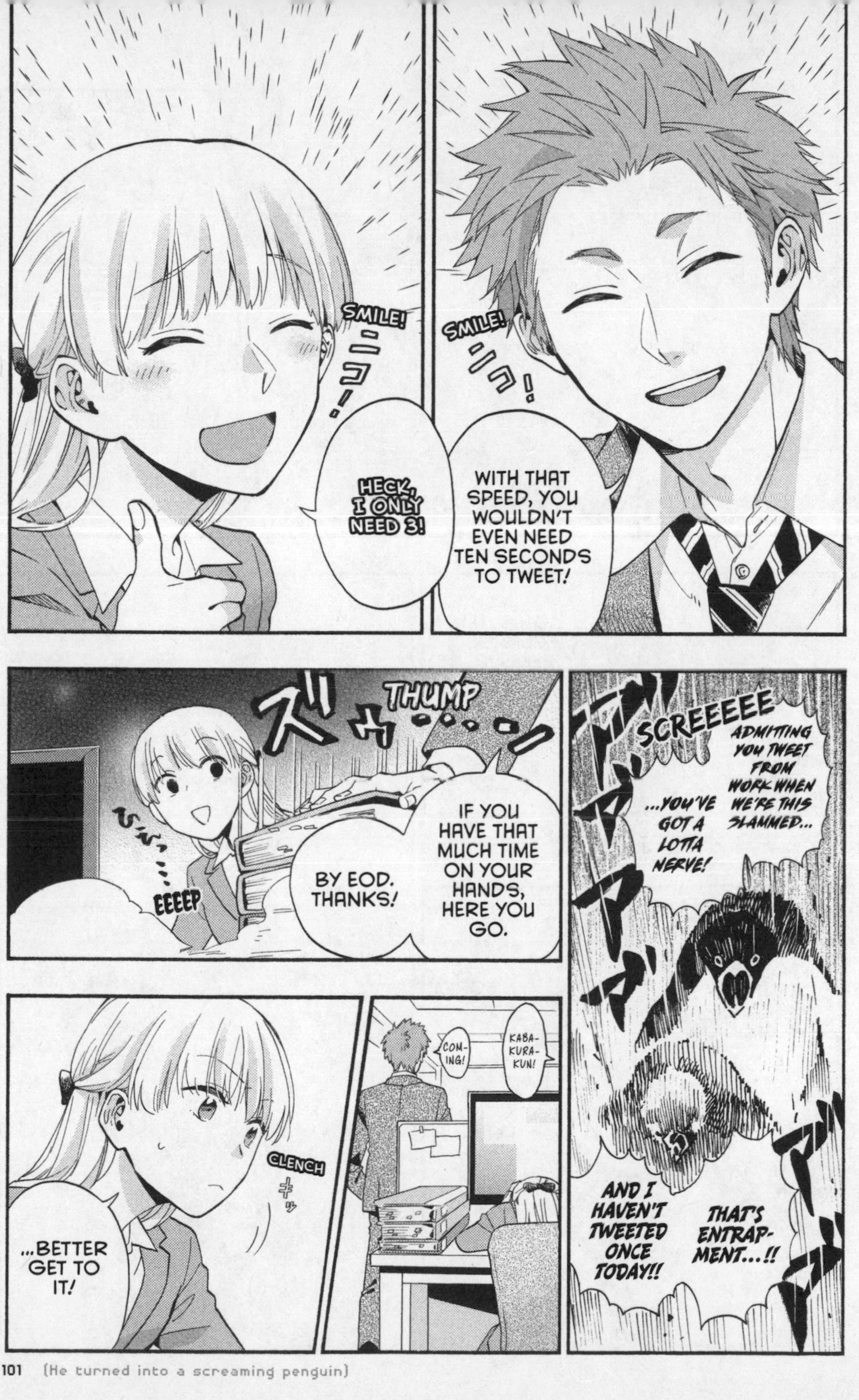
SMILE!
ニコッ!
WITH THAT SPEED, YOU WOULDN'T EVEN NEED TEN SECONDS TO TWEET!
SMILE!
ニコッ!
HECK, I ONLY NEED 3!
SCREEEEE
ADMITTING YOU TWEET FROM WORK WHEN WE'RE THIS SLAMMED...
...YOU'VE GOT A LOTTA NERVE!
THAT'S ENTRAPMENT...!!
AND I HAVEN'T TWEETED ONCE TODAY!!
THUMP
IF YOU HAVE THAT MUCH TIME ON YOUR HANDS, HERE YOU GO.
BY EOD. THANKS!
EEEEP
KABA-KURA-KUN!
COM-ING!
CLENCH
...BETTER GET TO IT!

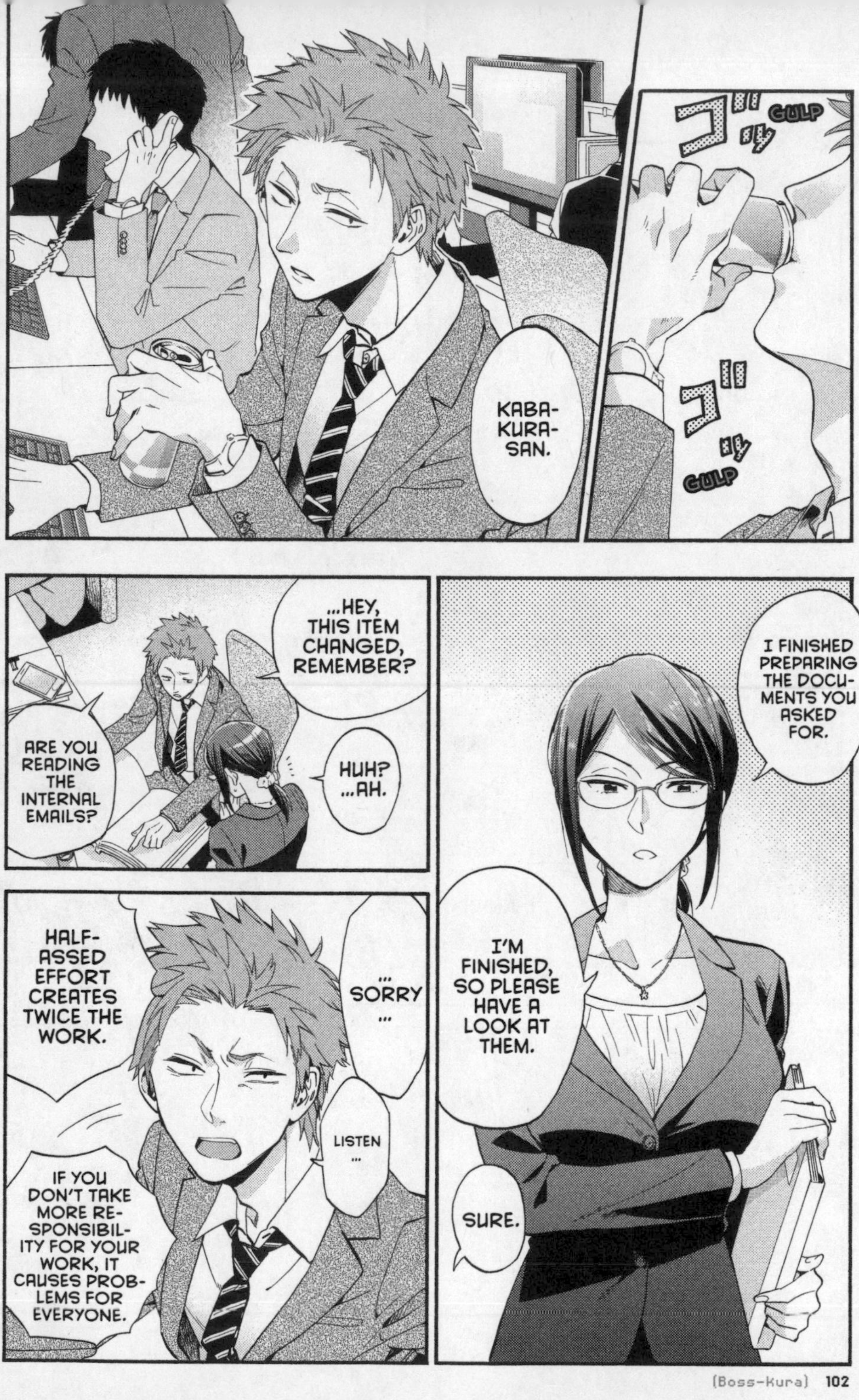
ゴッ
GULP
ゴッ
GULP
KABA-KURA-SAN.
I FINISHED PREPARING THE DOCU-MENTS YOU ASKED FOR.
I'M FINISHED, SO PLEASE HAVE A LOOK AT THEM.
SURE.
...HEY, THIS ITEM CHANGED, REMEMBER?
HUH? ...AH.
ARE YOU READING THE INTERNAL EMAILS?
... SORRY ...
HALF-ASSED EFFORT CREATES TWICE THE WORK.
LISTEN ...
IF YOU DON'T TAKE MORE RE-SPONSIBIL-ITY FOR YOUR WORK, IT CAUSES PROB-LEMS FOR EVERYONE.

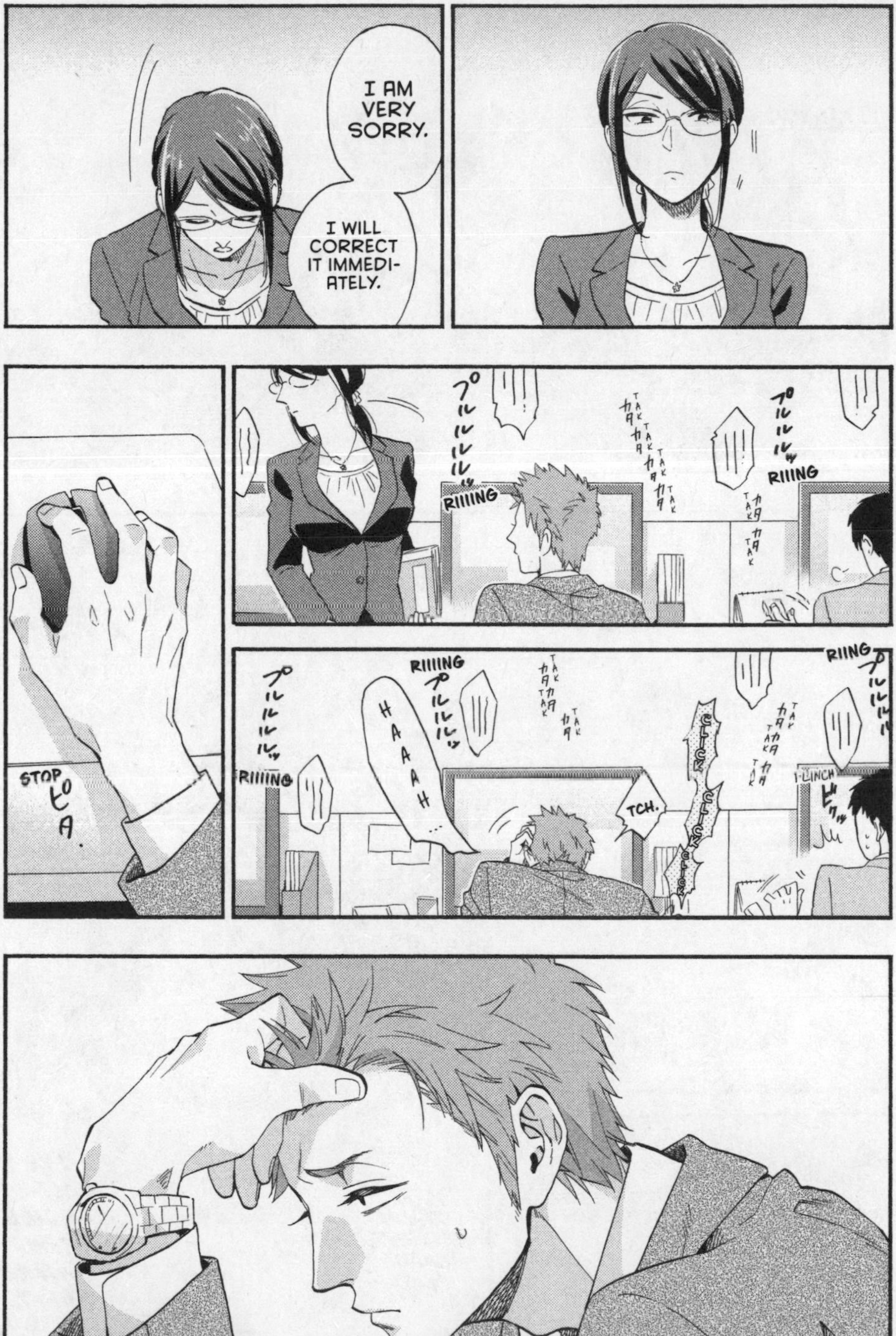
I AM VERY SORRY.
I WILL CORRECT IT IMMEDIATELY.
プルルルッ
RIIING
カタカタカタ
TAK TAK TAK
プルルルッ
RIIING
カタカタ
TAK TAK
RIING
プルルル
カタカタカタ
TAK TAK TAK
CLICK CLICK CLICK
I-LINCH
ビクッ
TCH.
カタカタカタ
TAK TAK TAK
RIIIING
プルルルッ
HAAAAH...
プルルルッ
RIIIING
STOP
ピタ.
(Well now it's weird)

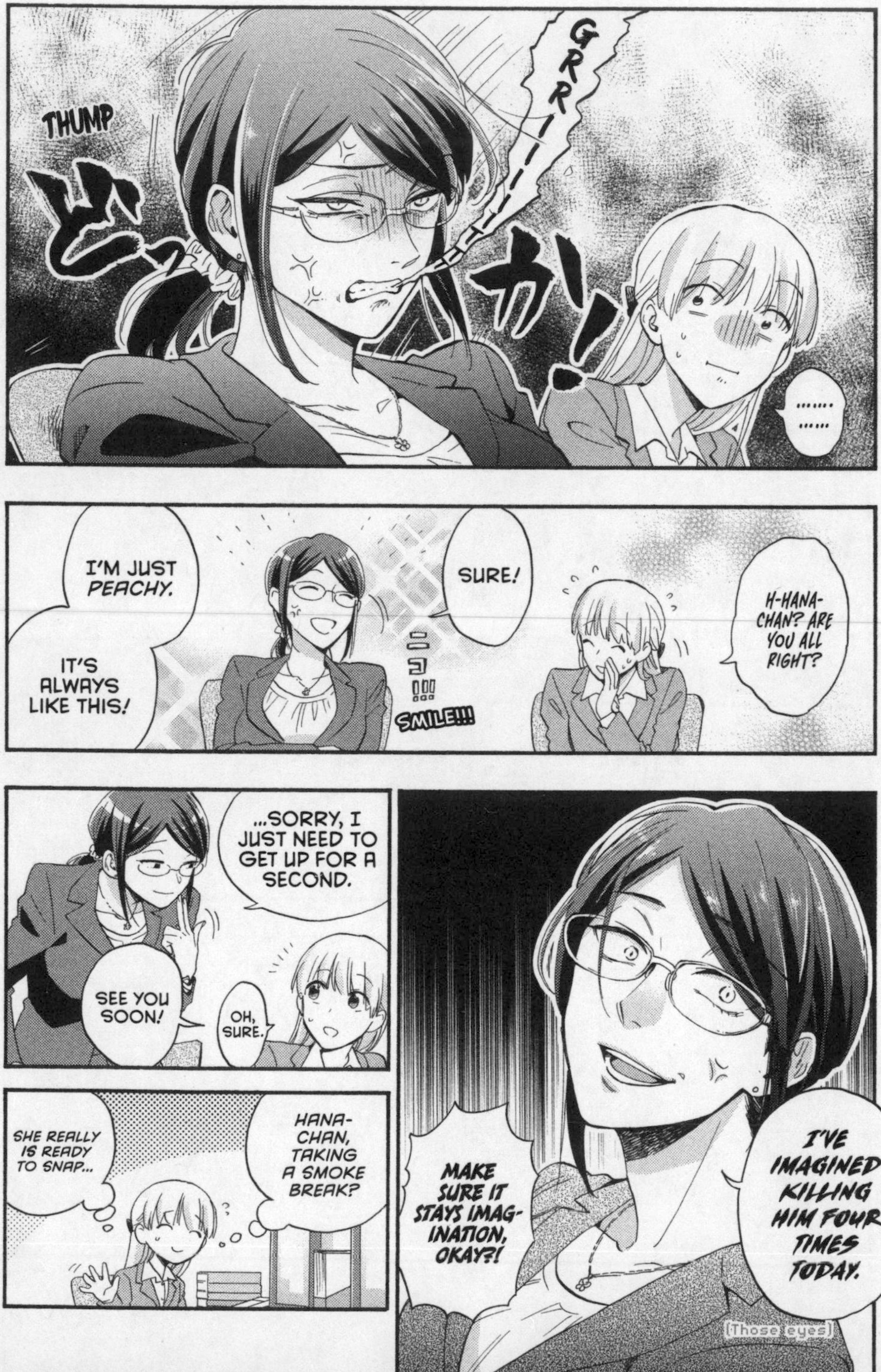
GRRR-----
THUMP
......
......
H-HANA-CHAN? ARE YOU ALL RIGHT?
SURE!
SMILE!!!
I'M JUST PEACHY.
IT'S ALWAYS LIKE THIS!
I'VE IMAGINED KILLING HIM FOUR TIMES TODAY.
MAKE SURE IT STAYS IMAGINATION, OKAY?!
(Those eyes)
...SORRY, I JUST NEED TO GET UP FOR A SECOND.
SEE YOU SOON!
OH, SURE.
HANA-CHAN, TAKING A SMOKE BREAK?
SHE REALLY IS READY TO SNAP...

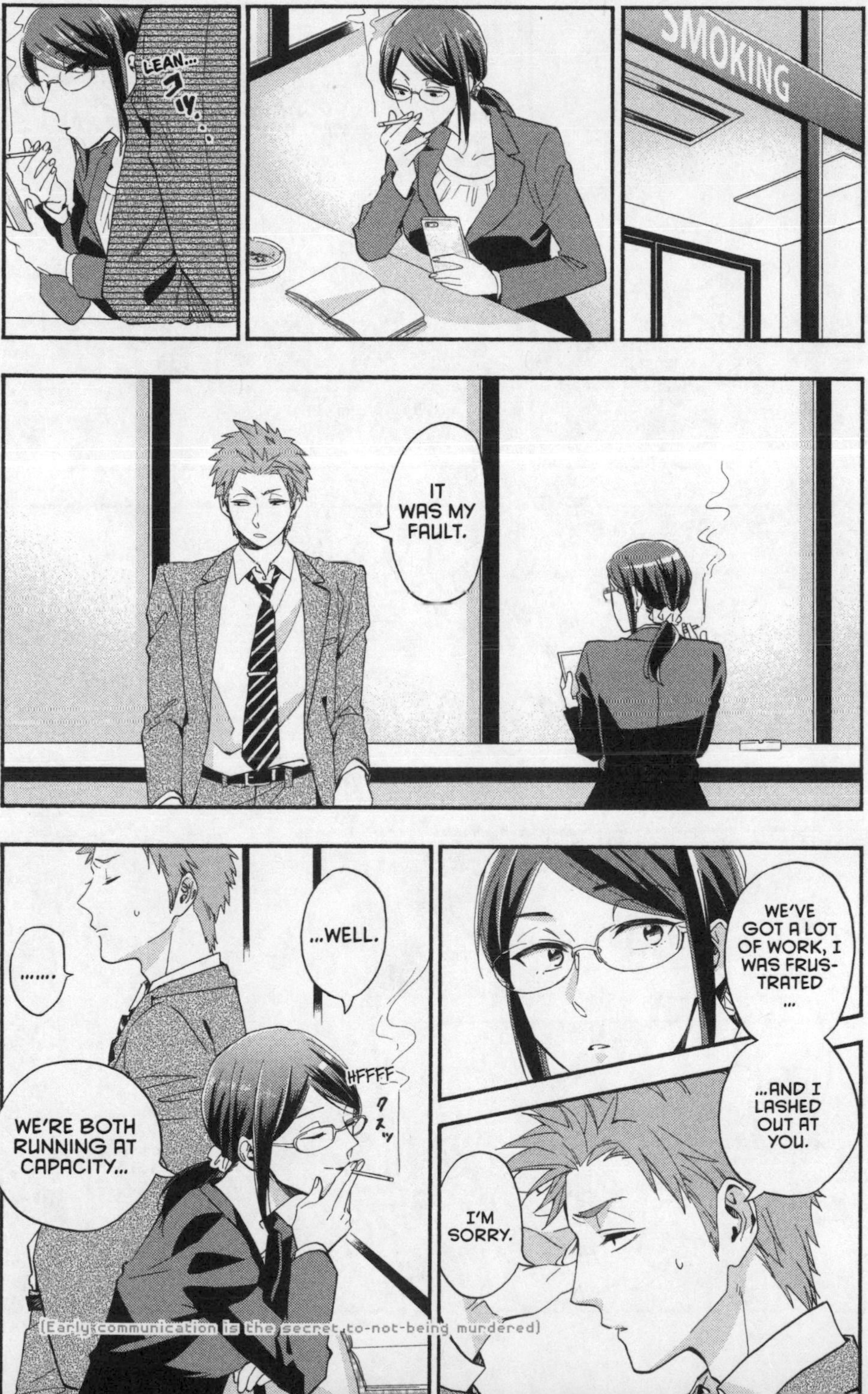
SMOKING
LEAN...
コィ...
IT WAS MY FAULT.
WE'VE GOT A LOT OF WORK, I WAS FRUS-TRATED ...
...AND I LASHED OUT AT YOU.
I'M SORRY.
...WELL.
....
HFFFF
クスッ
WE'RE BOTH RUNNING AT CAPACITY...
(Early communication is the secret to not being murdered)

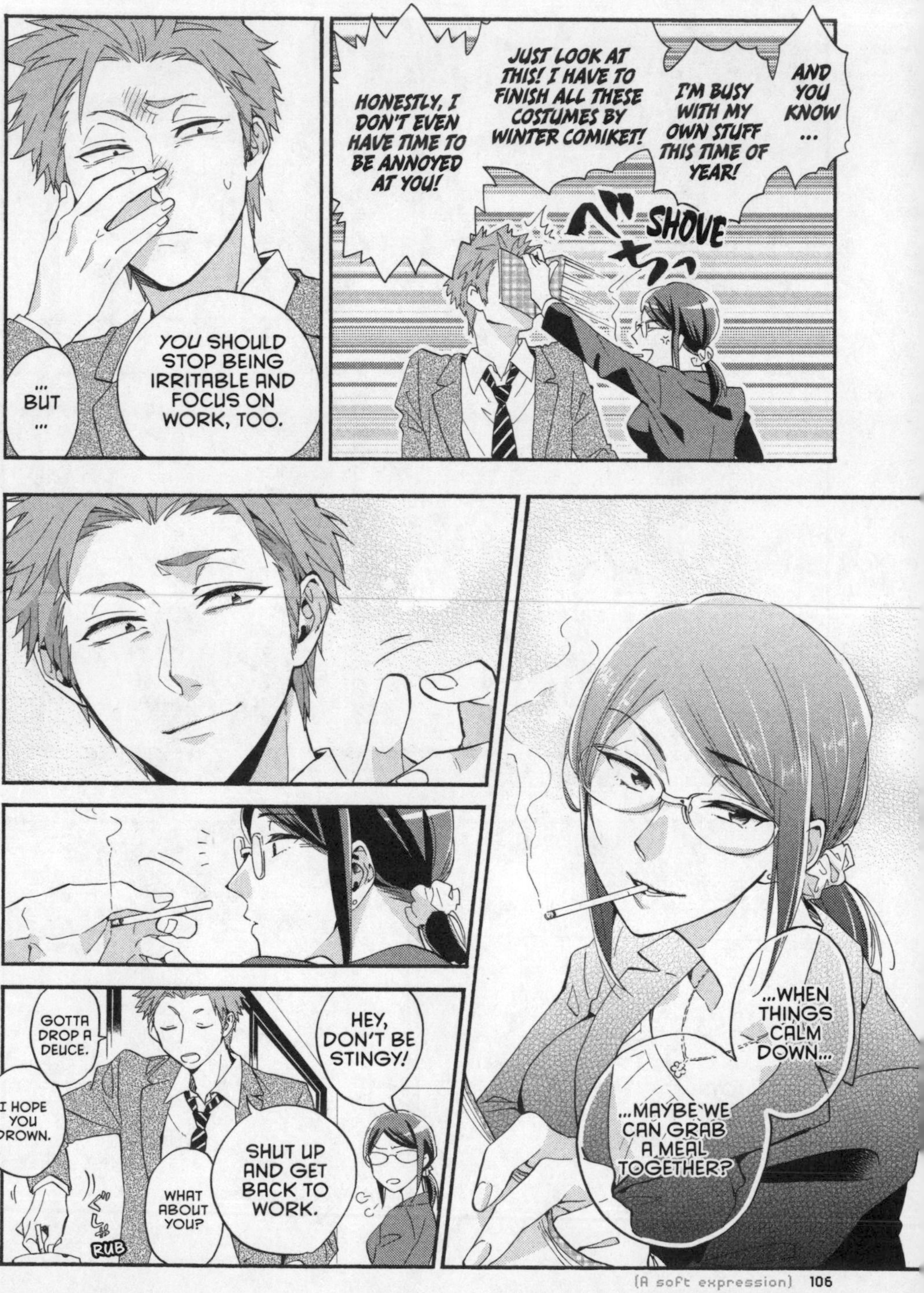
AND YOU KNOW ...
I'M BUSY WITH MY OWN STUFF THIS TIME OF YEAR!
JUST LOOK AT THIS! I HAVE TO FINISH ALL THESE COSTUMES BY WINTER COMIKET!
HONESTLY, I DON'T EVEN HAVE TIME TO BE ANNOYED AT YOU!
SHOVE
YOU SHOULD STOP BEING IRRITABLE AND FOCUS ON WORK, TOO.
... BUT ...
...WHEN THINGS CALM DOWN...
...MAYBE WE CAN GRAB A MEAL TOGETHER?
HEY, DON'T BE STINGY!
GOTTA DROP A DEUCE.
SHUT UP AND GET BACK TO WORK.
WHAT ABOUT YOU?
I HOPE YOU DROWN.
RUB

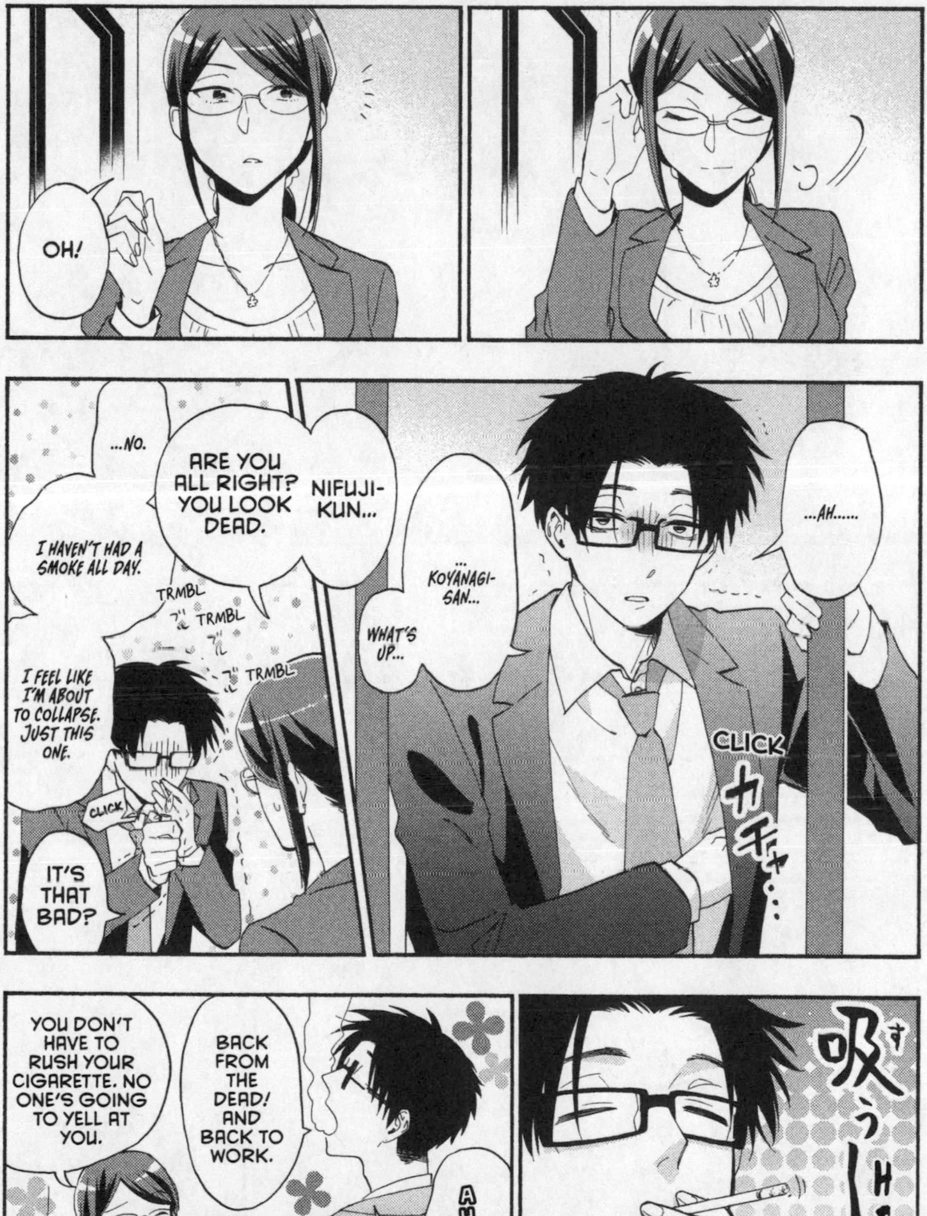
OH!
...AH......
...KOYANAGI-SAN...
WHAT'S UP...
CLICK
カチャ...
NIFUJI-KUN...
ARE YOU ALL RIGHT? YOU LOOK DEAD.
...NO.
I HAVEN'T HAD A SMOKE ALL DAY.
TRMBL
TRMBL
TRMBL
I FEEL LIKE I'M ABOUT TO COLLAPSE. JUST THIS ONE.
CLICK
IT'S THAT BAD?
吸う
HFFFF
AHHHHHHHH!
BACK FROM THE DEAD! AND BACK TO WORK.
YOU DON'T HAVE TO RUSH YOUR CIGARETTE. NO ONE'S GOING TO YELL AT YOU.

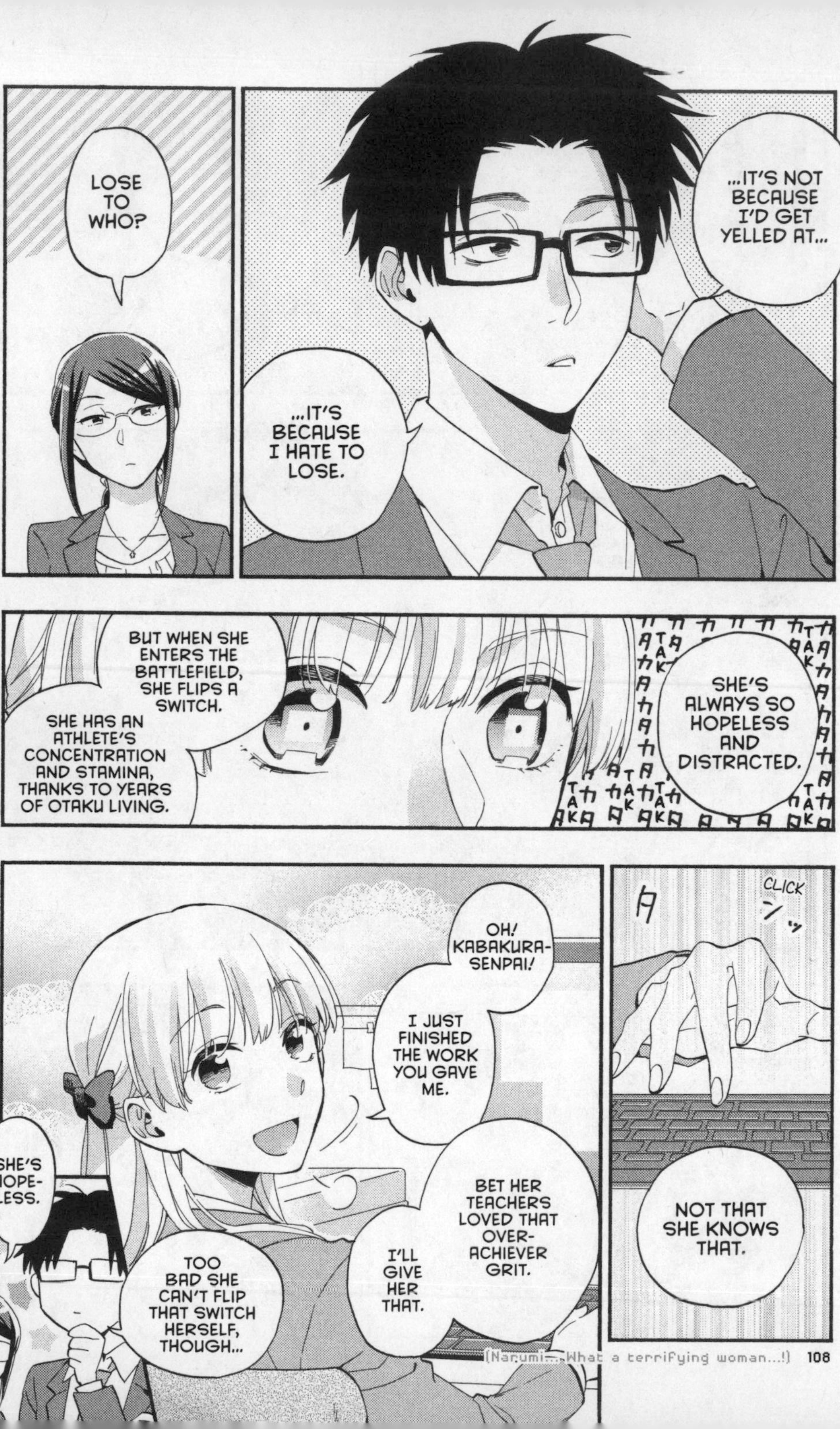
...IT'S NOT BECAUSE I'D GET YELLED AT...
...IT'S BECAUSE I HATE TO LOSE.
LOSE TO WHO?
SHE'S ALWAYS SO HOPELESS AND DISTRACTED.
TAK TAK TAK TAK
BUT WHEN SHE ENTERS THE BATTLEFIELD, SHE FLIPS A SWITCH.
SHE HAS AN ATHLETE'S CONCENTRATION AND STAMINA, THANKS TO YEARS OF OTAKU LIVING.
CLICK
NOT THAT SHE KNOWS THAT.
OH! KABAKURA-SENPAI!
I JUST FINISHED THE WORK YOU GAVE ME.
BET HER TEACHERS LOVED THAT OVER-ACHIEVER GRIT.
I'LL GIVE HER THAT.
TOO BAD SHE CAN'T FLIP THAT SWITCH HERSELF, THOUGH...
SHE'S HOPE-LESS.
(Narumi... What a terrifying woman...!)

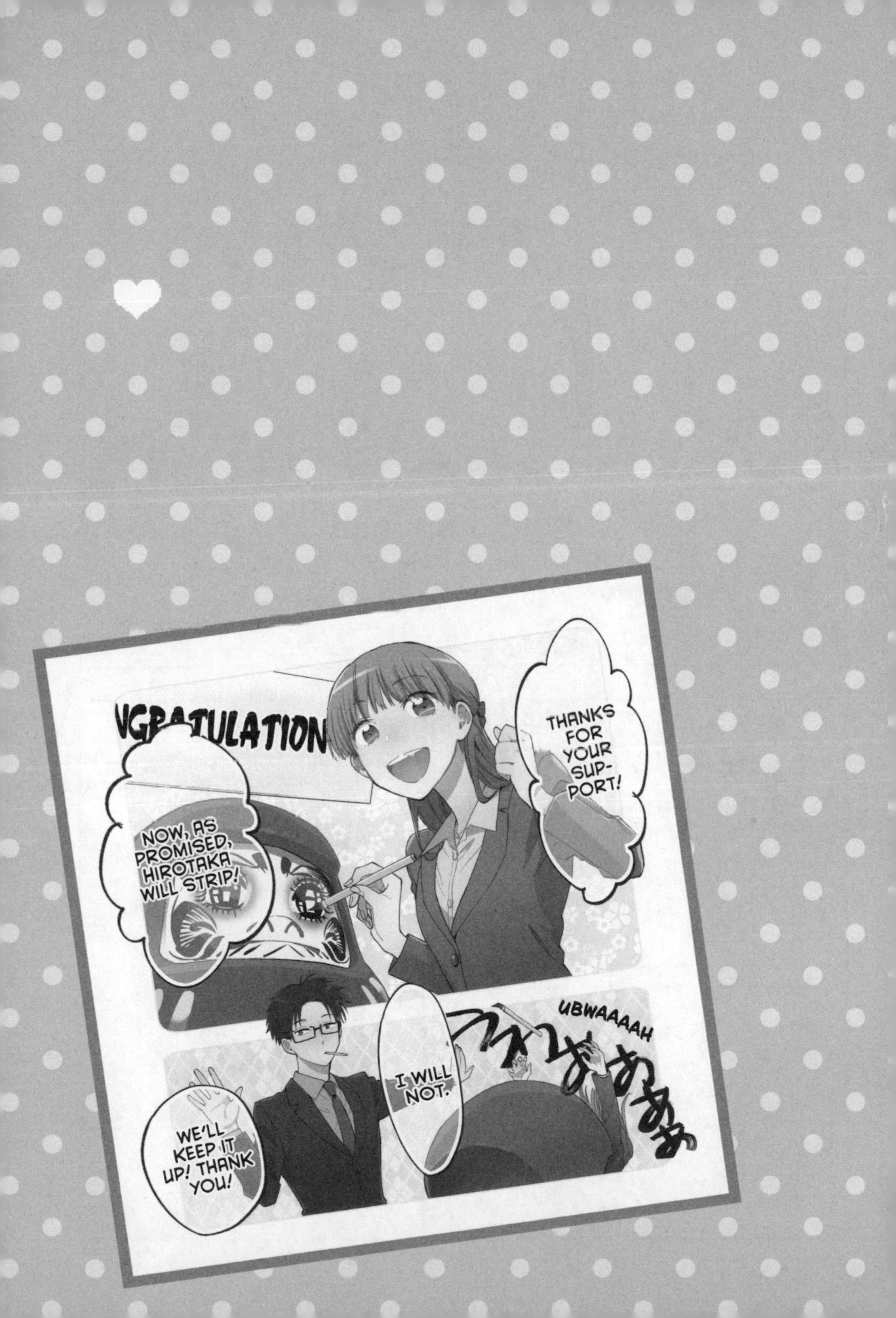
THANKS FOR YOUR SUP-PORT!
VGRATULATION
NOW, AS PROMISED, HIROTAKA WILL STRIP!
UBWAAAAH
I WILL NOT.
WE'LL KEEP IT UP! THANK YOU!

Episode....35

friends...3

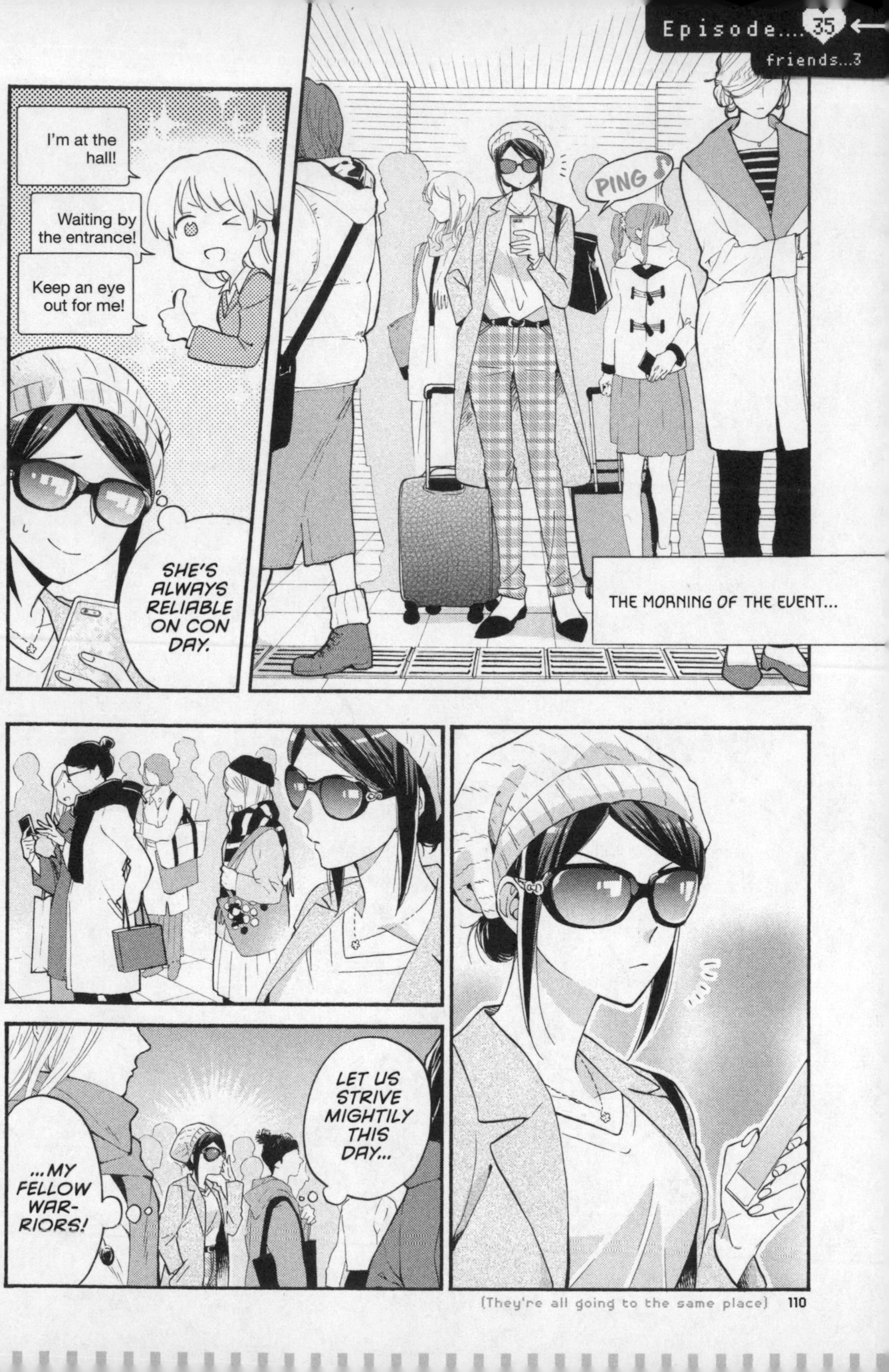
PING
THE MORNING OF THE EVENT...
I'm at the hall!
Waiting by the entrance!
Keep an eye out for me!
SHE'S ALWAYS RELIABLE ON CON DAY.
LET US STRIVE MIGHTILY THIS DAY...
...MY FELLOW WAR-RIORS!

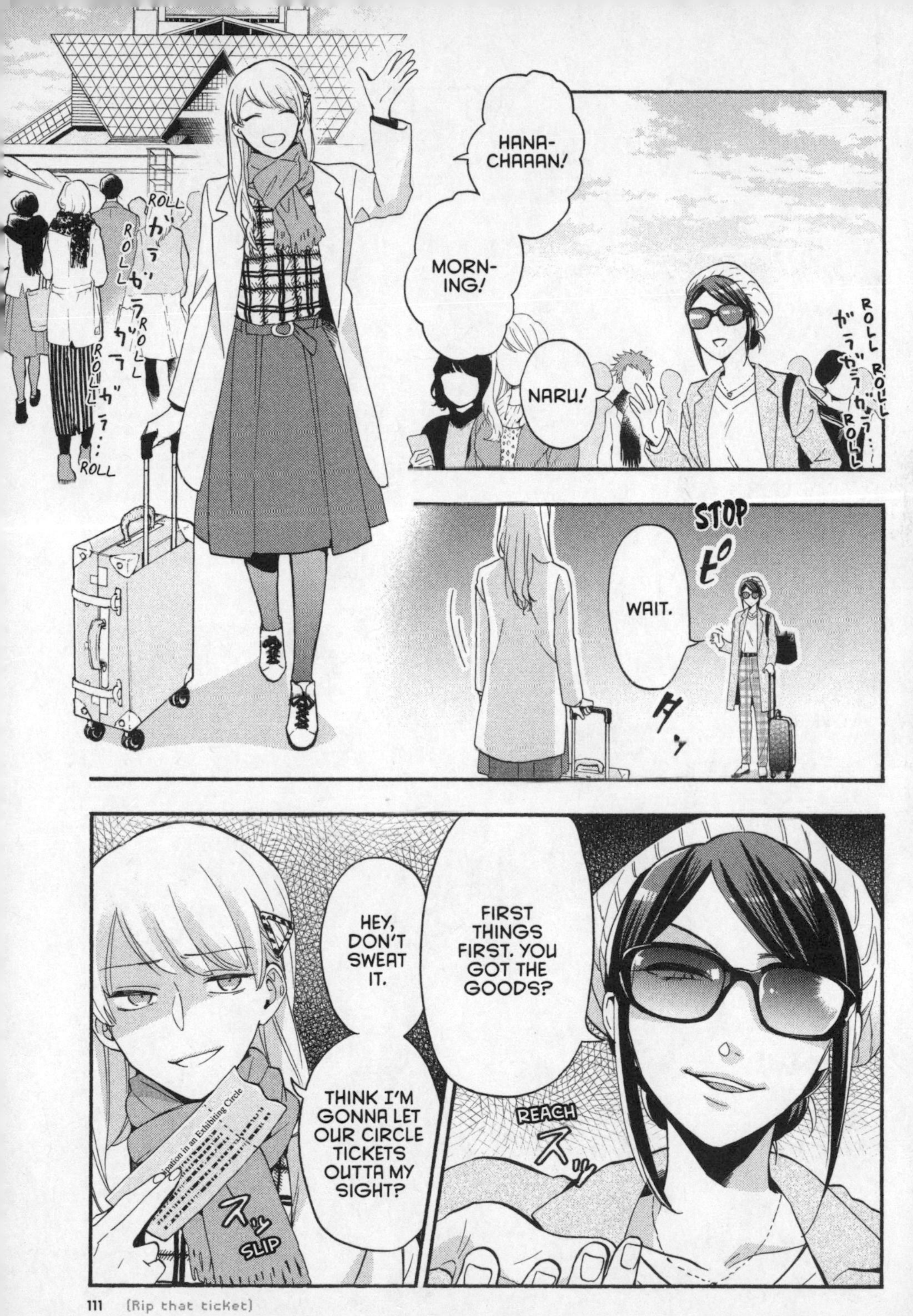
HANA-CHAAAN!
MORNING!
NARU!
ROLL ROLL
ROLL ROLL
STOP
WAIT.
ROLL
ROLL
ROLL
ROLL
ROLL
FIRST THINGS FIRST. YOU GOT THE GOODS?
REACH
HEY, DON'T SWEAT IT.
THINK I'M GONNA LET OUR CIRCLE TICKETS OUTTA MY SIGHT?
SLIP

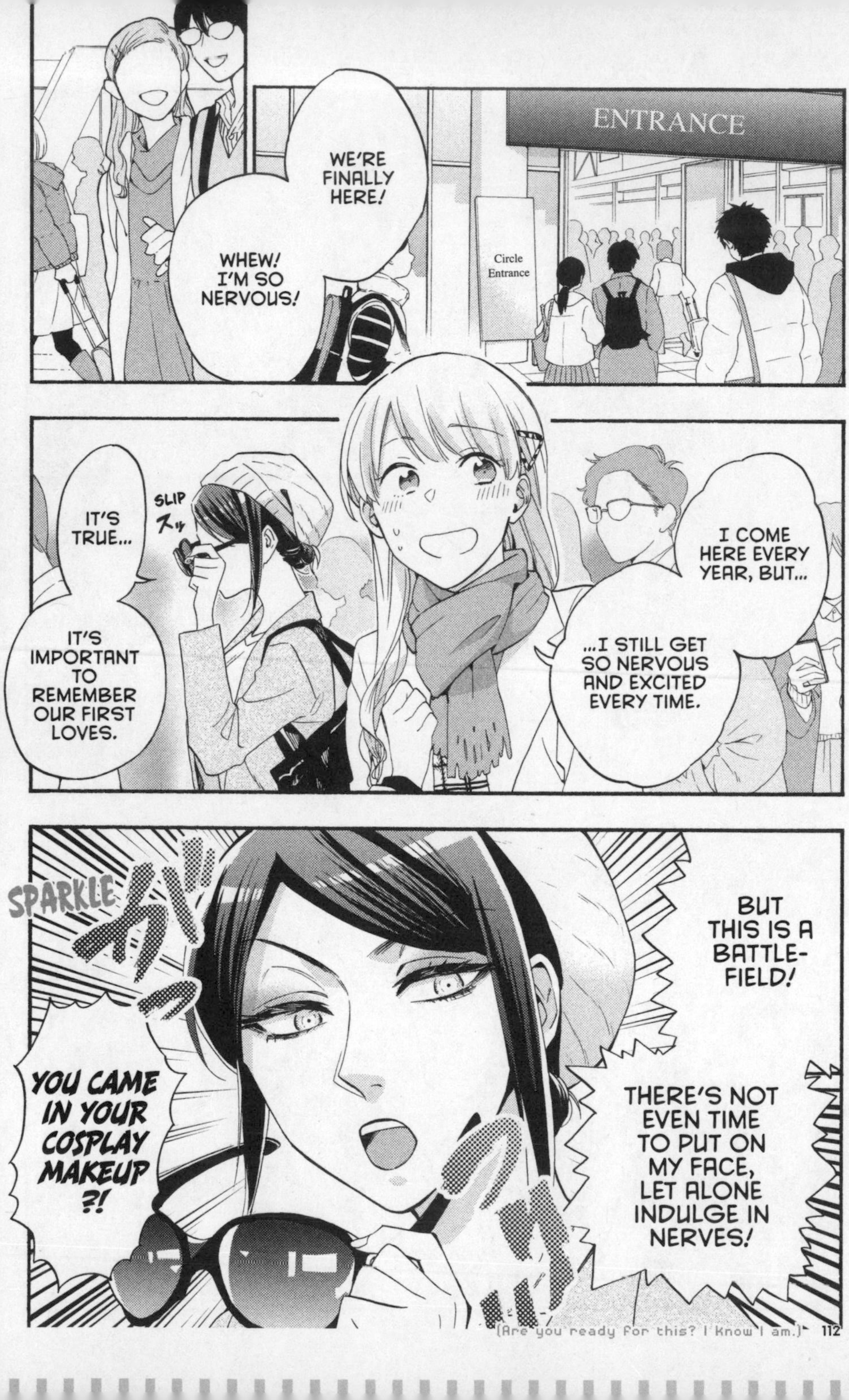
ENTRANCE
Circle Entrance
WE'RE FINALLY HERE!
WHEW! I'M SO NERVOUS!
I COME HERE EVERY YEAR, BUT...
...I STILL GET SO NERVOUS AND EXCITED EVERY TIME.
IT'S TRUE...
SLIP
スッ
IT'S IMPORTANT TO REMEMBER OUR FIRST LOVES.
BUT THIS IS A BATTLE-FIELD!
THERE'S NOT EVEN TIME TO PUT ON MY FACE, LET ALONE INDULGE IN NERVES!
SPARKLE
YOU CAME IN YOUR COSPLAY MAKEUP?!

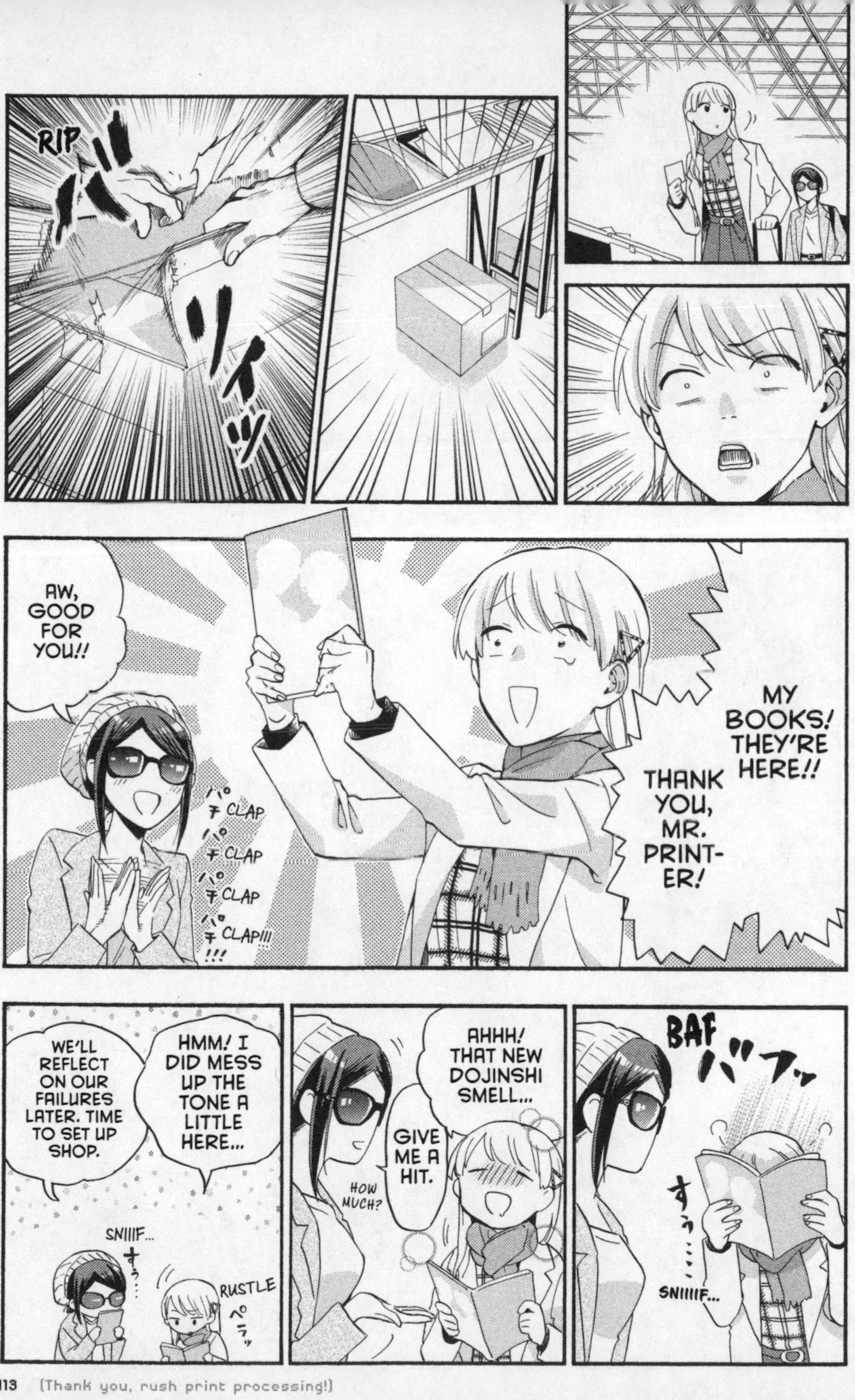

RIP
MY BOOKS! THEY'RE HERE!!
THANK YOU, MR. PRINTER!
AW, GOOD FOR YOU!!
CLAP
CLAP
CLAP
CLAP!!!
!!!
BAF
SNIIIIF...
AHHH! THAT NEW DOJINSHI SMELL...
GIVE ME A HIT.
HOW MUCH?
HMM! I DID MESS UP THE TONE A LITTLE HERE...
WE'LL REFLECT ON OUR FAILURES LATER. TIME TO SET UP SHOP.
SNIIIF...
RUSTLE

 (Thank you, rush print processing!)

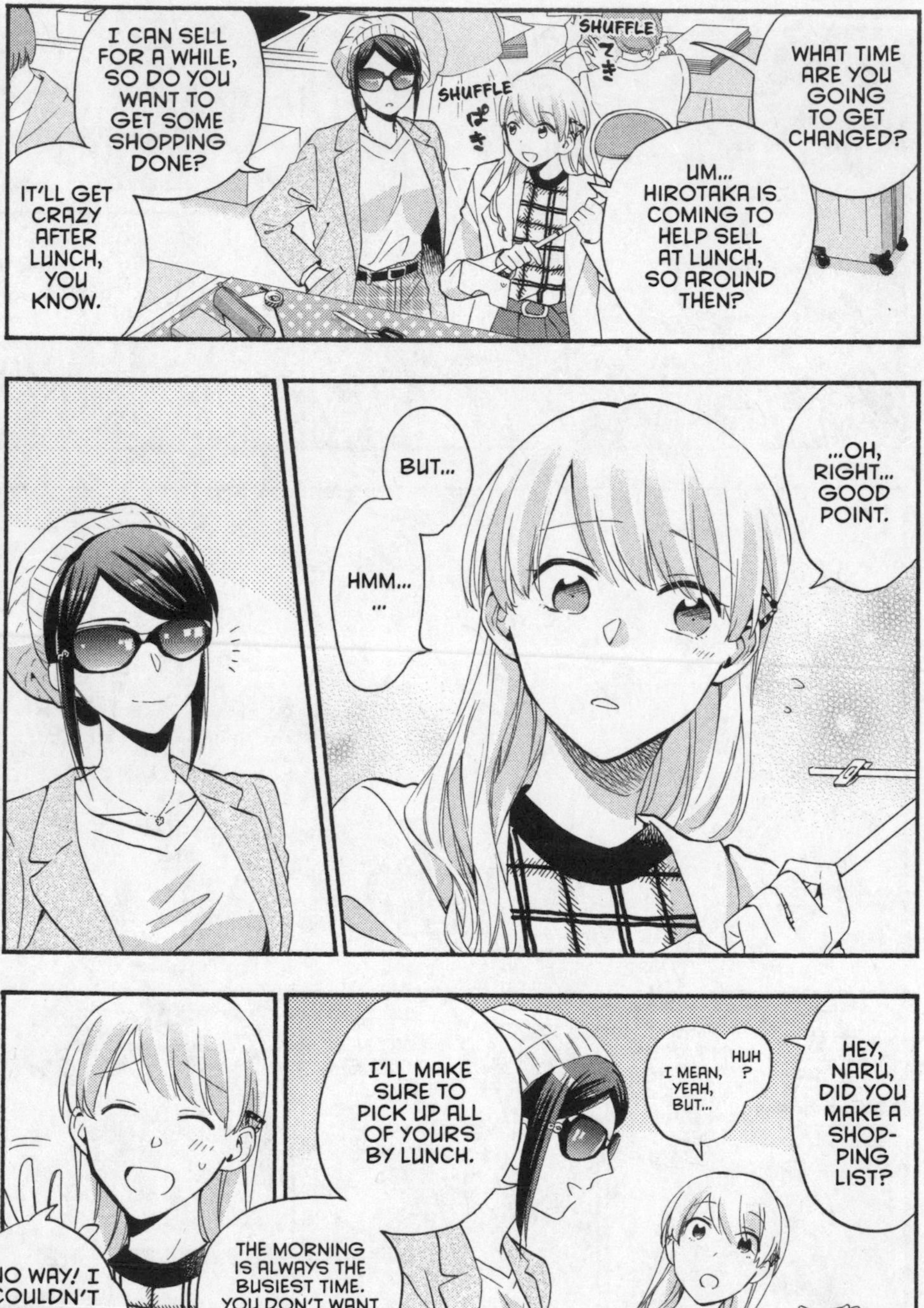
WHAT TIME ARE YOU GOING TO GET CHANGED?
SHUFFLE
SHUFFLE
UM... HIROTAKA IS COMING TO HELP SELL AT LUNCH, SO AROUND THEN?
I CAN SELL FOR A WHILE, SO DO YOU WANT TO GET SOME SHOPPING DONE?
IT'LL GET CRAZY AFTER LUNCH, YOU KNOW.
...OH, RIGHT... GOOD POINT.
BUT...
HMM... ...
HEY, NARU, DID YOU MAKE A SHOP-PING LIST?
HUH?
I MEAN, YEAH, BUT...
I'LL MAKE SURE TO PICK UP ALL OF YOURS BY LUNCH.
NO WAY! I COULDN'T ASK YOU TO DO THAT!
THE MORNING IS ALWAYS THE BUSIEST TIME. YOU DON'T WANT TO LEAVE THE BOOTH NOW.

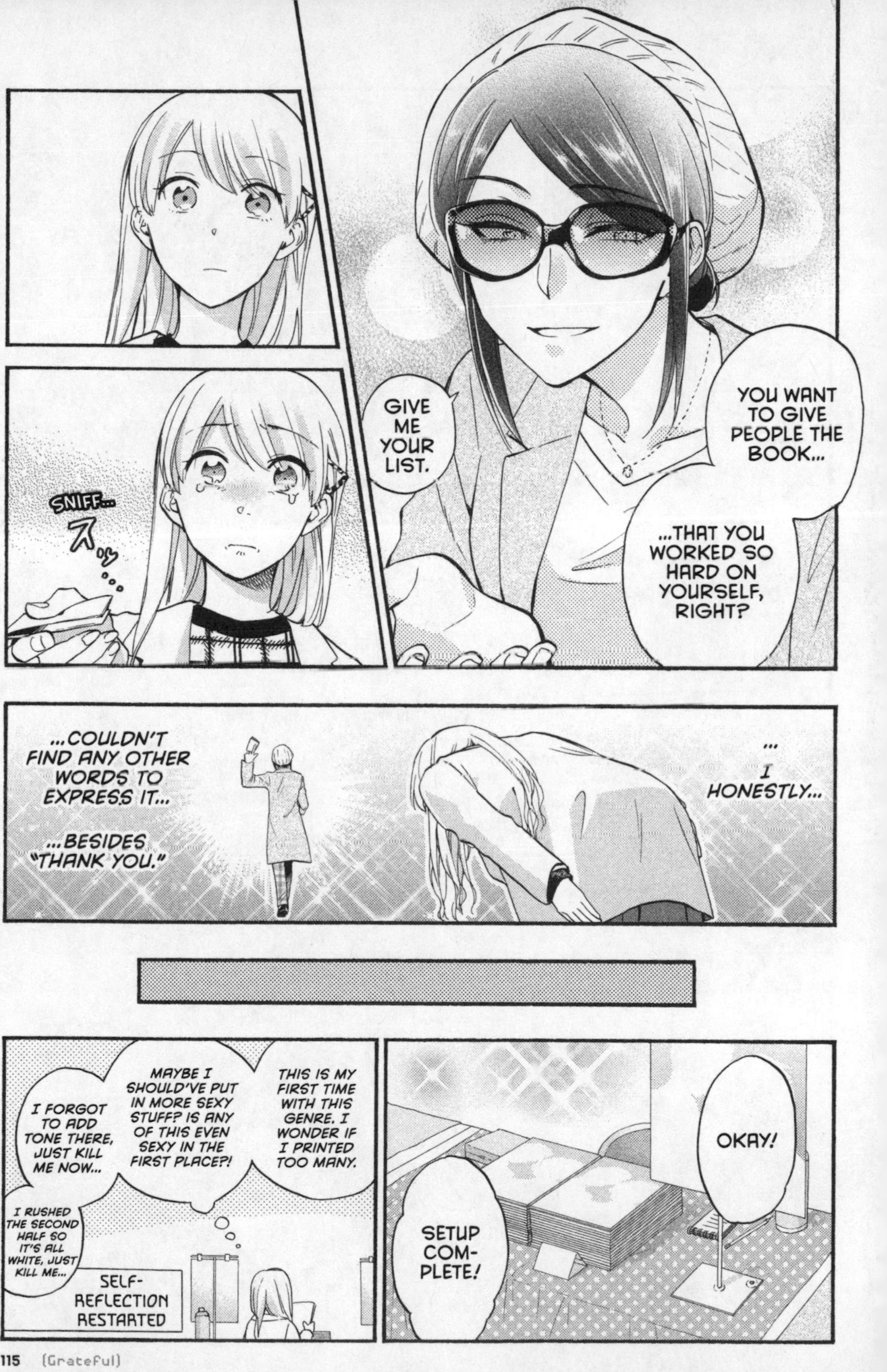
YOU WANT TO GIVE PEOPLE THE BOOK...
...THAT YOU WORKED SO HARD ON YOURSELF, RIGHT?
GIVE ME YOUR LIST.
SNIFF...
スッ
... I HONESTLY...
...COULDN'T FIND ANY OTHER WORDS TO EXPRESS IT...
...BESIDES "THANK YOU."
OKAY!
SETUP COM-PLETE!
THIS IS MY FIRST TIME WITH THIS GENRE. I WONDER IF I PRINTED TOO MANY.
MAYBE I SHOULD'VE PUT IN MORE SEXY STUFF? IS ANY OF THIS EVEN SEXY IN THE FIRST PLACE?!
I FORGOT TO ADD TONE THERE, JUST KILL ME NOW...
I RUSHED THE SECOND HALF SO IT'S ALL WHITE, JUST KILL ME...
SELF-REFLECTION RESTARTED

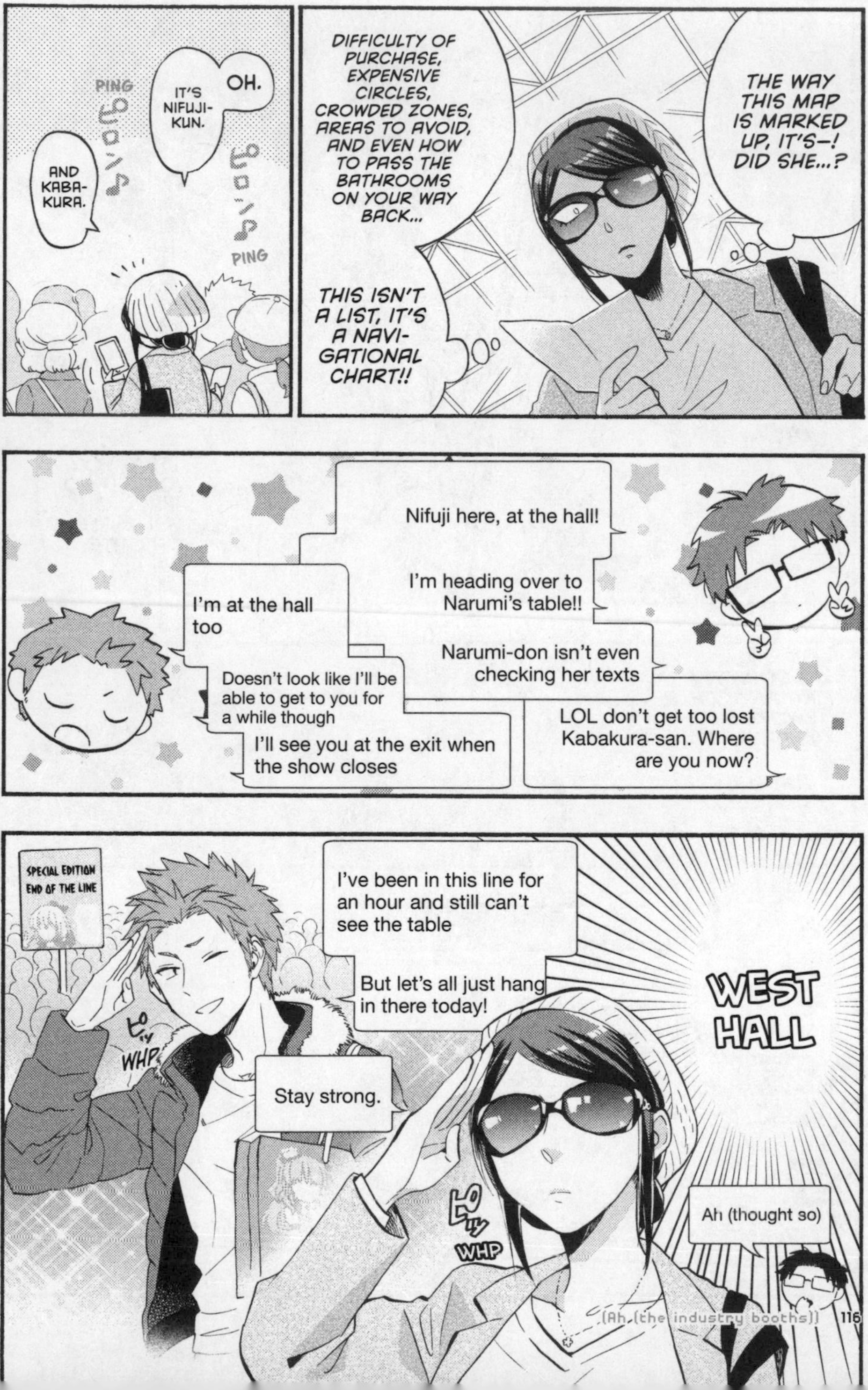
THE WAY THIS MAP IS MARKED UP, IT'S—! DID SHE...?
DIFFICULTY OF PURCHASE, EXPENSIVE CIRCLES, CROWDED ZONES, AREAS TO AVOID, AND EVEN HOW TO PASS THE BATHROOMS ON YOUR WAY BACK...
THIS ISN'T A LIST, IT'S A NAVIGATIONAL CHART!!
PING
OH.
IT'S NIFUJI-KUN.
PING
AND KABA-KURA.
Nifuji here, at the hall!
I'm heading over to Narumi's table!!
I'm at the hall too
Narumi-don isn't even checking her texts
Doesn't look like I'll be able to get to you for a while though
LOL don't get too lost Kabakura-san. Where are you now?
I'll see you at the exit when the show closes
WEST HALL
I've been in this line for an hour and still can't see the table
But let's all just hang in there today!
Stay strong.
SPECIAL EDITION END OF THE LINE
WHP
WHP
Ah (thought so)
(Ah (the industry booths))

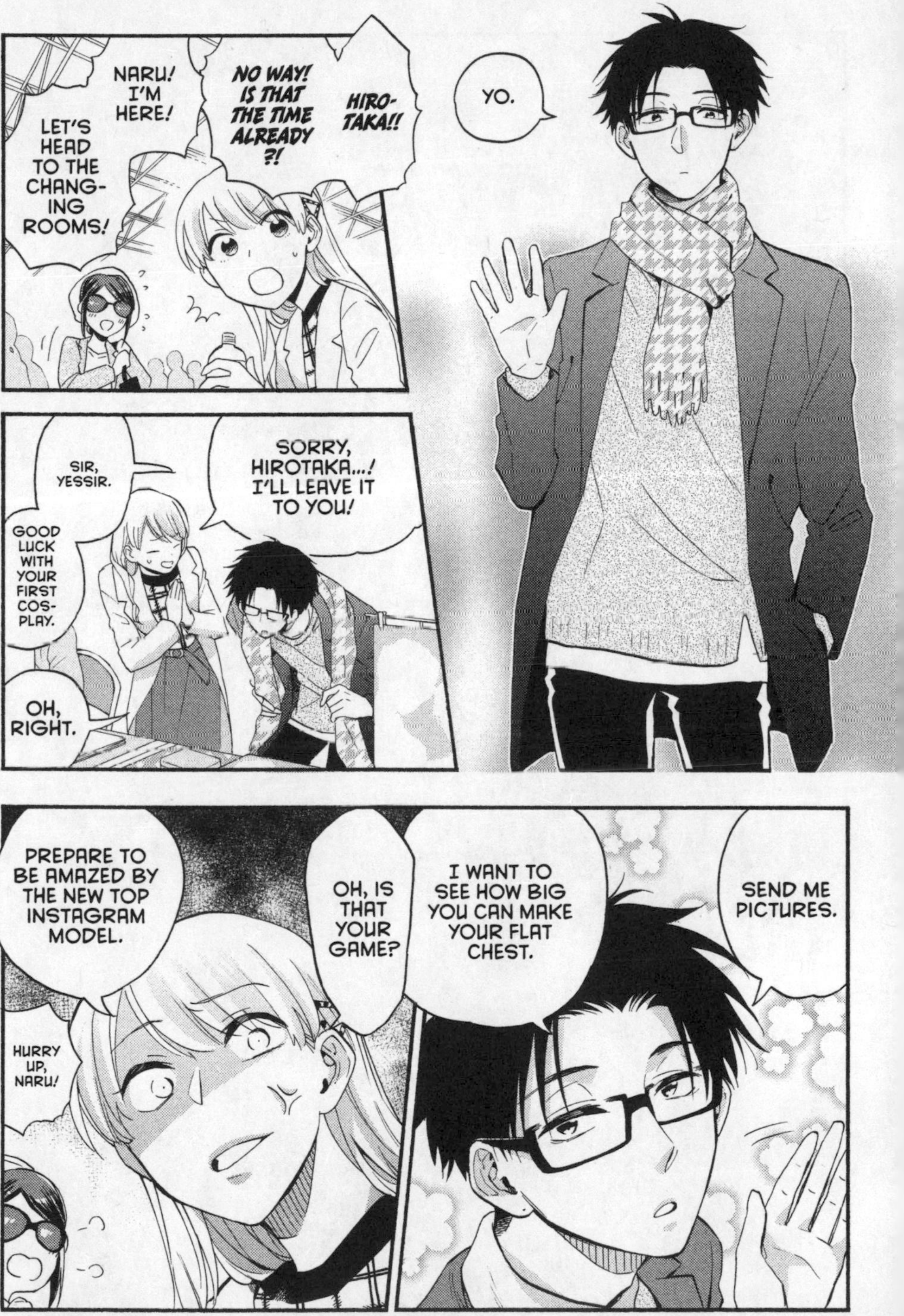
YO.
HIRO-TAKA!!
NO WAY! IS THAT THE TIME ALREADY ?!
NARU! I'M HERE!
LET'S HEAD TO THE CHANG-ING ROOMS!
SORRY, HIROTAKA...! I'LL LEAVE IT TO YOU!
SIR, YESSIR.
GOOD LUCK WITH YOUR FIRST COS-PLAY.
OH, RIGHT.
SEND ME PICTURES.
I WANT TO SEE HOW BIG YOU CAN MAKE YOUR FLAT CHEST.
OH, IS THAT YOUR GAME?
PREPARE TO BE AMAZED BY THE NEW TOP INSTAGRAM MODEL.
HURRY UP, NARU!

 (This is gonna end in tears for one of us)

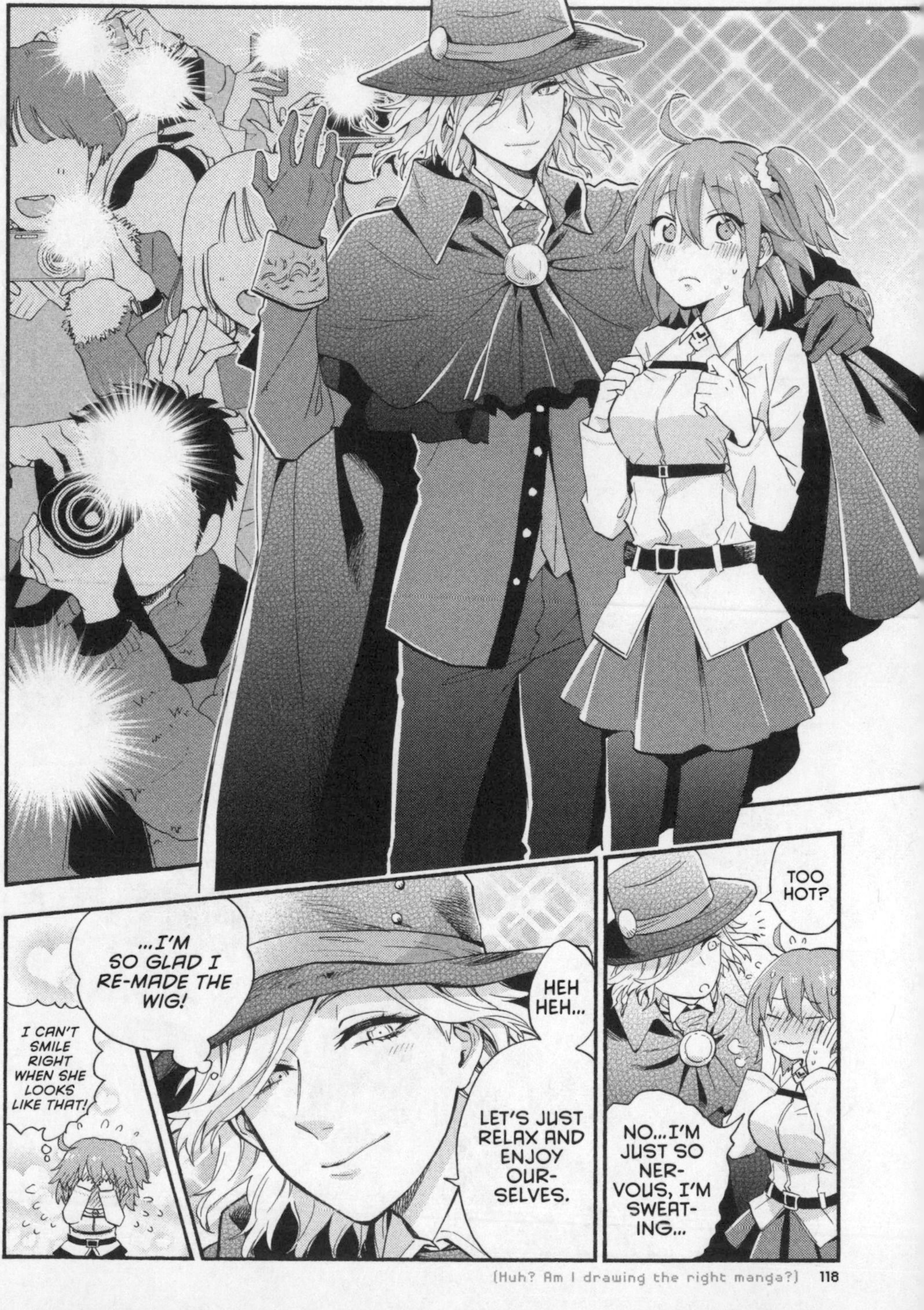
TOO HOT?
NO...I'M JUST SO NER-VOUS, I'M SWEAT-ING...
HEH HEH...
LET'S JUST RELAX AND ENJOY OUR-SELVES.
...I'M SO GLAD I RE-MADE THE WIG!
I CAN'T SMILE RIGHT WHEN SHE LOOKS LIKE THAT!

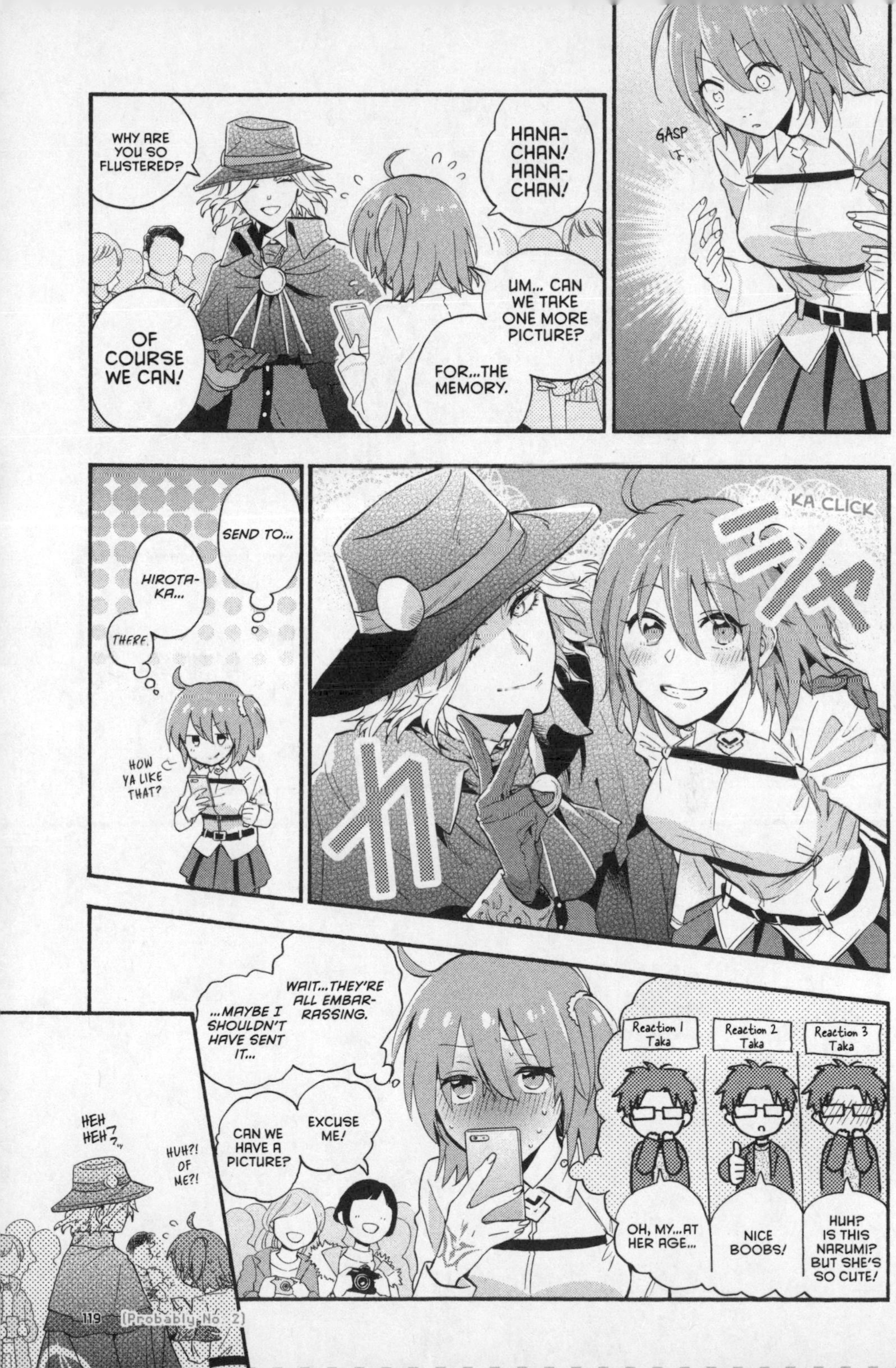
GASP
HANA-CHAN! HANA-CHAN!
WHY ARE YOU SO FLUSTERED?
UM... CAN WE TAKE ONE MORE PICTURE?
FOR...THE MEMORY.
OF COURSE WE CAN!
KA CLICK
SEND TO...
HIROTAKA...
THERE.
HOW YA LIKE THAT?
WAIT...THEY'RE ALL EMBARRASSING.
...MAYBE I SHOULDN'T HAVE SENT IT...
Reaction 3 Taka
HUH? IS THIS NARUMI? BUT SHE'S SO CUTE!
Reaction 2 Taka
NICE BOOBS!
Reaction 1 Taka
OH, MY...AT HER AGE...
EXCUSE ME!
CAN WE HAVE A PICTURE?
HUH?! OF ME?!
HEH HEH
(Probably No. 2)

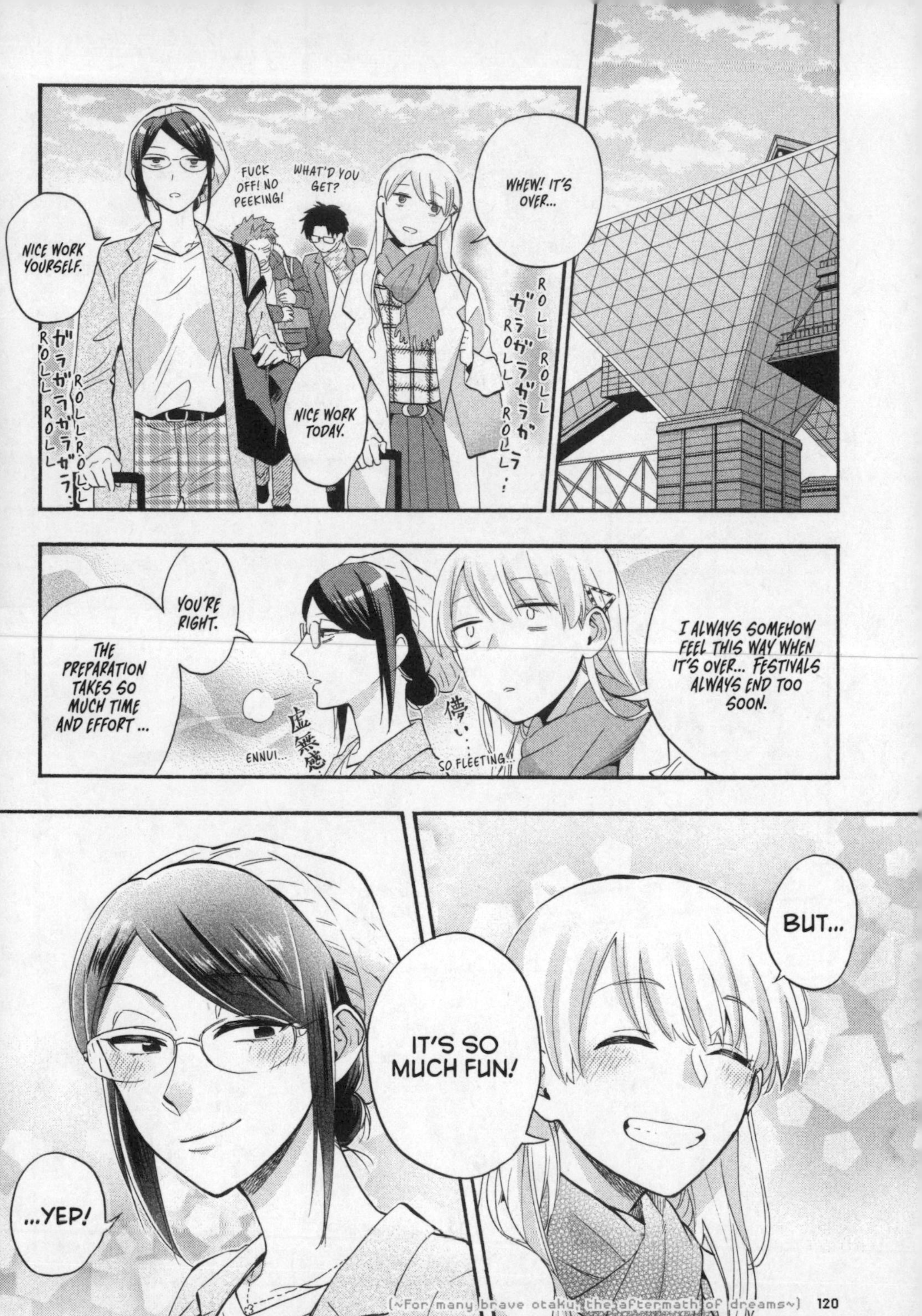
WHEW! IT'S OVER...
ROLL ROLL ROLL ROLL!
WHAT'D YOU GET?
FUCK OFF! NO PEEKING!
NICE WORK TODAY.
NICE WORK YOURSELF.
ROLL ROLL ROLL ROLL...
I ALWAYS SOMEHOW FEEL THIS WAY WHEN IT'S OVER... FESTIVALS ALWAYS END TOO SOON.
儚い...
SO FLEETING...
YOU'RE RIGHT.
THE PREPARATION TAKES SO MUCH TIME AND EFFORT ...
虚無感
ENNUI...
BUT...
IT'S SO MUCH FUN!
...YEP!

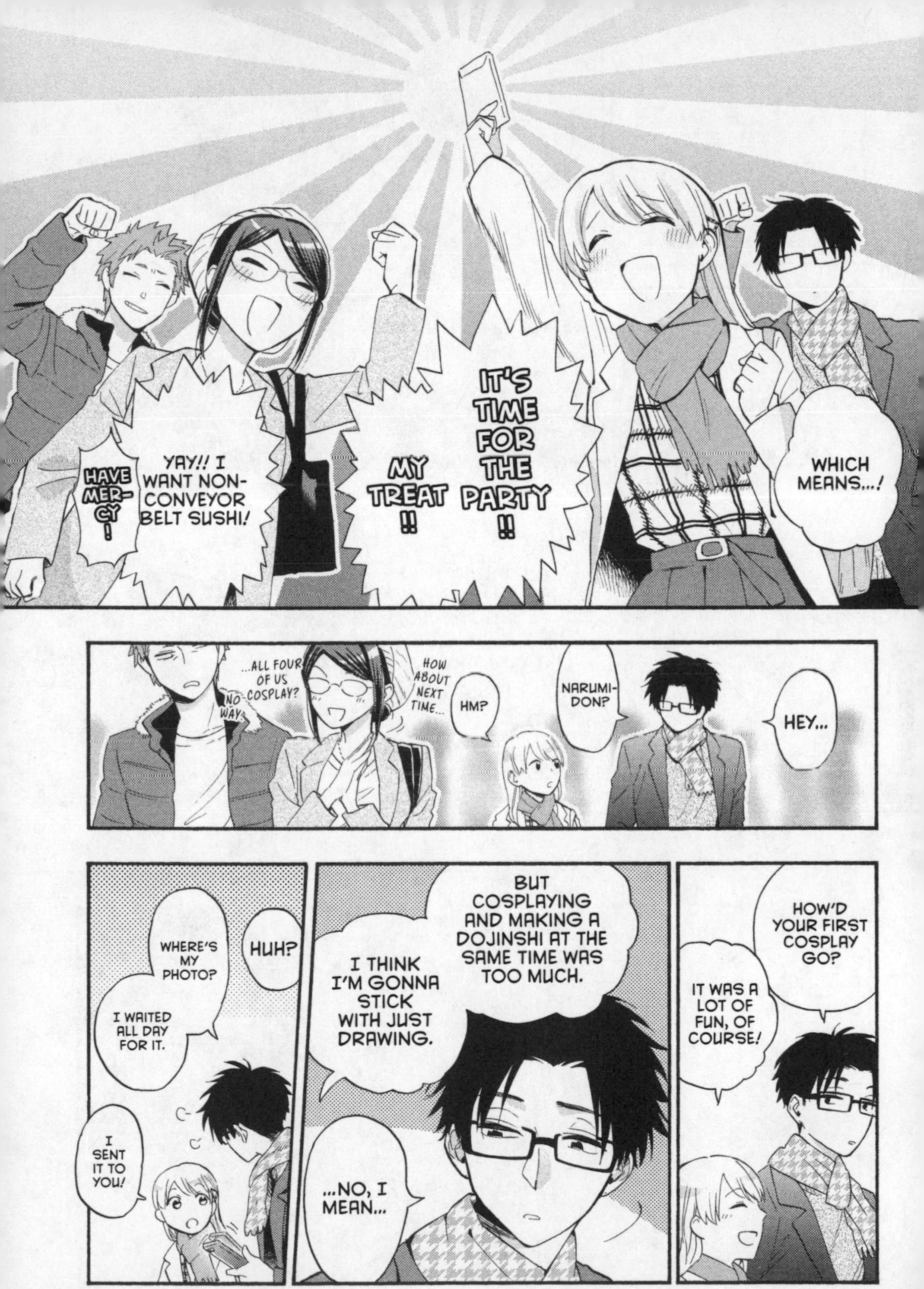
WHICH MEANS...!
IT'S TIME FOR THE PARTY!!
MY TREAT!!
YAY!! I WANT NON-CONVEYOR BELT SUSHI!
HAVE MERCY!
HEY...
NARUMI-DON?
HM?
HOW ABOUT NEXT TIME...
...ALL FOUR OF US COSPLAY?
NO WAY.
HOW'D YOUR FIRST COSPLAY GO?
IT WAS A LOT OF FUN, OF COURSE!
BUT COSPLAYING AND MAKING A DOJINSHI AT THE SAME TIME WAS TOO MUCH.
I THINK I'M GONNA STICK WITH JUST DRAWING.
...NO, I MEAN...
HUH?
WHERE'S MY PHOTO?
I WAITED ALL DAY FOR IT.
I SENT IT TO YOU!

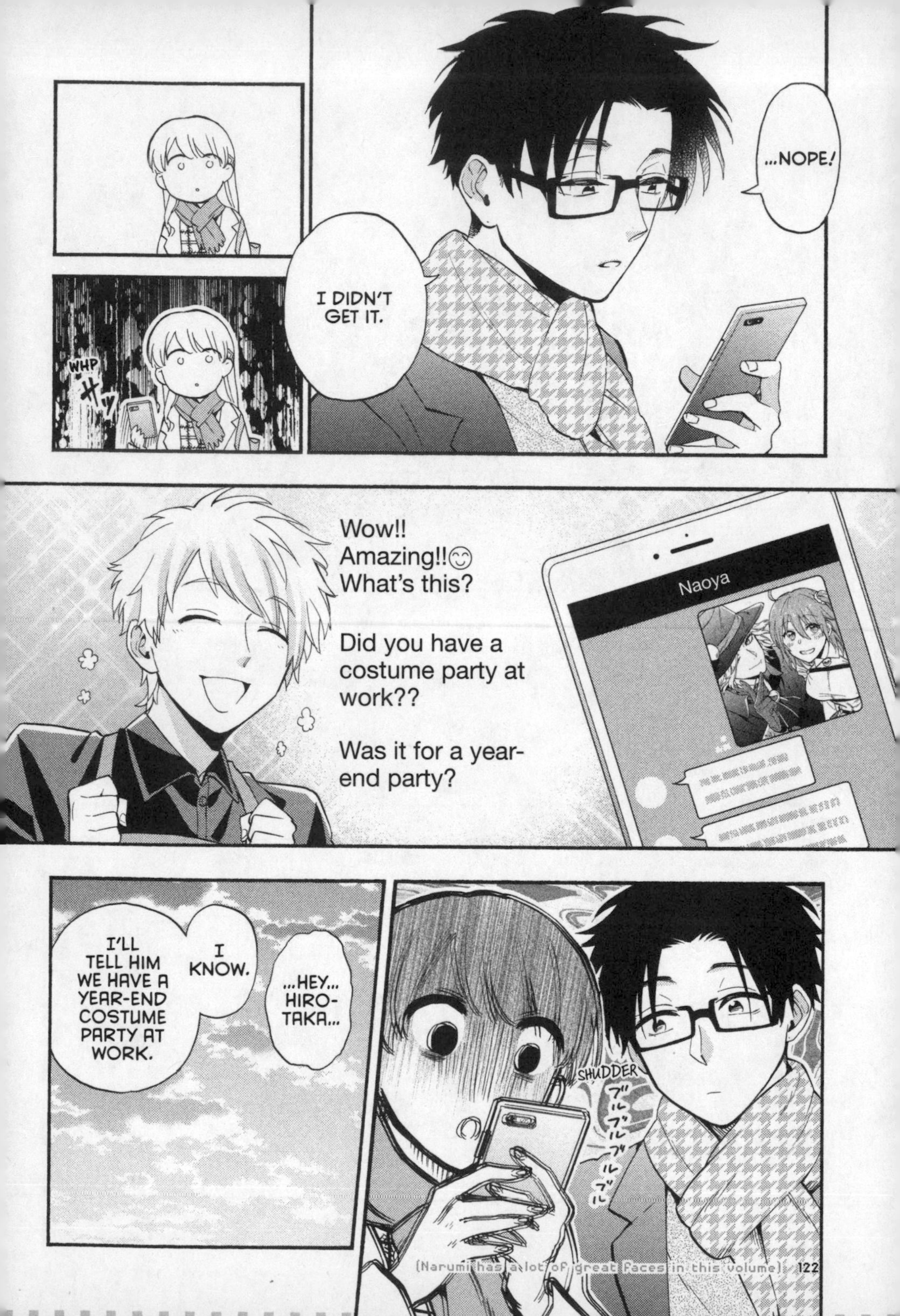
...NOPE!
I DIDN'T GET IT.
WHP
Naoya
Wow!!
Amazing!!☺
What's this?
Did you have a costume party at work??
Was it for a year-end party?
SHUDDER
...HEY... HIRO-TAKA...
I KNOW.
I'LL TELL HIM WE HAVE A YEAR-END COSTUME PARTY AT WORK.
(Narumi has a lot of great faces in this volume)

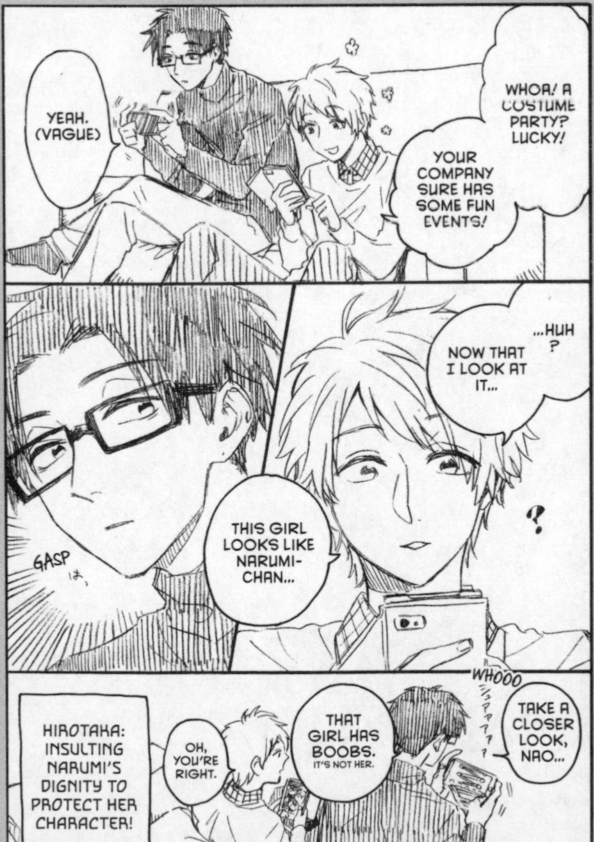
WHOA! A COSTUME PARTY? LUCKY!
YOUR COMPANY SURE HAS SOME FUN EVENTS!
YEAH. (VAGUE)
...HUH?
NOW THAT I LOOK AT IT...
THIS GIRL LOOKS LIKE NARUMI-CHAN...
GASP
は、
WHOOO
TAKE A CLOSER LOOK, NAO...
THAT GIRL HAS BOOBS. IT'S NOT HER.
OH, YOU'RE RIGHT.
HIROTAKA: INSULTING NARUMI'S DIGNITY TO PROTECT HER CHARACTER!

Wotakoi: Love is Hard for Otaku

▶CONTINUE

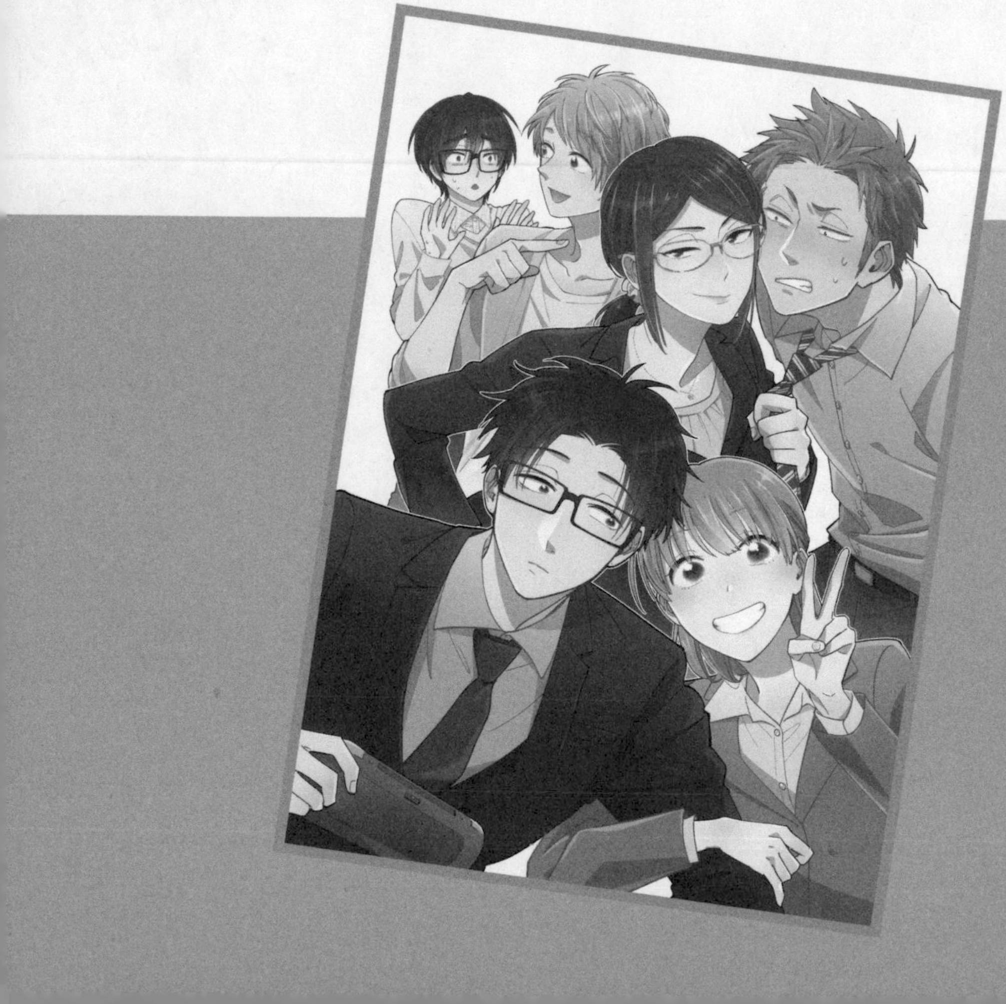

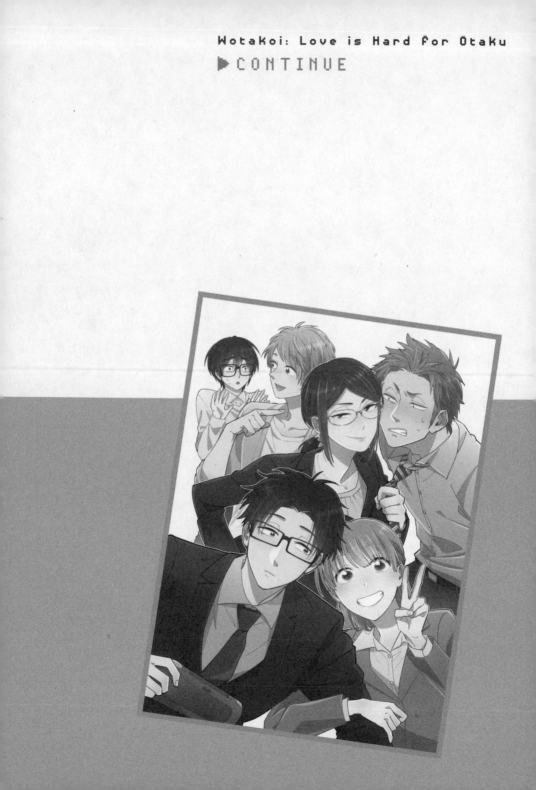

(｀д･´)

Afterword

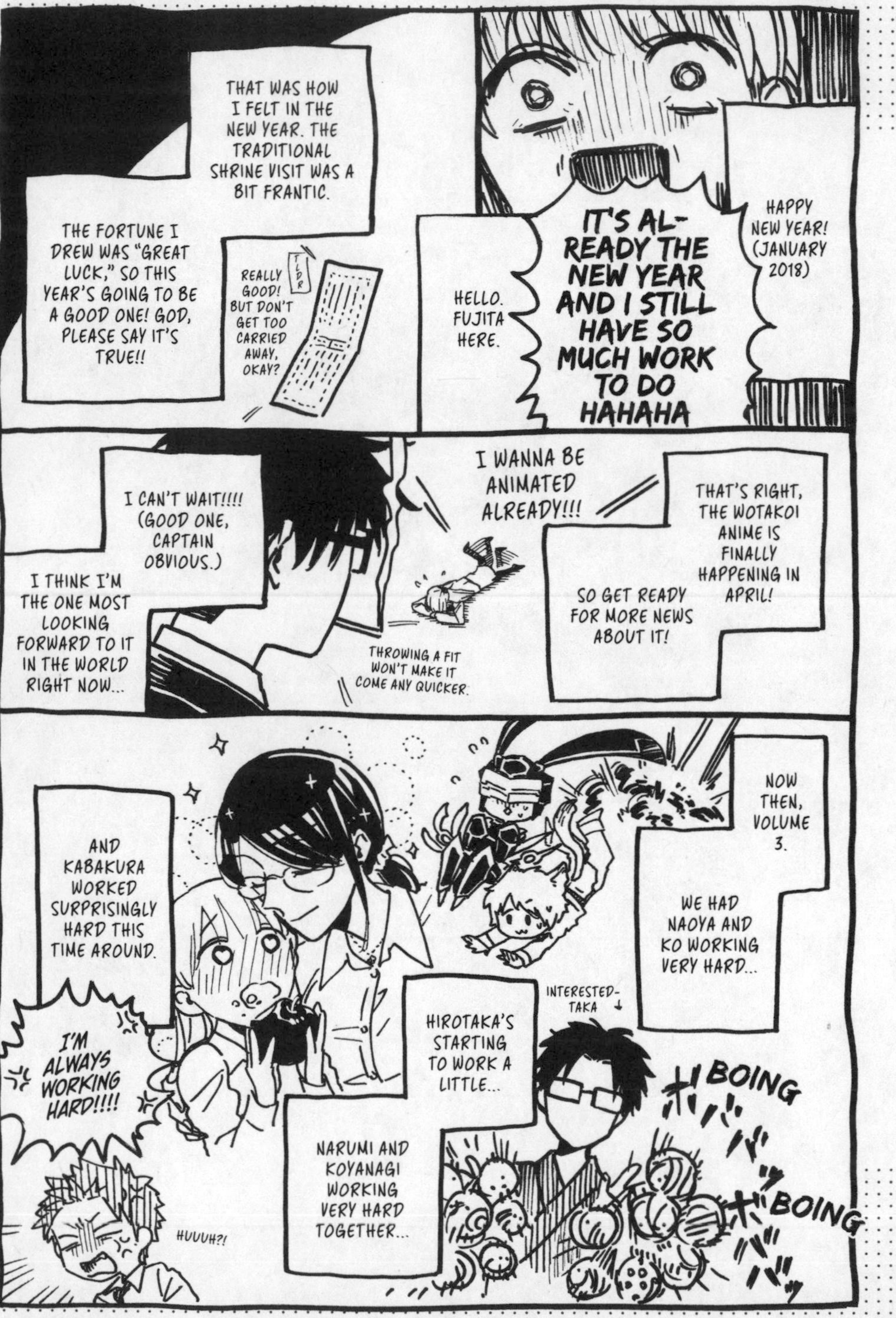
HAPPY NEW YEAR! (JANUARY 2018)
IT'S ALREADY THE NEW YEAR AND I STILL HAVE SO MUCH WORK TO DO HAHAHA
HELLO. FUJITA HERE.
THAT WAS HOW I FELT IN THE NEW YEAR. THE TRADITIONAL SHRINE VISIT WAS A BIT FRANTIC.
THE FORTUNE I DREW WAS "GREAT LUCK," SO THIS YEAR'S GOING TO BE A GOOD ONE! GOD, PLEASE SAY IT'S TRUE!!
TLDR
REALLY GOOD! BUT DON'T GET TOO CARRIED AWAY, OKAY?
THAT'S RIGHT, THE WOTAKOI ANIME IS FINALLY HAPPENING IN APRIL!
SO GET READY FOR MORE NEWS ABOUT IT!
I WANNA BE ANIMATED ALREADY!!!
THROWING A FIT WON'T MAKE IT COME ANY QUICKER.
I CAN'T WAIT!!!! (GOOD ONE, CAPTAIN OBVIOUS.)
I THINK I'M THE ONE MOST LOOKING FORWARD TO IT IN THE WORLD RIGHT NOW...
NOW THEN, VOLUME 3.
WE HAD NAOYA AND KO WORKING VERY HARD...
AND KABAKURA WORKED SURPRISINGLY HARD THIS TIME AROUND.
I'M ALWAYS WORKING HARD!!!!
HUUUH?!
INTERESTED-TAKA
HIROTAKA'S STARTING TO WORK A LITTLE...
NARUMI AND KOYANAGI WORKING VERY HARD TOGETHER...
BOING
BOING

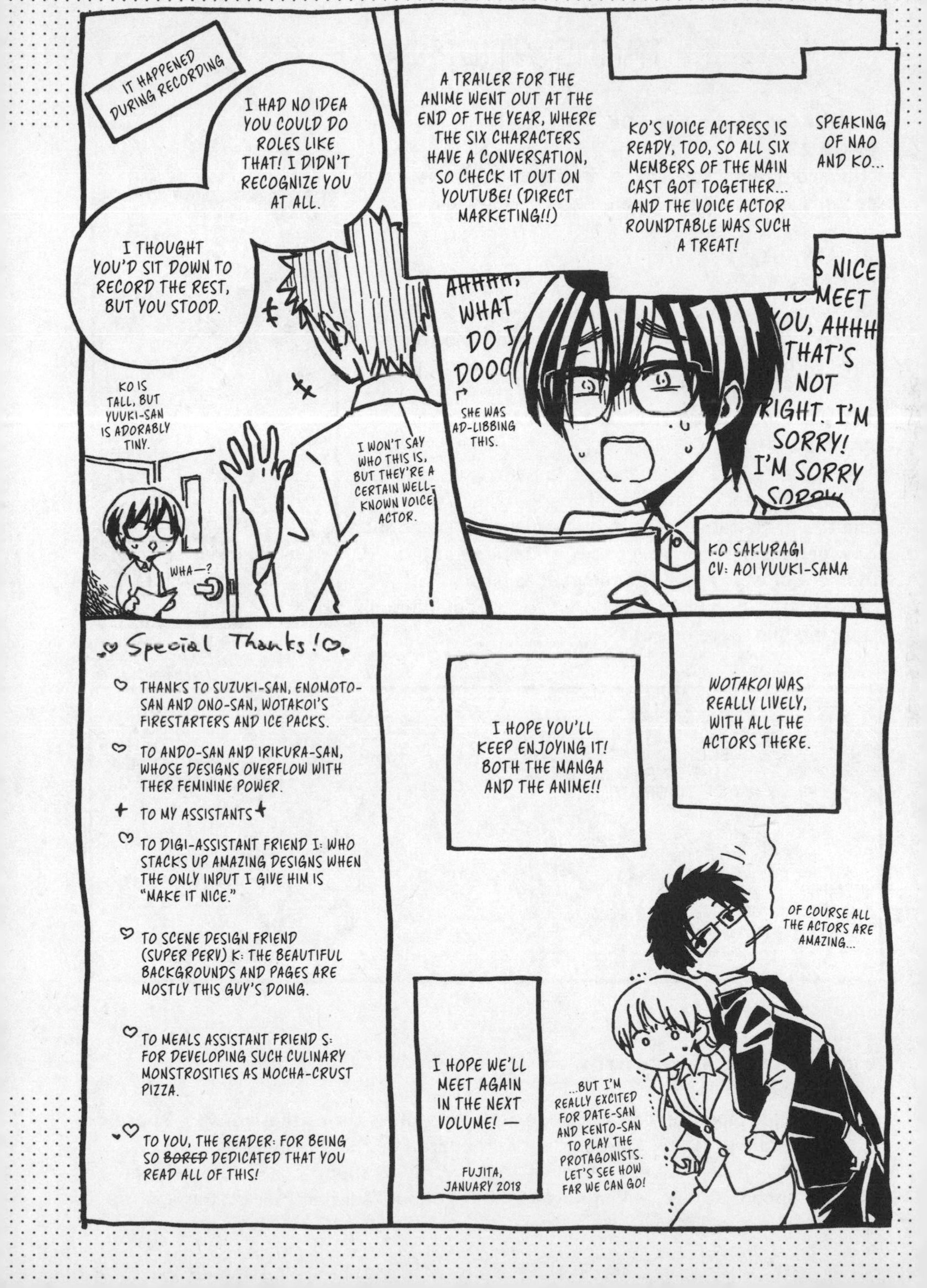
SPEAKING OF NAO AND KO...
KO'S VOICE ACTRESS IS READY, TOO, SO ALL SIX MEMBERS OF THE MAIN CAST GOT TOGETHER... AND THE VOICE ACTOR ROUNDTABLE WAS SUCH A TREAT!
A TRAILER FOR THE ANIME WENT OUT AT THE END OF THE YEAR, WHERE THE SIX CHARACTERS HAVE A CONVERSATION, SO CHECK IT OUT ON YOUTUBE! (DIRECT MARKETING!!)
S NICE MEET YOU, AHHH THAT'S NOT RIGHT. I'M SORRY! I'M SORRY
AHHHH, WHAT DO I DOOO
SHE WAS AD-LIBBING THIS.
KO SAKURAGI CV: AOI YUUKI-SAMA
IT HAPPENED DURING RECORDING
I HAD NO IDEA YOU COULD DO ROLES LIKE THAT! I DIDN'T RECOGNIZE YOU AT ALL.
I THOUGHT YOU'D SIT DOWN TO RECORD THE REST, BUT YOU STOOD.
I WON'T SAY WHO THIS IS, BUT THEY'RE A CERTAIN WELL-KNOWN VOICE ACTOR.
KO IS TALL, BUT YUUKI-SAN IS ADORABLY TINY.
WHA—?
WOTAKOI WAS REALLY LIVELY, WITH ALL THE ACTORS THERE.
I HOPE YOU'LL KEEP ENJOYING IT! BOTH THE MANGA AND THE ANIME!!
OF COURSE ALL THE ACTORS ARE AMAZING...
...BUT I'M REALLY EXCITED FOR DATE-SAN AND KENTO-SAN TO PLAY THE PROTAGONISTS. LET'S SEE HOW FAR WE CAN GO!
I HOPE WE'LL MEET AGAIN IN THE NEXT VOLUME! —
FUJITA, JANUARY 2018
Special Thanks!
THANKS TO SUZUKI-SAN, ENOMOTO-SAN AND ONO-SAN, WOTAKOI'S FIRESTARTERS AND ICE PACKS.
TO ANDO-SAN AND IRIKURA-SAN, WHOSE DESIGNS OVERFLOW WITH THER FEMININE POWER.
TO MY ASSISTANTS
TO DIGI-ASSISTANT FRIEND I: WHO STACKS UP AMAZING DESIGNS WHEN THE ONLY INPUT I GIVE HIM IS "MAKE IT NICE."
TO SCENE DESIGN FRIEND (SUPER PERV) K: THE BEAUTIFUL BACKGROUNDS AND PAGES ARE MOSTLY THIS GUY'S DOING.
TO MEALS ASSISTANT FRIEND S: FOR DEVELOPING SUCH CULINARY MONSTROSITIES AS MOCHA-CRUST PIZZA.
TO YOU, THE READER: FOR BEING SO BORED DEDICATED THAT YOU READ ALL OF THIS!

TRANSLATION NOTES

HANAKOM AND KABASOK,
PAGE 23

"Hanacom" and "Kabasok" are references to two major security companies in Japan, Secom and Alsok.

▶ TAIYAKI,
PAGE 23

Taiyaki is a Japanese pastry shaped like the *tai* fish. It's commonly sold as a street food, and is normally filled with red adzuki beans, custard, or chocolate.

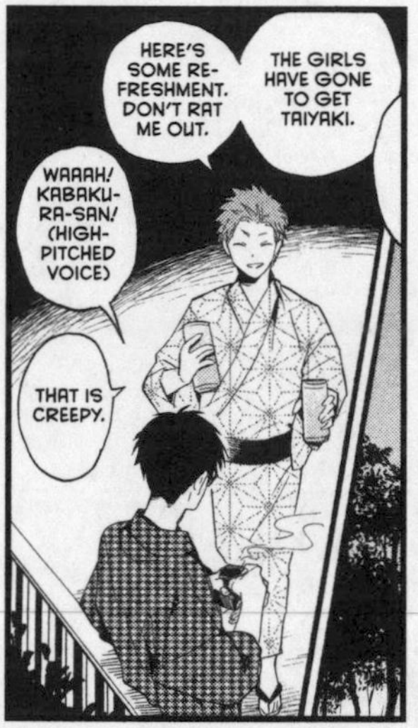
THE GIRLS HAVE GONE TO GET TAIYAKI.
HERE'S SOME RE-FRESHMENT. DON'T RAT ME OUT.
WAAAH! KABAKU-RA-SAN! (HIGH-PITCHED VOICE)
THAT IS CREEPY.

▼ I WANT TO GIVE IN...TO TEMPTATION...!,
PAGE 52

This is a reference to an episode in Kaiji, Nobuyuki Fukumoto's long-running gambling manga.
The titular character, a compulsive gambler, is confined on a gambling boat trying to pay off his debts. In a moment of weakness, he's tempted to blow all his money on luxurious food and drink, which could end up trapping him there forever.

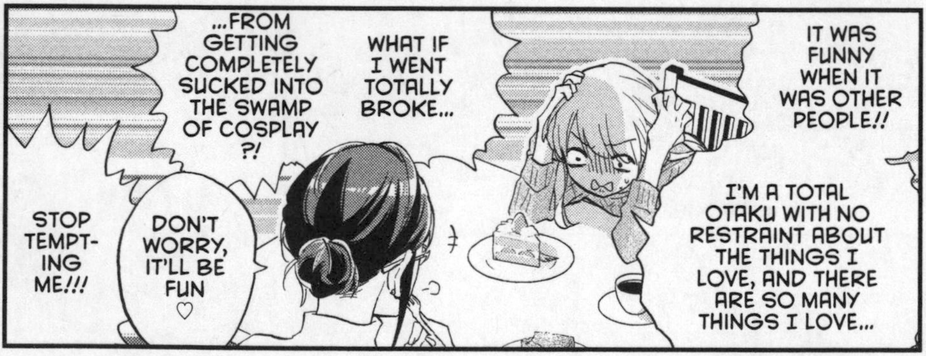
IT WAS FUNNY WHEN IT WAS OTHER PEOPLE!!
I'M A TOTAL OTAKU WITH NO RESTRAINT ABOUT THE THINGS I LOVE, AND THERE ARE SO MANY THINGS I LOVE...
WHAT IF I WENT TOTALLY BROKE...
...FROM GETTING COMPLETELY SUCKED INTO THE SWAMP OF COSPLAY?!
DON'T WORRY, IT'LL BE FUN ♡
STOP TEMPT-ING ME!!!

▼ OSHI/SASAGERU/TOUTOI,
PAGE 56

Koyanagi and Momose's conversation here uses three terms that are very specific to idol fandom in Japan. The term we've rendered as "my favorite idol" is *oshi*, which comes from the verb meaning "to push" or "to support." One's *oshi* is the idol one supports. Next, when Koyanagi talks about "adoring" her costume, she uses the word *sasageru*, which means "to exalt," or "to show devotion to"—but in the context of idol otaku, it refers to the performance of choreographed dances ("*otagei*") of adulation and enthusiasm they perform during live shows, from the audience, to show their support. Finally, the adjective *toutoi* (which we translated

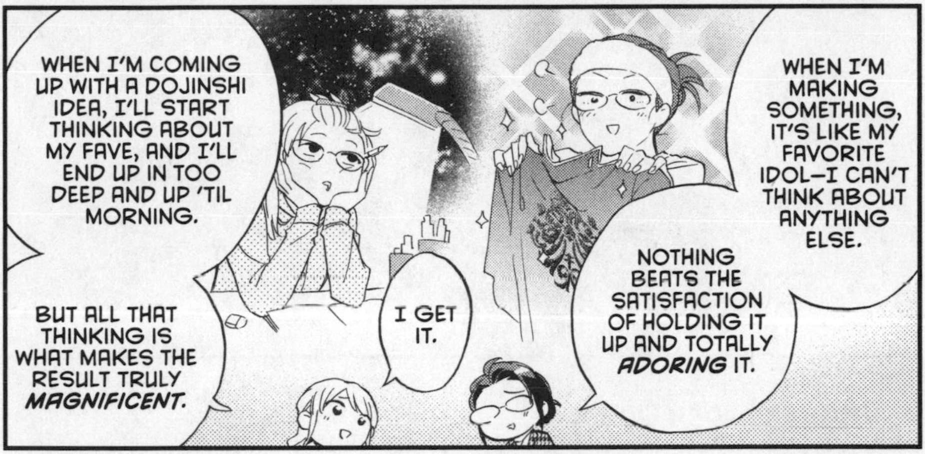
WHEN I'M MAKING SOMETHING, IT'S LIKE MY FAVORITE IDOL—I CAN'T THINK ABOUT ANYTHING ELSE.
NOTHING BEATS THE SATISFACTION OF HOLDING IT UP AND TOTALLY *ADORING* IT.
WHEN I'M COMING UP WITH A DOJINSHI IDEA, I'LL START THINKING ABOUT MY FAVE, AND I'LL END UP IN TOO DEEP AND UP 'TIL MORNING.
I GET IT.
BUT ALL THAT THINKING IS WHAT MAKES THE RESULT TRULY *MAGNIFICENT*.

as "magnificent") means "holy," "noble," or "sacred," and has recently come into favor as a term to describe the object of one's *oshi*.

**THE GATE OF TRUTH,
PAGE 56**

In Hiromu Arakawa's *Fullmetal Alchemist*, the Gate of Truth is the metaphysical source of all alchemical power—in much the same way that this primal enthusiasm is what powers Koyanagi and Momose's hobbies.

**▼ WOMEN WILL CRY, THAT'S JUST HOW IT IS,
PAGE 66**

Attack No. 1 was an influential shojo manga by Chikako Urano about high school volleyball players that ran in the late sixties. "Women will cry, that's just how it is! When suffering, when sorrowful" are lines from the anime version's opening theme.

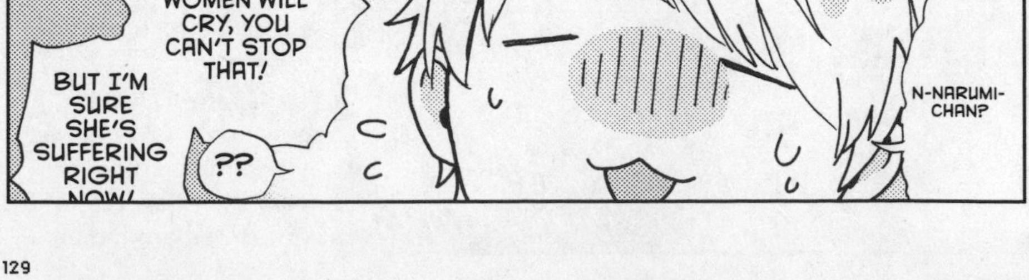
N-NARUMI-CHAN?
WOMEN WILL CRY, YOU CAN'T STOP THAT!
??
BUT I'M SURE SHE'S SUFFERING RIGHT NOW!

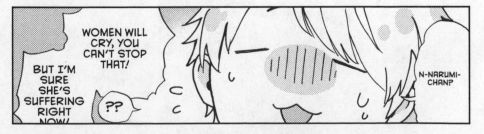

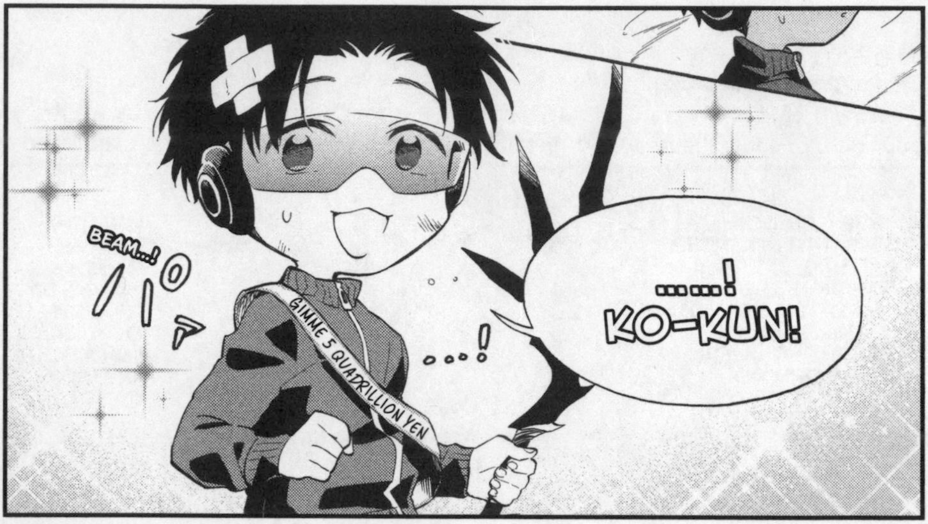

......!
KO-KUN!
...!
GIMME 5 QUADRILLION YEN
BEAM...!

▲ GIMME 5 QUADRILLION YEN, PAGE 76

Gosen-cho-en hoshii or "Gimme 5 Quadrillion Yen," is a semi-inexplicable Japanese twitter meme, originating with Twitter user and graphic designer @KSUWABE's chrome-styled lettering of the phrase.

QAWSEDRFTGYHUJIKOLP, PAGE 76

The keyboard-smashing here is a reverse-transcription of the Japanese meme "くぁwせdrftgyふじこlp", which is what the Microsoft Japanese input method produces when you run your fingers from left to right across the top two letter rows of a QWERTY keyboard. This particular meme goes back to at least 2005, and is typically used to indicate incoherent screaming. It's also called "fujiko," for the last three hiragana characters that appear in the string.

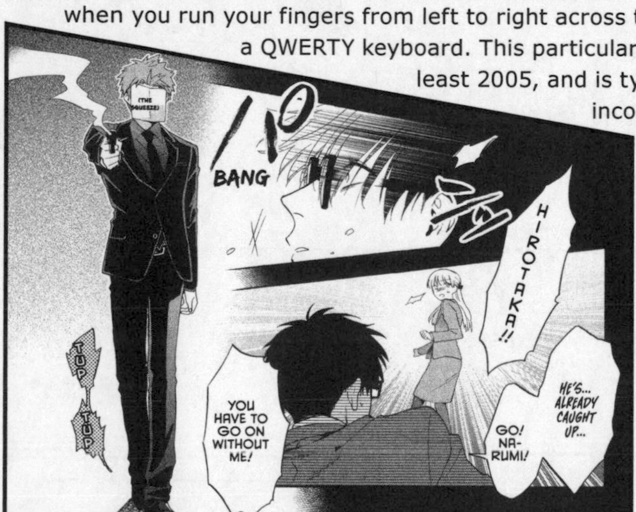

HIROTAKA!!
BANG
HE'S... ALREADY CAUGHT UP...
GO! NA-RUMI!
YOU HAVE TO GO ON WITHOUT ME!
TUP
TUP

◀ RUN FOR MONEY, PAGE 86

The Japanese reality TV show *Run for Money* was a variation on hide-and-seek, where contestants have to run around an area completing tasks while avoiding getting caught by "hunters," men in black suits and sunglasses (like Agents in *The Matrix*). The longer the players remain free, the more money they can win upon being the last person standing. *Cha$e*, an adaptation of this show, briefly ran on the SyFy network in 2008.

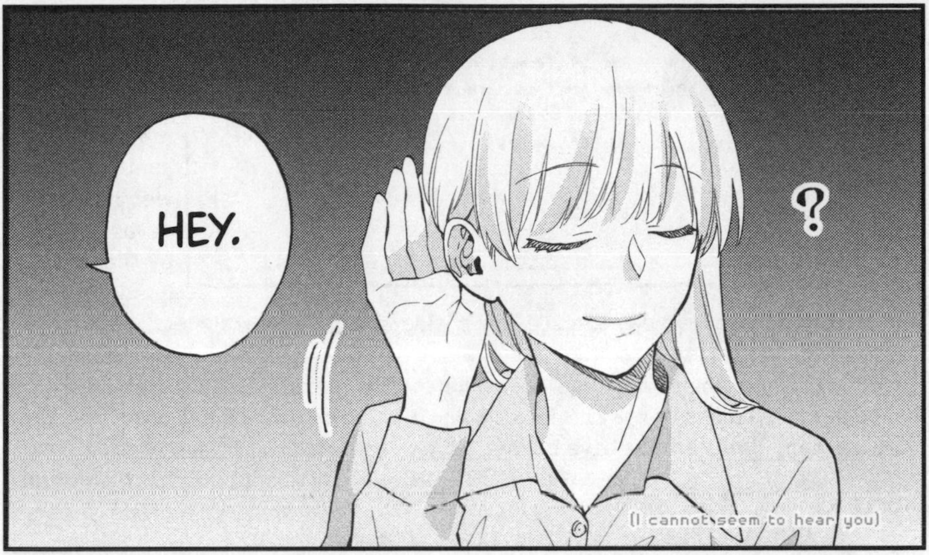
HEY.
?
(I cannot seem to hear you)

▲ I CANNOT SEEM TO HEAR YOU, PAGE 90

"I cannot seem to hear you" is the catchphrase of the eponymous protagonist of *Keiji*, an early nineties *Shonen Jump* manga about a flamboyant samurai in the early Edo period. The phrase has become something of a meme, used when someone is pretending not to hear something that they can obviously hear.

▶ SPLOOSH, PAGE 94

The word Hanako uses in the Japanese here is "*dochashiko*," which in turn is a derivation of the otaku adjective "*shikoi*." "*Shikoi*" comes from "*shiko shiko*," an onomatopoeia describing the sound of a man masturbating. *Shikoi* therefore describes something one is likely to pleasure oneself to, and is used by otaku of all genders. "Dochashiko" is an intensified variant, hence: "Sploosh."

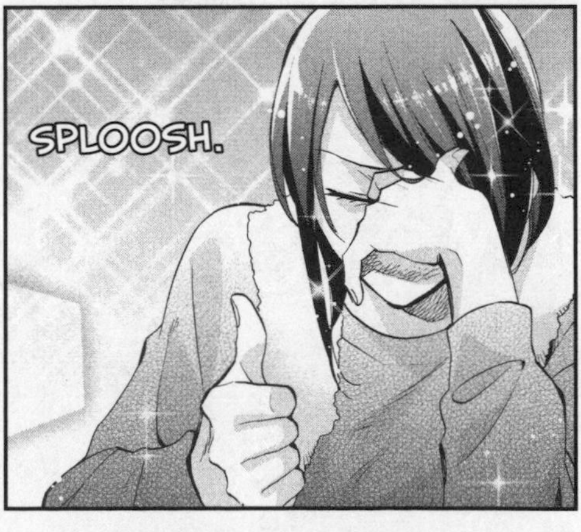
SPLOOSH.

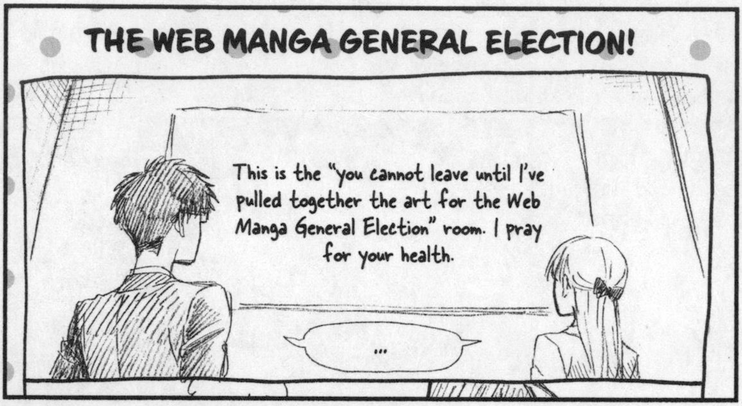
THE WEB MANGA GENERAL ELECTION!
This is the "you cannot leave until I've pulled together the art for the Web Manga General Election" room. I pray for your health.
...

◀ WEB MANGA GENERAL ELECTION, PAGE 96

The Web Manga General Election is a popularity contest for web comics in Japan run by the art hosting site Pixiv. *Wotakoi* won first place in 2017 by a wide margin. General elections, or "*sosenkyo*," have a long tradition in otaku circles—the idol group AKB48 holds *sosenkyo* to determine which member will headline major singles, with ballots included in CD copies of the previous single. In a fiendishly brilliant twist, you can vote as many times as you have ballots, which encourages fans to buy more than one copy of a single in order to support their favorites.

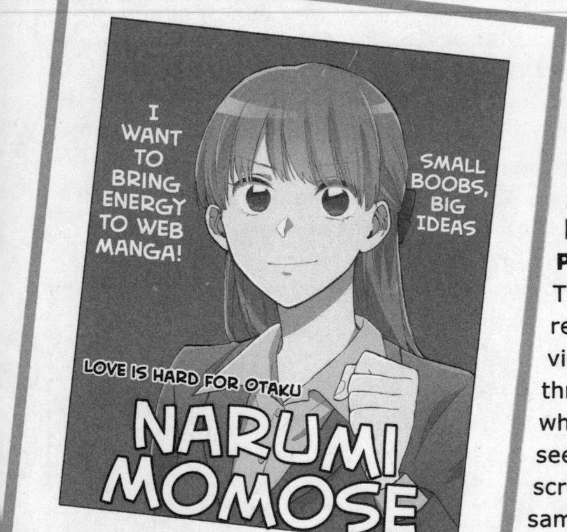
SMALL BOOBS, BIG IDEAS
I WANT TO BRING ENERGY TO WEB MANGA!
LOVE IS HARD FOR OTAKU
NARUMI MOMOSE
I DON'T THINK THIS IS WHAT THEY'RE LOOKING FOR.
WHO WROTE 'SMALL BOOBS'?
YOU DON'T THINK ??
Wotakoi
Wotakoi
?

◀ PAGE 98

This poster is a parody of the designs commonly seen in Japanese election campaign posters.

▶ PENGUINS, PAGE 101

This is a reference to a viral photo of three penguins who are all seeming to scream at the same chick. It became a meme when a twitter user put speech bubbles over it, inviting a wide variety of interpretations.

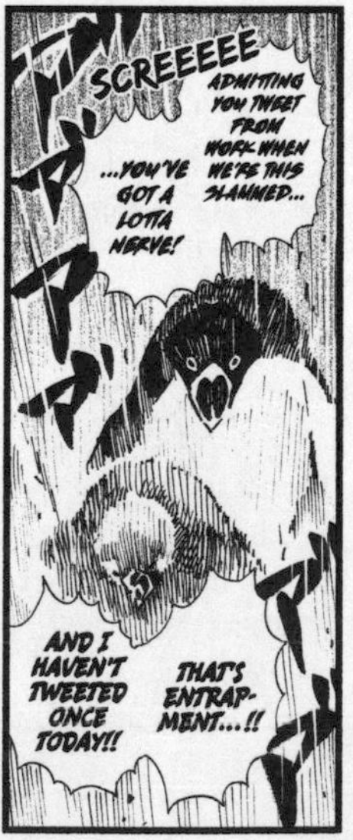
SCREEEEE
ADMITTING YOU TWEET FROM WORK WHEN WE'RE THIS SLAMMED...
...YOU'VE GOT A LOTTA NERVE!
THAT'S ENTRAP-MENT...!!
AND I HAVEN'T TWEETED ONCE TODAY!!

▶ **"THAT OVERACHIEVER GRIT," PAGE 108**

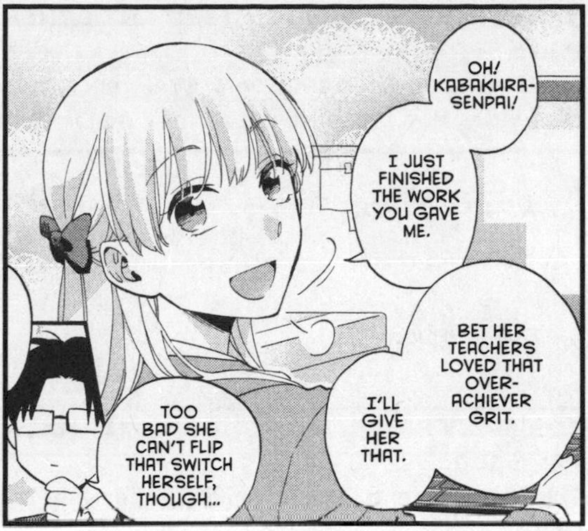
OH! KABAKURA-SENPAI!
I JUST FINISHED THE WORK YOU GAVE ME.
BET HER TEACHERS LOVED THAT OVER-ACHIEVER GRIT.
I'LL GIVE HER THAT.
TOO BAD SHE CAN'T FLIP THAT SWITCH HERSELF, THOUGH...

The term translated as "overachiever grit" here is "YDK," an acronym that derives from the phrase "*yareba dekiru ko*," roughly, "a kid who can do it, if they try." YDK was the theme of an ad campaign by Meiko Gijuku, a chain of after-school tutoring schools, which invited Twitter users to tweet their ideas for what YDK might mean. The most popular tweets were not exactly what Meiko Gijuku had in mind.

WHAT A TERRIFYING WOMAN...!, PAGE 108

This is a reference to a moment in Suzue Miuchi's classic 1970's shojo manga *Glass Mask*, when a famous actress realizes the acting potential of the protagonist.

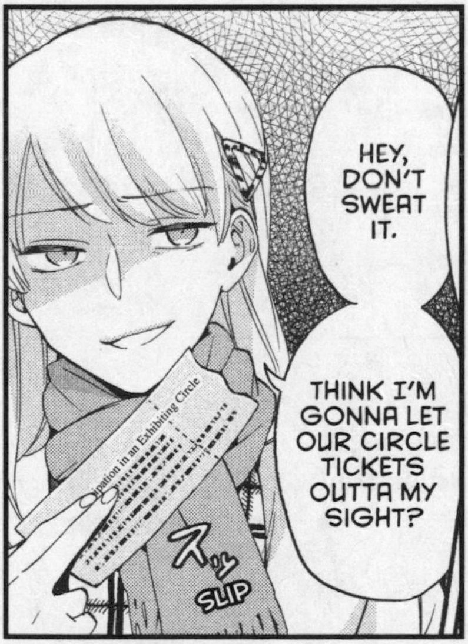
HEY, DON'T SWEAT IT.
THINK I'M GONNA LET OUR CIRCLE TICKETS OUTTA MY SIGHT?
SLIP

◀ **CIRCLE TICKET, PAGE 111**

A special pass given specially to dojinshi groups and individuals who are selling their work at events like Comic Market. It gives them early access to the venue to set up. General admission to Comic Market is free, but being in the venue early gives sellers the ability to check out the work of their fellow fans before the mob arrives.

ARE YOU READY FOR THIS?, PAGE 112

In Hirohiko Araki's *JoJo's Bizarre Adventure*, "Are you ready for this? I know I am," is part of a famous line spoken by the mobster Bruno Bucciarati.

WEST HALL, PAGE 115

Tokyo Big Sight, the venue that hosts Comic Market, is divided into the East and West Halls. The vast East Halls are where the fan-created dojinshi are sold, with the smaller (but still big) West Halls housing official industry booths.

▼ I HONESTLY COULDN'T FIND ANY OTHER WORDS TO EXPRESS IT, PAGE 115

Another *Jojo's Bizarre Adventure* reference, this is Johnny Joestar's line in Part 7, "Steel Ball Run," after the death of a major character.

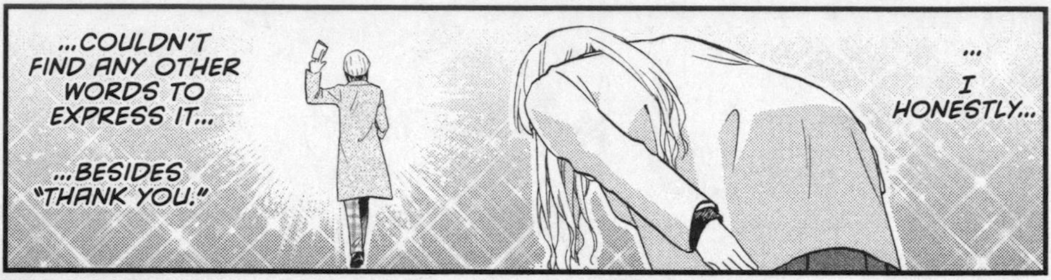

... I HONESTLY...
...COULDN'T FIND ANY OTHER WORDS TO EXPRESS IT...
...BESIDES "THANK YOU."

FOR MANY BRAVE OTAKU, THE AFTERMATH OF DREAMS, PAGE 120

This line is from a famous haiku by the 17th-century poet Matsuo Bashō. This is Donald Keene's translation of the original:

> The summer grasses—
> For many brave warriors
> The aftermath of dreams.

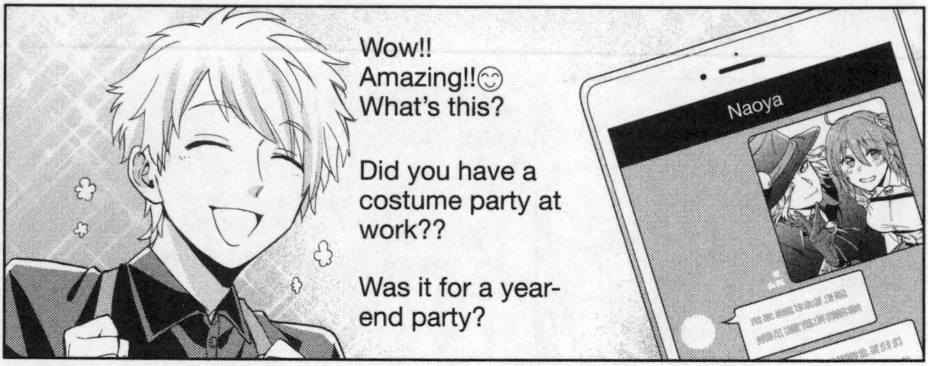

Naoya
Wow!! Amazing!!☺ What's this?
Did you have a costume party at work??
Was it for a year-end party?

▲ YEAR-END PARTY, PAGE 122

The term translated here as "year-end party" is "*bonenkai,*" which literally means "year-forgetting party." These office or school parties are typically held late in December, and tend to be raucous, beer-soaked, blowing-off-steam-type events.

▶ NEW YEAR'S SHRINE VISIT, PAGE 126

The new year is the most important holiday in Japan, and one of its traditions is "*hatsumode,*" the January 1st visit to a Shinto shrine. One of the more universal features is the drawing of your fortune on the year, the best of which is "*daikichi,*" or "great luck."

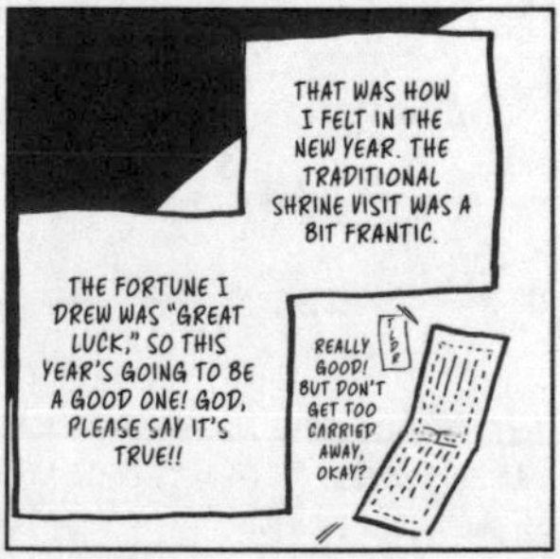

THAT WAS HOW I FELT IN THE NEW YEAR. THE TRADITIONAL SHRINE VISIT WAS A BIT FRANTIC.
REALLY GOOD! BUT DON'T GET TOO CARRIED AWAY, OKAY?
THE FORTUNE I DREW WAS "GREAT LUCK," SO THIS YEAR'S GOING TO BE A GOOD ONE! GOD, PLEASE SAY IT'S TRUE!!

WOTAKOI:
LOVE IS HARD FOR OTAKU

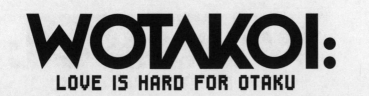

WOTAKOI:
LOVE IS HARD FOR OTAKU

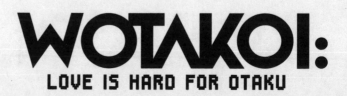

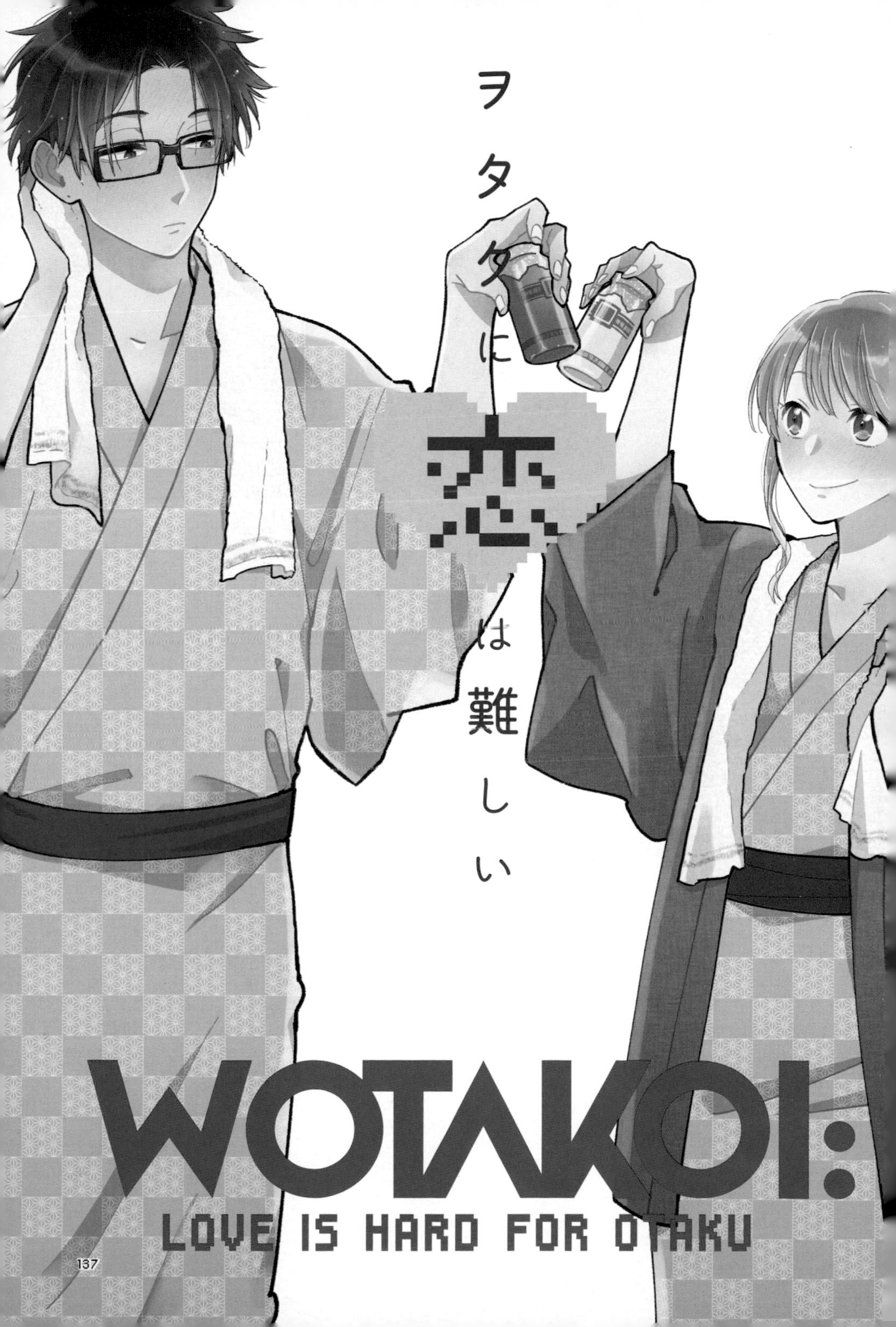
ヲタクに恋は難しい
WOTAKOI:
LOVE IS HARD FOR OTAKU

WOTAKOI:

LOVE IS HARD FOR OTAKU

FUJITA

Episode....39
trip...1

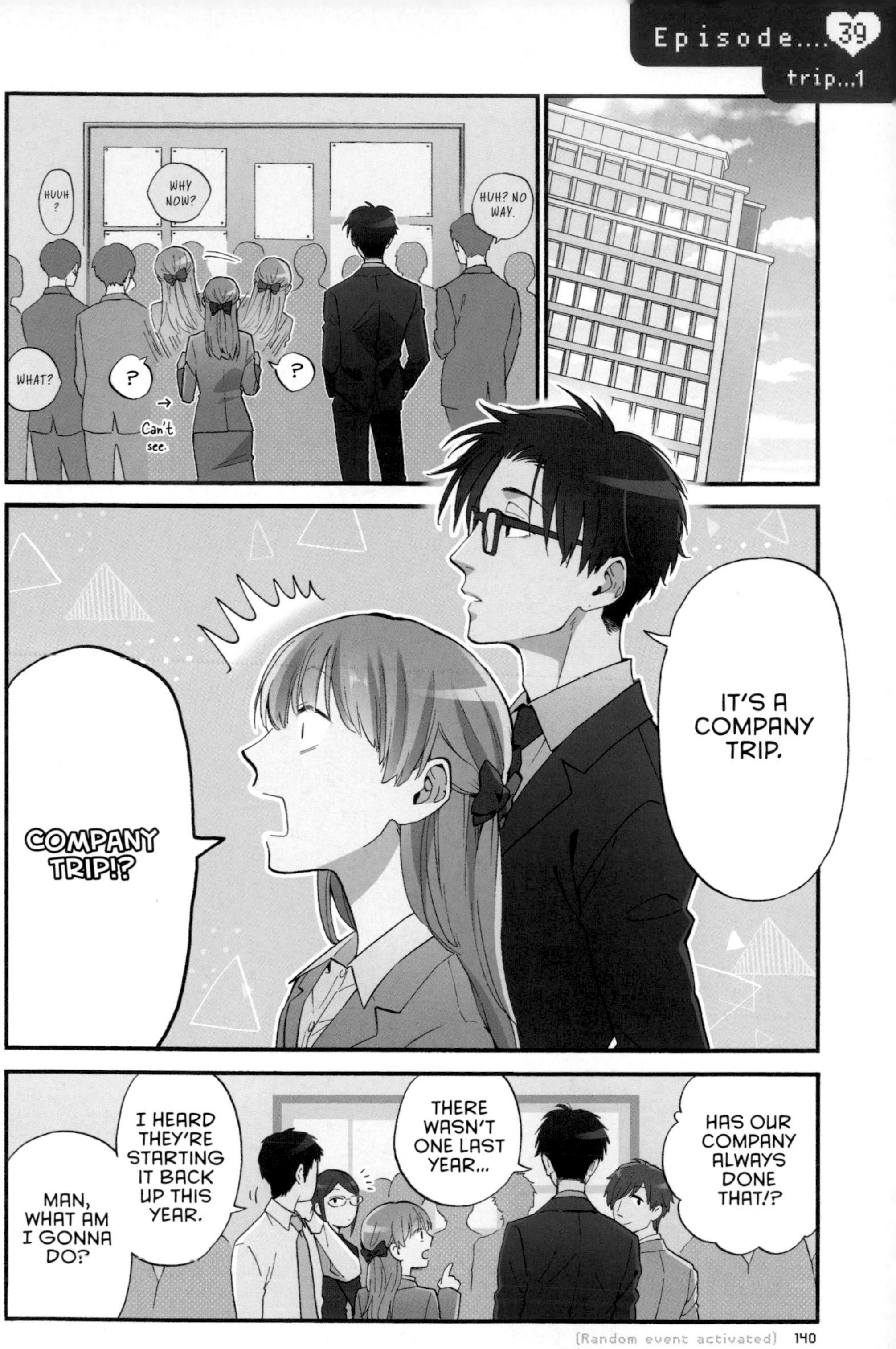

HUH? NO WAY.
WHY NOW?
HUUH?
?
?
WHAT?
→ Can't see.
IT'S A COMPANY TRIP.
COMPANY TRIP!?
HAS OUR COMPANY ALWAYS DONE THAT!?
THERE WASN'T ONE LAST YEAR...
I HEARD THEY'RE STARTING IT BACK UP THIS YEAR.
MAN, WHAT AM I GONNA DO?

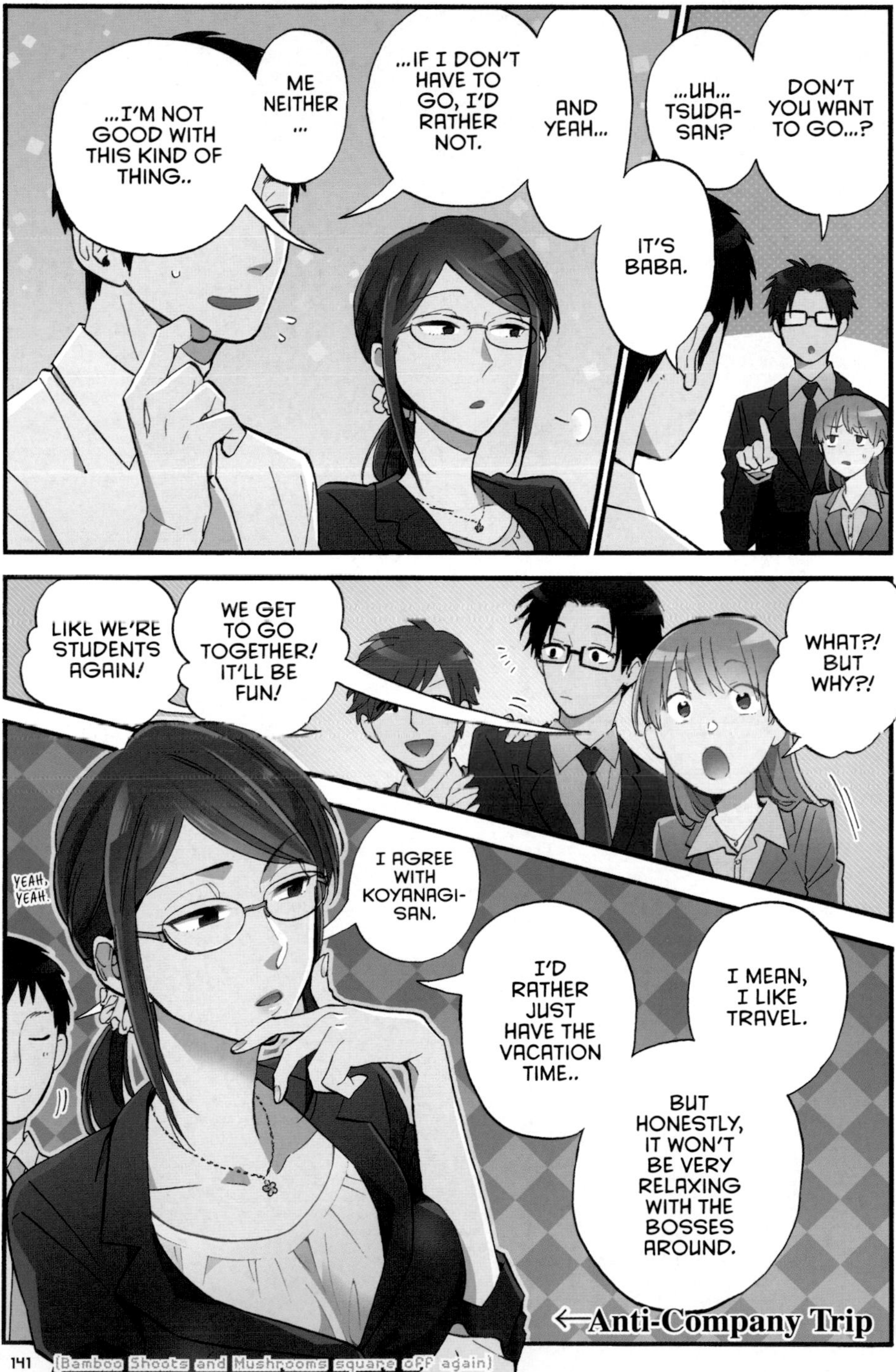
DON'T YOU WANT TO GO...?
...UH... TSUDA-SAN?
IT'S BABA.
AND YEAH...
...IF I DON'T HAVE TO GO, I'D RATHER NOT.
ME NEITHER ...
...I'M NOT GOOD WITH THIS KIND OF THING..
WHAT?! BUT WHY?!
WE GET TO GO TOGETHER! IT'LL BE FUN!
LIKE WE'RE STUDENTS AGAIN!
I MEAN, I LIKE TRAVEL.
BUT HONESTLY, IT WON'T BE VERY RELAXING WITH THE BOSSES AROUND.
I'D RATHER JUST HAVE THE VACATION TIME..
I AGREE WITH KOYANAGI-SAN.
YEAH, YEAH.
←Anti-Company Trip

 (Bamboo Shoots and Mushrooms square off again)

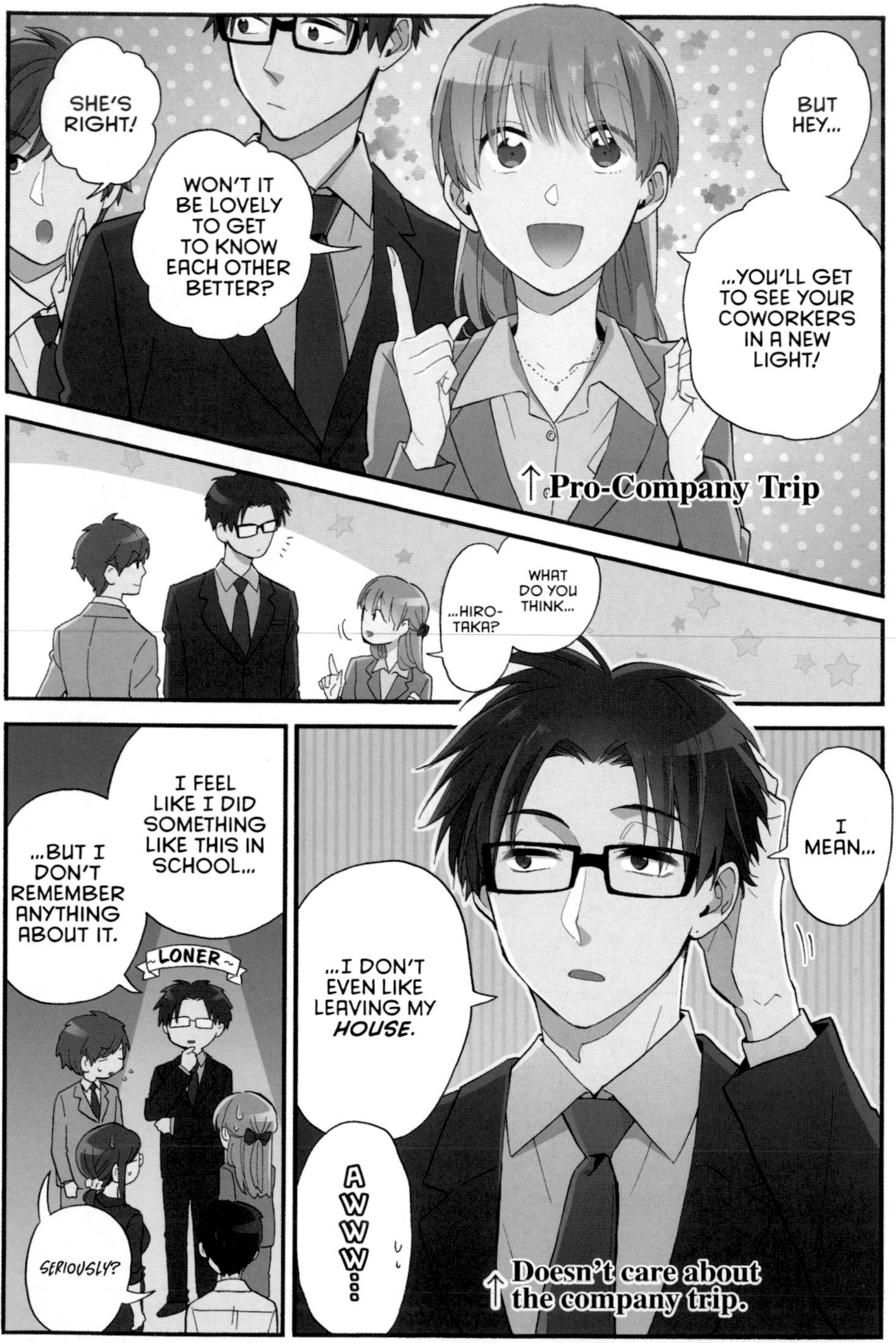
BUT HEY...
...YOU'LL GET TO SEE YOUR COWORKERS IN A NEW LIGHT!
WON'T IT BE LOVELY TO GET TO KNOW EACH OTHER BETTER?
SHE'S RIGHT!
↑ Pro-Company Trip
WHAT DO YOU THINK...
...HIRO-TAKA?
I MEAN...
...I DON'T EVEN LIKE LEAVING MY *HOUSE*.
AWWW...
↑ Doesn't care about the company trip.
I FEEL LIKE I DID SOMETHING LIKE THIS IN SCHOOL...
...BUT I DON'T REMEMBER ANYTHING ABOUT IT.
LONER
SERIOUSLY?

(The Final Faction, Stumps, remains)

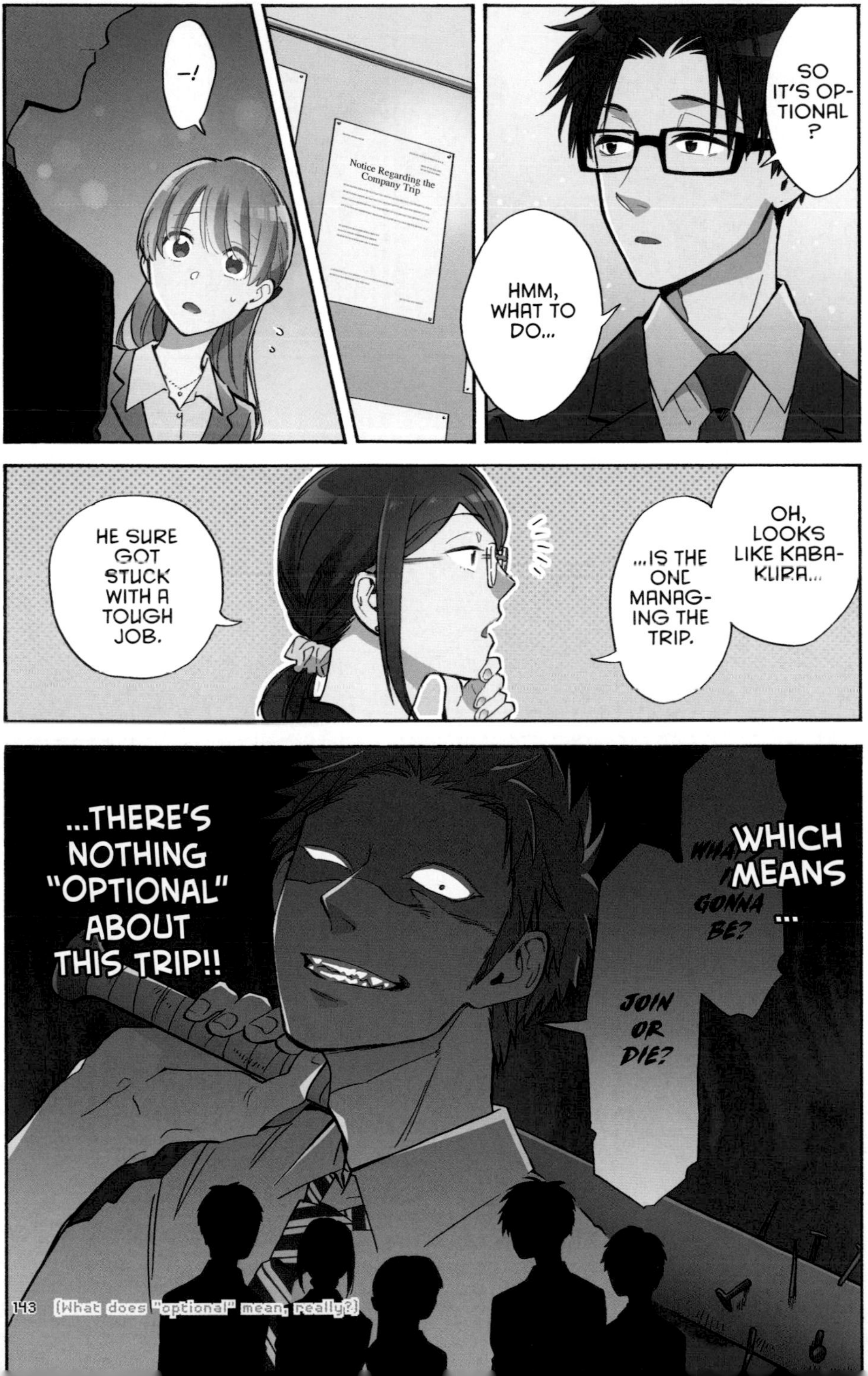
SO IT'S OPTIONAL?
HMM, WHAT TO DO...
Notice Regarding the Company Trip
—!
OH, LOOKS LIKE KABAKURA...
...IS THE ONE MANAGING THE TRIP.
HE SURE GOT STUCK WITH A TOUGH JOB.
WHICH MEANS...
...THERE'S NOTHING "OPTIONAL" ABOUT THIS TRIP!!
JOIN OR DIE?

(What does "optional" mean, really?)

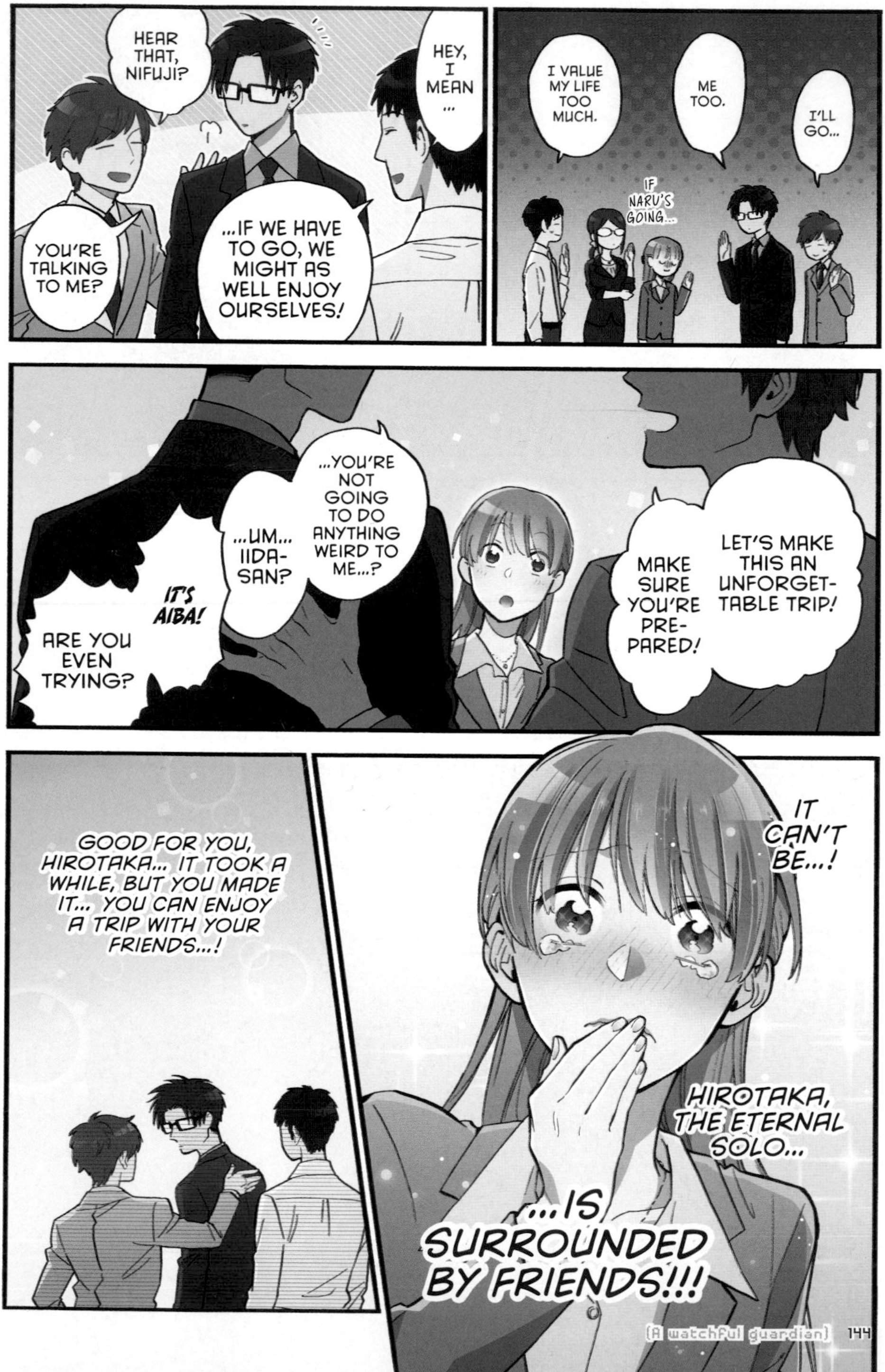
I'LL GO...
ME TOO.
I VALUE MY LIFE TOO MUCH.
IF NARU'S GOING...
HEY, I MEAN ...
...IF WE HAVE TO GO, WE MIGHT AS WELL ENJOY OURSELVES!
HEAR THAT, NIFUJI?
YOU'RE TALKING TO ME?
LET'S MAKE THIS AN UNFORGET-TABLE TRIP!
MAKE SURE YOU'RE PRE-PARED!
...YOU'RE NOT GOING TO DO ANYTHING WEIRD TO ME...?
...UM... IIDA-SAN?
IT'S AIBA!
ARE YOU EVEN TRYING?
IT CAN'T BE...!
HIROTAKA, THE ETERNAL SOLO...
...IS SURROUNDED BY FRIENDS!!!
GOOD FOR YOU, HIROTAKA... IT TOOK A WHILE, BUT YOU MADE IT... YOU CAN ENJOY A TRIP WITH YOUR FRIENDS...!

[A watchful guardian]

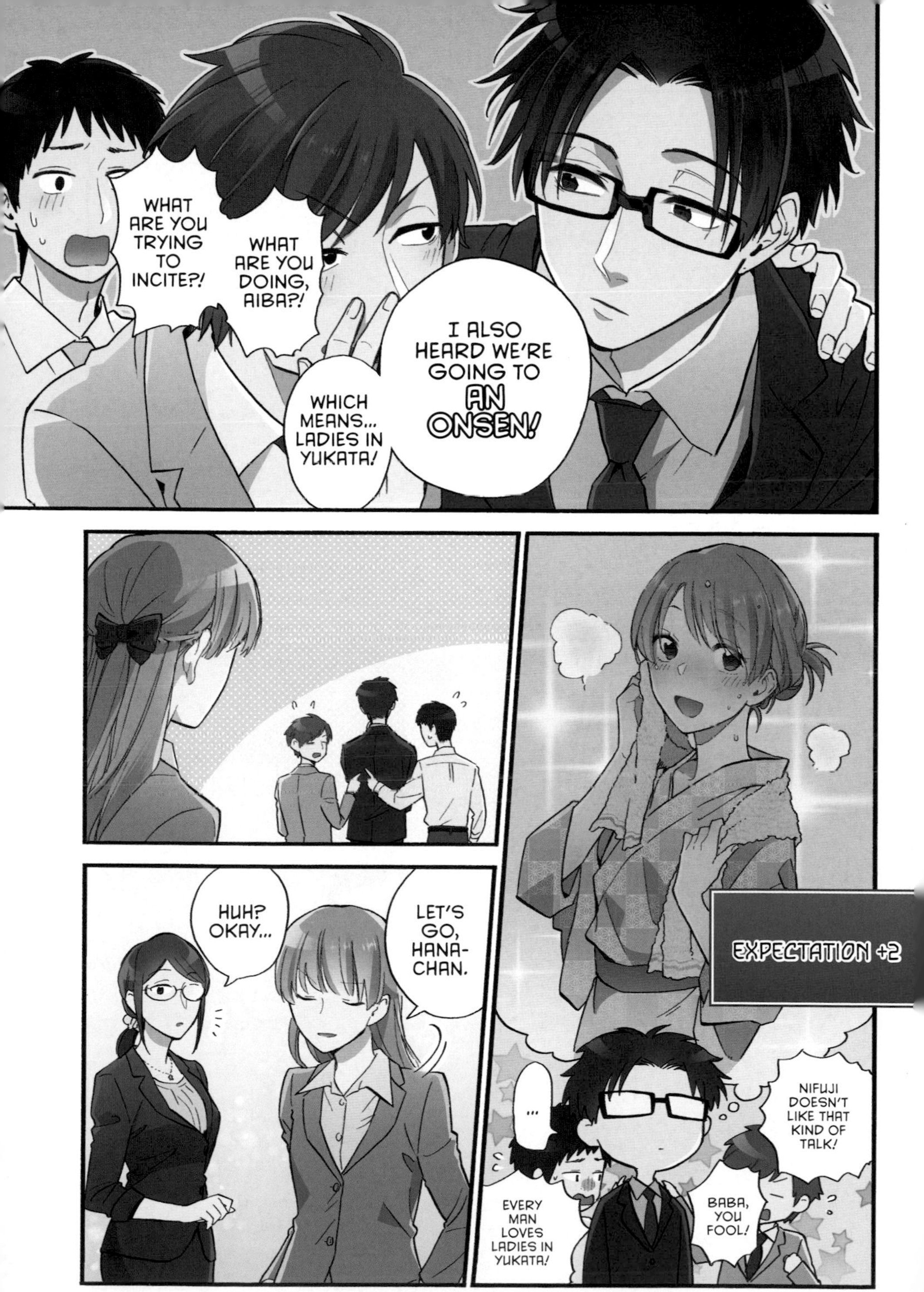

I ALSO HEARD WE'RE GOING TO AN ONSEN!
WHICH MEANS... LADIES IN YUKATA!
WHAT ARE YOU DOING, AIBA?!
WHAT ARE YOU TRYING TO INCITE?!
EXPECTATION +2
NIFUJI DOESN'T LIKE THAT KIND OF TALK!
...
BABA, YOU FOOL!
EVERY MAN LOVES LADIES IN YUKATA!
LET'S GO, HANA-CHAN.
HUH? OKAY...

 (Yukata after bath + nape of neck = raised expectations)

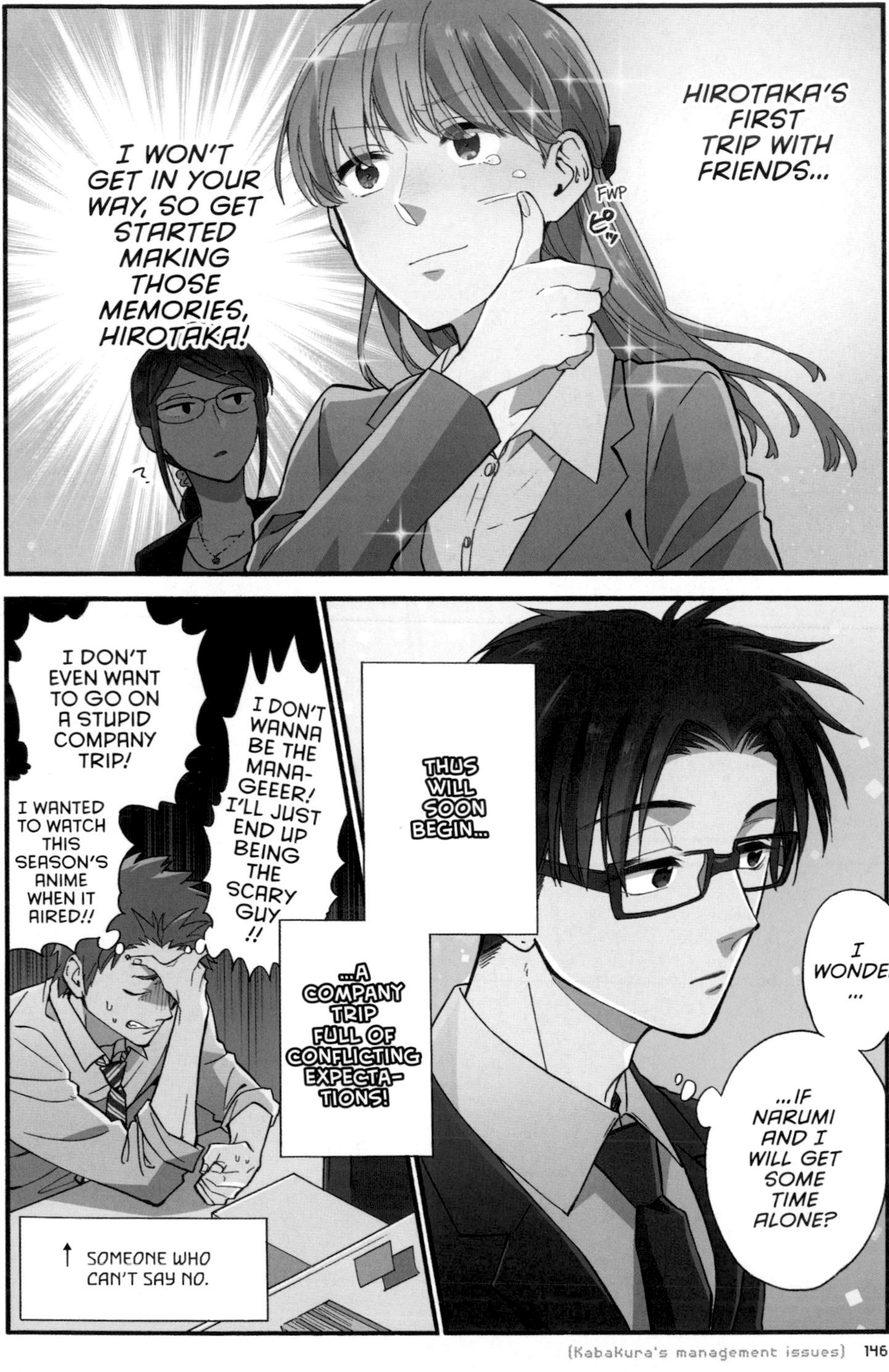
HIROTAKA'S FIRST TRIP WITH FRIENDS...
FWP
ピッ
I WON'T GET IN YOUR WAY, SO GET STARTED MAKING THOSE MEMORIES, HIROTAKA!
?
I WONDER...
...IF NARUMI AND I WILL GET SOME TIME ALONE?
THUS WILL SOON BEGIN...
...A COMPANY TRIP FULL OF CONFLICTING EXPECTATIONS!
I DON'T WANNA BE THE MANA-GEEER! I'LL JUST END UP BEING THE SCARY GUY!!
I DON'T EVEN WANT TO GO ON A STUPID COMPANY TRIP!
I WANTED TO WATCH THIS SEASON'S ANIME WHEN IT AIRED!!
↑ SOMEONE WHO CAN'T SAY NO.

(Kabakura's management issues)

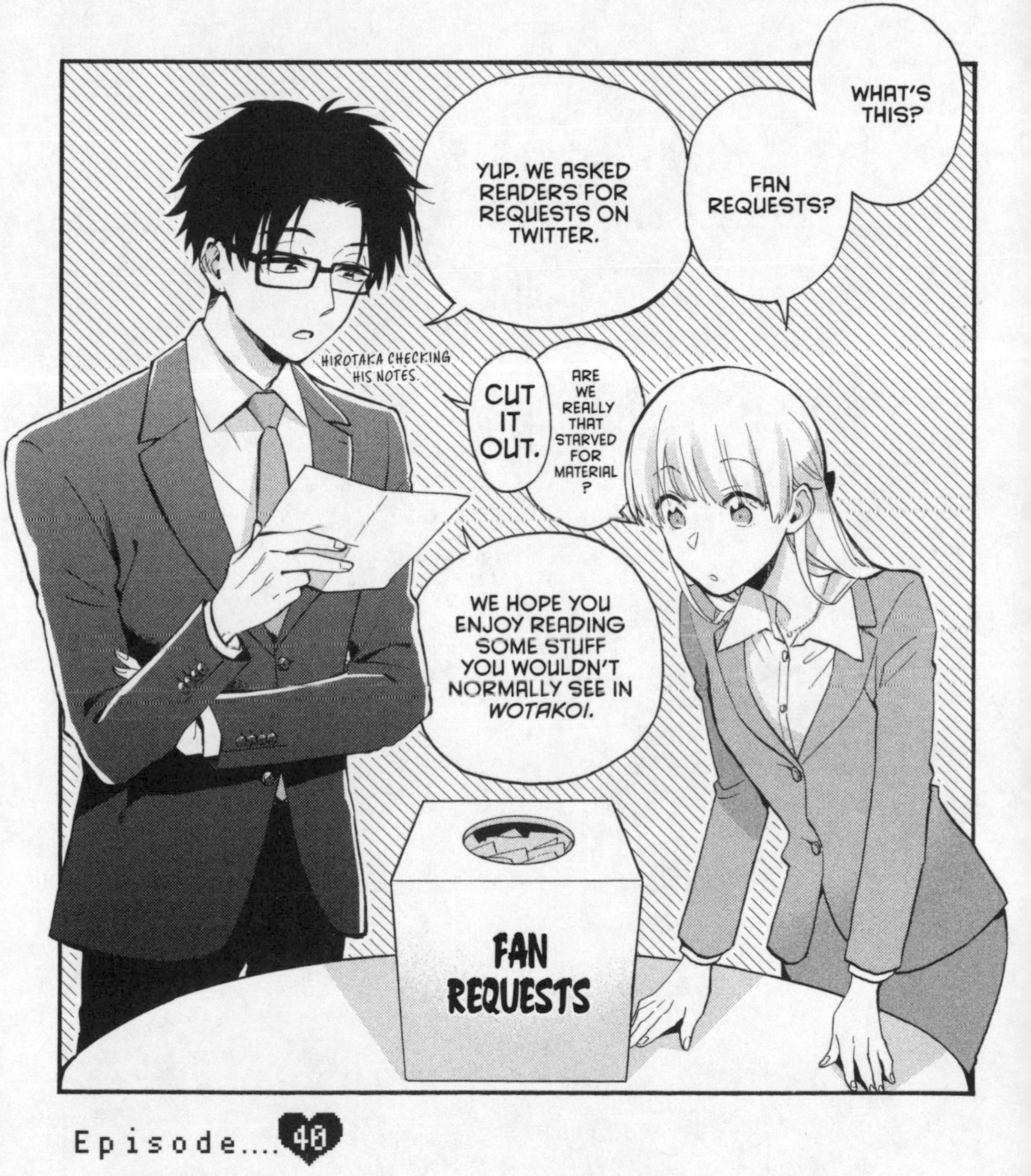
WHAT'S THIS?
FAN REQUESTS?
YUP. WE ASKED READERS FOR REQUESTS ON TWITTER.
ARE WE REALLY THAT STARVED FOR MATERIAL?
CUT IT OUT.
HIROTAKA CHECKING HIS NOTES.
WE HOPE YOU ENJOY READING SOME STUFF YOU WOULDN'T NORMALLY SEE IN *WOTAKOI*.
FAN REQUESTS

Episode....40

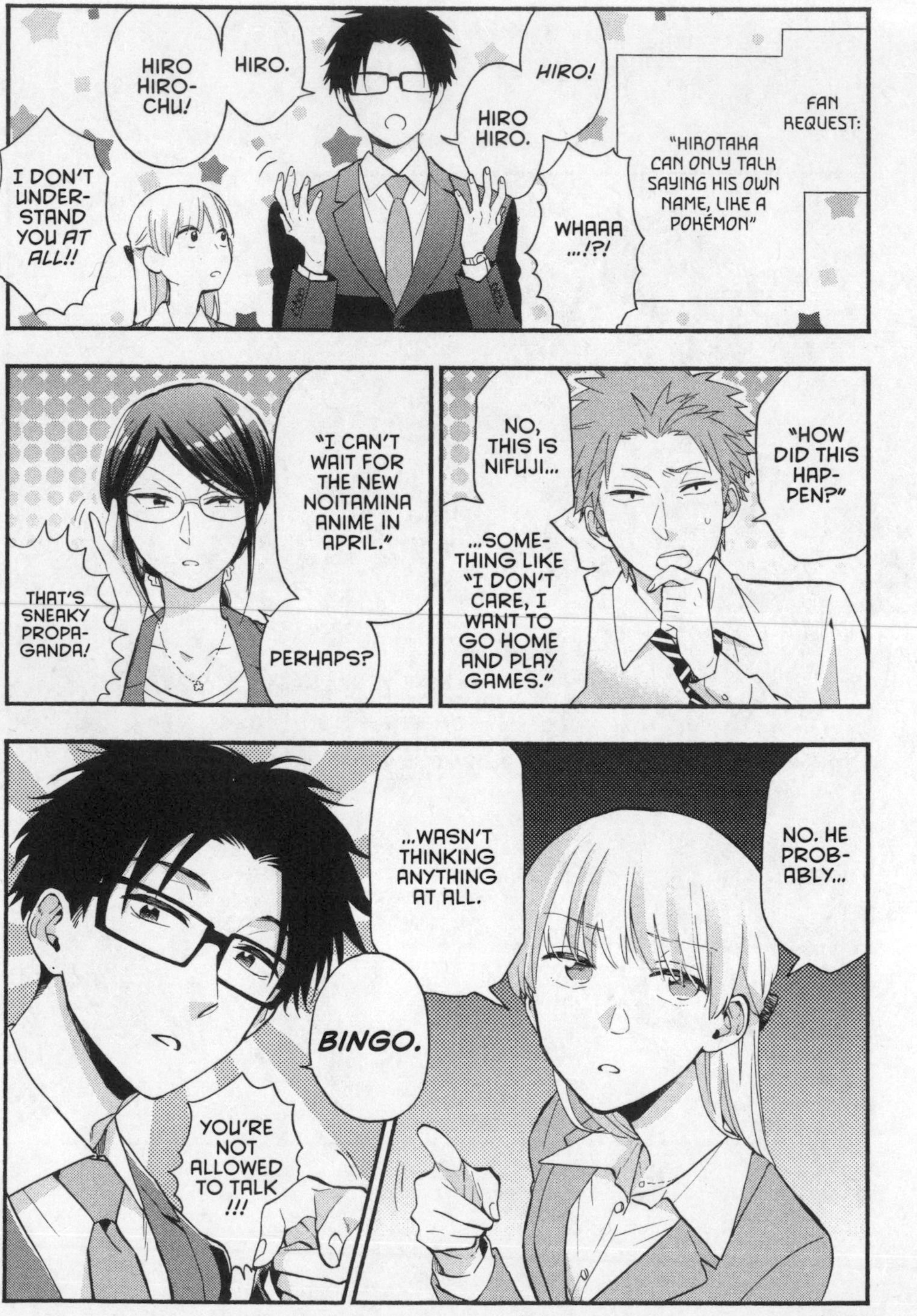
FAN REQUEST:
"HIROTAKA CAN ONLY TALK SAYING HIS OWN NAME, LIKE A POKÉMON"
HIRO!
HIRO HIRO.
WHAAA ...!?!
HIRO.
HIRO HIRO-CHU!
I DON'T UNDER-STAND YOU AT ALL!!
"HOW DID THIS HAP-PEN?"
NO, THIS IS NIFUJI...
...SOME-THING LIKE "I DON'T CARE, I WANT TO GO HOME AND PLAY GAMES."
"I CAN'T WAIT FOR THE NEW NOITAMINA ANIME IN APRIL."
PERHAPS?
THAT'S SNEAKY PROPA-GANDA!
NO. HE PROB-ABLY...
...WASN'T THINKING ANYTHING AT ALL.
BINGO.
YOU'RE NOT ALLOWED TO TALK !!!

(Sayonara, bye-bye, language skills)

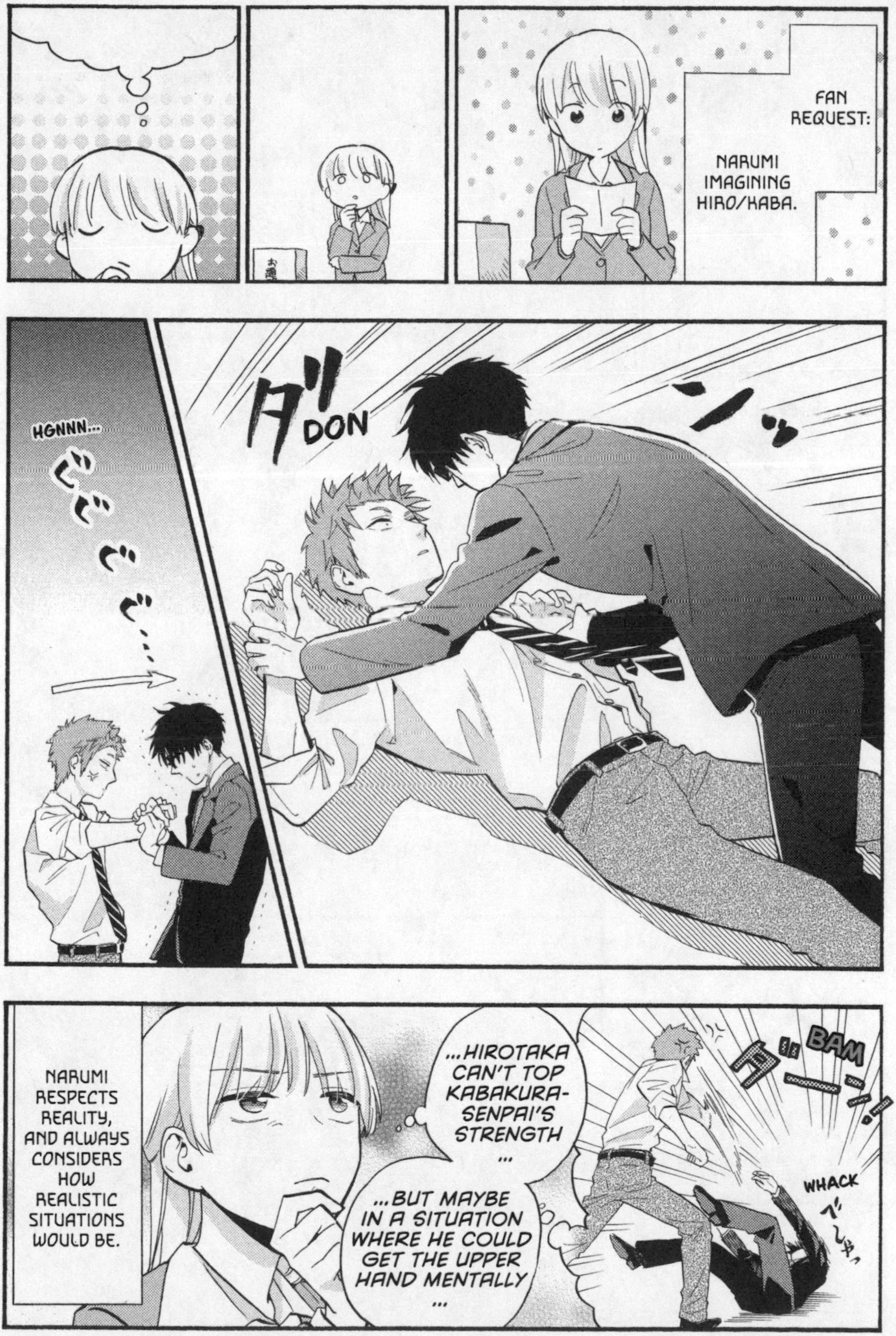
FAN REQUEST:
NARUMI IMAGINING HIRO/KABA.
DON
HGNNN...
BAM
WHACK
...HIROTAKA CAN'T TOP KABAKURA-SENPAI'S STRENGTH ...
...BUT MAYBE IN A SITUATION WHERE HE COULD GET THE UPPER HAND MENTALLY ...
NARUMI RESPECTS REALITY, AND ALWAYS CONSIDERS HOW REALISTIC SITUATIONS WOULD BE.

 (Someone who respects the original)

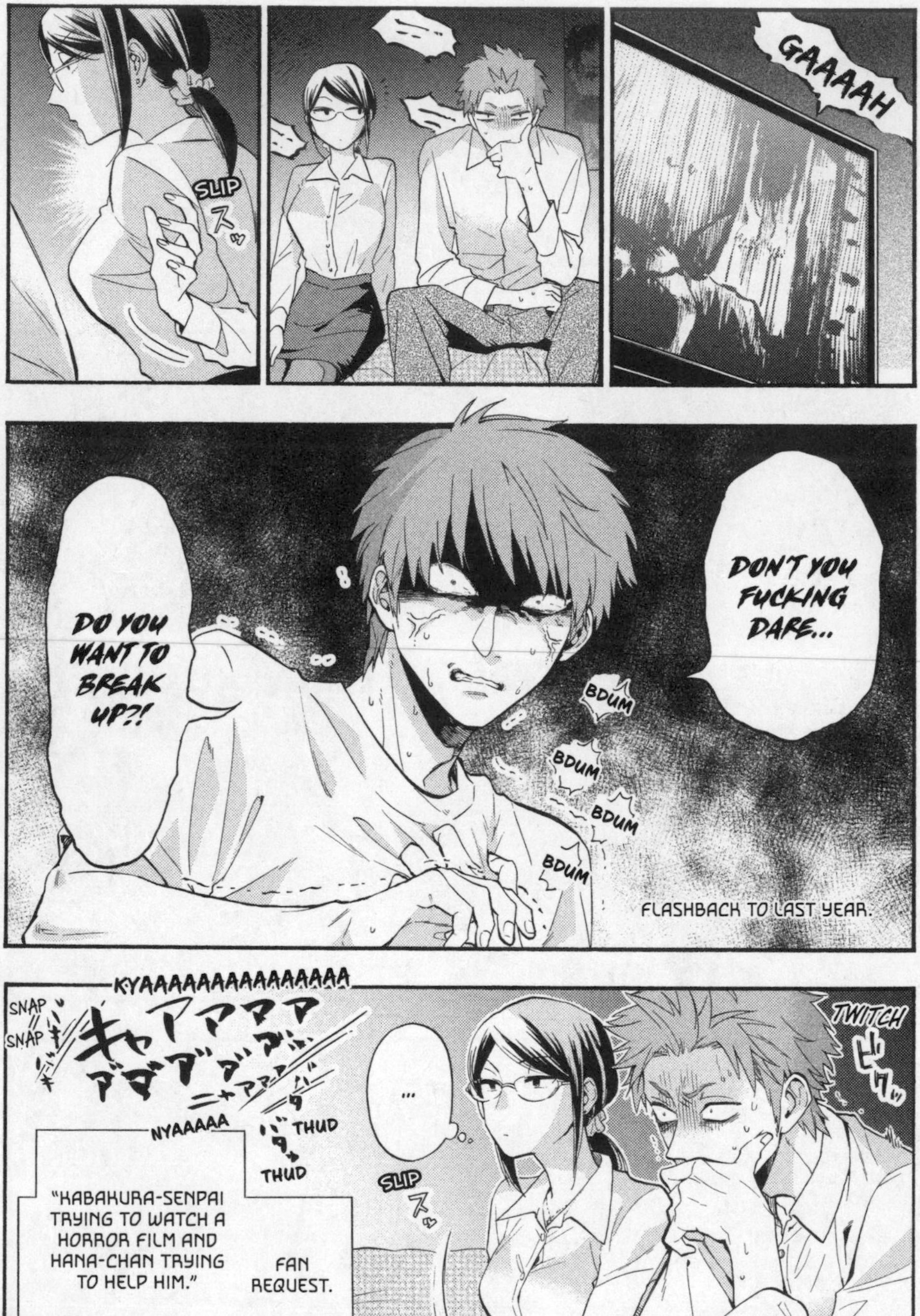
GAAAAH
SLIP
DON'T YOU FUCKING DARE...
DO YOU WANT TO BREAK UP?!
BDUM
BDUM
BDUM
BDUM
FLASHBACK TO LAST YEAR.
TWITCH
...
SLIP
KYAAAAAAAAAAAAAAA
SNAP
SNAP
NYAAAAA
THUD
THUD
"KABAKURA-SENPAI TRYING TO WATCH A HORROR FILM AND HANA-CHAN TRYING TO HELP HIM."
FAN REQUEST.

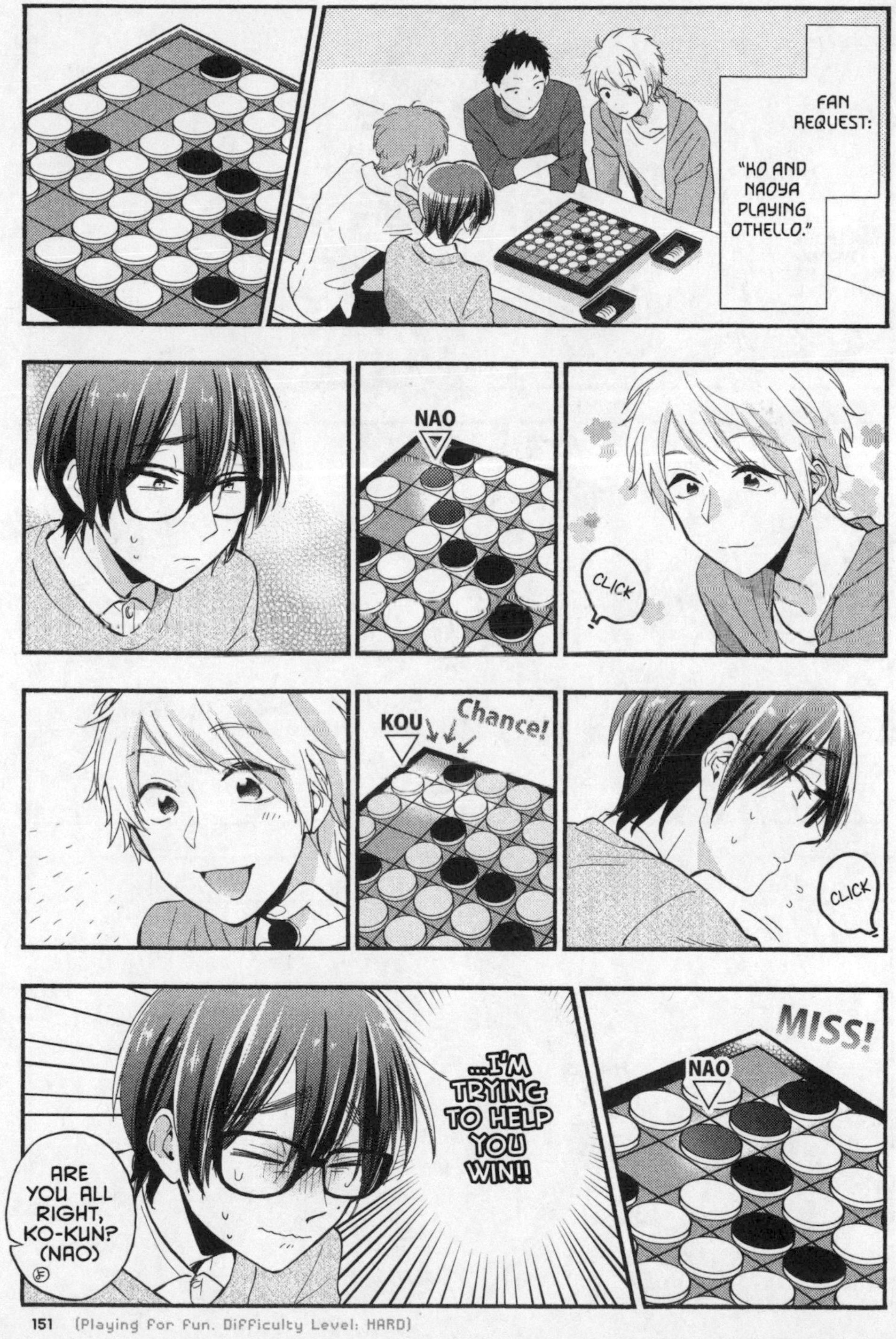
FAN REQUEST:
"KO AND NAOYA PLAYING OTHELLO."
CLICK
NAO
CLICK
KOU
Chance!
MISS!
NAO
...I'M TRYING TO HELP YOU WIN!!
ARE YOU ALL RIGHT, KO-KUN? (NAO)

(Playing for Fun. Difficulty Level: HARD)

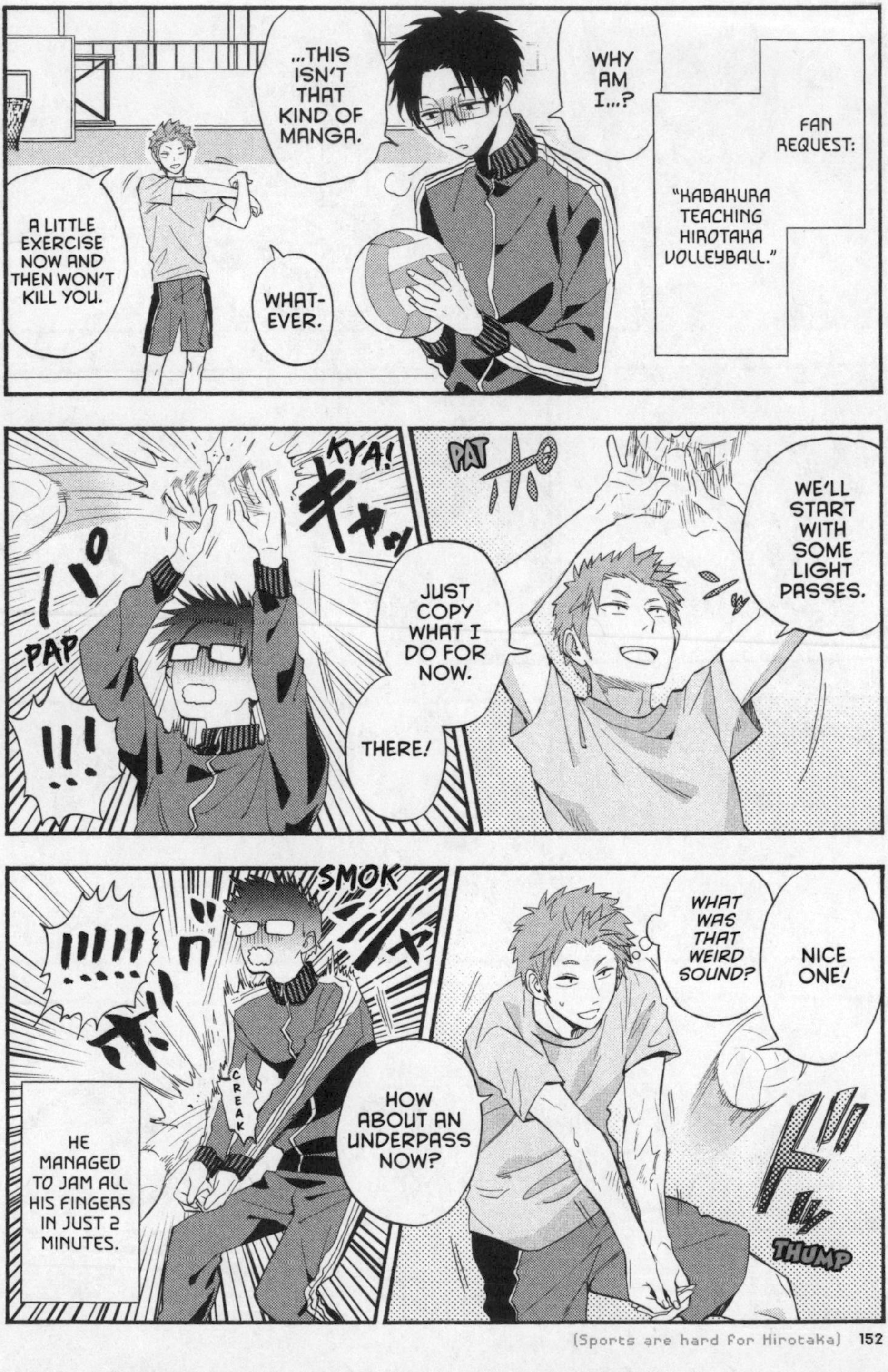
FAN REQUEST:
"KABAKURA TEACHING HIROTAKA VOLLEYBALL."
WHY AM I...?
...THIS ISN'T THAT KIND OF MANGA.
WHAT-EVER.
A LITTLE EXERCISE NOW AND THEN WON'T KILL YOU.
PAT
WE'LL START WITH SOME LIGHT PASSES.
JUST COPY WHAT I DO FOR NOW.
THERE!
KYA!
PAP
!!!
NICE ONE!
WHAT WAS THAT WEIRD SOUND?
HOW ABOUT AN UNDERPASS NOW?
THUMP
SMOK
CREAK
HE MANAGED TO JAM ALL HIS FINGERS IN JUST 2 MINUTES.
!!!!!!

(Sports are hard for Hirotaka)

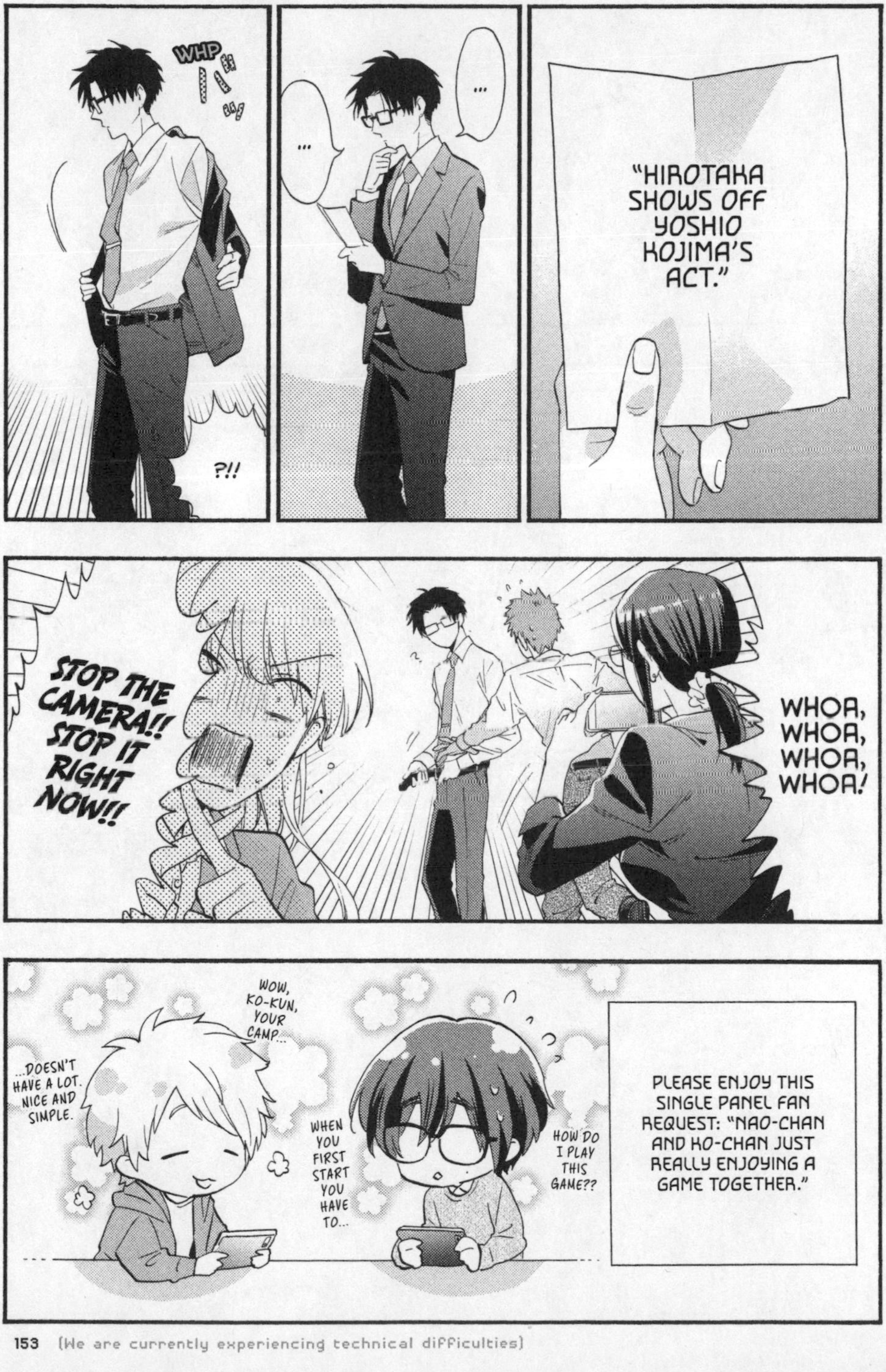
"HIROTAKA SHOWS OFF YOSHIO KOJIMA'S ACT."
...
...
WHP
?!!
WHOA, WHOA, WHOA, WHOA!
STOP THE CAMERA!! STOP IT RIGHT NOW!!
PLEASE ENJOY THIS SINGLE PANEL FAN REQUEST: "NAO-CHAN AND KO-CHAN JUST REALLY ENJOYING A GAME TOGETHER."
HOW DO I PLAY THIS GAME??
WOW, KO-KUN, YOUR CAMP...
WHEN YOU FIRST START YOU HAVE TO...
...DOESN'T HAVE A LOT. NICE AND SIMPLE.

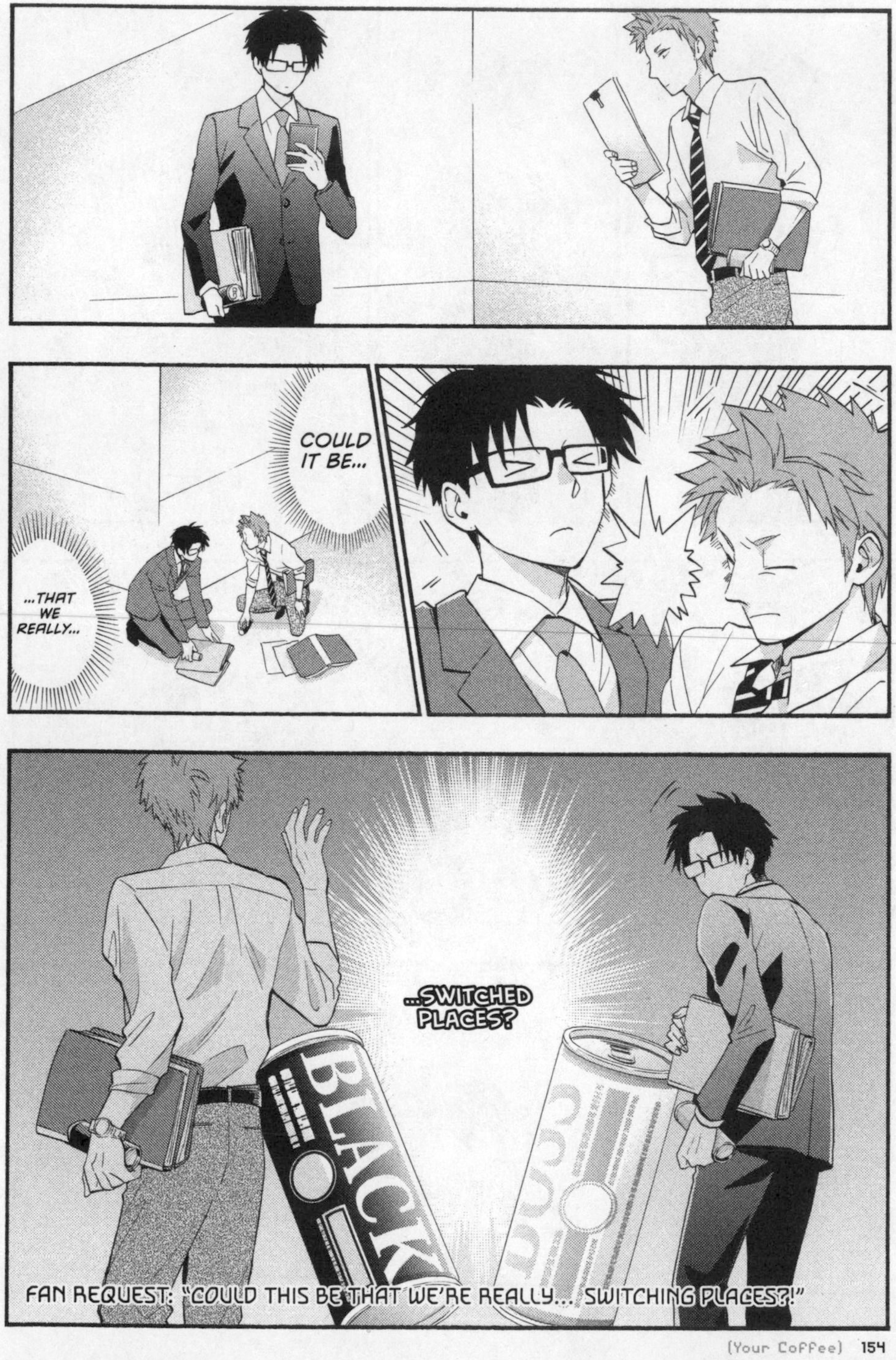
COULD IT BE...
...THAT WE REALLY...
...SWITCHED PLACES?
BLACK
FAN REQUEST: "COULD THIS BE THAT WE'RE REALLY... SWITCHING PLACES?!"

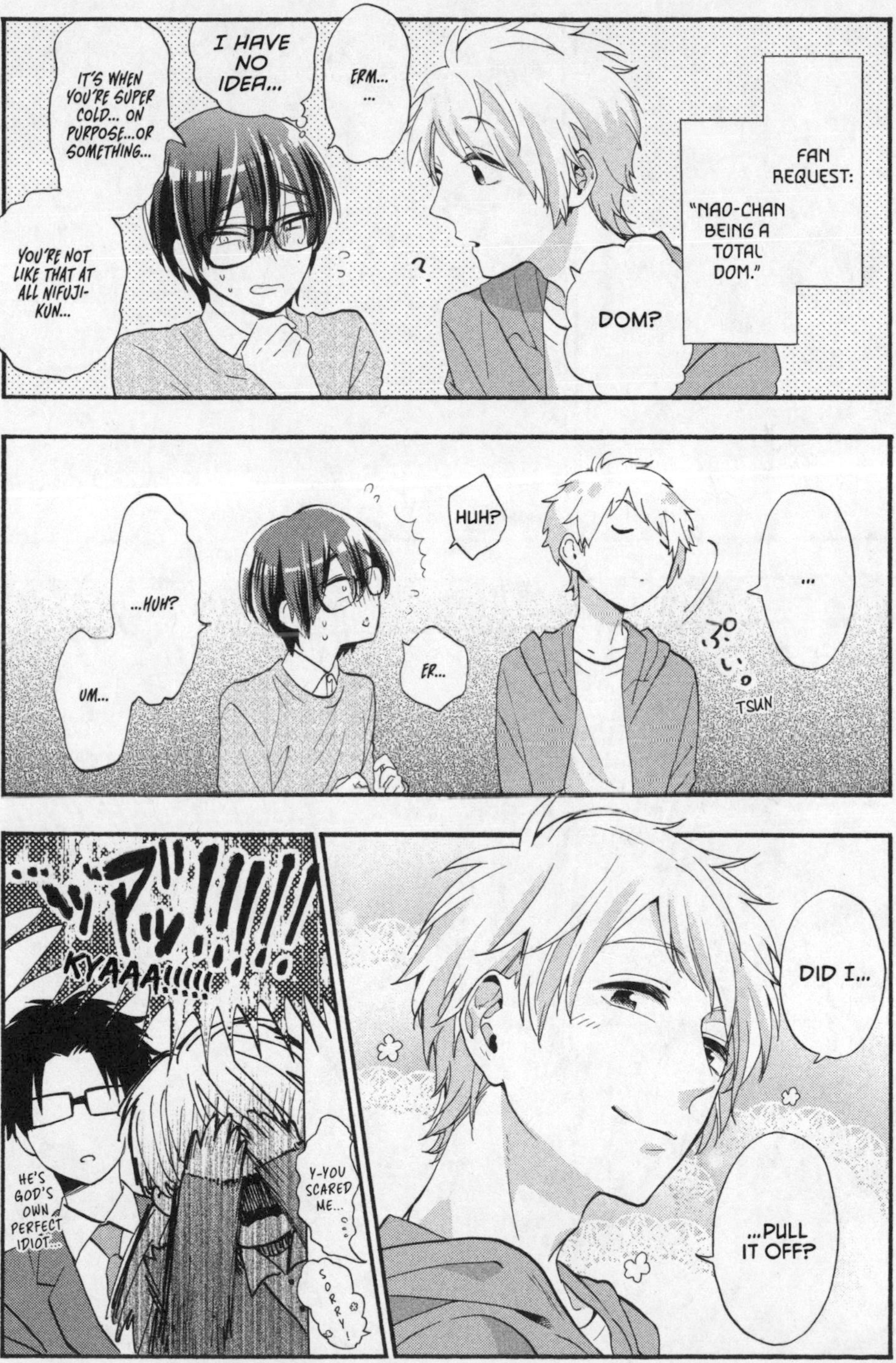
FAN REQUEST:
"NAO-CHAN BEING A TOTAL DOM."
DOM?
?
ERM... ...
I HAVE NO IDEA...
IT'S WHEN YOU'RE SUPER COLD... ON PURPOSE...OR SOMETHING...
YOU'RE NOT LIKE THAT AT ALL NIFUJI-KUN...
...
TSUN
HUH?
ER...
...HUH?
UM...
DID I...
...PULL IT OFF?
KYAAA!!!!!!
Y-YOU SCARED ME...
SORRY!
HE'S GOD'S OWN PERFECT IDIOT...

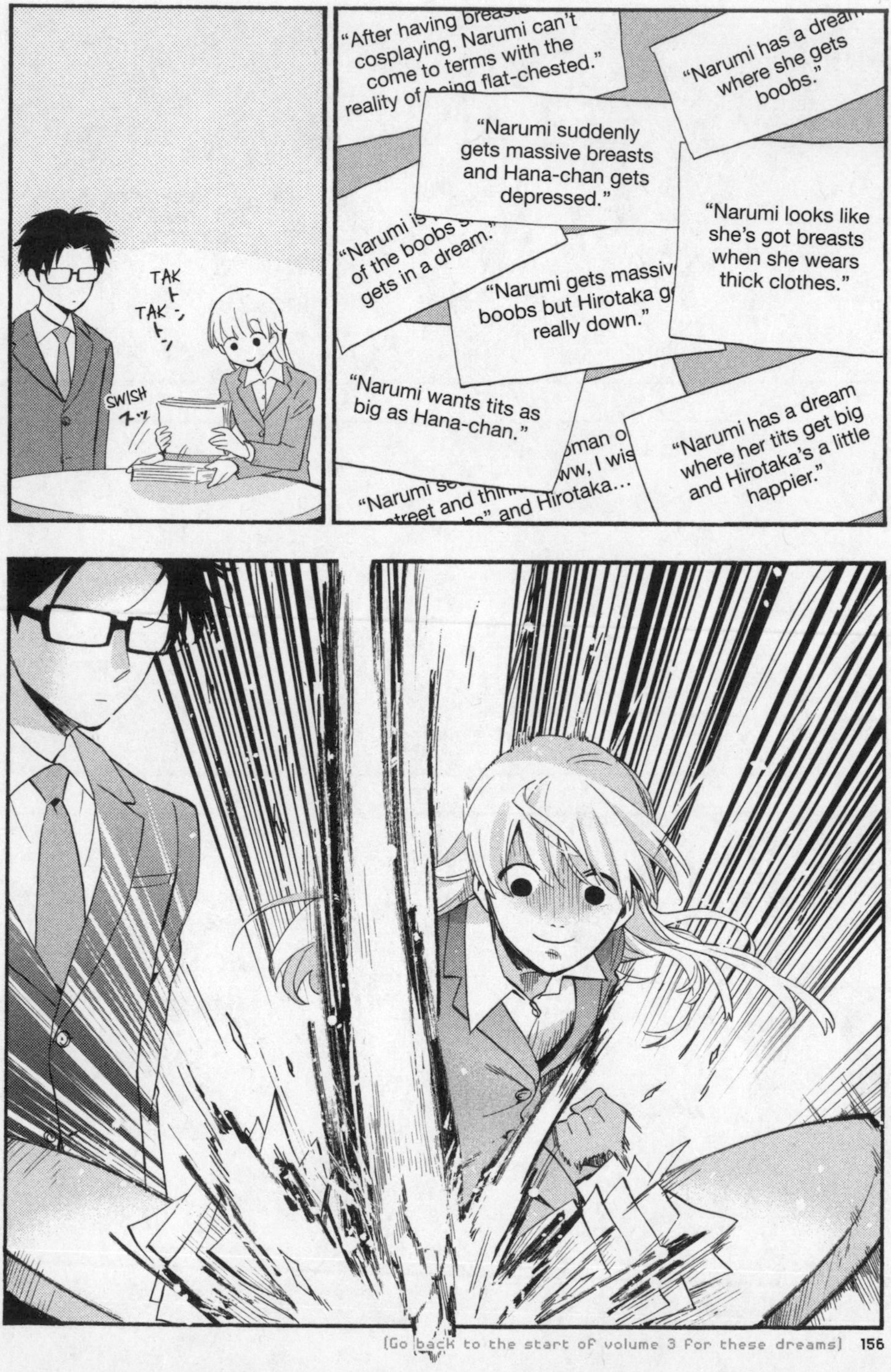
"Narumi has a dream where she gets boobs."
"After having breas cosplaying, Narumi can't come to terms with the reality of being flat-chested."
"Narumi suddenly gets massive breasts and Hana-chan gets depressed."
"Narumi looks like she's got breasts when she wears thick clothes."
"Narumi gets massive boobs but Hirotaka g really down."
"Narumi is of the boobs s gets in a dream."
"Narumi has a dream where her tits get big and Hirotaka's a little happier."
"Narumi wants tits as big as Hana-chan."
oman o ww, I wis
"Narumi se street and thin " and Hirotaka…
TAK
トン
TAK
トン
SWISH
スッ

(Go back to the start of volume 3 for these dreams)

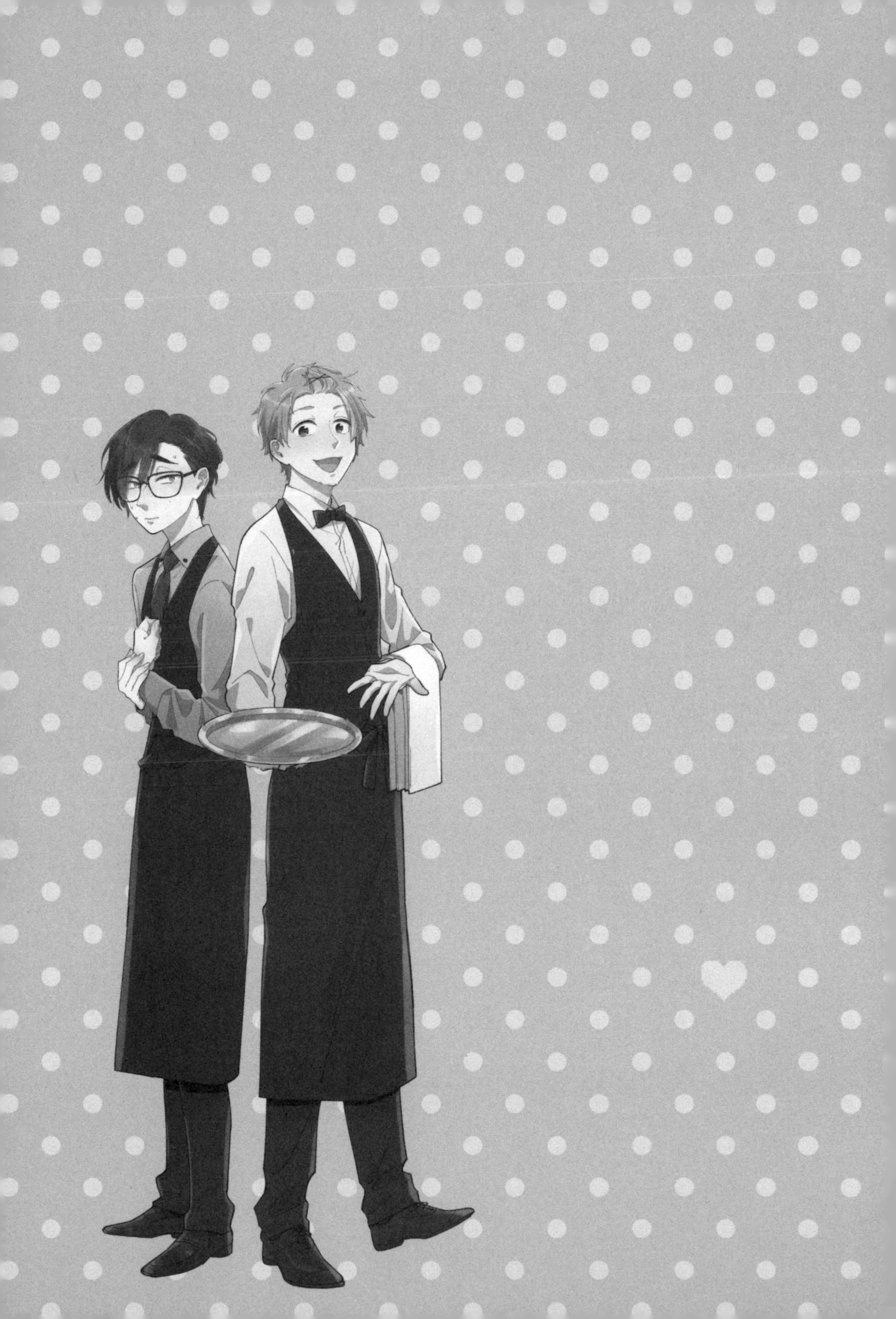

Narumi Momose

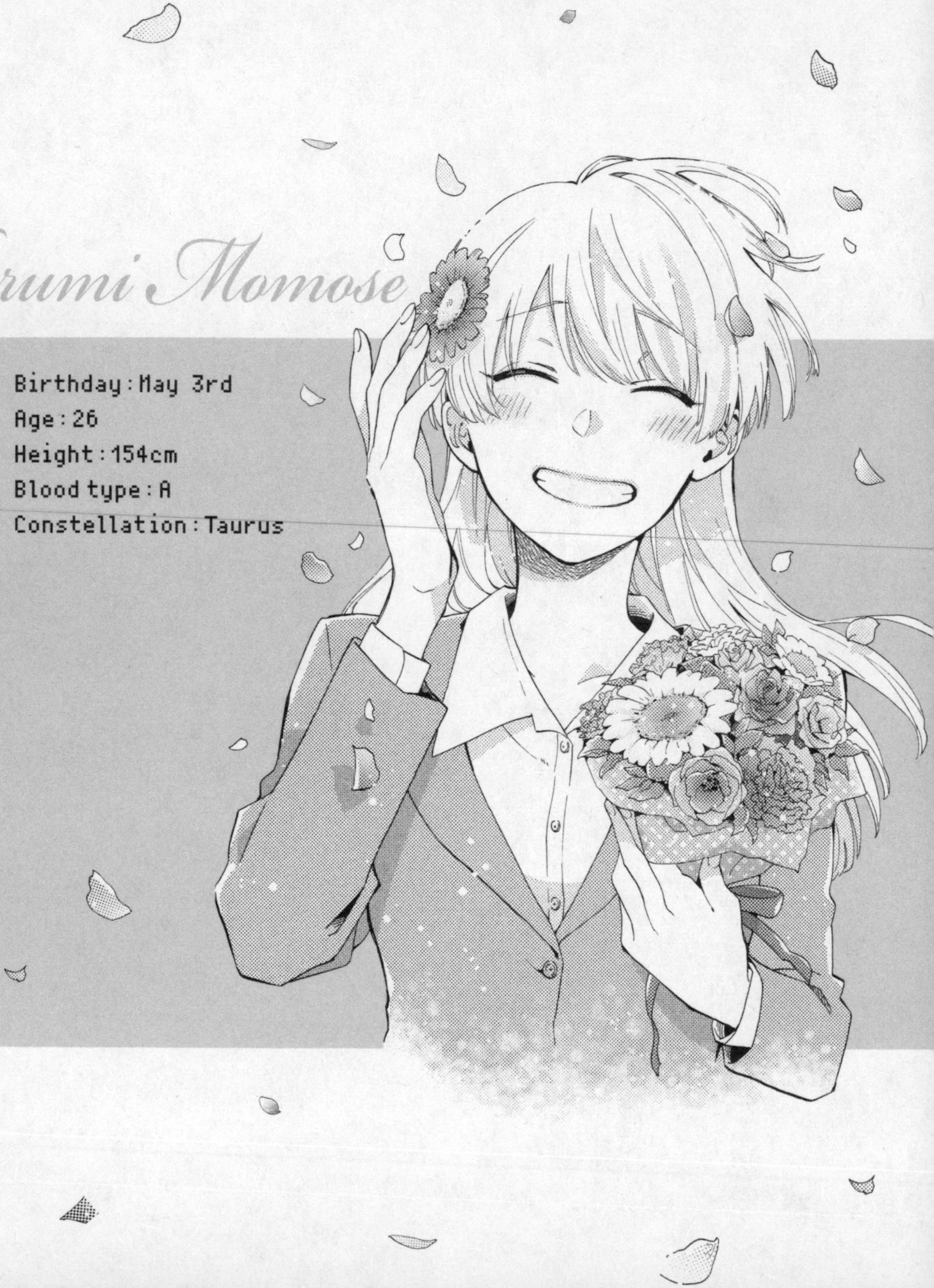

Birthday: May 3rd

Age: 26

Height: 154cm

Blood type: A

Constellation: Taurus

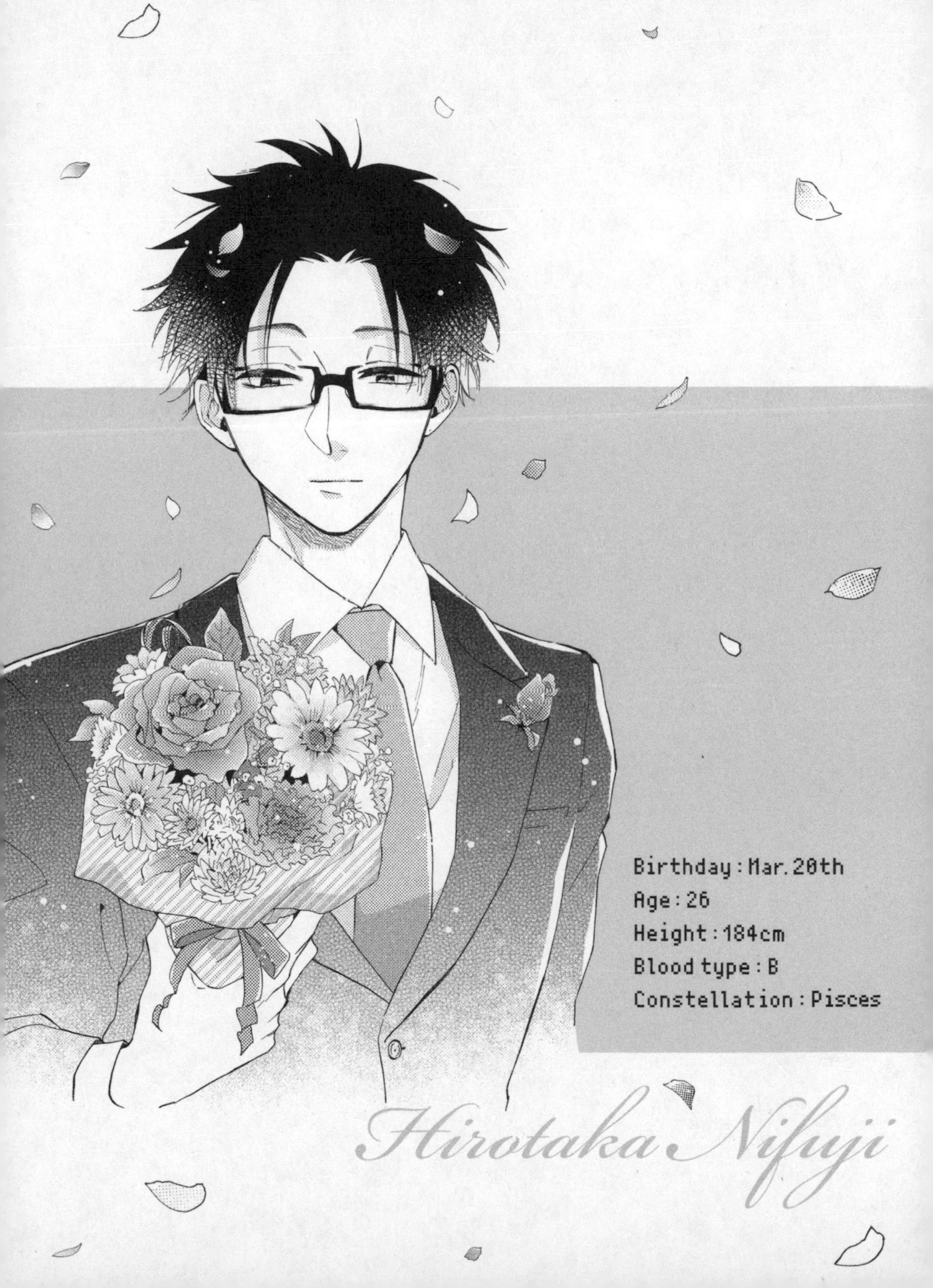
Birthday : Mar. 20th
Age : 26
Height : 184cm
Blood type : B
Constellation : Pisces
Hirotaka Nifuji

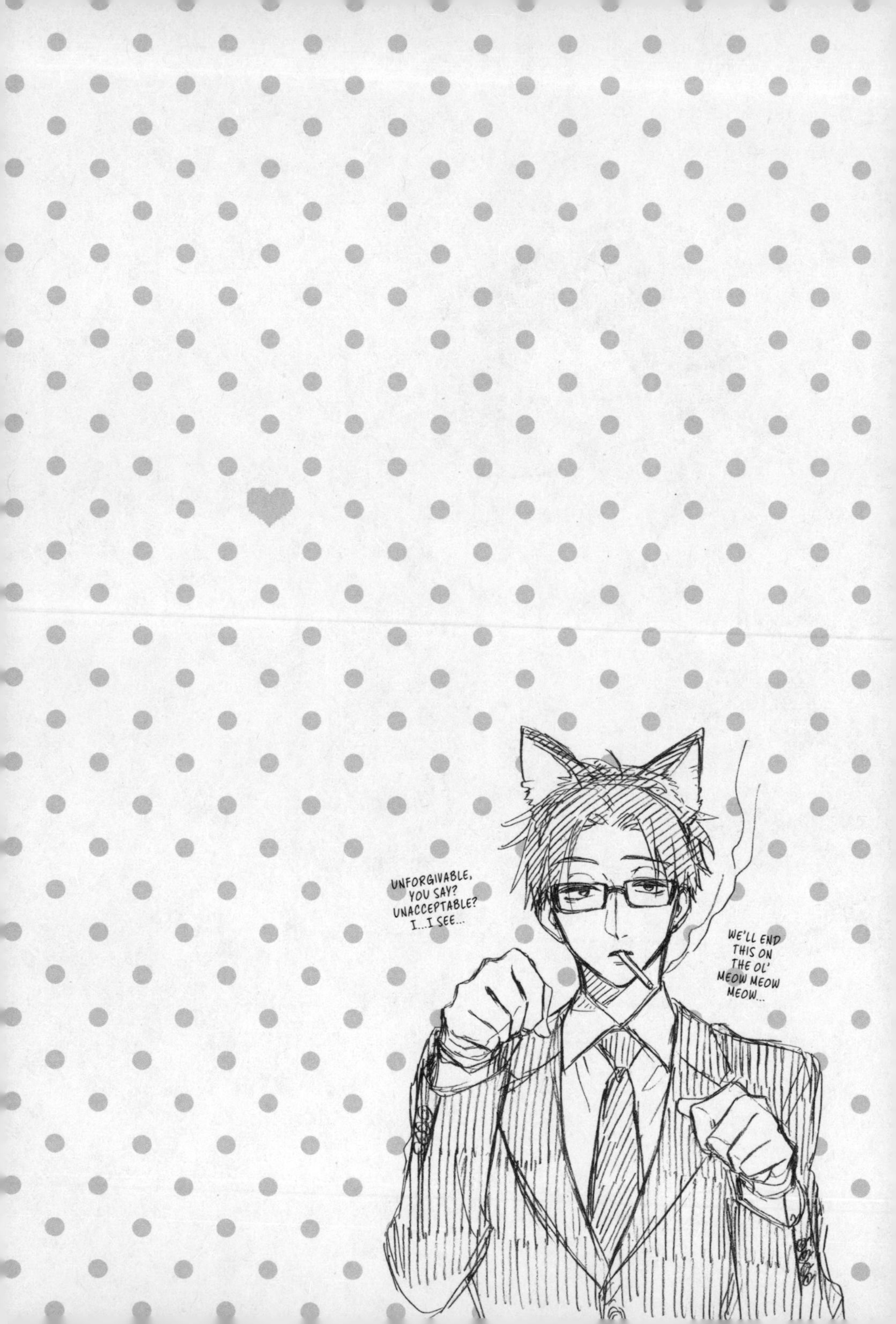
UNFORGIVABLE, YOU SAY? UNACCEPTABLE? I...I SEE...
WE'LL END THIS ON THE OL' MEOW MEOW MEOW...

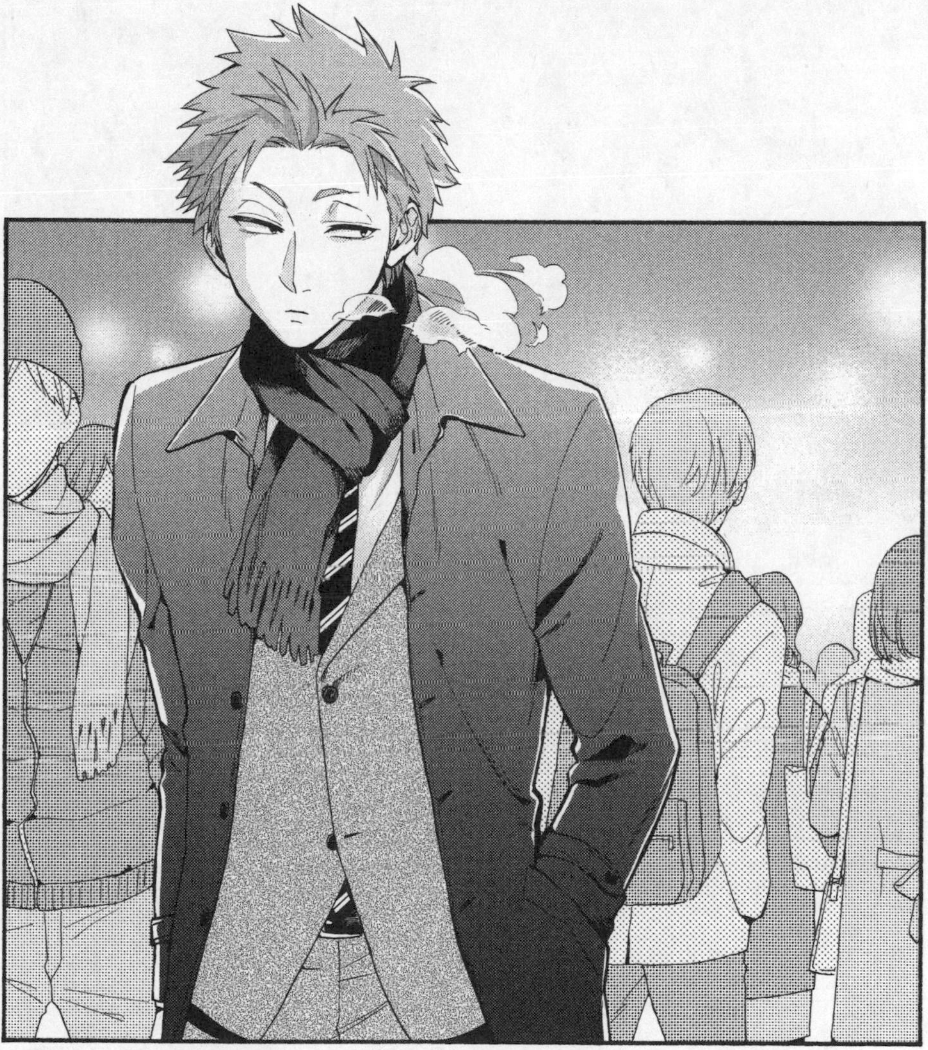

Episode.... 41

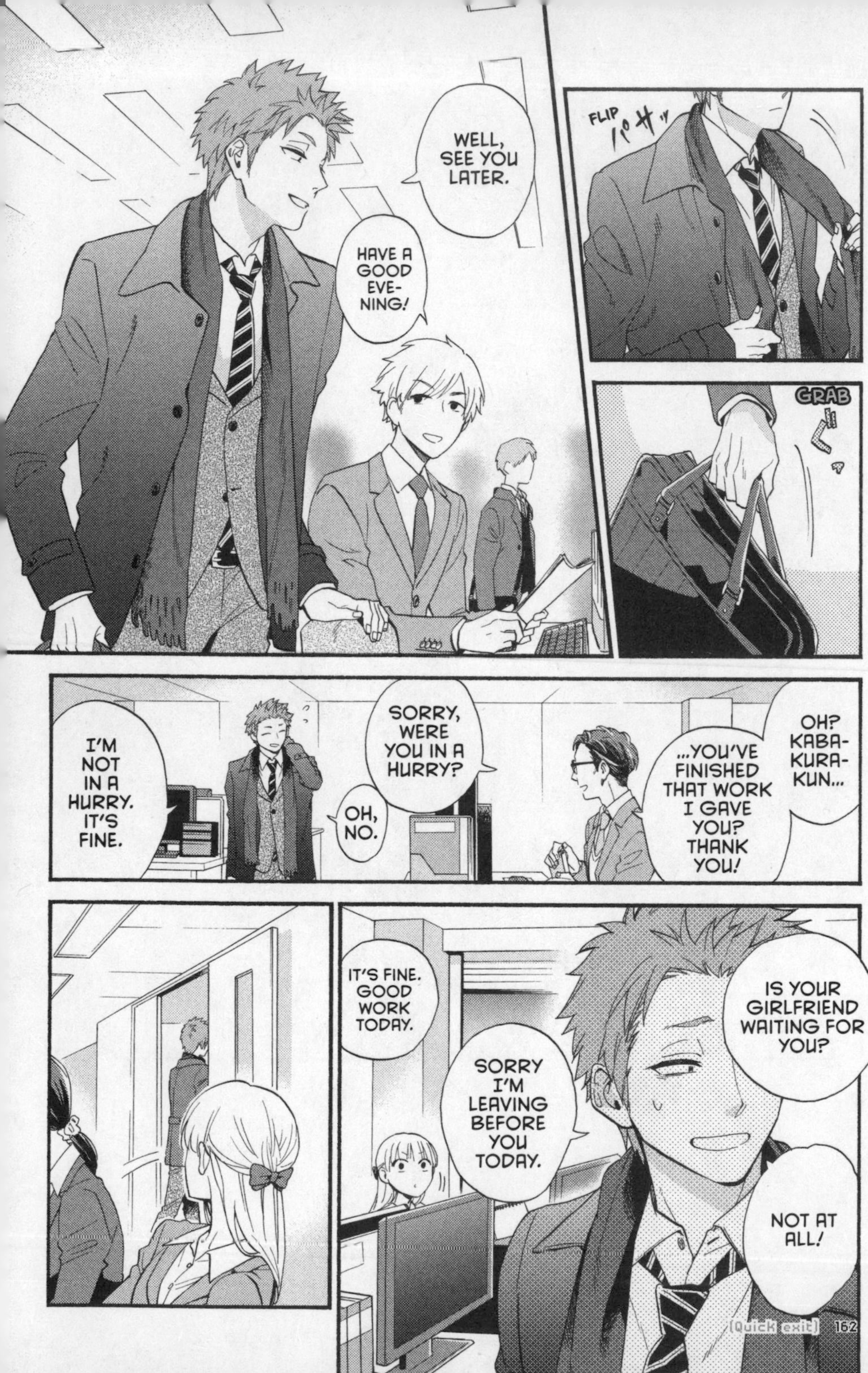
FLIP
GRAB
WELL, SEE YOU LATER.
HAVE A GOOD EVE-NING!
OH? KABA-KURA-KUN...
...YOU'VE FINISHED THAT WORK I GAVE YOU? THANK YOU!
SORRY, WERE YOU IN A HURRY?
OH, NO.
I'M NOT IN A HURRY. IT'S FINE.
IS YOUR GIRLFRIEND WAITING FOR YOU?
IT'S FINE. GOOD WORK TODAY.
SORRY I'M LEAVING BEFORE YOU TODAY.
NOT AT ALL!

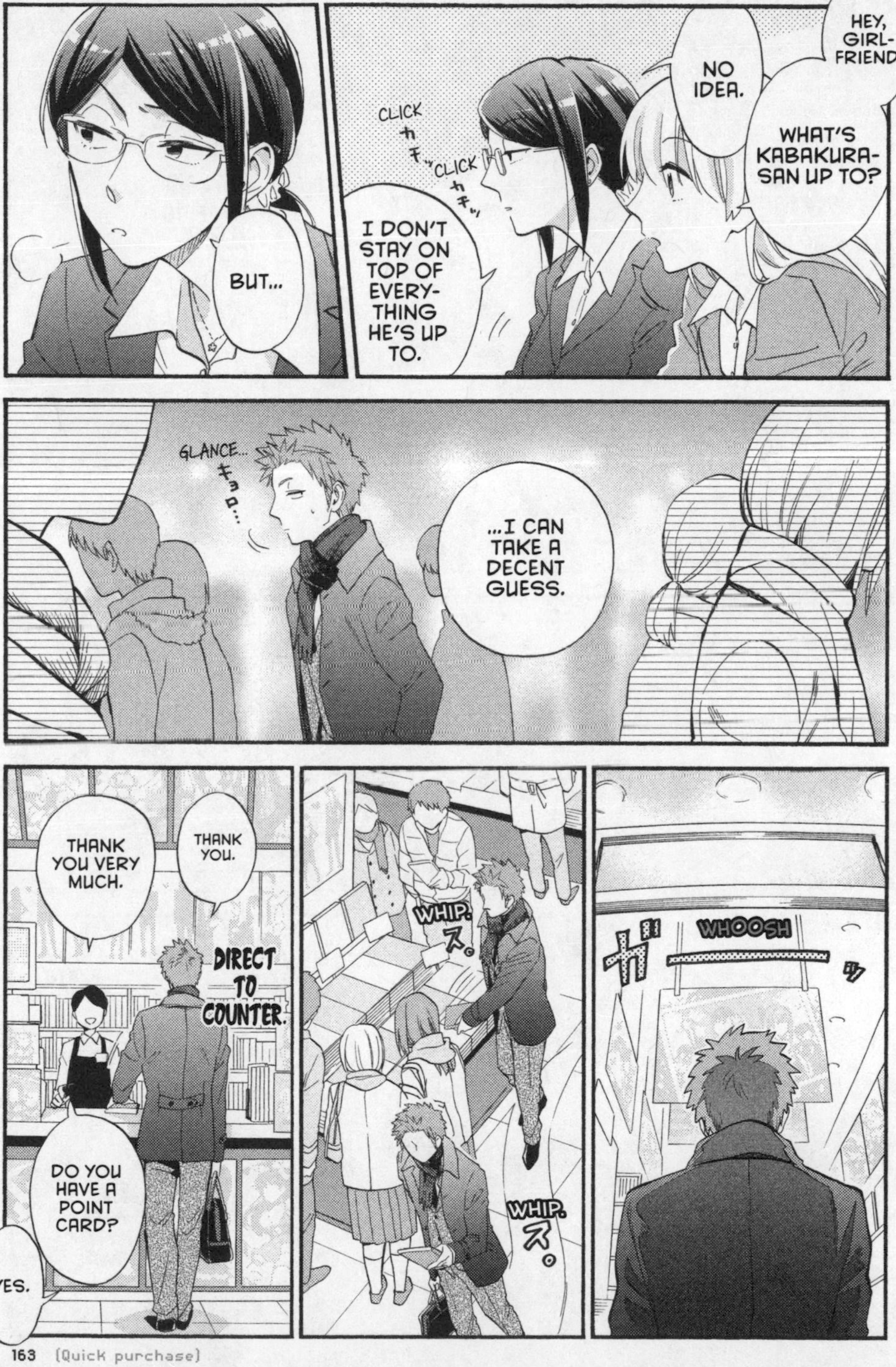
HEY, GIRL-FRIEND.
WHAT'S KABAKURA-SAN UP TO?
NO IDEA.
CLICK カチッ
CLICK カチッ
I DON'T STAY ON TOP OF EVERY-THING HE'S UP TO.
BUT...
...I CAN TAKE A DECENT GUESS.
GLANCE... キョロ...
WHOOSH
ガッ
WHIP. ス。
WHIP. ス。
THANK YOU.
THANK YOU VERY MUCH.
DIRECT TO COUNTER.
DO YOU HAVE A POINT CARD?
YES.

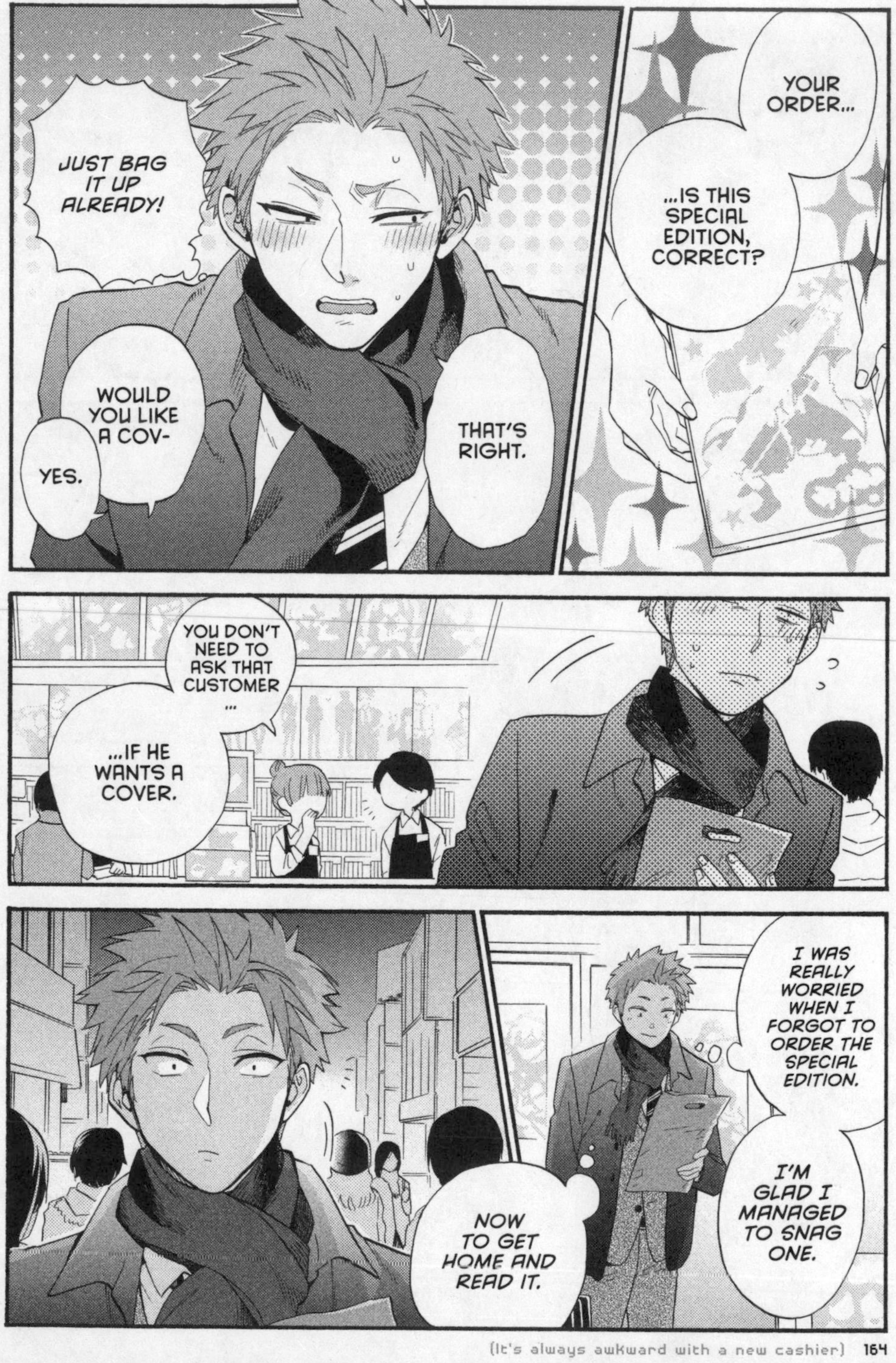
YOUR ORDER...
...IS THIS SPECIAL EDITION, CORRECT?
THAT'S RIGHT.
WOULD YOU LIKE A COV-
YES.
JUST BAG IT UP ALREADY!
YOU DON'T NEED TO ASK THAT CUSTOMER ...
...IF HE WANTS A COVER.
I WAS REALLY WORRIED WHEN I FORGOT TO ORDER THE SPECIAL EDITION.
I'M GLAD I MANAGED TO SNAG ONE.
NOW TO GET HOME AND READ IT.

(It's always awkward with a new cashier)

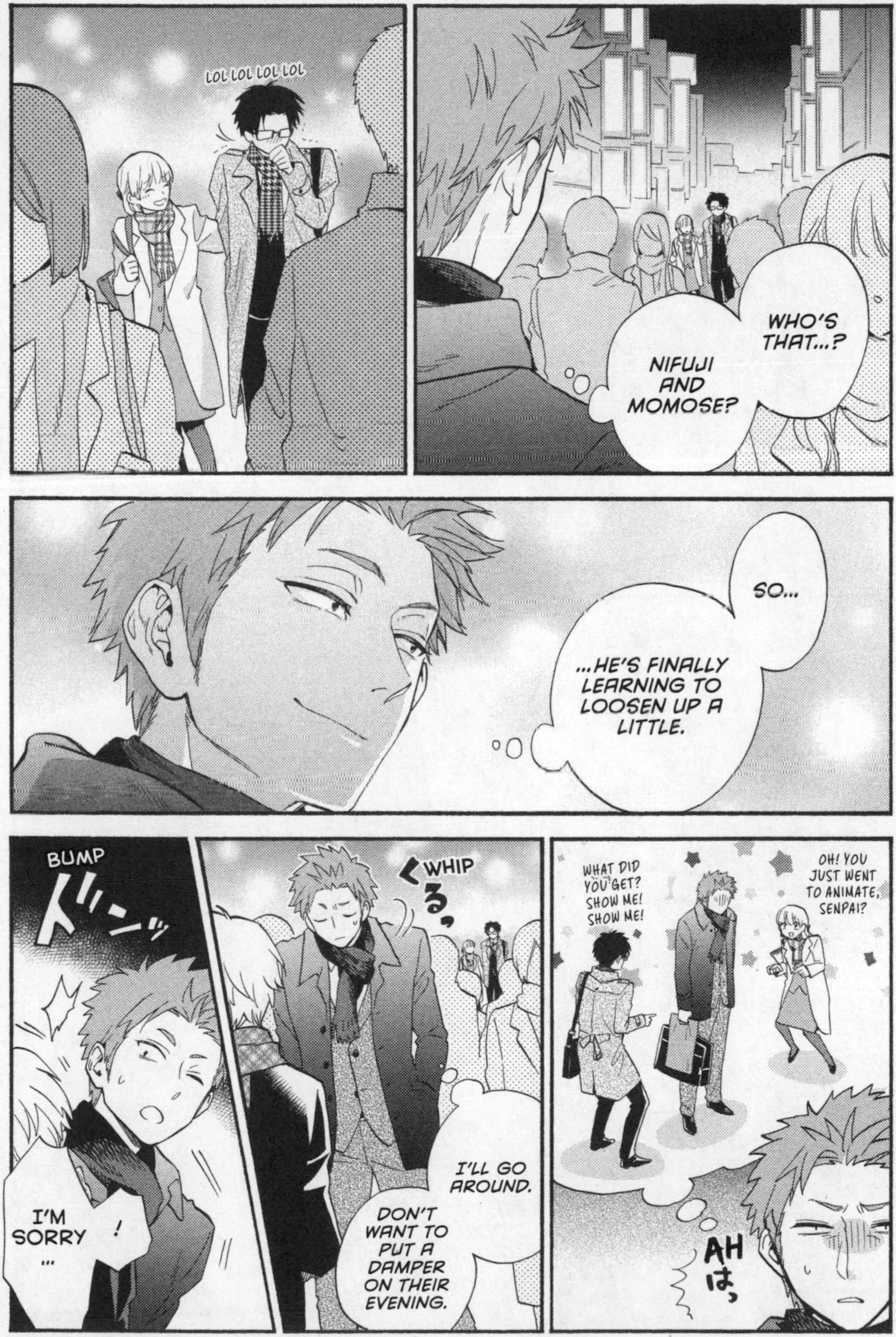
WHO'S THAT...?
NIFUJI AND MOMOSE?
LOL LOL LOL LOL
SO...
...HE'S FINALLY LEARNING TO LOOSEN UP A LITTLE.
OH! YOU JUST WENT TO ANIMATE, SENPAI?
WHAT DID YOU GET? SHOW ME! SHOW ME!
AH はっ
WHIP くるっ
I'LL GO AROUND.
DON'T WANT TO PUT A DAMPER ON THEIR EVENING.
BUMP ドンッ
I'M SORRY ...!

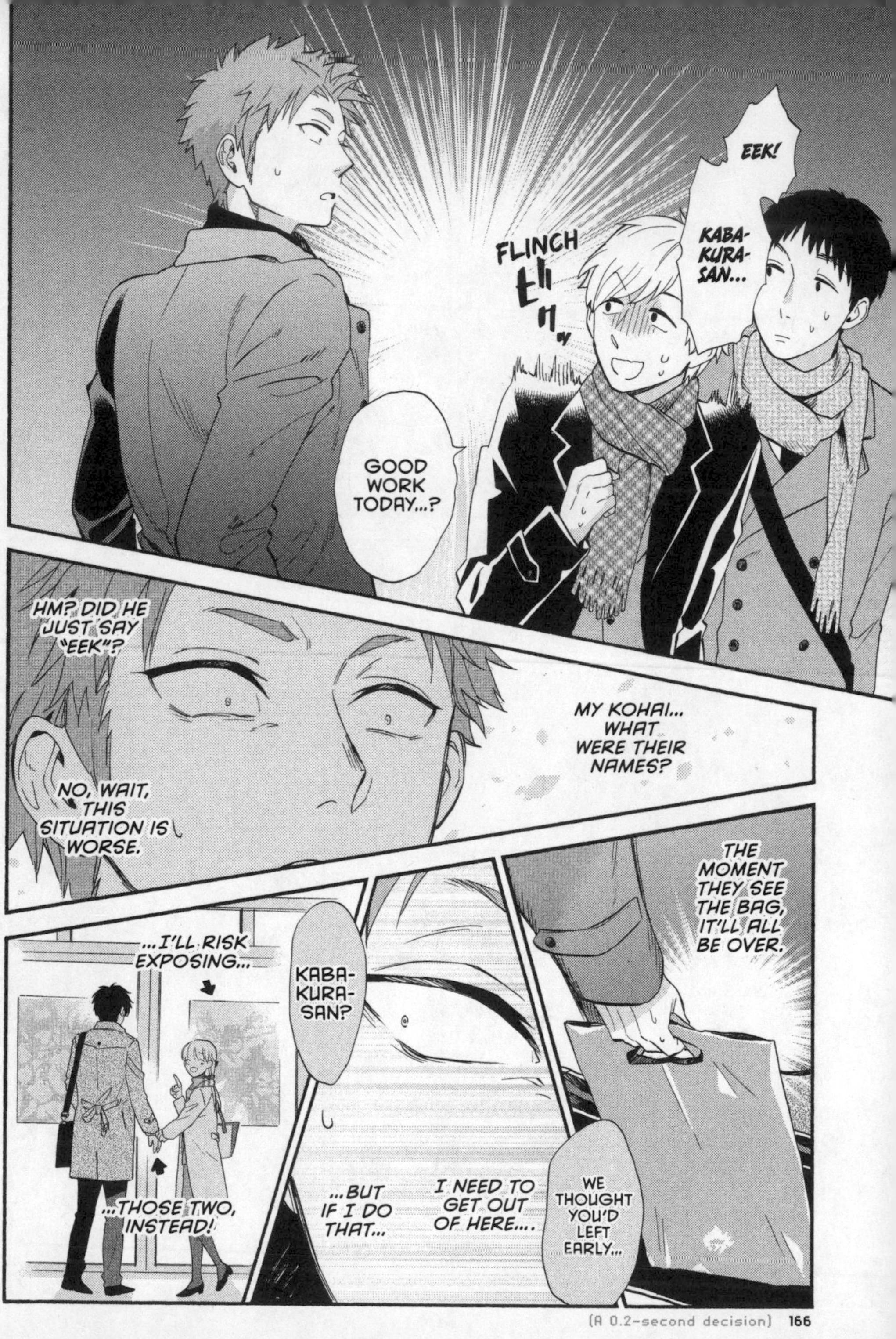
EEK!
KABA-KURA-SAN...
FLINCH
GOOD WORK TODAY...?
HM? DID HE JUST SAY "EEK"?
MY KOHAI... WHAT WERE THEIR NAMES?
NO, WAIT, THIS SITUATION IS WORSE.
THE MOMENT THEY SEE THE BAG, IT'LL ALL BE OVER.
WE THOUGHT YOU'D LEFT EARLY...
KABA-KURA-SAN?
I NEED TO GET OUT OF HERE....
...BUT IF I DO THAT...
...I'LL RISK EXPOSING...
...THOSE TWO, INSTEAD!

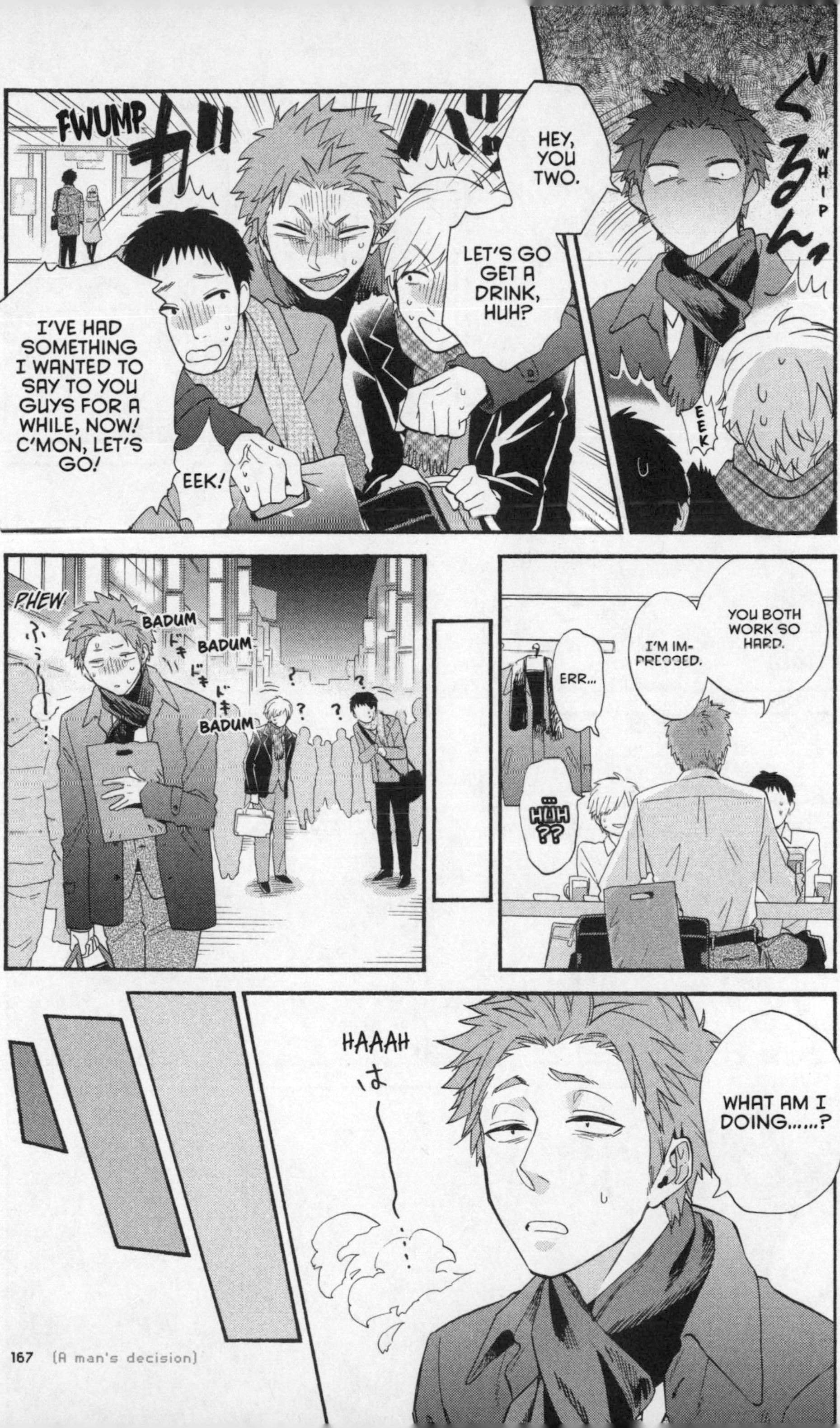
WHIP
HEY, YOU TWO.
LET'S GO GET A DRINK, HUH?
EEK
FWUMP
I'VE HAD SOMETHING I WANTED TO SAY TO YOU GUYS FOR A WHILE, NOW! C'MON, LET'S GO!
EEK!
YOU BOTH WORK SO HARD.
I'M IMPRESSED.
ERR...
...HUH??
PHEW
BADUM
BADUM
BADUM
HAAAH
WHAT AM I DOING......?

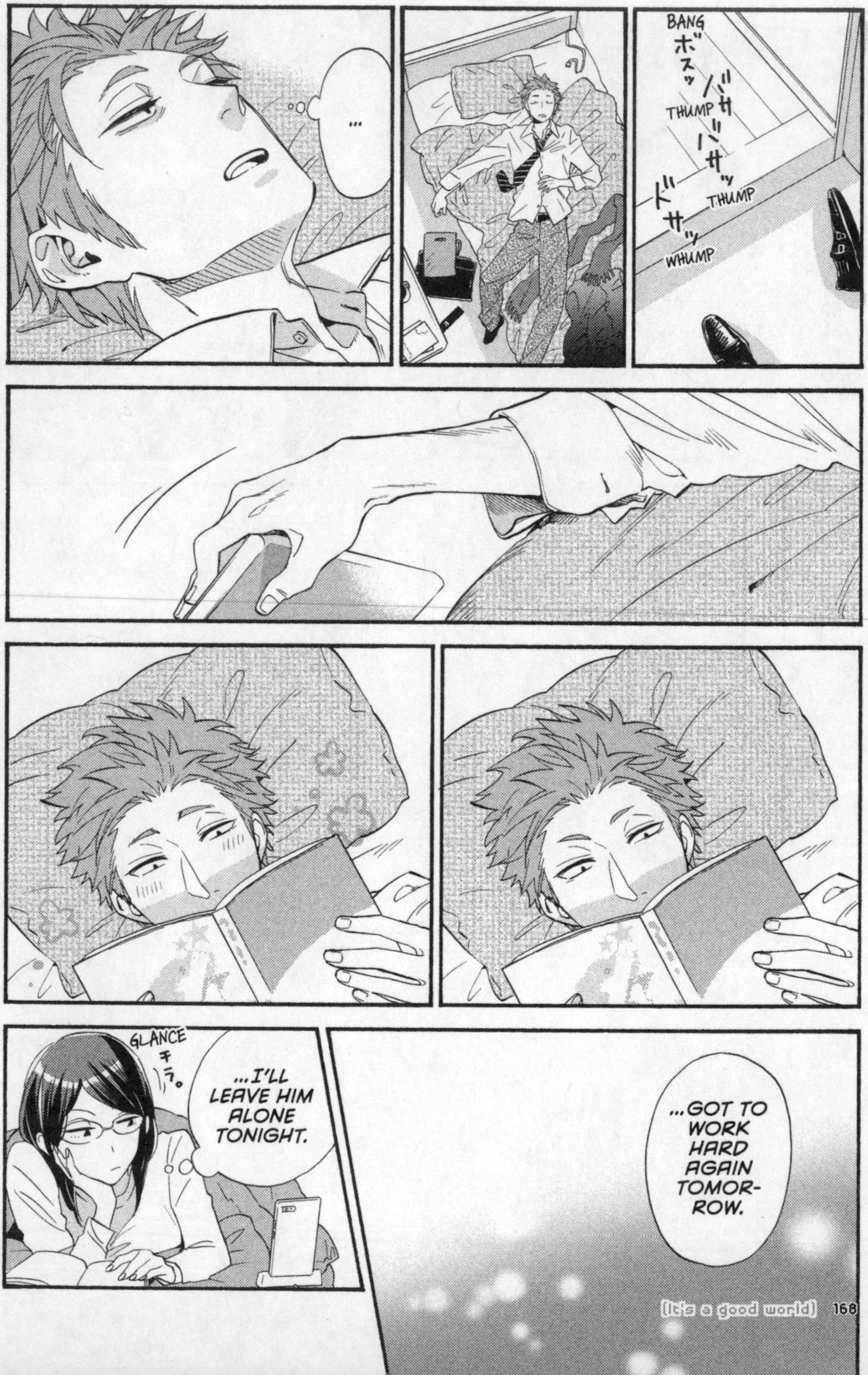
BANG
ボスッ
THUMP
バサッ
バサッ
THUMP
ドサッ
WHUMP
...
...GOT TO WORK HARD AGAIN TOMOR-ROW.
GLANCE
チラ。
...I'LL LEAVE HIM ALONE TONIGHT.

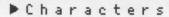

Kanako Koyanagi

Birthday : Aug.28th
Age : 27
Height : 167cm
Blood type : AB
Constellation : Virgo

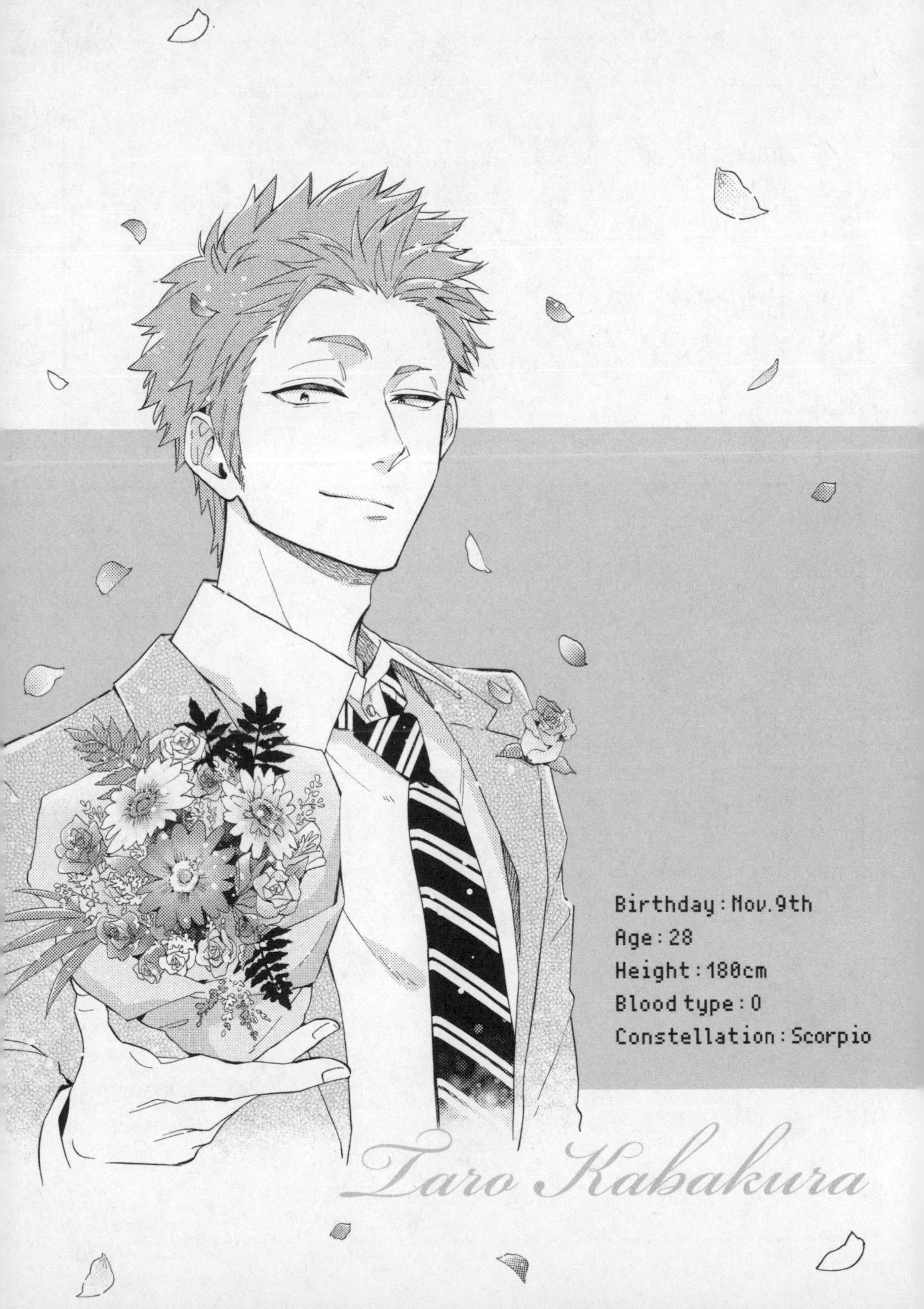
Birthday : Nov.9th
Age : 28
Height : 180cm
Blood type : O
Constellation : Scorpio
Taro Kabakura

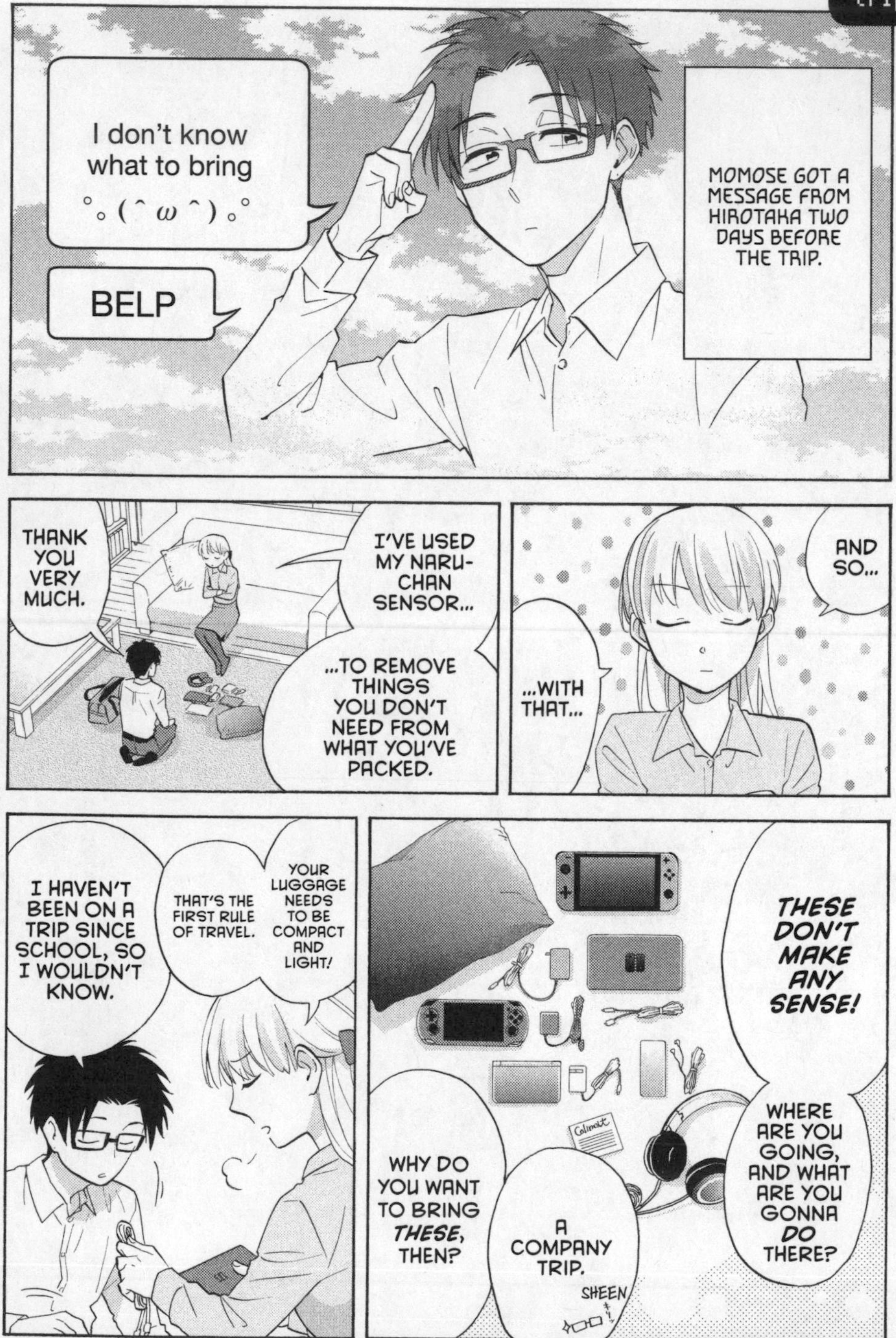
MOMOSE GOT A MESSAGE FROM HIROTAKA TWO DAYS BEFORE THE TRIP.
I don't know what to bring °。(ˆ ω ˆ) 。°
BELP
AND SO...
...WITH THAT...
I'VE USED MY NARU-CHAN SENSOR...
...TO REMOVE THINGS YOU DON'T NEED FROM WHAT YOU'VE PACKED.
THANK YOU VERY MUCH.
THESE DON'T MAKE ANY SENSE!
WHERE ARE YOU GOING, AND WHAT ARE YOU GONNA *DO* THERE?
A COMPANY TRIP.
WHY DO YOU WANT TO BRING *THESE*, THEN?
SHEEN
YOUR LUGGAGE NEEDS TO BE COMPACT AND LIGHT!
THAT'S THE FIRST RULE OF TRAVEL.
I HAVEN'T BEEN ON A TRIP SINCE SCHOOL, SO I WOULDN'T KNOW.

(You're amazing, Narumi-san!!)

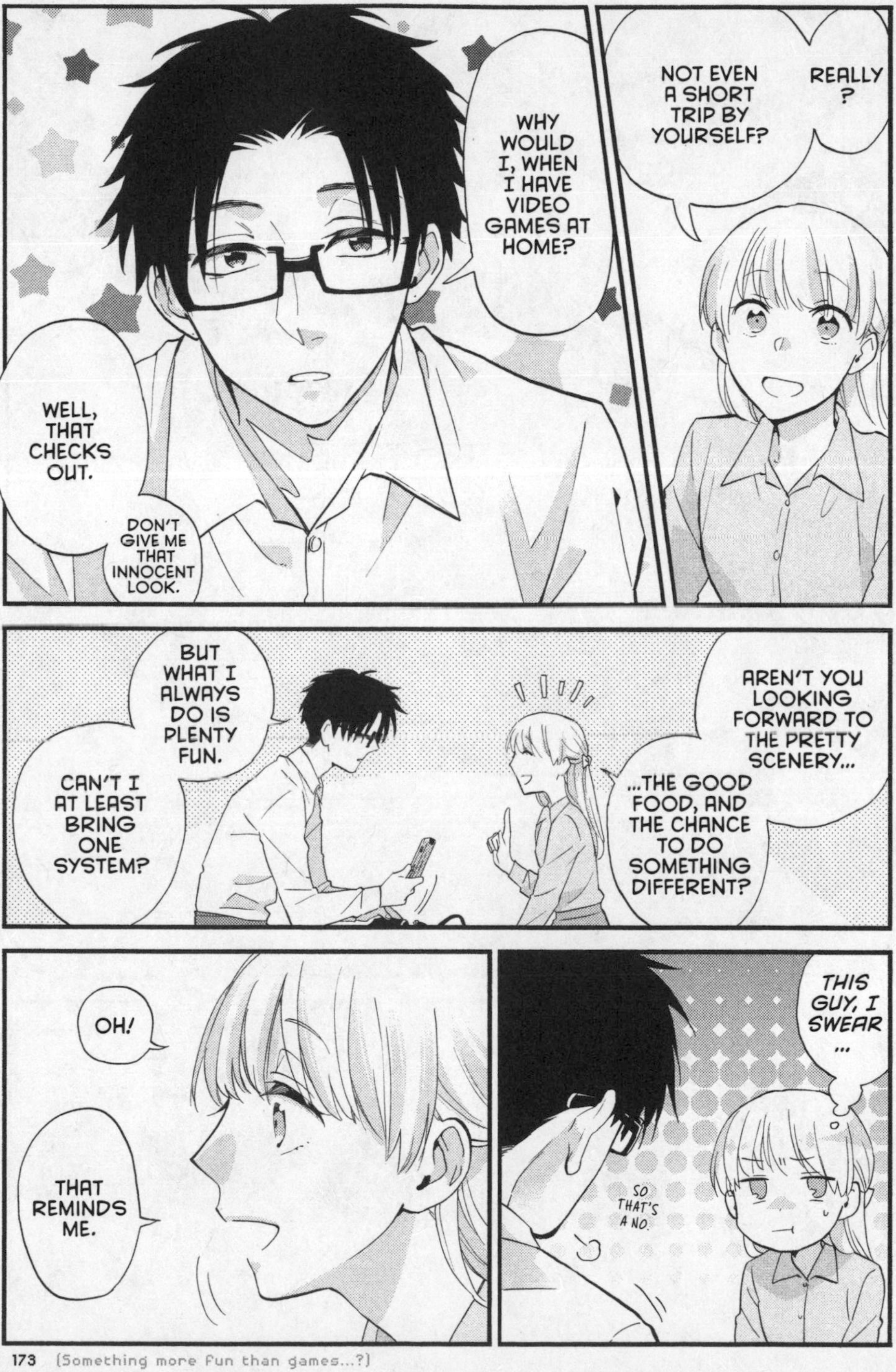
REALLY?
NOT EVEN A SHORT TRIP BY YOURSELF?
WHY WOULD I, WHEN I HAVE VIDEO GAMES AT HOME?
WELL, THAT CHECKS OUT.
DON'T GIVE ME THAT INNOCENT LOOK.
AREN'T YOU LOOKING FORWARD TO THE PRETTY SCENERY...
...THE GOOD FOOD, AND THE CHANCE TO DO SOMETHING DIFFERENT?
BUT WHAT I ALWAYS DO IS PLENTY FUN.
CAN'T I AT LEAST BRING ONE SYSTEM?
THIS GUY, I SWEAR...
SO THAT'S A NO.
OH!
THAT REMINDS ME.

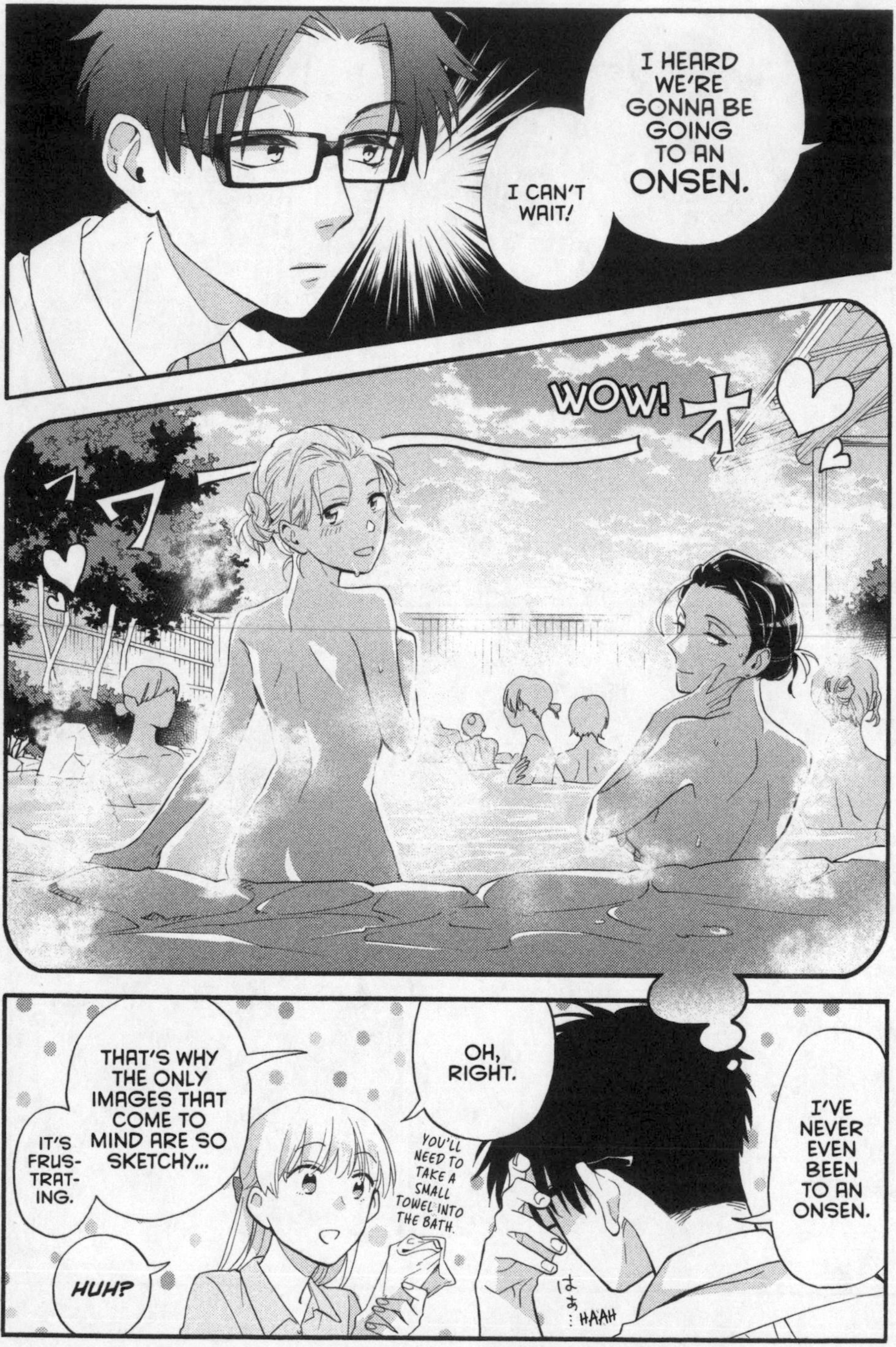
I HEARD WE'RE GONNA BE GOING TO AN ONSEN.
I CAN'T WAIT!
WOW!
I'VE NEVER EVEN BEEN TO AN ONSEN.
OH, RIGHT.
YOU'LL NEED TO TAKE A SMALL TOWEL INTO THE BATH.
THAT'S WHY THE ONLY IMAGES THAT COME TO MIND ARE SO SKETCHY...
IT'S FRUS-TRAT-ING.
HUH?
はぁ… HAAH

(He's actually got a good imagination)

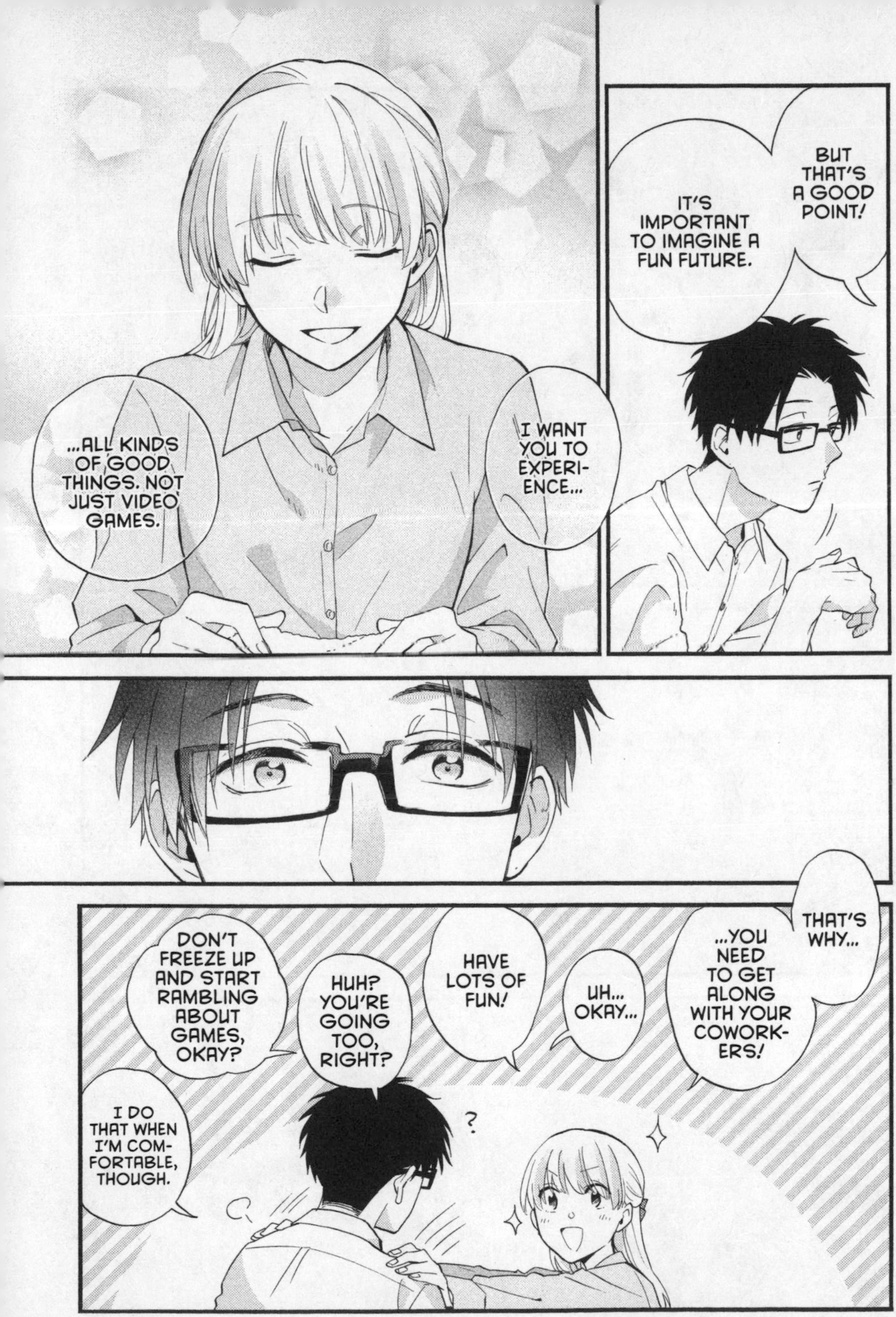
BUT THAT'S A GOOD POINT!
IT'S IMPORTANT TO IMAGINE A FUN FUTURE.
I WANT YOU TO EXPERIENCE...
...ALL KINDS OF GOOD THINGS. NOT JUST VIDEO GAMES.
THAT'S WHY...
...YOU NEED TO GET ALONG WITH YOUR COWORKERS!
UH... OKAY...
HAVE LOTS OF FUN!
HUH? YOU'RE GOING TOO, RIGHT?
DON'T FREEZE UP AND START RAMBLING ABOUT GAMES, OKAY?
?
I DO THAT WHEN I'M COMFORTABLE, THOUGH.

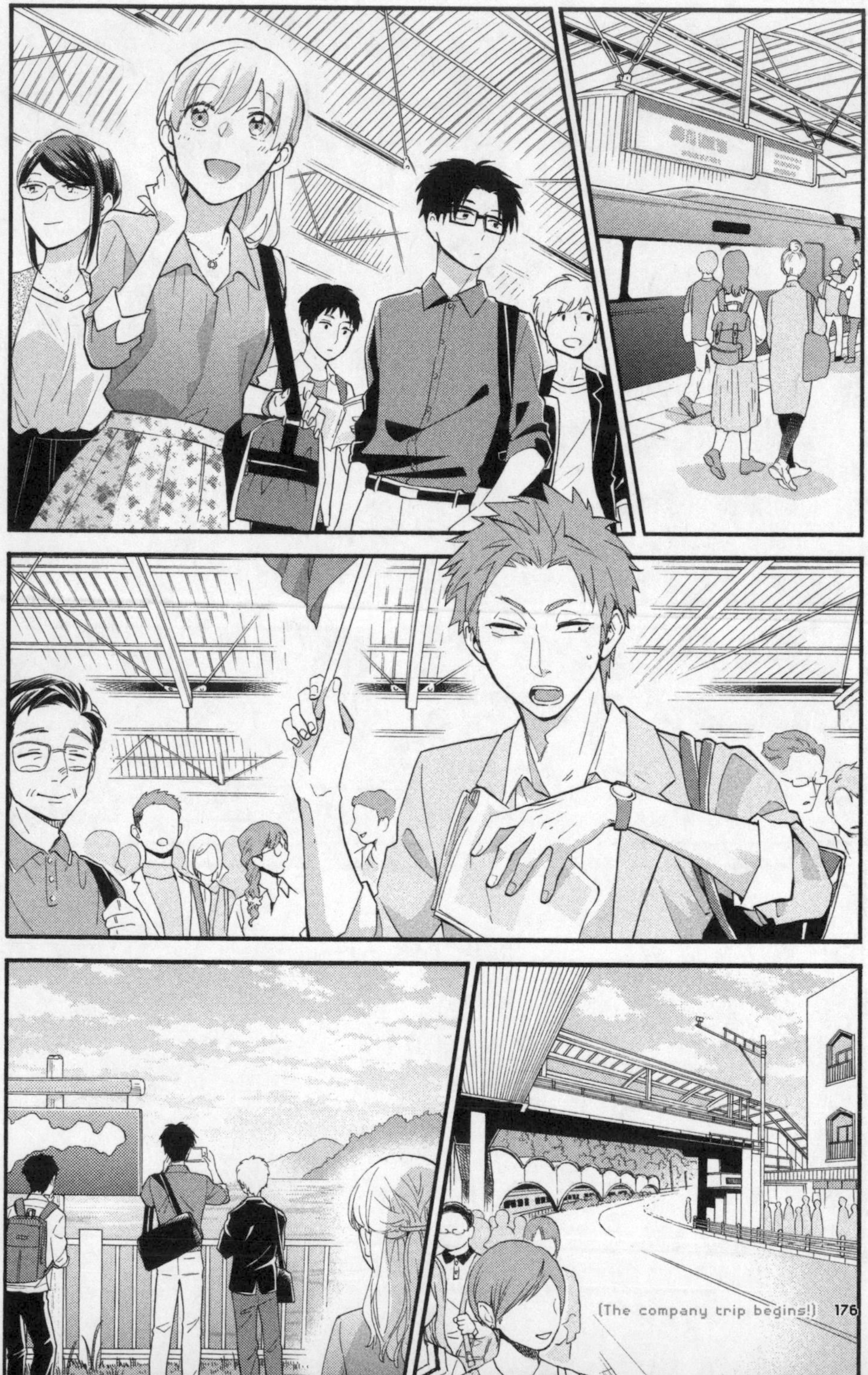
(The company trip begins!)

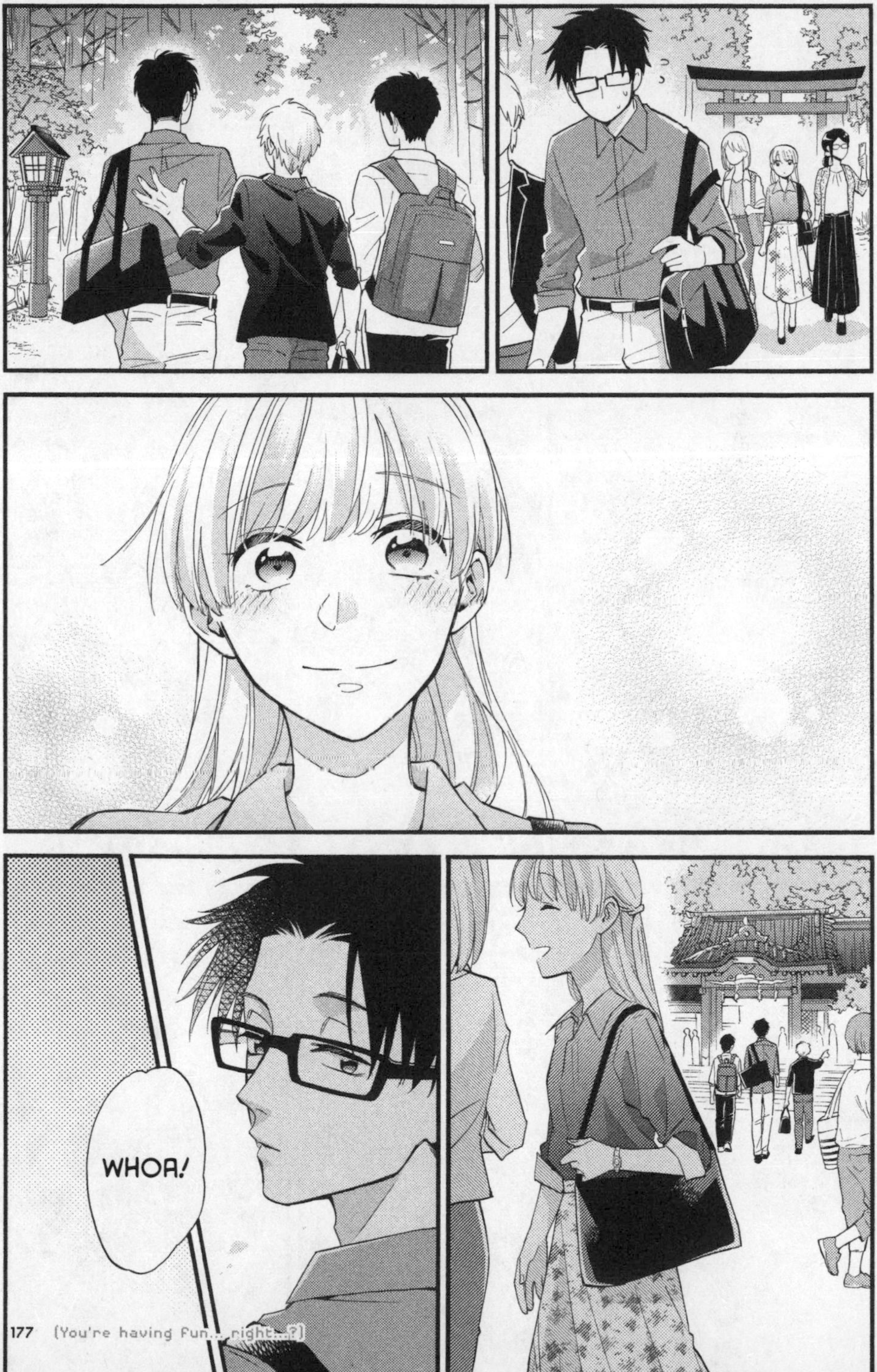
WHOA!

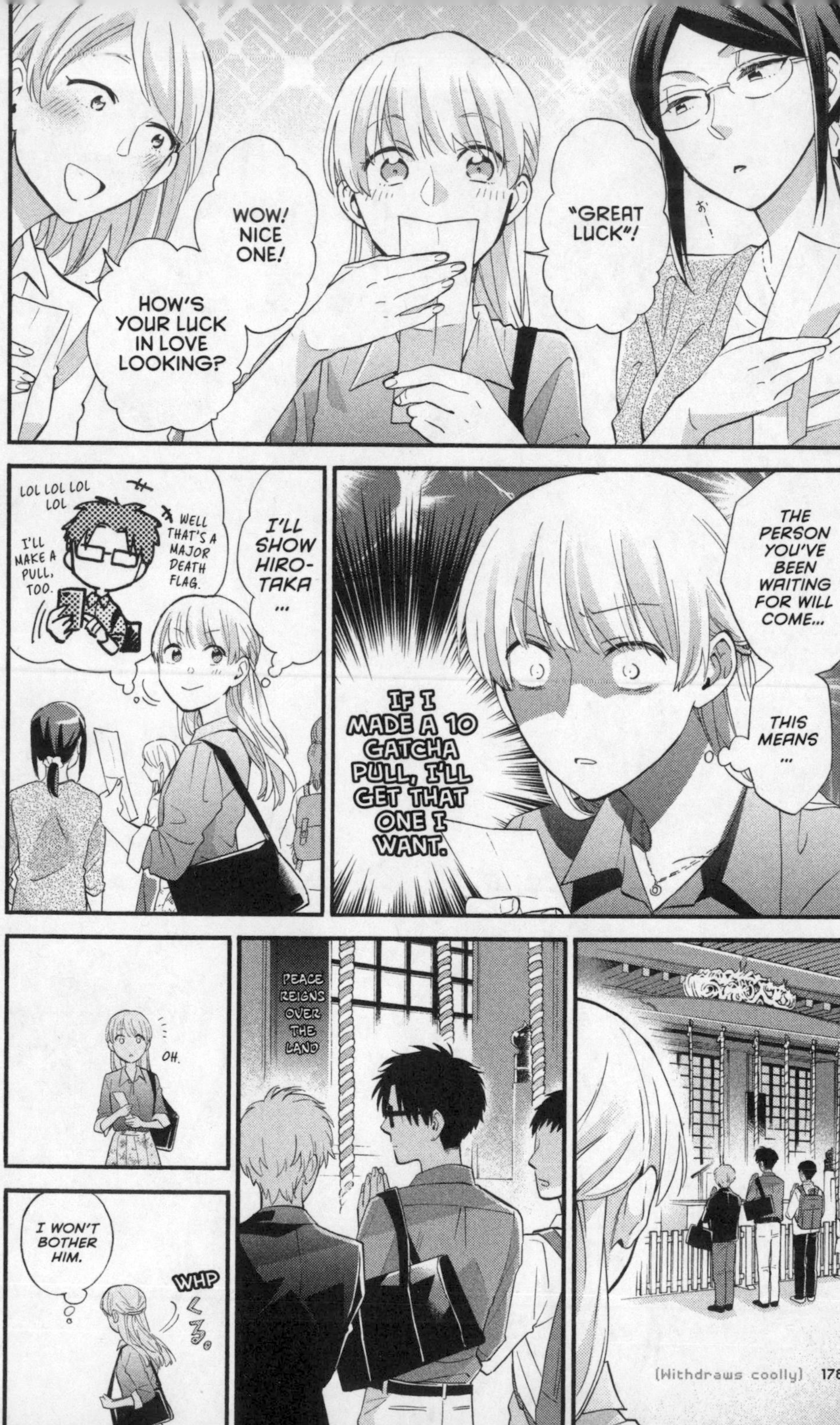
"GREAT LUCK"!
WOW! NICE ONE!
HOW'S YOUR LUCK IN LOVE LOOKING?
THE PERSON YOU'VE BEEN WAITING FOR WILL COME...
THIS MEANS ...
IF I MADE A 10 GATCHA PULL, I'LL GET THAT ONE I WANT.
I'LL SHOW HIRO-TAKA ...
WELL THAT'S A MAJOR DEATH FLAG.
LOL LOL LOL LOL LOL
I'LL MAKE A PULL, TOO.
PEACE REIGNS OVER THE LAND
OH.
I WON'T BOTHER HIM.
WHP
(Withdraws coolly)

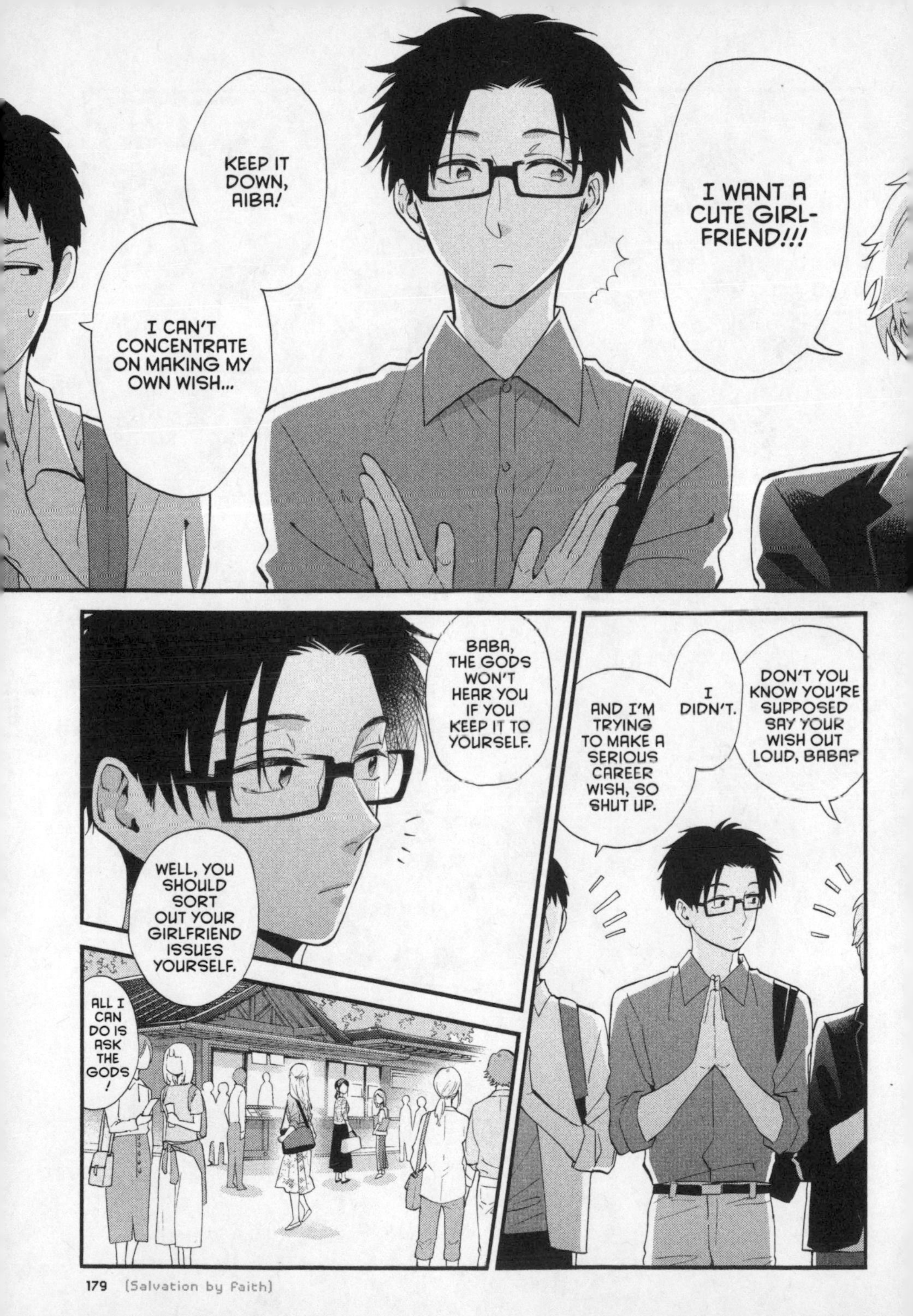
I WANT A CUTE GIRL-FRIEND!!!
KEEP IT DOWN, AIBA!
I CAN'T CONCENTRATE ON MAKING MY OWN WISH...
DON'T YOU KNOW YOU'RE SUPPOSED SAY YOUR WISH OUT LOUD, BABA?
I DIDN'T.
AND I'M TRYING TO MAKE A SERIOUS CAREER WISH, SO SHUT UP.
BABA, THE GODS WON'T HEAR YOU IF YOU KEEP IT TO YOURSELF.
WELL, YOU SHOULD SORT OUT YOUR GIRLFRIEND ISSUES YOURSELF.
ALL I CAN DO IS ASK THE GODS!

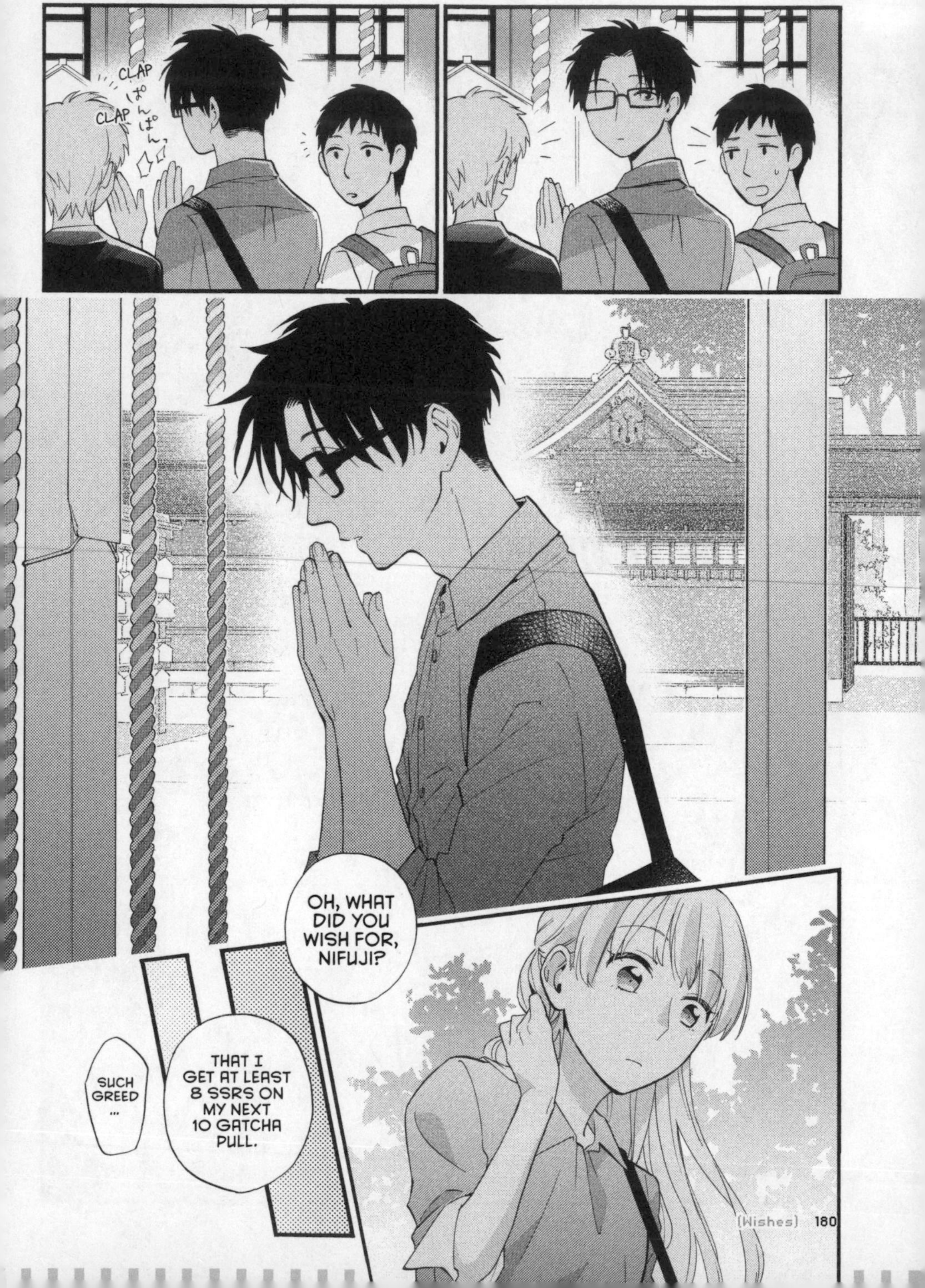
CLAP
CLAP
ぱんぱん
OH, WHAT DID YOU WISH FOR, NIFUJI?
THAT I GET AT LEAST 8 SSRS ON MY NEXT 10 GATCHA PULL.
SUCH GREED ...

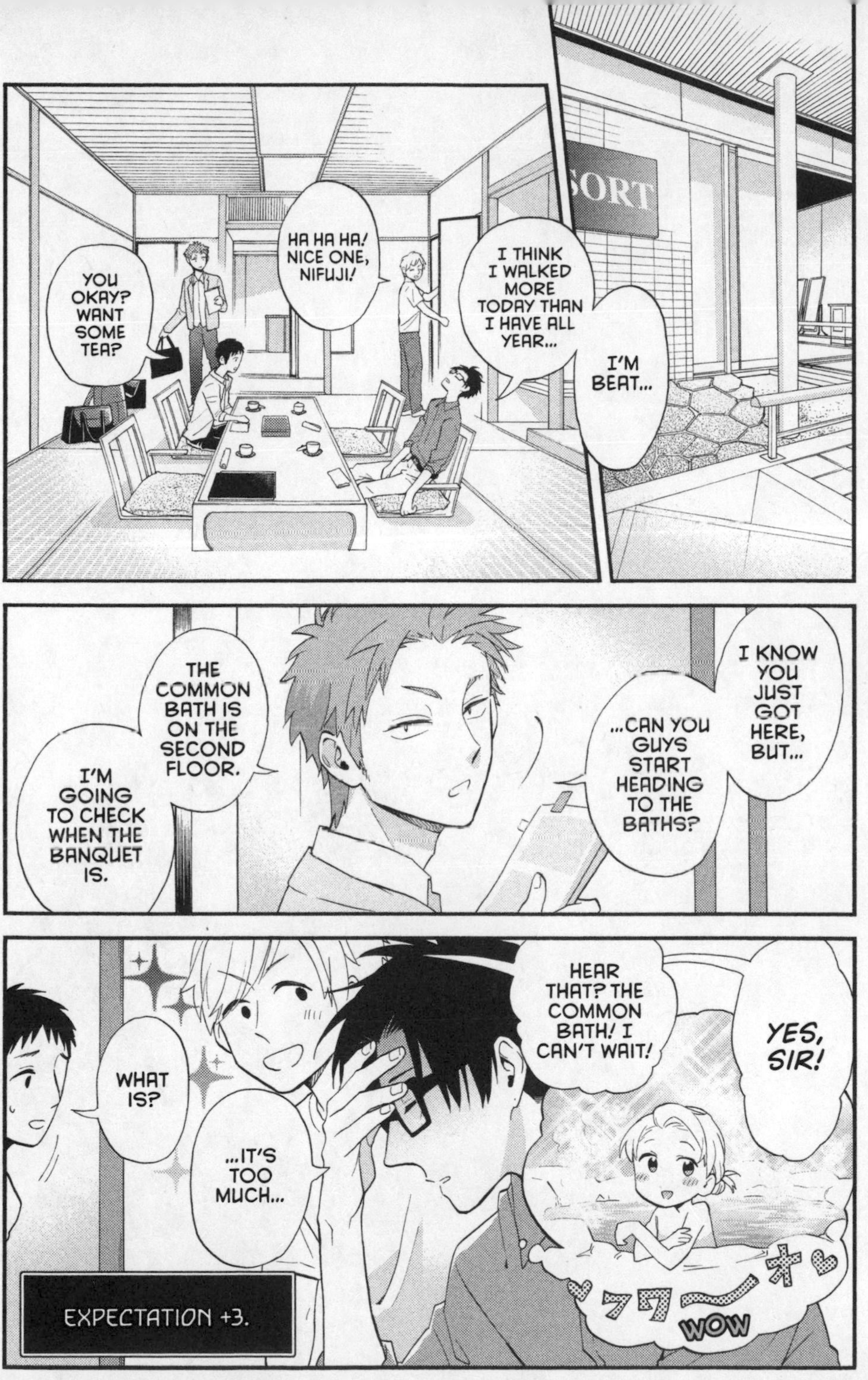
SORT
I'M BEAT...
I THINK I WALKED MORE TODAY THAN I HAVE ALL YEAR...
HA HA HA! NICE ONE, NIFUJI!
YOU OKAY? WANT SOME TEA?
I KNOW YOU JUST GOT HERE, BUT...
...CAN YOU GUYS START HEADING TO THE BATHS?
THE COMMON BATH IS ON THE SECOND FLOOR.
I'M GOING TO CHECK WHEN THE BANQUET IS.
YES, SIR!
HEAR THAT? THE COMMON BATH! I CAN'T WAIT!
WOW
...IT'S TOO MUCH...
WHAT IS?
EXPECTATION +3.

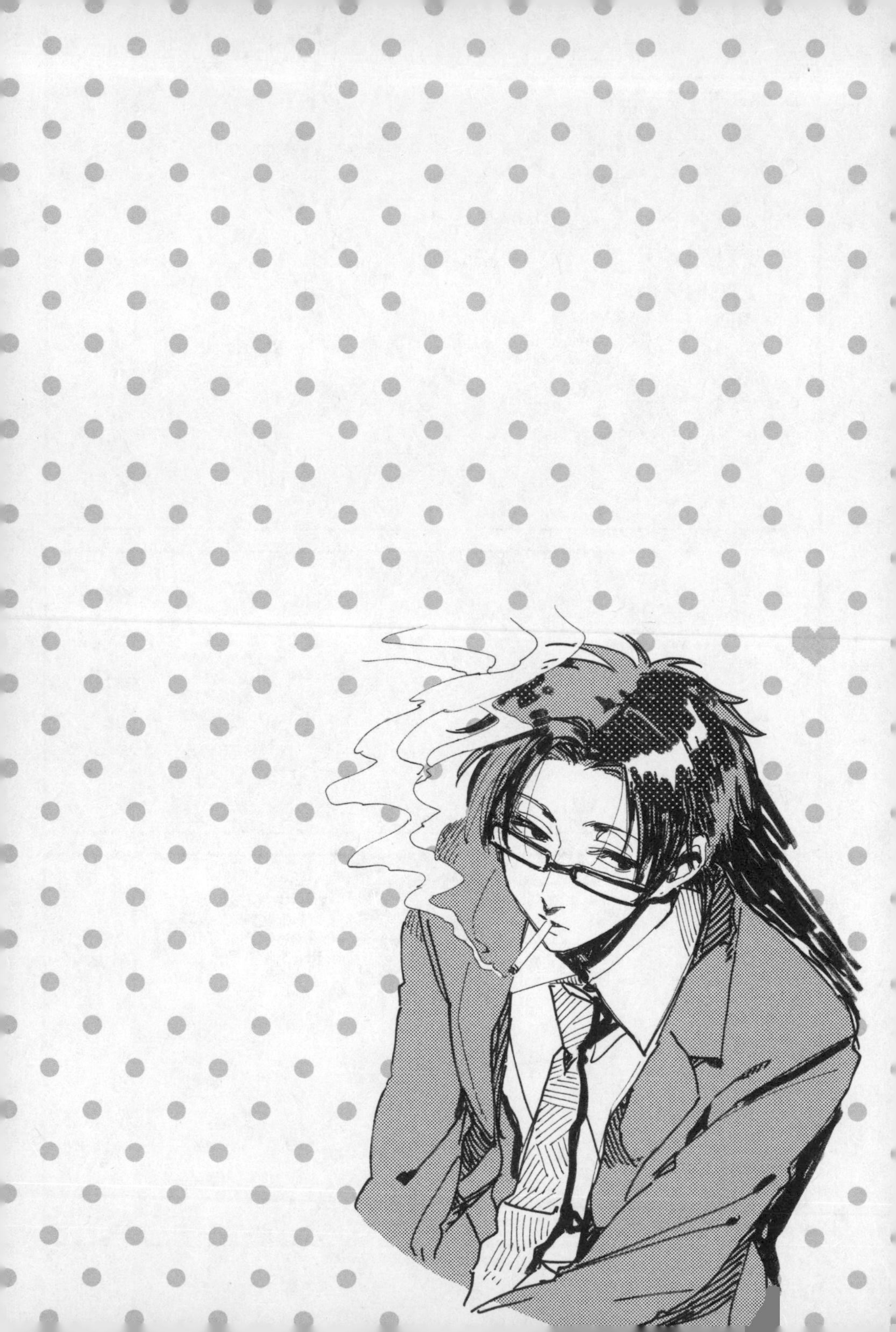

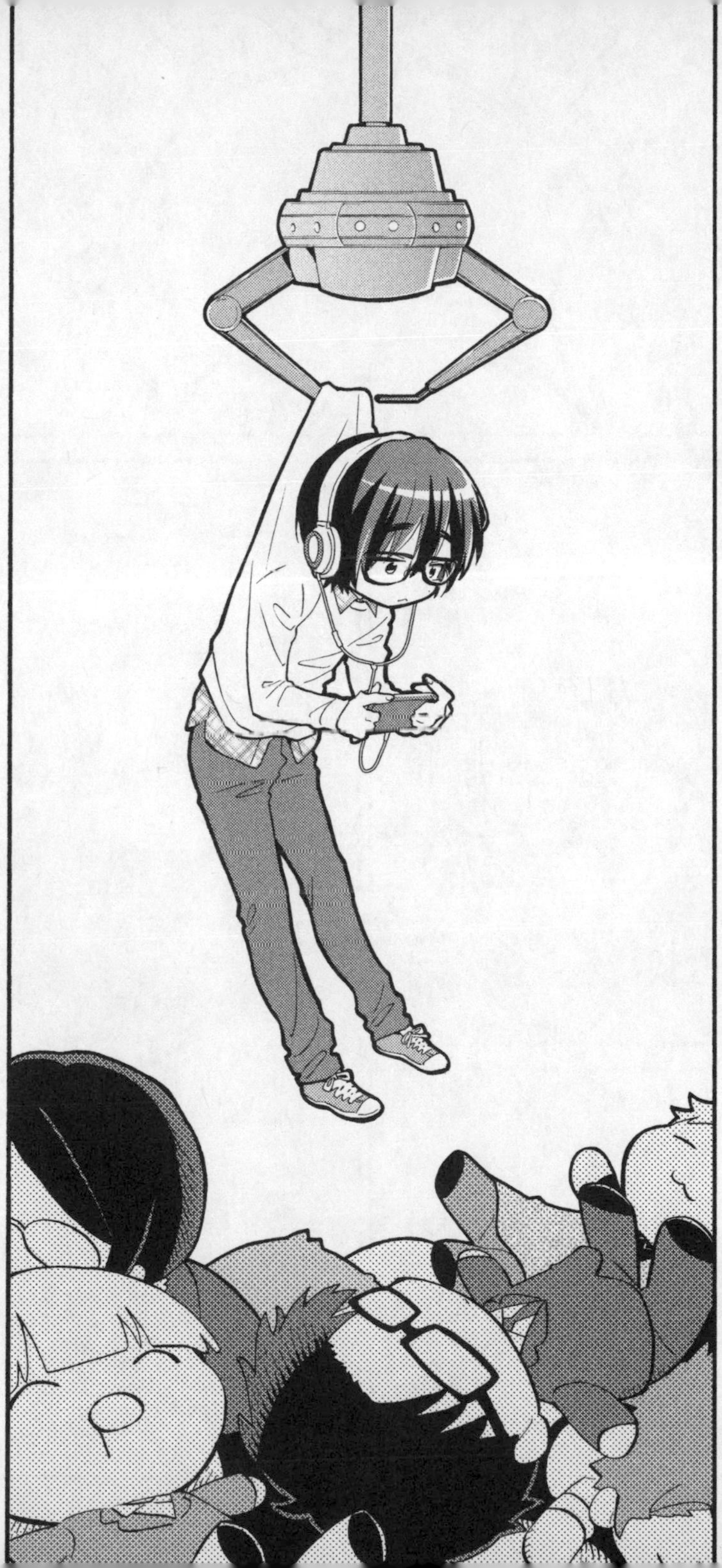

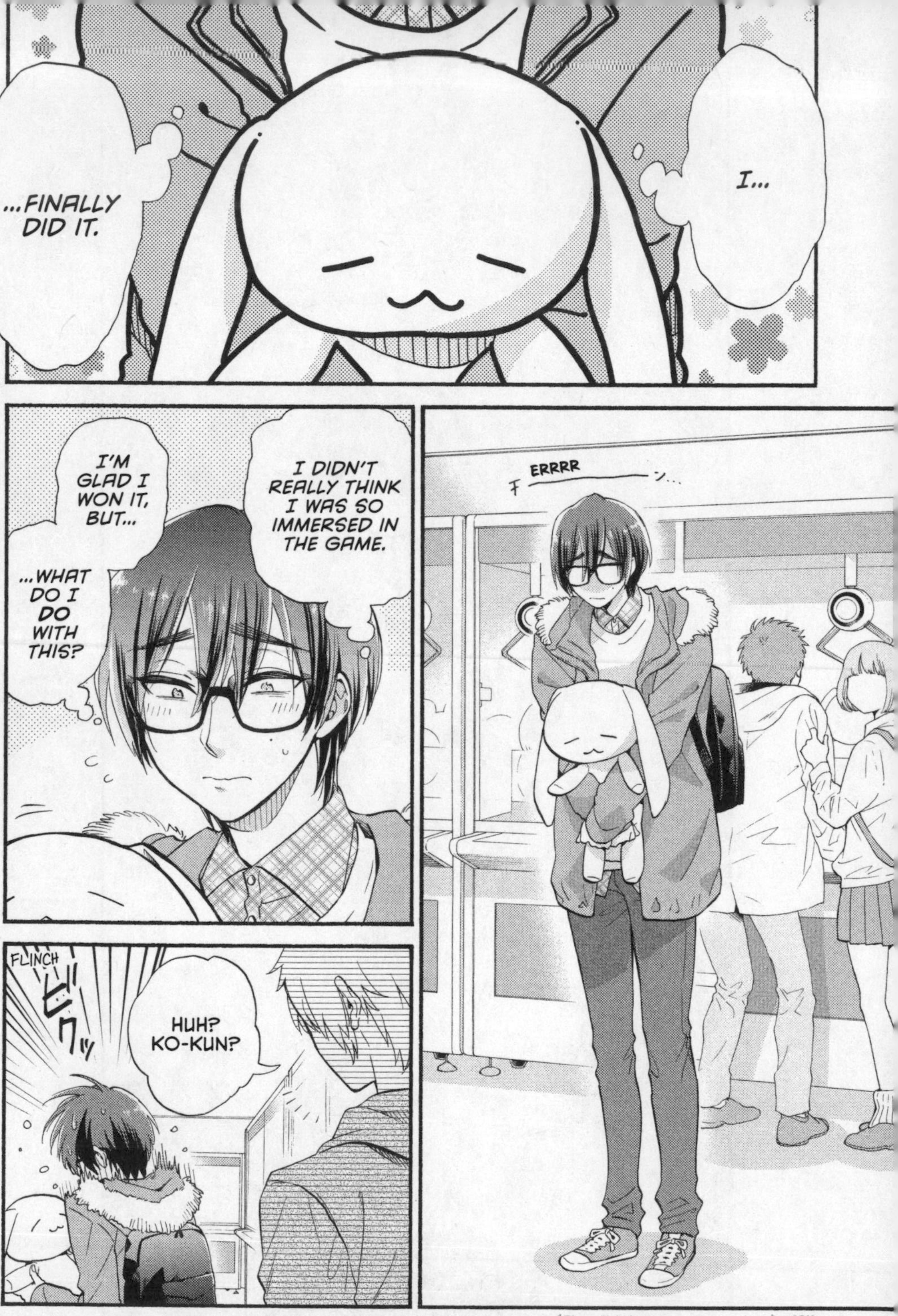
I...
...FINALLY DID IT.
ERRRR
I DIDN'T REALLY THINK I WAS SO IMMERSED IN THE GAME.
I'M GLAD I WON IT, BUT...
...WHAT DO I DO WITH THIS?
HUH? KO-KUN?
FLINCH

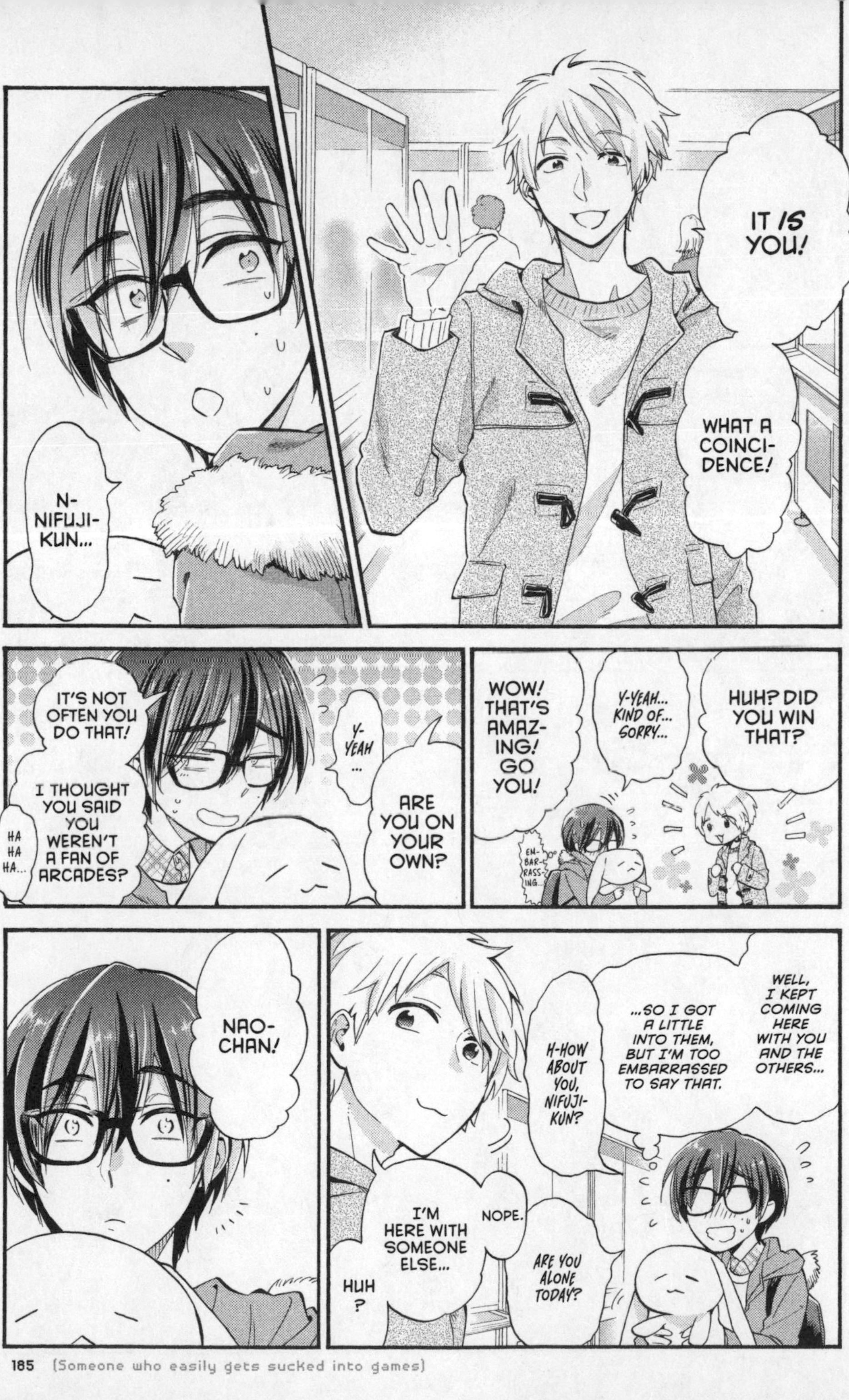
IT IS YOU!
WHAT A COINCIDENCE!
N-NIFUJI-KUN...
HUH? DID YOU WIN THAT?
Y-YEAH... KIND OF... SORRY...
WOW! THAT'S AMAZING! GO YOU!
EM-BAR-RASS-ING...
Y-YEAH...
ARE YOU ON YOUR OWN?
IT'S NOT OFTEN YOU DO THAT!
I THOUGHT YOU SAID YOU WEREN'T A FAN OF ARCADES?
HA HA HA...
WELL, I KEPT COMING HERE WITH YOU AND THE OTHERS...
...SO I GOT A LITTLE INTO THEM, BUT I'M TOO EMBARRASSED TO SAY THAT.
H-HOW ABOUT YOU, NIFUJI-KUN?
ARE YOU ALONE TODAY?
NOPE.
I'M HERE WITH SOMEONE ELSE...
HUH?
NAO-CHAN!

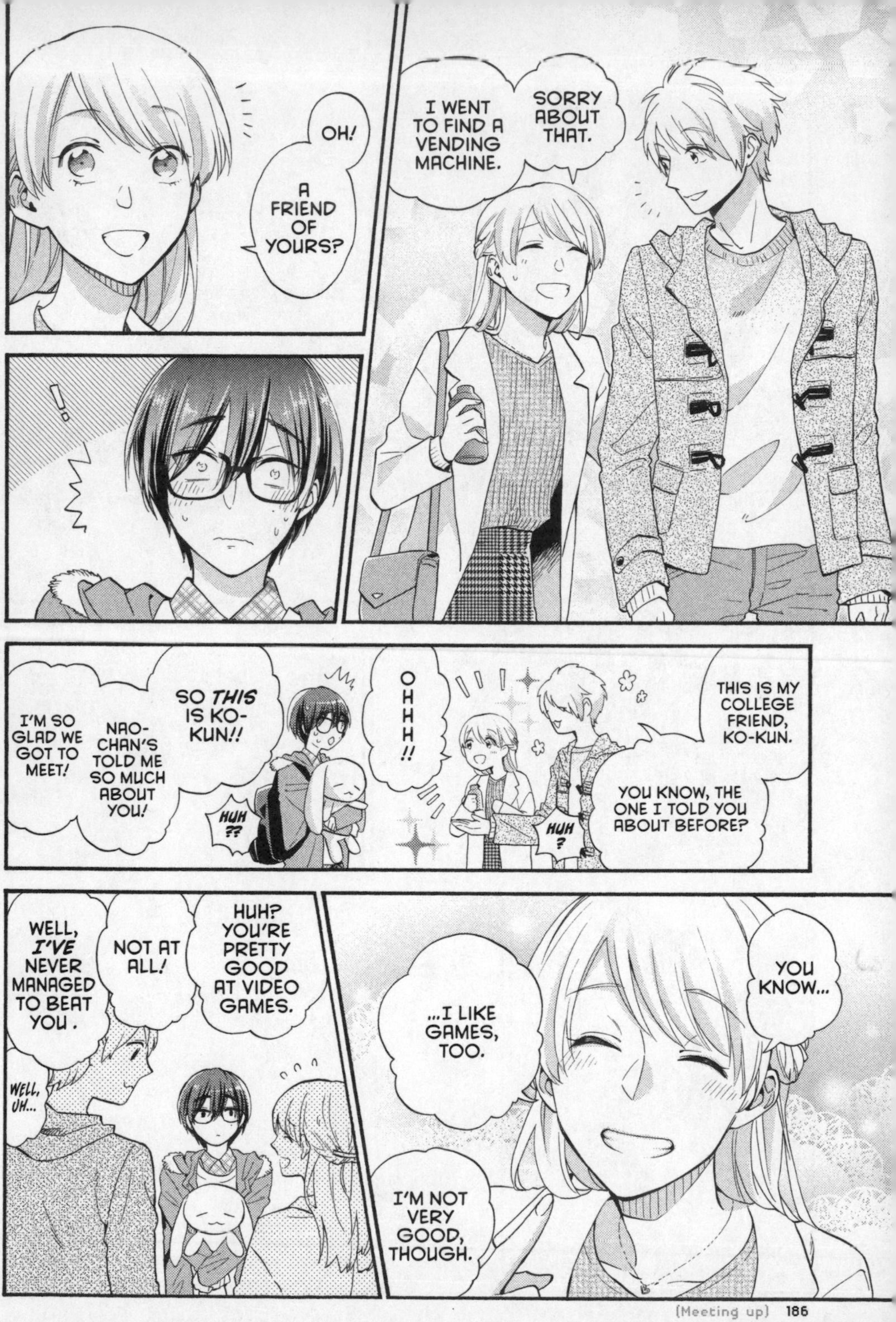
SORRY ABOUT THAT.
I WENT TO FIND A VENDING MACHINE.
OH!
A FRIEND OF YOURS?
!
THIS IS MY COLLEGE FRIEND, KO-KUN.
YOU KNOW, THE ONE I TOLD YOU ABOUT BEFORE?
HUH ?
OHHH!!
SO *THIS* IS KO-KUN!!
NAO-CHAN'S TOLD ME SO MUCH ABOUT YOU!
I'M SO GLAD WE GOT TO MEET!
HUH ??
YOU KNOW...
...I LIKE GAMES, TOO.
I'M NOT VERY GOOD, THOUGH.
HUH? YOU'RE PRETTY GOOD AT VIDEO GAMES.
NOT AT ALL!
WELL, *I'VE* NEVER MANAGED TO BEAT YOU.
WELL, UH...

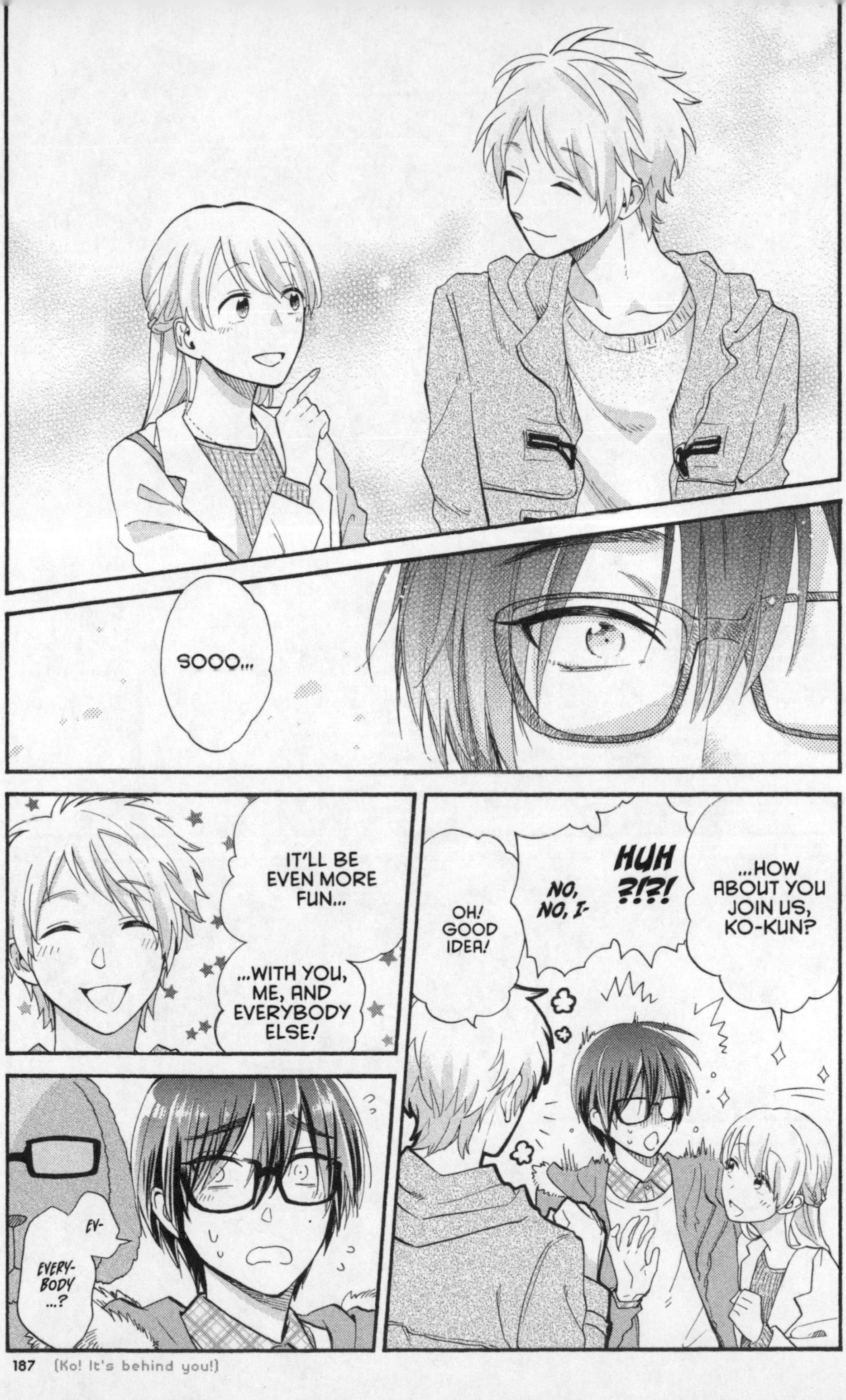
SOOO...
...HOW ABOUT YOU JOIN US, KO-KUN?
HUH ?!?!
NO, NO, I-
OH! GOOD IDEA!
IT'LL BE EVEN MORE FUN...
...WITH YOU, ME, AND EVERYBODY ELSE!
EV-
EVERY-BODY ...?

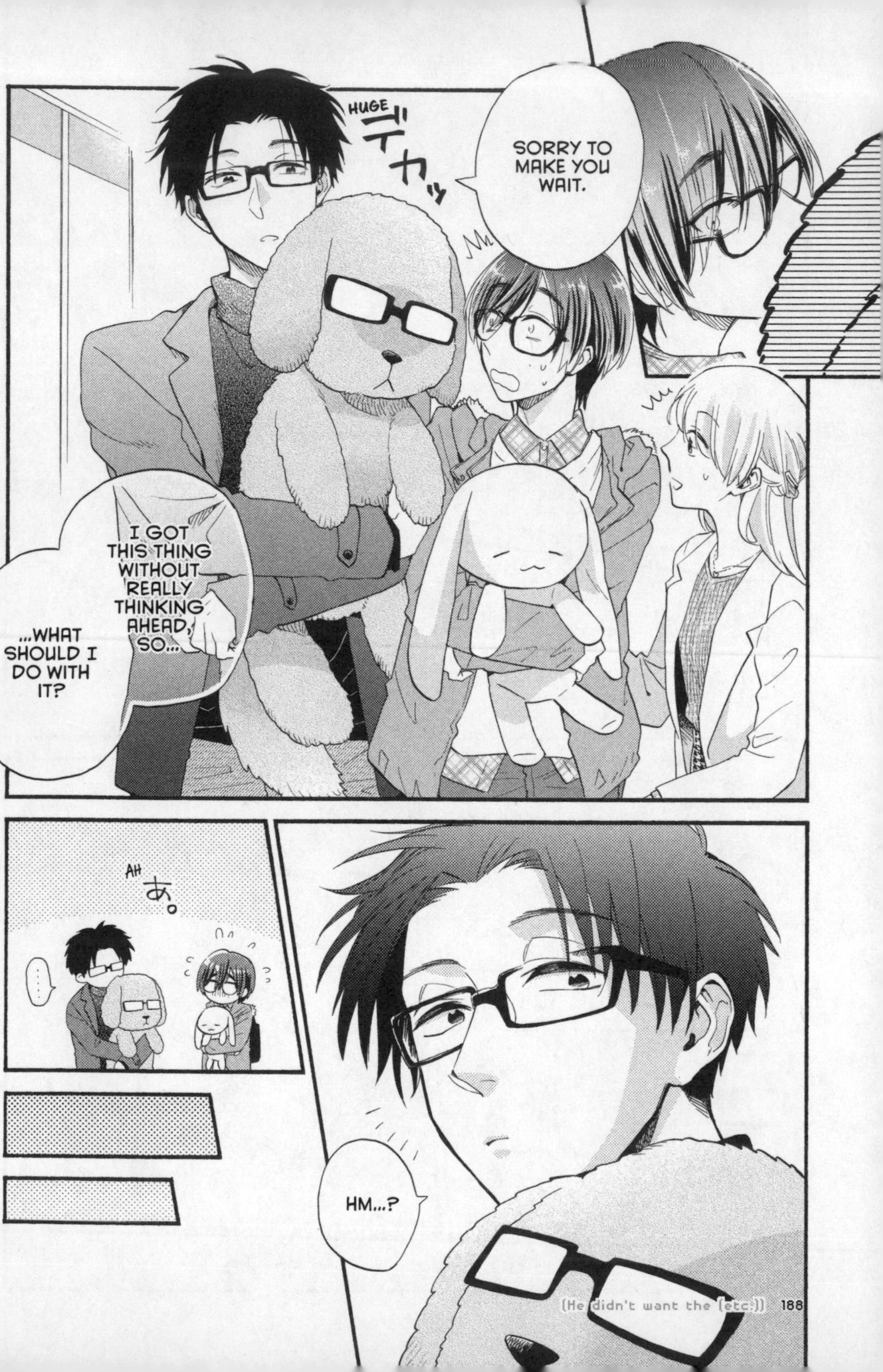
SORRY TO MAKE YOU WAIT.
HUGE
デカッ
I GOT THIS THING WITHOUT REALLY THINKING AHEAD, SO...
...WHAT SHOULD I DO WITH IT?
HM...?
AH
あ。
. . . . .

(He didn't want the [etc.])

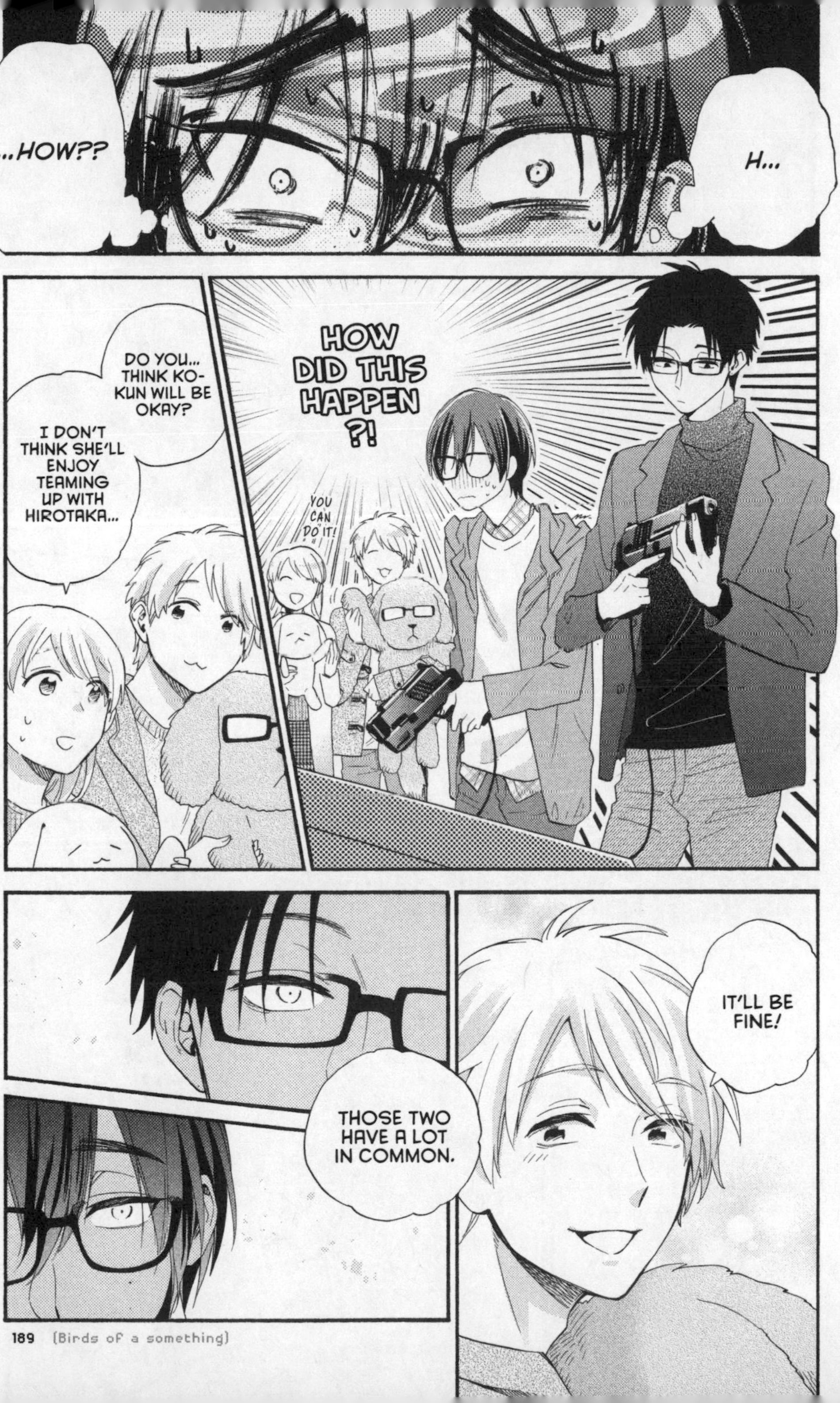
H...
...HOW??
HOW DID THIS HAPPEN?!
YOU CAN DO IT!
DO YOU... THINK KO-KUN WILL BE OKAY?
I DON'T THINK SHE'LL ENJOY TEAMING UP WITH HIROTAKA...
IT'LL BE FINE!
THOSE TWO HAVE A LOT IN COMMON.

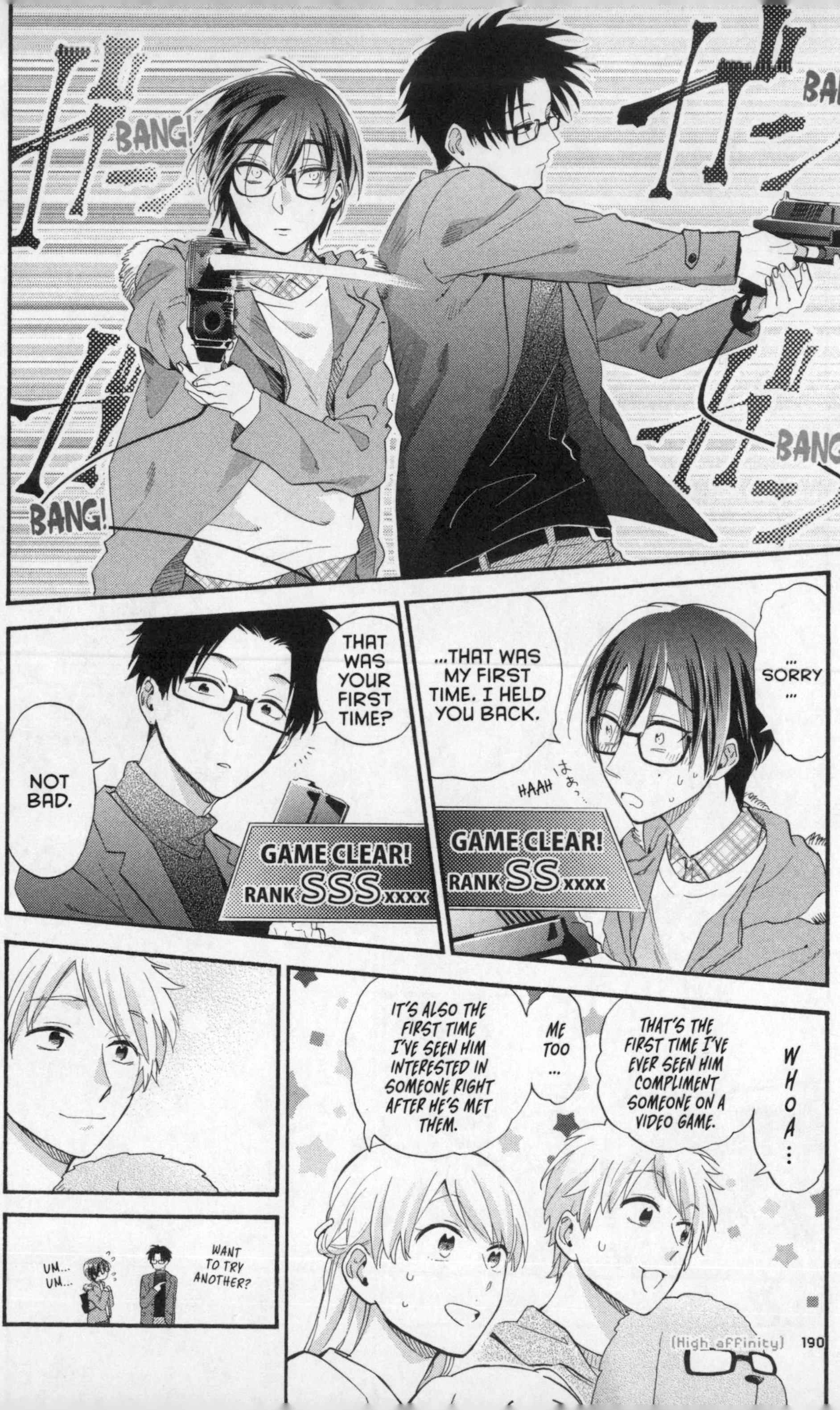
BANG!
BANG!
BANG!
BANG!
... SORRY ...
...THAT WAS MY FIRST TIME. I HELD YOU BACK.
HAAH はぁっ...
GAME CLEAR! RANK SS xxxx
THAT WAS YOUR FIRST TIME?
NOT BAD.
GAME CLEAR! RANK SSS xxxx
WHOA...
THAT'S THE FIRST TIME I'VE EVER SEEN HIM COMPLIMENT SOMEONE ON A VIDEO GAME.
ME TOO ...
IT'S ALSO THE FIRST TIME I'VE SEEN HIM INTERESTED IN SOMEONE RIGHT AFTER HE'S MET THEM.
WANT TO TRY ANOTHER?
UM... UM...
(High affinity)

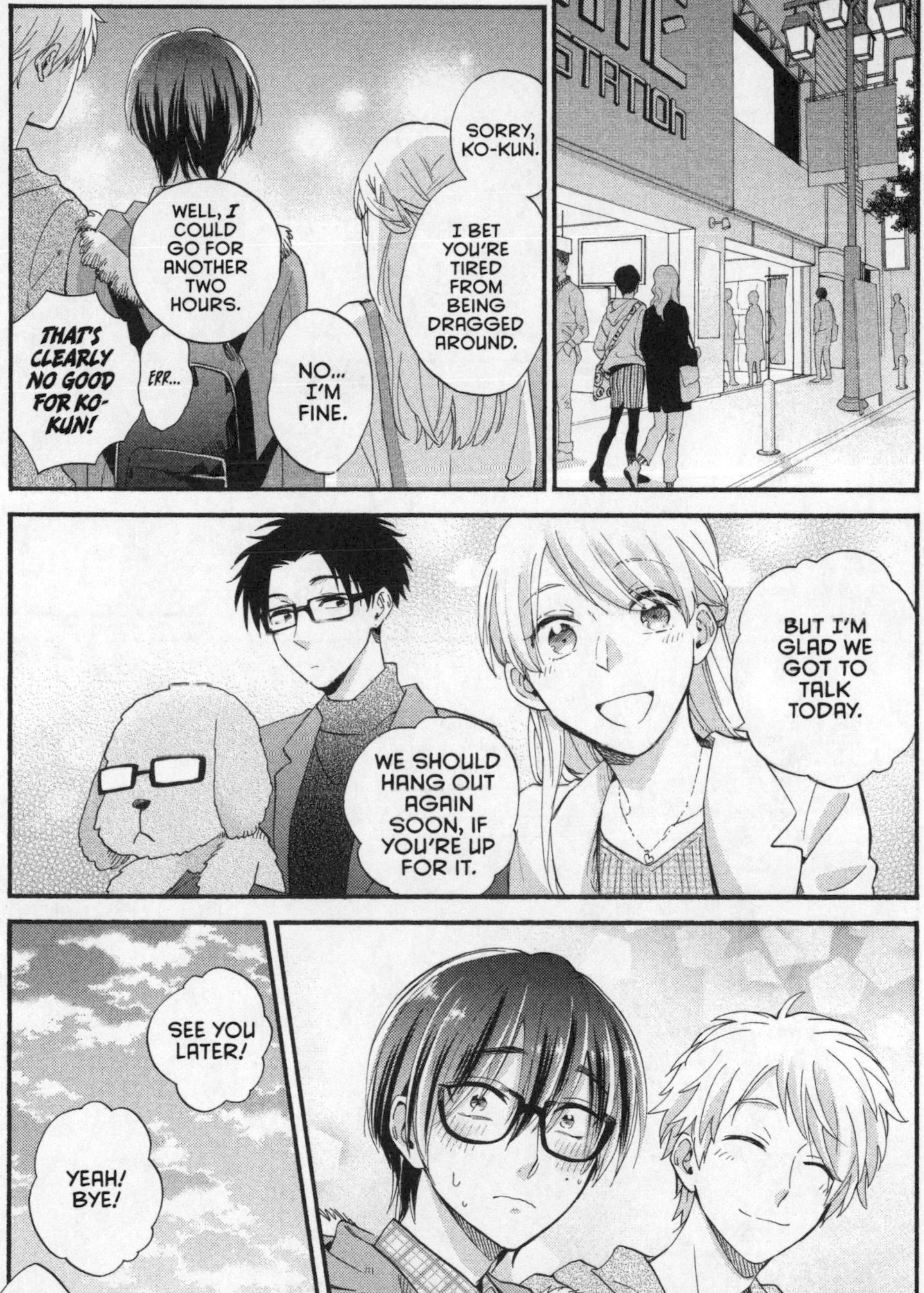
STATION
SORRY, KO-KUN.
I BET YOU'RE TIRED FROM BEING DRAGGED AROUND.
WELL, *I* COULD GO FOR ANOTHER TWO HOURS.
NO... I'M FINE.
ERR...
THAT'S CLEARLY NO GOOD FOR KO-KUN!
BUT I'M GLAD WE GOT TO TALK TODAY.
WE SHOULD HANG OUT AGAIN SOON, IF YOU'RE UP FOR IT.
SEE YOU LATER!
YEAH! BYE!
HUH?

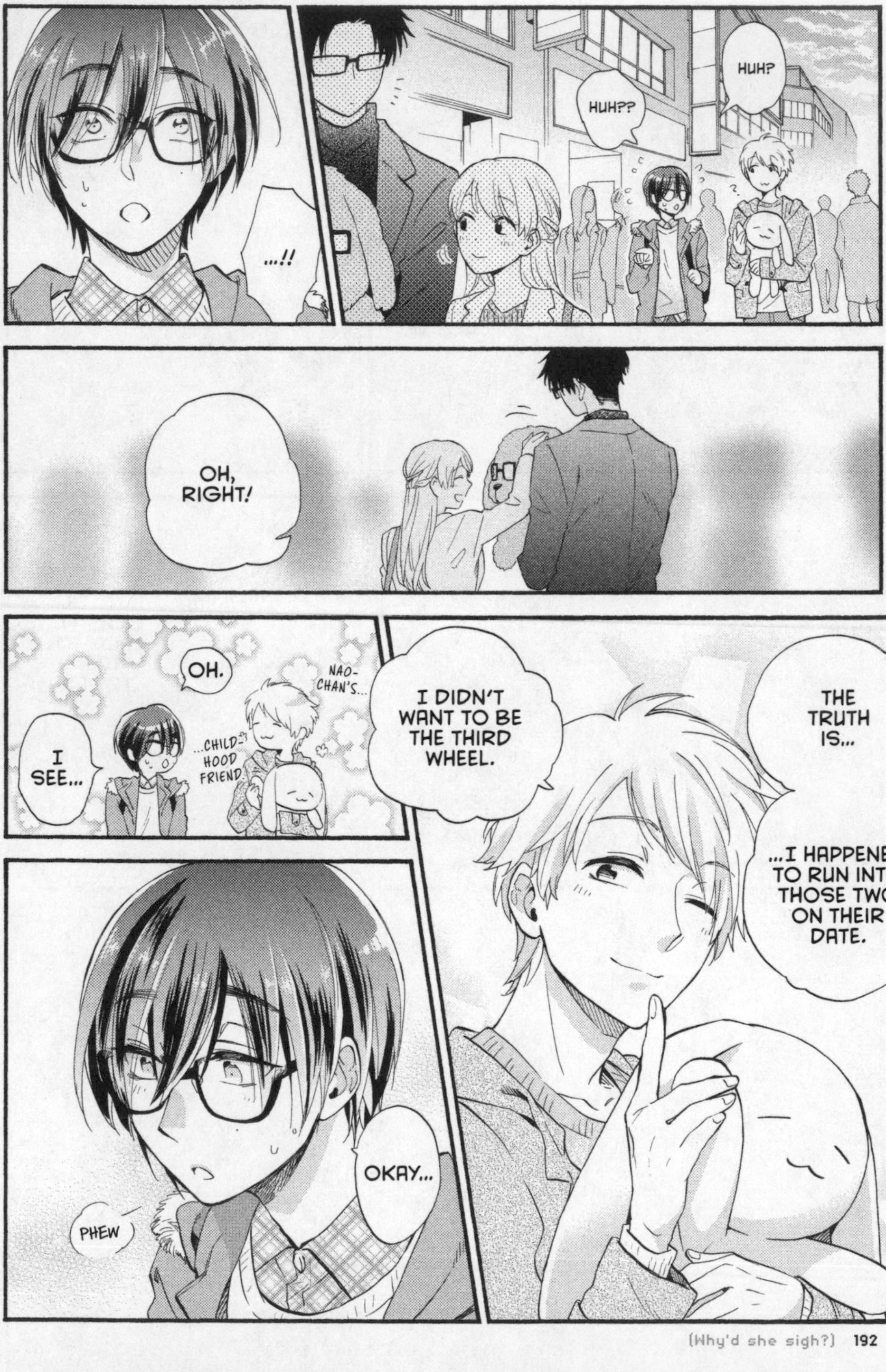
HUH?
HUH??
...!!
OH, RIGHT!
THE TRUTH IS...
...I HAPPENED TO RUN INTO THOSE TWO ON THEIR DATE.
I DIDN'T WANT TO BE THE THIRD WHEEL.
NAO-CHAN'S...
...CHILDHOOD FRIEND
OH.
I SEE...
OKAY...
PHEW

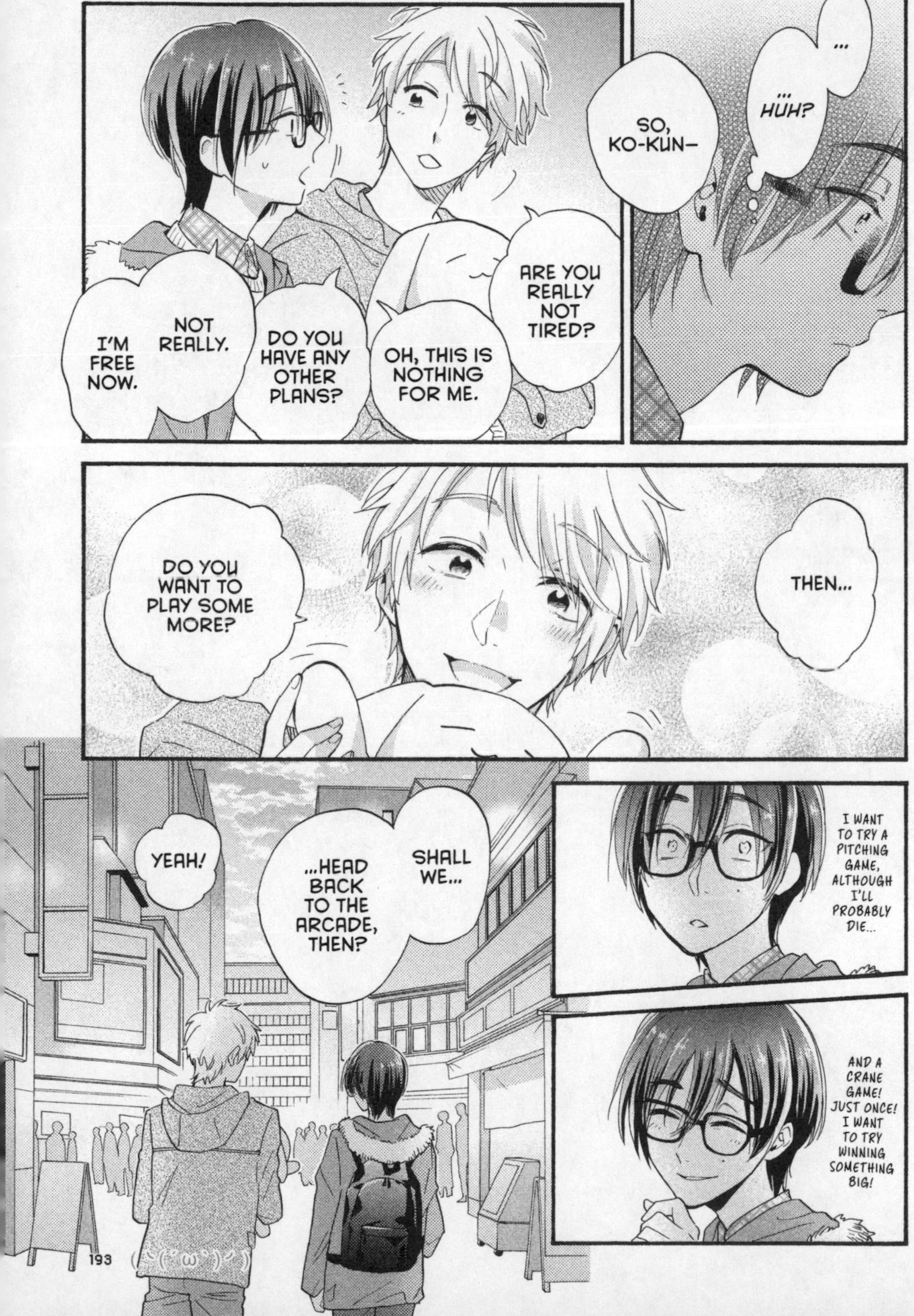
...
...HUH?
SO, KO-KUN–
ARE YOU REALLY NOT TIRED?
OH, THIS IS NOTHING FOR ME.
DO YOU HAVE ANY OTHER PLANS?
NOT REALLY.
I'M FREE NOW.
THEN...
DO YOU WANT TO PLAY SOME MORE?
I WANT TO TRY A PITCHING GAME, ALTHOUGH I'LL PROBABLY DIE...
AND A CRANE GAME! JUST ONCE! I WANT TO TRY WINNING SOMETHING BIG!
SHALL WE...
...HEAD BACK TO THE ARCADE, THEN?
YEAH!

Ko Sakuragi

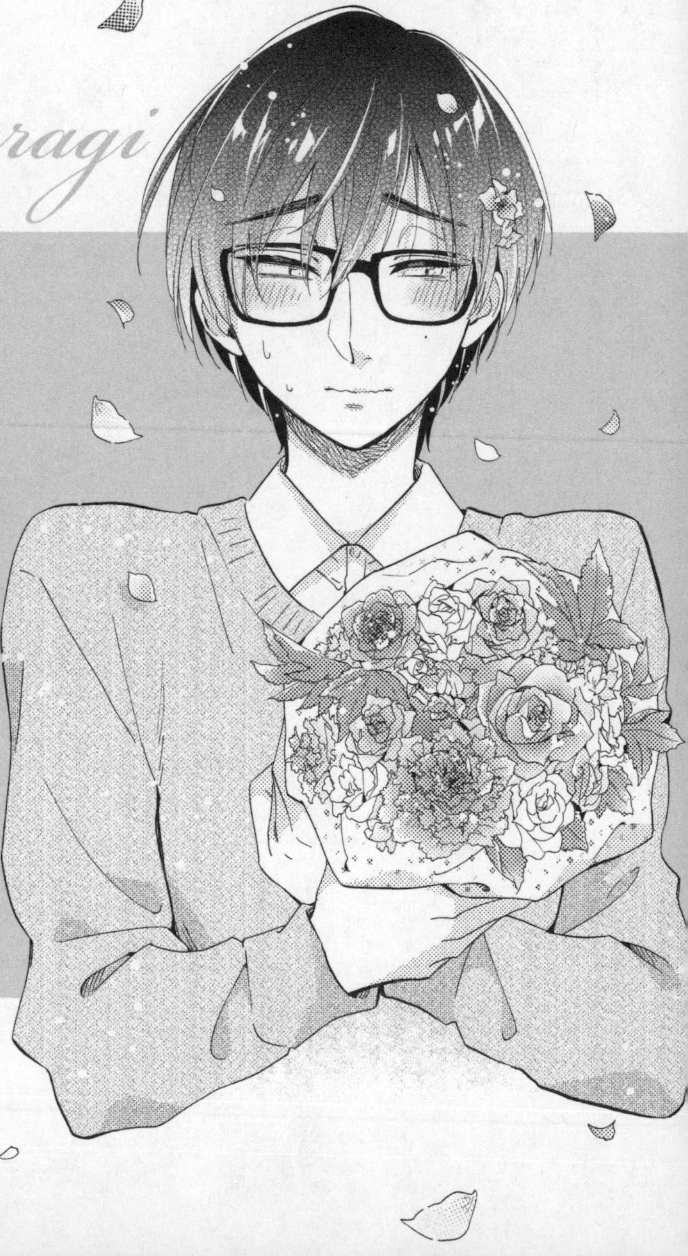

Birthday : Oct.15th

Age : 19

Height : 170cm

Blood type : A

Constellation : Libra

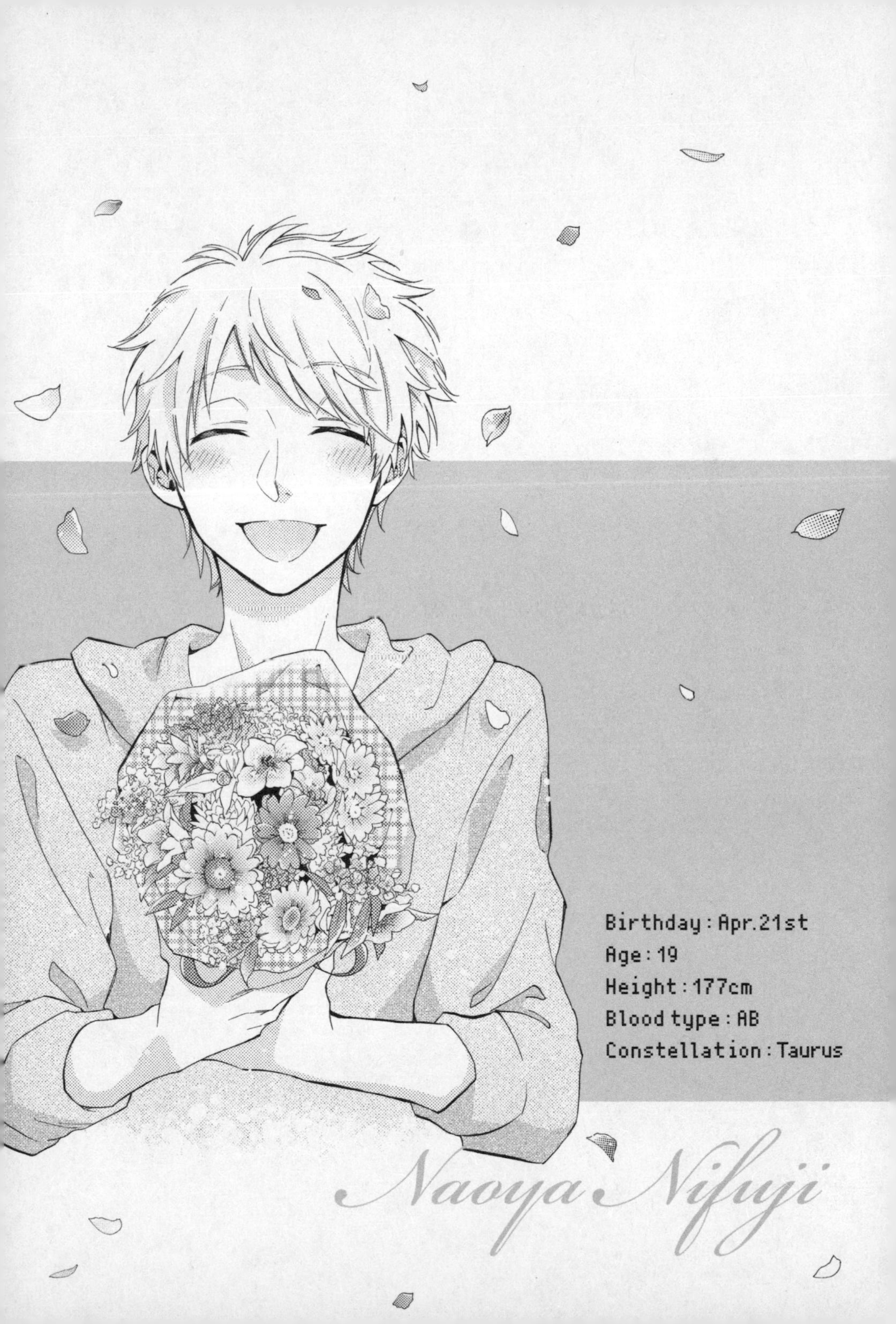
Birthday : Apr.21st
Age : 19
Height : 177cm
Blood type : AB
Constellation : Taurus
Naoya Nifuji

LOVE IS HARD FOR OTAKU

NAOYA

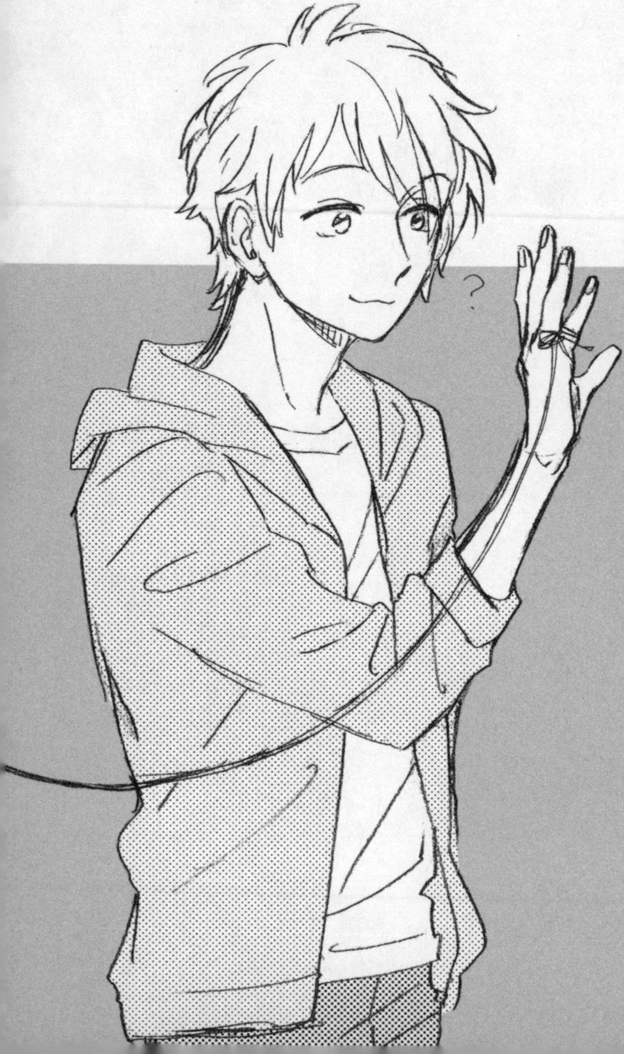

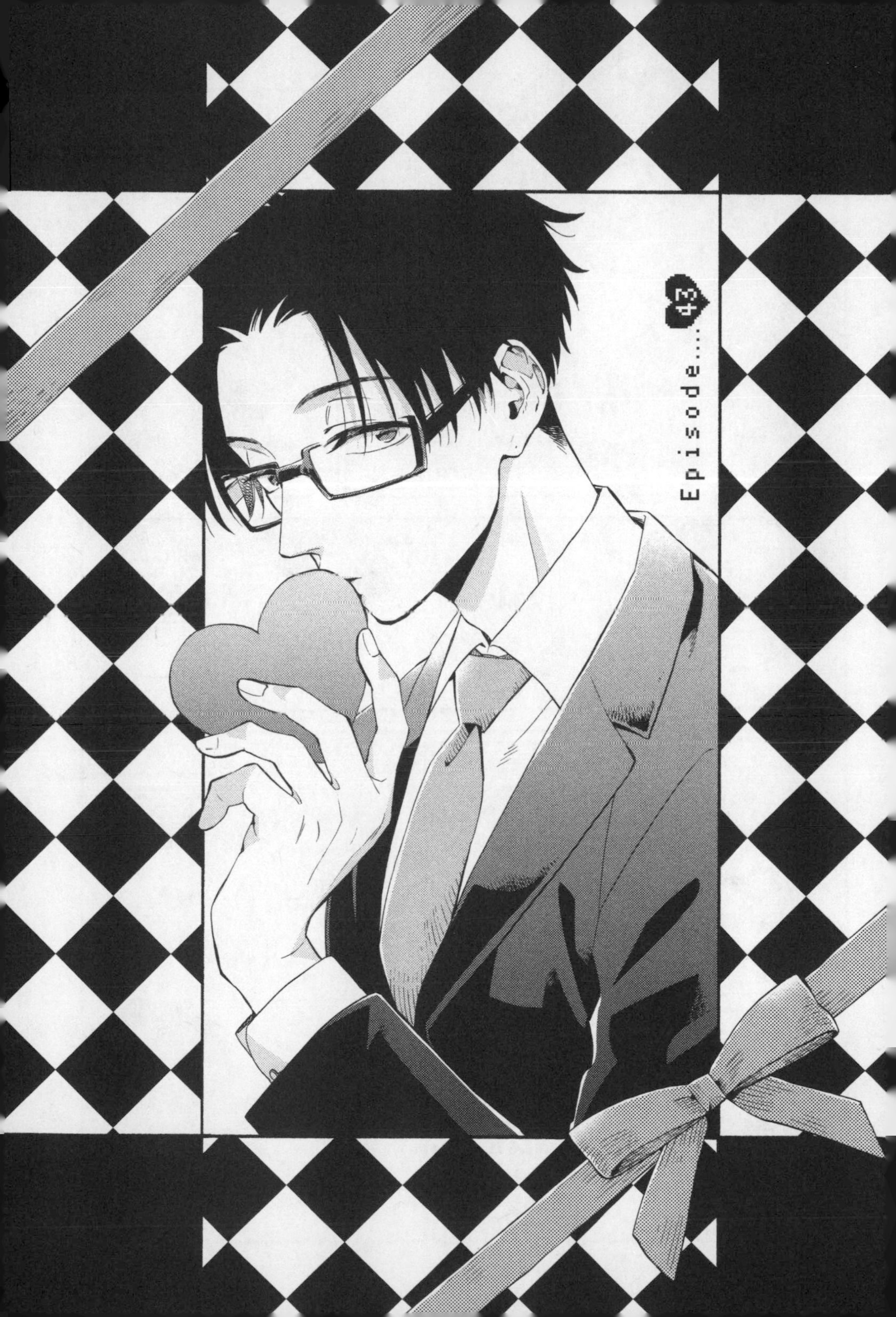
Episode.....43

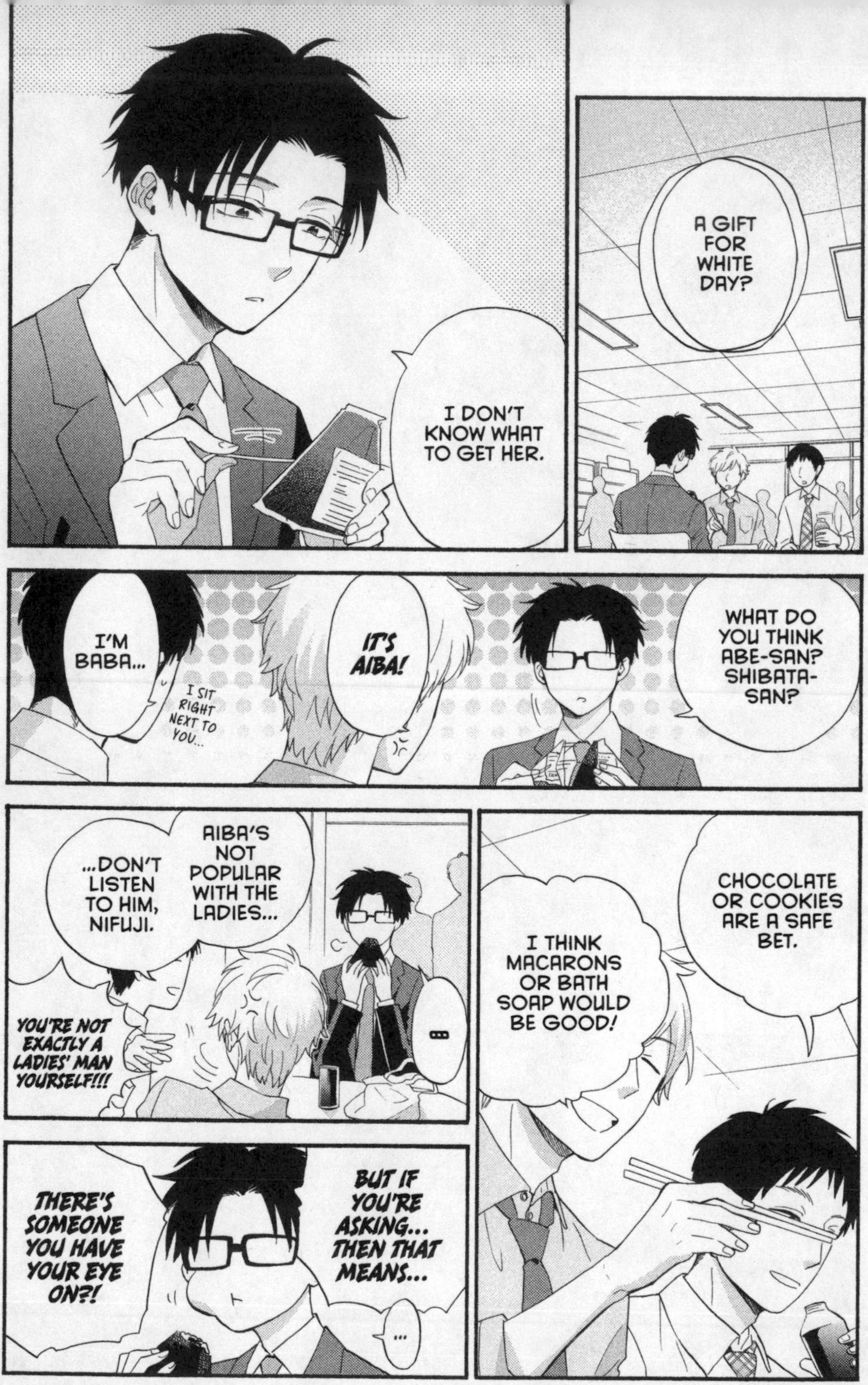
A GIFT FOR WHITE DAY?
I DON'T KNOW WHAT TO GET HER.
WHAT DO YOU THINK ABE-SAN? SHIBATA-SAN?
IT'S AIBA!
I'M BABA...
I SIT RIGHT NEXT TO YOU...
CHOCOLATE OR COOKIES ARE A SAFE BET.
I THINK MACARONS OR BATH SOAP WOULD BE GOOD!
AIBA'S NOT POPULAR WITH THE LADIES...
...DON'T LISTEN TO HIM, NIFUJI.
YOU'RE NOT EXACTLY A LADIES' MAN YOURSELF!!!
...
BUT IF YOU'RE ASKING... THEN THAT MEANS...
THERE'S SOMEONE YOU HAVE YOUR EYE ON?!
...

(He got some of their names right)

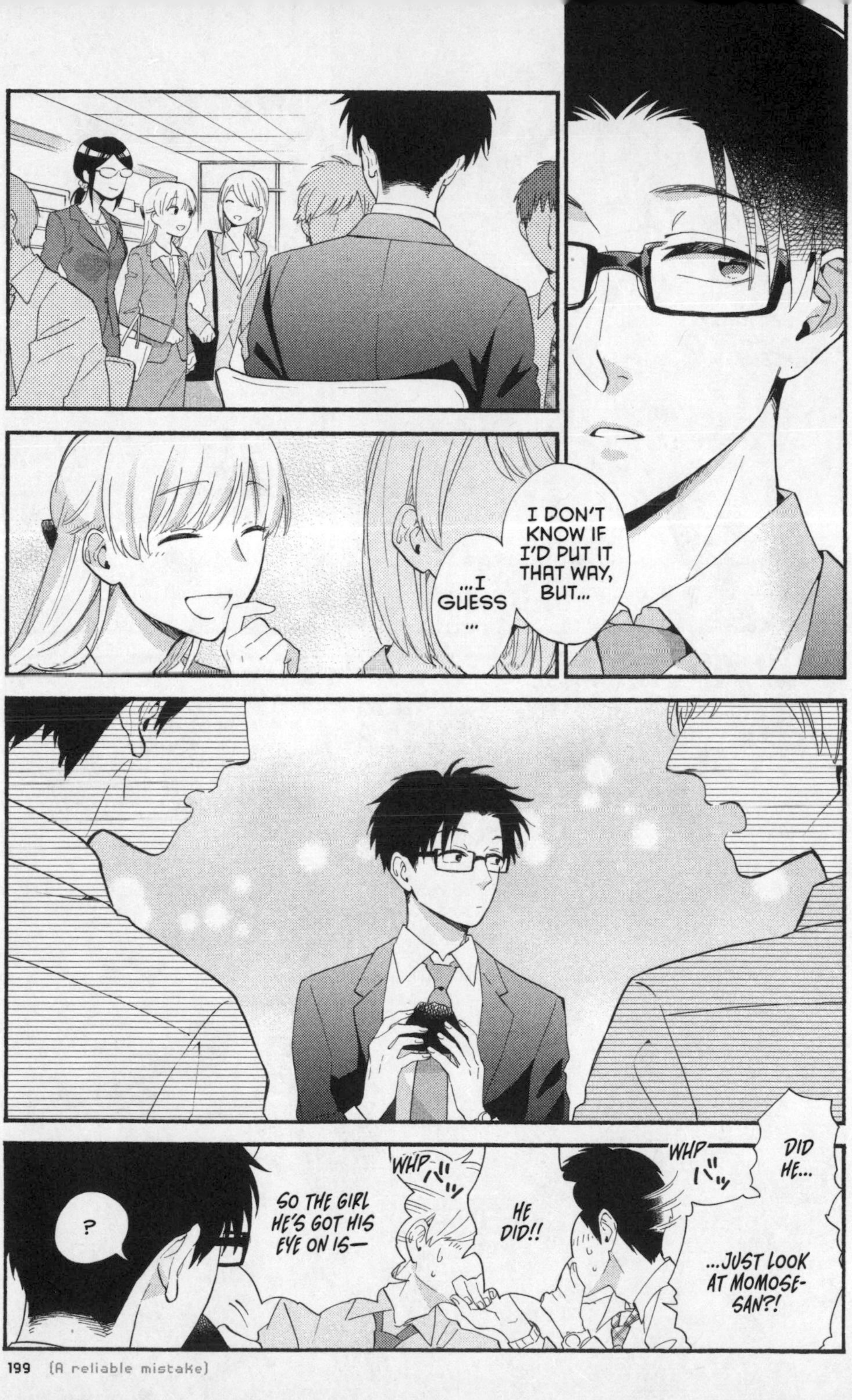
I DON'T KNOW IF I'D PUT IT THAT WAY, BUT...
...I GUESS...
DID HE...
...JUST LOOK AT MOMOSE-SAN?!
WHP バッ
HE DID!!
WHP バッ
SO THE GIRL HE'S GOT HIS EYE ON IS—
?

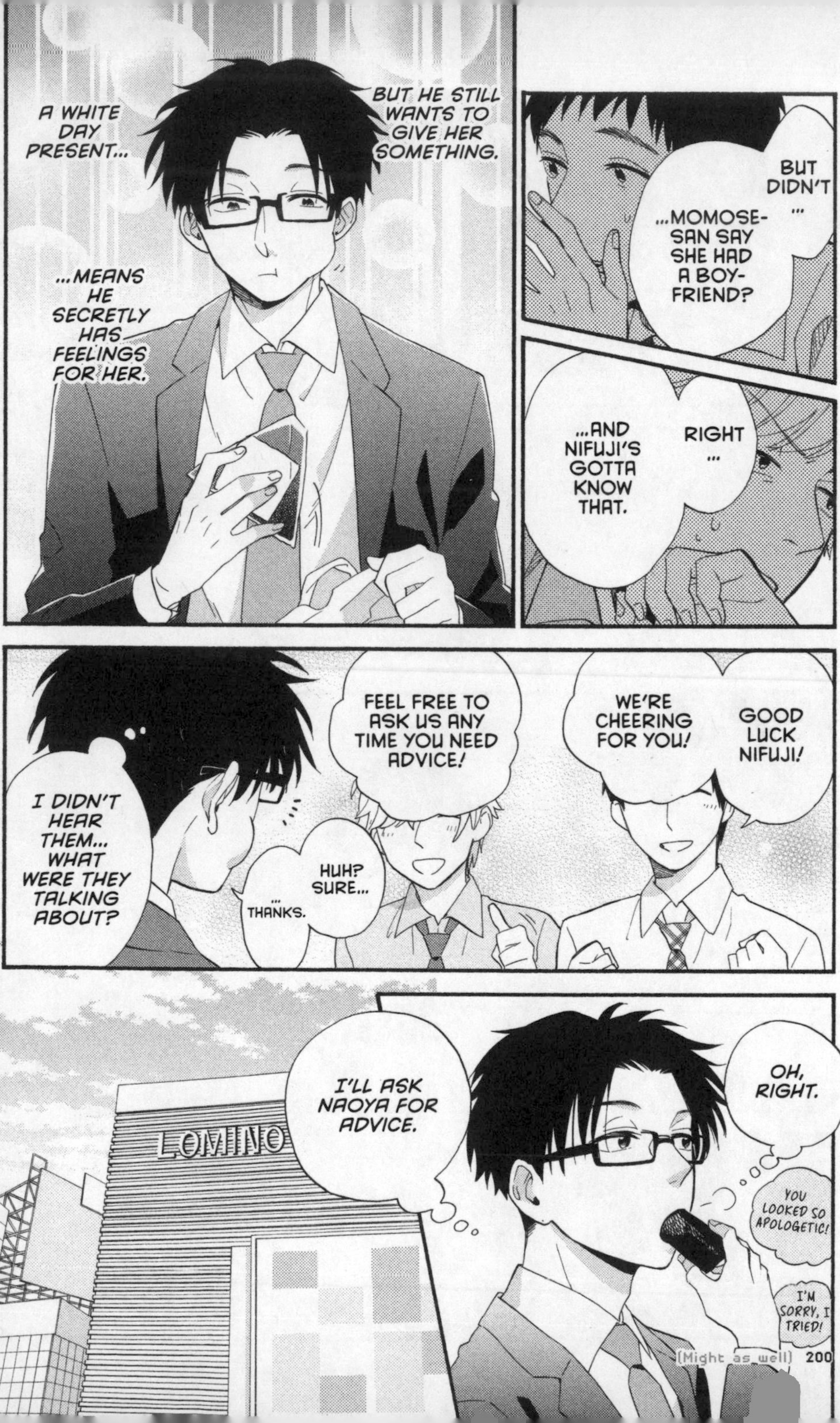
BUT DIDN'T ...
...MOMOSE-SAN SAY SHE HAD A BOY-FRIEND?
RIGHT ...
...AND NIFUJI'S GOTTA KNOW THAT.
A WHITE DAY PRESENT...
...MEANS HE SECRETLY HAS FEELINGS FOR HER.
BUT HE STILL WANTS TO GIVE HER SOMETHING.
GOOD LUCK NIFUJI!
WE'RE CHEERING FOR YOU!
FEEL FREE TO ASK US ANY TIME YOU NEED ADVICE!
HUH? SURE...
... THANKS.
I DIDN'T HEAR THEM... WHAT WERE THEY TALKING ABOUT?
OH, RIGHT.
YOU LOOKED SO APOLOGETIC!
I'M SORRY, I TRIED!
I'LL ASK NAOYA FOR ADVICE.
LOMINO

[Might as well]

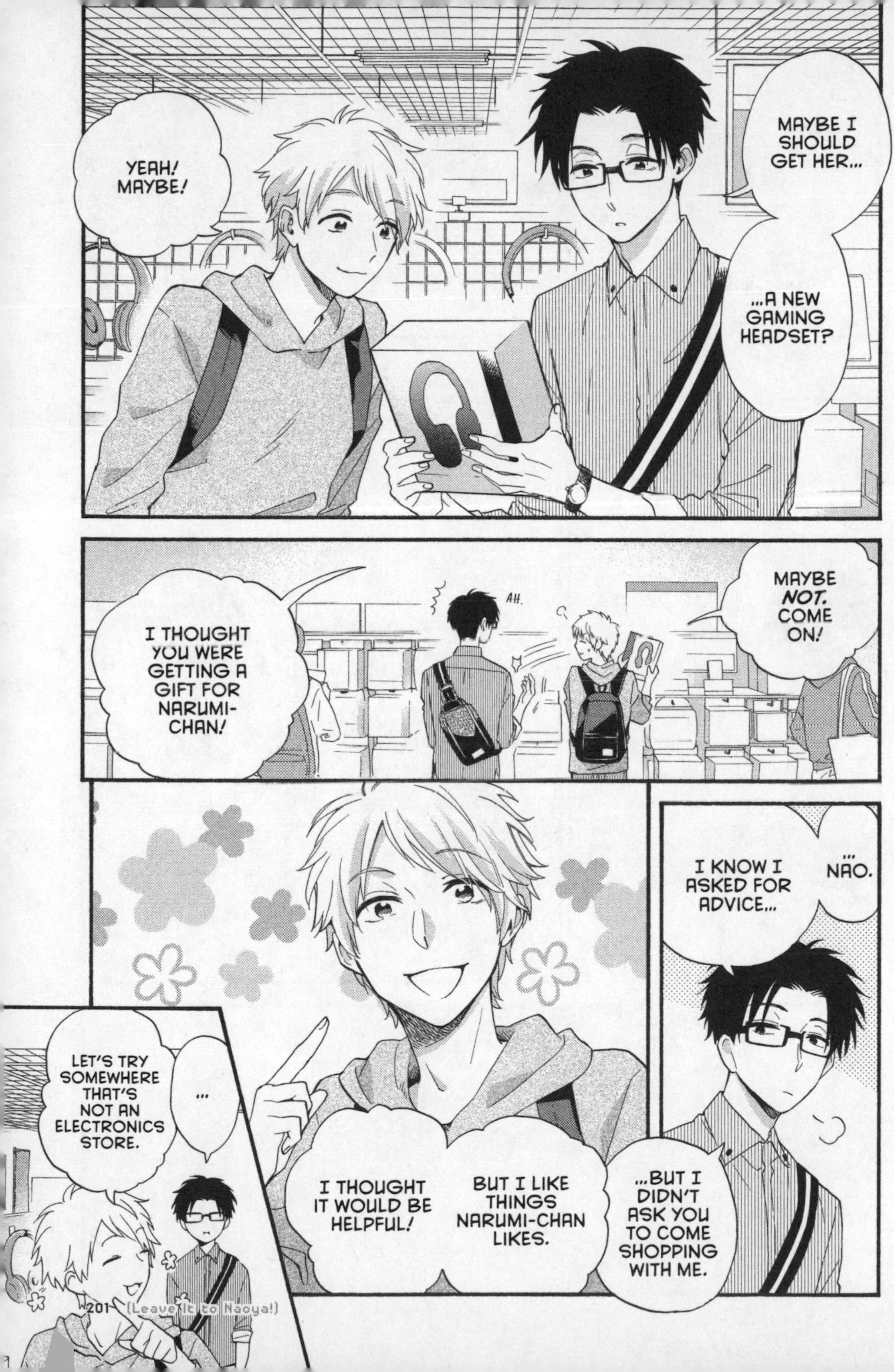
MAYBE I SHOULD GET HER...
...A NEW GAMING HEADSET?
YEAH! MAYBE!
MAYBE *NOT.* COME ON!
AH.
I THOUGHT YOU WERE GETTING A GIFT FOR NARUMI-CHAN!
... NAO.
I KNOW I ASKED FOR ADVICE...
...BUT I DIDN'T ASK YOU TO COME SHOPPING WITH ME.
BUT I LIKE THINGS NARUMI-CHAN LIKES.
I THOUGHT IT WOULD BE HELPFUL!
...
LET'S TRY SOMEWHERE THAT'S NOT AN ELECTRONICS STORE.

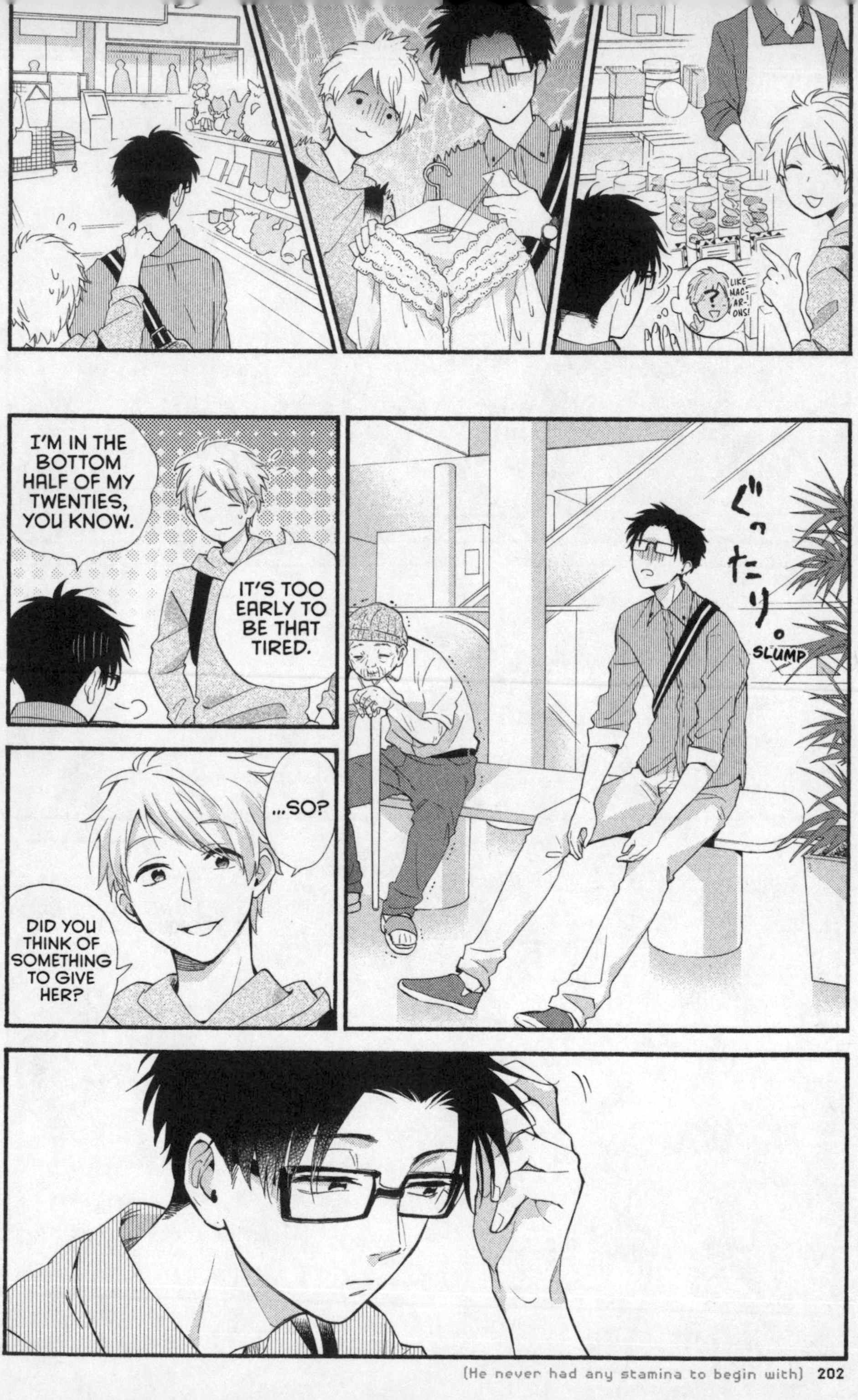
LIKE MAC-AR-ONS!
ぐったり。
SLUMP
I'M IN THE BOTTOM HALF OF MY TWENTIES, YOU KNOW.
IT'S TOO EARLY TO BE THAT TIRED.
...SO?
DID YOU THINK OF SOMETHING TO GIVE HER?

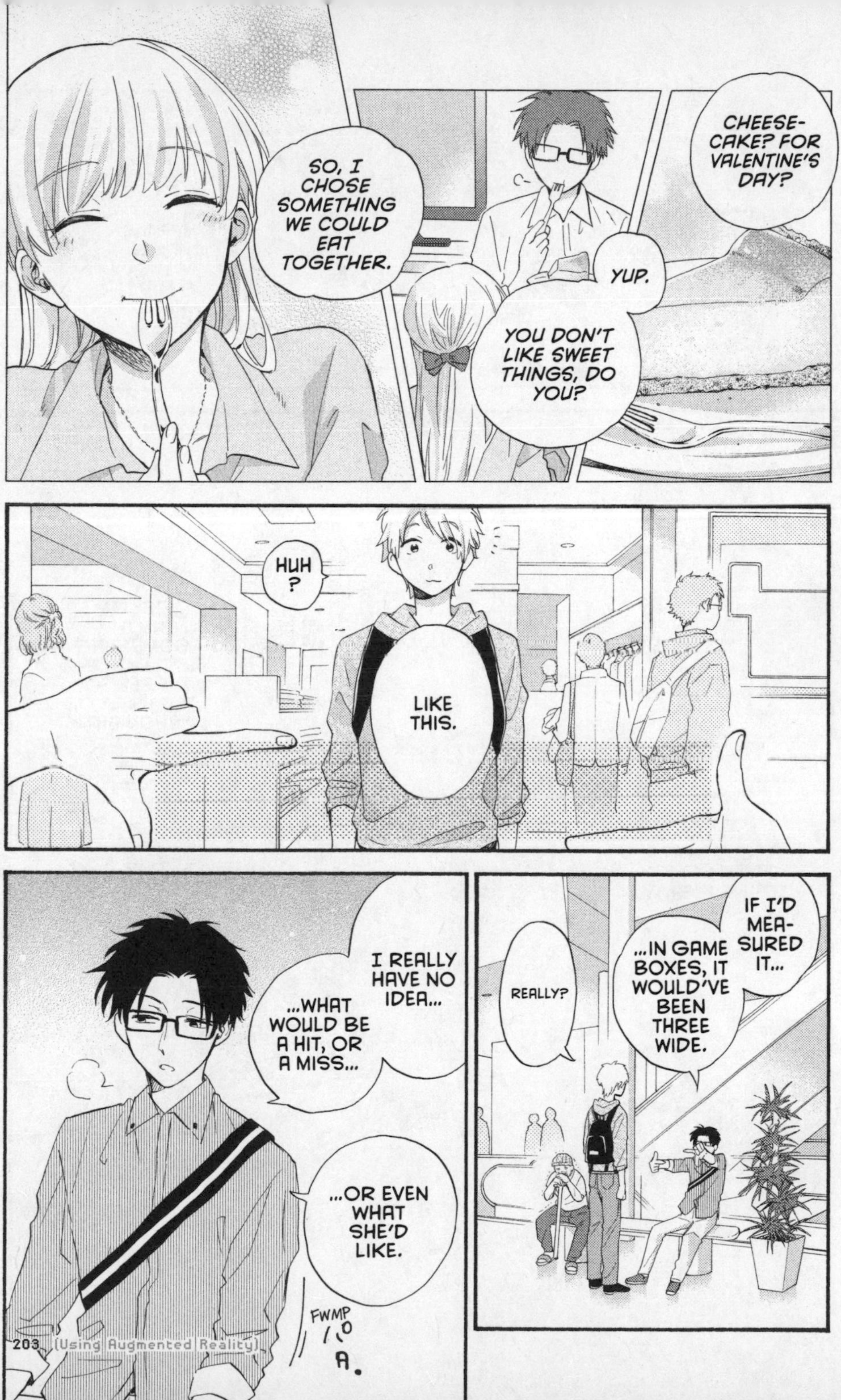
CHEESE-CAKE? FOR VALENTINE'S DAY?
YUP.
YOU DON'T LIKE SWEET THINGS, DO YOU?
SO, I CHOSE SOMETHING WE COULD EAT TOGETHER.
HUH?
LIKE THIS.
IF I'D MEA-SURED IT...
...IN GAME BOXES, IT WOULD'VE BEEN THREE WIDE.
REALLY?
I REALLY HAVE NO IDEA...
...WHAT WOULD BE A HIT, OR A MISS...
...OR EVEN WHAT SHE'D LIKE.
FWMP

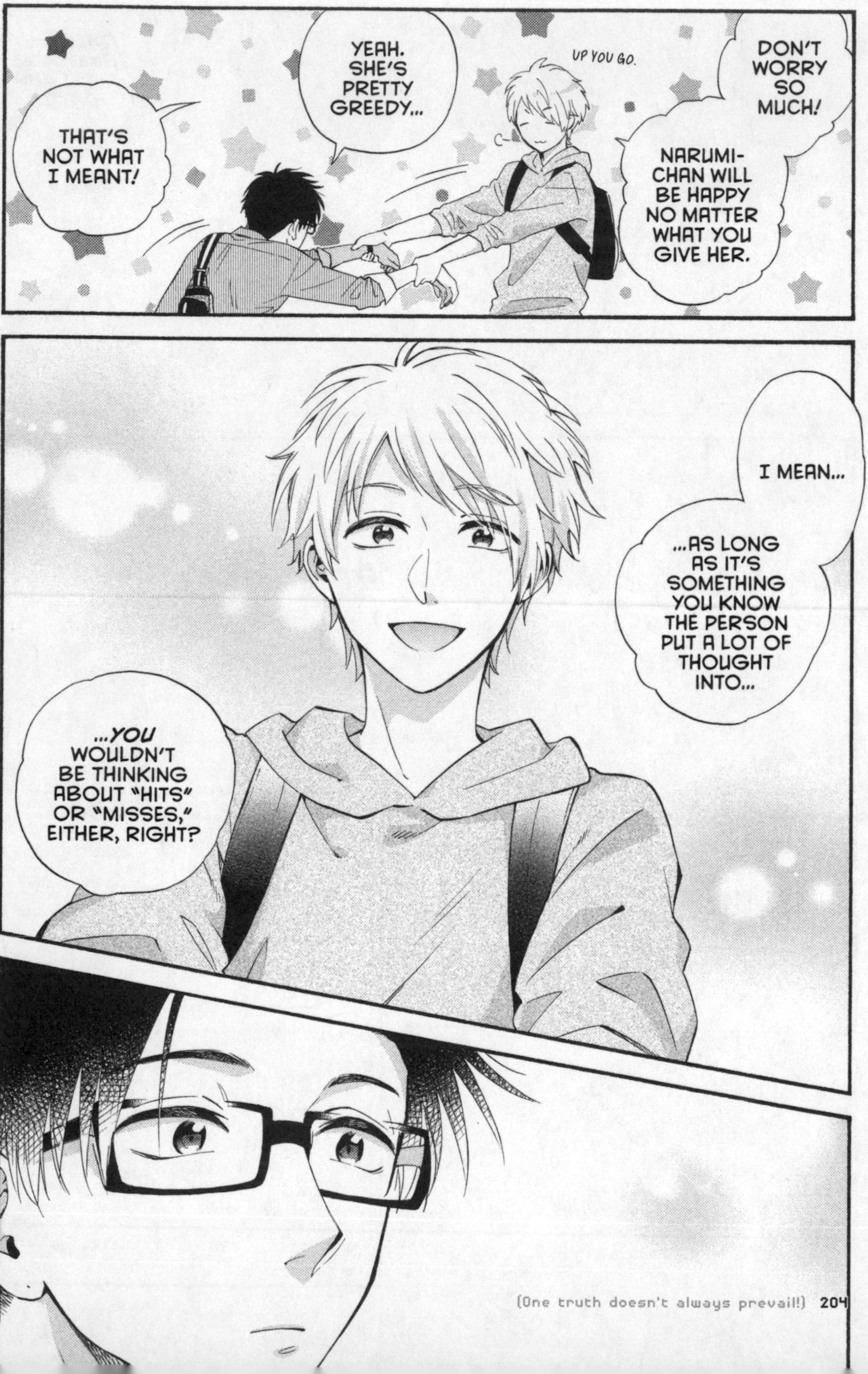
DON'T WORRY SO MUCH!
NARUMI-CHAN WILL BE HAPPY NO MATTER WHAT YOU GIVE HER.
UP YOU GO.
YEAH. SHE'S PRETTY GREEDY...
THAT'S NOT WHAT I MEANT!
I MEAN...
...AS LONG AS IT'S SOMETHING YOU KNOW THE PERSON PUT A LOT OF THOUGHT INTO...
...*YOU* WOULDN'T BE THINKING ABOUT "HITS" OR "MISSES," EITHER, RIGHT?

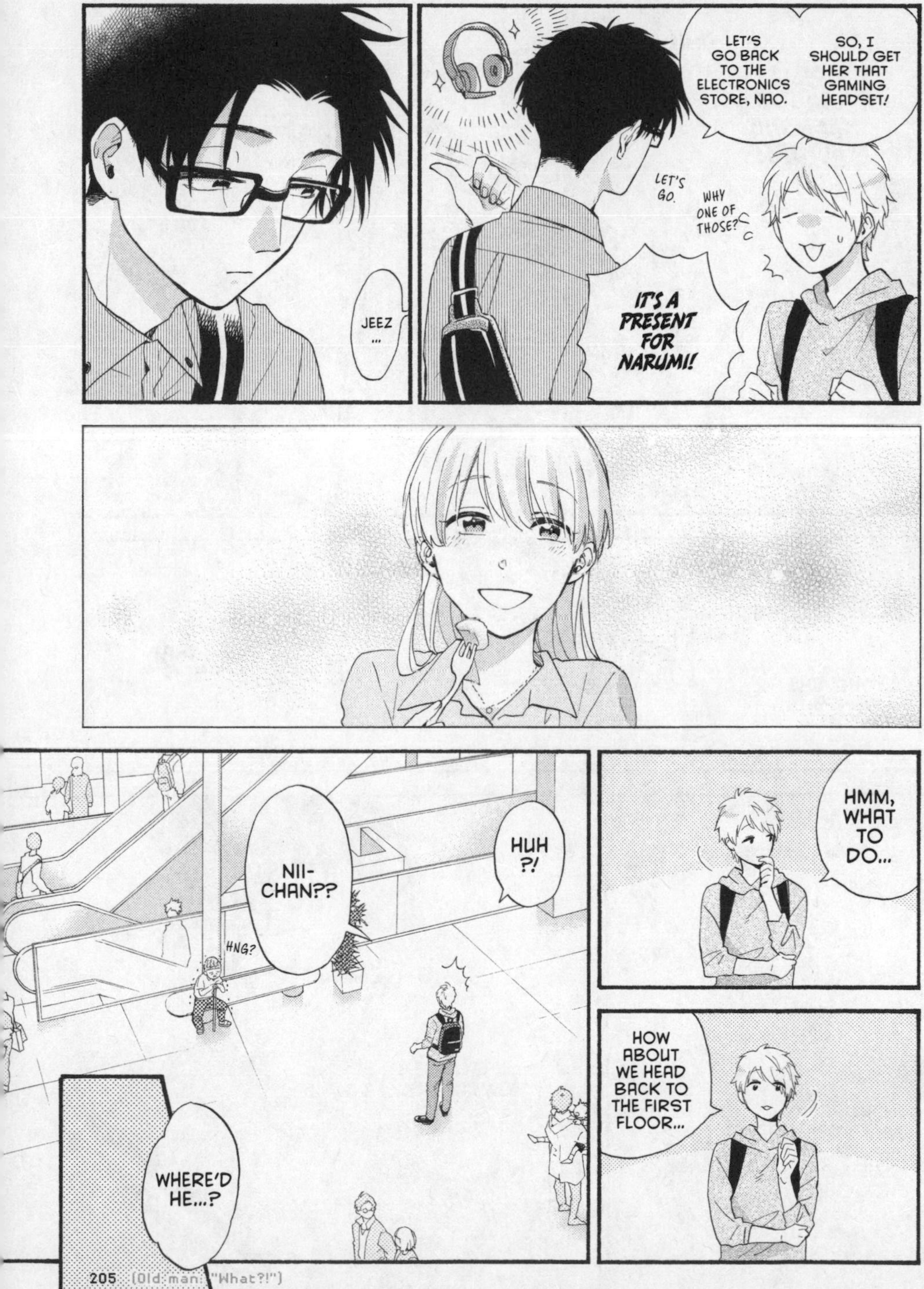
SO, I SHOULD GET HER THAT GAMING HEADSET!
LET'S GO BACK TO THE ELECTRONICS STORE, NAO.
LET'S GO.
WHY ONE OF THOSE?
IT'S A PRESENT FOR NARUMI!
JEEZ ...
HMM, WHAT TO DO...
HOW ABOUT WE HEAD BACK TO THE FIRST FLOOR...
HUH ?!
NII-CHAN??
HNG?
WHERE'D HE...?

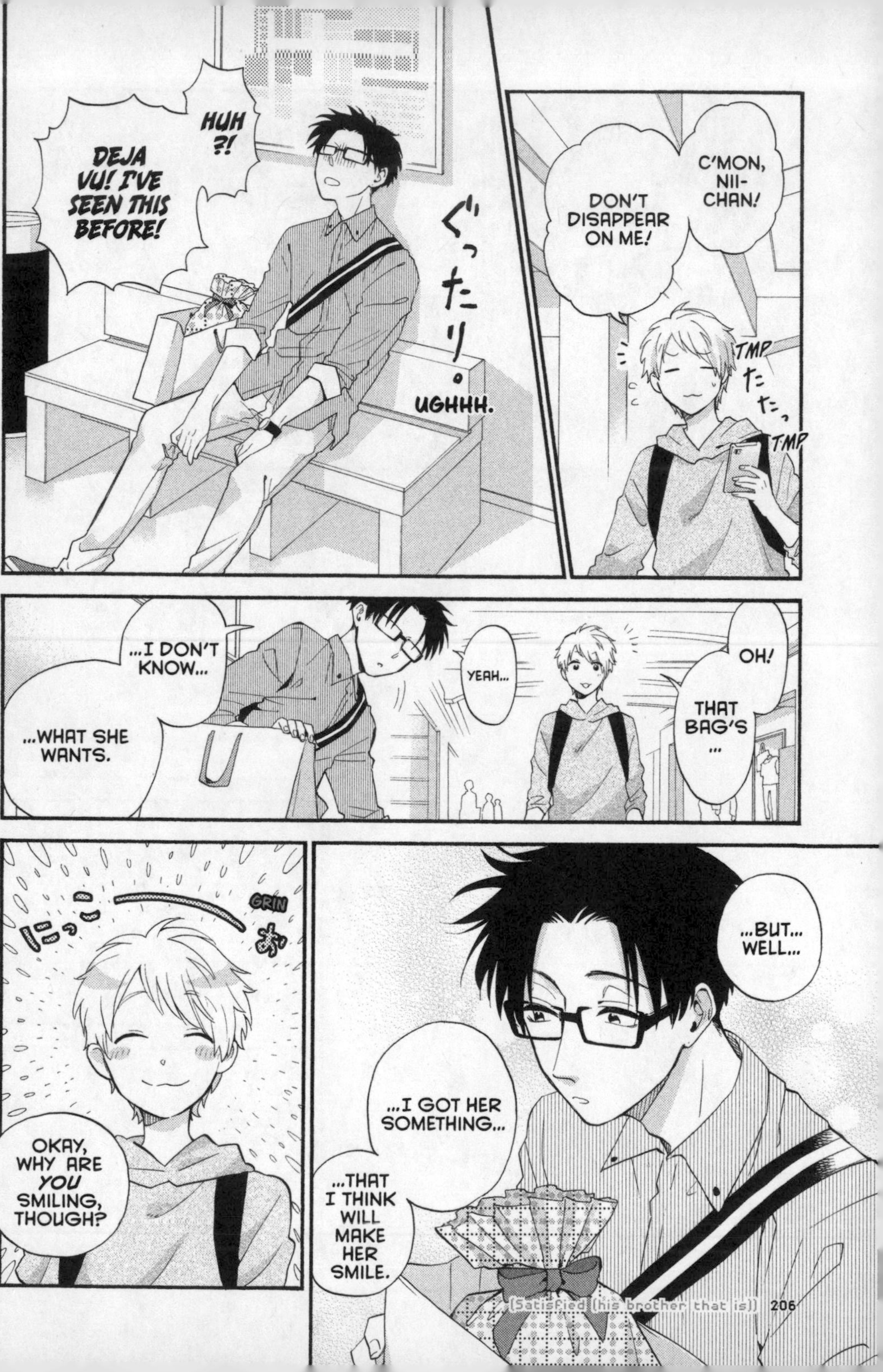
C'MON, NII-CHAN!
DON'T DISAPPEAR ON ME!
TMP
たたっ
TMP
HUH ?!
DEJA VU! I'VE SEEN THIS BEFORE!
ぐったり。
UGHHH.
OH!
THAT BAG'S ...
YEAH...
...I DON'T KNOW...
...WHAT SHE WANTS.
...BUT... WELL...
...I GOT HER SOMETHING...
...THAT I THINK WILL MAKE HER SMILE.
GRIN
にっこー
OKAY, WHY ARE *YOU* SMILING, THOUGH?
(Satisfied (his brother that is))

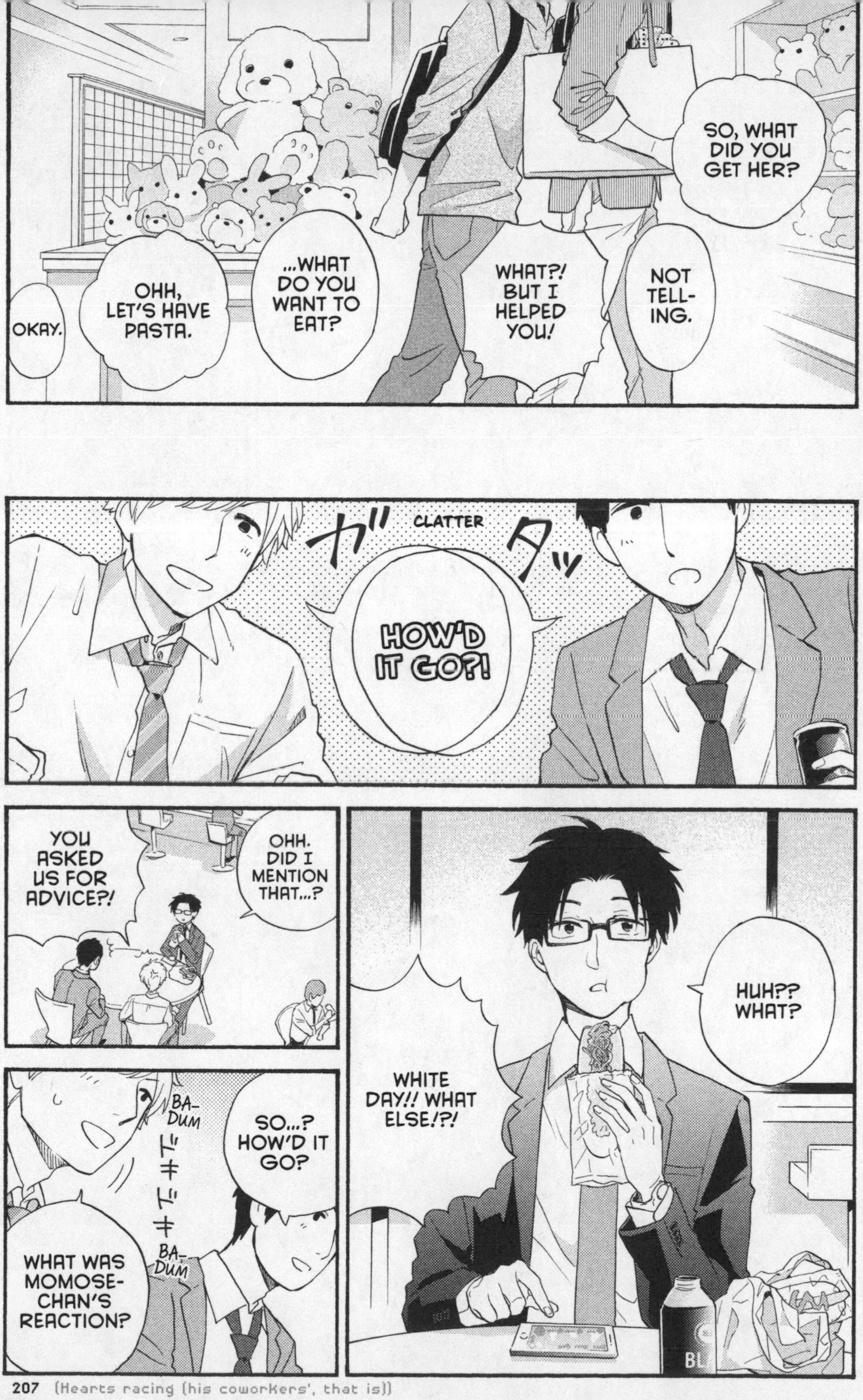
SO, WHAT DID YOU GET HER?
NOT TELLING.
WHAT?! BUT I HELPED YOU!
...WHAT DO YOU WANT TO EAT?
OHH, LET'S HAVE PASTA.
OKAY.
CLATTER
HOW'D IT GO?!
HUH?? WHAT?
WHITE DAY!! WHAT ELSE!?!
OHH. DID I MENTION THAT...?
YOU ASKED US FOR ADVICE?!
SO...? HOW'D IT GO?
BA-DUM
BA-DUM
WHAT WAS MOMOSE-CHAN'S REACTION?

 (Hearts racing (his coworkers', that is))

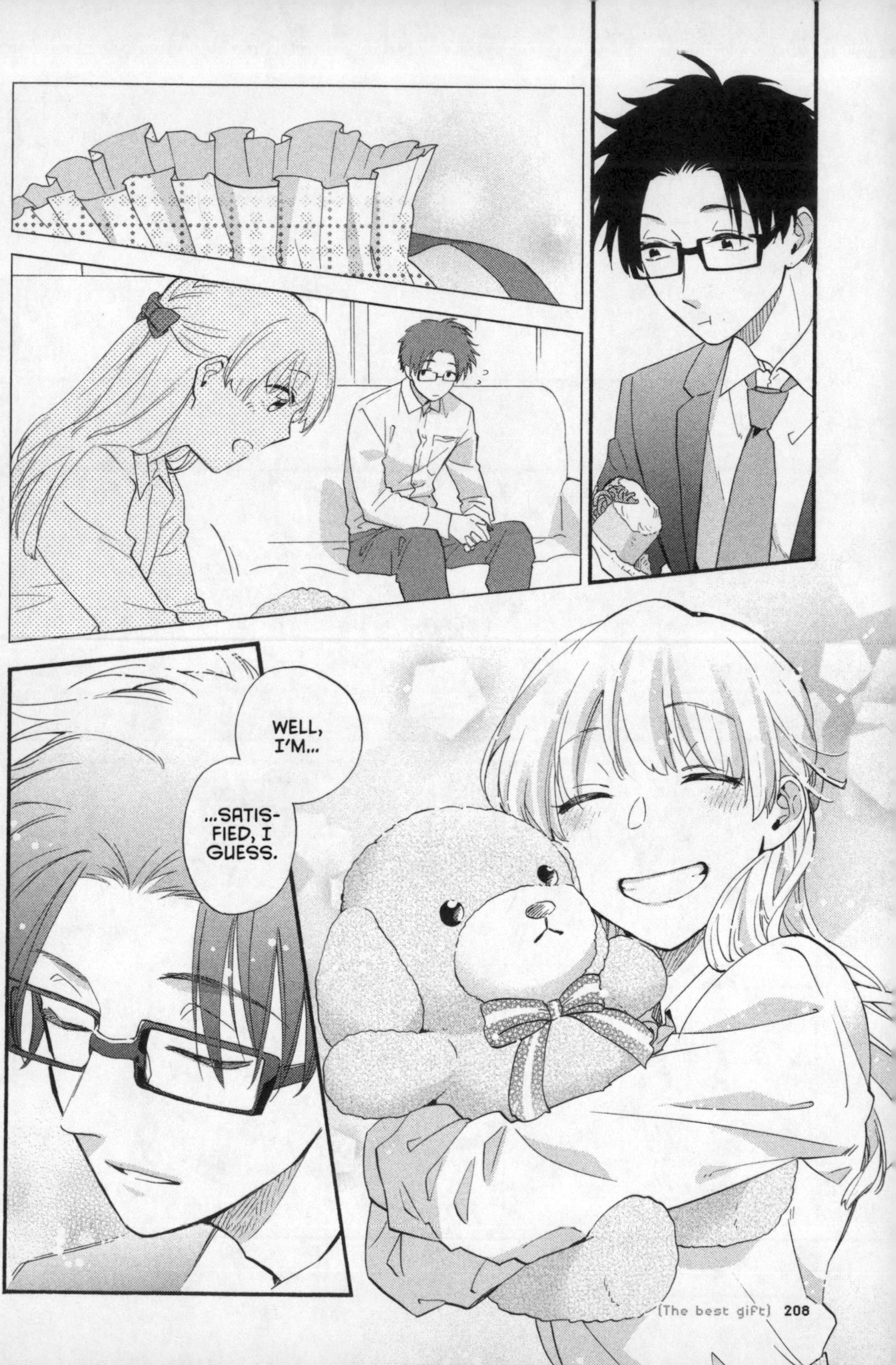
WELL, I'M...
...SATIS-FIED, I GUESS.

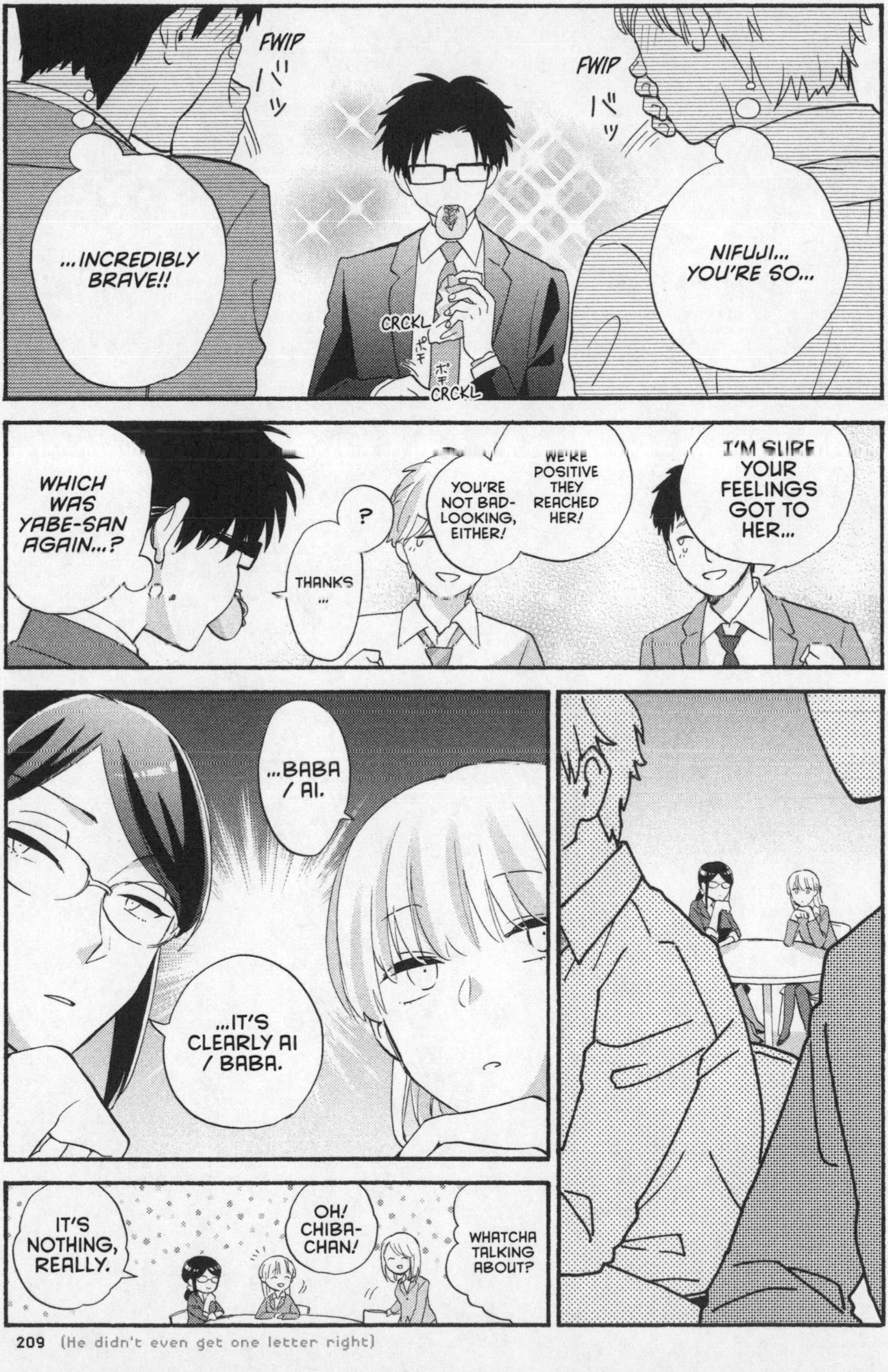
FWIP
バッ
FWIP
バッ
NIFUJI... YOU'RE SO...
...INCREDIBLY BRAVE!!
CRCKL
ポキ
ポキ
CRCKL
I'M SURE YOUR FEELINGS GOT TO HER...
WE'RE POSITIVE THEY REACHED HER!
YOU'RE NOT BAD-LOOKING, EITHER!
?
THANKS...
WHICH WAS YABE-SAN AGAIN...?
...BABA / AI.
...IT'S CLEARLY AI / BABA.
WHATCHA TALKING ABOUT?
OH! CHIBA-CHAN!
IT'S NOTHING, REALLY.

LOVE IS HARD FOR OTAKU

▶CONTINUE

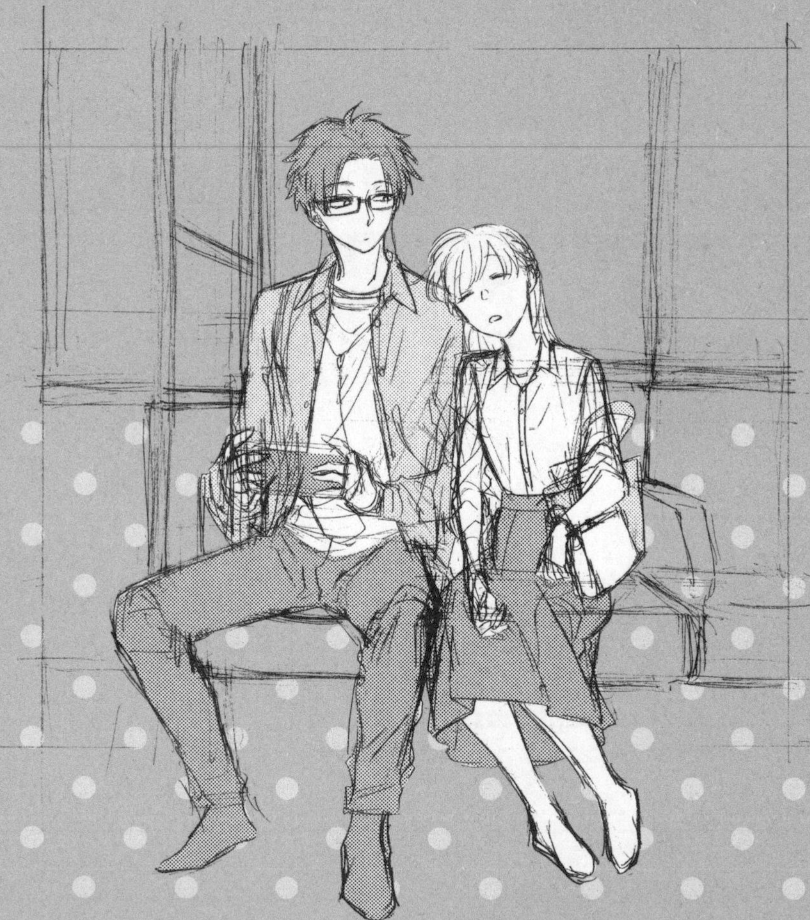

(σ´・ω・)

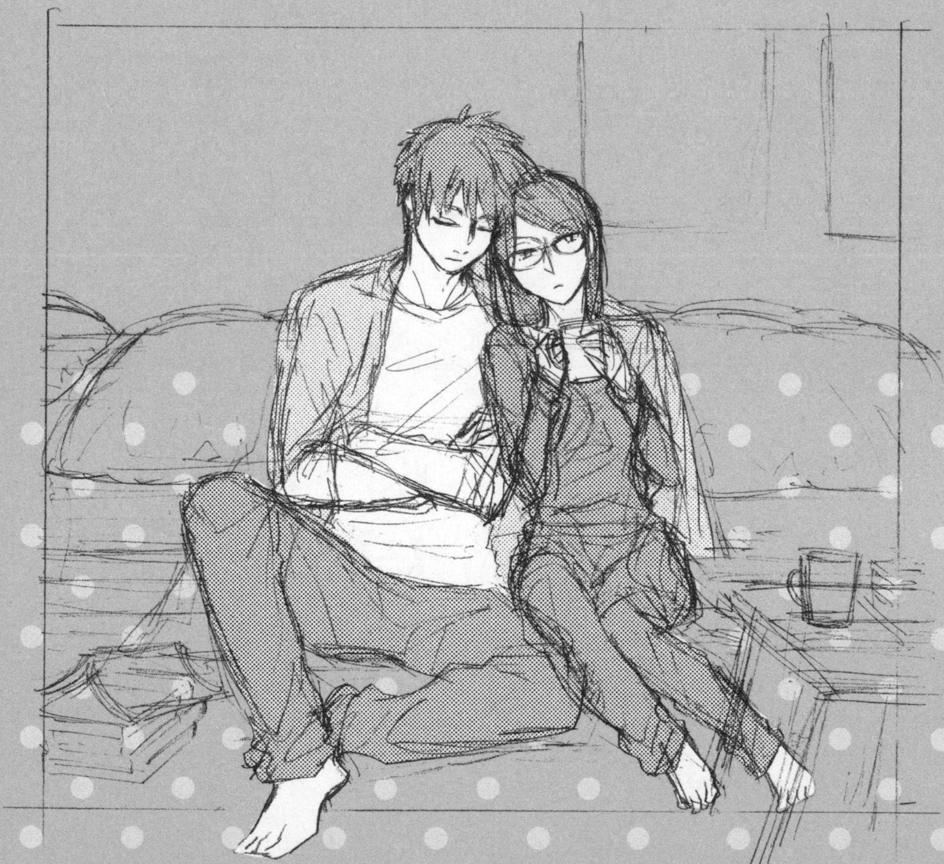

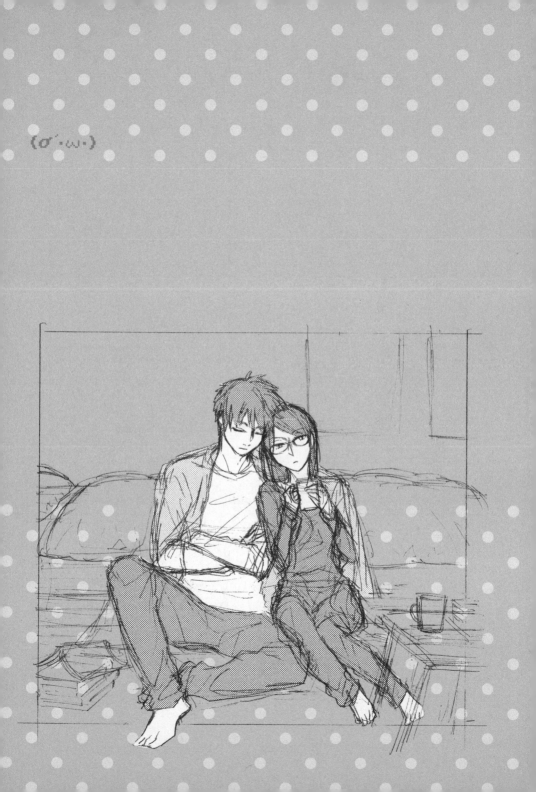

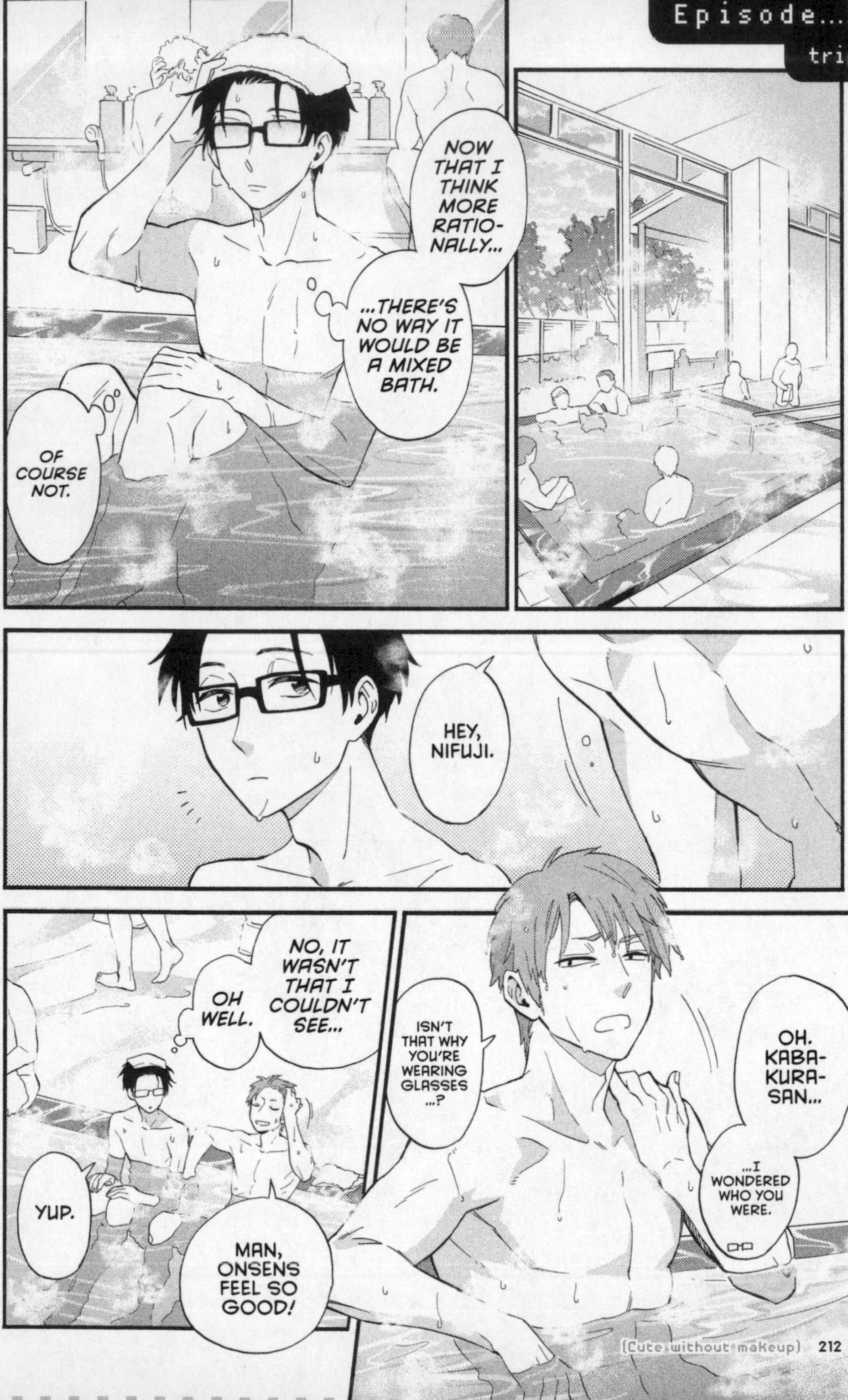
NOW THAT I THINK MORE RATIONALLY...
...THERE'S NO WAY IT WOULD BE A MIXED BATH.
OF COURSE NOT.
HEY, NIFUJI.
OH. KABAKURA-SAN...
...I WONDERED WHO YOU WERE.
ISN'T THAT WHY YOU'RE WEARING GLASSES...?
NO, IT WASN'T THAT I COULDN'T SEE...
OH WELL.
MAN, ONSENS FEEL SO GOOD!
YUP.

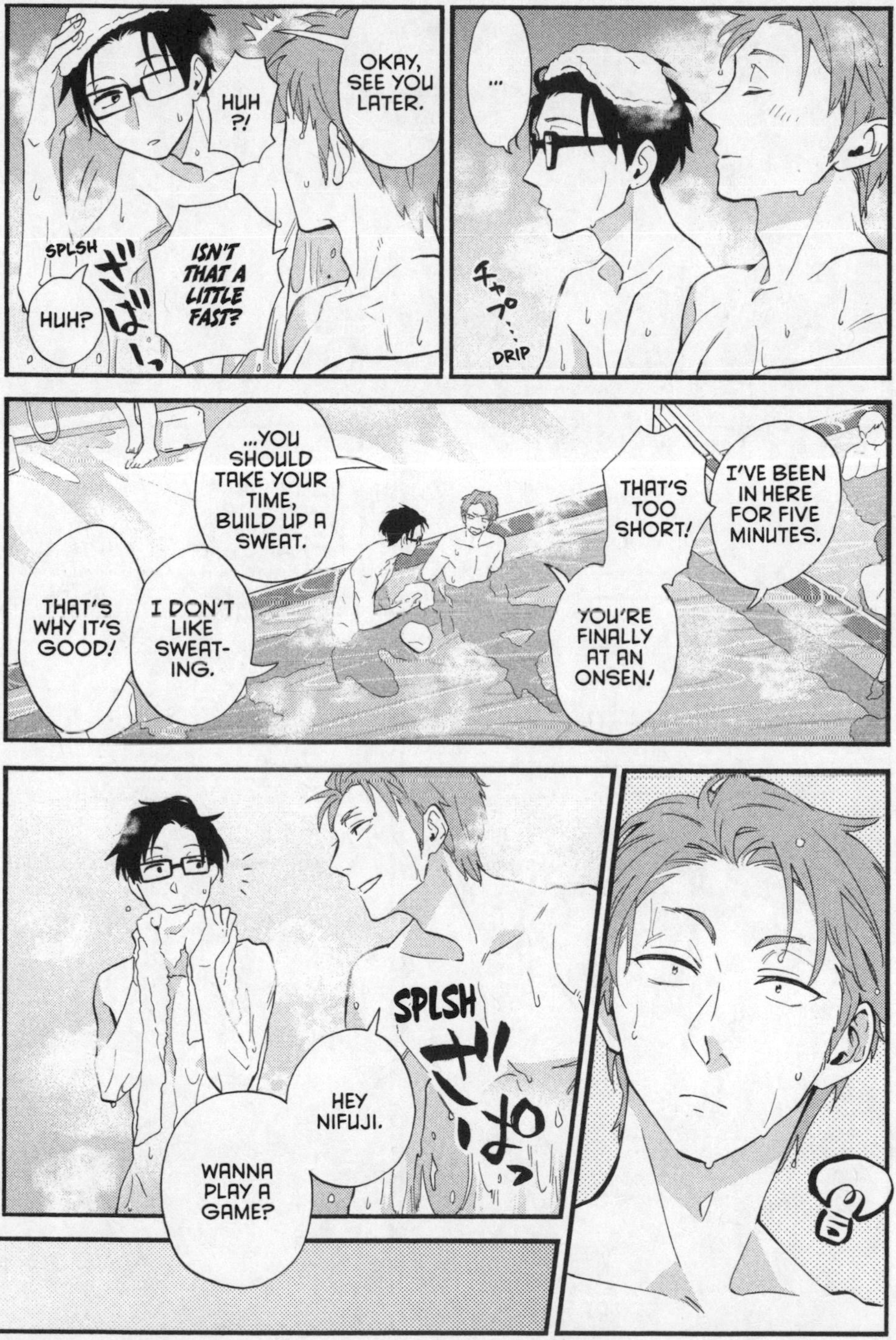
...
DRIP
OKAY, SEE YOU LATER.
HUH ?!
ISN'T THAT A LITTLE FAST?
SPLSH
HUH?
I'VE BEEN IN HERE FOR FIVE MINUTES.
THAT'S TOO SHORT!
YOU'RE FINALLY AT AN ONSEN!
...YOU SHOULD TAKE YOUR TIME, BUILD UP A SWEAT.
I DON'T LIKE SWEAT-ING.
THAT'S WHY IT'S GOOD!
SPLSH
HEY NIFUJI.
WANNA PLAY A GAME?

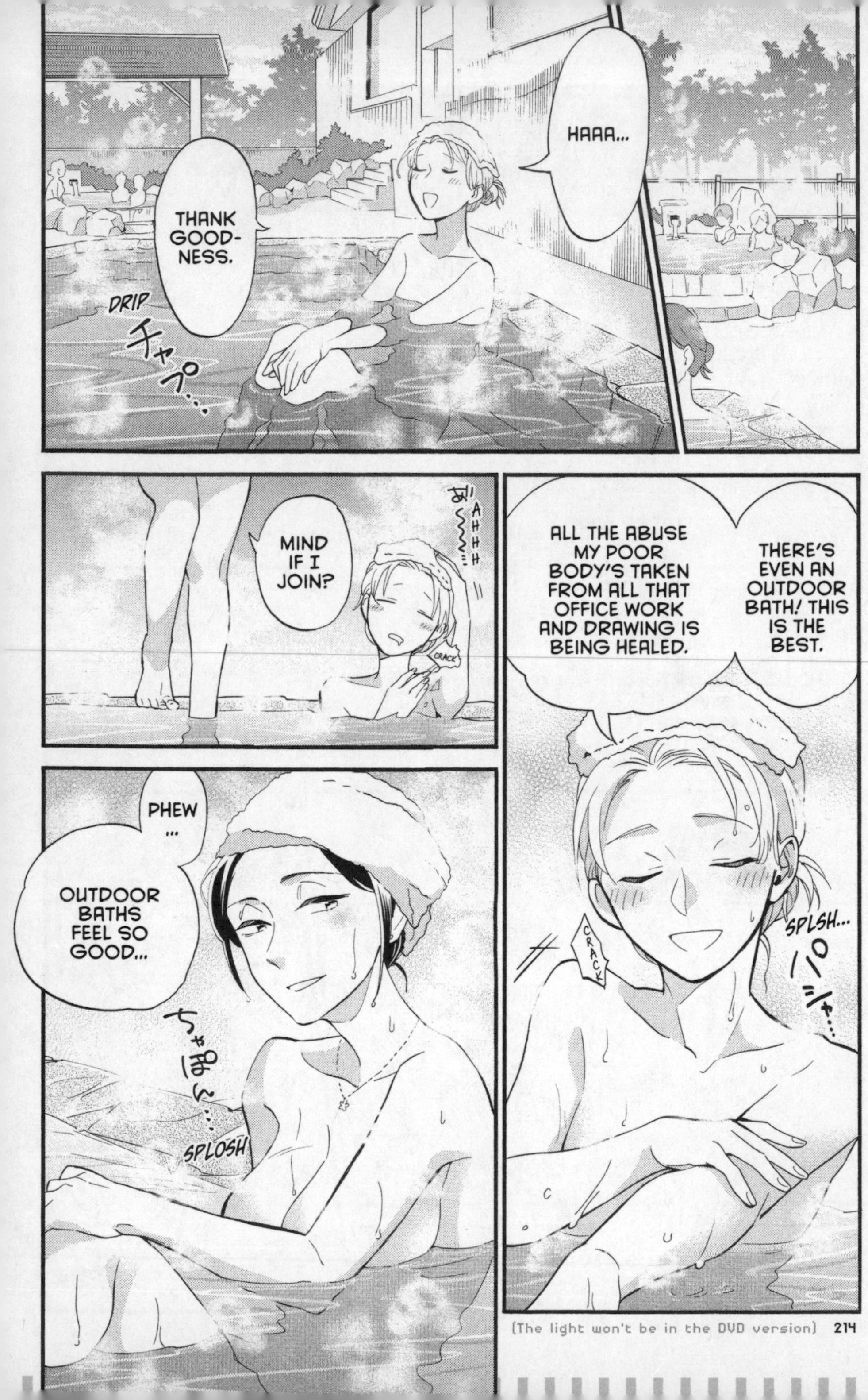
HAAA...
THANK GOODNESS.
DRIP
チャプ…
THERE'S EVEN AN OUTDOOR BATH! THIS IS THE BEST.
ALL THE ABUSE MY POOR BODY'S TAKEN FROM ALL THAT OFFICE WORK AND DRAWING IS BEING HEALED.
CRACK
SPLSH...
パシャ…
あ〜〜…
AHHHH
MIND IF I JOIN?
CRACK
PHEW ...
OUTDOOR BATHS FEEL SO GOOD...
ちゃぽん…
SPLOSH

(The light won't be in the DVD version)

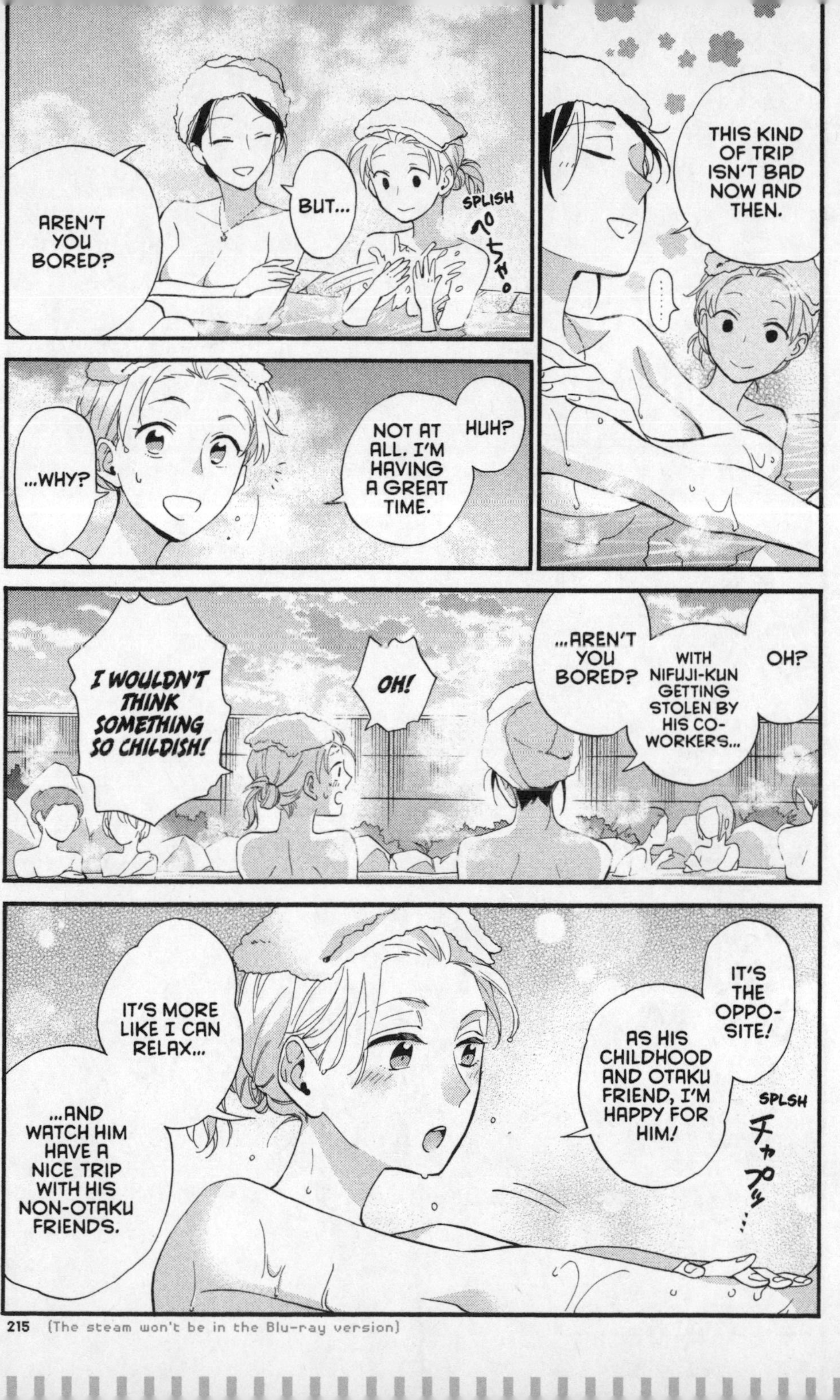
THIS KIND OF TRIP ISN'T BAD NOW AND THEN.
......
SPLISH
ぺちゃ。
BUT...
AREN'T YOU BORED?
HUH?
NOT AT ALL. I'M HAVING A GREAT TIME.
...WHY?
OH?
WITH NIFUJI-KUN GETTING STOLEN BY HIS CO-WORKERS...
...AREN'T YOU BORED?
OH!
I WOULDN'T THINK SOMETHING SO CHILDISH!
IT'S THE OPPOSITE!
AS HIS CHILDHOOD AND OTAKU FRIEND, I'M HAPPY FOR HIM!
SPLSH
チャプッ...
IT'S MORE LIKE I CAN RELAX...
...AND WATCH HIM HAVE A NICE TRIP WITH HIS NON-OTAKU FRIENDS.

 (The steam won't be in the Blu-ray version)

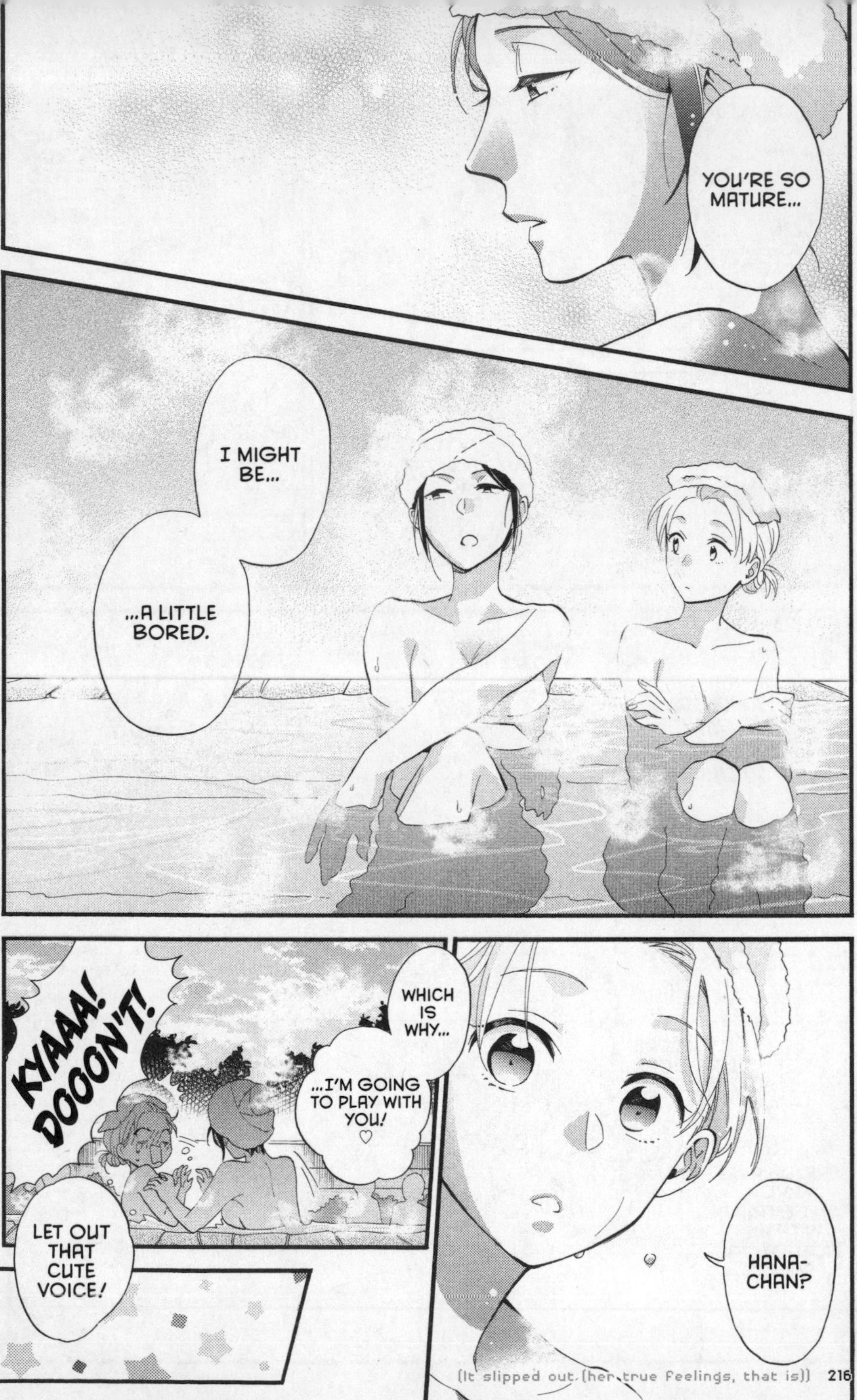
YOU'RE SO MATURE...
I MIGHT BE...
...A LITTLE BORED.
HANA-CHAN?
WHICH IS WHY...
...I'M GOING TO PLAY WITH YOU! ♡
KYAAA! DOOON'T!
LET OUT THAT CUTE VOICE!

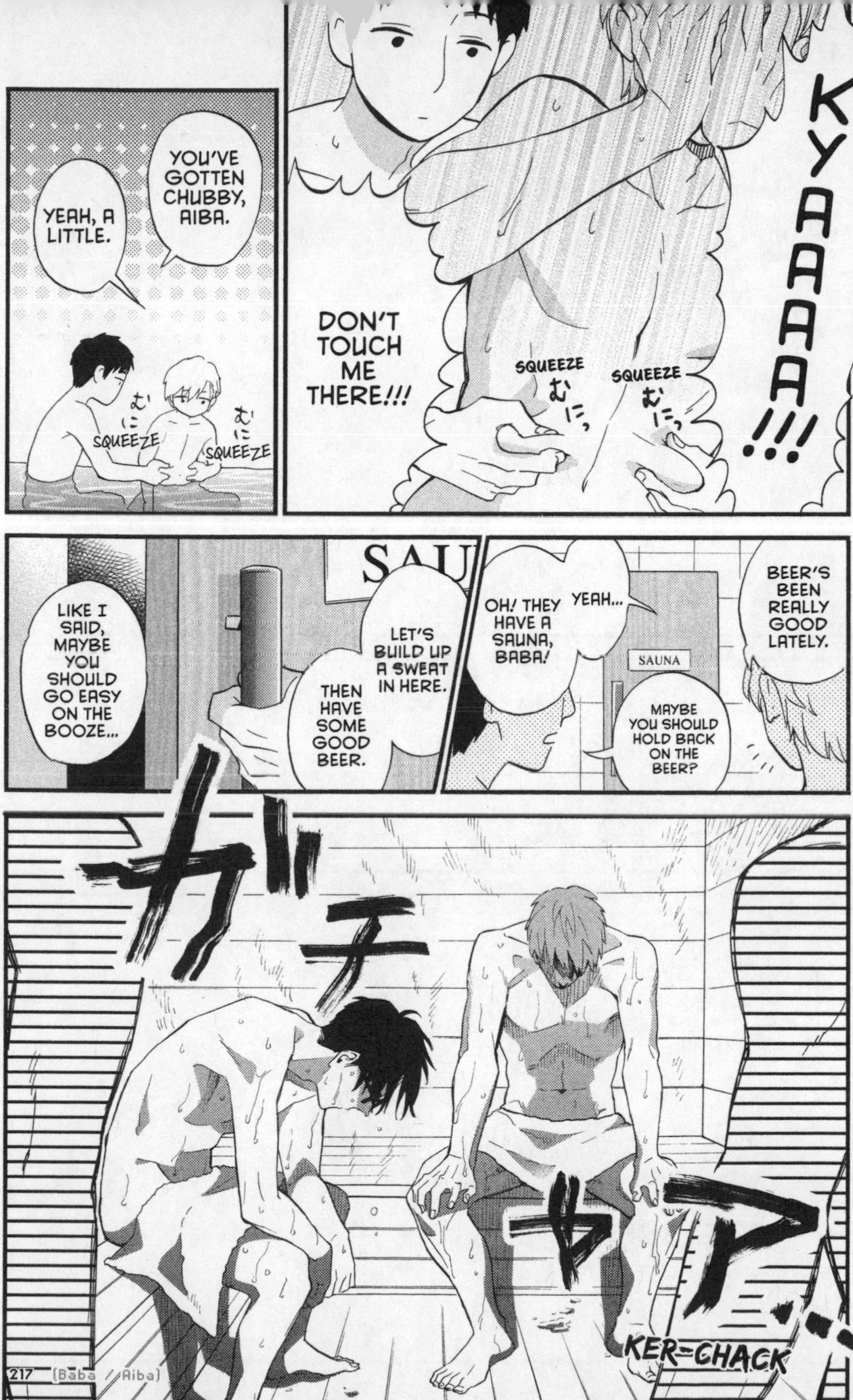
KYAAAAA!!!
DON'T TOUCH ME THERE!!!
SQUEEZE むにっ
SQUEEZE むにっ
YOU'VE GOTTEN CHUBBY, AIBA.
YEAH, A LITTLE.
むに SQUEEZE
むに SQUEEZE
BEER'S BEEN REALLY GOOD LATELY.
MAYBE YOU SHOULD HOLD BACK ON THE BEER?
OH! THEY HAVE A SAUNA, BABA!
YEAH...
SAUNA
SAU
LET'S BUILD UP A SWEAT IN HERE.
THEN HAVE SOME GOOD BEER.
LIKE I SAID, MAYBE YOU SHOULD GO EASY ON THE BOOZE...
ガチャ…
KER-CHACK

SAUNA
KA-CLNK
WAS THAT ...
...AIBA AND BABA JUST NOW?
DUNNO ...
I'M TOO HOT TO CARE.
YEAH.
HEY, KABA-KURA-SAN?
THIS IS ENOUGH, RIGHT? THIS "SAUNA-OFF" ISN'T MUCH OF A GAME.
YOU DON'T MOVE MUCH, DO YOU?
A SWEAT SOME-TIMES CAN BE GOOD.

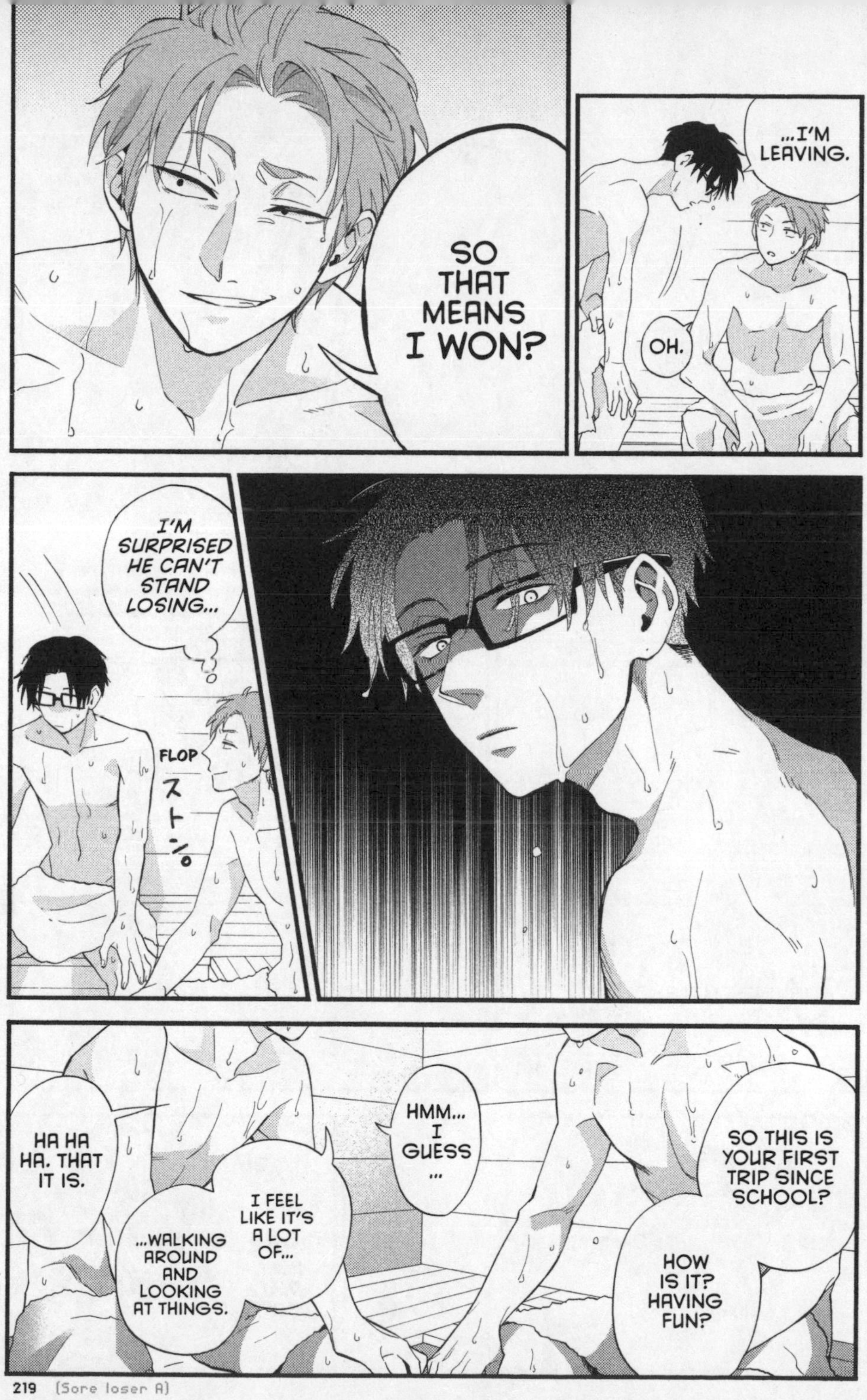
...I'M LEAVING.
OH.
SO THAT MEANS I WON?
I'M SURPRISED HE CAN'T STAND LOSING...
FLOP
ストン。
SO THIS IS YOUR FIRST TRIP SINCE SCHOOL?
HOW IS IT? HAVING FUN?
HMM... I GUESS...
I FEEL LIKE IT'S A LOT OF...
...WALKING AROUND AND LOOKING AT THINGS.
HA HA HA. THAT IT IS.

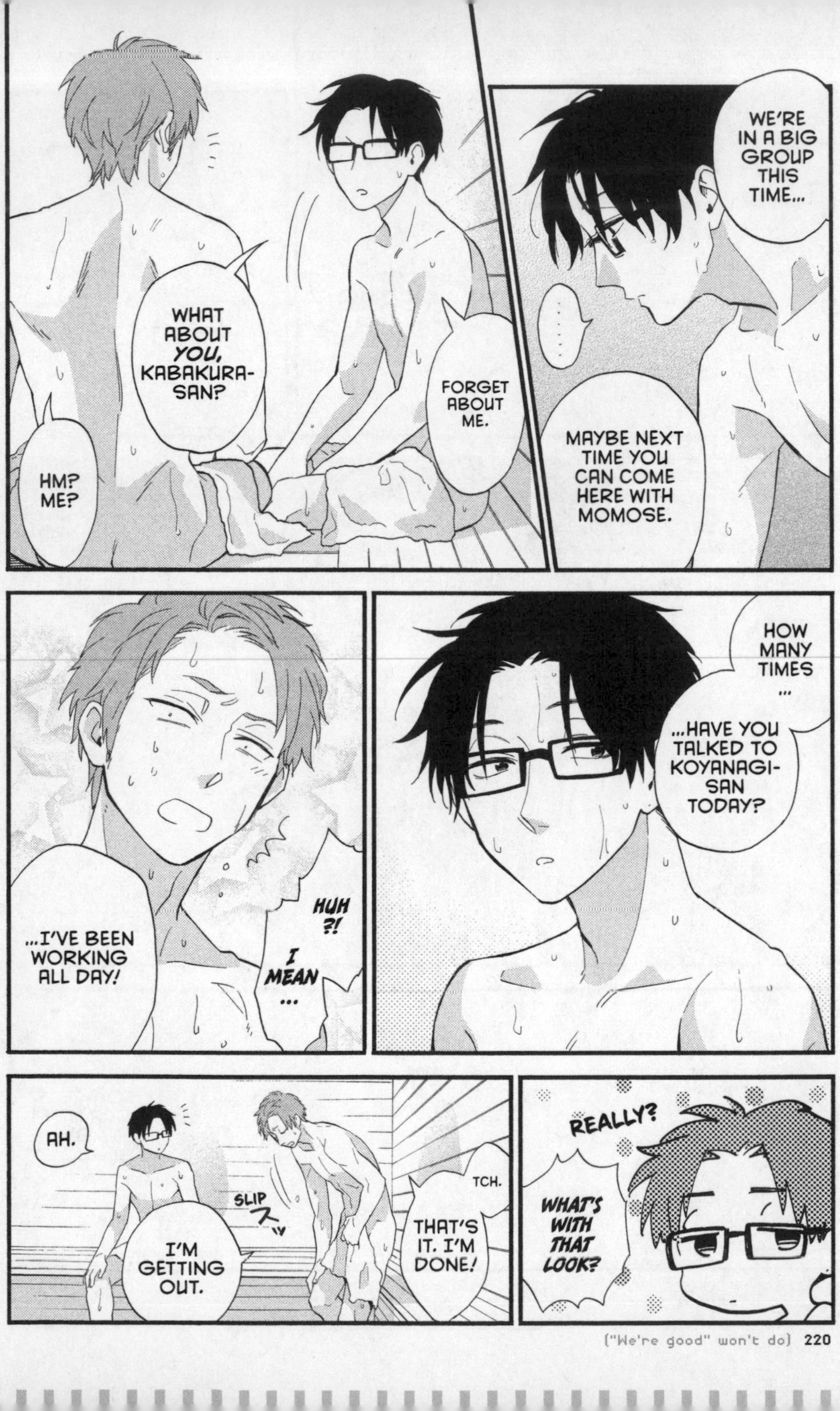
WE'RE IN A BIG GROUP THIS TIME...
......
MAYBE NEXT TIME YOU CAN COME HERE WITH MOMOSE.
FORGET ABOUT ME.
WHAT ABOUT *YOU,* KABAKURA-SAN?
HM? ME?
HOW MANY TIMES ...
...HAVE YOU TALKED TO KOYANAGI-SAN TODAY?
HUH ?!
I MEAN ...
...I'VE BEEN WORKING ALL DAY!
REALLY?
WHAT'S WITH THAT LOOK?
TCH.
THAT'S IT. I'M DONE!
SLIP
ス
AH.
I'M GETTING OUT.

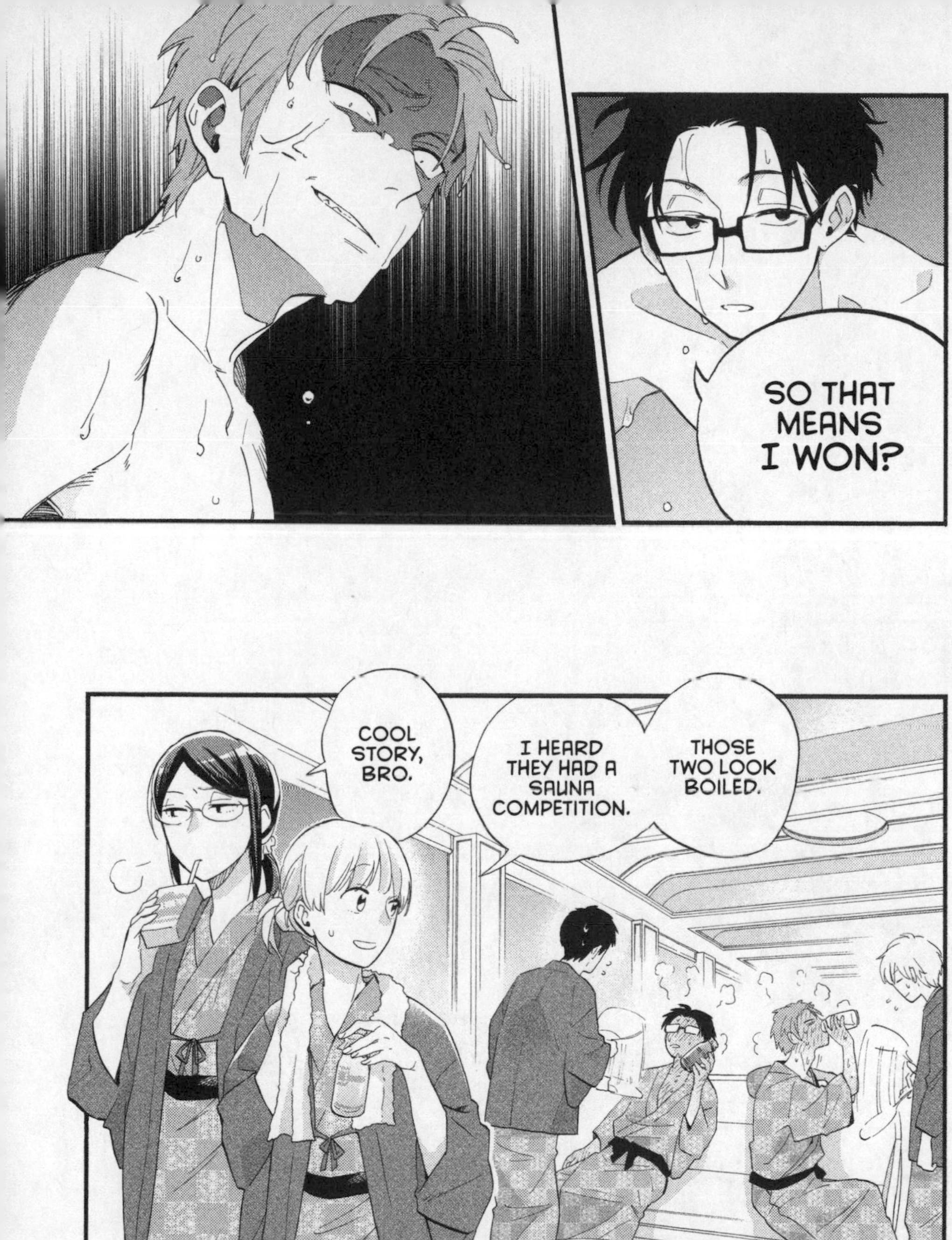
SO THAT MEANS I WON?
THOSE TWO LOOK BOILED.
I HEARD THEY HAD A SAUNA COMPETITION.
COOL STORY, BRO.

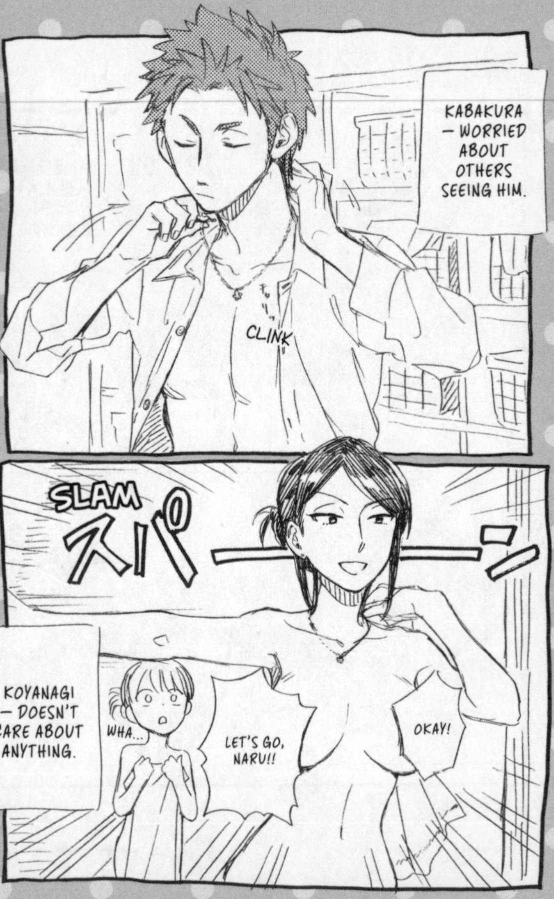
KABAKURA — WORRIED ABOUT OTHERS SEEING HIM.
CLINK
SLAM
スパーーン
OKAY!
LET'S GO, NARU!!
WHA...
KOYANAGI — DOESN'T CARE ABOUT ANYTHING.

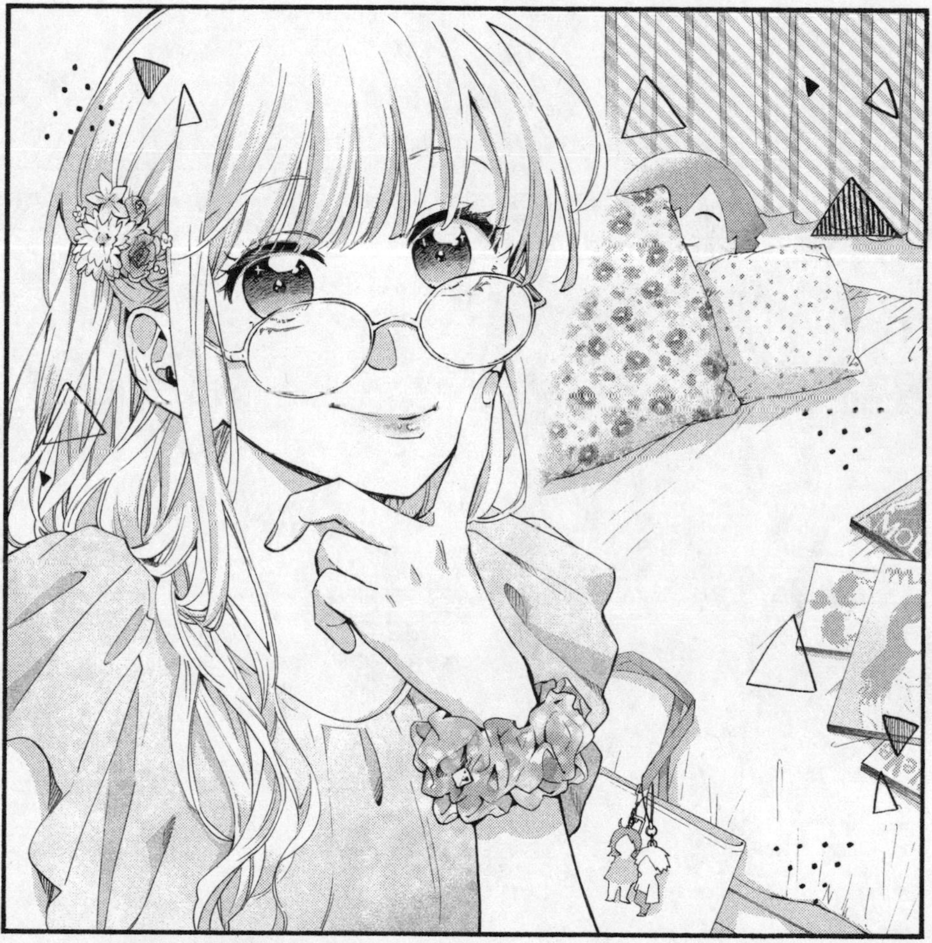

Episode.... 44

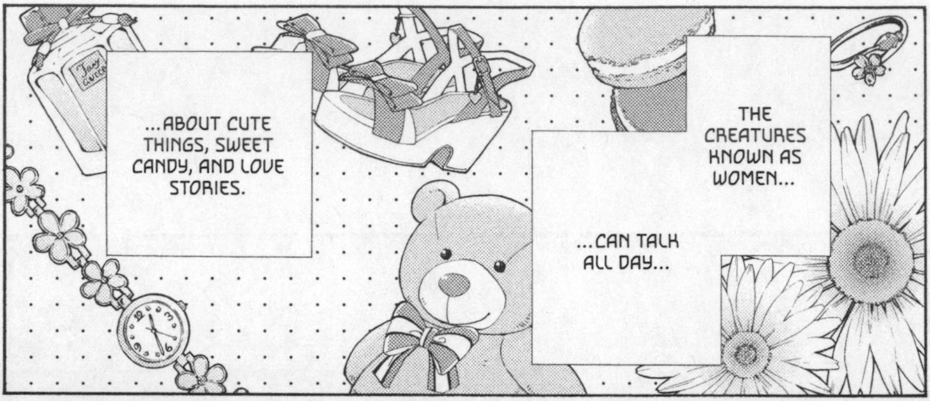
THE CREATURES KNOWN AS WOMEN...
...CAN TALK ALL DAY...
...ABOUT CUTE THINGS, SWEET CANDY, AND LOVE STORIES.

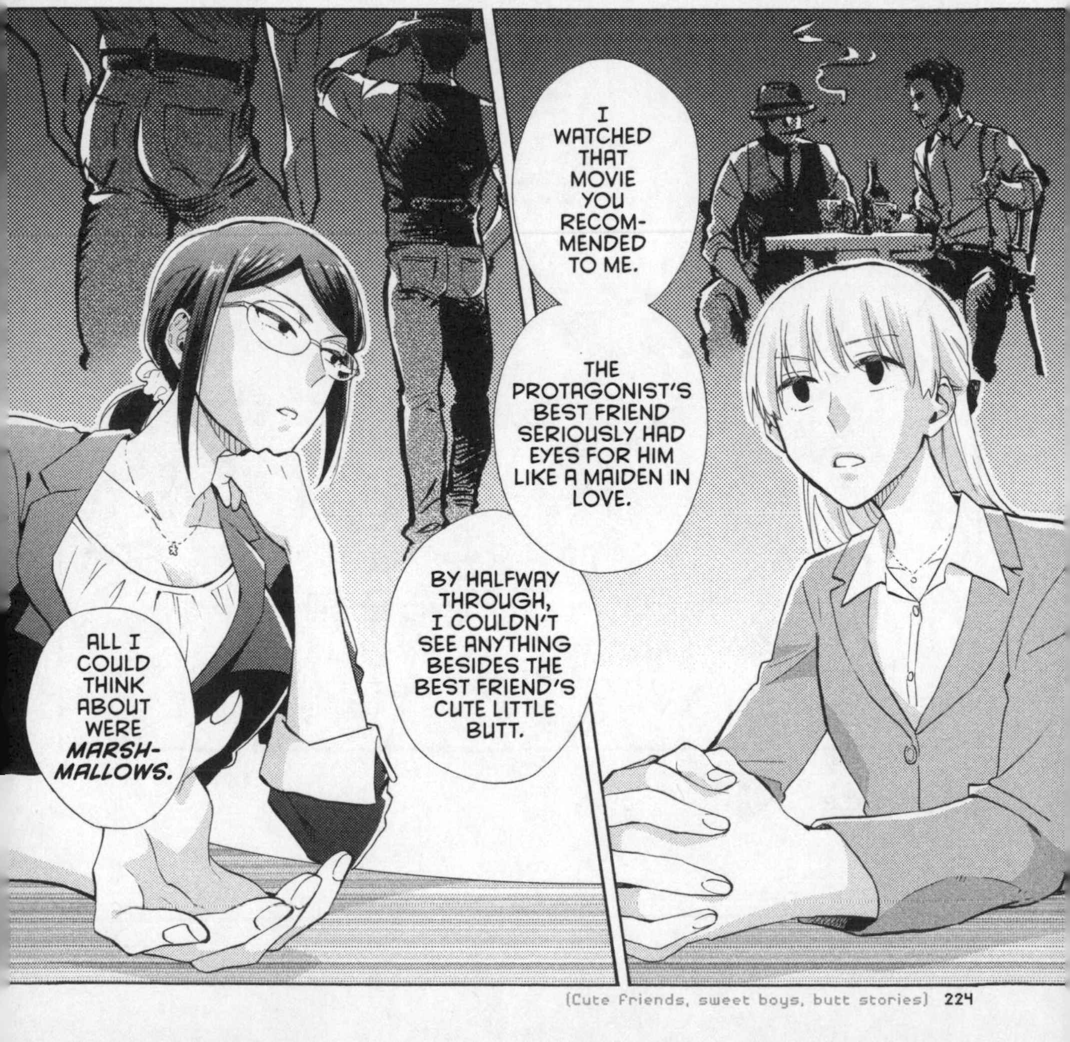
I WATCHED THAT MOVIE YOU RECOMMENDED TO ME.
THE PROTAGONIST'S BEST FRIEND SERIOUSLY HAD EYES FOR HIM LIKE A MAIDEN IN LOVE.
BY HALFWAY THROUGH, I COULDN'T SEE ANYTHING BESIDES THE BEST FRIEND'S CUTE LITTLE BUTT.
ALL I COULD THINK ABOUT WERE *MARSHMALLOWS.*

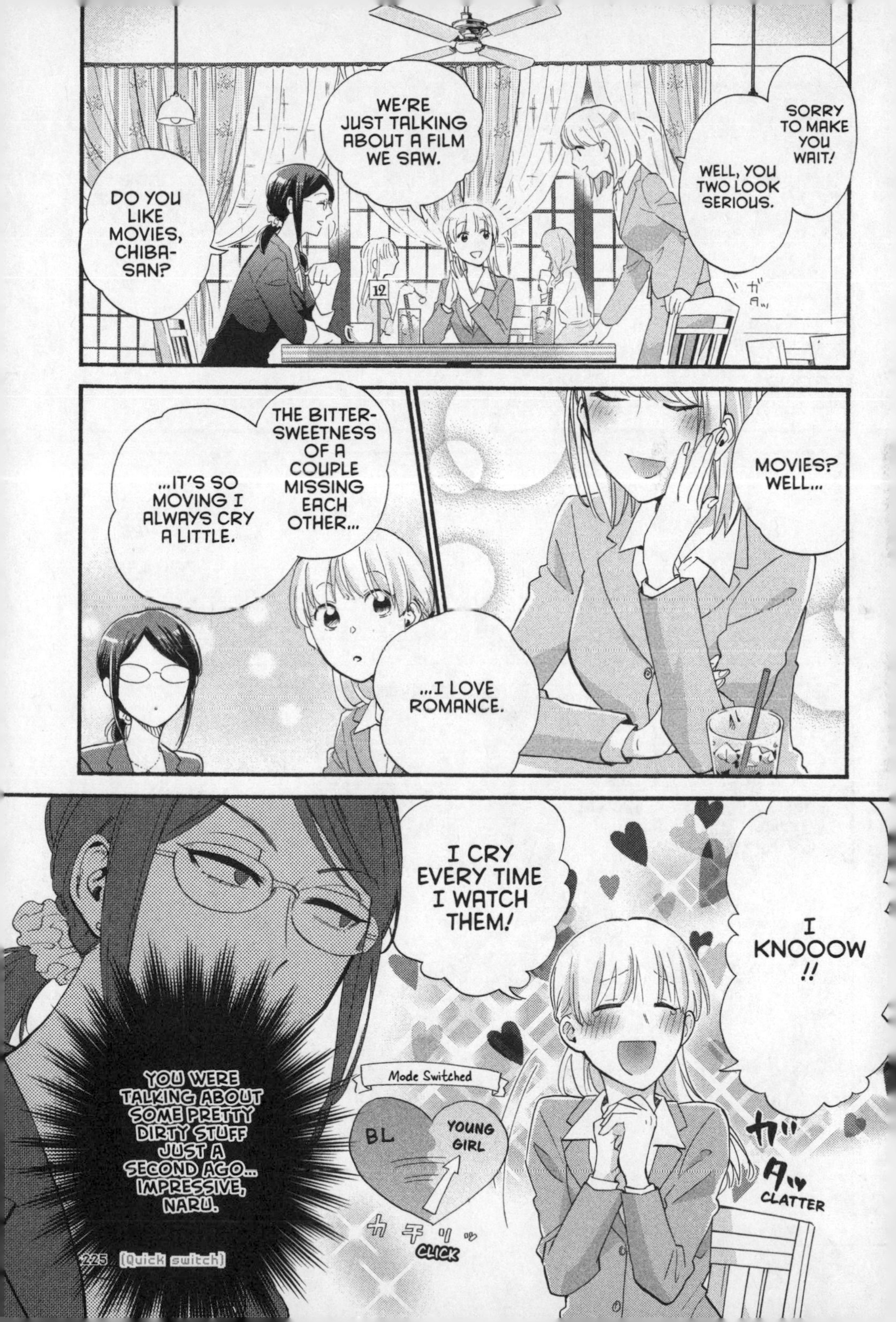
SORRY TO MAKE YOU WAIT!
WELL, YOU TWO LOOK SERIOUS.
WE'RE JUST TALKING ABOUT A FILM WE SAW.
DO YOU LIKE MOVIES, CHIBA-SAN?
MOVIES? WELL...
...I LOVE ROMANCE.
THE BITTER-SWEETNESS OF A COUPLE MISSING EACH OTHER...
...IT'S SO MOVING I ALWAYS CRY A LITTLE.
I KNOOOW!!
I CRY EVERY TIME I WATCH THEM!
CLATTER
Mode Switched
BL
YOUNG GIRL
CLICK
YOU WERE TALKING ABOUT SOME PRETTY DIRTY STUFF JUST A SECOND AGO... IMPRESSIVE, NARU.

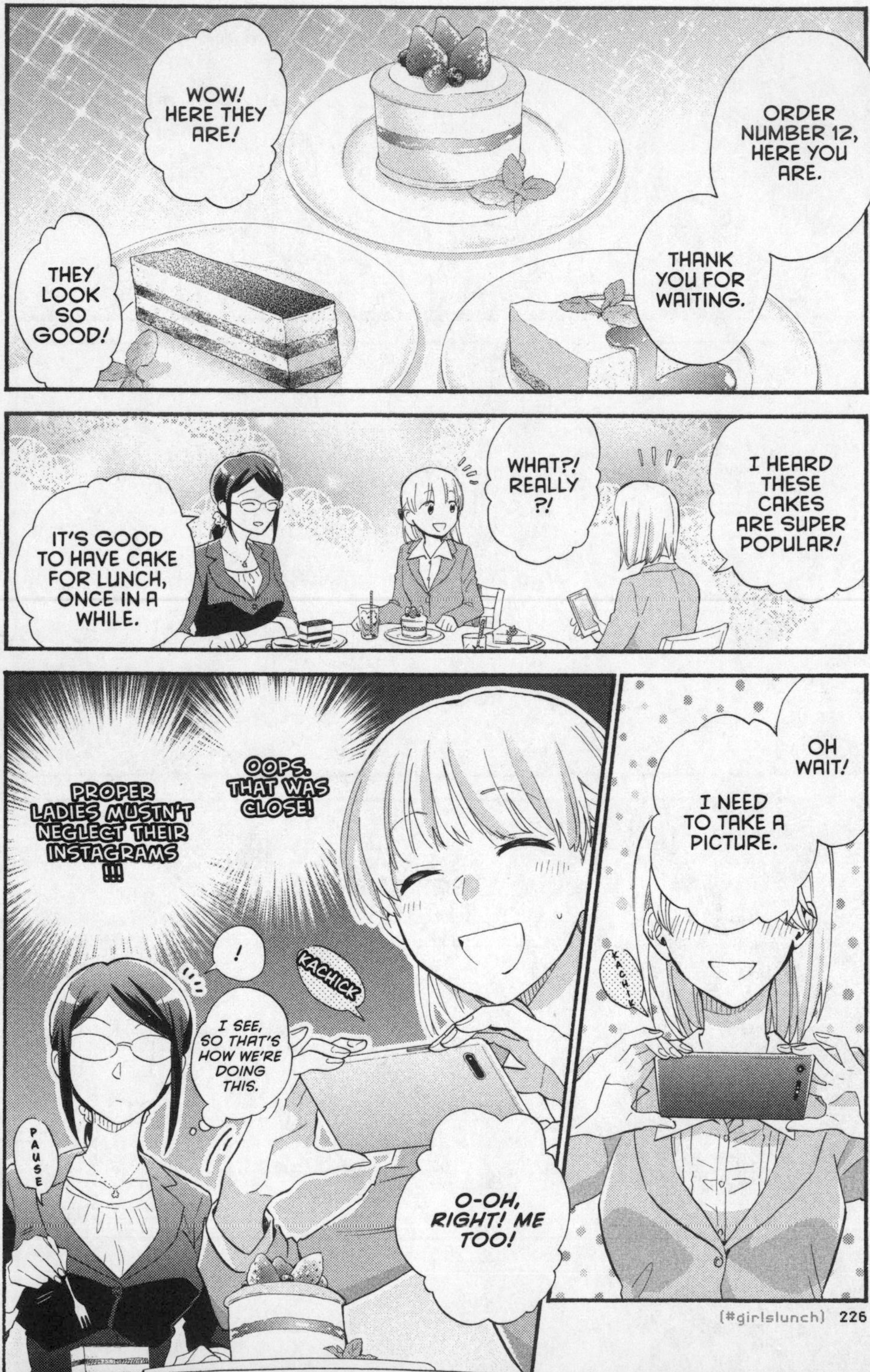
ORDER NUMBER 12, HERE YOU ARE.
THANK YOU FOR WAITING.
WOW! HERE THEY ARE!
THEY LOOK SO GOOD!
I HEARD THESE CAKES ARE SUPER POPULAR!
WHAT?! REALLY?!
IT'S GOOD TO HAVE CAKE FOR LUNCH, ONCE IN A WHILE.
OH WAIT!
I NEED TO TAKE A PICTURE.
KACHIK
OOPS. THAT WAS CLOSE!
PROPER LADIES MUSTN'T NEGLECT THEIR INSTAGRAMS!!!
KACHICK
!
I SEE, SO THAT'S HOW WE'RE DOING THIS.
O-OH, RIGHT! ME TOO!
PAUSE

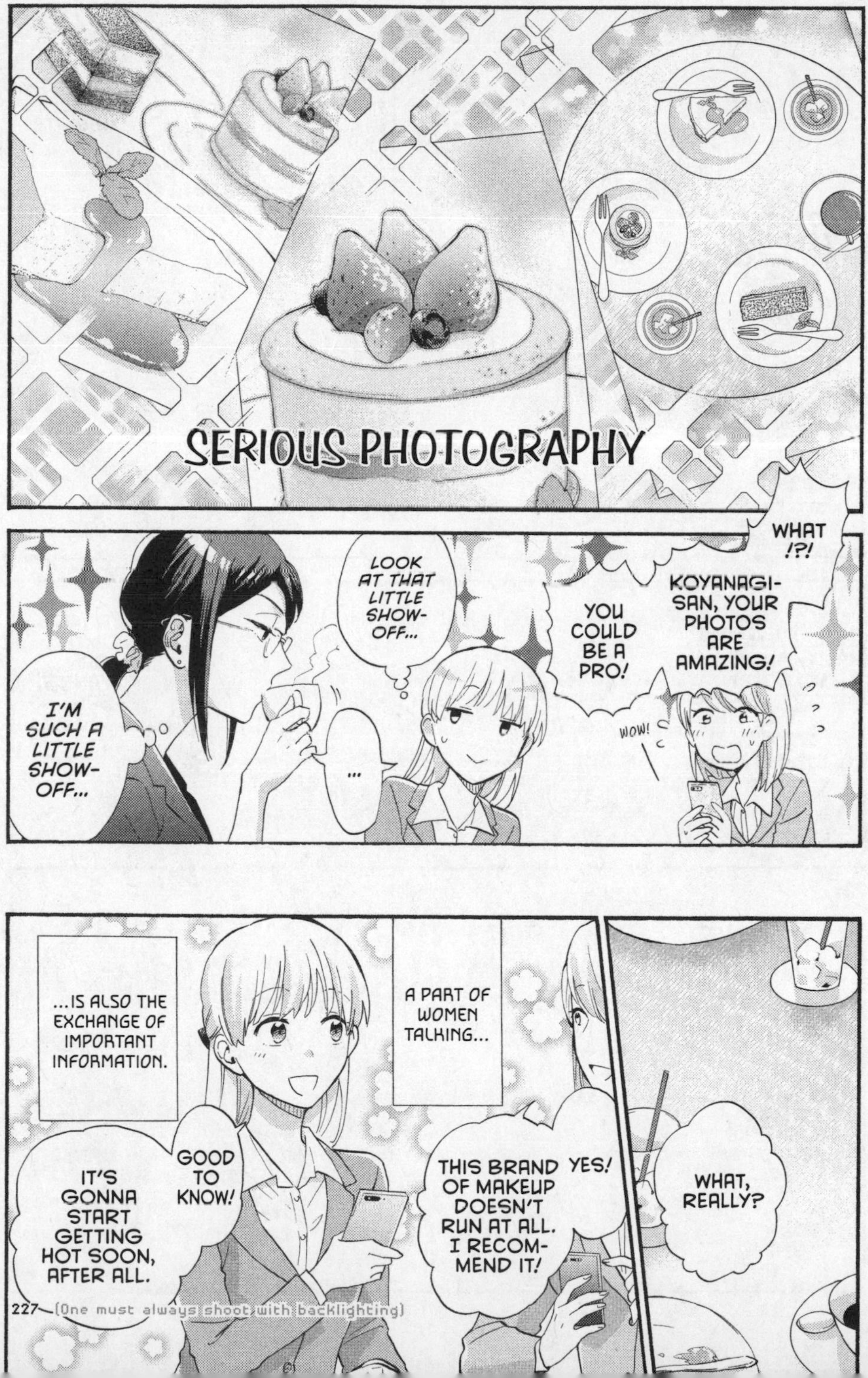
SERIOUS PHOTOGRAPHY
WHAT !?!
KOYANAGI-SAN, YOUR PHOTOS ARE AMAZING!
WOW!
YOU COULD BE A PRO!
LOOK AT THAT LITTLE SHOW-OFF...
...
I'M SUCH A LITTLE SHOW-OFF...
WHAT, REALLY?
YES!
A PART OF WOMEN TALKING...
THIS BRAND OF MAKEUP DOESN'T RUN AT ALL. I RECOMMEND IT!
...IS ALSO THE EXCHANGE OF IMPORTANT INFORMATION.
GOOD TO KNOW!
IT'S GONNA START GETTING HOT SOON, AFTER ALL.

(One must always shoot with backlighting)

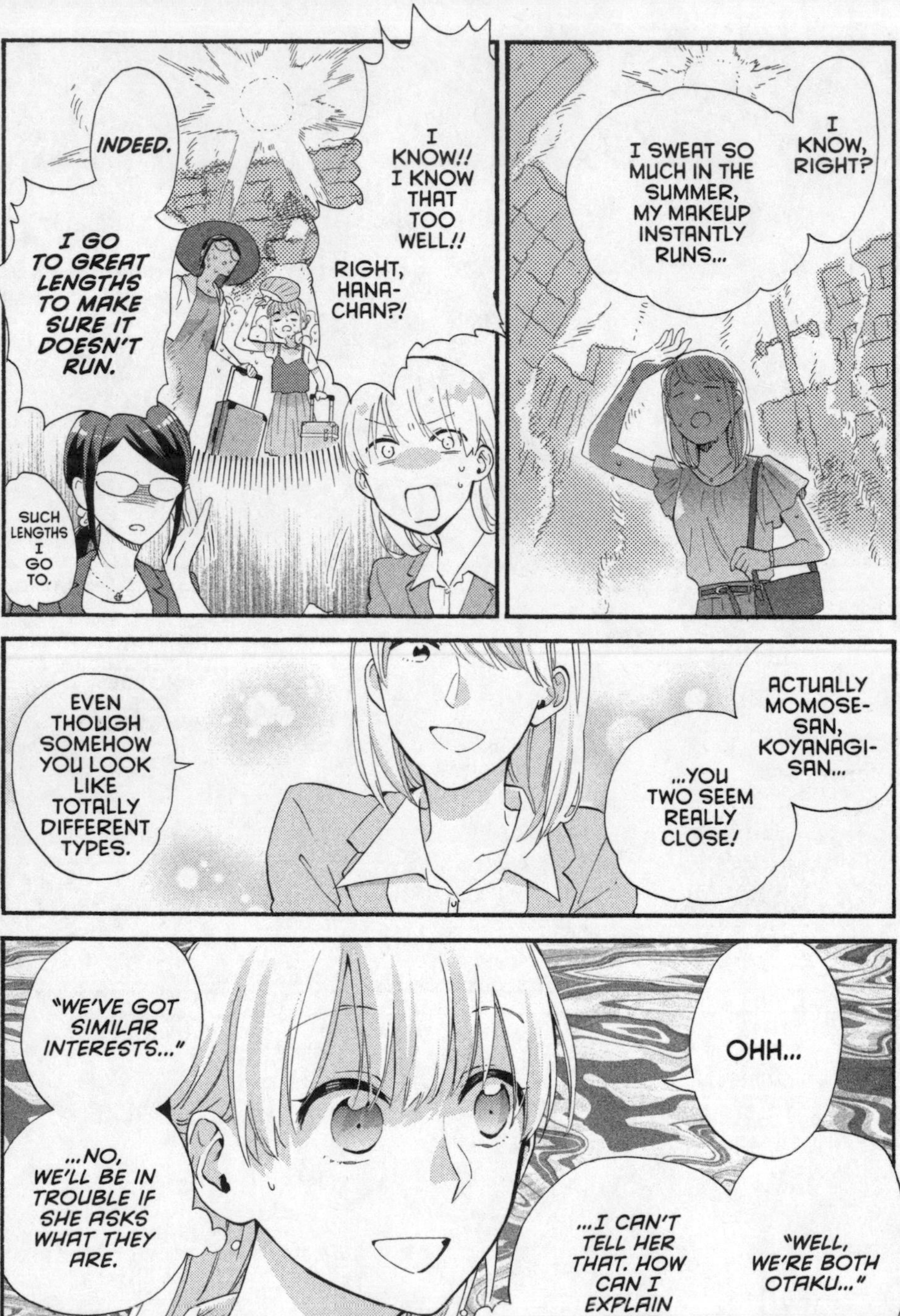
I KNOW, RIGHT?
I SWEAT SO MUCH IN THE SUMMER, MY MAKEUP INSTANTLY RUNS...
I KNOW!! I KNOW THAT TOO WELL!!
RIGHT, HANA-CHAN?!
INDEED.
I GO TO GREAT LENGTHS TO MAKE SURE IT DOESN'T RUN.
SUCH LENGTHS I GO TO.
ACTUALLY MOMOSE-SAN, KOYANAGI-SAN...
...YOU TWO SEEM REALLY CLOSE!
EVEN THOUGH SOMEHOW YOU LOOK LIKE TOTALLY DIFFERENT TYPES.
OHH...
"WELL, WE'RE BOTH OTAKU..."
...I CAN'T TELL HER THAT. HOW CAN I EXPLAIN THIS?
"WE'VE GOT SIMILAR INTERESTS..."
...NO, WE'LL BE IN TROUBLE IF SHE ASKS WHAT THEY ARE.

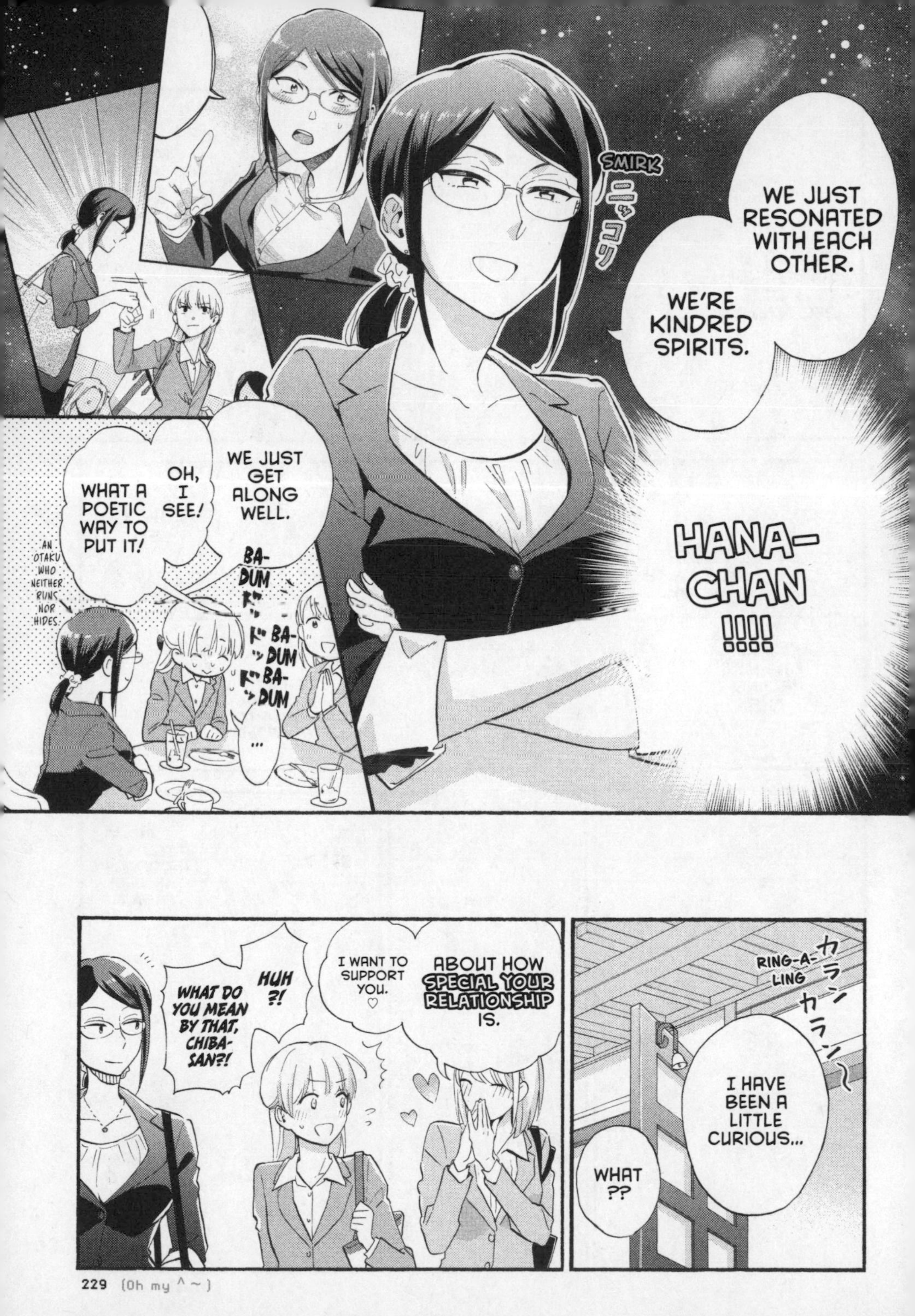
SMIRK
WE JUST RESONATED WITH EACH OTHER.
WE'RE KINDRED SPIRITS.
HANA-CHAN!!!!
WE JUST GET ALONG WELL.
OH, I SEE!
WHAT A POETIC WAY TO PUT IT!
AN OTAKU WHO NEITHER RUNS NOR HIDES.
BA-DUM BA-DUM BA-DUM
...
RING-A-LING
I HAVE BEEN A LITTLE CURIOUS...
WHAT??
ABOUT HOW SPECIAL YOUR RELATIONSHIP IS.
I WANT TO SUPPORT YOU. ♡
HUH?!
WHAT DO YOU MEAN BY THAT, CHIBA-SAN?!

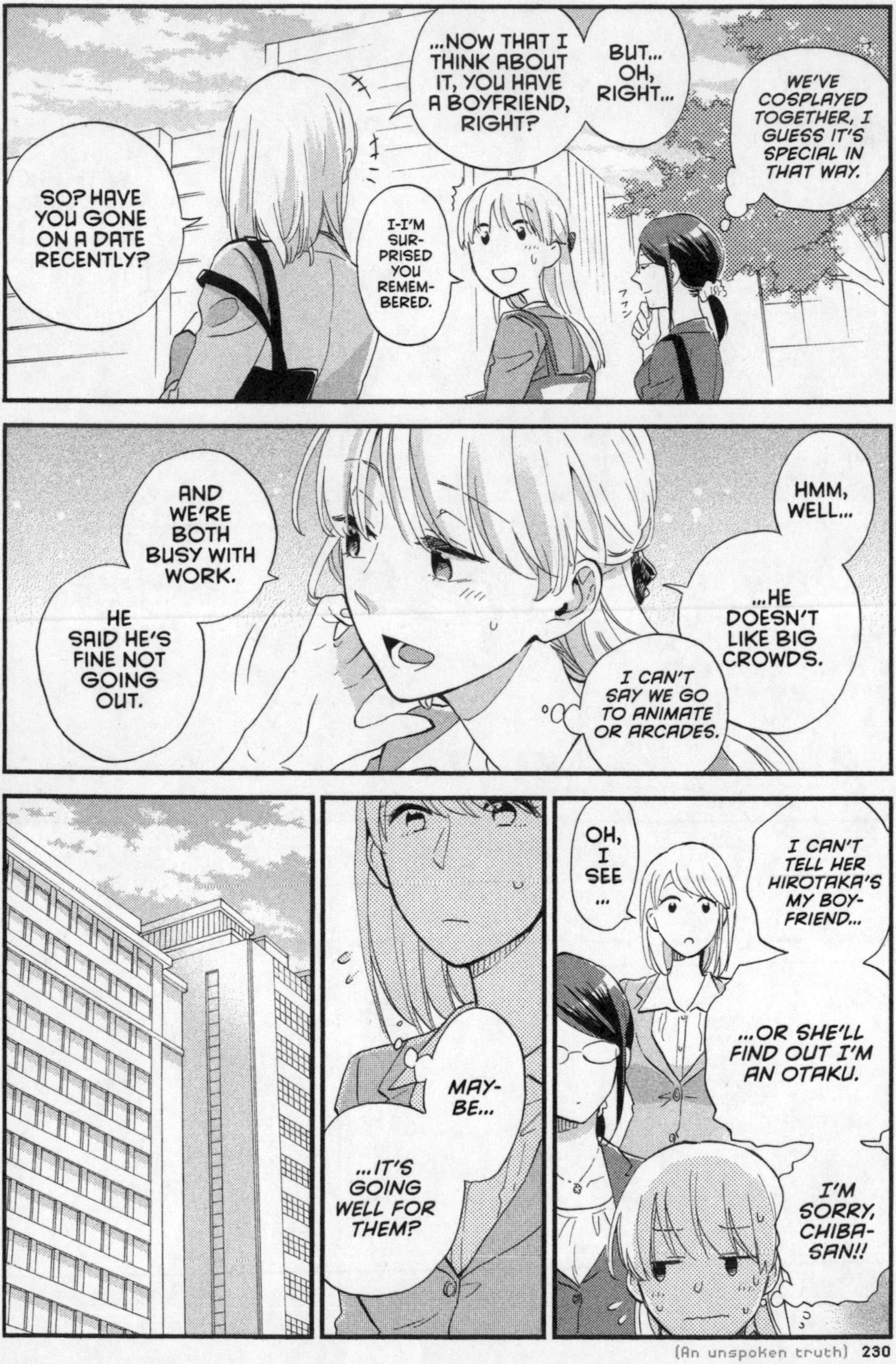
WE'VE COSPLAYED TOGETHER, I GUESS IT'S SPECIAL IN THAT WAY.
BUT... OH, RIGHT...
...NOW THAT I THINK ABOUT IT, YOU HAVE A BOYFRIEND, RIGHT?
I-I'M SURPRISED YOU REMEMBERED.
SO? HAVE YOU GONE ON A DATE RECENTLY?
HMM, WELL...
...HE DOESN'T LIKE BIG CROWDS.
I CAN'T SAY WE GO TO ANIMATE OR ARCADES.
AND WE'RE BOTH BUSY WITH WORK.
HE SAID HE'S FINE NOT GOING OUT.
I CAN'T TELL HER HIROTAKA'S MY BOYFRIEND...
OH, I SEE...
...OR SHE'LL FIND OUT I'M AN OTAKU.
I'M SORRY, CHIBA-SAN!!
MAYBE...
...IT'S GOING WELL FOR THEM?

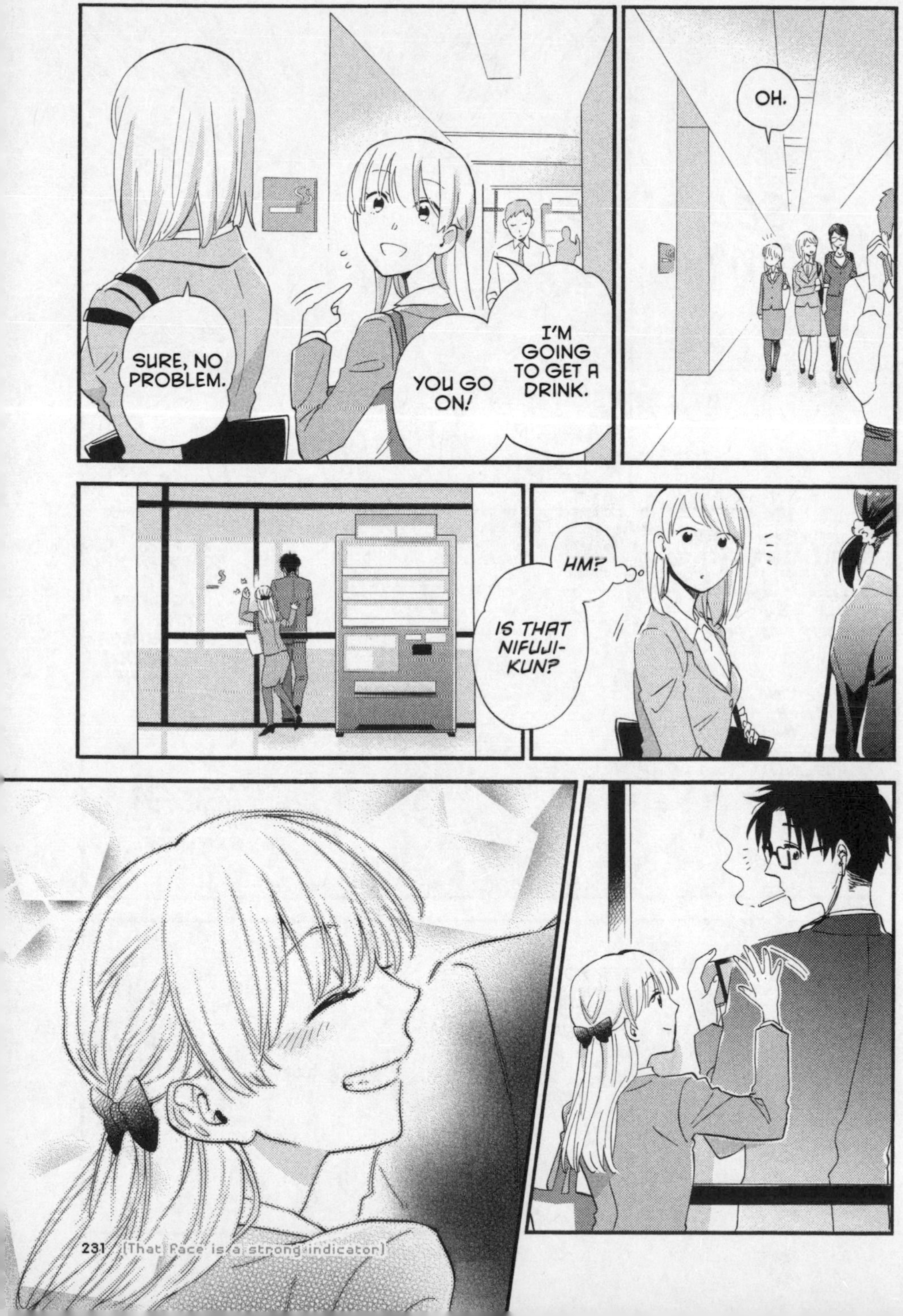
OH.
I'M GOING TO GET A DRINK.
YOU GO ON!
SURE, NO PROBLEM.
HM?
IS THAT NIFUJI-KUN?

I SEE, NOW!

HE'S COOL, HARD TO READ, AND DOESN'T HAVE MANY FRIENDS. SHE CAN'T HELP BUT FALL FOR HIM.

THE ONE YOU'RE DESTINED TO BE WITH WON'T NECESSARILY BE YOUR FIRST!!

IF HER BOYFRIEND WON'T GO ON PROPER DATES, OF COURSE SHE'D WORRY ABOUT WHETHER HE REALLY LOVES HER.

THEN SHE RUNS INTO HER CHILDHOOD FRIEND, AND IT FEELS LIKE FATE.

WOMEN...

...LOVE GETTING WORKED UP OVER THINGS, TOO.

YOU'RE ALLOWED TO BE HAPPY!

HUH?

WHAT ARE YOU DOING, CHIBA-CHAN?

BA-DUM

BA-DUM

DON'T YOU WORRY, MOMOSE-SAN...!

...I'M CHEER-ING FOR YOU!

(Another member joins her guardian corps) 232

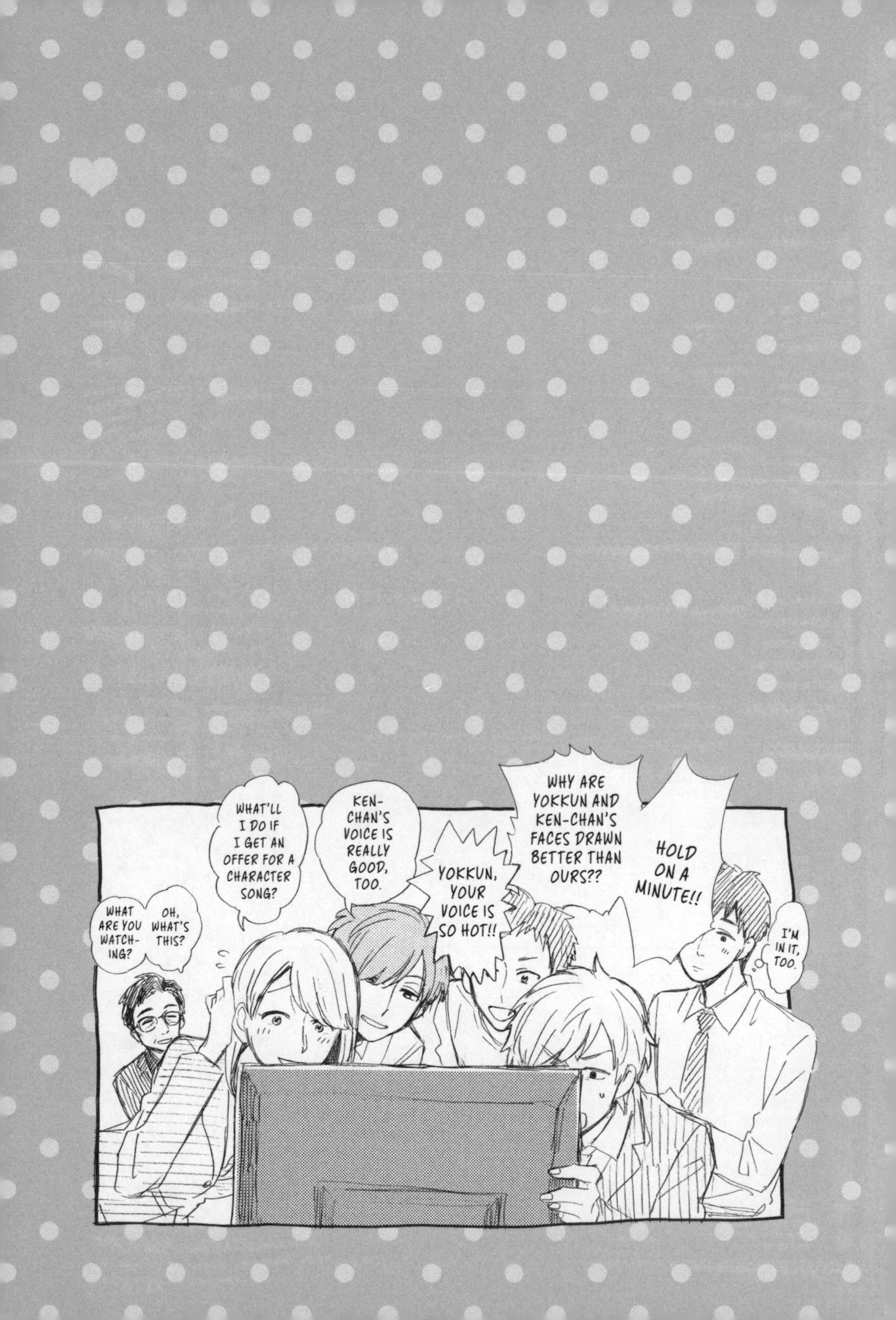
HOLD ON A MINUTE!!
I'M IN IT, TOO.
WHY ARE YOKKUN AND KEN-CHAN'S FACES DRAWN BETTER THAN OURS??
YOKKUN, YOUR VOICE IS SO HOT!!
KEN-CHAN'S VOICE IS REALLY GOOD, TOO.
WHAT'LL I DO IF I GET AN OFFER FOR A CHARACTER SONG?
OH, WHAT'S THIS?
WHAT ARE YOU WATCHING?

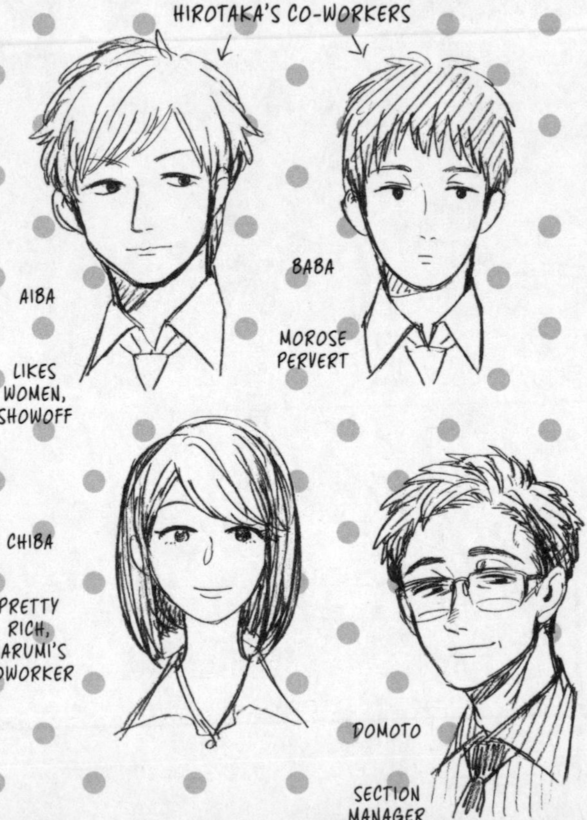
HIROTAKA'S CO-WORKERS
BABA
MOROSE PERVERT
AIBA
LIKES WOMEN, SHOWOFF
DOMOTO
SECTION MANAGER
CHIBA
PRETTY RICH, NARUMI'S COWORKER

Episode.... 45

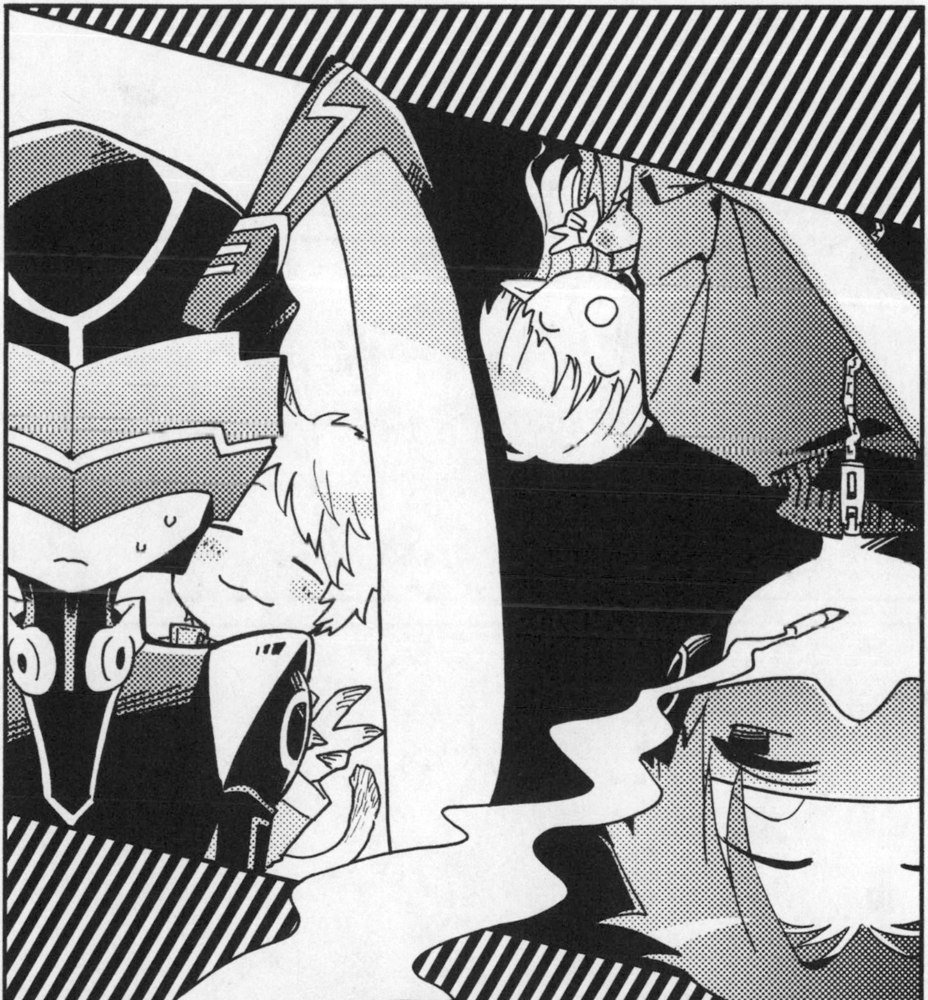

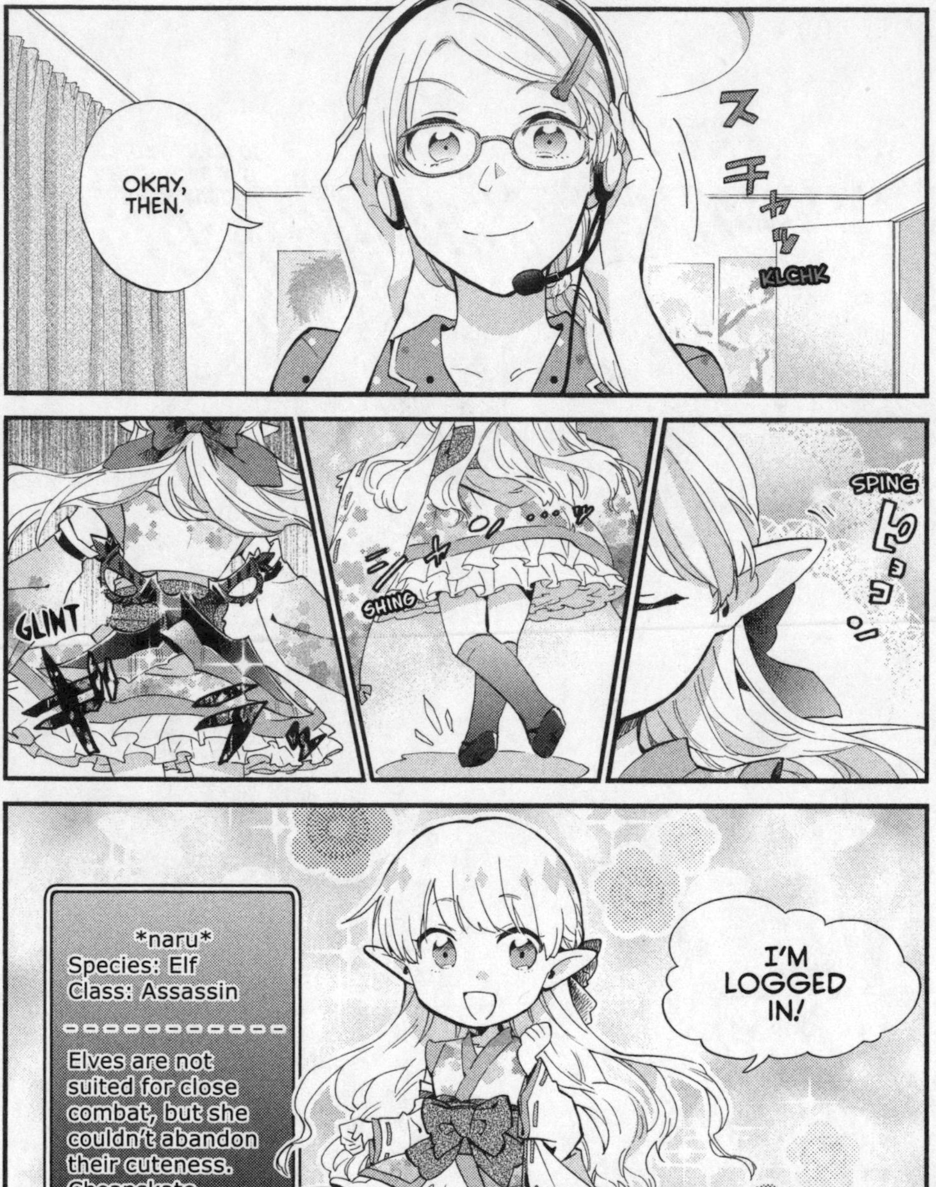
KLCHK
OKAY, THEN.
SPING
SHING
GLINT
I'M LOGGED IN!
naru
Species: Elf
Class: Assassin
Elves are not suited for close combat, but she couldn't abandon their cuteness. Cheapskate.

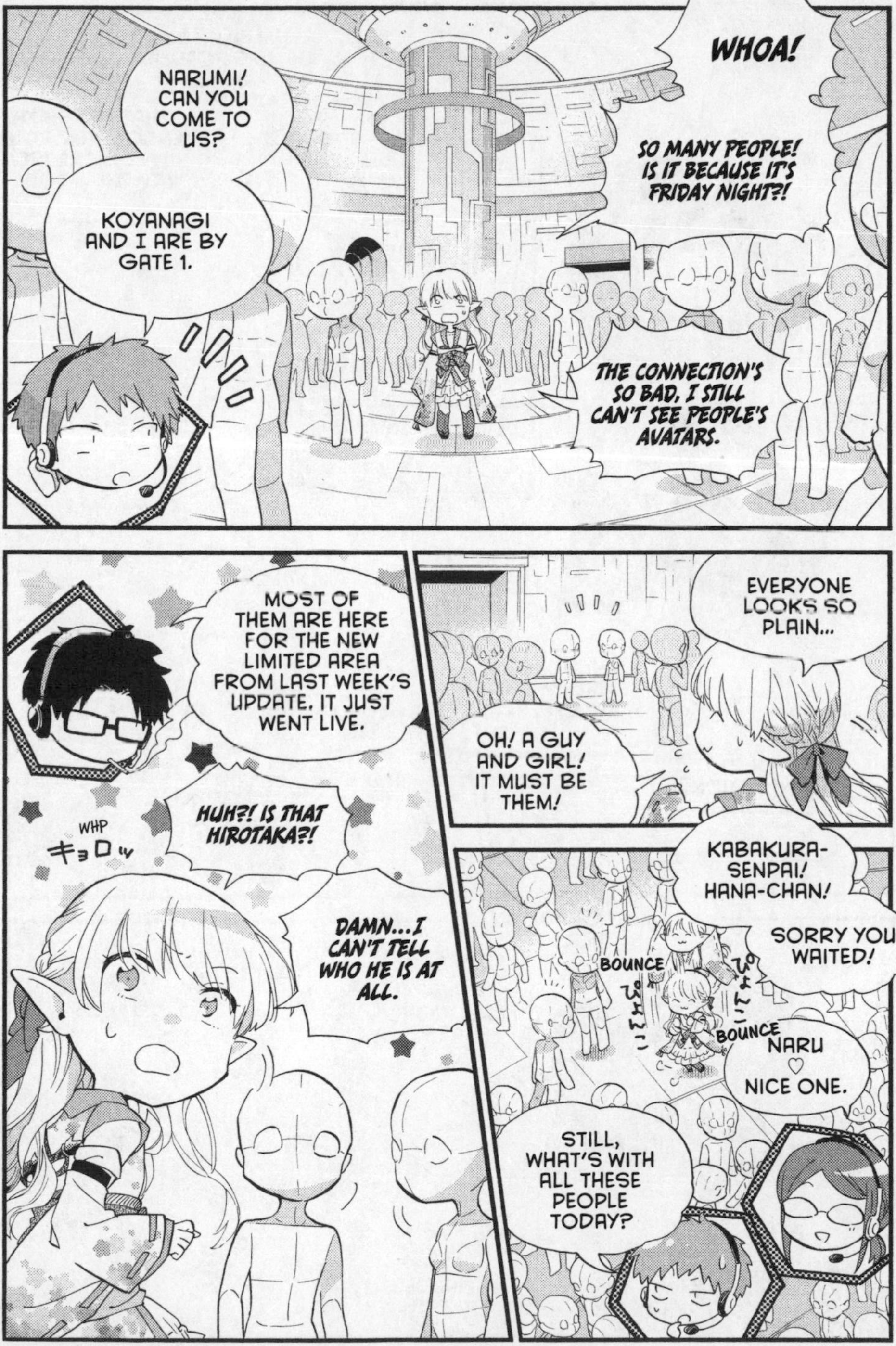
WHOA!
SO MANY PEOPLE! IS IT BECAUSE IT'S FRIDAY NIGHT?!
THE CONNECTION'S SO BAD, I STILL CAN'T SEE PEOPLE'S AVATARS.
NARUMI! CAN YOU COME TO US?
KOYANAGI AND I ARE BY GATE 1.
EVERYONE LOOKS SO PLAIN...
OH! A GUY AND GIRL! IT MUST BE THEM!
KABAKURA-SENPAI! HANA-CHAN!
SORRY YOU WAITED!
BOUNCE
BOUNCE
NARU ♡ NICE ONE.
STILL, WHAT'S WITH ALL THESE PEOPLE TODAY?
MOST OF THEM ARE HERE FOR THE NEW LIMITED AREA FROM LAST WEEK'S UPDATE. IT JUST WENT LIVE.
HUH?! IS THAT HIROTAKA?!
WHP
キョロッ
DAMN... I CAN'T TELL WHO HE IS AT ALL.

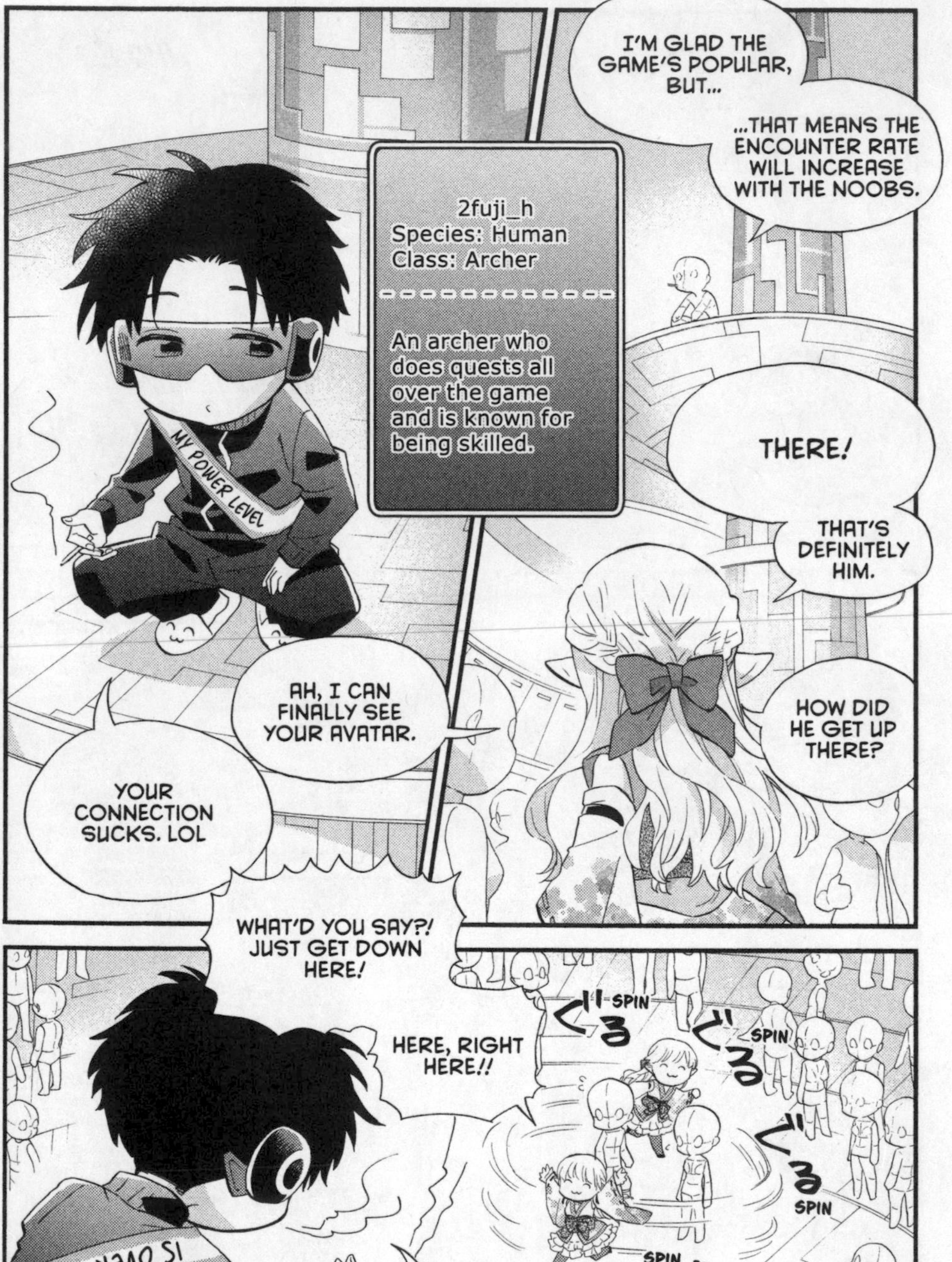
I'M GLAD THE GAME'S POPULAR, BUT...
...THAT MEANS THE ENCOUNTER RATE WILL INCREASE WITH THE NOOBS.
THERE!
THAT'S DEFINITELY HIM.
HOW DID HE GET UP THERE?
2fuji_h
Species: Human
Class: Archer
An archer who does quests all over the game and is known for being skilled.
MY POWER LEVEL
AH, I CAN FINALLY SEE YOUR AVATAR.
YOUR CONNECTION SUCKS. LOL
WHAT'D YOU SAY?! JUST GET DOWN HERE!
SPIN
SPIN
HERE, RIGHT HERE!!
SPIN
SPIN
IS OVER 9000
HMM? NARUMI, THAT'S...

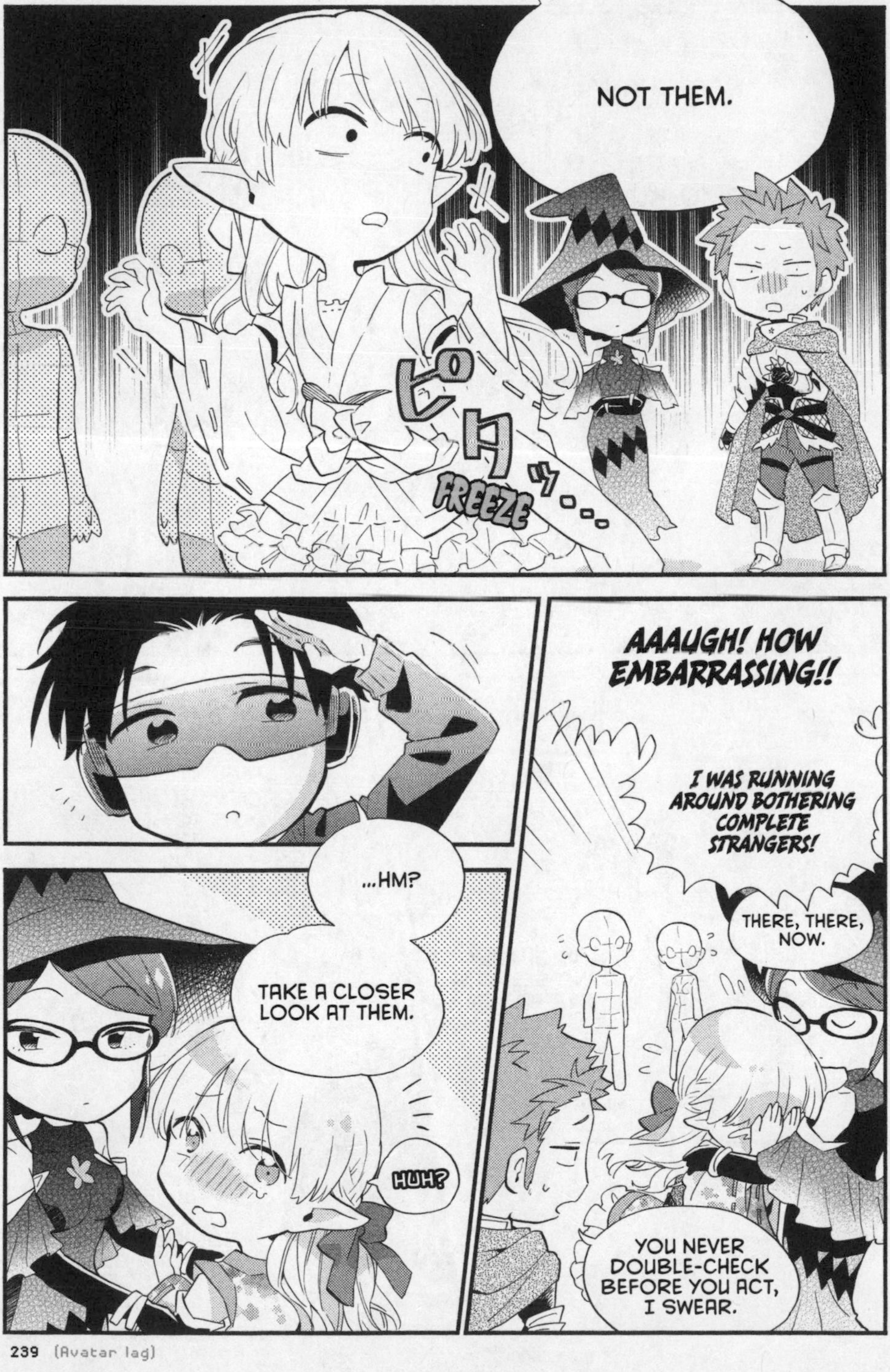
NOT THEM.
ピクッ
FREEZE
AAAUGH! HOW EMBARRASSING!!
I WAS RUNNING AROUND BOTHERING COMPLETE STRANGERS!
THERE, THERE, NOW.
YOU NEVER DOUBLE-CHECK BEFORE YOU ACT, I SWEAR.
...HM?
TAKE A CLOSER LOOK AT THEM.
HUH?

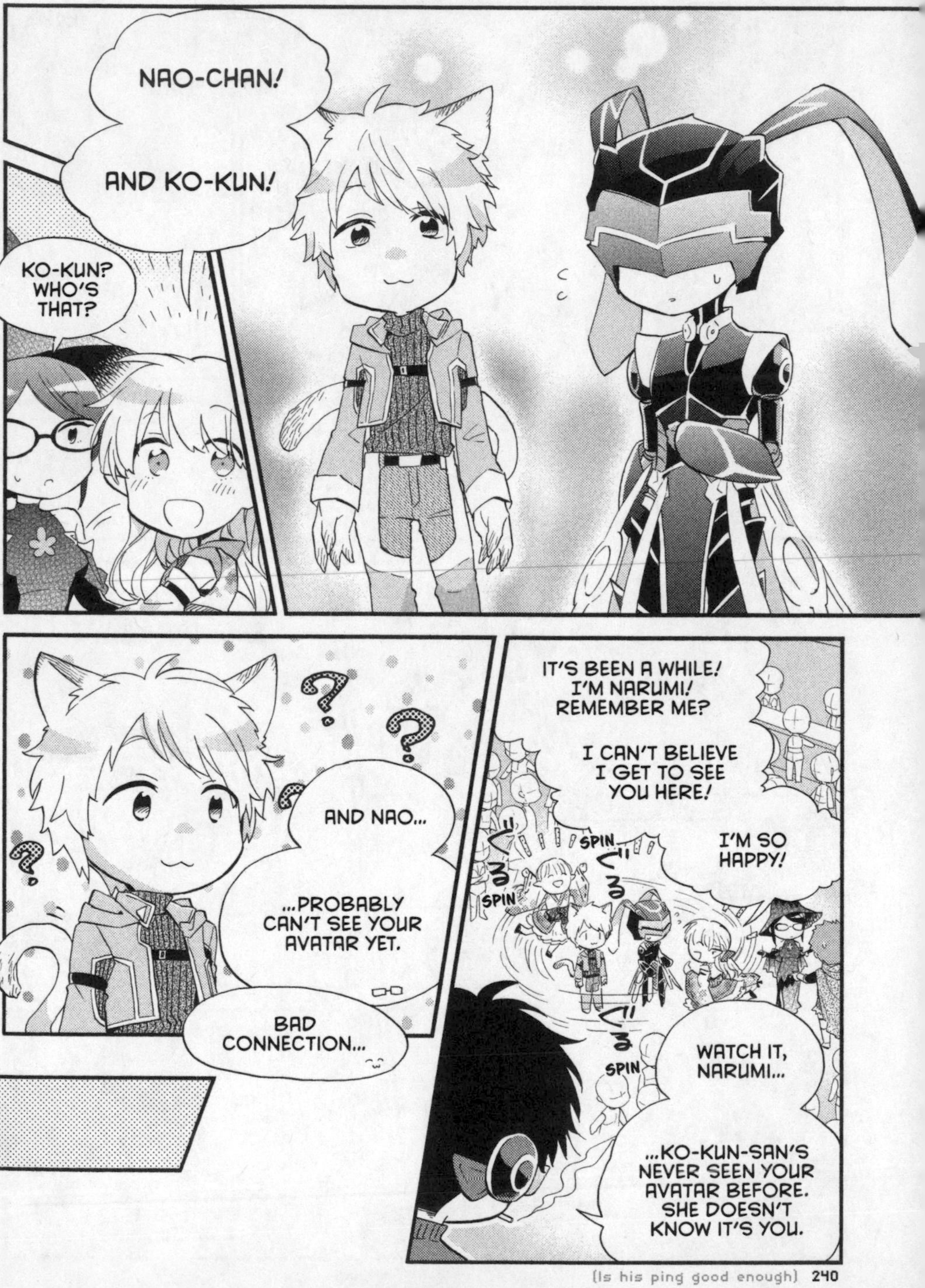
NAO-CHAN!
AND KO-KUN!
KO-KUN? WHO'S THAT?
IT'S BEEN A WHILE! I'M NARUMI! REMEMBER ME?
I CAN'T BELIEVE I GET TO SEE YOU HERE!
I'M SO HAPPY!
SPIN
SPIN
SPIN
WATCH IT, NARUMI...
...KO-KUN-SAN'S NEVER SEEN YOUR AVATAR BEFORE. SHE DOESN'T KNOW IT'S YOU.
AND NAO...
...PROBABLY CAN'T SEE YOUR AVATAR YET.
BAD CONNECTION...

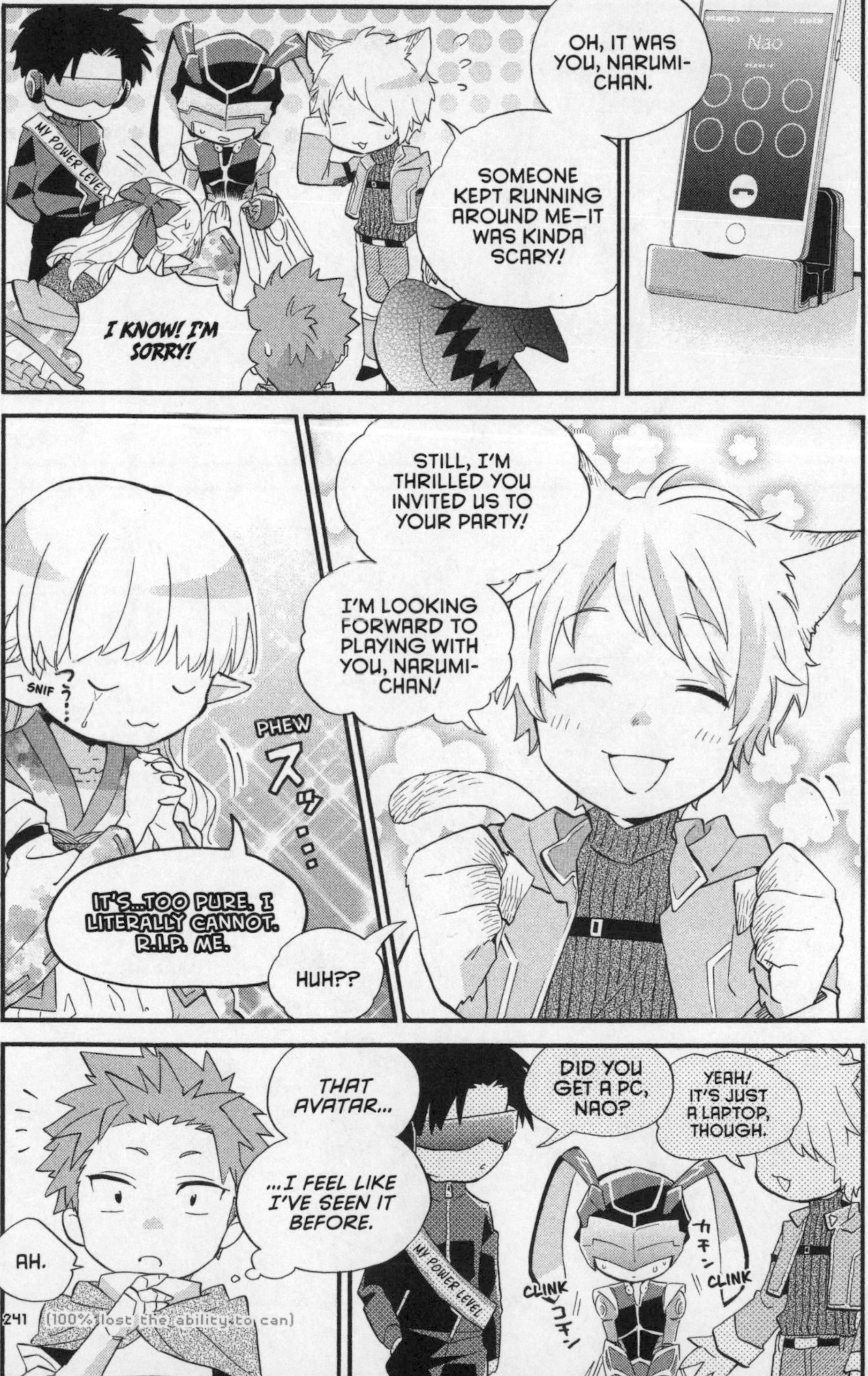
Nao
OH, IT WAS YOU, NARUMI-CHAN.
SOMEONE KEPT RUNNING AROUND ME—IT WAS KINDA SCARY!
MY POWER LEVEL
I KNOW! I'M SORRY!
STILL, I'M THRILLED YOU INVITED US TO YOUR PARTY!
I'M LOOKING FORWARD TO PLAYING WITH YOU, NARUMI-CHAN!
HUH??
SNIF
PHEW
スッ...
IT'S...TOO PURE. I LITERALLY CANNOT. R.I.P. ME.
DID YOU GET A PC, NAO?
YEAH! IT'S JUST A LAPTOP, THOUGH.
カチン
CLINK
コチン
CLINK
MY POWER LEVEL
THAT AVATAR...
...I FEEL LIKE I'VE SEEN IT BEFORE.
AH.
(100% lost the ability to can)

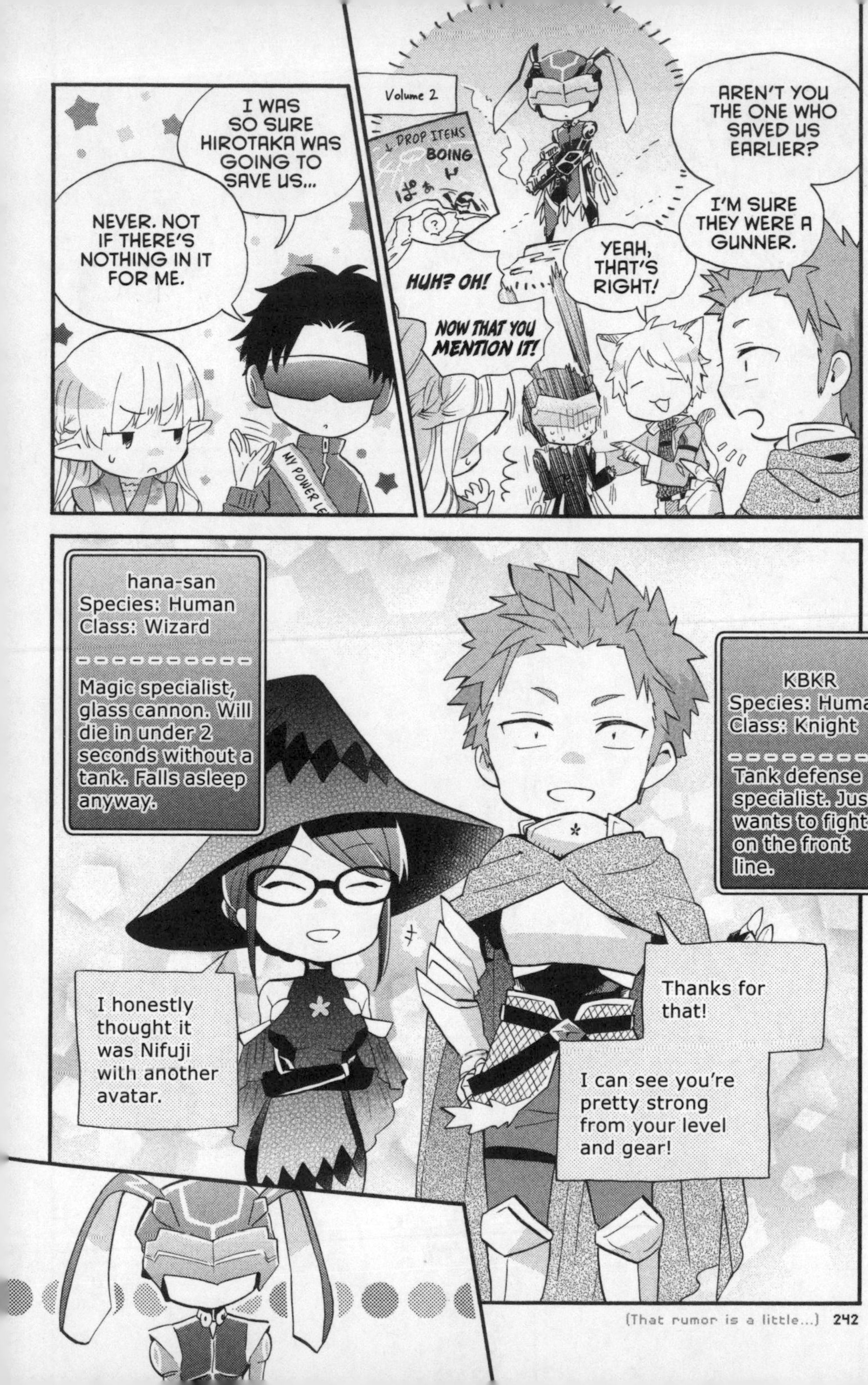
AREN'T YOU THE ONE WHO SAVED US EARLIER?
I'M SURE THEY WERE A GUNNER.
YEAH, THAT'S RIGHT!
Volume 2
DROP ITEMS
BOING
HUH? OH!
NOW THAT YOU MENTION IT!
I WAS SO SURE HIROTAKA WAS GOING TO SAVE US...
NEVER. NOT IF THERE'S NOTHING IN IT FOR ME.
KBKR
Species: Human
Class: Knight
Tank defense specialist. Just wants to fight on the front line.
hana-san
Species: Human
Class: Wizard
Magic specialist, glass cannon. Will die in under 2 seconds without a tank. Falls asleep anyway.
Thanks for that!
I can see you're pretty strong from your level and gear!
I honestly thought it was Nifuji with another avatar.

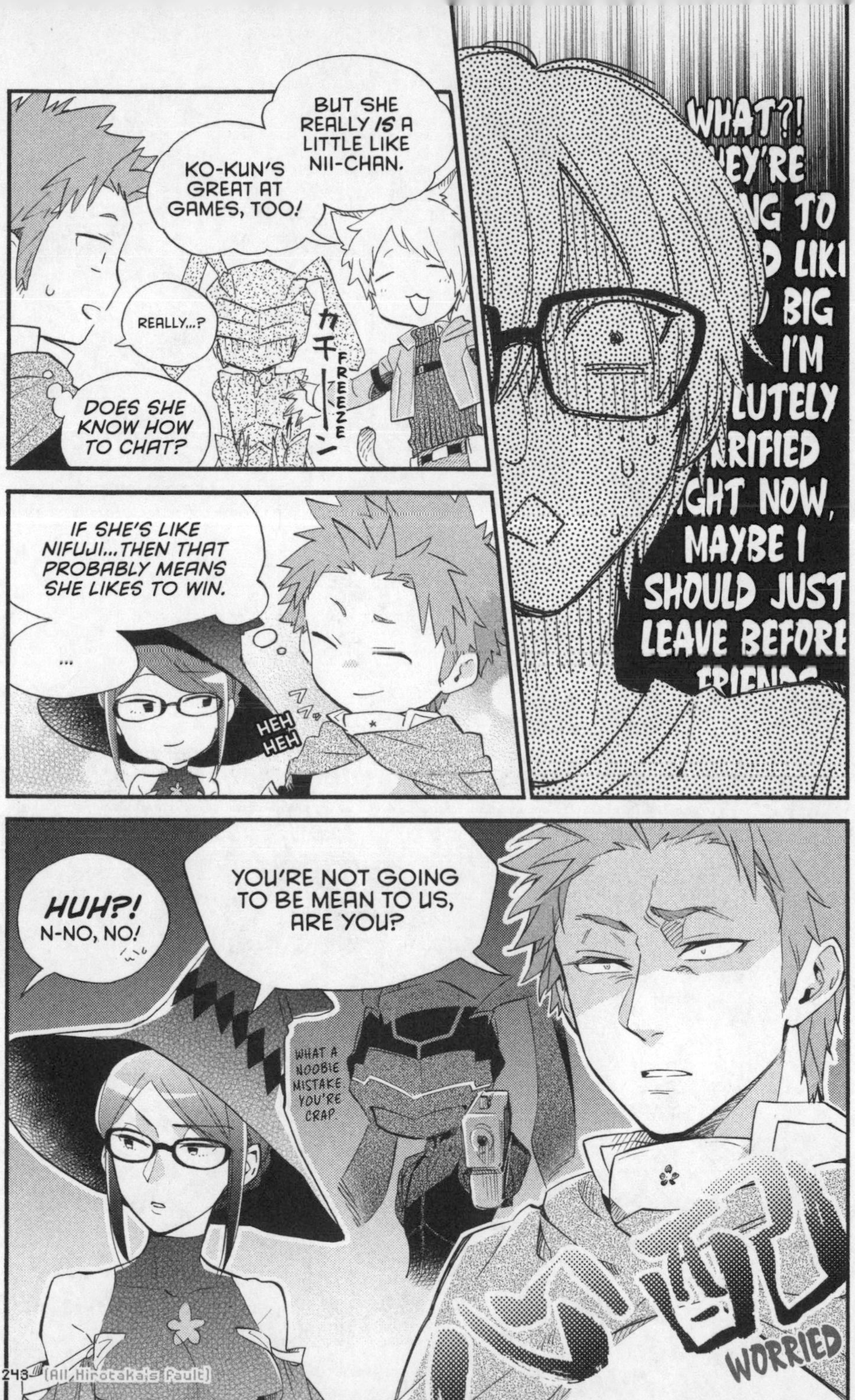
WHAT?!
EY'RE
NG TO
D LIKI
BIG
I'M
LUTELY
RIFIED
GHT NOW,
MAYBE I
SHOULD JUST
LEAVE BEFORE
BUT SHE REALLY *IS* A LITTLE LIKE NII-CHAN.
KO-KUN'S GREAT AT GAMES, TOO!
REALLY...?
DOES SHE KNOW HOW TO CHAT?
FREEZE
IF SHE'S LIKE NIFUJI...THEN THAT PROBABLY MEANS SHE LIKES TO WIN.
...
HEH HEH
YOU'RE NOT GOING TO BE MEAN TO US, ARE YOU?
HUH?! N-NO, NO!
WHAT A NOOBIE MISTAKE YOU'RE CRAP.
WORRIED

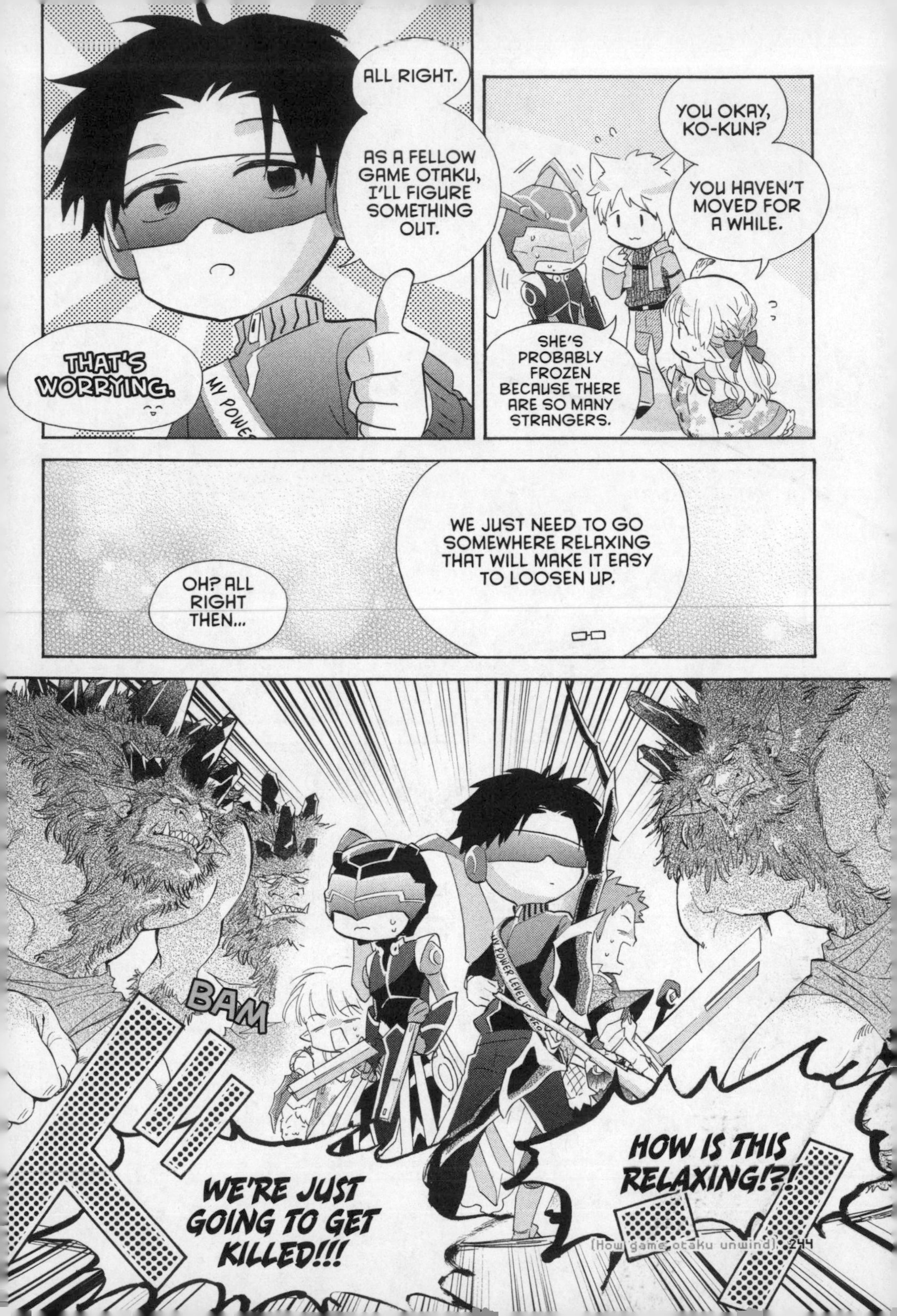
YOU OKAY, KO-KUN?
YOU HAVEN'T MOVED FOR A WHILE.
SHE'S PROBABLY FROZEN BECAUSE THERE ARE SO MANY STRANGERS.
ALL RIGHT.
AS A FELLOW GAME OTAKU, I'LL FIGURE SOMETHING OUT.
THAT'S WORRYING.
WE JUST NEED TO GO SOMEWHERE RELAXING THAT WILL MAKE IT EASY TO LOOSEN UP.
OH? ALL RIGHT THEN...
BAM
HOW IS THIS RELAXING!?!
WE'RE JUST GOING TO GET KILLED!!!
(How game otaku unwind)

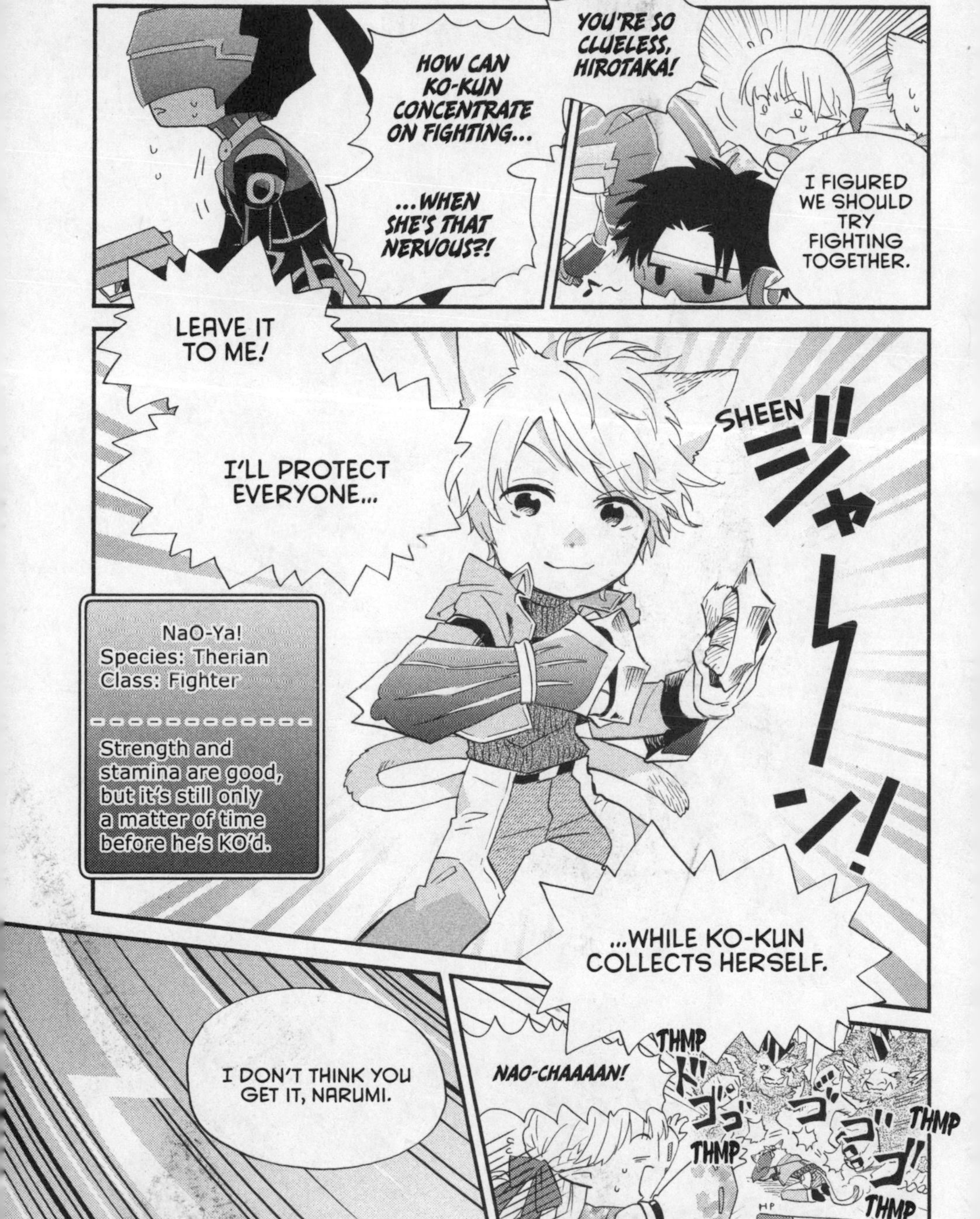
I FIGURED WE SHOULD TRY FIGHTING TOGETHER.
YOU'RE SO CLUELESS, HIROTAKA!
HOW CAN KO-KUN CONCENTRATE ON FIGHTING...
...WHEN SHE'S THAT NERVOUS?!
LEAVE IT TO ME!
I'LL PROTECT EVERYONE...
SHEEN
ジャーン!
NaO-Ya!
Species: Therian
Class: Fighter
Strength and stamina are good, but it's still only a matter of time before he's KO'd.
...WHILE KO-KUN COLLECTS HERSELF.
NAO-CHAAAAN!
THMP
THMP
THMP
THMP
HP
I DON'T THINK YOU GET IT, NARUMI.

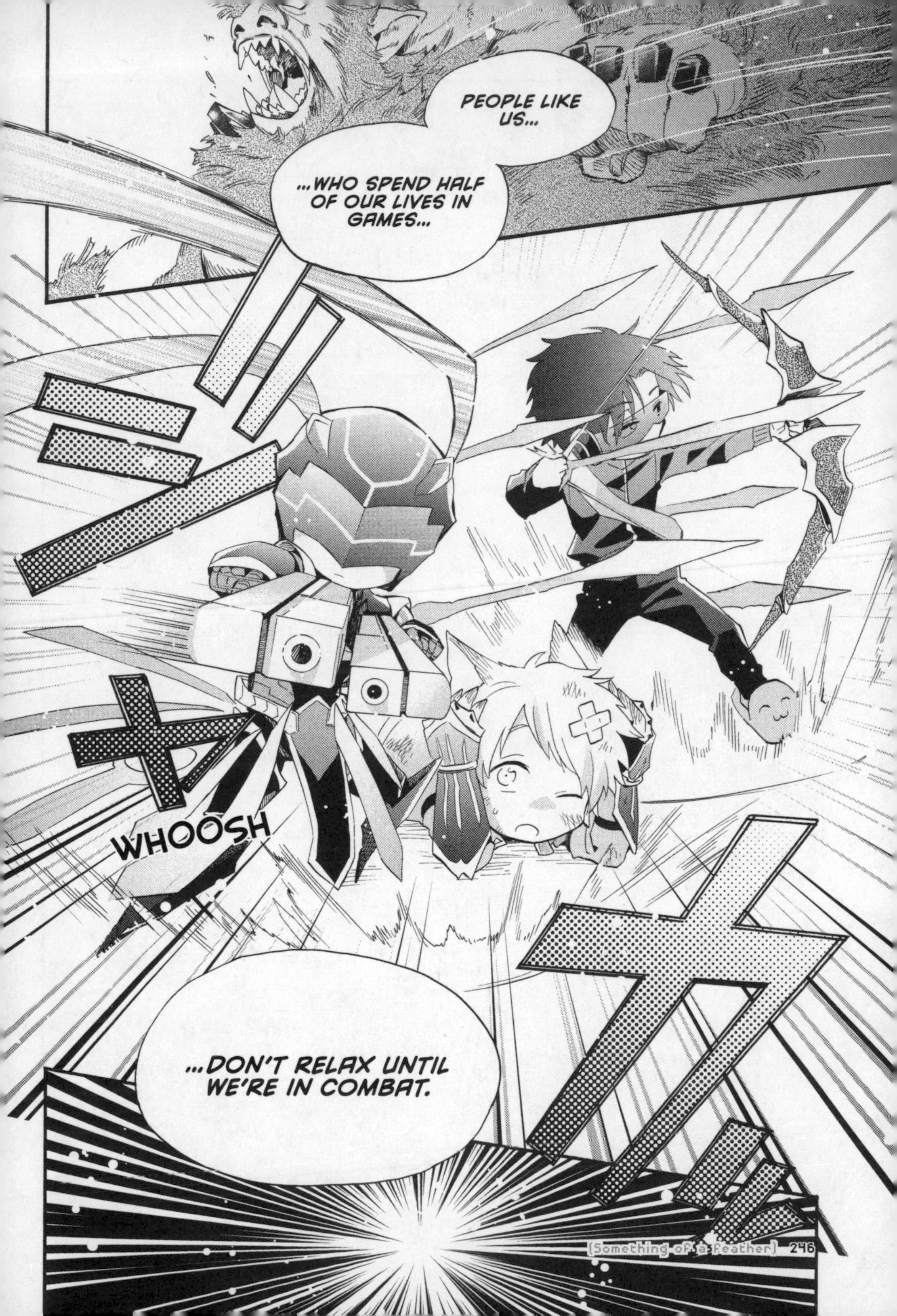
PEOPLE LIKE US...
...WHO SPEND HALF OF OUR LIVES IN GAMES...
WHOOSH
...DON'T RELAX UNTIL WE'RE IN COMBAT.

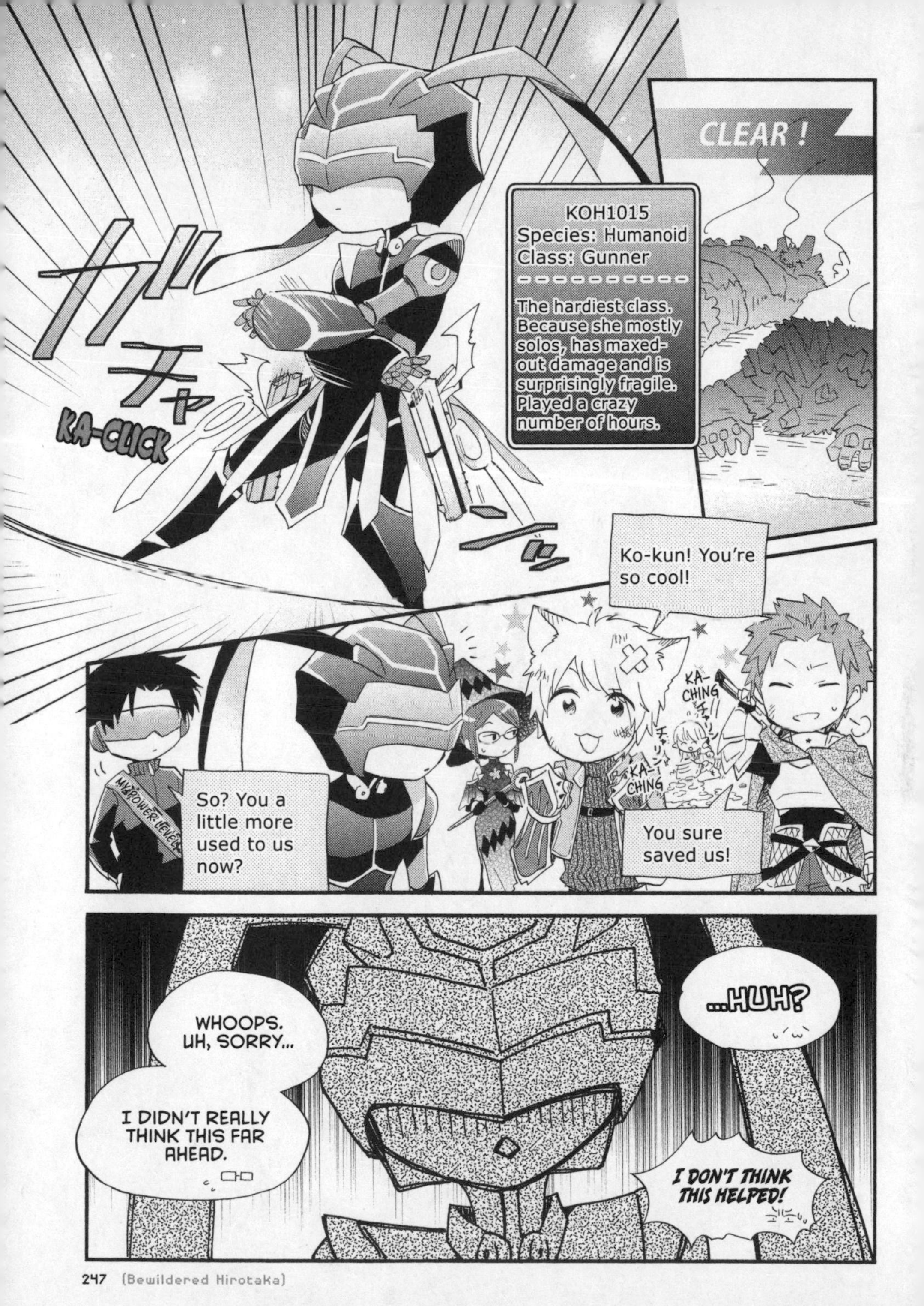
CLEAR !
KOH1015
Species: Humanoid
Class: Gunner
The hardiest class. Because she mostly solos, has maxed-out damage and is surprisingly fragile. Played a crazy number of hours.
KA-CLICK
Ko-kun! You're so cool!
KA-CHING
KA-CHING
You sure saved us!
MY POWER LEVELS
So? You a little more used to us now?
...HUH?
I DON'T THINK THIS HELPED!
WHOOPS. UH, SORRY...
I DIDN'T REALLY THINK THIS FAR AHEAD.

LOVE IS HARD FOR OTAKU ко

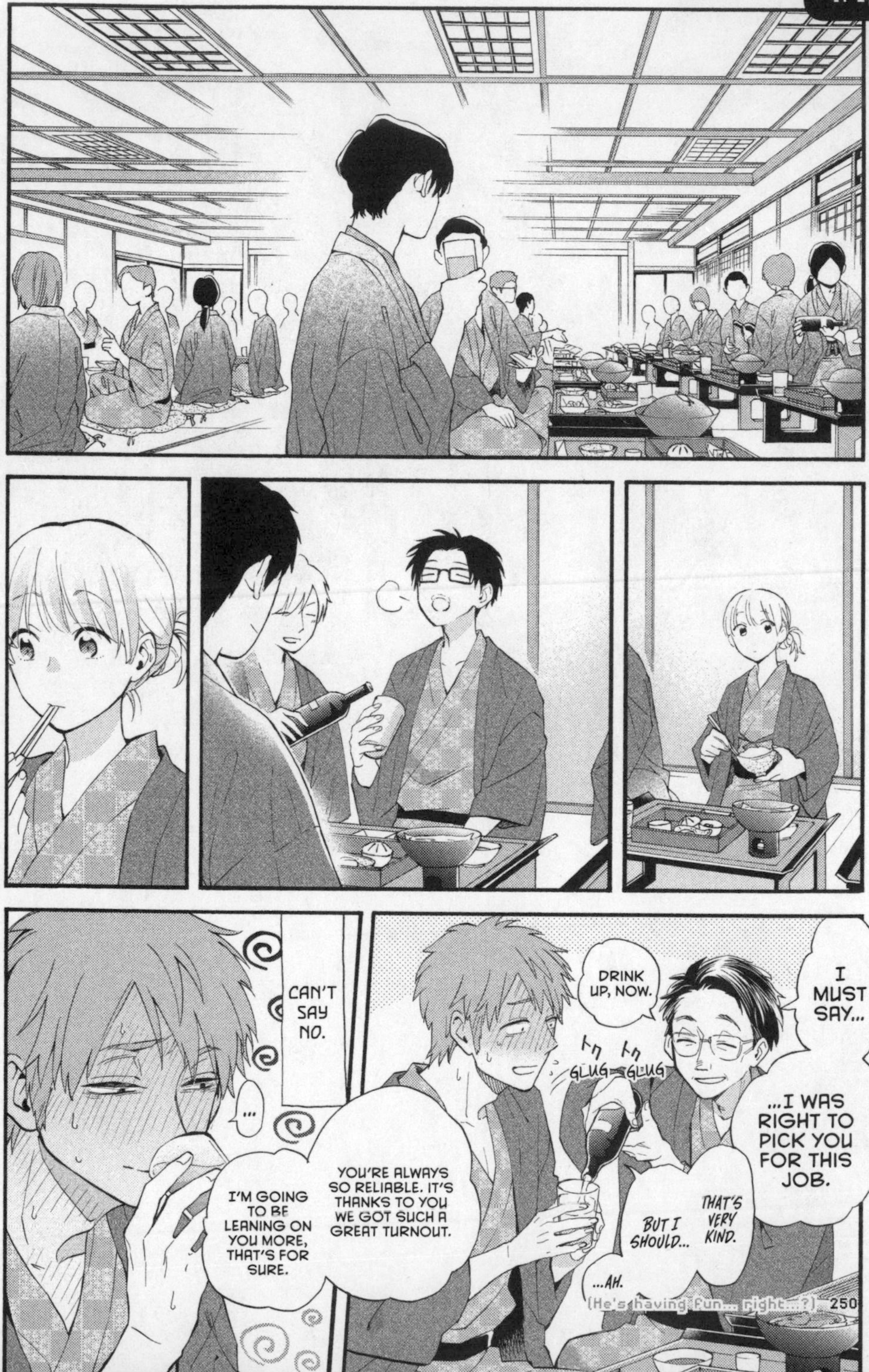
I MUST SAY...
...I WAS RIGHT TO PICK YOU FOR THIS JOB.
DRINK UP, NOW.
トク トク
GLUG GLUG
THAT'S VERY KIND.
BUT I SHOULD...
...AH.
YOU'RE ALWAYS SO RELIABLE. IT'S THANKS TO YOU WE GOT SUCH A GREAT TURNOUT.
I'M GOING TO BE LEANING ON YOU MORE, THAT'S FOR SURE.
CAN'T SAY NO.
...

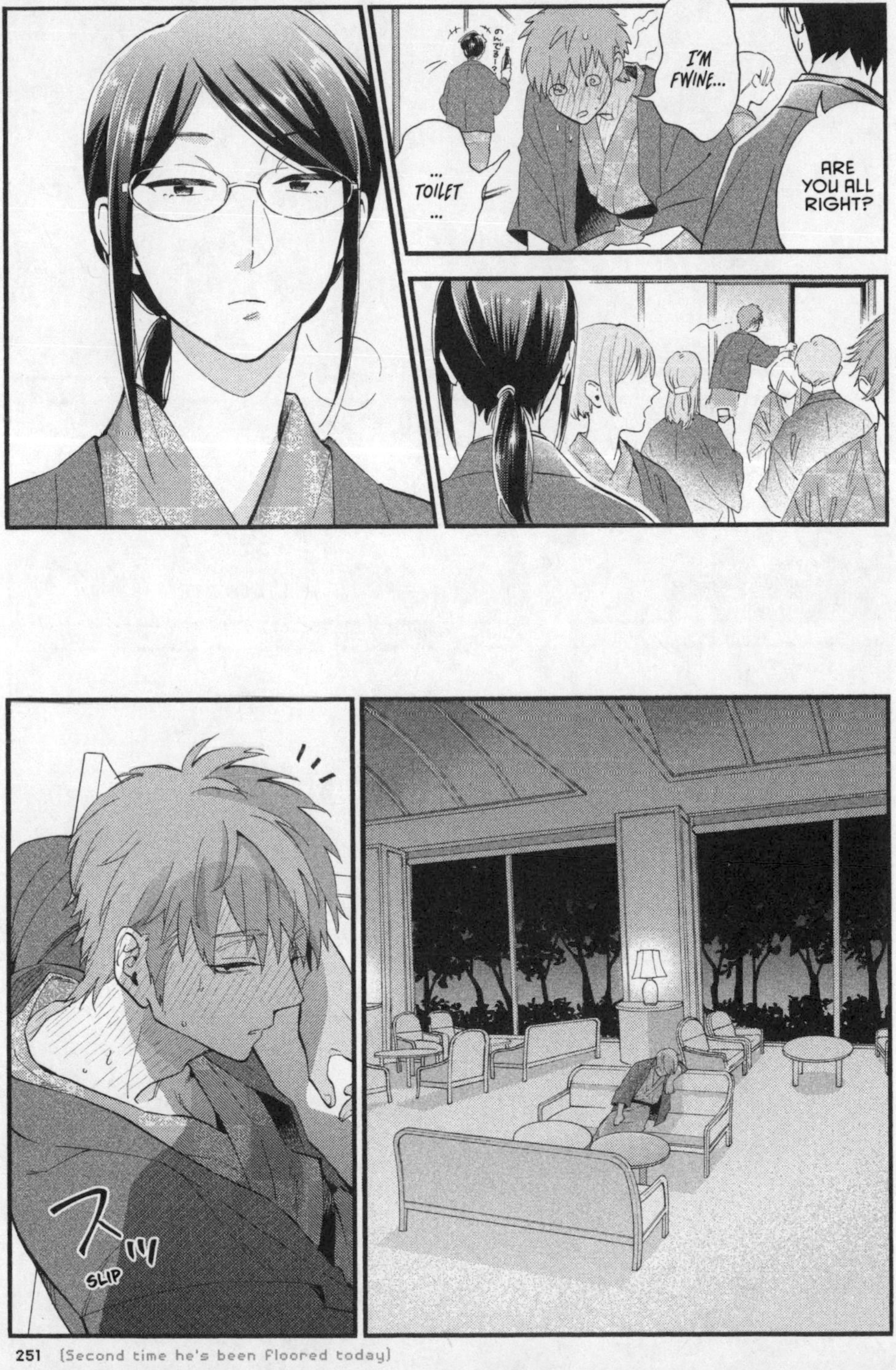
ARE YOU ALL RIGHT?
I'M FWINE...
... TOILET ...
スッ
SLIP

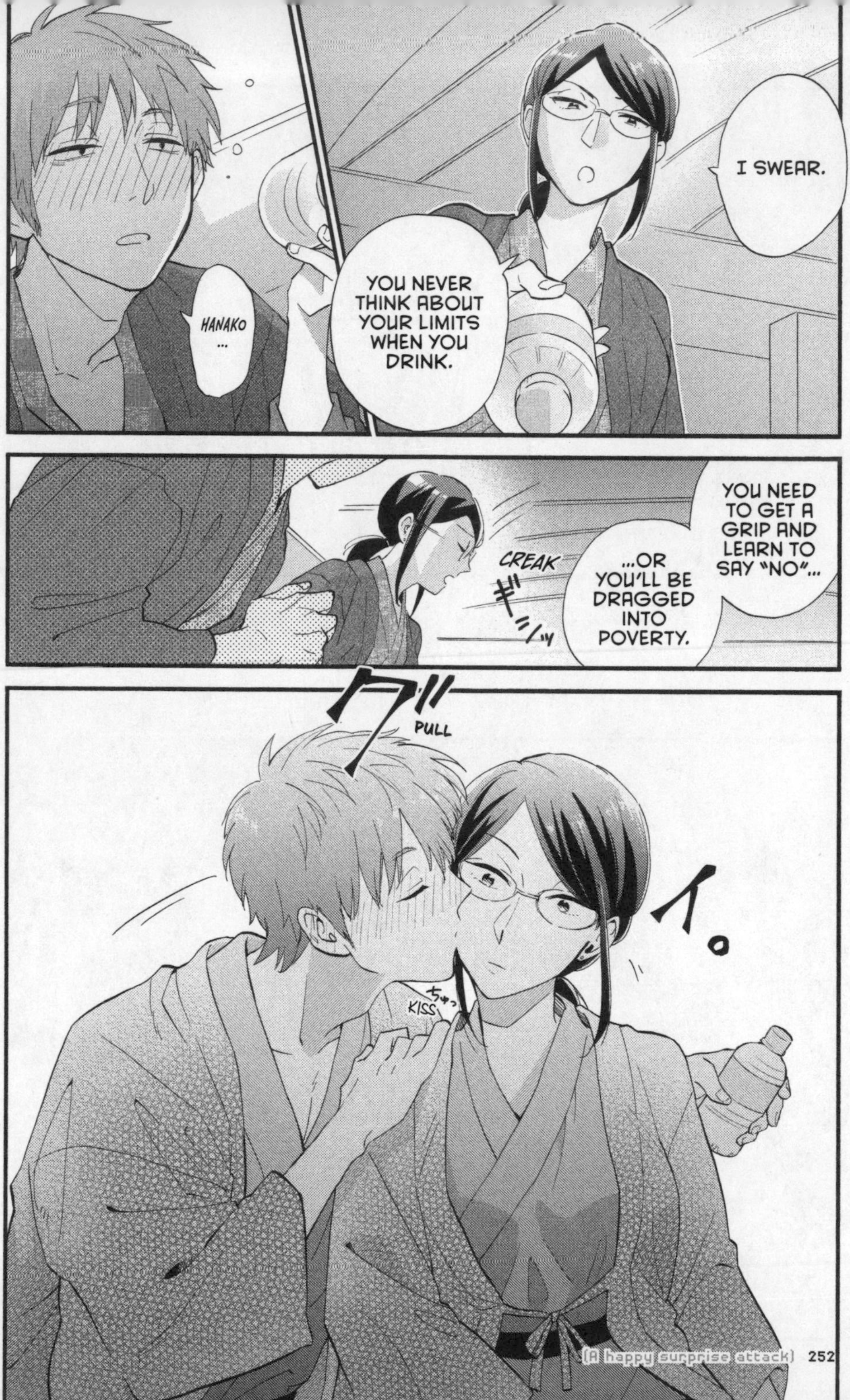
I SWEAR.
YOU NEVER THINK ABOUT YOUR LIMITS WHEN YOU DRINK.
HANAKO ...
YOU NEED TO GET A GRIP AND LEARN TO SAY "NO"...
...OR YOU'LL BE DRAGGED INTO POVERTY.
CREAK
ギシッ
グイ
PULL
イ。
ちゅっ
KISS

[A happy surprise attack]

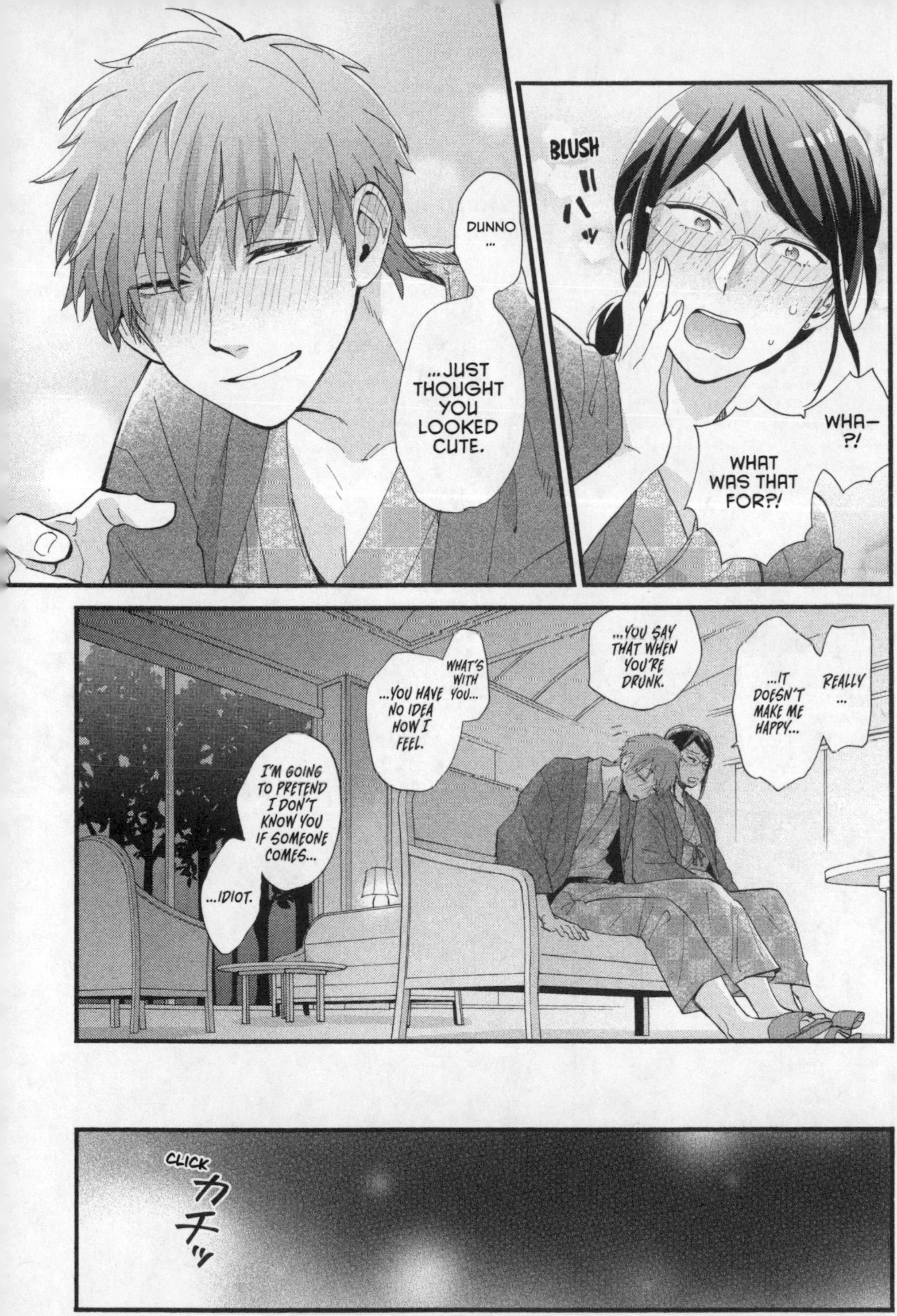
BLUSH
WHA—?!
WHAT WAS THAT FOR?!
DUNNO...
...JUST THOUGHT YOU LOOKED CUTE.
REALLY...
...IT DOESN'T MAKE ME HAPPY...
...YOU SAY THAT WHEN YOU'RE DRUNK.
WHAT'S WITH YOU...
...YOU HAVE NO IDEA HOW I FEEL.
I'M GOING TO PRETEND I DON'T KNOW YOU IF SOMEONE COMES...
...IDIOT.
CLICK
カチッ

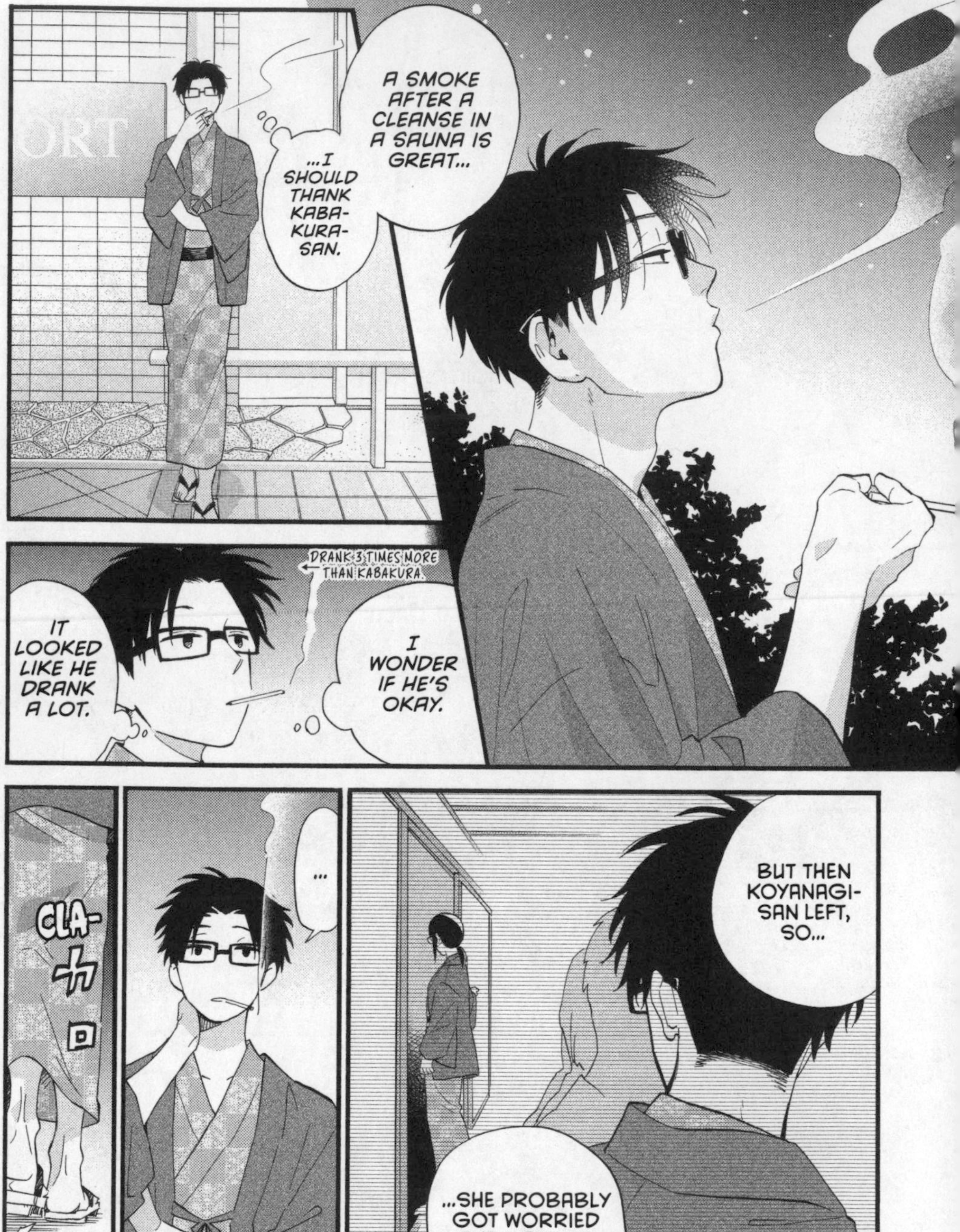
A SMOKE AFTER A CLEANSE IN A SAUNA IS GREAT...
...I SHOULD THANK KABAKURA-SAN.
I WONDER IF HE'S OKAY.
DRANK 3 TIMES MORE THAN KABAKURA.
IT LOOKED LIKE HE DRANK A LOT.
BUT THEN KOYANAGI-SAN LEFT, SO...
...SHE PROBABLY GOT WORRIED AND WENT TO LOOK FOR HIM.
...
CLA-
CLAK

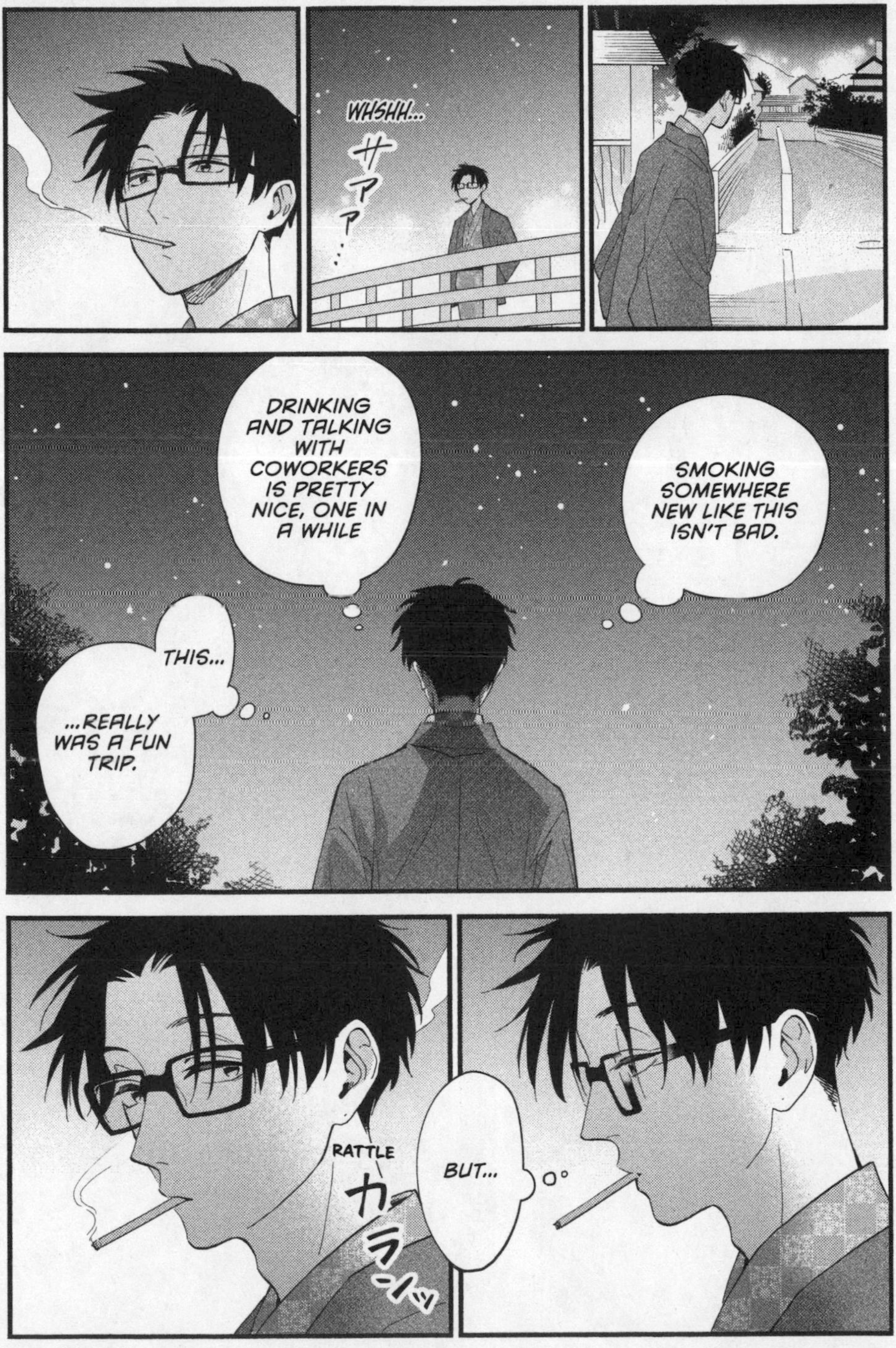
WHSHH...
サアァ...
SMOKING SOMEWHERE NEW LIKE THIS ISN'T BAD.
DRINKING AND TALKING WITH COWORKERS IS PRETTY NICE, ONE IN A WHILE
THIS...
...REALLY WAS A FUN TRIP.
BUT...
RATTLE
カラーンッ

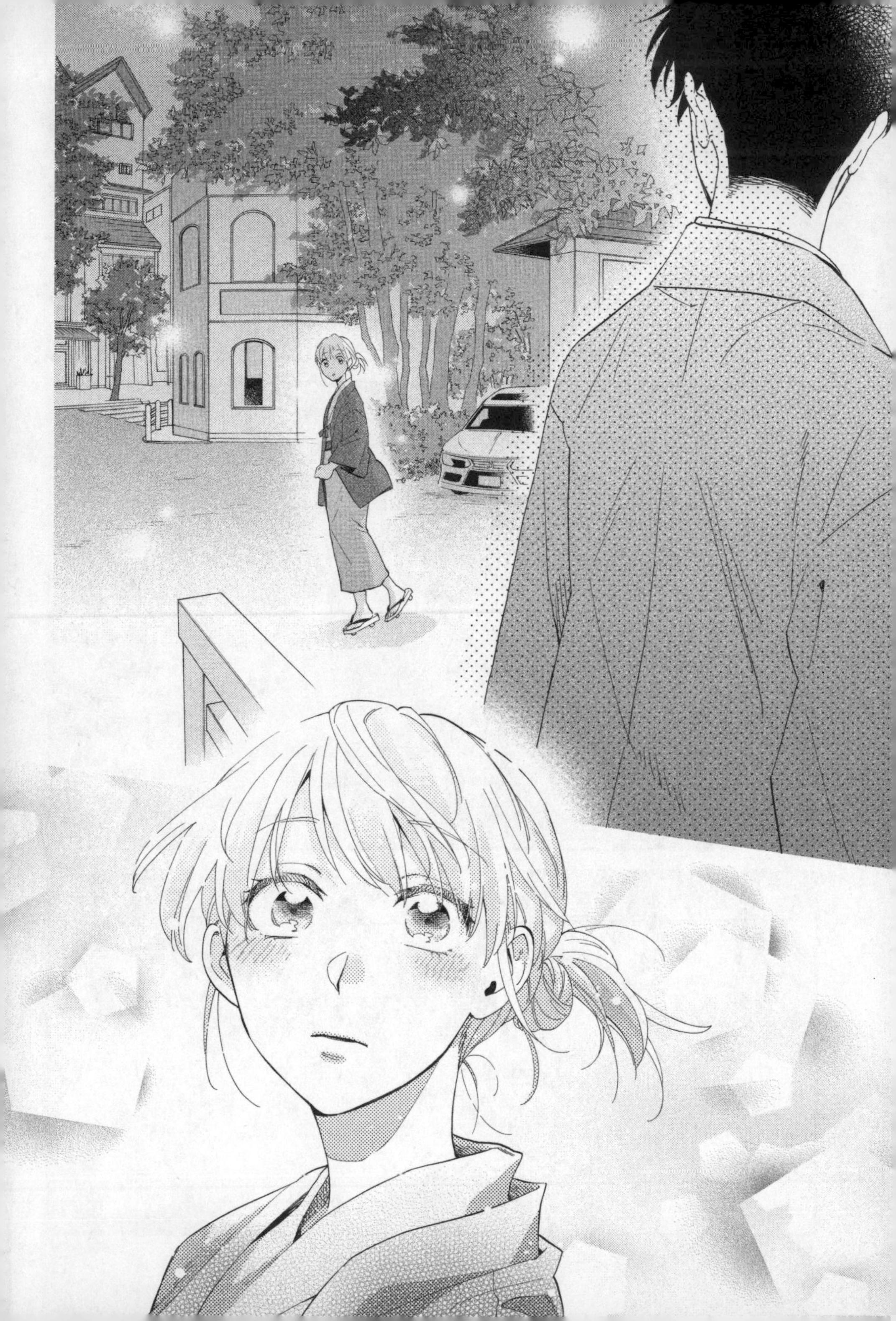

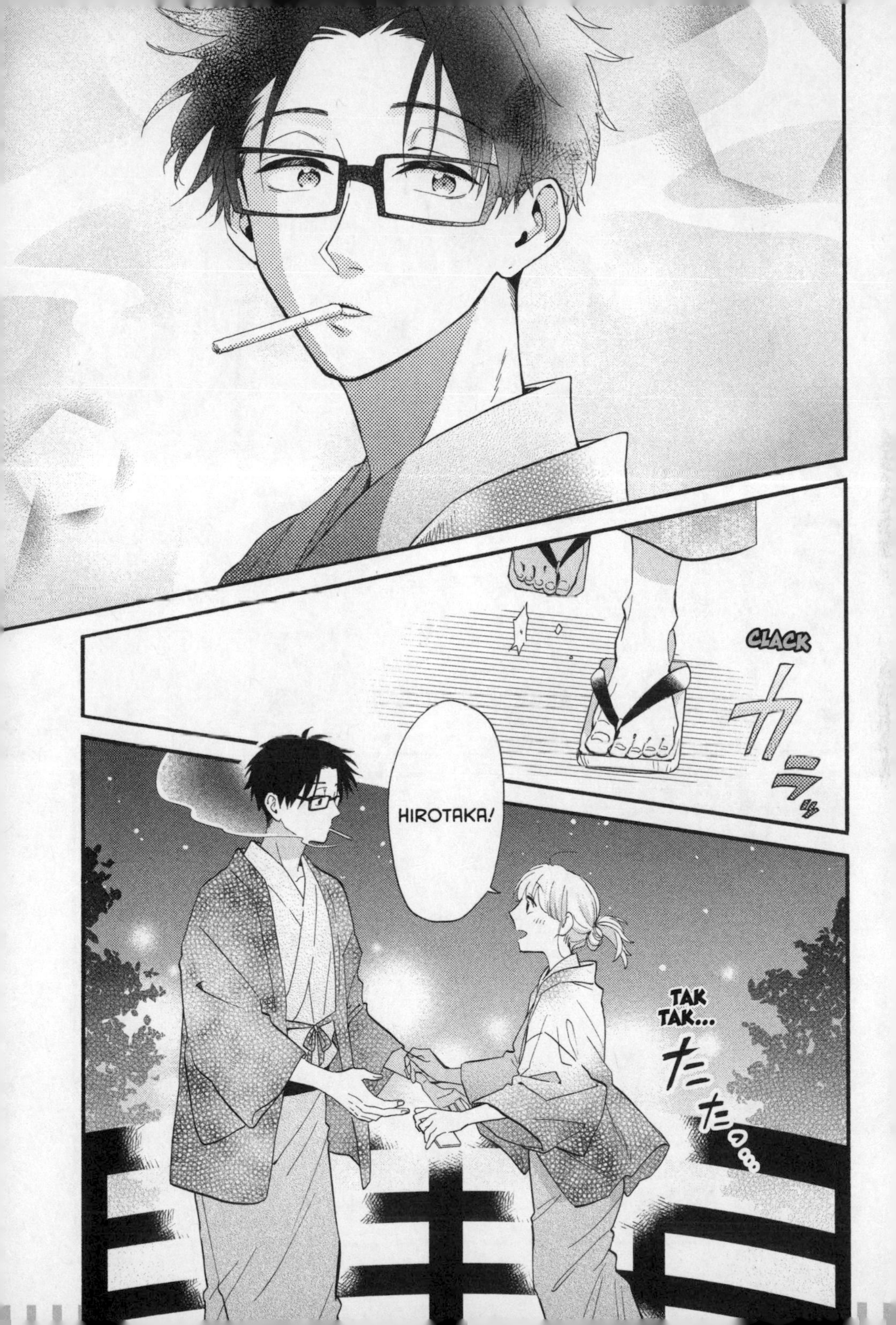
CLACK
カラッ
HIROTAKA!
TAK TAK...
たたっ...

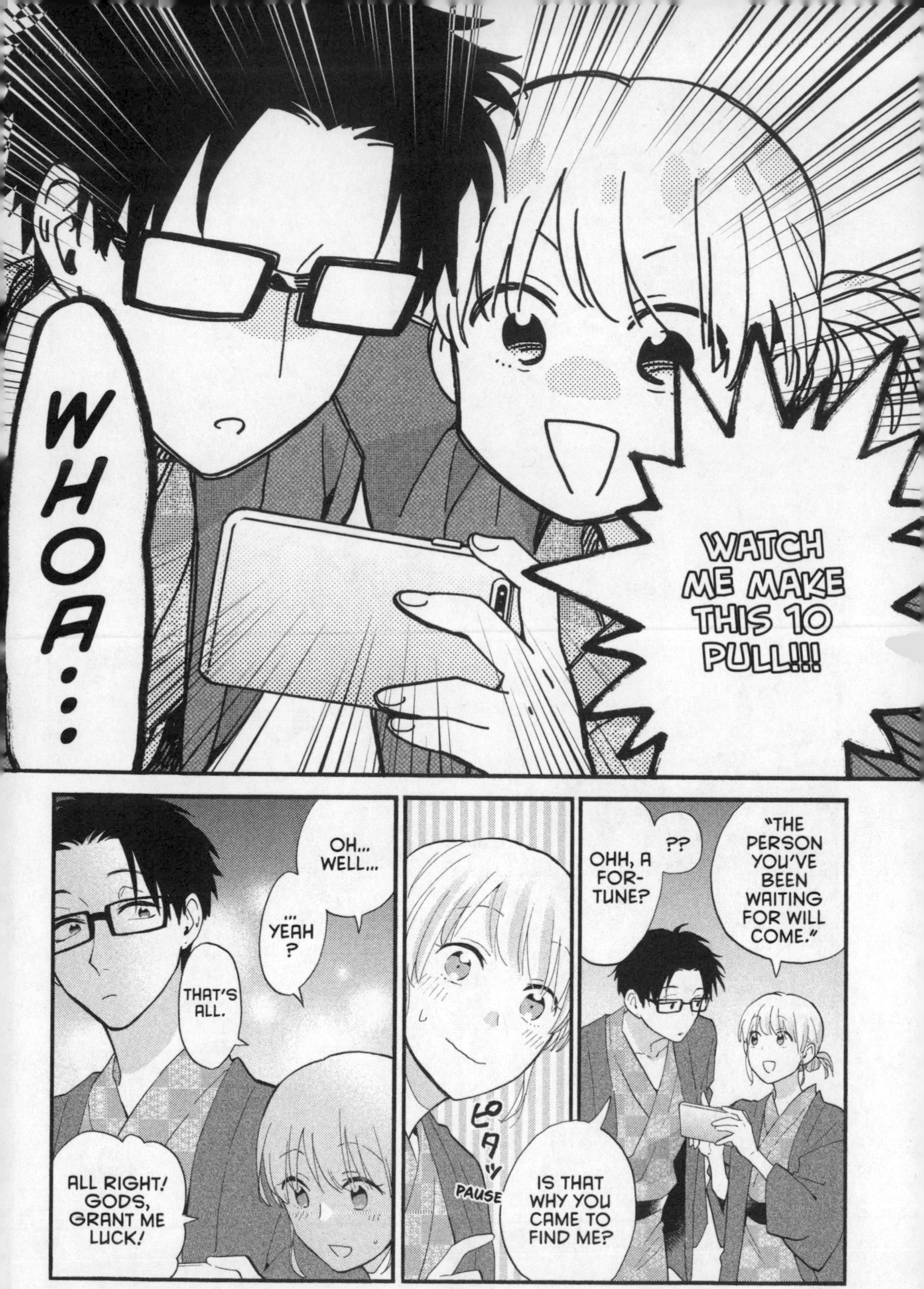
WATCH ME MAKE THIS 10 PULL!!!
WHOA...
"THE PERSON YOU'VE BEEN WAITING FOR WILL COME."
??
OHH, A FOR-TUNE?
ピタッ
PAUSE
IS THAT WHY YOU CAME TO FIND ME?
OH... WELL...
...YEAH?
THAT'S ALL.
ALL RIGHT! GODS, GRANT ME LUCK!

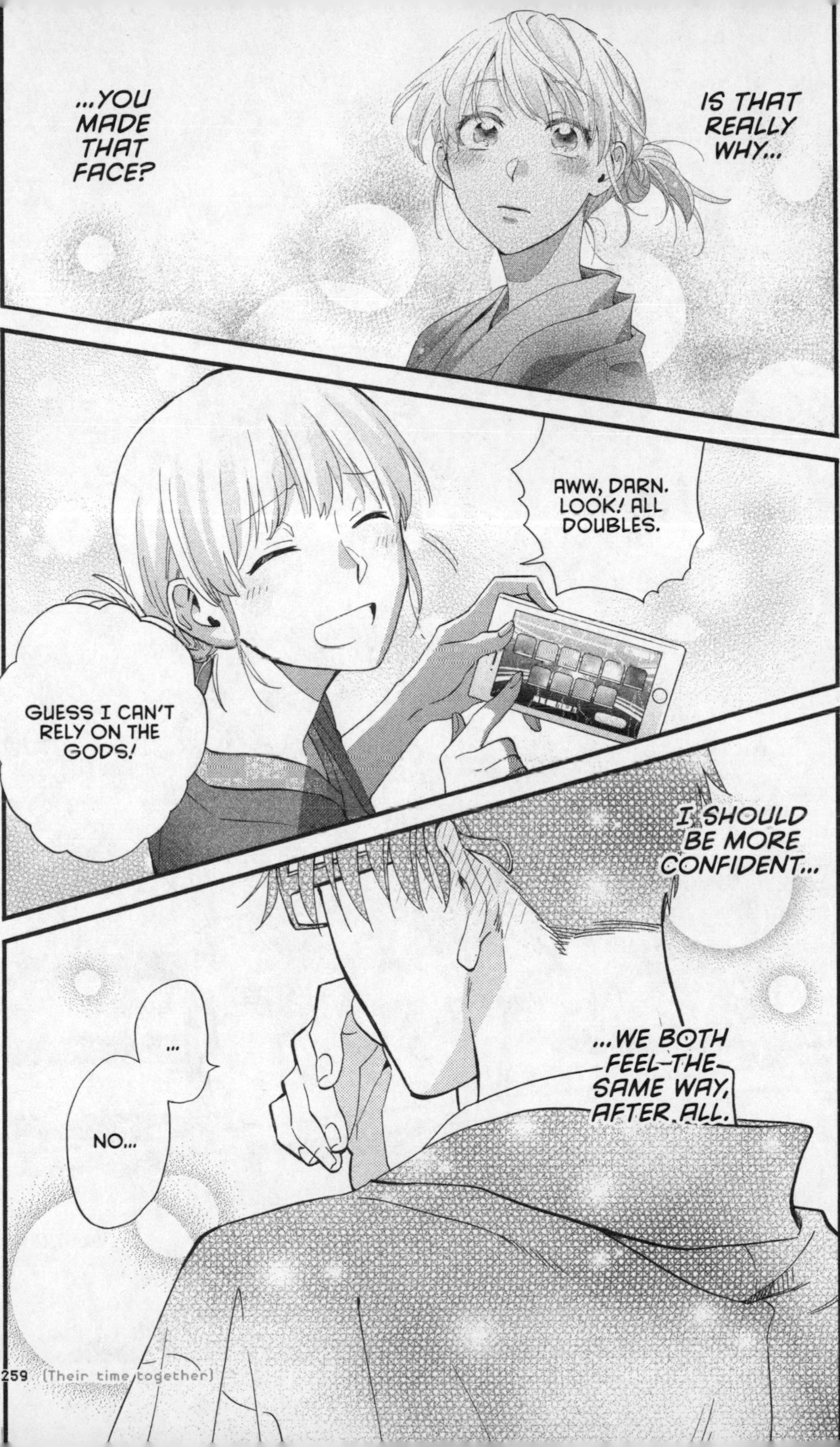
IS THAT REALLY WHY...
...YOU MADE THAT FACE?
AWW, DARN. LOOK! ALL DOUBLES.
GUESS I CAN'T RELY ON THE GODS!
I SHOULD BE MORE CONFIDENT...
...WE BOTH FEEL THE SAME WAY, AFTER ALL.
...
NO...

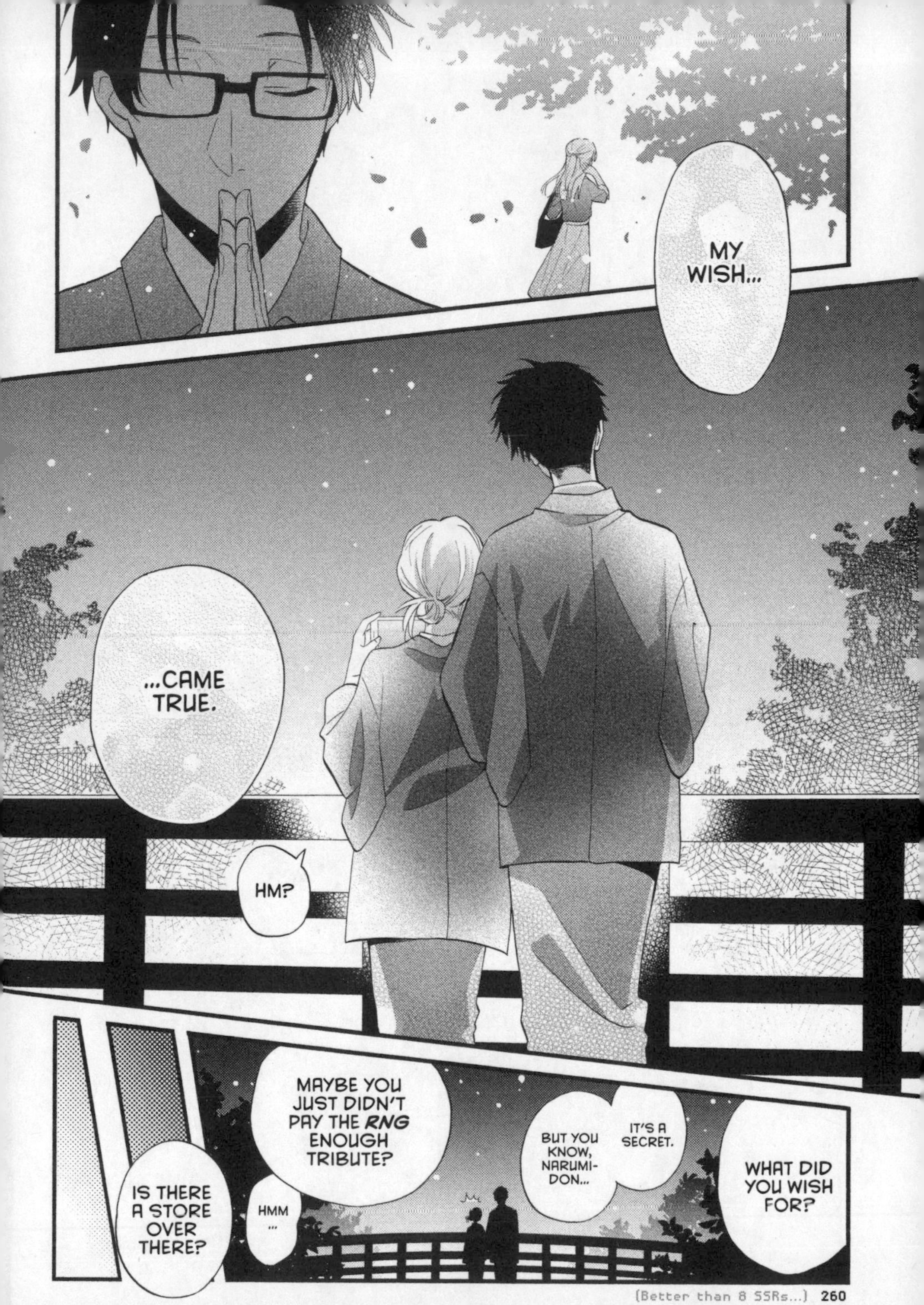
MY WISH...
...CAME TRUE.
HM?
WHAT DID YOU WISH FOR?
IT'S A SECRET.
BUT YOU KNOW, NARUMI-DON...
MAYBE YOU JUST DIDN'T PAY THE *RNG* ENOUGH TRIBUTE?
HMM ...
IS THERE A STORE OVER THERE?

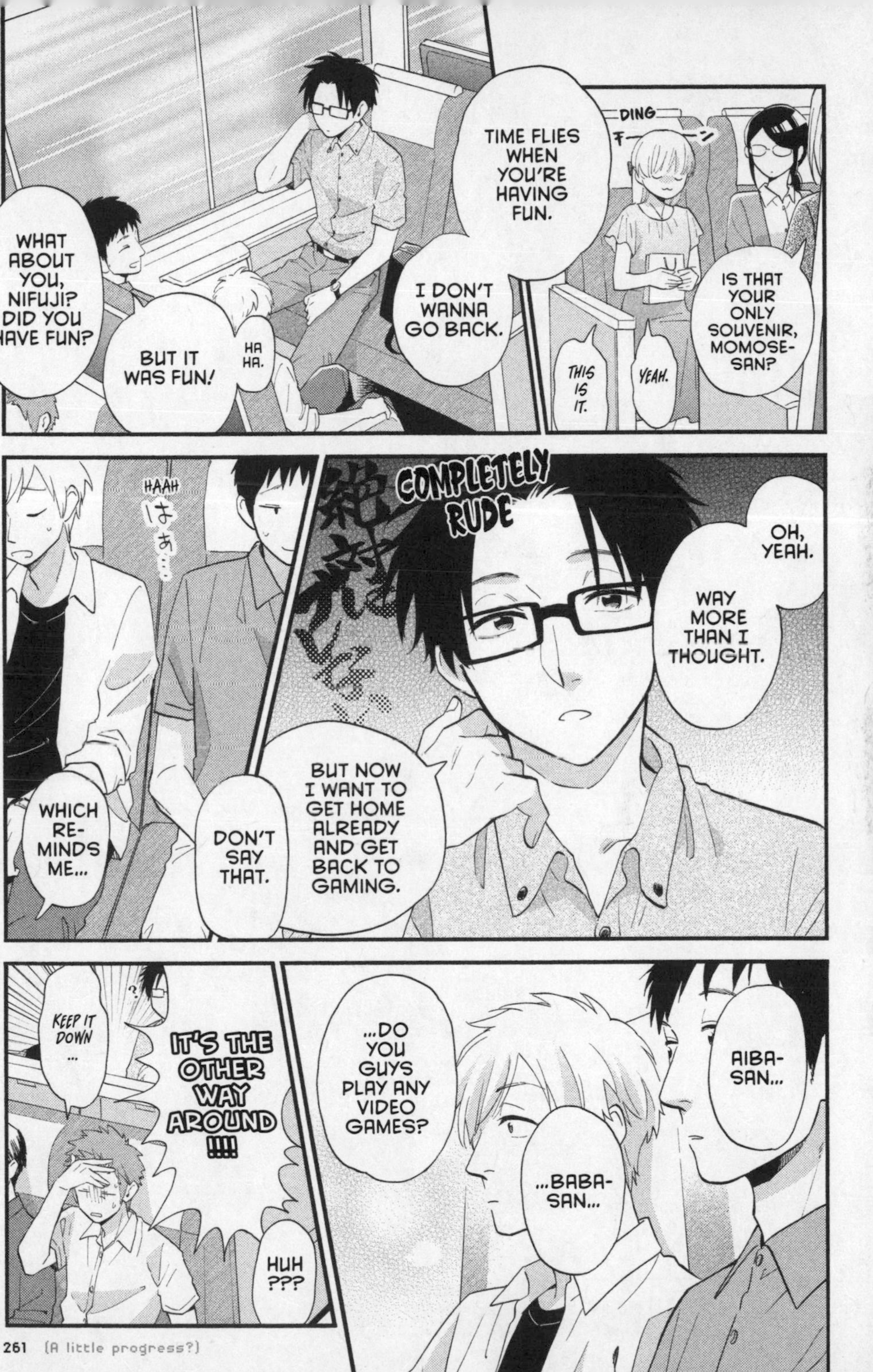
DING
チーン
IS THAT YOUR ONLY SOUVENIR, MOMOSE-SAN?
YEAH.
THIS IS IT.
TIME FLIES WHEN YOU'RE HAVING FUN.
I DON'T WANNA GO BACK.
HA HA.
BUT IT WAS FUN!
WHAT ABOUT YOU, NIFUJI? DID YOU HAVE FUN?
COMPLETELY RUDE
OH, YEAH.
WAY MORE THAN I THOUGHT.
BUT NOW I WANT TO GET HOME ALREADY AND GET BACK TO GAMING.
HAAH
はぁ…
DON'T SAY THAT.
WHICH RE-MINDS ME...
AIBA-SAN...
...DO YOU GUYS PLAY ANY VIDEO GAMES?
...BABA-SAN...
IT'S THE OTHER WAY AROUND!!!!
KEEP IT DOWN...
HUH???

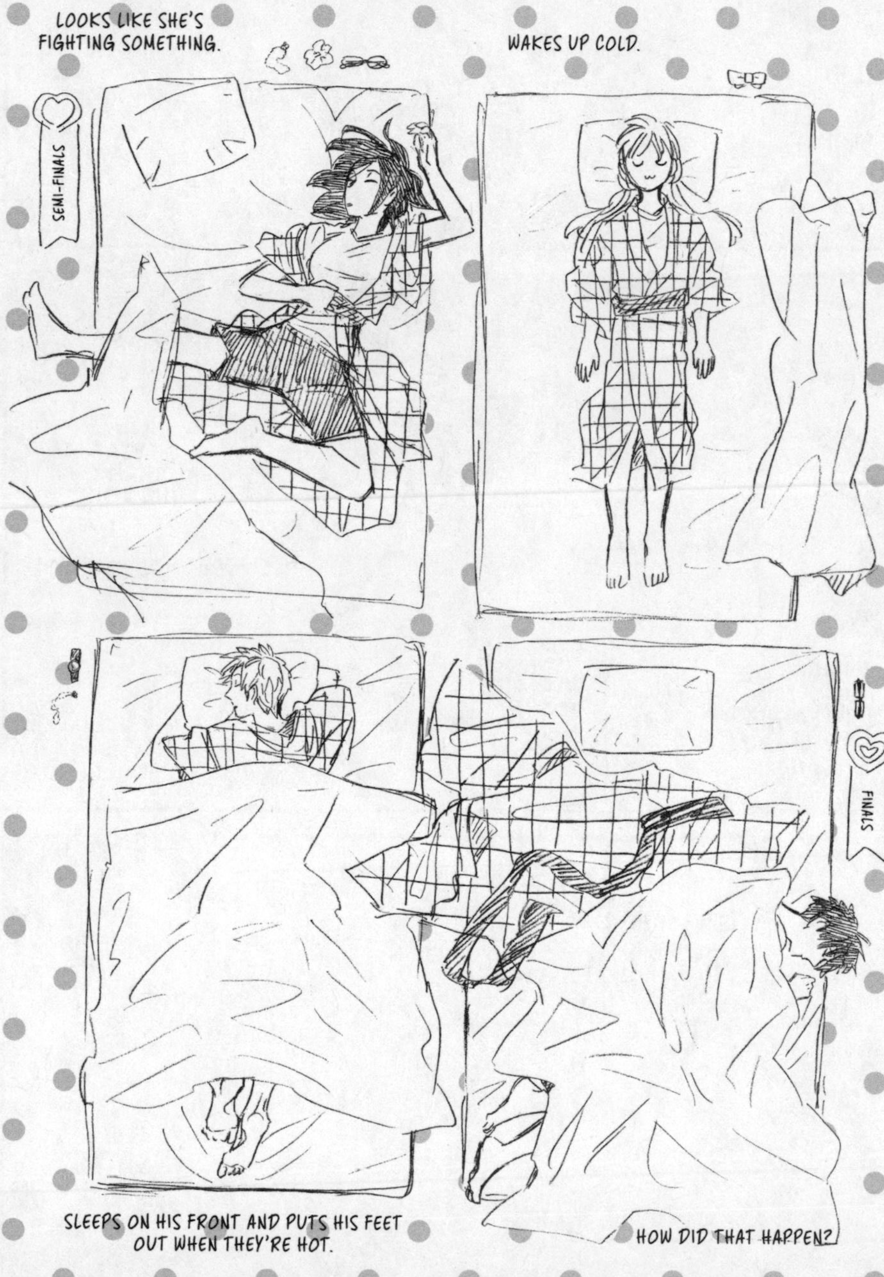
WAKES UP COLD.
LOOKS LIKE SHE'S FIGHTING SOMETHING.
SEMI-FINALS
FINALS
HOW DID THAT HAPPEN?
SLEEPS ON HIS FRONT AND PUTS HIS FEET OUT WHEN THEY'RE HOT.

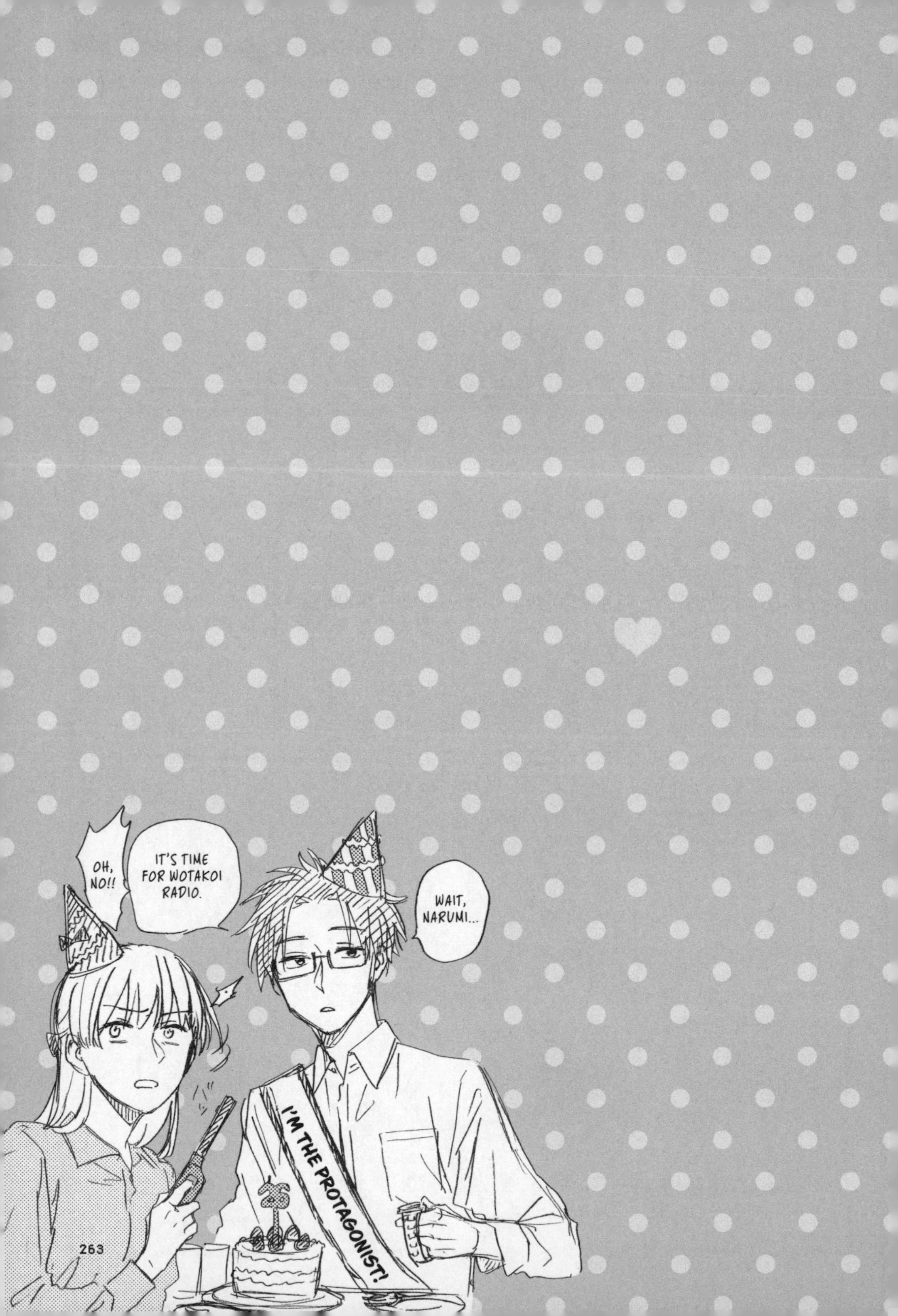
WAIT, NARUMI...
IT'S TIME FOR WOTAKOI RADIO.
OH, NO!!
I'M THE PROTAGONIST!

Afterword

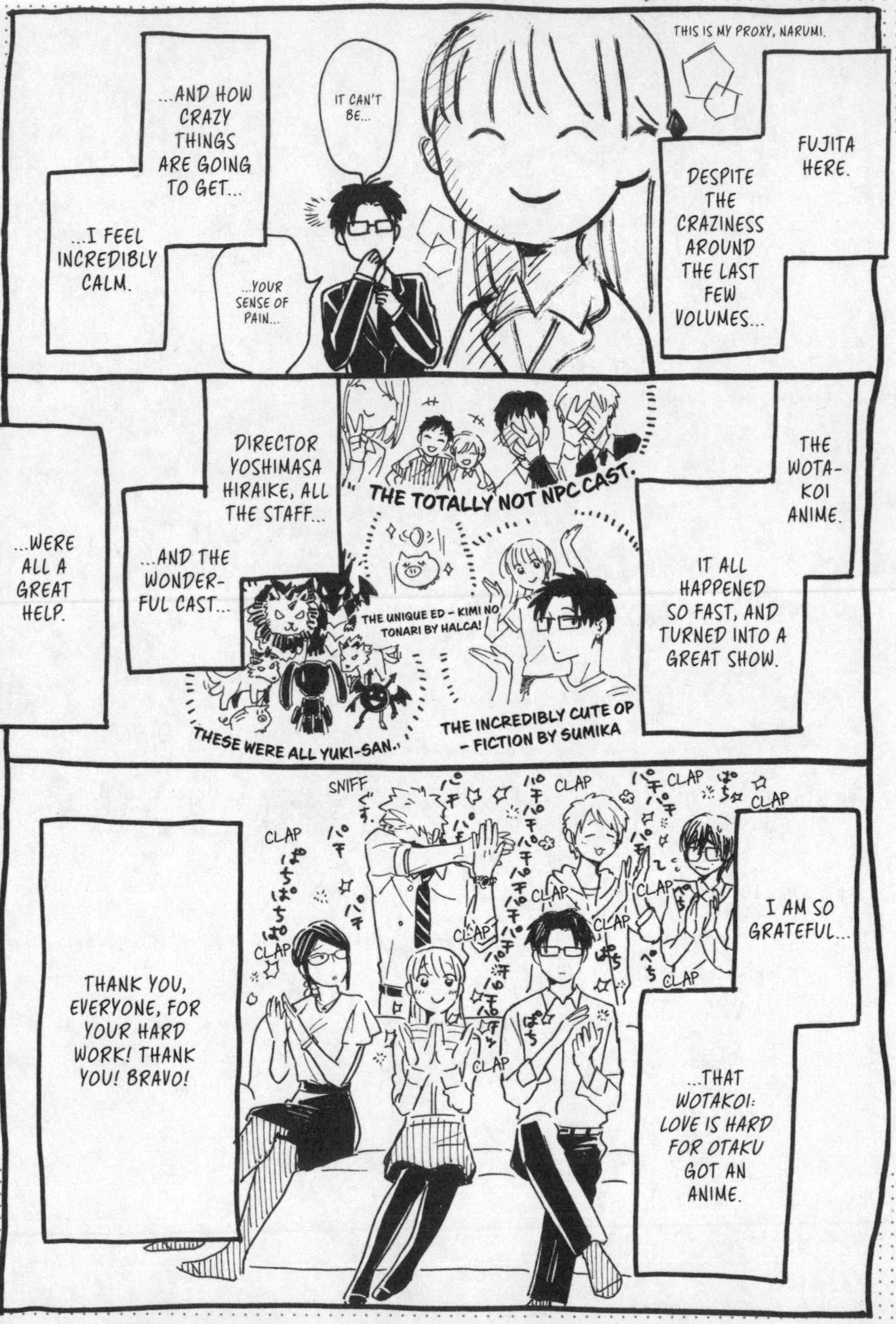
THIS IS MY PROXY, NARUMI.
FUJITA HERE.
DESPITE THE CRAZINESS AROUND THE LAST FEW VOLUMES...
IT CAN'T BE...
...YOUR SENSE OF PAIN...
...AND HOW CRAZY THINGS ARE GOING TO GET...
...I FEEL INCREDIBLY CALM.
THE WOTA-KOI ANIME.
IT ALL HAPPENED SO FAST, AND TURNED INTO A GREAT SHOW.
THE TOTALLY NOT NPC CAST.
THE UNIQUE ED - KIMI NO TONARI BY HALCA!
THE INCREDIBLY CUTE OP - FICTION BY SUMIKA
THESE WERE ALL YUKI-SAN.
DIRECTOR YOSHIMASA HIRAIKE, ALL THE STAFF...
...AND THE WONDERFUL CAST...
...WERE ALL A GREAT HELP.
I AM SO GRATEFUL...
...THAT WOTAKOI: LOVE IS HARD FOR OTAKU GOT AN ANIME.
CLAP
パチ
CLAP
SNIFF
CLAP
CLAP
THANK YOU, EVERYONE, FOR YOUR HARD WORK! THANK YOU! BRAVO!

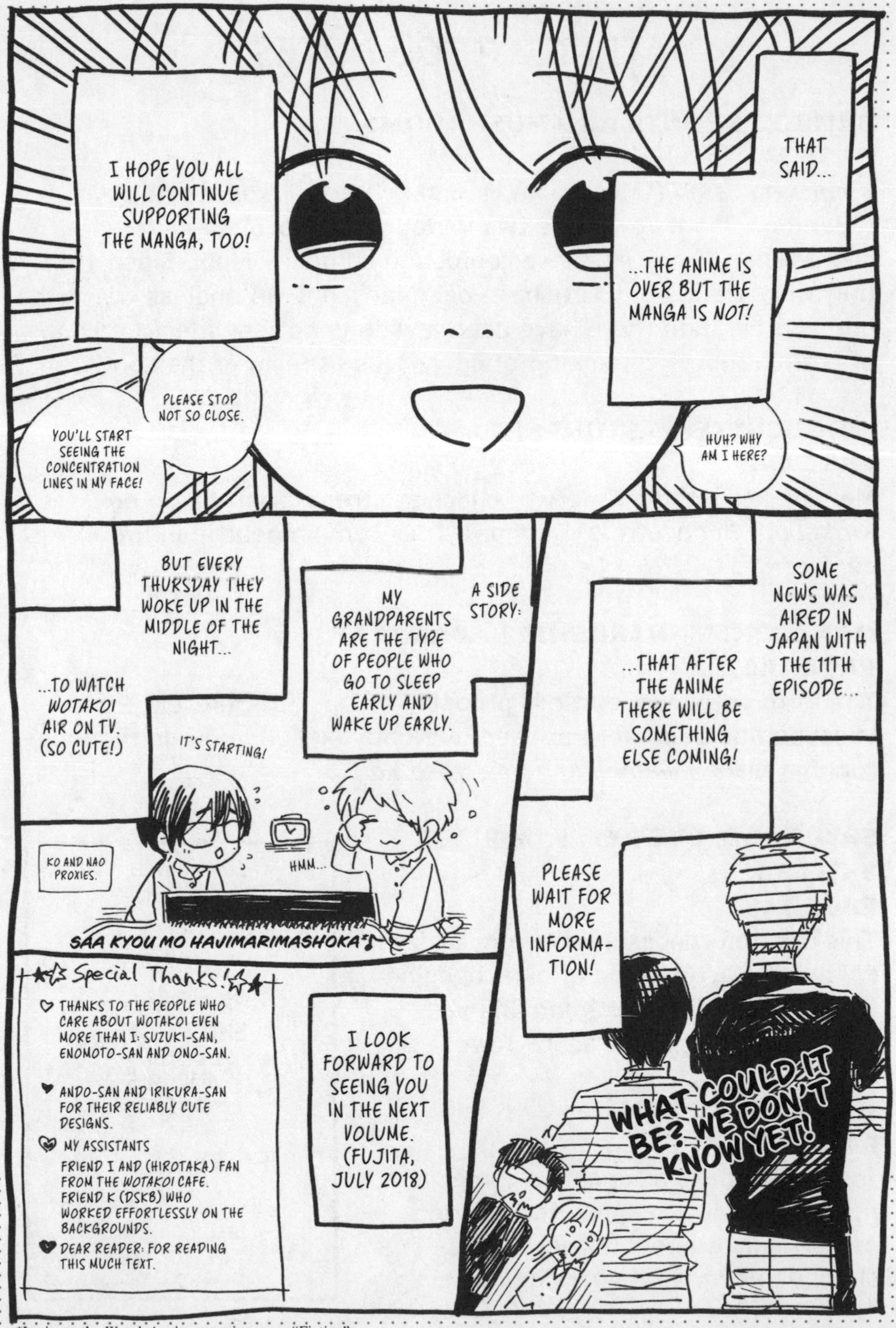
THAT SAID...
...THE ANIME IS OVER BUT THE MANGA IS NOT!
I HOPE YOU ALL WILL CONTINUE SUPPORTING THE MANGA, TOO!
HUH? WHY AM I HERE?
PLEASE STOP NOT SO CLOSE.
YOU'LL START SEEING THE CONCENTRATION LINES IN MY FACE!
SOME NEWS WAS AIRED IN JAPAN WITH THE 11TH EPISODE...
...THAT AFTER THE ANIME THERE WILL BE SOMETHING ELSE COMING!
PLEASE WAIT FOR MORE INFORMATION!
WHAT COULD IT BE? WE DON'T KNOW YET!
A SIDE STORY:
MY GRANDPARENTS ARE THE TYPE OF PEOPLE WHO GO TO SLEEP EARLY AND WAKE UP EARLY.
BUT EVERY THURSDAY THEY WOKE UP IN THE MIDDLE OF THE NIGHT...
...TO WATCH WOTAKOI AIR ON TV. (SO CUTE!)
IT'S STARTING!
HMM...
KO AND NAO PROXIES.
SAA KYOU MO HAJIMARIMASHOKA*!
I LOOK FORWARD TO SEEING YOU IN THE NEXT VOLUME. (FUJITA, JULY 2018)
Special Thanks!
THANKS TO THE PEOPLE WHO CARE ABOUT WOTAKOI EVEN MORE THAN I: SUZUKI-SAN, ENOMOTO-SAN AND ONO-SAN.
ANDO-SAN AND IRIKURA-SAN FOR THEIR RELIABLY CUTE DESIGNS.
MY ASSISTANTS
FRIEND I AND (HIROTAKA) FAN FROM THE WOTAKOI CAFE.
FRIEND K (DSKB) WHO WORKED EFFORTLESSLY ON THE BACKGROUNDS.
DEAR READER: FOR READING THIS MUCH TEXT.

*Lyrics to the *Wotakoi* anime opening song, "Fiction"

TRANSLATION NOTES

BAMBOO SHOOTS AND MUSHROOMS, PAGE 141

Kinoko no Yama ("Mushroom Mountain") and *Takenoko no Sato* ("Bamboo Shoot Town) are two varieties of chocolate-covered cookie snack from Japanese confection company Meiji. Since 1980, the two varieties of treats have been locked in an endless war with one another, and there have been a wide variety of special editions of both products commemorating various aspects of the conflict.

WOODCUTTER'S STUMPS, PAGE 142

Meiji makes a third variety of chocolate treat called *Kikori no Kirikabu*, "Woodcutters' Stumps." They remain neutral in the conflict.

MANAGEMENT HARDSHIP KABAKURA, PAGE 146

The form of this page title is probably an obscure reference to the idiosyncratic titling format used by Nobuyuki Fukumoto in the long-running manga *Gambling Apocalypse Kaiji*.

SAYONARA, BYE BYE, LANGUAGE SKILLS, PAGE 148

This title references a lyric from "Mezase, Pokémon Master!", the original opening theme to the first *Pokémon* anime: "Sayonara, bye bye, Masara Town."

▶ YOSHIO KOJIMA, PAGE 153

Yoshio Kojima is a Japanese comedian famous for always appearing—during performances and interviews alike—in a skimpy Speedo-style bathing suit.

"HIROTAKA SHOWS OFF YOSHIO KOJIMA'S ACT."

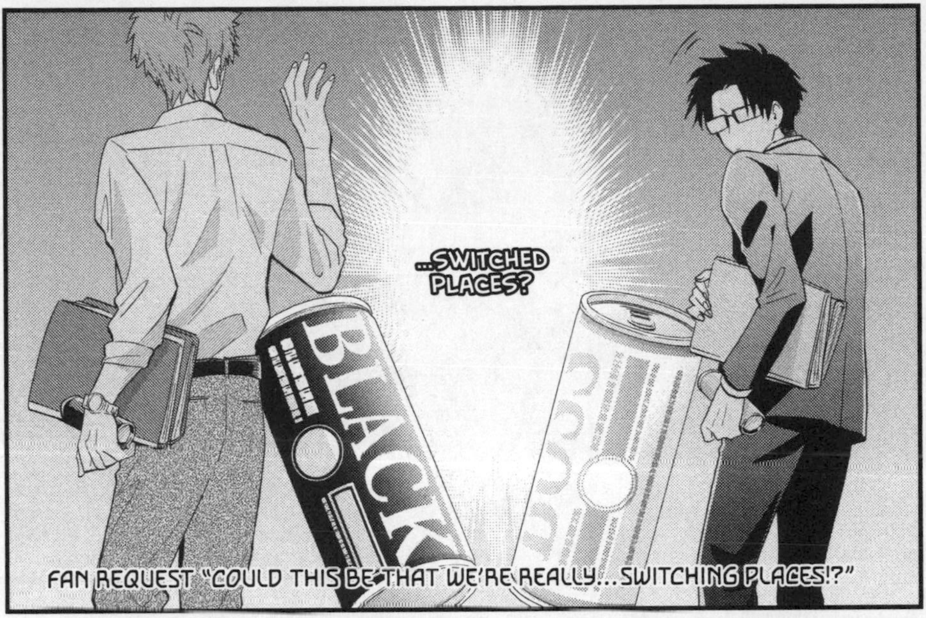
...SWITCHED PLACES?
BLACK
FAN REQUEST "COULD THIS BE THAT WE'RE REALLY... SWITCHING PLACES!?"

▲ COULD IT BE THAT WE REALLY SWITCHED PLACES?, PAGE 154

This is a quote from *Your Name*, Makoto Shinkai's 2016 animated film.

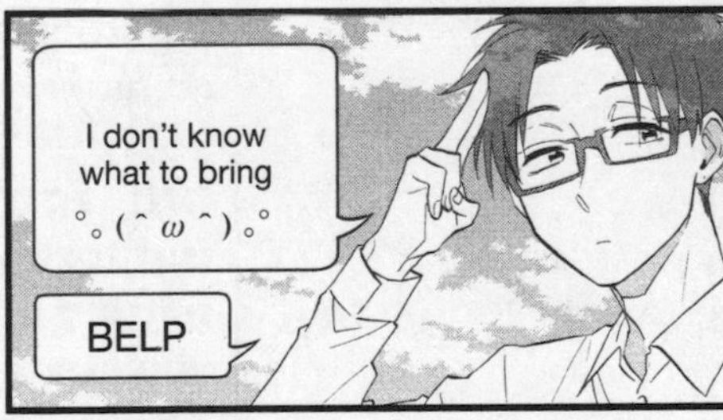
I don't know what to bring °｡(ˆωˆ)｡°
BELP

▶ BELP / YOU'RE AMAZING, NARUMI-SAN, PAGE 172

BELP (or "*Bosukete*") in the original Japanese, is a meme that originated with a joke from Kyosuke Usuta's manga *Sexy Commando Gaiden: You're amazing! Masaru-san.* Captured members of the titular commandoes use a device to contact their boss for a rescue, but the device truncates the message from "*Bosu, tasukete!*" ("Boss, help!") to "*Bosukete*" (notionally, "Belp!"). However, the Boss sees the "belp" message and inexplicably concludes that it must be an abbreviation meaning "Boss, please don't run, just walk quickly and come help us!"

▶ WITHDRAWS COOLLY, PAGE 178

This refers to a line from *Jojo's Bizarre Adventure*, spoken by Robert E. O. Speedwagon, in reference to himself: "Speedwagon withdraws coolly."

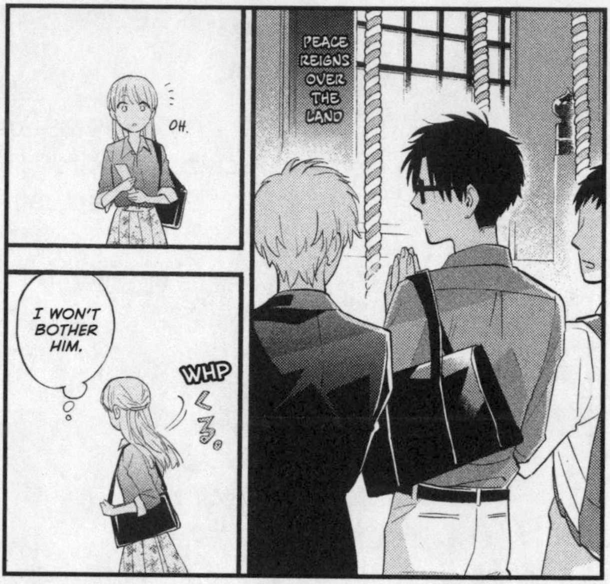
PEACE REIGNS OVER THE LAND
OH.
I WON'T BOTHER HIM.
WHP

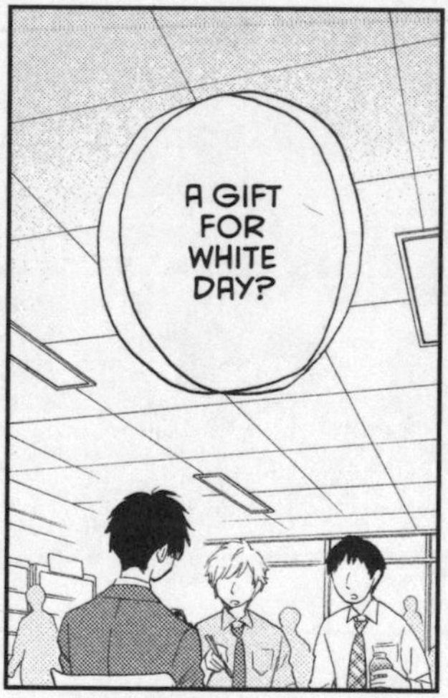
A GIFT FOR WHITE DAY?

◀ WHITE DAY PAGE 198

On Valentine's Day in Japan, women (and only women) give chocolate to men. Men are notionally expected to reciprocate a month later, on "White Day," March 14th, commonly with white chocolate.

ONE TRUTH DOESN'T ALWAYS PREVAIL!, PAGE 204

This is a twist on Jimmy Kudo's famous catchphrase from *Case Closed!* The original is, of course, "Only one truth prevails!"

THEY'RE COMING IN FROM BELOW! WATCH OUT!, PAGE 237

This is a reference to a line spoken by the puzzlingly named character Combat Echizen in the 1996 Sega Saturn light gun shooter *Death Crimson*. Echizen shouts "They're coming in from above! Watch out!" as the player is actually descending a staircase, the surrealism of which is only bolstered by the game's terrible graphics. The phrase "They're coming in from [direction]! Watch out!" has since become a meme.

I LITERALLY CANNOT, PAGE 240

PHEW
スッ...
SNIF
IT'S...TOO PURE. I LITERALLY CANNOT. R.I.P. ME.

In the original Japanese, Naru's line here is "*Toutomi Hideyoshi*," a reference that requires some unpacking. As mentioned in the note for page 56, "*Toutoi*" Is an adjective meaning "holy" or "sacred," but which has come into otaku usage as a hyperbolic way to describe something incredibly cute, charming, or otherwise attractive. The noun version of toutoi would be toutomi, ("holyness"), which is in turn phonetically similar to Toyotomi, the family name of one of the three great unifiers of Japan, the 16th century feudal lord Toyotomi Hideyoshi. As such, saying "Toutomi Hideyoshi" is a pun along the lines of something like "Babe-raham Lincoln." Usage of "Toutomi Hideyoshi" as a meme may be attributable to a 2017 tweet from voice actress Eriko Matsui suggesting the joke. Our translation elides the content of the joke and focuses on Naru's overstatement and Nao's lack of comprehension.

WOTAKOI:
LOVE IS HARD FOR OTAKU

Kinichiro Imamura isn't a bad guy, really, but on the first day of high school his narrow eyes and bleached blonde hair made him look so shifty that his classmates assumed the worst. Three years later, without any friends or fond memories, he isn't exactly feeling bittersweet about graduation. But after an accidental fall down a flight of stairs, Kinichiro wakes up three years in the past... on the first day of high school! School's starting again—but it's gonna be different this time around!

Vol. 1-3 now available in **PRINT** and **DIGITAL**!
Vol. 4 coming August 2018!

Find out **MORE** by visiting:
kodanshacomics.com/MitsurouKubo

ABOUT **MITSUROU KUBO**

Mitsurou Kubo is a manga artist born in Nagasaki prefecture. Her series *3.3.7 Byoshi!!* (2001–2003), *Tokkyu!!* (2004–2008), and *Again!!* (2011–2014) were published in *Weekly Shonen Magazine*, and *Moteki* (2008–2010) was published in the seinen comics magazine *Evening*. After the publication of *Again!!* concluded, she met Sayo Yamamoto, director of the global smash-hit anime *Yuri!!! on ICE*. Working with Yamamoto, Kubo contributed the original concept, original character designs, and initial script for *Yuri!!! on ICE*. *Again!!* is her first manga to be published in English.

ANIME COMING SUMMER 2018

The award-winning manga about what happens inside you!

"Far more entertaining than it ought to be... What kid doesn't want to think that every time they sneeze, a torpedo shoots out their nose?"

—Anime News Network

Strep throat! Hay fever! Influenza! The world is a dangerous place for a red blood cell just trying to get her deliveries finished. Fortunately, she's not alone. She's got a whole human body's worth of cells ready to help out! The mysterious white blood cell, the buff and brash killer T cell, the nerdy neuron, even the cute little platelets—everyone's got to come together if they want to keep you healthy!

Cells at Work!

はたらく細胞

By Akane Shimizu

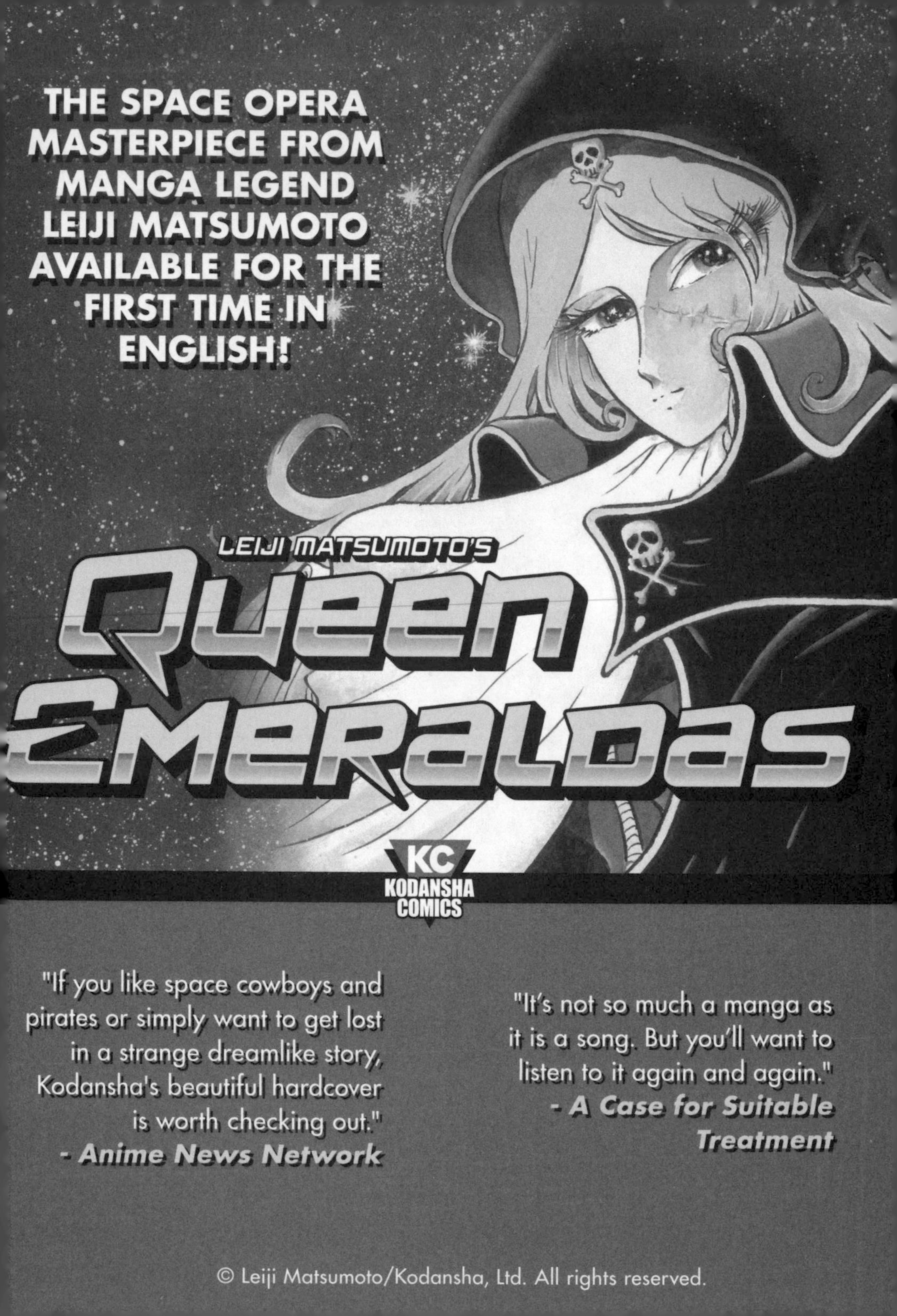
THE SPACE OPERA MASTERPIECE FROM MANGA LEGEND LEIJI MATSUMOTO AVAILABLE FOR THE FIRST TIME IN ENGLISH!
LEIJI MATSUMOTO'S
Queen Emeraldas
KC
KODANSHA COMICS

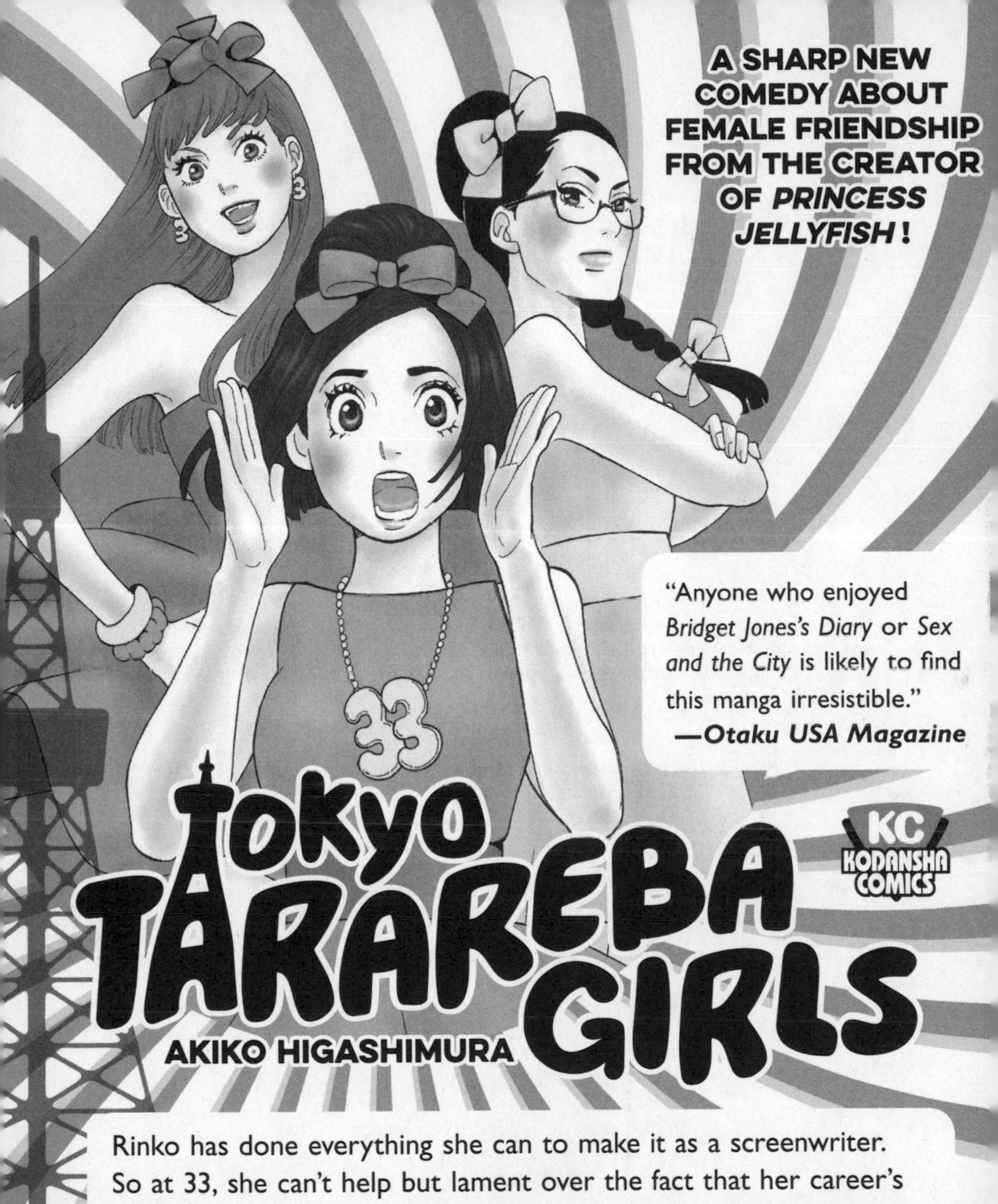

Tokyo TARAREBA GIRLS

AKIKO HIGASHIMURA

Rinko has done everything she can to make it as a screenwriter.
So at 33, she can't help but lament over the fact that her career's
plateaued, she's still painfully single, and spends most of her nights
drinking with her two best friends. One night, drunk and delusional,
Rinko swears to get married by the time the Tokyo Olympics roll
around in 2020. But finding a man—or love—may be a cutthroat,
dirty job for a romantic at heart!

A Kodansha Comics Trade Paperback Original.

Wotakoi: Love is Hard for Otaku volume 3 copyright © 2018 Fujita
English translation copyright © 2018 Fujita

All rights reserved.

Published in the United States by Kodansha Comics, an imprint of Kodansha USA Publishing, LLC, New York.

Publication rights for this English edition arranged through Kodansha Ltd., Tokyo.

First published in Japan in 2018 by Ichijinsha Inc., Tokyo. as *Wotaku ni koi ha muzukashi* volumes 5 & 6

ISBN 978-1-63236-706-8

Printed in the United States of America.

www.kodansha.us

9 8 7 6 5

Translation: Jennifer O'Donnell
Lettering: AndWorld Design
Editing: Paul Starr
Kodansha Comics edition cover design: Phil Balsman